S0-BDL-988

PRAY TELL

A HADASSAH GUIDE TO JEWISH PRAYER

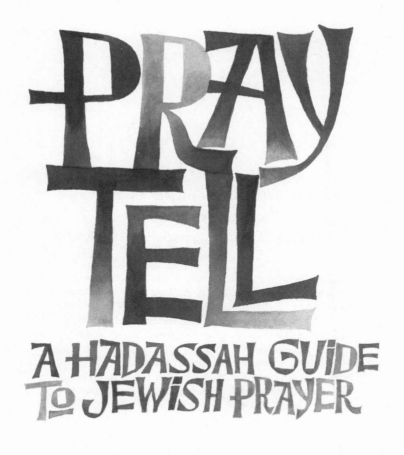

PRAY TELL
A HADASSAH GUIDE TO JEWISH PRAYER

by Rabbi Jules Harlow

with Tamara Cohen
Rochelle Furstenberg
Rabbi Daniel Gordis
& Leora Tanenbaum

edited by Claudia R. Chernov and Carol Diament

HADASSAH
The Women's Zionist Organization of America, Inc.

JEWISH LIGHTS PUBLISHING
Woodstock, Vermont

Pray Tell: A Hadassah Guide to Jewish Prayer

© 2003 by Hadassah

The Women's Zionist Organization of America, Inc.

All rights reserved. No part of this book may be
reproduced or transmitted in any form or by any means,
electronic or mechanical, including photocopying, recording,
or by any information storage and retrieval system,
without permission in writing from the publisher.

For information regarding permission to reprint
material from this book, please mail or fax your request in
writing to Jewish Lights Publishing, Permissions Department,
at the address/fax number listed below.

Library of Congress Cataloging-in-Publication Data is available.

ISBN 1-58023-163-2

10 9 8 7 6 5 4 3 2 1

Manufactured in the United States of America

Design: Tina R. Malaney

Cover Illustration: Ilene Winn-Lederer

Published by JEWISH LIGHTS Publishing
A Division of LongHill Partners, Inc.
Sunset Farms Offices, Route 4
P.O. Box 237
Woodstock, VT 05091
Tel: (802) 457-4000   Fax: (802) 457-4004
www.jewishlights.com

Contents

FOREWORD

Carol Diament

For me, prayer is a mechanism deep inside my soul, one that allows me to disclose my innermost sensibilities and yearnings. Although I do not experience this every time I am in a synagogue, I felt this way about prayer during the entire High Holy Day season following September 11, 2001. Even on Sukkot, during the reading of *Hallel,* the phrase from Psalm 118 "From the depths I call You" brought to mind not the depths of despair but feelings of confidence that heartfelt prayer would ultimately be answered. The meaning of that phrase from Psalms is one subject among many that I debated with Rabbi Jules Harlow, the premier author of the guide.

Why did Hadassah choose Rabbi Harlow as *Pray Tell's* primary exegist? Most important, he has superlative credentials as a scholar and translator of Jewish liturgy. Jules Harlow is the editor of the Conservative movement's acclaimed *Siddur Sim Shalom*, first published in 1985. His English translations of the Hebrew and Aramaic prayers are both beautiful and accurate. Though they are not strictly literal, the interpretations closely adhere to the originals, and are based on deep and intimate knowledge of Rabbinic sources.

Rabbi Harlow, however, is strongly opposed to many recent feminist changes to the traditional liturgy. In 1994, the Rabbinical Assembly decided to include the names of the *imahot,* the matriarchs, in the *Amidah* blessings, a change for which earlier Conservative Jewish feminists had pleaded, and one that enabled contemporary Conservative Jewish women to claim their share in prayer. Even though the 1994 edition of *Siddur Sim Shalom* is based almost entirely on Rabbi Harlow's translations from the

1985 edition, the addition of the *imahot* was incompatible with his principles, and the later edition of *Siddur Sim Shalom* no longer bears Rabbi Harlow's name on its title page.

Rabbi Harlow has long supported other feminist ideals, including synagogue leadership roles for both women and men, rigorous Jewish education for girls, women publicly reading from the Torah, and women being counted in the *minyan* (prayer quorum). Still, he said, "The inclusion of the *imahot* violates the liturgical and the literary integrity of the classic text. It also breaks the close link between the language of the Bible and the language of the prayer book." Rabbi Harlow felt that changing the *siddur* to include the *imahot* had momentous implications. For one thing, the phrases that were added to the *Amidah* appear nowhere in the Bible or the Talmud, though the phrases that refer to the *avot* (patriarchs) are found in the Bible and Talmud. For another, invoking the God of the matriarchs creates a rupture with Jewish congregations the world over who pray using the traditional liturgy.

I argued with Rabbi Harlow. I feel that the women of the Bible are absent from the liturgy, and that this absence has had a profound impact on women's perceptions. Growing up in an observant Orthodox home in the 1940s and 1950s, I had always known of the dichotomy between the public roles of men and women in Jewish practice and ritual. These inequities tore at my very being. Unlike my brother, I was never called to the Torah as a bat mitzvah. By adding the matriarchs to the liturgy, we publicly acknowledge women as part of the historic Jewish people. Furthermore, changing the words of the *Amidah* is not equivalent to changing the words of the Bible. The *siddur* has always been relatively flexible, and it is able to accommodate necessary additions. Unlike the Bible, the *siddur* has always been in flux. Innovations, such as *Kabbalat Shabbat* in the 16th century, become traditional over time.

The question remains: Why did I choose Rabbi Harlow as the primary author of a book published by a women's organization? Moreover, why did I choose him for a book produced by the National Jewish Education Department, which has strong feminist leanings? Why did I choose a writer who is opposed both to the inclusion of the *imahot* and to the use of gender-neutral language when referring to God in English?

I chose Rabbi Harlow because his translations of the traditional Hebrew liturgy offer a middle ground between the literalism and the male-gender language of recent Orthodox translations and the extensive deletions and reworkings of the Reform and Reconstructionist liturgies. I hoped that, by choosing a middle ground, *Pray Tell* would become more accessible to Jews of all denominations.

Unit One of *Pray Tell* presents English translations and explanations of the traditional Hebrew and Aramaic liturgy. It can be used by Jews of every denomination to broaden and deepen their understanding of traditional Jewish liturgy. In addition to Rabbi Harlow's text—which is, at times, a line-by-line explication of the meaning of the *siddur*—marginal commentary is included for all nine chapters of Unit One. Today's finest scholars and theorists have wrestled with Rabbi Harlow's text, and their meditations, critiques, and amplifications offer readers a diverse and expansive dialogue on prayer, on Judaism, and on women and men. Like the pages of the Talmud, *Pray Tell* is a polemic, a dispute in the name of Heaven *(makhloket leshem Shamayyim)*.

Unit Two of *Pray Tell* presents some of the "big picture" issues that Jews confront today. Chapters 10 and 11 deal respectively with non-Orthodox and Orthodox women's prayer (which includes both Yiddish and Ladino prayers of our foremothers). Chapter 10, on feminism's impact on Jewish prayer over the last 30 years, presents eloquent arguments in favor of changing the language of the *siddur*. Some feminists view the traditional Hebrew liturgy—and English translations such as Rabbi Harlow's—as sexist. For them, the image of God as a male King, who sits on a throne and judges humanity, is alienating. Some of these feminists feel that adding feminine language—God as Queen, God as Mother—makes the concept of the divine inclusive, and this allows them to embrace Jewish prayer.

Other feminists, myself included, object to changing the Hebrew language that refers to God. The traditional Hebrew of the *siddur* unites Jews everywhere. Although I, and other Jewish feminists, welcome changes in the English translations and though I welcome original prayers and new feminist rituals (alongside new understandings of Jewish women's roles), I believe that public, communal Hebrew prayer should remain largely fixed. As Rabbi Harlow argues, traditional Hebrew prayer, even today, is shared by Jews in all countries of the world. I pray with greatest intensity when the words are familiar and link me to earlier generations and to Jews in Israel and elsewhere.

I believe, too, that traditional conceptions of God include attributes that are neither masculine nor feminine; both women and men are wise, strong, merciful. For me, God transcends gender. I am uncomfortable with feminist rewriting of Hebrew language that addresses or refers to God. While changing references to the Jewish people, both to our ancestors and to Jews today, is—for me—a necessary change, changing the way we refer to God is, in my mind, not authentically Jewish. The Bible describes God using physical terms with masculine gender: *Melekh* or King, *Adon* or Lord. Yet, as Rabbi Harlow points out, the Bible also uses feminine imagery in referring to God. None of these descriptions or images of God in the Bible imply God is either masculine or feminine. Some people would assign specific attributes to masculine or feminine aspects of God, but such narrow definitions tend to create and reinforce stereotypes that are misleading because of God's unique and genderless nature. Tampering with the original Hebrew eliminates the nuances of the multi-dimensional meaning of God.

I dare not depart from this emotional issue without mentioning Marcia Falk, who is at the forefront of rewriting the traditional Hebrew prayers. She believes that masculine-gender language must be changed, but merely adding feminine language is not the answer. God is neither male nor female; instead God encompasses all and exists everywhere. For Falk, God is not a being that rules over humanity, but a presence that exists within every aspect of creation. Falk's Hebrew prayers use a multiplicity of images—frequently of feminine gender—yet they exclude no one; they allow everyone to share in the experience of communicating with God in a sacred, meaningful way.

Chapters 12 and 13 of Unit Two were added after September 11, 2001. In August 2001, a month before the attack on the United States, Hadassah held its 88th Convention in Jerusalem, and Rabbi Daniel Gordis spoke to an auditorium full of delegates about the relationship between Zionism and Judaism. Rabbi Gordis had left a prestigious position at the University of Judaism in Los Angeles to go on *aliyah* with his young family. When asked how he could continue to live in Israel under such ominous conditions, when he could easily return to the United States, he answered: "The Jewish people have seen very dark days in the past, have seen dark days in the present, and will see them in the future. But we know where our home is. We will do whatever we need to do to raise children and grandchildren who will be committed to say, *am Yisrael ḥai.*" After my return home and the terrible events of September, I knew that Rabbi Gordis would be right person to write about prayer in response to evil. I believe you will find Rabbi Gordis's chapter extraordinary. It plumbs the depths of the *siddur* and explains some of the emotional and intellectual ways in which Hebrew prayer grapples with evil and suffering.

The missing voice in *Pray Tell* had been the Israeli voice, especially the voice of the large majority of Israeli Jews who define themselves as secular. These Israelis are numerically the principal voice of the Jewish State, yet many of them reject Jewish religion. How do they express their spiritual yearnings? Do they pray at all? Rochelle Furstenberg, a literary scholar and frequent contributor to *Hadassah Magazine,* wrote Chapter 12, "Israeli Poetry as Prayer." She told me: "I loved doing this assignment. Whatever is special about Jewish values is also special about Jewish prayer and Hebrew poetry." Israeli poetry provides a rich tapestry of meaning, woven of threads from the Bible and the *siddur*, as well as from modern culture. Anguish and pain can be found in the verses, yet at the same time the verses reveal hope and faith in the Jewish people and the Jewish State. Indeed, many Israeli poems also reveal continuing faith in God.

Before closing, I must clarify two aspects of this guide to Jewish prayer that might lead to confusion. First, *Pray Tell* presents the Hebrew prayers of the traditional *siddur* only in translation, yet it presents the Israeli poems of Chapter 12, as well as a few modern prayers, in both Hebrew and English. This is because the established Hebrew prayers are easy to find in a *siddur* in any synagogue or Jewish library, whereas Israeli poems and modern Hebrew prayers are not quite so easily located.

Second, the marginal commentary appears as sidebars, and, at times, a comment on a particular sentence or paragraph of the main text will not appear on the same page as that text. In these cases, the sidebar appears on the page facing the main text.

The Jewish Education Department's recent publications have covered Jewish and Zionist thought, Hebrew language and literature, and Jewish family education. *Pray Tell* brings to a close the Jewish women's education trilogy that began in 1997 with *Jewish Women Living the Challenge*. That first book was a compendium of essays—on abortion, breast cancer, aging, interfaith marriage, contemporary women's rituals, and many other topics. *Moonbeams: A Hadassah Rosh Hodesh Guide*, the second volume in the trilogy, provided a course of study for Rosh Hodesh groups.

Pray Tell, the third book of the trilogy, is not a *siddur*. It is a guide to the *siddur*. It will help you understand and make sense of the prayer book. Use this guide to lead a study group together with others who want to learn. Take it with you to the synagogue, and place it underneath your *siddur*. As the service progresses, you can turn the pages of the *siddur*—any *siddur*—and follow along in *Pray Tell* to learn the meaning, history, and interpretations of communal prayer. Or read *Pray Tell* at home to learn at your own pace. No matter how you choose to use this book, your understanding of Jewish prayer will be enhanced. Our greatest hope is that all of our prayers will be answered.

Acknowledgments

Many people have contributed to the creation of *Pray Tell*. Rabbi Jules Harlow is the explicator *par excellence* of Unit One, the guide to the prayer book. His illuminating translation and commentary are our primary texts. I also want to thank the commentators in the marginal texts, both those who wrote specifically for Hadassah and those who allowed us to use their writings. As you read the guide, you will see that we have included the ideas of some of the finest and most inspirational of today's Jewish scholars. To them, I offer my profound appreciation. The disputes were learning experiences for all involved.

The Jewish Education Department is thrilled to be working with Jewish Lights Publishing in our efforts to reach beyond Hadassah's membership to the broader Jewish community.

Kudos to Tamara Cohen, Leora Tanenbaum, Vanessa Paloma, Rochelle Furstenberg, and Rabbi Daniel Gordis who wrote informative chapters for Unit Two of *Pray Tell*. A special thank you also to Renée Septimus and Mordehi Horowitz for their initial translations of the Hebrew prayers of Yael Levine, and to Tova Hartman-Halbertal for reading and commenting on Chapter 11.

I am grateful to Ilene Winn-Lederer, who created the cover art. Thank you as well to Tina Malaney, whose typographical design of this immensely difficult guide made my vision of "a dispute in the name of Heaven" a reality, and to Deborah Meisels for proofreading the entire book.

My deepest gratitude is to Claudia Chernov, senior editor of the Jewish Education Department. She chose many of *Pray Tell's* marginal texts with the aim of including—in the words of Rabbi Harlow—"something to offend everyone." Her aim, however, was to make *Pray Tell* interesting and provocative. Claudia is fascinated by disputes and controversies about liturgy.

I also owe thanks to Carol Winer, director of Hadassah's National Creative Services Department, for her help with the cover art and for working out all design questions with the artist and the book designer. Sincere thanks as well to Agnes Gregorio, for her 11th hour design assistance.

I am grateful to Bonnie Dimun, Ed.D., director of the Leadership, Education, and Training Center of Hadassah, for expediting this important project.

My thanks also to Jamie Reiffel, assistant general counsel of Hadassah, for her knowledge and invaluable assistance.

Finally, I am grateful to Leora Tanenbaum, assistant editor of the Jewish Education Department, and Rachel Schwartz, former assistant director, for their critical reading of this work. Rachel's penchant for detail and her accuracy have always proved to be invaluable. Courtney Hanauer, current assistant director, oversaw all final production issues, contributed commentary in sections of *Pray Tell*, and could be always counted on to step in when added research was needed and administrative duties in the office were heavy. Thanks are also due to Elissa Groskin, project manager, Ilana Horowitz, administrative assistant, and Miriam Miller, librarian, for their careful reading of the manuscript. I am grateful as well to Ilana, Leora, and Courtney, who were given the difficult task of obtaining permission to reprint previously published works. Last but not least, I wish to thank Sandra King, Hadassah National chair of the Jewish Education Department, whose support, encouragement, insight, and understanding sustain all of us in the Department.

INTRODUCTION TO THE PRAYER BOOK

Rabbi Jules Harlow

Our understanding and appreciation of Jewish prayer grow with our knowledge of the words, structure, and themes of the Jewish prayer book, the *siddur*. This translation and commentary are steps on the path toward gaining such knowledge.

Before taking any steps on that path, however, we pause to reflect on a question that would take more than a book to answer: What is the purpose of prayer? Though knowing and understanding the words of the prayer book are important, we must also go beyond the words; we must realize that the words are only a way.

Why pray? There are many answers to this question. They include a question that many believers would ask in response: "How could I *not* pray?" A committed Jew prays because prayer is one of the Jew's many obligations (*mitzvot*).

As loyal servants, of course, we should obey the commands of our Sovereign. Yet even the most loyal and devoted servant must, at one time or other, ponder the question of purpose.

Reflecting on the question, I favor the approach suggested by Rabbi Louis Jacobs, who attempts to answer why a Jew should fulfill *any* of the *mitzvot*.[1] He points out that in ancient Babylonia, the sage Rav taught that the commandments were given to refine human character, to ennoble humanity, to have a positive impact on our lives. Rav offered a brief lesson. "What does it matter to the Holy One if a cow is slaughtered in front at the neck (according to ritual law) or stabbed in the back of the neck (not according to ritual law)?" The goal of this particular *mitzvah*—the kosher slaughter of an animal—is to teach about care and compassion. ▦ Jewish ritual slaughter prescribes taking the life of the animal in the most painless way possible. If the lesson stops with careful attention to the details of ritual slaughter, we may be obeying the letter of the law but we are not led to the basic purpose of fulfilling the law—avoiding cruelty in our relations with all creatures, animal and human alike. Hence, observing the dietary laws is meant to influence human character so that we act with compassion.

The medieval philosopher Nahmanides, in his discussion of the purpose of worship (commentary on Deuteronomy 22:6), arrives at the same conclusion. The proper worship of God should have a beneficial impact on human character, leading us to exemplify virtues in our lives, and bring us closer to perfection, to being God-like in our behavior.

The Creator demands the worship of His creatures. ◉ The purpose of the demand, however, is not to send praise heavenward. Nahmanides teaches that fulfilling the demand is for the benefit of humanity. Fulfilling *mitzvot* can keep us from doing harm and from acquiring negative character traits. Worshiping God, the Creator, should remind us of His creatures, including ourselves. Through worship, we aspire to understand God's ways as we strive to draw nearer to God. Although prayer is addressed to God, a basic purpose of prayer is to improve human behavior and thought, to enhance the quality of the human spirit.

Prayer should be an elevating experience. Although prayer often concerns basic human needs, prayer allows us to reach out toward the highest, the infinite, the Creator of the universe. ▨ We dare to confront our Creator, though we are mortal creatures of flesh and blood.

Remember that the words are only a way. The medieval philosopher Bahya Ibn Pakuda wrote that one who is "employed in those duties in which both the heart and the body are involved, such as prayer and praising God, blessed be He, should empty himself of all matters appertaining

▦ Vegetarians, of course, have another attitude about this. The laws of kosher slaughter assume that a decision has been made to consume meat.—*JH*

◉ All beings long for the very source of their origin. Every plant, every grain of sand, every lump of earth, small creatures and big ones, the heavens above and the angels, every substance together with its particles—all of them are longing, yearning, panting to attain the state of holy perfection. Humans suffer all the time from this homesickness of the soul and it is in prayer that it is cured. When praying, humanity feels at one with the whole creation, and raises it to the very source of blessing and life.—*Rav Abraham Isaac Kook* [2]

▨ Prayer serves many functions, in fact, every function and its opposite: It is a safety hatch when one is overcome by fear or dread, anger or need. It calls forth a generosity of the human spirit. Prayer reminds us not to take totally for granted that which we all must presume as we go about our business—the gifts of life, health, love, and good fortune…. Prayer is a sensation of community; but it is also a feeling of intense loneliness, and aloneness with God…. Prayer adds routine and organization to life; it is also orientation away from everyday life, a momentary stepping out of time and of motion.—*Blu Greenberg* [3]

to this world or the next and should empty his heart of every distracting thought, after first cleansing himself" (*Duties of the Heart* 8:3). According to Baḥya, we also should keep our distance from unpleasant smells and other unpleasantness during prayer. We should consider to whom we direct our prayers; we should ponder the words of the prayers and their meaning. The words of prayers are like the husk covering grain, and reflection on their meaning is like the kernel. Prayer itself is like the body, and reflection on its meaning is like the spirit. ✳ If we merely utter the words of prayers while thinking about matters other than prayer, it is like a body without a spirit, a husk without a kernel; the body is present but the heart is absent. Baḥya wrote that, of such people, Scripture says: "This people has drawn near to me with its mouth, and honors Me with its lips, but has kept its heart far from Me" (Isaiah 29:13).

In the words of Maimonides, if you pray merely by moving your lips while facing a wall, and at the same time think about your business, your buying and selling, or if you read the Torah with your tongue while your heart is set on the build-ing of your house and does not consider what you read; and similarly in all cases in which you perform a com-mandment merely with your limbs—as if you were digging a hole in the ground or hewing wood in the forest— without reflecting either on the meaning of that action or on the One from whom the commandment proceeds or on the purpose of the action, you should not think that you have achieved the end. Rather, Maimonides stated (*Guide of the Perplexed* III:51), you will then be similar to those of whom it is said, "You (God) are present in their mouths and far from their thoughts" (Jeremiah 12:2).

✳ Worship is a turning of the whole being toward that which we affirm as ultimately real and valuable. Humble in the face of a spiritual reali-ty whose essence we cannot "know," we speak in metaphors. Our "truth" is a truth of the heart no less than of the mind. The "facts" we assert are those of the hopeful spirit. But we believe that the spiritual reality within us corresponds to a spiritual reality beyond us, and in worship we hope to bring the two realities into communion.—*Rabbi Chaim Stern*[4]

❖ [Such questions are] not new; nor are they unique to our times. Since the beginnings of the development of Jewish prayer, our rabbis and lay people have asked similar questions and have made sure—through ➤

None of this is easy or simple. We must try to go beyond the words, yet we must start with words. Only when we are familiar with the words of prayer will we be able to reach beyond them and attain ultimate goals.

One more question to ponder: How do we make prayer our own when almost all of the words we utter are not our own? The words are from the Bible, from Rabbinic Sages, and from later authorities. As Abraham Joshua Heschel taught, Jewish prayer is an act of listening. The self is silent; the spirit of the people Israel speaks. We listen to what the classic words convey.

Still, how can I express my deepest personal feelings with the words of a formula that I did not write? ❖ The use of a common expression can help us to answer the question. "I love you." These words constitute a formula of sorts, one that I did not invent. If, however, I do not say those words to the people I love, and if I do not hear them, what am I? Those three words—I love you—can be as meaningful or as meaningless as we show them to be through the way that we live. When we invest ourselves in those "three little words," when our actions reflect our love, then that familiar formula has meaning.

The same is true with the words of prayer. ▦ We must invest ourselves in them, heart and soul, as we listen to what the words convey.[5]

The translations and commentaries in the following nine chapters do not include all passages of the prayer book, although they present most of the basic selections for weekdays and the Sabbath. Jewish prayer and its commentaries constitute a vast literature that is central to Jewish life and tradition.

Almost every classic post-Biblical Jewish work begins with a discussion of Jewish prayer. The Mishnah, compiled in the third century, begins with a section on prayer, *Brakhot* (Blessings), and the Talmud, since it is based on the Mishnah, also begins with the tractate *Brakhot*. The major legal compilations, or law codes—from the *Mishneh Torah* of Maimonides in 12th-century Egypt to the *Arba Turim* of Rabbi Jacob Ben Asher in 14th-century Morocco, to the *Shulhan Arukh* of Rabbi Isaac Luria with the notes of Rabbi Moses Isserles in 16th-century Poland—all teach us about prayer at or near the beginning.

We read prayers in the Bible, but the Bible itself does not begin with prayer. The ancient Rabbis, our teachers *par excellence*, put prayer at the forefront of Judaism, and they developed the classic texts of Jewish prayer,

praying and straying—that the community responds with authenticity and thoughtful change. [Comparing the prayers printed in the *siddur* with the prayers we say when we speak to God in our own voices] captures the tension between *keva*, the fixed order of the familiar prayers, and *kavanah*, the deep, heartfelt, spontaneous intention and attention with which we endow the words. I believe that Jewish prayer was always meant to be a mix of *keva* and *kavanah*, as each possesses a unique and potentially powerful purpose. *Keva* grounds us, brings us home, allows us to access the genius of our ancestors, and build community through the comfort of shared knowledge, melodies, and traditions. *Kavanah* empowers us to see each ancient word as new again, draws us to open our hearts, inspires us to be at once vulnerable and strong as we draw close to God.—*Rabbi Judy B. Shanks*[6]

▦ I used to value *kavanah* (intentional, spontaneous prayer) over *keva* (fixed, standard liturgy). Over the years, however, I have said the fixed liturgy three times a day, every day, and at times a verse of the *siddur* will jump out at me, suddenly invested with personal meaning because of its direct and immediate relevance to my life. Both the verse and my life then take on new significance, because of the interaction between them. I see the verse in a new light—and the moment in my life is refracted through the verse. This interaction between the words of the liturgy and the events of my life has happened many times. For me, saying the fixed liturgy is very personal. Reciting these words that were composed by others is like looking through a scrapbook of my life.—*Rabbi Paula Reimers*[7]

✹ The core of the traditional Hebrew liturgy became standardized in the Talmudic and Geonic periods, from about 200 until roughly 1000. Even then, a creative struggle emerged between the proponents of fixed prayer and those who composed spontaneous, heartfelt words of devotion. To enable their congregations to recite the fixed prayers with meaning and sincerity, *paytanim* (liturgical poets) served as prayer ➤

often using words of the Bible as their starting point. Jewish prayer, like Judaism itself, is not Biblical; it is Rabbinic.

The prayer book incorporates many extra-Biblical passages as well as generous citations of Biblical passages. These latter include about 50 chapters from the Book of Psalms as well as selections of verses from Exodus, Deuteronomy, Chronicles, many of the Prophets, and other books of the Bible.

Although we may attain a commendable state of devotion in worship and an admirable understanding of services, prayer will never be without its problems, including problems of faith. Some people believe that we can solve these problems by composing new prayers, by teaching new melodies with which to sing new as well as traditional prayers, or by breathing new life into the classic prayers. ✹ None of these approaches should be ignored. A more basic goal, however, is breathing new life into ourselves. As Rabbi Heschel taught, we must learn how to approach a word, how to dwell in silence upon a thought. The words of prayer represent commitments. To pray, we must commit ourselves. Heart and soul, we must invest ourselves in the words that we utter, with all the intensity at our command. ✳ Still, we must be attentive not only to the words of the prayer; we must be aware that we stand in the presence of God.

leaders and wrote original poems (*piyyuttim*) that explained and interpreted the standard prayers. The *piyyut* (poem) generally preceded a segment of prayer, and it directed the congregation to the content and intent of that segment, and often to its application to contemporary problems. The verses were unique in their cadences, alliterations, and rhyme patterns, and they were often put to music, for the *paytanim* were the early cantors. Thus the sounds, rhythms, and the music of the *piyyut* would heighten the listeners' emotions, even as the content inspired their thoughts. Although many *piyyuttim* were lost and others were ignored or neglected in later eras, a number of *piyyuttim* became incorporated into the standard liturgy, particularly into the liturgy for Rosh Hashanah and Yom Kippur.—*Claudia Chernov*

✳ How can we invest ourselves in the words of prayer when, to us, the words make no sense or, worse, are obviously untrue? How do we bring our heart and soul into the words of a formula when that formula violates the dictates of our heart and soul? Orthodox and Conservative Jews tend to reinterpret such words, often using metaphor or some type of schematic classification, so that the ultimate meaning remains acceptable even when the words are troubling. In addition (as Rabbi Daniel Gordis points out in Chapter 13), the prayer book itself contains many contradictory statements and images. Hence, Orthodox and Conservative Jews may indeed say some words whose literal meanings are confusing or difficult to accept, but such Orthodox and Conservative Jews will emphasize some very different words of prayer. Reform and Reconstructionist Judaism, however, have taken another approach to the meaning of the words of prayers. Starting in the late 18th century, a number of German rabbis began to systematically reform—that is, rewrite—the traditional liturgy. Although some of those early Reform changes have since been reconsidered and the traditional words of liturgy restored, many other early changes have endured and have now become standard in Reform prayer books. The Reconstructionist movement, begun in the early 20th century in America, has also systematically reformulated the prayer book, stressing the need for consistency and rational honesty during prayer. More recently, feminist Jews within the liberal denominations have also stressed the need for praying only when the words can be said with honesty and sincerity, and thus for praying in a way that values female as well as male experience. (Refer to Chapter 10.) Poet Marcia Falk, author of an alternative prayer book, asks: "Why should we be willing to hold one set of beliefs as our truths while we articulate something very different in worship? If we do not try to touch our deepest faith—our most truthful truths—in prayer, then where?"[8]—*Claudia Chernov*

Here is a story about the words of prayer. A rabbi was about to begin an official visit to a synagogue when he hesitated. He then refused to enter. When his disciples questioned his strange behavior, the rabbi answered, "The synagogue is filled with words of prayer." His disciples thought this was a compliment; it seemed to be great praise. Why did the rabbi refuse to enter? He explained that the words of prayer filled the synagogue because the words had not risen to heaven. They were stripped of love and joy. The words had been uttered without feeling, without reverence. The synagogue was full of prayer whose words were going nowhere.[9]

May these thoughts help each of us to elevate our own words of prayer beyond the physical space we occupy as we say them.

Acknowledgments

Most of the translations in this commentary are based on an earlier work of mine, which has been published in the standard edition of *Siddur Sim Shalom*.[10] I am grateful to The Rabbinical Assembly for extending permission to make use in this volume of those translations, into which I have incorporated many changes based on new understandings of texts as well as matters of style.

Some of the commentary was written while I was at the Shalom Hartman Institute in Jerusalem. I am grateful to the Institute and to its director, Rabbi David Hartman, for the opportunities afforded me at that unique place of learning and pluralism.

Two members of the staff of Hadassah have been especially helpful. The suggestions of Claudia Chernov, as editor, have led to improvements in the style and content of my original manuscript. The director of Hadassah's Department of Education, Dr. Carol Diament, has always been supportive and encouraging. Together we have produced a volume on prayer that includes more than one point of view. Finally, the text has benefited from the reactions and insights of Navah Harlow and Ilana Harlow.

On Translations and Other Textual Differences

The commentary and other texts in this volume present differences of belief, often concerning language about God, often concerning other issues. Just as there are many approaches to life within the Jewish community, there are many paths in prayer. That this produces differences should not be surprising. In spite of substantial differences, however, all the views of communities and individuals presented here are informed by a desire to relate to God through prayer in a manner that reflects their deepest commitments and concerns. In spite of the divisive potential of differences, the reality of this sincere desire should encourage us to live together as a united community with tolerance for the views of others. We cannot be true to God, or to each other, if we are not true to ourselves. We cannot live someone else's life, or expect others to live ours. Condescension or coercion in relating to others is not acceptable, especially in an area so sensitive and so personal as prayer. The search that we share should bind us together in spite of conclusions that differ.

1. Louis Jacobs, *A Jewish Theology* (New York: Behrman House, 1973).

2. Rav Abraham Isaac Kook, cited in *"Tefillat Hasachar": Abridged Siddur for Tel Yehudah and other Hashachar Functions* (New York: Hadassah Zionist Youth Commission), page 36. Rav Kook (1864–1935) exerted great influence on Jewish thought as a Talmudist, philosopher, and mystic.

3. Blu Greenberg, *How To Run a Traditional Jewish Household* (New York: Simon & Schuster, 1983), pages 137–138.

4. Rabbi Chaim Stern, *Shaarei Tefillah, Gates of Prayer: The New Union Prayerbook* (New York: Central Conference of American Rabbis, 1975), page xi.

5. For more on personal prayer, see pages 104–105 on words to be recited at the conclusion of the *Amidah* and page 134 on words to be recited when lighting Shabbat or Festival candles.

6. Rabbi Judy B. Shanks, "Ask the Rabbi," *Reform Judaism* 29:2 (winter 2000), page 94.

7. Rabbi Paula Reimers copyright © 2003.

8. Marcia Falk, *The Book of Blessings: New Jewish Prayers for Daily Life, the Sabbath, and the New Moon Festival* (New York: HarperCollins, 1996; paperback edition, Boston: Beacon, 1999), page 421. See also www.marciafalk.com.

9. This story has been told about Rabbi Israel Baal Shem Tov and about Rabbi Levi Yitzchak of Berditchev.

10. Copyright © 1985 by The Rabbinical Assembly.

OUTLINE OF SERVICES

Shaharit—Morning Service

Birkhot Hashahar—Morning Blessings
Pesukei DeZimra—Verses of Song
Barkhu—Call to Prayer
Kriat Shema
    1m. Creation
    2m. Revelation
    Kriat Shema
    3m. Redemption
Amidah
    (19 blessings on weekdays, 7 blessings on Shabbat and Festivals)
Kriat HaTorah—Torah Service
    (only on Monday, Thursday, Shabbat, Festivals, and Rosh Hodesh)
Musaf—Additional Service
    (only on Shabbat, Festivals, and Rosh Hodesh)
Concluding passages, including *Aleinu*

Minhah—Afternoon Service

Ashrei (Psalm 145)
Amidah
    (19 blessings on weekdays, 7 blessings on Shabbat and Festivals)
Aleinu

Maariv—Evening Service

Barkhu—Call to Prayer
Kriat Shema
    1e. Creation
    2e. Revelation
    Kriat Shema
    3e. Redemption
    4e. Peace and Protection
Amidah
    (19 blessings on weekdays, 7 blessings on Shabbat and Festivals)
    (*Kiddush* is added on Shabbat and Festivals)
Havdalah
    (only on Saturday night)
Aleinu

UNIT ONE:

TRADITIONAL LITURGY OF THE SIDDUR

BY RABBI JULES HARLOW

THE BLESSING

Do not take the world for granted

If you want to know what Jews believe (especially what Jews *should* believe), study the Jewish prayer book. The words of the prayer book form the core of Jewish religion, and they reflect the essence of what it means to be a Jew. ▒ Franz Rosenzweig declared that the prayer book will ever be "the sum and substance of the whole of historical Judaism, its handbook and memorial tablet."[1]

We recite one of the best-known blessings—indeed some of the most familiar words in all of Jewish prayer—before eating bread: "Blessed are You, Lord our God, King of the universe who brings forth bread

▒ I regard the old Jewish *siddur* as the most important single Jewish book—a more personal expression, a closer record, of Jewish sufferings, Jewish needs, Jewish hopes and aspirations, than the Bible itself. For one thing the Bible is too grand and universal to be exclusively Jewish (as Shakespeare is not the typical Englishman), and for another whatever is quintessentially needed for daily use has been squeezed out of it into the prayer book and so made our daily own. And if you want to know what Judaism is—the question which has no answer if debated on the plane of intellectual argument—you can find it by absorbing that book. The Jewish soul is mirrored there as nowhere else, mirrored or rather embodied there: the individual's soul in its private sorrows, and the people's soul in its historic burdens, its heroic passion and suffering, its unfaltering faith, through the ages.—*Henry Slonimsky*[2]

from the earth." ▣ These words constitute the blessing known as *hamotzi* (Hebrew for "who brings forth"), which is one of the Hebrew words the blessing contains: *Barukh Attah Adonai, Eloheinu Melekh haolam, hamotzi lehem min haaretz*. This blessing *(brakhah)* is only one of Judaism's many blessings *(brakhot)*.

The Hebrew liturgical formula known as a *brakhah* is a basic unit of Jewish prayer, and it expresses a specific reaction to the world. Some people think of blessings as prayers uttered on someone's behalf, and some think of blessings as prayers that ask for something. (And some people, unfortunately, never think of blessings at all.) In Judaism, however, a *brakhah* proclaims the blessedness of God, and it expresses gratitude.

The Hebrew *brakhah* formally articulates our gratitude

▣ A message of this blessing struck me with full force for the first time on a farm in Iowa. Reciting these words there made me reflect that our ancestors were much more aware of and much closer to the soil than most Jews are today. It also served to renew my awareness of the partnership between Creator and creature which this blessing assumes. For the blessing is not recited over untreated wheat or other grain, the Creator's gift. It is recited over baked bread, a result of the divine/human partnership.—JH

⊛ The Babylonian Talmud, *Menahot* 43b states: "Rabbi Meir used to say, It is incumbent on each person to bless God in one hundred blessings daily, as written in Deuteronomy 10:12, 'And now, Israel, what *(mah)* does *Adonai* your God require of you?'" Rabbi Meir here ➤

and praise. It provides us with a way of saying "thank you" to our Creator. The Talmud teaches, "It is forbidden to benefit from this world without uttering a *brakhah*" (Babylonian Talmud, *Brakhot* 35a–b). We did not bring this world into being, and it is not ours: "The earth is the Lord's, and the fullness therein" (Psalms 24:1). God has allowed us to benefit from it, and we must not take its blessings for granted. The Talmud continues: "Anyone who benefits from this world without uttering a *brakhah* has transgressed" (Babylonian Talmud, *Brakhot* 35a–b). Such a person has enjoyed a gift without saying "thank you."

When we recite a *brakhah*, we express not only our gratitude for a specific gift. Reciting a *brakhah* reflects our awareness of the bounty the world holds for us. Rabbi Abraham Joshua Heschel taught: "The surest way to suppress our ability to understand the meaning of God and the importance of worship is to take things for granted."[3] He went even further by declaring: "Indifference to the sublime wonder of living is the root of sin."

Peter Davison, a modern poet, also has given us a reminder:

> There's only one surprise—
> to be alive—and that
> may be forgotten daily
> if daily not remembered.[4]

Whether we recite one *brakhah* or one hundred *brakhot* ⊛ each day, the experience can heighten our awareness of the wonders in our daily lives and help us to respond to them with gratitude. Since reciting a *brakhah* reflects an awareness of what has been given to us, we could call a *brakhah* a not-taking-for-granted. We need to reinforce this lesson daily, since too often we do take things for granted.

Allow me to share a personal example. During a hospital stay I was fed only intravenously for several days following surgery. My first solid meal was mashed potatoes and asparagus spears. In my mind's eye, I still can see the grains of salt on the asparagus. I savored every morsel and I vowed that never again would I take anything for granted. Two or three days later I complained that the tea was not hot enough. Members of my family breathed a sigh of relief and said, "He's returning to normal."

To spend our lives enthusiastically acclaiming the wonders of the world would be unnatural. Yet if we never acknowledge the good things that are ours, we are ungrateful, and we can become deadened to an awareness of life's precious gifts. Reciting a *brakhah* helps to restore the balance. ❈

What words should a *brakhah* contain? In what form do we express our awareness and our gratitude? For an answer, we turn first to the Bible. From our examination, we shall see that the *brakhah* has not always existed in its present form. The *brakhot* we recite result from development within Jewish tradition.[6]

interprets the word "what" or *mah* as though it were *me'ah*, which means "one hundred." Hence, Rabbi Meir's interpretation: Israel, one hundred [is the number of blessings that] *Adonai* your God requires of you.—JH

❈ Jewish prayer is prayer that uses the idiom of the Hebrew Bible and reflects the Jewish soul. It is prayer that expresses the basic values of the Jewish people and affirms the central articles of Jewish faith. It is prayer that reflects our historical experiences and gives expression to our future aspirations. When the prayer of a Jewish person does not reflect one of these components, he may be praying, but it cannot be said that he is praying as a Jew.

A Jew may choose his own words when praying to God; but when he uses the words of the *siddur*, he becomes part of a people. He identifies with Jews everywhere who use the same words and express the same thoughts. He affirms the principal of mutual responsibility and concern. He takes his place at the dawn of history as he binds himself to Abraham, Isaac, and Jacob. He asserts his rights to a Jewish future in this world and to personal redemption in the world to come.

Whatever is special about Jewish theology, whatever is special about Jewish values, whatever is special about Jewish history—is also special about Jewish prayer.

One final thought. Attending synagogue services and praying are often thought of as one and the same. It is assumed that a person who does one also does the other. This assumption should be valid, but it is not, especially today. One may pray, and pray daily, but do so privately, outside the framework of the synagogue. On the other hand, there are those who come to the synagogue to attend the services but do not engage in prayer. They come in response to an invitation by a host family to join it in celebrating a bar mitzvah or some other event. They come to watch, not to pray. There is hardly a rabbi who has not at one time experienced the empty feeling of having a packed synagogue consisting mostly of people who sit politely and quietly, watching services, sometimes not even bothering to open a prayer book. These people may be "attending services," but they are not participating in prayer. Being a spectator at a Jewish worship service is not the same as being a worshiper. To be a worshiper requires a certain involvement, if only to answer "Amen" at certain points, if only for the heart to feel that it wants to be a part of what is being said.— *Rabbi Hayim Halevy Donin* [5]

If you tried to find examples of the *brakhah* in the Bible, your search would fail. The Bible, however, does contain the beginnings of what has become the traditional *brakhah* formula. In the Bible we read about individuals who reacted to God's world by uttering praise in a specific way. Consider the following examples.

In the Book of Genesis, Abraham sends his servant, Eliezer, to find a proper mate for Isaac, Abraham's son. Eliezer seeks a sign from heaven that will help him to identify the appropriate young woman. After the servant finds her, what does he say? How does he express his gratitude?

Blessed is the Lord
the God of my master Abraham
who has not withheld His steadfast love from my master. (Genesis 24:26–27)

Barukh Adonai
Elohei adoni Avraham
asher lo azav ḥasdo vaamito me'im adoni.

Soon after Moses and the Israelites emerge from Egyptian slavery, Moses meets his father-in-law, Jethro. Moses tells Jethro about the miraculous events that the Israelites have encountered on their journey from slavery to redemption, including everything that the Lord had done to Pharaoh in Egypt. How does Jethro respond?

Blessed is the Lord
who saved you from the hands of the Egyptians. (Exodus 18:10)

Barukh Adonai
asher hitzil etkhem miyad Mitzrayim.

King David encounters a man of great wealth, by the name of Naval, and requests that he supply provisions for the king's troops. Naval refuses. David prepares to attack Naval and his followers. Naval's wife Abigail hears about the possible confrontation and rushes to dissuade David. After Abigail convinces David that he should not attack, how does David express his relief?

Blessed is the Lord
the God of Israel
who sent you this day to meet me. (I Samuel 25:32)

Barukh Adonai
Elohei Yisrael
asher shlaḥekh bayom hazeh likrati.

After a complicated battle for succession, Solomon sits on his father's throne. How does David express gratitude?

**Blessed is the Lord
the God of Israel
who has given this day one to sit on my throne,
and my eyes have seen it. (I Kings 1:48)**

*Barukh Adonai
Elohei Yisrael
asher natan hayom yoshev al kisi ve'einai ro'ot.*

The ancient Israelites in Babylon yearn to return to Jerusalem. King Artaxerxes grants their leader Ezra permission to ascend to Jerusalem with appropriate offerings, along with materiel for rebuilding the Temple. How does Ezra react?

**Blessed is the Lord
the God of our ancestors
who has put this into the heart of the king to beautify the House of the Lord
which is in Jerusalem. (Ezra 7:27)**

*Barukh Adonai
Elohei avoteinu
asher natan kazot belev hamelekh lefaer et beit Adonai
asher biYrushalayim.*

Ruth, a widow, travels to the land of Israel with her mother-in-law Naomi, whose husband and sons have died. Without adequate means for survival, Ruth and Naomi require the assistance of what was known as a redeeming kinsman. Boaz fulfills this role, and he also marries Ruth. Ruth gives birth to a child, and the Israelite women express to Naomi their happiness.

**Blessed is the Lord
who has not withheld from
you a redeeming kinsman.
(Ruth 4:14)**

*Barukh Adonai
asher lo hishbit lakh go'el.*

▦ The pattern, "Blessed is the Lord" followed by a descriptive phrase, does not exist in all Biblical prayers. For example, Moses prays for his stricken sister Miriam: "Please, God, heal her" (*El na, refa na lah*, Numbers 12:13). Many psalms also beseech God directly, "Answer me, *Adonai*, according to Your great steadfastness" (Psalm 69:17). —JH

These examples show us the beginnings of a fixed pattern in the *brakhah*. A very short phrase ("Blessed is the Lord") begins a declaration, and a phrase describing God follows. ▦ This descriptive phrase varies from blessing to blessing according to each situation. Let's review some of the examples.

Blessed is the Lord / the God of my master Abraham
Blessed is the Lord / who saved you
Blessed is the Lord / the God of Israel
Blessed is the Lord / the God of our ancestors
Blessed is the Lord / who has not withheld from you

We find this pattern in both Biblical and early Rabbinic literature, as Professor Yosef Heinemann points out. In the Talmud we see the pattern in an incident from the life of Rabbi Yohanan ben Zakkai. He hears Rabbi Elazar ben Arakh, a student, deliver a brilliant public lesson on the prophet Ezekiel's vision, and Rabbi Yohanan ben Zakkai is overwhelmed with pleasure. How does he express his gratitude? "Blessed is the Lord, the God of Israel, who has given a son to Abraham our father, one who knows how to speculate and investigate and expound on the mystical vision of the divine chariot." *Barukh Adonai, Elohei Yisrael, shenatan ben leAvraham avinu she'yode'a lehavin ulehakor ulidrosh bemaaseh merkavah* (Babylonian Talmud, *Hagigah* 14b).

All of these examples use the same first phrase—"Blessed is the Lord" *(Barukh Adonai)*. That phrase, however, differs from the first phrase in the *brakhah* formula we use today. The examples in the Bible and Talmud make declarations *about* God. The *brakhah* that we use today addresses God directly: "Blessed are You" *(Barukh Attah)*. We see this in *hamotzi*: "Blessed are You *(Barukh Attah)*, Lord our God, King of the universe who brings forth bread from the earth."

Though we now take this second-person blessing for granted, it was a radical departure from standard usage in the Bible. The second-person address in a blessing occurs only twice in the *Tanakh*, the Hebrew Bible:

Blessed are You, Lord; teach me Your laws. (Psalms 119:12)

And David blessed the Lord in the presence of the entire assemblage. David said, "Blessed are You, Lord, the God of Israel, our Father, now and forever." ▨ **(I Chronicles 29:10)**

▨ The verse "Blessed are You, Lord, the God of Israel, our Father, now and forever" appears at the beginning of a passage that has been incorporated into the early part of the Morning Service.—JH

Why did the ancient Sages change the *brakhah* formula? Why did they alter the Bible's typical declaration about God to develop the *brakhah*, in which a person speaks directly to God? Professor Heinemann answers:

> Undoubtedly this gives expression to the inclination to give prayer, even fixed prayer, the quality of turning directly to God as in a conversation in which is revealed the intimate and personal relationship between the one who prays and his God.

With the addition of the word "You" *(Attah)*, the predominant Biblical formula ("Blessed is the Lord") changes to direct confrontation with God ("Blessed are You, Lord").

The change became a fixed part of Jewish liturgy over the course of time, and involved much discussion and argument. The Talmud recounts that two Sages of the third century, Rav and Shmuel, debated the addition of the word "You" to the *brakhah* formula (Jerusalem Talmud, *Brakhot* 12:4). Rav insisted that a *brakhah* include "You," as he maintained that we turn directly to God in a *brakhah*. Rav cites Psalms 16:8 as support: "I have set the Lord *before me* always" (Jerusalem Talmud, *Brakhot* 9:1). Rav's doctrine is theologically bold, and reflects the desire for a personal relationship with God. Mere creatures can address their Creator directly. Shmuel, however, maintained that a *brakhah* need not include *Attah*; when it does, it places mere mortals in too intimate a relationship with the Creator of the universe.

Apparently, before their debate, Jews used several different formulas for *brakhot*. All Jews have a religious obligation to utter a *brakhah* at the appropriate time, but what words should we use? If expressing gratitude is the main idea, perhaps the specific words do not matter. We learn, though, from the debate between Rav and Shmuel, that the words are important indeed. The Sages agreed on the need to establish a norm, a legal standard to which all must adhere, but they initially differed about the wording of that norm. Ultimately, Jewish law followed Rav's opinion. Thus, if we do not include the word *Attah* or "You," we do not fulfill our obligation to recite a *brakhah*. A person who recites words that differ from the established norm may have uttered something admirable, but has not fulfilled his or her religious obligation.

The opinion of Shmuel also found its way into the *brakhah* formula. (Decisions in Jewish legal tradition often reflect both sides to a debate.) The last part of the obligatory wording of the *brakhah*, following the mention of God as King of the universe, refers to God in the third person, thereby following the Bible's pattern. To consistently conform to Rav's opinion, we would state the entire *brakhah* in the second person. For example, "Blessed are You, Lord our God, King of the universe, for You bring forth bread from the earth." Instead, the *brakhah* as we know it is grammatically confusing. It switches from addressing God in the second person ("You") to referring to God in the third person ("who brings forth").

Scholars have discussed the inconsistent grammar of the *brakhah* for centuries. Simḥah ben Samuel, author of the 11th-century French *Maḥzor*

Vitry, ▦ compares the wording of the *brakhah* to the wording one uses in the presence of royalty. First we speak directly to the King (in the second person, as in "Your Majesty"). Later we use language that shows even more respect, maintaining distance, speaking as through an intermediary (in the third person, as in "His Majesty"). The author of *Mahzor Vitry* chooses the *brakhah* recited before drinking wine to illustrate.

▦ The *Mahzor Vitry* is a compilation of the liturgy and the laws governing the entire yearly cycle of prayer, as well as scholarly commentary and Rabbinic legends about the prayers. The *Mahzor Vitry* also includes laws for kosher slaughter, marriage, the Sabbath, and several other matters. Simhah ben Samuel, the author, was a disciple of Rashi (Rabbi Solomon ben Isaac, 1040–1105). Vitry is a town in northern France.—*JH*

✹ David ben Joseph Abudarham wrote a commentary on Jewish prayer, *Sefer Abudarham,* in 1340 in Seville. He stated that the customs of prayer among Jews varied from country to country, "and most of the people do not understand the words of the prayers, nor do they know the correct ritual procedures and the reasons for them."[7] His work contains a special section listing the rules that apply to *brakhot.*—*JH*

✼ Rabbi David Abudarham [states that] God is revealed in His actions of creation, which we can behold, but is hidden within Himself and cannot be seen. God, in essence, is beyond our comprehension. He is called *Ein Sof*—the Infinite. Therefore, we have this change from second to third person, from the unknown to the known. The mystery of the Being of God is beyond human comprehension, the domain of the universe is the creation of God and that area is for man to study in the sciences. In one sentence, we have a religious philosophy.— *Rabbi Leonard B. Gewirtz*[8]

> We say, "Blessed are You, Lord our God, King of the universe who creates (*borei*—third person) the fruit of the vine." …We do not say, "Blessed are You, Lord, who have created (*shebarata*—second person) the fruit of the vine." Thus, after we have addressed God directly ("Blessed are You") we must relate to Him as if through an intermediary ("who creates").

We find another explanation of the grammatical peculiarity of the *brakhah* in the writings of the 14th-century Spanish authority, Abudarham. ✹ He taught that the blessing's structure teaches us about the nature of God, who is both revealed to and concealed from mortals. God is revealed in His deeds and God is concealed by the mystery of His divinity, ✼ which is difficult or impossible for mortals to grasp. The *brakhah* formula reflects the nature of human beings as well.

> Mortals are a combination of body and soul. From the perspective of the human soul, it is appropriate for a person to cleave to his Maker, always standing before Him. From the perspective of the human body, however, a mortal cannot stand before God. Therefore the *brakhah,* uttered by mortals, uses language that is both direct [in the second person] and concealed [in the third person].

Dr. Max Kadushin, a twentieth-century scholar, considered such explanations inadequate. He wrote: "The attempt to make an idea specific when the Rabbis [of the Talmud] have not done so often results in the misinterpretation of a Rabbinic idea." Dr. Kadushin notes that the Rabbis in the

Talmud did not explain the change from second person to third person either rationally or philosophically, because they did not have a rational or a philosophical apprehension of God. They had, according to Dr. Kadushin, a mystical apprehension of God. When the medieval authorities discuss the *brakhah,* they understand the use of the second person and the third person as two separate ways of relating to God. Thus, they need to account for the change from second person to third person by associating each with a different idea.

Dr. Kadushin maintains, however, that the *brakhah* deals with what can only be described as a mystical consciousness, the consciousness of a relationship like no other, that is, the relationship of Creator and creature, immortal God and mortal human beings. The mystical consciousness is expressible to a point, but in a manner in which no other relationship is expressible.

> The *brakhah* formula thus enables the Rabbis and the people as a whole to express their consciousness of relationship to God.... It was nothing short of religious genius first to have achieved the *brakhah* formula and then to have made it the basic element of the prayers.[9]

The *brakhah* also requires an explicit statement of God's sovereignty. Thus the *brakhah* includes the words *Melekh haolam* ("King of the universe"). In the Babylonian Talmud, Rabbi Yohanan declared that, to meet the legal requirement, every *brakhah* must include that statement (*Brakhot* 40b). Discussions about this requirement refer to a verse from Psalm 145 (known in the prayer book as *Ashrei)*: "I will exalt You, my God, the King."[10] From the time of the Bible, the image of God as Sovereign, as King, has resonated in Jewish liturgy. The daily use of the image constantly reminds us that we owe ultimate allegiance only to God, ✳ not to a person, a nation, or a concept. According to Professor Heinemann and other scholars, the requirement grew out of a response to the idolatrous worship of the Roman emperor. The shapers of Jewish tradition considered such worship a perversion, and they demanded that Jews affirm daily that there is only one true Sovereign, and it is not Caesar.

Contemporary Jews have difficulty assigning such power and glory to the

✳ I will never forget the first time I was able to *daven* after my daughter's birth. In my recovery from a surgical delivery, I was too weak to *daven* for a full week after the baby's birth—a very long hiatus from *davenning* for me. When I was able to hold the *Siddur* in my hands once again, on the second Shabbat of my daughter's life, I found myself reaching out to a different God than ever before. I found myself talking not to an image of God as the God of law and command and blame, an image I had known so well throughout my childhood and rabbinic training. At that moment, I called out to God as the giver of life, the God of mothers and children, of love and care and nourishment, a God who would understand that there was sanctity in nursing and diaper changing and rocking and comforting as surely as there was sanctity in my encounter with the *siddur.* That night, for the first time in my life, I encountered a feminine image of God, who rejoiced in the birth of my daughter and my own rebirth as a mother. This is a gift that will be with me forever.— *Rabbi Amy Eilberg*[11]

word "king," because kings and emperors today serve merely as figure-heads. The designation "king" seems inadequate, since it is today assigned to individuals who no longer hold absolute power. ▣ (This objection applies equally to the words "sovereign" and "ruler," which many substitute for "king" in prayer book trans-lations.) Nonetheless, to continue the tradition begun in the Bible and maintained by the ancient Rabbis and succeeding generations, we continue to use the word *Melekh* (King) in Hebrew prayer as an image of God's dominion and supremacy.

Translations in many prayer books substitute "the Eternal" for "Lord" and "Sovereign" or "Ruler" for "King." Translators make these substitutions to eliminate references to gender in English, hence avoiding the words "King" and "Lord," which are masculine in gender. They also prefer to avoid the pro-nouns "He," "Him," and "His." Those who pray in Hebrew using these prayer books, however, continue to use Hebrew gender-specific words such as *Melekh* (King) as well as the masculine gender pronouns, because Hebrew has no words that are gender neutral. (For further discussion of this topic, see Chapter 10, pages 205–219.)

In the slightly longer version of the *brakhah* that we recite before ful-filling a commandment *(mitzvah)*, we add a phrase that articulates anoth-er dimension of the relationship between God and the people Israel. After the words "Blessed are You, Lord our God, King of the universe," we add "who made us holy through His commandments" *(asher kiddshanu bemitzvotav)*. ✸ In Judaism, the condition of being holy is available to all. The Jewish religion does not limit holiness to elders, scholars, the strin-gently pious, or any other special category. Since Biblical times, God has commanded the entire people Israel to be a holy people *(am kadosh)*. We are to attain that status by fulfilling the *mitzvot*, the commandments. Each of us can be as holy as we allow ourselves to be. Reciting *asher kiddshanu bemitzvotav* should remind us of the connection between God, holiness, and our lives, and of the many ways (through the performance and fulfill-ment of *mitzvot*) that we may attain holiness. The Bible teaches us how to be human and holy,[13] a concept that post-Biblical literature and tradi-tion continue to expand.

▣ [Kol Haneshamah, *the Reconstructionist prayer book, replaces both the English and the Hebrew phrase for "King of the world" in the bless-ings that begin the* Shaharit *service.*] The familiar introductory formula for blessings, which includes the phrase *melekh haolam*/sovereign of the world, was adopted by the Rabbis during the Talmudic era and uni-versally accepted by later Jews. Substituting another Rabbinic phrase, *hai haolamim*/life of all the worlds, expresses the idea that as Judaism continues to evolve, alternatives to the ancient metaphor of God as divine ruler should emerge.... The "worlds" to which *hai haolamim* refers may be the many universes that each of us inhabits, the vast spaces that surround our world, or the infinite depths that fill the human heart. We proclaim that God is the single flow of life that inhabits and unifies them all.—*Rabbi Arthur Green*[12]

✸ Other English versions of *asher kiddshanu bemitzvotav* include "who sanctified us with His commandments" and "whose commandments (or *mitzvot*) add holiness to our lives."—*JH*

Asher kiddshanu bemitzvotav. These words should also remind us that a Jew in prayer is never alone, for these words are phrased in the first-person plural—"who made US holy." The plural here reinforces the fourth Hebrew word of the *brakhah—Eloheinu,* "OUR God." Even alone, without anyone else nearby, a Jew prays in the first-person *plural,* praising our God (not *my* God) who made us holy (not who made *me* holy). Whenever and wherever we utter a *brakhah,* we affirm our connection with the people Israel as well as with our Creator, and with the entire people Israel throughout the world and throughout time.

The *brakhah* recited while putting on a *tallit* (prayer shawl) furnishes an example of a *brakhah* recited before fulfilling a commandment. "Blessed are You, Lord our God, King of the universe who has made us holy through His commandments, commanding us to wrap ourselves in *tzitzit.*" (*Tzitzit* are the ritual fringes at the four corners of the prayer shawl. *Barukh Attah Adonai Eloheinu Melekh haolam, asher kiddshanu bemitzvotav vetzivanu lehitatef batzitzit.)*

The *brakhot* recited before eating bread or before drinking wine or grape juice are examples of *birkhot hane-henin,* blessings recited before enjoying food, drink, or fragrances. ✳ When smelling a mixture of fragrant spices, one says:

Blessed are You, Lord our God, King of the universe who creates different kinds of spices. (*Barukh Attah Adonai Eloheinu Melekh haolam, borei minei vesamim.)*

Most complete Jewish prayer books contain a section that lists such blessings as well as *brakhot* that we recite in response to natural phenomena ✳ and to events in our lives. For example, when hearing thunder or experiencing a storm, we say:

Blessed are You, Lord our God, King of the universe whose power and might fill the world. (*Barukh Attah Adonai Eloheinu Melekh haolam, shekoho u-gevurato malei olam.)*

✳ Ideally, every act and pleasure should be undertaken with an awareness that it is God who is being served and God who dispenses to us our needs and desires. In order to help inculcate this awareness in the Jewish people, the Sages, from the time of Ezra and his court, composed the various blessings and ordained the occasions upon which they must be recited. The very fact that the day is filled with events that require blessings provides constant inspiration. The thinking person [is] drawn ever closer to the loving God by the awareness that every delicious morsel and soothing drink affords a fresh opportunity to recognize and thank the Giver of all.—*Rabbi Nosson Scherman*[14]

✳ The dominion granted to humanity in the creation story [of Genesis] properly entails tending the land loaned to us by God rather than exploiting the land for our own gain. When we recognize that we are only tenants on this earth, bound together with the rest of its creatures in an enduring covenant, we gain a deep appreciation for the beauty and complexity of the natural world. Our Jewish tradition affirms that covenant—and the sense of awe and thanksgiving it inspires—through a series of *brakhot* or blessings. By saying *brakhot,* we acknowledge our covenantal responsibility and assert that the creation points to the presence of a Creator…. The very first section of the entire Mishnah is called *Brakhot.* It is … the source of most of the *brakhot* over nature's wonders.—*Rabbi Daniel B. Fink*[15]

When seeing a rainbow, one refers to the covenant that God made with Noah after the flood, and says:

Blessed are You, Lord our God, King of the universe who remembers the covenant, is faithful to the covenant, and keeps His promise. (*Barukh Attah Adonai Eloheinu Melekh haolam, zokheir habrit vene'eman bivrito vekayam bemaamaro.*)

When seeing fruit trees blossoming for the first time each year, one says:

Blessed are You, Lord our God, King of the universe whose world lacks nothing, who created in it beautiful creatures and beautiful trees for mortals to enjoy. (*Barukh Attah Adonai Eloheinu Melekh haolam, shelo hisar baolamo davar, uvara vo briyyot tovot ve'ilanot tovim lehannot bahem bnei adam.*)

When seeing creatures of unusual beauty, one says:

Blessed are You, Lord our God, King of the universe who has such in His world. (*Barukh Attah Adonai Eloheinu Melekh haolam, shekkakhah lo baolamo.*)

When seeing a person who possesses outstanding Jewish religious scholarship, one says:

Blessed are You, Lord our God, King of the universe who has shared His wisdom with those who revere Him. (*Barukh Attah Adonai Eloheinu Melekh haolam, shehalak mehokhmato lire'av.*)

When seeing a person who possesses outstanding scholarship in secular subjects, one says:

Blessed are You, Lord our God, King of the universe who has given of His wisdom to flesh and blood. (*Barukh Attah Adonai Eloheinu Melekh haolam, shennatan mehokhmato l'vasar vadam.*)

When seeing a head of state, one says:

Blessed are You, Lord our God, King of the universe who has given of His glory to flesh and blood. (*Barukh Attah Adonai Eloheinu Melekh haolam, shennatan mikkvodo l'vasar vadam.*)

When hearing good news, one says:

Blessed are You, Lord our God, King of the universe, the essence of goodness who brings goodness. (*Barukh Attah Adonai Eloheinu Melekh haolam, hattov vehammetiv.*)

When hearing bad news, one says:

Blessed are You, Lord our God, King of the universe, the true Judge. *(Barukh Attah Adonai Eloheinu Melekh haolam, dayan ha'emet.)*

The *dayan ha'emet* blessing is also recited by a mourner just before a funeral. The blessing thus differs from the other blessings in that it does not reflect gratitude. Instead it articulates the acceptance of God's decrees, which are beyond human understanding.

Before wearing new clothes, before eating a seasonal fruit in a new season, upon reciting *kiddush* on the first night of a Festival, and upon reaching a significant occasion in life, one says:

Blessed are You, Lord our God, King of the universe who has kept us in life and sustained us and helped us to reach this time. *(Barukh Attah Adonai Eloheinu Melekh haolam, shehehe'yanu vikimanu vehigiyanu lazman hazeh.)*

Most *brakhot* that are part of formal liturgical services are longer than one or two lines, as we shall see in the following chapters.

QUESTIONS FOR FURTHER STUDY AND REFLECTION

1. Define and explain what a *brakhah* is, both in the narrowest sense and in the broadest sense. How would you teach a child about a *brakhah*?
2. Have you wanted to thank God? When? Have you wanted to challenge God with a question? Why?
3. Grammatically, the *brakhah* directly confronts God. What does this direct confrontation mean to you?
4. What does the image of God as King or as Sovereign mean to you? Is there a different image of God that has greater meaning for you? If there is, explain its meaning for you. (Consider these questions again after reading Chapter 10, "Women's Spiritual Alternatives.")
5. Jews believe that human beings are created in the image of God. How would you explain this concept to a child? How would you explain it to a non-Jew?
6. What does "holiness" mean?
7. How would you incorporate more holiness into your life and the life of your family?
8. The *brakhah* is a response to life. Why should anyone care to respond to life?
9. "The words of the prayer book form the core of Jewish religion, and they reflect the essence of what it means to be a Jew." Many Jews would assert that the Torah, not the prayer book, reflects the essence of Jewish religion. For example, the Torah is much more ancient than the prayer

book, and its words are attributed to God. In addition, the text of the Torah has remained unchanged over millennia. The same cannot be said for the prayer book. Which book do you place at the heart of the Jewish religion?

1. Cited in *Franz Rosenzweig: His Life and Thought* by Nahum M. Glatzer (Philadelphia: Jewish Publication Society, 1953), page 251.

2. Henry Slonimsky, *Essays* (Cincinnati/Chicago: Hebrew Union College Press/Quadrangle, 1967) page 120; reprinted in *Gates of Prayer: The New Union Prayerbook: Weekdays, Sabbaths, and Festivals, Services and Prayers for Synagogue and Home* (New York: Central Conference of American Rabbis, 1975), page 6.

3. Abraham Joshua Heschel, *God in Search of Man: A Philosophy of Judaism* (New York: Farrar, Straus & Cudahy, 1955), page 43.

4. Peter Davison, "After Being Away" in *Pretending to Be Asleep* (New York: Atheneum, 1970), page 3. See also Peter Davison, *The Poems of Peter Davison, 1957-1995* (New York: Knopf, 1995).

5. Rabbi Hayim Halevy Donin, *To Pray As a Jew* (New York: Basic Books/Harper-Collins, 1980), page 7.

6. The following examples from the Bible and from Rabbinic literature are found in Joseph Heinemann, *Prayer in the Talmud: Forms and Patterns* (Berlin, New York: Walter de Gruyter, 1977), chapter three.

7. *Sefer Abudarham*, cited by Zvi Avneri and editors, "Abudarham, David ben Joseph," *Encyclopaedia Judaica*, volume 2, page 181.

8. Rabbi Leonard B. Gewirtz, "Jewish Theology in One Sentence: The *B'rakhah*," *Shofar* 30:10 (June 2001); at www.akse.org/200106/page8.html. *Shofar* is the newsletter of Adas Kodesch Shel Emeth Congregation of Delaware.

9. Max Kadushin, *The Rabbinic Mind* (New York: Jewish Theological Seminary, 1952), pages 269-270.

10. Jerusalem Talmud, *Brakhot* 9:1.

11. Amy Eilberg, "The Gifts of First Fruits" in *Four Centuries of Jewish Women's Spirituality*, Ellen M. Umansky and Dianne Ashton, eds. (Boston: Beacon Press, 1992), page 284.

12. Rabbi Arthur Green, "Commentary" and "Derash" in *Kol Haneshamah: Shabbat Vehagim*, 3rd ed. (Wyncote, PA: Reconstructionist Press, 1996), page 153.

13. Words ascribed to Abraham Joshua Heschel.

14. Rabbi Nosson Scherman, commentary on "Blessings" in *The ArtScroll Siddur: Weekday/Sabbath/Festival* (Brooklyn: Mesorah, 1984), page 224.

15. Rabbi Daniel B. Fink, "Creation, Covenant and Ecology" in *Judaism and Ecology: A Hadassah Study Guide in Cooperation with Shomrei Adamah, Keepers of the Earth* (New York: Hadassah, 1993), pages 29-30.

SHAHARIT, THE MORNING SERVICE

To tell of Your love each morning

Daily routine can overwhelm our appreciation of the miraculous, yet each of us experiences the miraculous every day. Through early morning prayer, we greet each day with gratitude for our daily renewal in the continuing miracle of life. Prayer begins as soon as we awaken from sleep.

I am grateful to You *(modeh/modah ani lefanekha)*, living, enduring King, for restoring my soul to me in compassion. Great is Your faithfulness.

God's faithfulness is great, but so is human suffering, and this often challenges our faith. Though the prayer book excels in praise of God, it also includes passages that express this challenge. Psalm 90 (page 33), for example, articulates questions about afflictions and the brevity of human life. In spite of life's misfortunes, Judaism does not succumb to despair.[1] Rabbi Aharon Roth (Reb Arele, of Jerusalem, 1894–1944) taught that when an individual finds prayer impossible at a particular time, silence is also an appropriate response.[2] Silence is preferable to violating our intellectual or spiritual integrity.

BIRKHOT HASHAHAR (MORNING BLESSINGS)

This passage is to be recited upon entering a sanctuary.

How lovely are your sanctuaries, people of Jacob, your prayer houses, descendants of Israel. ▨ Your great love inspires me to enter Your house, to worship in Your holy sanctuary. I love Your house, the place of Your glory. Before my Maker do I bow in worship, bending the knee. I pray that this be an acceptable time for my prayer. God, Your love is great; answer me with Your true deliverance.

▨ "How lovely are your sanctuaries … your prayer houses" is an interpretive translation of Numbers 24:5. The Hebrew was first uttered by the non-Israelite prophet, Balaam, who had been hired to curse the people Israel. Some authorities opposed the inclusion in the prayer book of any words that he uttered. Jewish liturgy includes them nevertheless, since he, who set out to curse, ended by praising the Israelites. A Rabbinic source states that Balaam changed his mind after noticing the layout of the Israelite camp, which ensured privacy for each family, reflecting their sense of moral propriety. A literal translation of the verse reads: "How lovely are your *tents*, O Jacob, your *dwellings*, O Israel." The translation here, appropriate for the setting of prayer in a synagogue, is based on an interpretation of the verse in the Babylonian Talmud, *Sanhedrin* 105b.—JH

Early in the Morning Service, whether alone or with a congregation, we recite blessings while putting on *tallit* (prayer shawl) and *tefillin*. Psalms 104:1–2 offers words for reflection before putting on the *tallit*.

Let my whole being praise the Lord who is clothed in splendor and majesty, wrapped in light as in a garment, unfolding the heavens as a curtain.

As we put on the *tallit*, we recite a blessing:

Blessed are You, Lord our God, King of the universe who has made us holy through His commandments, commanding us to wrap ourselves in *tzitzit*.

When we look at the *tzitzit* (fringes) on the corners of the *tallit*, we should be reminded of all the *mitzvot* (commandments), as the Bible states: "Thus you will remember to observe all My commandments and be holy to your God" (Numbers 15:40).

In recent years many women, as well as men, have taken upon themselves the obligation to wear *tzitzit*. According to some Rabbinic sources, *tzitzit* were worn in Talmudic times by women and men, and some Rabbis stated that women are required to fulfill the commandment of *tzitzit*.[3] According to the *Shulḥan Arukh*, women are not obligated to wear *tzitzit* (*Oraḥ Ḥayyim* 17:2). A note there (by Rabbi Moses Isserles, the *Rema*) explains that women are nevertheless *permitted* to wear *tzitzit* if they wish, and should recite the appropriate blessing. He continues, though, by stating that women should *not* wear *tzitzit*.

Some women today wear *tzitzit* on a standard *tallit*. ✹ Others fulfill the commandment by wearing a colorful shawl or a cape-type garment to which *tzitzit* are attached. One image that remains in my mind symbolizes something of the significance of women wearing a *tallit*. Several years ago, at an egalitarian *minyan*, I watched with fascination as a young girl played with the *tzitziyot* (plural of *tzitzit*) on the *tallit* of her mother. That youngster is growing up with a set of assumptions that differ even from those of her mother's childhood. Many people remember playing with the *tzitziyot* on the *tallit* of their fathers or grandfathers only. We have witnessed and are witnessing irreversible changes in attitudes and assumptions on the part of both men and women.

> ✹ When I *daven* in *tallit* and *tefillin*, I am not trying to make a feminist gesture or prove that I can "pray like a man." I began to observe these *mitzvot* out of a desire to serve God by fulfilling God's commandments. It never occurred to me that the need to be reminded of God's presence in regular, concrete ways was limited to men. I felt, and still feel, that every *mitzvah* I perform strengthens the bond between me and my Creator.—*Dvora E. Weisberg*[4]

Following a meditation, we wind the *tefillin* designated for the hand seven times around the arm while reciting:

Blessed are You, Lord our God, King of the universe who has made us holy through His commandments, commanding us to put on *tefillin*.

Before we wrap *tefillin* for the hand around the middle fingers and the hand, we put on *tefillin* designated for the head while reciting:

Blessed are You, Lord our God, King of the universe who has made us holy through His commandments, commanding us about the *mitzvah* of *tefillin*.

After we have placed *tefillin* on our head, we recite:

Blessed be God's sovereignty throughout all time.

As we wind the hand *tefillin* strap around the middle fingers we recite verses from Hosea 2:21–22.

I will betroth you to Me forever, I will betroth you with righteousness, with justice, with love, and with compassion. I will betroth you to Me with faithfulness, and you shall love the Lord.

Tefillin are a sign of the covenant between God and the people Israel (a covenant that includes women as well as men). *Tefillin* symbolize the deep mutual affection and devotion between Creator and creature. We do not wear *tefillin* on Shabbat or Festivals, because these days themselves are signs of the covenant.[5]

We express gratitude for the gift of the body.

Blessed are You, Lord our God, King of the universe who has fashioned the human being with wisdom, creating diverse ducts and diverse veins. It is well known before Your glorious throne that should one of them open or one of them close it would be impossible to live, to stand in Your presence. ▦ Blessed are You, Healer of all flesh who performs wonders.[6]

▦ This blessing expresses wonder at the simple but necessary functioning of the human body. We do not need to stand before any greater wonder of nature than our own bodies in order to appreciate the intricacy and beauty with which our world is endowed. A sense of awe at our own creation is a starting point of prayer.—*Rabbi Arthur Green*[7]

⊛ [In her Morning Blessing, Marcia Falk expresses thankfulness for awakening after sleep:]
The breath of my life
will bless,

the cells of my being
sing

in gratitude,
reawakening.
          —*Marcia Falk*[8]

▨ *Barukh Attah Adonai, hamahazir neshamot lifgarim metim* is the Hebrew for "Blessed are You, Lord who restores souls to lifeless bodies." In context, the blessing refers not to resurrection of the dead *(metim)* but simply to the daily revival of the body after sleep.—*JH*

✳ The first section of [the *Shaharit* service] belongs to the World of Action [the first of four worlds described in Kabbalistic lore; the World of Action corresponds to the physical world] in every sense, serving as a means of preparation for reaching the higher levels. It contains benedictions of thanksgiving related to everyday matters *(Birkhot Hashahar)*, ➤

After blessings of gratitude and praise for the gift of Torah, we read and reflect on a few short passages from the Bible and Rabbinic literature (not reproduced here). Then we express gratitude for the gift of the soul.

My God, the soul which You have given me is pure. You created it in me, You breathed it into me and You maintain it within me. In the future You will take it from me, to restore it to me in time to come. So long as the soul is within me, I give thanks to You, ⊛ Lord my God and God of my ancestors, Master of all worlds, Lord of all souls. Blessed are You, Lord who restores souls to lifeless bodies. ▨

The Christian doctrine of original sin is alien to Jewish thought. Some writers have suggested that the phrase "original virtue" better reflects the Jewish teachings on human origins and potential, even as the Jewish perspective maintains that humans are less than perfect. Each human soul, at the beginning, reflects the purity of the Creator (Babylonian Talmud, *Brakhot* 10a). Each human being has a fresh start in life, with no reflection or intimation of sinfulness.

The Talmud provides the source for a group of blessings that we recite as we begin each new day (Babylonian Talmud, *Brakhot* 60b).✳

When hearing the sound of the rooster, one should say, "Blessed the One who has given the rooster ▓ intelligence to distinguish between day and night." [Some prefer the translation "who enables His creatures to distinguish between day and night."] When opening the eyes, one should say, "Blessed the One who gives sight to the blind." When sitting up [after having been comparatively motionless during sleep] one should say, "Blessed the One who releases the bound." While getting dressed one should say, "Blessed the One who clothes the naked." When stretching up one should say, "Blessed the One who raises the downtrodden." When putting one's feet on the ground one should say, "Blessed the One who establishes the land upon the water." When walking one should say, "Blessed the One who directs the steps of mortals" [literally, of man]. When putting on one's shoes one should say, "Blessed the One who has provided for all my needs." ✺ When putting on a belt one should say, "Blessed the One who girds the people Israel with strength." When putting on headgear one should say, "Blessed the One who crowns the people Israel with glory." When putting on *tzitzit* [that is, the *tallit*], one should say, "Blessed the One who has made us holy with His *mitzvot*, commanding us to wrap ourselves in *tzitzit*." When putting *tefillin* on the arm one should say, "Blessed the One who made us holy with His *mitzvot*, commanding us to put on *tefillin*." When putting *tefillin* on the head one should say, "Blessed the One who made us holy with His *mitzvot*, commanding us about the *mitzvah* of *tefillin*." When rinsing the hands one should say, "Blessed the One who made us holy with His *mitzvot*, commanding us to rinse the hands." When rinsing the face one should say, "Blessed the One ▓ who removes sleep from my eyes and slumber from my eyelids."

words of meditation, [and] selections from the Bible and the Talmud…. In general, the main purpose of this section is to begin the day and to enter into prayer by reading words of Torah. There is little here for spiritual elevation as such; it is mostly a means of preparation for prayer. The Mishnah records that in olden times, pious men used to spend an hour before worship in preparing their hearts for prayer (*Brakhot* 5:1). In a similar spirit, our Sages have said in the Talmud that "one does not stand up to pray either in a mood of laziness, or mirth … nor in trivial occupation, but only in a state of joy in performing a *mitzvah* [commandment]."—*Rabbi Adin Steinsaltz*[9]

▓ The Hebrew of the blessing that distinguishes day from night—*asher natan lasekhvi vinah lehav*h*in ben yom uven lailah*—is based on Job 38:36, *mi natan lasekhvi vinah*, literally "who has given to the heart understanding," and which has nothing to do with roosters. The Hebrew *sekhvi* means "heart," which was believed to be the organ of understanding and intelligence, by means of which we are able to discern the passage from night to day each morning. Since the word *sekhvi* in Arabic means "rooster" some authorities decided that the *brakhah* be associated with hearing the rooster in the morning. As a result, many translators understand that the *brakhah* refers to the rooster's intelligence.—*JH*

✺ Because the person who is barefoot cannot go about to earn wages, the Rabbis of the Talmud associate putting on our shoes with the fulfillment of our material needs.—*JH*

▓ Though the Talmud reads, "Blessed the One," the prayer book replaces it with the formula "Blessed are You, Lord our God, King of the universe." The Rabbis who composed Jewish liturgy determined that every blessing must address God directly (as "You") and refer to God as King.—*JH*

Some authorities insisted that each of the *brakhot* listed in this Talmud passage be recited only while carrying out the action described. That, however, did not become Jewish practice (except for the blessings on *tallit, tefillin,* and the rinsing of hands and face). Maimonides, among others, declared that the *brakhot* must be recited publicly in the synagogue, because most Jews lacked the education that would have enabled them to recite the *brakhot* alone at home. Consequently, these *brakhot* begin our public Morning Service. ▨ The leader of the service recites them, and to each *brakhah* those assembled answer "Amen."

Three additional early morning *brakhot*, not mentioned in the Talmudic passage from *Brakhot* 60b, have become a matter of controversy within the Jewish community:

▨ The transference of these blessings [that celebrate such acts of awakening as focusing the eyes, sitting up, and stretching] to the public worship service (ninth century) disengaged the blessing and the particular act of awakening with which it was joined. In their public setting, the morning blessings took on a new level of meaning. Removed from the acts of awakening, individual activities became metaphors for Godly action. The blessing "who clothes the naked" ceased to be a pointed acknowledgment of personal possessions and personal protection. Instead it became a celebration of God as the power that prompts the care and nurturance of humankind. The blessing "who raises the lowly" ceased to be a blessing over the renewal of physical mobility and became a blessing of the divine presence manifest in actions that raise the bodies and elevate the spirits of those who are low.—*Steven Sager* [10]

✺ In the rigidly stratified society in which these prayers [*Birkhot Hasha<u>h</u>ar*] originated, people were less conscious of identity than of status. Thus, the original forms of these prayers expressed the thankfulness of the most privileged members of the community—free Jewish males—that they did not have the less privileged status of women, slaves, or non-Jews.

The blessings we now use affirm that since we embody the divine image, we are all intrinsically valuable. To degrade or enslave others ➤

Blessed are You, Lord our God, King of the universe who has not made me a woman *(shelo asani ishah)*.

Blessed are You, Lord our God, King of the universe who has not made me a slave *(shelo asani aved)*.

Blessed are You, Lord our God, King of the universe who has not made me a gentile *(shelo asani goy)*.

Many have opposed these *brakhot* because they imply that individuals in the three categories—women, slaves and non-Jews—are of an inferior status. Others have opposed the *brakhot* because they are stated in the negative. No one finds satisfaction in the explanation that women, slaves, and non-Jews have fewer obligations which they are commanded to fulfill than Jewish men—who therefore express gratitude for the privilege of fulfilling a larger number of *mitzvot*.

The Conservative and Reconstructionist movements have changed these *brakhot* in their prayer books, and substitute three *brakhot* that bless God for having "created me in His image" *(she'asani betzalmo)*, "for having created me a Jew" *(she'asani Yisrael)*, and "for having created me free" *(she'asani ben/bat <u>h</u>orin)*. ✺ ▨ The Reform *Gates of Prayer* includes two of these revised blessings in the Shabbat service, and the newest Reform *siddur* will include its own version of all three. Orthodox

prayer books continue to use the three *brakhot* as first introduced on page 22. They also add a *brakhah* to be recited by women to replace the first:"Blessed are You, Lord our God, King of the universe who has created me according to His will." ✳ *Barukh Attah Adonai Eloheinu Melekh ha'olam she'asani kirtzono.*

Following the list of short blessings, the Talmud passage concludes with an extended prayer that has been incorporated almost entirely into *Birkhot Hashahar.* 🕮

May it be Your will, Lord my God, to make me feel at home with Your Torah and to make me cling to Your commandments. Bring me not to sin or transgression, to temptation or disgrace. Subdue my evil impulse to Your service. Keep me far from wicked people and wicked companions. Help me cleave to the good impulse and to good companions in Your world. Today and every day help me find grace, kindness, and compassion in Your sight and in the sight of all who see me, and grant me a full measure of kindness. Blessed are You, Lord who grants a full measure of kindness to His people Israel.

The Morning Service continues with several passages; only one of them is included in this volume.

is to deface the image of God. We are created free just as our Creator is free. We are capable of choice, of invention, and of transformation in our lives and in our world. We also give thanks for our particular identity as Jews. God, who creates our common humanity, also cherishes human diversity. Each people is unique and precious.—*Rachel Adler* [11]

🕮 The Conservative movement introduced these blessings—"created me in His image," "created me a Jew," and "created me free"—in 1946 in the Sabbath and Festival Prayer Book.—JH

✳ The blessing "who has created me according to His will" was introduced in medieval times, and is not found in the Talmud. In the 19th century, an Orthodox scholar in Germany, Avraham Berliner, suggested that one *brakhah* be recited instead of the three controversial ones: Blessed are You, Lord our God, King of the universe who has made me a Jew *(she'asani Yisrael).* This formulation is found in the Talmud as well as in later sources (replacing the negative: who has not made me a *goy*). Apparently, Berliner felt that reciting it would obviate the necessity of reciting the other, negative, *brakhot* under discussion as well as the *brakhah* formulated for women.—JH

🕮 Creating Sacred Space

The morning blessings (*Birkhot Hashahar*) repeatedly thank God for returning our souls to us, for enabling us after a night of sleep to rise and conduct spiritual lives once again. In the *modeh ani* we say, "You have restored my soul with mercy," and in the *Elohai* passage we reiterate that theme, "So long as the soul is within me I give thanks to You, my God." The morning blessings include as well the blessings over Torah study (*birkhot haTorah*): With our souls re-engaged, we can now proceed to the study of sacred literature. All of these blessings set the tone and prepare us for the act of prayer. Along with the actual recital of the prayers comes a law that has fallen into neglect, how one physically creates preparedness. This preparation is an integral part and objective of the morning blessings.

Maimonides recommends eight acts that create physical preparedness for prayer. Perhaps we can call this the creation of sacred space soon to be filled with sacred words. One must stand, face the Temple of old in Jerusalem when directing one's prayers, make sure one's body is in no discomfort and that one is properly dressed. In addition, one should prepare a physical space that is conducive to prayer, make sure one's voice is able to project the prayers, and make sure that one is able to prostrate and bow in the appropriate places ➤

You [God] are the One existing before creation and since creation, in this world and in the world to come. Show the holiness of Your being through those who hallow You, show the holiness of Your being throughout Your world; with Your deliverance raise us to dignity and strength. Praised are You, Lord, manifesting Your holiness to all humanity.

(*Mishneh Torah, Laws of Prayer* 5:1). In describing what is meant by preparing a place conducive to prayer, Maimonides cites the Talmud (*Brakhot* 27a), which requires a space of four cubits (about six feet) between people engaged in prayer. Allowing that much space would require quite a dramatic change in synagogue architecture, but the principle underlying the law is, nevertheless, important. Although our prayers are recited in the voice of the community, our posture should be one of the individual. Privacy of thought, and ensuring that we extend that sense of privacy to others, is an important way that we prepare for prayer. Creating a spiritual force field or white space around us means both that other people cannot enter and that we have made room around us to share that space with God alone.

The *Shulhan Arukh* expresses this prayer requirement in the negative rather than the positive: It is "forbidden to pass another engaged in prayer within four cubits" when walking in front of another individual (*Orah Hayyim* 102:4). We must be careful not to distract others from the difficult task of entering the realm of prayer. The Talmud (*Brakhot* 31b) bases this ruling on Hannah's statement in I Samuel 1:26; she identifies herself to the high priest Eli when she brings her son, Samuel, to him for a lifetime of service: "Please, my lord. As you live, my lord, I am the woman who stood here beside you and prayed to the Lord." By saying that Hannah stood beside Eli and prayed, the Talmud infers that Eli respected Hannah's prayer space. Even within close physical proximity to others, we should be able to mentally transport ourselves elsewhere if others are respectful of our "four cubits" or personal sacred space.

Creating personal sacred space and respecting that of others is one of the great challenges of contemporary synagogue life. Because the synagogue is the hub of the Jewish community, it fulfills an important social role. However, the social dimension can sometimes obstruct the privacy that authentic prayer demands. We may not always be sensitive to the genuine need of the person beside us to pray, and we may invade his or her sacred space with our mundane banter. Conversely, we may ourselves feel uncomfortable looking too pious; we may be distracted by the joy of seeing friends or by new, attractive suits or by the late arrival of a fellow congregant. Our services may be conducted with so much emphasis on group activity that we fail to find in an hour's time one minute of quiet mental repose. It is then that we may have to wait until the community leaves and we find ourselves alone in the pews with the light of the *ner tamid* as our only company; only then will we locate some personal sacred space. In a striking statement, the Sages of the Talmud declared that upon the destruction of the Temple, God occupies only four cubits of Jewish law in this world (*Brakhot* 8a). Most commentators understand that this represents a ➤

Orthodox and Conservative prayer books present excerpts from classical Jewish literature at this point. Orthodox prayer books include Biblical and Rabbinic passages about sacrificial offerings. Recent Conservative prayer books substitute other Rabbinic passages here. In both instances, the passages are followed by the recitation of *Kaddish DeRabbanan*.[12]

PESUKEI DEZIMRA— VERSES OF SONG

The second section of every Morning Service is called *Pesukei DeZimra* (Verses of Song or Passages of Psalmody). What do we sing about? Basically, we sing in praise of God. Though we emphasize praise of God throughout the prayer book, in this section the theme is most pervasive. ▨ This is especially true for the main section of *Pesukei DeZimra*, Psalms 145 through 150 (pages 39–46). Praise and its repetition create difficulties for many people. Does God require such repetitive reassurance that His attributes are praiseworthy? Does God wish us to resemble robots, repeating praises we have already offered? We often hear the complaint that the prayer book represents God as a cosmic egomaniac, a being who can never receive enough compliments. For people whose tastes run to understatement, the repetition of praise is an unattractive aspect of Jewish prayer.

Praise in the prayer book, however, is not a matter of giving compliments or feeding a divine ego. ✹ As the British Catholic author C. S. Lewis noted, all enjoyment overflows into praise. The world rings with praise, including lovers praising their beloved,

readers their favorite poet, walkers praising the countryside, players praising their favorite game—praise of weather, wines, dishes, actors, horses, colleges, countries, historic personages, children, flowers, mountains, rare stamps, rare beetles, even sometimes politicians or scholars. I had not noticed how the humblest, and at the same time most balanced and capacious minds, praised most, while the cranks, misfits, and malcontents praised least....

Just as men spontaneously praise whatever they value, so they spontaneously urge us to join them in praising it: "Isn't she lovely? Don't you think that magnificent?" The Psalmists, in telling everyone to praise God, are doing what all men do when they speak of what they care about.... I think we delight to praise what we enjoy because the praise not merely expresses but completes the enjoyment; it is its appointed consummation. It is not out of compliment that lovers keep on telling one another how beautiful they

change in our relationship to God in the absence of the Temple. Without prayer, we find God in our engagement in study. But what about the limitation of God in this statement? How can God only occupy four cubits of space in a world in which all belongs to Him? I understand those four cubits to be the very same four cubits that each individual is granted as her or his designated sacred space. If God is no longer present in expansive ritual spaces, then we must make room for God in our own four cubits.

Despite the challenge this ancient law poses, it can help us in our daily prayers to be more conscious of the need to physically prepare a quiet place, a place of solitude and contemplation. Each morning when we rise and thank God for the return of our souls, we must nurture a reflective home for that soul for the duration of our morning prayers. When we have succeeded on focusing ourselves, we can begin to reflect outward as our collective prayers demand of us. In the words of Martin Buber: "To begin with oneself but not to end with oneself. To start with oneself but not to aim at oneself. To comprehend oneself but not be preoccupied with oneself."—*Erica Brown*

▓ *Pesukei DeZimra*—sentences of song in praise of God of nature, God of justice, God of Torah, and God of Israel—themes that echo throughout our liturgy. Why are we prescribed to sing these praises first thing in the morning? According to Jewish teachings, angels sing in the heavenly courts all day long, especially in the morning. Some angels exist only to sing. We aspire to be like angels, and the liturgy encourages our angelic behavior. First thing in the morning, we emulate angels, so that we may operate from our higher selves for the rest of the day. The *Pesukei DeZimra* encourage us to sing out our praise and gratitude, to affirm God and our appreciation of God's majesty, before we move into the prayers of community. *Barukh She'amar* opens the *Pesukei DeZimra* with themes of the beginning of the world. The section continues with Psalms 148, 149, and 150—naming the angels and depicting ecstatic music and dancing in God's sanctuary. In other words, we move from earth to heaven, bridging the distance with song.—*Rabbi Rayzel Raphael*

✹ This section [*Pesukei DeZimra*], corresponding to the World of Formation or the World of Angels [the second of four worlds described in Kabbalistic lore], is meant to arouse the spirit.... *Pesukei DeZimra* may be seen as made up of two main parts: the first consists of praise and glorification of God's work in the world, based mainly on the Psalms (particularly Psalms 145–150); the second part involves praise for His redemptive acts in history, and for the loving kindness shown to our forefathers.... All of *Pesukei DeZimra* are words of poetry that ➤

25

appeal mainly to the emotions. Beyond their descriptive contents, they are hymns of praise for all of God's creation and for His loving kindness to Israel. The recital of these passages is meant to sweep the worshiper into also participating in this song of thanksgiving.—*Rabbi Adin Steinsaltz*[13]

▨ There are two types of prayer-state generally described in Ḥasidic sources. *Qatnut,* the "lower" or ordinary state in which one generally begins [one's] prayers, is opposed to *gadlut,* the "greater" or expanded state of mystical consciousness. Prayer recited while in a state of *qatnut* may contain within it great devotion; it is generally the simple prayer devotion of giving oneself to God and accepting [God's] will. It may contain both the love of God and [human] awe before [God's] presence, the two essential qualities for authentic prayer in Ḥasidism. In *qatnut,* however, [a person] is not transported beyond [the self, does] not "ascend" to a world where consciousness is transformed or where self-awareness is transcended.

The ascent from this state to that of *gadlut* is one of the central themes of Ḥasidic prayer literature. While the simple devotions of the *qatnut* state are highly valued, the true goal of the worshiper is to enter that world where "[one] may come to transcend time," where "distinctions between 'life' and 'death,' 'land' and 'sea,' have lost their meaning." [The worshiper] seeks to "concentrate so fully on prayer that he [or she] no longer is aware of [the] self ... to step outside [the] body's limits." Rapturous descriptions of the state of *gadlut* abound in Ḥasidic writings.

The first step in the attainment of *gadlut* is the involvement of the entire self in the act of worship. There must be no reservation, no holding back of a part of the person. The body is to be involved along with the soul in the act of prayer: the rhythmic movement of the body, the sometimes loud outcry of the voice, the training of the eye to the page—all these externals are aids, in the first stages of prayer, to the involvement of the entire self.

As the ecstatic power of this involvement begins to overwhelm [the worshiper, he or she] may begin to dispense with the externals, one by one, as he [or she] feels ready to do so. [The] body may become still, [one's] shouts may become a whisper, and [the worshiper] may put the book aside and see the letters of [the] prayer with the mind's eye alone.

At this point the winged ascent of the soul and word to the upper worlds begins in earnest. Prayer must ever be accompanied by the love and fear of God, the two emotions Jewish teachers had long seen as the "wings" that allow one's prayer to ascend to God. Each moment of true prayer contains within it the moment of standing before the Lord at Sinai, when the consuming love of God and the total awe before [God's] tremendous power were most fully combined.—*Rabbi Arthur Green and Barry W. Holtz*[15]

are; the delight is incomplete until it is expressed. It is frustrating to have discovered a new author and not to be able to tell anyone how good he is; to come suddenly, at the turn of the road, upon some mountain valley of unexpected grandeur and then to have to keep silent because the people with you care for it no more than for a tin can in the ditch; to hear a good joke and to find no one to share it with.... This is so even when our expressions are inadequate, as of course they usually are. But what if one could really and fully praise even such things to perfection— utterly "get out" in poetry or music or paint the upsurge of appreciation which almost bursts you? Then indeed the object would be fully appreciated and our delight would have attained perfect development. The worthier the object, the more intense this delight would be.[14]

The words of Abraham Joshua Heschel also provide insight that can enhance our prayer, especially the Verses of Song:

The beginning of prayer is praise. The power of worship is song. First we sing, then we understand. First we praise, then we believe. Praise and song open our eyes to the grandeur of reality that transcends the self. ▨ Song restores the soul; praise repairs the spiritual deficiency. To praise is to make Him present to our minds, to our hearts, to vivify the understanding that beyond all questions, protests, and pain at God's dreadful silence, are His mercy and humility. We are stunned when we try to think of His essence; we are exalted when intuiting His presence....

Worship is more than paying homage. To worship is to join the cosmos in praising God. The whole cosmos, every living being, sings, the psalmists insist. Neither joy nor sorrow but song is the ground-plan of being. It is the quintessence of life. To praise is to call forth the promise and the presence of the divine. We live for the sake of a song. We praise for the privilege of being. Worship is the climax of living. There is no knowledge without love, no truth without praise. At the beginning was the song, and praise is man's response to the never-ending beginning. The alternative to praise is disenchantment, dismay.[16]

The recitation of Psalm 30 immediately precedes *Pesukei DeZimra*.

Psalm 30

A Psalm of David, a song for the dedication of the House.

I exalt You, Lord, for You lifted me up and have not let my foes rejoice over me. Lord my God, I cried out to You and You have healed me. Lord, You brought me up from the grave, You saved my life lest I go down to the abyss. Sing to the Lord, all His faithful ones, and praise His holy name. His wrath is for a moment; His graciousness lasts a lifetime. Weeping may linger for a night, but joy comes in the morning. I once thought, while at my ease, that I never could be shaken. For Lord, in Your graciousness You made me firm as a mighty mountain. But when You hid Your face I was terrified. To You, Lord, did I call; to my Lord did I plead. "What profit is there in my death, in my going down to the abyss? Will the dust acknowledge You? Will it declare Your faithfulness? Hear, O Lord, and be gracious to me; Lord, be my help." You changed my mourning into dancing, stripping my sackcloth to clothe me with gladness, that I might sing Your glory ceaselessly; Lord my God, forever will I thank You.

The title of Psalm 30, "song for the dedication of the House" (that is, the Temple), does not relate to its content, gratitude to God for healing. The content, however, speaks for Judaism in its entirety as it affirms life and optimism in the face of danger. The psalmist praises God with gratitude, in spite of the sorrow and despair that have burdened his life. This can encourage all of us who may at times resist uttering the unqualified praise of God.

According to the Mishnah, in ancient times the Levites[17] sang this Psalm when the Israelites brought the first fruits of the harvest to the Temple (*Bikkurim* 3:4). Perhaps the Levites chose this Psalm to reinforce the concept that an individual's prosperity and physical welfare have their source in God. Then, in later times, Psalm 30 was designated for recitation only on *H*anukkah, which commemorates the rededication of the Temple (probably because of the word "dedication" in its first verse, in Hebrew *hanukkat habayit*). Finally, the Rabbis placed this Psalm in the daily

Morning Service, perhaps because of the statement that "joy comes in the morning." The word for joy *(rinah)* is also associated with singing, appropriate for a passage that precedes Verses of Song *(Pesukei DeZimra)*.

When a *minyan* is present, mourners and those observing *yahrzeit* recite the Mourner's *Kaddish* after Psalm 30.[18] The section known as Verses of Song *(Pesukei DeZimra)* then begins with the following blessing. Customarily, all stand to recite it.

Barukh She'amar

Blessed the One with whose word the world came into being. Blessed is He. Blessed is the Creator. Blessed the One whose word is deed, whose decree is fulfillment. Blessed the One who has mercy for the world and mercy for its people. Blessed the One who rewards those who revere Him. Blessed the One who lives forever, who abides eternally. Blessed the One who redeems and saves, blessed is His name. 🔅 Blessed are You, Lord our God, King of the universe, merciful Father, praised by His people, extolled and glorified by His faithful servants. With the songs of Your servant David shall we praise You, Lord our God, lauding and singing, exalting, extolling, and praising You, celebrating Your glory. We proclaim Your sovereignty, our King, singular, ever-living God, exalted, glorified King whose great name lives forever. Blessed are You, Lord, King who is praised with psalms of exaltation.

🔅 In many prayer books, *Barukh She'amar* is split into two paragraphs. The first one, ending with "blessed is His name," resonates with the many repetitions of the word *barukh*, blessed. Repetition is a tool often used in prayer and poetry to express an abundance of praise or an infinite amount of feeling. At the end of *Hallel*, for example, we repeat verses in praise of God as a way to compensate for our inability to adequately extol God. Similarly, we open the *Pesukei DeZimra* with a tribute to God's greatness by repeating the word *barukh*. The second part of *Barukh She'amar*, beginning with "Blessed are You, Lord our God, King of the universe, merciful Father," announces that we will continue our praise of God, lauding and exalting through the Psalms of David.—*Rebecca Boim Wolf*

⚙ The Book of Psalms *(Tehillim* in Hebrew) … is found in *Ketuvim*, the third section of the *Tanakh* (Jewish Bible). *Ketuvim* (Writings) is a miscellany of various and varied literature, including the Song of Songs, the Book of Esther, … Proverbs, and Job. What these works have in common is that they are not sacred history…nor are they accounts of divine revelation…. Rather, books of *Ketuvim* are religious teachings, or intended for use in worship settings. Psalms fits both of these criteria.

The Book of Psalms is made up of 150 individual poetic compositions. Each psalm is separate and discrete, and is often referred to as ➤

A commentary on prayer from 16th-century Palestine instructs us to begin *Barukh She'amar* sweetly and gently in song, concentrating upon each and every word.[19] This instruction could inform our approach to many of our prayers.

Pesukei DeZimra includes complete chapters and selected verses from the Book of Psalms, ⚙ as well as verses and longer passages added from other books of the Bible, such as the following.

Chronicles I 16:8–36

Praise the Lord, invoke His name, declare His deeds among the nations. Sing to Him, make music to Him, discuss all His wonders. Exult in His holy name, let the hearts of those who seek the Lord rejoice. Turn to the Lord, to His might, ✄ seek His presence continually. Remember the wonders He has done, His marvels and His pronounced judgments. Descendants of Israel, His servant, descendants of Jacob, His chosen, He is the Lord our God; everywhere on earth are His judgments. Remember His covenant always, the word He gave for a thousand generations, the covenant He made with Abraham, His oath to Isaac, the decree He confirmed with Jacob, an eternal covenant with Israel, saying: "To you I give the land of Canaan as your inherited portion." Then you were few in number, not many at all, sojourners there, wandering from nation to nation, from one kingdom to another. He allowed no one to oppress them and on their account He reproved kings: "Touch not My anointed ones, harm not My prophets." Sing to the Lord, all people on earth; spread news of His deliverance day after day. Tell of His glory among the nations, His wonders among all peoples. For great is the Lord and praiseworthy indeed, awesome is He above all gods. For all the gods of the nations are but idols, and the Lord made the heavens. Majesty and glory attend Him, splendor and delight are in His presence. Ascribe to the Lord, families of nations, ascribe to the Lord glory and might. Ascribe to the Lord the glory due His name, lift up an offering and come before Him; bow to the Lord in sacred splendor. Tremble in His presence, all people on earth. The world stands firm, it cannot be shaken. Let the heavens rejoice and the earth be glad; proclaim among the nations that the Lord is King. Let the sea roar, and all it contains; let the fields, and all that they hold, exult. Then all the trees of the forest will sing for joy before the Lord who is coming to rule the earth. Praise the Lord, for He is good; His steadfast love is forever. Declare: Deliver us, God, our deliverer; gather us and save us from the nations, that we may acclaim Your holy name, that we may triumph in Your praise.

Blessed is the Lord, God of Israel, forever and forever. And all the people said, "Amen" and "Praise the Lord."

a chapter in the book.... The Book of Psalms is best appreciated as a collection of religious poems, or even prayers of varying poetic quality, although for the most part the quality is compellingly, even dauntingly, high.... We can get the most from the Book if we treat the various psalms individually, rather than try to force the entire work into an ideological unity.... The Book of Psalms [does] not say just *one* thing. The psalms say many things, which is what makes [them] so complex, as well as so rewarding. — *Rabbi Daniel F. Polish*[20]

✄ The Rabbis interpret "Turn to the Lord, to His might," as referring to God's presence as manifest in the Holy Ark of the covenant. Chronicles I 16:1 states: "They brought in the Ark of God, and they set it up inside the tent that David had pitched for it, and they sacrificed burnt offerings and offerings of well-being before God."—JH

Our ancient ancestors recited these words in celebration when the Holy Ark was brought up to the City of David. Our people's history has always been an important theme in Jewish prayer, then as now. Jewish history begins with Abraham's covenant with God, a covenant that God confirmed again with Abraham's descendants, Isaac and Jacob (also known as Israel). Succeeding generations faced adversity in their wandering, yet they maintained the covenant. These verses from Chronicles praise God for His protection and deliverance; they invite people everywhere and all of creation to join a swelling chorus of praise.

Verses from Psalms

Exalt the Lord our God and bow at His footstool; ▦ He is holy. Exalt the Lord our God, bow toward His holy mountain, for the Lord our God is holy.[21] And He, being merciful, grants atonement for sin and does not destroy. He excels in restraining His wrath, and will not let His rage be all-consuming.[22] Lord, withhold not Your tender mercies from me; let Your unfailing love forever protect me.[23] Remember Your compassion and faithfulness, Lord, for they have been forever.[24] Ascribe might to God, whose majesty extends over Israel, whose might is in the heavens. God, You are awesome in Your sanctuaries; the God of Israel gives strength and courage to the people; blessed is God.[25] God of retribution, Lord, God of retribution, appear! Arise, Judge of the earth, give the arrogant what they deserve.[26] The Lord is the source of salvation; may Your blessing be on Your people. Selah.[27] The Lord of Hosts is with us; the God of Jacob is our refuge. Selah.[28] Lord of Hosts, happy the one who trusts in You.[29] Lord, help! King, answer us when we call![30]

Help and bless Your people, Your heritage; tend and sustain them forever.[31] We wait with hope for the Lord; He is our help and our shield. In Him do our hearts rejoice for we trust in His holy name. Extend Your faithfulness to us, Lord, for we have hoped in You.[32] Show us Your kindness and grant us Your deliverance.[33] Rise up to help us; redeem us because of Your faithfulness.[34] "I am the Lord your God who brought you up out of the land of Egypt. Hold your mouth wide open, and I will fill it.[35] Happy the people who have it so, happy the people whose God is the Lord.[36] I have trusted in Your steadfast love; my heart rejoices in Your deliverance. I will sing to the Lord, for He has been bountiful with me.[37]

▦ A free translation of "bow at His footstool" is: "worship at His Temple."—JH

On Shabbat and on Festivals, we add several passages to *Pesukei DeZimra* here. Those days, with their more relaxed schedule, allow more time for prayer and reflection than is available during the week. The additional passages begin with Psalm 19 and continue to the end of Psalm 93 (see page 38).

Psalm 19

For the leader. A psalm of David. The heavens tell the glory of God, the sky bespeaks His handiwork. One day to another spreads the word, one night to another shares the knowledge. There are no words, there is no speech; not one sound is heard. Yet their message spreads throughout the earth, their statement to the end of the world. In the heavens He placed a tent for the sun who goes out like a bridegroom from his wedding chamber, rejoicing like a champion to run the course. From one end of the heavens it rises, and its circuit arches over to the other end; nothing escapes its heat. ❂ The Torah of the Lord is perfect, renewing the spirit. The teaching of the Lord is dependable, making wise the simple. The injunctions of the Lord are just, gladdening the heart. The commandment of the Lord is clear, brightening the eyes. Reverence for the Lord is pure, enduring forever. The laws of the Lord are true, all of them upright. ✳ More attractive are they than gold, the finest gold, and sweeter than honey, drippings from the honeycomb. Truly your servant strives to fulfill them; to obey them brings great reward. Yet who can know all of one's errors? Clear me of unknown faults. And keep Your servant from willful sins; let them not master me. Then shall I be free of blame, cleared of grave transgression. May the words of my mouth and the meditations of my heart be acceptable to You, Lord, my Rock and my Redeemer.

❂ Nature, for the psalmist, is never taken at purely face value. Rather, a particular element … is selected, and exhibited, as evidence for the divine. That nature is never an end in itself is seen … in Psalm 19. The first seven verses point primarily … to the order of the heavens, an order that betokens the power of their Creator. "One day to another… one night to another" (verse 3): The ordered cycle is constant and never-changing, and rouses David [the psalmist] to the sense of the miraculous. Yet … how are verses 8 to 15 ["The Torah of the Lord is perfect" to "the laws of the Lord are true"] integrated with the first half of the [psalm]? It is only when we realize the importance of the seemingly perfunctory "glory of God" (verse 2) that the latter verses are seen as pointing to that same object as do the first seven verses, namely God, who establishes both physical order and Torah, which is "perfect," "right," and "true."—*Gerald J. Blidstein*[38]

✳ Immediately following the description of heaven and sun or, more accurately, hard upon the greatness of God as it is revealed through the heavens and the sun, there ensues the praise of God as the giver of the Torah. Some commentators build a bridge between these two segments by saying "Great as is this unveiling of God in nature, still greater is the revelation of God in scripture."[39] But this is not at all what the verse says. It is not the intention of the psalm to show any preference for the one over the other. For God manifests Himself in both, in nature and in Torah. Yet one might say that the manifestation through Torah is more comprehensible, clearer. The great English philosopher Lord Bacon succeeded magnificently in expressing this thought in the following words: "The heavens indeed tell the glory of God, but not His will."

When the heavens declare the glory of God, the heart is filled with wonder and thankfulness. Perhaps in this way the heavens teach humanity how we too can express the glory of God. But they do not teach us … how to conduct our lives, nor do they help us to clear a path for ourselves in our lives. This the Torah does….

Rabbi David Kim*h*i and other commentators believe that the poet connects the praise of the Torah with the description of the sun because both give light and warmth to the world, the latter in the physical universe, and the former in the world of human activity…. Kim*h*i says, "Why does he join the idea of the law [the Torah] with that of the sun? His meaning is that … as the heavens and the sun benefit the world and through them the world continues to exist, so is the law, which is 'perfect' and restores the soul."—*Nehama Leibowitz*[40]

The very existence of creation's wonders—like the sky above us—attests to God's glory. Creation, renewed daily, reflects the Creator; we praise both creation and the Creator here, as we do in other psalms (including those recited for *Kabbalat Shabbat*). Revelation—the gift of Torah and its laws—also attests to God's glory. In Psalm 19, we celebrate both creation and Torah as unique divine gifts that enhance the lives of God's human creatures.

Psalm 34

A song of David, when he feigned madness at the court of Abimelekh, who expelled him, so he left.[41] I bless the Lord at all times, His praise is always in my mouth. In the Lord do I rejoice; let the humble hear and be glad. Extol the Lord with me, let us exalt His name together. I sought out the Lord and He answered me; He saved me from all my frights. Those who looked to Him became radiant; they could not be doleful. Here was a lowly person who cried out and the Lord hearkened, delivering him from all of his woes. The angel of the Lord camps near those who fear Him, and rescues them. Have the sense to see that the Lord is good; ▨ happy the one who takes refuge in Him. Let His devoted people fear the Lord, for those who fear Him lack nothing. Even young lions[42] may starve and famish, but those who seek the Lord will not lack any good thing. Come along, students,[43] listen to me, for I will teach you about fearing the Lord. Do you desire life, would you love years of good fortune? Then keep your tongue from evil, your lips from speaking deceit. Turn from evil and do what is good, seek peace and pursue it. The eyes of the Lord are on the righteous; His ears are open to their cry. The face of the Lord is set against evildoers, to erase their memory from the earth. When the righteous cry out the Lord hearkens; from all of their woes He saves them. The Lord is near the broken-hearted; the crushed in spirit He delivers. Many are the woes of the righteous, but the Lord will save him from them all, keeping all his bones intact; not one of them will be broken. Their own misdeeds are death to the wicked; those who hate the righteous shall be ruined. The Lord redeems the life of His servants; none will be ruined who take refuge in Him.

▨ The phrase *ki tov*—"that [the Lord] is good"—which appears in verse 9 [of Psalm 34], has an interesting history. It is the same phrase we encounter in the first chapter of Genesis, where God at the end of each day of creation looks at the handiwork of that day and sees *ki tov*—that it was good. A little later in Genesis, the same phrase is associated with the first act of human disobedience: When Eve looked at the fruit of the tree she had been forbidden to eat, she saw that in appearance it was good (*ki tov*) to eat (Genesis 3:6). From that perception flowed the actions that would leave their imprint on the condition of human life for all generations to follow…. We could imagine that the act of praising God in this Psalm is intended as atonement for the act of disobedience in the Genesis story.—*Rabbi Daniel F. Polish* [44]

The first letters of verses 2 through 22 spell out the Hebrew alphabet.[45] This device is also a feature of Psalm 145, discussed later in this section. Verses 13 through 15 (starting in Hebrew with the letters *mem, nun,* and *samekh*) seem to bear the Psalm's main message: "Do you desire life, would you love years of good fortune? Then keep your tongue from evil, your lips from speaking deceit. Turn from evil and do good, seek peace and pursue it." In the meditation recited at the conclusion of the *Amidah,* we include an adaptation of verse 14, "Keep your tongue from evil" (see pages 104–105).

Psalm 90

A prayer of Moses, the man of God. Lord, our refuge have You been from generation to generation. Before the mountains were born, before You brought forth the earth, the world, forever and ever, You are God. You return human beings to dust, saying, "Return, mortals." Truly, a thousand years are in Your sight like a passing day, like a watch in the night.[46] You plunge them into sleep; in the morning they are like grass that springs up afresh; in the morning it renews itself, at nightfall it dries up and withers. Surely we are consumed by Your anger, by Your wrath do we expire. You set our transgressions before You, our secret sins in the light of Your Presence. Surely all our days pass away in Your wrath; our years are spent like a sigh. The length of our life numbers three score and ten; four score years, if granted the strength. Even their splendor contains toil and trouble; time passes quickly, we fly away. Who can understand the power of Your wrath, or Your fearsome anger? Teach us truly to make our days count, that we may attain a heart of wisdom. Turn, Lord! How long? Show concern for Your servants. Satisfy us in the morning with Your steadfast love, ✺ that we may sing happily all of our days. Make us happy for the length of our affliction, equal to the years we have seen misfortune. Then Your

✺ "Satisfy us in the morning with Your steadfast love," is a plea that each morning we will be reminded not only of life's brevity, but assured of God's love.—*JH*

good works will be seen by Your servants, Your glory by their children. May the blessing of the Lord our God be upon us; may we see the work of our hands prosper, may the work of our hands truly prosper.

Only here and in Deuteronomy (33:1), just before his death, does the Bible call Moses "man of God." This Psalm opens with praise of creation and its long-lasting wonders, which leads to thoughts about the brevity of human life that too often is afflicted by misfortune. Misfortune, like joy, has its source in God. We rarely search to understand how good fortune comes our way, and we fail in our attempts to grasp how misfortune can come from God, who loves and cares for us. We cry out for help in understanding, and we plead for an end to our trouble. We seek God's blessing so that we can make a contribution of our own, one that will endure and prosper. The psalmist will not succumb to despair, in spite of harsh reality.[47]

Psalm 91

The Most High abides in secret; Shaddai dwells in a shadow of darkness. I say to the Lord: You are my sheltering refuge, my God in whom I trust.

He will save you from the fowler's trap, from deadly pestilence. With His pinions will He protect you, and under His wings will you find shelter; His faithfulness is a shield round about you. Have no fear of terror by night, of the arrow that flies by day, of pestilence that walks in darkness, or of destruction that rages at noon. ▦ A thousand enemies may drop at your left, ten thousand at your right, but no harm will befall you. You have only to open your eyes to see the recompense of the wicked.

For You, Lord, my refuge, have made the most high shelter a haven for Your Presence.

No evil shall befall you, no affliction shall approach your dwelling. He even will command His angels to guard you in all of your paths. With their hands will they lift you, lest you stumble on a stone. ✹ On cubs and cobras will you step, tread on young lions and serpents.

Since he delights in Me I will deliver him, I will protect him since he knows Me by name. When he calls to Me I will answer, with him will I be in time of trouble, rescuing and honoring him. With long life will I satisfy him, and show him My salvation. With long life will I satisfy him, and show him My salvation.

▦ [We read] Psalm 91 [during] the Sabbath morning prayers. [Before September 11, 2001] I used to rush through this one, which speaks of God as a "refuge" from various terrors.... During the weeks that America trembled at the thought of anthrax (or smallpox) in our "tents," those references to ... "pestilence" were a comfort. [Today,] we can understand a little better the conditions of peril that our ancestors keenly felt and to which Jewish prayer so powerfully addresses itself. Those conditions explain why Jews of earlier generations were able to fulfill a *mitzvah* [commandment] that we have, or had, a difficult time taking seriously. As Maimonides writes in the *Mishneh Torah*, a Jew who doesn't actively look forward to the ultimate redemption, the coming of the Messiah, has missed the point of much of the rest of Jewish practice and belief (*Hilkhot Melakhim* 11:1). We are not intended to regard this world with complacency and satisfaction. That's why, three times daily in the *Amidah* prayer, we petition God for the reinstitution of King David's monarchy, with all that entails by way of "breaking [the Lord's] enemies." This is hard stuff for a modern American Jew, who tends to feel rather satisfied with life as it is.—*David Klinghoffer*[48]

✹ Verses 11–12 of Psalm 91 ["He even will command His angels to guard you...."] convey a lovely image of God protecting the psalmist—and us. This image has caused this psalm to be characterized by many as "a Psalm of Protection." ... In Psalm 91:2 we come upon the word *beta*ḥ ("trust"), the sense of absolute confidence in God. This word, which sounds one of the most important themes in the Book of Psalms, appears in some variant over 50 times in the 150 psalms.—*Rabbi Daniel F. Polish*[49]

Psalm 135

Halleluyah. Praise the name of the Lord; give praise, servants of the Lord who stand in the house of the Lord, in the courts of the house of our God. Praise the Lord, since the Lord is good; sing to His name since it is pleasant. For the Lord has chosen Jacob for His own, the people Israel as His prized treasure.

Surely I am aware that the Lord is great, greater than all gods. All that the Lord desires He does, in the heavens and on earth, in the seas and in all the depths. He makes clouds rise from the end of dry land, sends lightning for the rain, brings out the wind from His treasuries. He smote the firstborn of Egypt, from man to beast, sent signs and wonders in the midst of Egypt, warning Pharaoh and all of his servants. He smote many nations and slew mighty kings— Sihon King of the Amorites, Og King of Bashan, and all of the kings in Canaan. ❈ He gave their land as a heritage, a heritage for Israel His people. Lord, Your name lives forever; Lord, Your fame through all generations. Surely the Lord will provide for His people, making peace with His servants. The idols of the nations are silver and gold, the work of human hands. They have a mouth but cannot speak, eyes they have but cannot see, ears they have but cannot hear, there is not even breath in their mouths. Those who make them will be like them, whoever trusts in them. House of Israel, bless the Lord. House of Levi, bless the Lord. You who fear the Lord, bless the Lord. "Blessed is the Lord from Zion, dwelling in Jerusalem. Halleluyah."

❈ *[Psalm 135 includes images of God as destroying and slaying. These images are deeply troubling to many who pray. In contrast, the well-known Psalm 23, which begins "The Lord is my shepherd," presents a more satisfactory image. Rabbi Lawrence Hoffman analyzes our reactions:]* Psalm 23 has done rather well for moderns. We like the idea of a comforting protective deity, so despite the fact that we may never see shepherds any more, we retain a vague sense of how they protect their flocks....

We should ask ourselves, however, whether the psalmist thought that God was an actual shepherd or was just drawing an analogy. Surely the psalmist was being metaphorical. The psalmist could hardly have believed that God inhabited the Judean hills with a shepherd's crook in hand. The King James translator, too, was certainly not arguing that God had moved to a British country pasture. It was the metaphor that mattered, and both writers were fully appreciative of metaphor in human life.

It follows, then, that other divine descriptions were intended equally metaphorically. Yet, for some reason, when we come across descriptions of God that please us less than the shepherd's image, we make the mistake of thinking that the negative ones were intended literally.

When the Israelites walk successfully across the dry bed of the Red Sea and observe their Egyptian pursuers perishing in the water, Moses and all of Israel sing the Song of the Sea. "God is a man of war!" they shout. "He has drowned Pharaoh's chariots and their riders in the sea!" (Exodus 15:3–4). We are less comfortable with a warlike deity and wonder how the Bible could attribute warrior-like vengefulness to the same God who, elsewhere, is a shepherd, or—to take other similar instances of divine compassion—a God who "opens your hand and satisfies the hunger of every living thing" (Psalm 145:20), or who "watches over strangers and upholds the widow and the orphan" (Psalm 146:10). All these passages are part of traditional Jewish liturgy, but surely both their original Biblical authors and the later prayer book editors who used them meant to express the way we perceive God's actions rather than to describe God's essential characteristics. God saves us in battle. God cares about widows (who in antiquity had no means of support) and orphans (who still today suffer more than most of us are willing or even able to admit).

I do not mean to say that every ancient expression needs to be ➤

35

Psalm 135, like I Chronicles 16 (page 29), reflects God's involvement in the temporal history of the people Israel. Verses in the middle of the Psalm reinforce the wisdom of allegiance to God and point to the folly of those nations who trust in idols. Although most of this Psalm is addressed to the people Israel, the next-to-last verse emphasizes universal concern, for faith knows no borders. It calls upon *all* who fear the Lord, not only Israelites and the Levites among them, to praise Him. The last verse then states a theme found throughout Jewish liturgy, that God dwells in Zion, which is another name for Jerusalem.

retained in our current books of prayer, or that understanding the context in which metaphors of God arise makes every metaphor automatically acceptable. But we need not throw out every one, either. What we decide to do in any given case is a measured judgment that balances our regard for tradition against the extent to which a given description of God has become dysfunctional for worship or even, judged by today's standards, actually immoral. Each movement handles the matter differently.

Orthodox and Conservative Judaism expect their adherents to pray in Hebrew and to know what the Hebrew means, though not necessarily pondering the meaning of each and every word. Most worshipers cannot do that, but that is the ideal. Worship is all in Hebrew, therefore, and because of the pace with which it is prayed, problems inherent in the meaning of specific images do not stand out as much as they do in Reform and Reconstructionist Judaism. In Reform and Reconstructionist synagogues, people read at least some of the liturgy in English, or are likely at least to consult the English translation that accompanies the Hebrew and to ponder the meaning of the English. These movements need to worry more about the impact of the English on modern sensitivities. Also, their founders, Isaac Mayer Wise and Mordecai Kaplan, left them a tradition of never praying anything, even in Hebrew, that you cannot say also in English, so these two movements have been especially apt to alter imagery that they find offensive.—*Rabbi Lawrence A. Hoffman* [50]

▩ God is the loving Source of all life.

God is the life force that created the world through love. Whenever we take time to examine a flower and notice the details of its perfection, peel an artichoke, rake leaves, or see a sunset, we are reminded of the beauty of life and the creative imagination that resides with God. The care of each detail shows the amount of love.

This metaphor translates easily for us. If we take time, if we give our children, friends, aging parents our full attention, if we really listen to them, we give our love. And that loving attention attracts other love—the energy of love collects and reproduces itself. We reproduce in love as do flowers.

What then is prayer? Prayer is intentional magnification; it increases the love force in the universe. When we use our instrument—the body—through words, songs, chants, and movement, we stimulate and gather the ➤

Psalm 136

**Praise the Lord for He is good,
His steadfast love is forever.
Praise the God of gods, His
steadfast love is forever.** ▩
**Praise the Lord of lords;
His steadfast love is forever;
who alone works great
wonders,
His steadfast love is forever;
who made the heavens with
wisdom,
His steadfast love is forever;
who stretched the earth above
the waters,
His steadfast love is forever;
who made the great lights,
His steadfast love is forever;
the sun for ruling by day,
His steadfast love is forever;
the moon and the stars for
ruling by night,
His steadfast love is forever;
who smote Egypt
through their firstborn,
His steadfast love is forever;**

and brought Israel
out of their midst,
His steadfast love is forever;
with a strong hand
and an outstretched arm,
His steadfast love is forever;
who split the Sea of Reeds,
His steadfast love is forever;
who brought the people Israel
through it,
His steadfast love is forever;
who threw Pharaoh and his
army into the Sea of Reeds,
His steadfast love is forever; ✹
who led His people through the
wilderness,
His steadfast love is forever;
who smote great kings,
His steadfast love is forever;
who slew mighty kings,
His steadfast love is forever;
Sihon King of the Amorites,
His steadfast love is forever;

love force to flow more evenly in the world. Then we can direct it with intention (*kavanah*). Tears add their own potency to the love force— just as water is a conductor of electrical energy.

We must first engage the energy, the love force, God. Traditionally we have engaged God through acknowledgment, using words of praise: "God, You are great." Then we amplify the acknowledgment through song, the *Pesukei DeZimra.* (We intensify the acknowledgment with the *Shema,* which reminds us to love with heart, soul, and might, deepen the acknowledgment with the *Amidah,* and finally send it out to the world with the *Aleinu.*) Our job is to use our instrument to the best of our ability—that is, we must keep the body in shape, ready to move more love force, and direct it where needed, especially for healing and repair of the world.—*Rabbi Rayzel Raphael*

✹ We also recite Psalm 136 during the *Hallel* section of the Passover Seder. Because the Psalm includes a recounting of the exodus and the Israelites' entrance into Israel, it is particularly appropriate for the Seder night.—*Rebecca Boim Wolf*

✻ The "righteous" and the "upright" in this verse refer to all who gather together to pray, not to a special, limited category of people.—*JH*

and Og King of Bashan, **His steadfast love is forever;**
and gave their land as a heritage, **His steadfast love is forever;**
a heritage to Israel His servant, **His steadfast love is forever;**
who remembered us in our abasement, **His steadfast love is forever;**
and rescued us from our adversaries, **His steadfast love is forever;**
who gives bread to all flesh, **His steadfast love is forever.**
Praise the God of the heavens; His steadfast love is forever.

Psalm 136, like the preceding Psalm, focuses on God in the history of the people Israel. The Psalm briefly sketches that history to Israel's entrance into the promised land, and it praises God for the wonders of creation, as well as for constancy and dependability. Originally, this Psalm was probably a call and response, with a leader chanting the first part of each verse and those assembled chanting the last.

Psalm 33

Sing for joy to the Lord, you righteous; for the upright it is pleasant to praise Him. ✻ Praise the Lord with the lyre, with the ten-stringed harp[51] sing to Him. Sing to Him a new song; play sweetly with resounding sounds. For the word of the Lord is reliable, every one of His deeds is dependable. He loves what is

right and just; the Lord's steadfast love fills the earth. By the word of the Lord the heavens were made, with the breath of His mouth all their array. He gathers the waters of the sea like a mound, stores the depths in vaults. All people on earth should fear the Lord, all who live in the world should hold Him in awe. For He decreed and it was, He commanded and it came to be. The Lord annuls the plans of nations; abrogates the designs of peoples. The plans of the Lord will endure forever, the designs of His heart throughout the ages. Happy the nation whose God is the Lord, the people He has chosen as His own heritage. From the heavens the Lord looks out, beholding all mortals. From the place of His dwelling does He gaze upon all who live on earth. He fashions the hearts of them all, He discerns all of their deeds. Kings are not saved by great armies, warriors are not rescued by great strength. Horses are a false hope for deliverance; in spite of their great power they provide no escape. You can see that the eye of the Lord is on those who fear Him, those who hope in His steadfast love to save them from death, to keep them alive during famine. We longingly wait for the Lord; He is our help and our shield. For in Him do our hearts rejoice, with trust in His holy name. May Your steadfast love embrace us, as we have hoped in You.

On Shabbat, we follow the recitation of Psalm 33 with Psalms 92 and 93. For the texts and for comments, see pages 129-131 in the service for *Kabbalat Shabbat,* which also includes them. Psalms 92 and 93 conclude the passages that we add on Shabbat and Festivals, which began with Psalm 19. We recite the selections that follow both on Shabbat and on weekdays.

Verses from Psalms and elsewhere

May the glory of the Lord last forever, may the Lord rejoice in His works.[52] May the name of the Lord be blessed, now and forever. From the rising of the sun to its setting the name of the Lord is praised. Exalted beyond all nations is the Lord, beyond the heavens is His glory.[53] Lord, Your name lives forever; Lord, Your fame through all generations.[54] The Lord has established His throne in the heavens; His sovereignty rules over all.[55] Let the heavens rejoice and the earth be glad; proclaim among the nations that the Lord is King.[56] The Lord was King, the Lord is King, the Lord shall be King for ever and ever. The Lord shall be King for ever and ever; the nations will vanish from His land.[57] The Lord annuls the plans of nations, abrogates the designs of peoples.[58] Many are the designs in a human heart, but the plan of the Lord shall be fulfilled.[59] The plans of the Lord will come to be forever, the designs of His heart throughout the ages. For He decreed and it was; He commanded and it came to be.[60] For the Lord has chosen Zion, He desired it for His throne.[61] The Lord has chosen Jacob for His own, the people Israel as His prized treasure.[62] For the Lord will not abandon His people, He will not forsake His own heritage.[63] And He, being merciful, grants atonement for sin and does not destroy. He excels in restraining His wrath, and will not let His rage be all-consuming.[64] Lord, deliver! King, answer us when we call![65]

Ashrei

Psalms 84:5

Happy are they who dwell in Your house; forever shall they praise You. *Selah*. ▨

Psalms 144:15

Happy the people who have it so, happy the people whose God is the Lord.

Psalm 145

A song of praise, of David.
I exalt You, my God, the King;
I will bless Your name forever
and ever.
Every day will I bless You,
and praise Your name
forever and ever.
Great is the Lord
and praiseworthy indeed;
His greatness is beyond measure.
One generation to another shall laud Your works,
telling of Your mighty deeds.
The splendid glory of Your majesty and reports of Your wonders will I tell.
People shall recount the power of Your awesome acts,
and I will tell of Your greatness.
They shall spread the fame of Your great goodness,
and sing of Your faithfulness.
Gracious and merciful is the Lord, patient and abounding in steadfast love.
The Lord is good to all; His mercy extends to all His works.
All Your works shall praise You, Lord, and Your faithful ones shall bless You.
They shall tell the glory of Your sovereignty, and speak of Your power,
To declare His power to mortals, the glorious splendor of His sovereignty.
Your sovereignty is everlasting, Your dominion endures for all generations.
The Lord supports all who stumble, and raises all who are bowed down.
The eyes of all await You, and You give them their food in its time.
You open Your hand and provide for all that live with favor. ✹
Generous is the Lord in all His paths, and faithful in all His deeds.
The Lord is near to all who call Him, to all who call upon Him truly.
He satisfies those who fear Him, He hearkens to their cry and saves them.
The Lord watches over all who love Him, but all the wicked will He destroy.
My mouth shall speak the Lord's praise;
let all flesh bless His holy name forever and ever.

▨ The Hebrew word *selah* appears at the end of many verses in the Book of Psalms. Its precise meaning remains a puzzle. Various scholars understand it as a musical instruction, a liturgical response by worshipers, or a sign denoting a pause; others say it means "forever." —JH

✹ Another translation of Psalm 145, verse 16, reads: "You open Your hand and satisfy every living thing with favor."—JH

Psalms 115:18

We shall praise the Lord now and always. Halleluyah!

Psalm 145 is the only psalm to begin with the Hebrew word for psalm, *tehillah,* "a psalm of David" (translated above as "a song of praise"). We generally refer to this psalm, however, as *Ashrei,* the first word in each of the two verses that precede it in the prayer book. Those verses are Psalms 84:5 and 144:15. Also, in the prayer book verse 18 of Psalm 115 always follows Psalm 145.

In fourth-century Palestine, Rabbi Elazar bar Ravina declared that whoever says Psalm 145 every day is assured of a place in the world to come. What was the singular attraction of this psalm, out of all 150 psalms? The Sages of the Talmud (*Brakhot* 4b) answer this question: Psalm 145 is a special psalm both in style and in content. Stylistically, the first letter of each verse is part of an acrostic of the Hebrew alphabet, from *alef* to *tav*. ▨ Other psalms, however, are also arranged as an acrostic of the alphabet (Psalm 34, for example), so the style alone is not unique. The content of Psalm 145 stresses God's goodness and mercy. Other psalms, however, do the same. For example, Psalms 136:25 declares that God "provides food for all flesh." The uniqueness of Psalm 145 lies in the combination of unusual style and content. It is, in other words, the only alphabetic acrostic in the Bible that stresses God's goodness and mercy.

Furthermore, verse 16 of Psalm 145 states: "You open Your hand and provide for all that live with favor." The Talmud declares that this Psalm should be recited three times daily *because* it contains this verse (*Brakhot* 4b). Synagogue customs highlight the centrality of verse 16. While reciting this verse, Ashkenazim touch the forehead (or, on weekdays, the *tefillin*) with the fringes *(tzitzit)* of the prayer shawl *(tallit)* and then kiss the fringes, and Sephardim extend their open hands, palms up. Verse 16 encapsulates the psalm's theme of God's merciful concern for all, and the verse also highlights the practicality of the Jewish approach. ✪ According to Jewish teachings, helping the needy should not remain a task only for God, nor should helping the needy remain merely a noble thought from the Bible. Our prayers should be more than words. ▨ They should influence how we live, and they should

---

▨ An alphabetic acrostic serves as an aid to the memory. This device also reflects the psalmist's decision to employ a specified, limited framework to express the unlimited and inexpressible praise of God.—JH

✪ A Rabbinic comment on "You open Your hand and provide for all that live with favor" states that the wonder of the daily provision of sustenance exceeds the wonder of the final redemption (*Midrash Rabbah, Genesis* 20:9).—JH

▨ Because [the verse "You open Your hand and provide for all that live with favor"] is the core verse of the psalm, a reason for its being chosen in the first place, according to the Talmud, it must be said with ➤

govern our relationships with other people. According to some theologians, thinking that our prayers will influence our Creator is the height of *hutzpah*. Instead, the words we utter in prayer should cause *us* to change. They should encourage us to follow God's ways, for example, by opening our own hands to the needy.

The word "happy" (*ashrei*), which appears three times in the first two verses of *Ashrei*, refers to those who are truly blessed, regardless of changing circumstances or moods: "Happy are they who dwell (literally: 'sit') in Your house." Some interpret this phrase as applying to those who spend time in meditation and private devotions at the synagogue ("Your house") before public services, preparing themselves for full and meaningful participation. Such preparation is one goal of *Pesukei DeZimra*.

Psalm 145 begins with an individual extolling God ("I exalt You"). In a mounting crescendo of praise, the Psalm resounds among all the faithful and then among all creatures. Like a lover who sings about the beauty of the beloved, calling upon others to join in a chorus of praise, the individual believer will not be content until the world joins in praising the Creator of all. The number of those praising God expands, but the praise begins with the individual. Even the last verse, which calls upon all flesh to join in praising God, begins with the individual: "My mouth shall speak the Lord's praise." This focus on each individual's relationship with God characterizes Jewish religion. Some other religions idealize the depersonalization of relationships with divinity, striving to de-emphasize, if not erase, each human being's unique personality. Such religions teach that one must forego individuality in order to participate in spiritual life. Judaism teaches that each person relates to God directly as an individual.

Yet the Jewish religion obligates us to participate in the life of the community. Jews recite certain prayers only in the presence of a community, *never* when alone, and these prayers focus on the dimension of holiness (see comments on *minyan*, pages 90 and 185–186; see also sidebar on pages 160–161). Thus, an individual attains the holiest state in prayer in the presence of a community. Still, any Jew can pray directly to her or his Creator, without intermediaries and without the presence of a congregation.

In Psalm 145, praise begins with one individual ("I exalt You"), yet the psalm ultimately focuses on the entire human community ("let all flesh bless"). The Psalm emphasizes God's mercy for all creatures, and it

the *kavanah* (the thought in one's mind) that God's providence extends over all living beings in order to sustain them. If it is not said with that *kavanah*, it must be repeated, for without attending to God's beneficence at this point, one has not fulfilled the requirement of saying *Pesukei DeZimra*. Along with that *kavanah* regarding God's goodness, I believe it is fitting to add the personal intention of imitating God's ways in this respect, for the Talmud tells us, "As God clothes the naked ... so must you clothe the naked. As God visited the sick, so must you visit the sick" (*Sotah* 14a). Similarly, therefore, as God sustains those who are hungry, so must we.—*Daniel Landes*[66]

expresses the universal acclaim of God. The Hebrew word *kol*, meaning "all," ⊠ repeated 17 times in the psalm, highlights this universal focus.

We have noted that Psalm 145 is an acrostic, each verse beginning with a letter of the alphabet, in order. However, one letter is missing. No verse begins with the letter *nun*. Why is one letter missing? By skipping the letter *nun* in the acrostic, Psalm 145 avoids negative associations with a Biblical verse that *does* begin with *nun*. This is verse 2 of chapter 5 from the prophet Amos: "Fallen *(noflah)*, not to rise again, is the maiden Israel." ✺ Avoiding the negative seems to be an after-the-fact explanation, yet it typifies a Jewish attitude that seeks to avoid unpleasant or disheartening associations in the prayer book.

Teachers cherish this explanation even though some ver-

⊠ Scholars have pointed out that in the system known as *gematria*, which assigns numerical values to the letters of the Hebrew alphabet, the number 17 corresponds to the word "good" *(tov)*. In our translation, the word "every" in line three ("Every day will I bless You") is a translation of the Hebrew for "all" *(bekhol)*. —JH

✺ Were a verse beginning with the letter *nun* included, it would come between these two verses: "Your sovereignty is everlasting, Your dominion endures for all generations" and "The Lord supports all who stumble, and raises all who are bowed down." Amos 5:2 reads: *Noflah lo tossif kum betulat Yisrael*. Some sources point out that this verse could have been retained if read with a break after the third Hebrew word. This would yield, "She shall fall no more; arise, maiden Israel." Furthermore, the following verse, starting with the letter *samekh*, declares that God supports and raises those who fall. —JH

sions of Psalm 145 do include a verse beginning with the letter *nun*. For example, a manuscript of the Bible from the 14th century (known as the Kenicott Bible) includes a *nun* verse written in the margin alongside the psalm: "Faithful *(ne'eman)* is the Lord in all of His works, and loving in all of His deeds." In the Dead Sea scrolls (dating from about the first century), we read a similar verse beginning with *nun* within the psalm itself: "Faithful *(ne'eman)* is God *(Elohim)* in all of His works and loving in all of His deeds." (Nonetheless, Psalm 145 in the Hebrew Bible and in the Jewish prayer book remains as transmitted, lacking a verse for the letter *nun*.)

A close reading of the eighth verse of Psalm 145 offers a lesson about the Jewish view of God's mercy as well as a glimpse of Biblical interpretation within the Bible itself. "Gracious and merciful is the Lord, patient and abounding in steadfast love." Verse 8 constitutes a commentary on a passage from the Book of Exodus that articulates the attributes of God. Exodus 34:6 begins: "The Lord, the Lord, a God gracious and merciful, patient and abounding in love *and truth*."[67] Psalm 145, however, deletes "truth," because the psalm emphasizes the mercy of God. It avoids the implication that God is a strict judge, which the word "truth" suggests. Thus, verse 8 of Psalm 145 interprets, rather than merely cites, God's attributes as presented in Exodus 34:6.

Some students of religion (generally non-Jews) declare that the God of the Hebrew Bible is vengeful. Psalm 145, among other Biblical passages, however, clearly stresses love as a value. Verse 9, for example, emphasizes God's goodness, and extends that goodness universally to all of God's creatures. Yet the Psalm also embraces strict justice, as reflected in one of the final verses, stating that God will destroy the wicked. Compassion does not abolish the distinction between goodness and wickedness; however, in God's universe the primary obligation to take action against the wicked lies with God. Judaism teaches that in a normal human life, both the extremes of goodness and of evil exist. The challenge to humanity is to follow the model of God's mercy, so long as that does not put human life at risk.

The word Halleluyah concludes verse 18 of Psalm 115, which the compilers of the liturgy placed after the last line of Psalm 145 to conclude *Ashrei*. The word Halleluyah connects *Ashrei* with Psalms 146 through 150, because these five psalms each begin and end with "Halleluyah." Jews recite *Ashrei* and then Psalms 146 through 150 (the final five chapters in the Book of Psalms) in the Morning Service every day. The Talmud (*Shabbat* 118b) refers to these selections with the statement, "May it be my good fortune to be among those who complete *Hallel* psalms of praise each day."

Psalm 146

Halleluyah! Praise the Lord, O my soul. I would praise the Lord all my life. I will sing to my God while I live. Trust not in the powerful, in the mortal who cannot save. When his breath departs, he returns to dust; on that day his plans perish. ❋ Happy the one whose help is the God of Jacob, whose hope is the Lord his God, the Maker of heaven and earth, the seas and all that is in them, who keeps faith forever, maintains justice for the oppressed, provides bread for the hungry. The Lord releases the bound, the Lord gives sight to the blind. The Lord raises those bowed down. The Lord loves the righteous. The Lord watches over the stranger, supports the orphan and the widow, but frustrates the way of the wicked. The Lord shall reign forever, Your God, Zion, through all generations. Halleluyah!

❋ This psalm [Psalm 146], together with the next one, affirms the popular saying, attributed to the architect Le Corbusier, that "God is in the details." We are here cautioned against trusting in earthly princes, whose designs will perish with them. Rather, we are called upon to give our allegiance only to the "Maker of heaven and earth, the seas and all that [is in them, who keeps faith forever]," for God's perspective, unlike that of mortal rulers, transcends the utilitarian calculus of those in power. As sovereign of the universe, God can afford to take notice of even the lowliest subjects: the oppressed, the hungry, the captive, the blind, the bent over, the stranger, the orphan, and the widow. Only an unassailable ruler can attend to the endless minor details of governance while at the same time upholding his duty to thwart "the way of the wicked."—*Ellen Frankel*[68]

The descriptions of divine activity in Psalm 146 recall words of the prophet Jeremiah: "I the Lord act with kindness, justice, and equity in the world; for in these do I delight" (9:23). God is not an abstraction. Earth is the site of God's actions, which serve as models for human behavior, according to the Rabbis. The principles of universal concern and social consciousness are rooted in the Bible and developed in post-Biblical Jewish life and literature.

The eternal God, "Maker of heaven and earth," is dependable, in contrast to limited mortals. Therefore, the assembled declare their acceptance of God's sovereignty in the final verse: "The Lord shall reign forever."[69] This verse also appears in *Kedushah* (see pages 90–94).

Psalm 147

Halleluyah! It is good to sing to our God; it is pleasant, for praise becomes Him. The Lord, builder of Jerusalem, will gather the dispersed of Israel. The Healer of the broken-hearted binds up their wounds. He reckons the number of the stars, giving names to them all. Great is our Lord with power abundant; His understanding is beyond human reckoning. The Lord supports the humble, casts the wicked to the ground. Chant to the Lord with gratitude, to the strings of a lyre sing to our God who covers the heavens with clouds, provides rain for the earth, makes mountains put forth greenery, who gives the beasts their food, gives young ravens what they cry for. Not in the strength of horses does He delight,[70] nor is He drawn to the power of mortals. The Lord is drawn to those who fear Him, to those who await His steadfast love. Jerusalem, laud the Lord; Zion, praise Your God. For He has strengthened the bars of your gates, and has blessed your children in your midst. He has set peace as your border, and shall satisfy you with choice wheat. He sends His word to the earth, how quickly His command issues forth. He sends forth snow like wool, scatters frost like ashes. He casts down hail stones like crumbs; who can withstand His frigid blasts? He sends forth a command and melts them; He stirs the wind and the waters flow. He declared His commands to Jacob, His laws and statutes to the people Israel. This He did not do for other nations, and His statutes they know not. Halleluyah!

Psalm 148

Halleluyah! Praise the Lord from the heavens. Praise Him on high. Praise Him, all His angels; praise Him, all His heavenly array. Praise Him, sun and moon, praise Him all shining stars. Praise Him, highest heavens, and the waters above the heavens. Let them praise the name of the Lord, at whose command they were created. He made them to endure forever, established an order that will not change. Praise the Lord, all on earth: sea monsters and all ocean depths, fire and hail, snow and smoke, stormy wind that fulfills His command, all mountains and hills, all fruit trees and cedars, all beasts and cattle, creeping creatures, winged birds, all earthly kings and nations, all princes and earthly judges, young men and maidens alike, elders and the young. Let them praise

the name of the Lord, for His name alone is exalted, His splendor encompasses earth and heavens. ❈ He has exalted the horn of His people, praising all of His faithful, Israel, the people drawn close to Him. Halleluyah!

The last lines of this psalm (starting "Let them praise the name of the Lord") are chanted by the congregation toward the end of the Torah Service (pages 162-163).

Psalm 149

Halleluyah! Sing to the Lord a new song, let His praise resound where the faithful assemble. Let the people Israel rejoice in their Maker, let the children of Zion exult in their King. Let them praise His name in dance, with timbrel and lyre let them sing to Him. For the Lord cherishes His people, He crowns the humble with triumph. Let the faithful exult in glory, let them sing upon their couches ❂ with the praise of God in their throats and a double-edged sword in their hands, to bring retribution to the nations, to bring punishment upon the peoples, to bind their kings in chains, their nobles with chains of iron, carrying out the judgment decreed against them. This is glory for all of His faithful. Halleluyah!

"Sing to the Lord a new song." At one time, this song indeed was new. (The phrase recurs several times in the Book of Psalms, in Psalm 33, for exam-

▨ Rabbi Levi Yitzhak of Berditchev (1740–1810) … draws a teaching from Genesis 2:4, "These are the generations of the heavens and the earth when they were created—on the day the Lord, God, made earth and heaven." He notes that when God created the universe, God made the heavens first, but, as we learn from the reversed order of the end of the verse, this is not *our* goal. This same order of earth followed by heaven in Psalm 148 ["His splendor encompasses earth and heavens"] teaches us that the earth must come first. Our responsibility is to realize, that is, *make real,* the divine potential in the ordinary, physical reality of this world. Any beginning student of religion can easily see how to find God's majesty in the heavens and make them holy, but can we do the same for our everyday, mundane reality?—*Lawrence Kushner and Nehemia Polen*[71]

❂ In the verse, "let them sing upon their couches," the Hebrew word *mishkevotam* ("couches") can also be translated as "beds." *Etz Yosef* explains: "The righteous will thank God for allowing them to go to bed without fear of danger and attack."[72] As the terrorist attacks in Israel and America have taught us, we must also thank God whenever we are able to live life without fear of danger and attack. Today, when children live in war zones, we, who live in peace, must thank God for allowing us to sleep soundly and for protecting us from day to day.—*Courtney Hanauer*

▨ Throughout time, God has presented us with different challenges and problems. And in the 21st century, in the aftermath of September 11, 2001, as the Palestinian *intifada* continues, we feel how timely Psalm 149 is today. No longer is this the psalm of the future—rather it is our anthem now. More accurately, King David's song from ages ago is our new song, our new hymn. How, why? As Rabbi Harlow notes, we make prayers or psalms new by increasing our awareness. As decades turn into generations, we heighten our sense of connection even as our people face new problems. Yet we never lose faith that with each new challenge, a solution will also be provided. "Sing to the Lord a new song." The psalm will never be stale or staid, but will always have new meaning—for each one of us and for the Jewish people. —*Courtney Hanauer*

ple, on pages 37-38.) How can such a demand constantly be fulfilled? Whenever we invest ourselves in a psalm or in a prayer in a different way, we can make it new. ▨ We often become aware of a new aspect of the words, a new dimension of meaning, because of a new experience, because of something we have seen or heard. An awareness of what our life lacks, of something that threatens our welfare, a reawakening to beauty and wonder in the world, to blessings that we take for granted, can help us to break out of routine repetition. A new or fresh awareness can lead to a new song even though the words are the same. Self-renewal should have precedence over liturgical renewal.

The setting of this psalm may be the celebration of an Israelite military victory. Some understand that this psalm will be sung in the future, at the time of victory over forces of evil.

Psalm 150

Halleluyah! Praise God in His sanctuary, praise Him in the vault of heaven, His stronghold. Praise Him for His mighty deeds, praise Him for His abundant greatness. Praise Him with blasts of the shofar, praise Him with harp and lyre. Praise Him with timbrel and dance, ▦ praise Him with lute and pipe. Praise Him with clashing cymbals, praise Him with resounding cymbals. ⊛ Let all that breathes praise the Lord. Halleluyah! Let all that breathes praise the Lord. Halleluyah!

▦ "Praise Him with timbrel and dance" recalls the Song at the Sea. Exodus 15:20 states: "Then Miriam the prophetess, Aaron's sister, took a timbrel in her hand, and all the women went out after her in dance with timbrels." —JH

⊛ Worship with musical instruments and dance is an ancient Jewish practice, evidenced by this Psalm and [Psalm 149]. Since fixing things is prohibited on the Sabbath, Festivals, and High Holy Days, instruments that can easily be fixed by the player should not be used then, but on all other days instruments are certainly permissible. Dance, too, is an ancient Jewish mode of worship. In the 19th and early 20th centuries, Jews eschewed dance and most instruments in their worship, but these forms are increasingly reappearing.—*Rabbi Elliot N. Dorff* [73]

After 149 psalms lauding, exalting, petitioning, and adoring God in words through good times and bad, the psalmist confronts the inadequacy of words. In chapter 150, the psalmist goes beyond words to music, a wordless language of the soul, for an adequate expression of love and joy, gratitude and praise. In the last verse, too, it would seem that not words but the breath of God's creatures best expresses God's praise.

Concluding responses from the Book of Psalms

Blessed is the Lord forever. Amen and Amen.[74] Blessed from Zion is the Lord who dwells in Jerusalem. Halleluyah![75] Blessed is the Lord God, God of the people Israel, who alone does wonders. Blessed is His glorious name forever. His glory fills the whole world. Amen and Amen.[76]

I Chronicles 29:10–13

And David blessed the Lord in the presence of the entire congregation, saying: Blessed are You, Lord, God of Israel our Father, forever and ever. Yours are greatness and power, splendor and triumph and majesty, all that is in heaven or on earth. Yours, O Lord, is sovereignty, Yours is preeminence above all. Riches and honor have their source in You, and You rule over all. Power and might are in Your hand; You have the power to strengthen and encourage. We gratefully acclaim You now, our God, and praise Your name in its splendor.

These verses from Chronicles include an excerpt from a prayer uttered by King David. In it, David speaks about building the Temple, a privilege that only his son King Solomon will be allowed to fulfill. David declares that no mortal can truly give a gift to God, since everything has its source in God. "It is Your gift that we have given You. For we are sojourners with You, mere transients like our fathers." David's prayer addresses God directly in a formal blessing (blessed are You), one of only two instances in the Bible that do so.[77]

Nehemiah 9:6–11

You alone are the Lord, You created the heavens, the highest heavens and all their array, the land and everything on it, the seas and everything in them. You sustain them all in life; the array of the heavens worships You. You are the Lord God who chose Abram and brought him out of Ur of the Chaldeans, giving him his name of Abraham, finding his heart true to You.

  You made a covenant with Him, to give the land of the Canaanite, the Hittite, the Amorite, the Perizite, the Jebusite, and the Girgashite to his descendants, and You kept Your promise, for You are just. You saw the suffering of our ancestors in Egypt, and You heard their cry at the Sea of Reeds. You sent signs and wonders against Pharaoh and all of his servants and all the people of his land, for You knew of their shameless behavior toward our ancestors. You made a name for Yourself that endures to this day. You split the sea for them and they passed through it as on dry land. But their pursuers did You cast into the depths, like a stone into turbulent waters.

Once again the prayer book reviews the past of the people Israel, from Abraham and his relationship to God and to the land, through the wonders that accompanied the descendants of Abraham, Isaac, and Jacob in their liberation from Egypt. The next two passages celebrate that liberation.

Exodus 14:30–31

Thus the Lord saved Israel that day from the hand of the Egyptians, and Israel saw the Egyptians dead on the shore of the sea. When the people Israel saw the

great power that the Lord had used against the Egyptians, the people feared the Lord and they believed in the Lord and in His servant Moses.

God created us and shaped our history. Here the prayer book includes a passage from the Book of Exodus that celebrates the people Israel's liberation from Egypt and stresses the theme of redemption in the future. This is one of the most ancient Biblical poems, known as The Song at the Sea and as The Song of Moses.

Exodus 15:1–18

Then Moses and the people Israel sang this song to the Lord, ▨ saying:

I will sing to the Lord,
who has triumphed gloriously.
Horse and driver
has He hurled into the sea.
The Lord is my strength
and my might.
He is my deliverance.
This is my God
and I glorify Him,

▨ The Song at the Sea is often referred to as *Az Yashir* "Then [Moses] sang," the first two words of the song. According to Jewish folklore, men or women who wish to get married should recite The Song at the Sea with special *kavanah*, intention, because, as the Talmud states, God's task of pairing men and women in compatible unions is more difficult than the splitting of the Sea of Reeds (*Sanhedrin* 22a, *Sotah* 2a).—*Rebecca Boim Wolf*

the God of my father and I exalt Him.
The Lord, the warrior, the Lord is His name.
Pharaoh's chariots and army has He cast into the sea.
His choice captains have sunk in the Sea of Reeds.
The depths cover them; down they went in the deep like a stone.
Your right hand, Lord, singular in strength,
Your right hand, Lord, shatters the enemy.
With Your great might You destroy those who rise against You;
You let loose Your fury and consume them like straw.
In the rush of Your rage the waters were raised,
they stood like a wall, the depths congealed in the heart of the sea.
The enemy said: "I will pursue, overtake, and divide the plunder;
I will devour them, I will bare my sword,
with my bare hands will I subdue them."
You loosed the wind, the sea covered them;
like lead they sank in the swelling waters.
Who is like You, Lord, among the mighty?
Who is like You, majestic in holiness,
awesome in splendor, working wonders?
You stretched out Your right hand, the earth swallowed them.
In Your love You led this people You redeemed,
in Your strength You guided them to Your holy habitation.
Nations hear and they tremble, panic grips the dwellers of Philistia.

The clans of Edom are alarmed, the tribes of Moab are seized with trembling.
All those who live in Canaan are terrified.
Fear and dread descend upon them;
Your overwhelming might makes them still as stone
Until Your people, Lord, until
this people You have redeemed
pass peacefully over.
Lead them to Your very own
mountain and plant them there,
the place You made
for dwelling, Lord,
the sanctuary, Lord,
which You have established.
The Lord shall reign
throughout all time.
The Lord shall reign
throughout all time.

Concluding verses

For sovereignty is the Lord's; He rules the nations.[78] Deliverers shall rise on Mount Zion to judge Mount Esau, and the Lord shall be sovereign.[79] And the Lord shall be King of all the earth. On that day the Lord shall be One and His name One.[80]

Pesukei DeZimra precedes the core sections of the service—*Kriat Shema* and its blessings, and the *Amidah*—because we should recite those core sections only after appropriate preparation. The verses of *Pesukei DeZimra* help to prepare us. When we take the words to heart and reflect upon their meaning, we can approach the most important parts of the service in an appropriate spirit, freely and openly, starting the new day with devotion. For many people, the length of this section is overwhelming. ✹ The remedy is to focus on one's own relationship to the words of the Psalms

✹ Some Jews don't belong in synagogues. I actually know a lovely man who fainted every time he went inside one. On the other hand, some Jews are quite pleased with things just as they are. They see the synagogue as a place of community. In it they experience friendship, support, and the good feeling that comes from worshiping in a style that feels right.

But there is a third group that finds it as difficult to live *with* the synagogue as to live *without* it.

There are two groups of these people. One is composed of people who are looking for a place to make Jewish religious discoveries. The other is a more amorphous group of people who simply find themselves dissatisfied with some or all of the following: the style of the services, the rabbi, the other congregants, the decorum, the lack of decorum, the liturgy. At many points these groups merge by their vague longings for something different. If you belong to either group, you probably want to glow a little when you leave the synagogue. You want to be lightly touched by something you don't quite understand but know is very powerful. You want some sense of the aliveness of Torah. You may be flirting with Jewish observance, though it doesn't quite make sense to you yet. Or it makes a little sense, but you would like it to make a lot more sense for all the trouble it causes you. You need the synagogue to help you along. How are you going to grow in a synagogue full of good people with slightly shriveled souls who seem to love responsive readings?

If you are in the first group, know that it can be hard to make serious Jewish religious discoveries in a synagogue today. That is because most of the regulars in the synagogue near where you live have settled into comfortable patterns of behavior. They are married people looking for areas of stability in a too-complicated world. They want the relationships between themselves to be relatively predictable. That is not an evil wish. It only means that your average synagogue goers are not likely to be engaged in the Grand Quest. They are not searching for what is Absolutely True, at least not anymore.

They are trying to raise children, make a living, keep up with the mortgage payments, and somehow remain reliable, committed members of the Jewish community. They are much more heavily committed to concreteness than to spirituality. It is a good thing for all of us that ➤

and other Biblical excerpts, and perhaps to concentrate on a single phrase or on only a few phrases. Hence we might treat the section between *Barukh She'amar* (page 28) and *Nishmat* (below) as an anthology, and select only a limited number of texts to recite. Better a small amount of text recited with proper attention and devotion than a great deal of text without them! A congregation could vary the selection day to day, but should always include Psalm 145, *Ashrei*.

The following long poem, *Nishmat*, serves as a prelude to the concluding blessing of *Pesukei DeZimra*. *Nishmat*, which we recite only on Shabbat and on Festivals, extends and expands upon the praise of God. On weekdays, we conclude *Pesukei DeZimra* with *Yishtabah* (page 52).

they are there, too, or there wouldn't *be* a synagogue for the religious adventurers to want to improve.

If you are only an occasional attender who expects the synagogue to launch your prayers heavenward, then forgive me but I have to give you a brief lecture. It is reasonable to want the synagogue to provide you with an environment in which true prayer is possible. It is not reasonable to expect the synagogue to provide you with a spiritual iron lung, to do for you what you cannot do for yourself. The essential work must be done by you. All that you can hope the synagogue will do is give you a small boost, help you along, provide you with a few people who are trying to accomplish what you are. You couldn't swim the English Channel as a three-times-a-year swimmer, and you are not very likely to get high in the synagogue if you only appear *there* three times a year.

But what if you *are* a serious religious searcher who has tried often and long; what if you are *not* just a passing *kvetch*? How then can the synagogue help you find what you are looking for?

First of all, you have got to understand the acoustic principles of synagogues. Formal synagogues are very quiet—usually *too* quiet for my taste—but less formal synagogues, which are usually the more traditional ones, are zoned for sound. Knowing that, you should locate yourself to suit your mood. People who want to talk sit in the back rows. People who really want to *daven* sit forward. If you sit very far back you will probably only hear talk about the stock market or the ball games.

One of the characteristics of many synagogues is that the worship moves along rapidly. Just when you want to dive in and really work through an issue that the prayer book has suggested, the congregation is already moving on. Don't be intimidated. If you aren't ready to move on, don't. Stay as long as you need to, whenever you wish. Try limiting yourself to a verse or two and really work at them in order to rediscover life in words that have died. You may want to stand and sit with the rest of the congregation, at least if people do those things all at the same time in your synagogue, but don't be hurried through the text.

Recognize that the traditional *siddur* contains a lot more than just prayers in the ordinary sense of the word. It is a veritable liturgical anthology. You can learn from it, fight with it, be infuriated by it. It is variously meditative, didactic, polemical, philosophical, poetic, historical; but whatever it is, it is always exceedingly busy. It can argue with you, offer consolation, raise questions, and offer answers. It has a lot of material that can keep you going if the creativity of your own head or soul has dried up.—*Rabbi Richard J. Israel* [81]

Nishmat

The breath of all that lives praises Your name, Lord our God. The force that drives all flesh exalts and glorifies You, our King, always. Forever and forever You are God. Without You we have no one to rescue and redeem us, to save us and sustain us, to show us mercy in disaster and distress. We have no King but You. God of beginnings and endings, God of all creatures, Lord of all ages, extolled in praise abundant, He guides His world with steadfast love, His creatures with mercy. The Lord neither slumbers nor sleeps, stirring the sleeping, waking the slumbering, giving speech to the speechless, freeing

the fettered, supporting the falling, raising those bowed down. You alone do we gratefully acknowledge.

Could song fill our mouth as water fills the sea
And could joy flood our tongue like its countless waves,
Could our lips utter praise as limitless as sky
And could our eyes shed the light of sun and moon,
Could we soar with arms like eagle's wings
And could our feet match the swiftness of wild deer,
Never could we fully state our gratitude,
Lord our God and God of our ancestors,
In our attempt to bless Your name,
For one ten-thousandth of the multitude of blessings
You have granted to our ancestors and us.

From Egypt You redeemed us, Lord our God, from the house of bondage You delivered us. In famine You nourished us, in prosperity You sustained us. You saved us from the sword, delivered us from pestilence, and rescued us from severe and lingering disease. To this day have Your mercies helped us, and Your steadfast love has not forsaken us. Abandon us not, Lord our God, forever.

Therefore the limbs that You formed for us, the soul-force and spirit You have breathed into us, the tongue You have put in our mouth, surely shall acknowledge, bless, praise, laud, exalt, extol, sanctify, and enthrone You as our King. For every mouth shall acknowledge You, every tongue pledge devotion to You, every knee bend to You, every erect body bow to You, every heart revere You, every fiber of our being shall sing to Your name. Thus it is written: "All my bones exclaim: Lord, who is like You, saving the weak from those more powerful, the weak and the needy from those who rob them!"[82] Who is like You, who can equal You, who can be compared to You, great, mighty, and awesome God, God supreme, Creator of heaven and earth? We praise You, laud You, and glorify You and we bless Your holy name, as it is written: "A Song of David. Let my very being bless the Lord; let all that is within me bless His holy name."[83]

On Festivals, the cantor or leader of the service begins formal chanting with the following passage, which expands upon words from the previous passage: "great, mighty, and awesome God." We will again recite these same adjectives in the first blessing of the *Amidah* (see page 83).

God through the vastness of Your power, great through the glory of Your name, mighty forever and awesome through Your awesome works—You are King, enthroned aloft on high.

On Shabbat, the cantor or leader of the service begins formal chanting with the following:

Shokhein Ad

Dwelling in eternity,[84] exalted and holy is His name. And it is written: "Sing for joy to the Lord, you righteous; it is fitting for the upright to praise Him."[85] By the mouth of the upright are You praised, by the words of the righteous are You blessed, by the tongue of the faithful are You exalted, and in the heart of the holy are You hallowed.

In the multitude of assembled throngs of Your people the House of Israel shall Your name be glorified in song, our King, in every single generation. For it is the duty of all creatures before You, Lord our God and God of our ancestors, to acknowledge, praise, laud, glorify, exalt, beatify, bless, adore, and single out with acclamation, adding to all the words in the songs and praises of David, the son of Jesse, Your anointed servant.

We fulfill our obligation to praise God by reciting the words in the prayer book, many of them from psalms attributed to King David. The last phrase of the passage above points out that even when we do, something is lacking. We must add our own words, our personal contribution. We must express what is in our own hearts and souls. Without that, our praise of God is incomplete.

With *Shokhein Ad* and the *Nishmat* passage above, we conclude the additional section for Shabbat and Festivals that began with *Nishmat*. The following blessing is the formal conclusion of *Pesukei DeZimra*. It is customary to stand while reciting it, as we stood for *Barukh She'amar*, the first formal blessing of *Pesukei DeZimra*.

Yishtaba<u>h</u>

Praised be Your name forever, our King, God, great and holy King in heaven and on earth. For song and adoration, praise and psalmody, become You, might and dominion, triumph, greatness and strength, psalm and splendor, holiness and sovereignty, blessings and acclamations, now and forever. Blessed are You, Lord God, King great in adoration, God of acclamations, Lord of wonders, who delights in song and psalmody, King, God, eternal life of the universe.

This concluding blessing of *Pesukei DeZimra* presents the sum and substance of its theme: the praise of God. Fifteen words of praise (from "song and adoration" to "blessings and acclamations") express the core of this blessing. The number 15 holds rich associations in Jewish tradition. There are 15 Psalms of Ascent in the Book of Psalms.[86] They correspond to the 15 steps leading to the sanctuary of the ancient Temple, steps on which the choir of the Levites would stand. There are 15 Hebrew words in the Priestly Blessing,[87] in which the *kohanim* bless the people Israel in the name of God. Thus, as the priests bless us through the number 15, we use the same number to praise God. Finally, the number 15 enjoys special status because of its relationship to one of God's names. To understand this you must be aware of *gematria*, a system that assigns a numerical value to every Hebrew letter, beginning with 1 for the first letter of the alphabet, *alef.* In this system, *Yah,* one of the names of God, has the numerical value of 15, creating a special association between that number and holiness. ▩

▩ *Yah* is spelled *yod* (10) *hei* (5). The number 15 is integral to other selections in the prayer book as well; for example, we recite 15 blessings each morning at the core of *Birkhot Hashahar* (pages 18–24).—*JH*

Following the conclusion of *Pesukei DeZimra,* we recite *Hatzi Kaddish.* The cantor or leader of the service then formally calls the congregation to prayer.

Barkhu

[Leader:]
Bless the Lord, the source of blessing.
[The congregation responds:]
Blessed be the Lord, the source of blessing, forever and ever.

This call to prayer is followed immediately by *Kriat Shema* and its blessings (see Chapter 3).

QUESTIONS FOR FURTHER STUDY AND REFLECTION

1. How do you begin each day? Does your early morning routine include any words of prayer? If not, why not?
2. Do you ever set aside time to reflect on the meaning of your actions and your life? If so, how do you do it? If not, why not? If you should decide to try it, how would you go about it?
3. The *tallit* and *tefillin* physically remind us of the covenant between God and the Jewish people. How could you become more aware of the covenant in your life? How would you teach a child about the covenant between God and the people Israel? How would you go about designing your own *tallit*?
4. Do you tend to take your life and the world in which you live for granted? How could you begin to change that "taking for granted" to an appreciation of life?
5. Do you tend to use prayer for emergencies only? That is, do you pray only when a loved one is ill or suffering, or only when mourning a death? What comfort does prayer offer in those times? Contrast this with the way in which prayer affects you during non-emergencies.
6. Consider the three morning *brakhot* concerning women, slaves, and non-Jews. Which of the various approaches to saying these *brakhot* do you prefer? Why?

1.   For further discussion, see Chapter 3, pages 61–63, and Chapter 4 on the 18th blessing of the *Amidah,* pages 101–102.

2.   Rabbi Aharon Roth, *Shomer Emunim* cited by Steven S. Schwarzschild, "Silence and Speech Before God," *Judaism*, Summer 1961, pages 195 ff.

3.   Babylonian Talmud, *Menahot* 43a; *Sifrei Numbers* 115.

4.   Dvora E. Weisberg, "On Wearing *Tallit* and *Tefillin*" in *Daughters of the King: Women and the Synagogue,* Susan Grossman and Rivka Haut, eds. (Philadelphia: Jewish Publication Society, 1992), page 283.

5.   On *Tisha b'Av* in the morning, we wear neither *tallit* nor *tefillin* because such adornment is inappropriate while commemorating the destruction of the ancient Temples in Jerusalem. We do, however, wear *tallit* and *tefillin* at the Afternoon Service on that day.

6.   This blessing is discussed in the Babylonian Talmud, *Brakhot* 60b.

7.   Rabbi Arthur Green, commentary in *Kol Haneshamah: Shabbat Vehagim* (Wyncote, PA: Reconstructionist Press, 1994), page 162.

8.   Marcia Falk, *The Book of Blessings: New Jewish Prayers for Daily Life, the Sabbath, and the New Moon Festival* (New York: HarperCollins, 1996; paperback edition, Boston: Beacon, 1999), page 10. See also www.marciafalk.com.

9.   Rabbi Adin Steinsaltz, *A Guide to Jewish Prayer* (New York: Schocken, 2000; original Hebrew publication, Tel Aviv: Miskal, 1994), page 88.

10. Steven Sager, commentary in *Kol Haneshamah: Shabbat Vehagim* (Wyncote, PA: Reconstructionist Press, 1994), page 160.

11. Rachel Adler, commentary in *Kol Haneshamah: Shabbat Vehagim,* page 160.

12. For a discussion of all forms of *Kaddish*, see Chapter 8.

13. Rabbi Adin Steinsaltz, *A Guide to Jewish Prayer,* page 89.

14. C. S. Lewis, *Reflections on the Psalms* (New York: Harcourt, Brace & World, 1958), pages 94–96.

15. Arthur Green and Barry W. Holtz, *Your Word Is Fire: The Hasidic Masters on Contemplative Prayer* (New York: Paulist Press, 1977), pages 11–13. The citations within Green and Holtz's text are "not directly to be found in any single Hasidic source," but are "culled from the advice of various masters" (Green and Holtz, page 11).

16. Abraham Joshua Heschel, "On Prayer," in *Conservative Judaism* 25:1 (Fall 1970).

17. During ancient times, the Levites, one of the tribes of Israel, served as Temple functionaries.

18. For discussion of *Kaddish*, see chapter 8.

19. *Sefer Seder Hayom*, by Moshe ibn Makhir.

20. Rabbi Daniel F. Polish, *Bringing the Psalms to Life: How to Understand and Use the Book of Psalms* (Woodstock, VT: Jewish Lights, 2000), pages 1–2.

21. Psalms 99:5, 9.

22. Psalms 78:38.

23. Psalms 40:12.

24. Psalms 25:6.

25. Psalms 68:35, 36.

26. Psalms 94:1, 2.

27. Psalms 3:9.

28. Psalms 46:8.

29. Psalms 84:13.

30. Psalms 20:10.

31. Psalms 28:9.

32. Psalms 33:20-22.

33. Psalms 85:8.

34. Psalms 44:27.

35. Psalms 81:11.

36. Psalms 144:15.

37. Psalms 13:6.

38. Gerald J. Blidstein, "Nature in 'Psalms,'" *Judaism,* 1964, page 34; cited in Nehama Leibowitz, *Leader's Guide to the Book of Psalms* (New York: Hadassah Education Department, 1971), page 30.

39. W. Graham Scroggie, *The Psalms* (London, 1965); cited in Nehama Leibowitz, *Leader's Guide to the Book of Psalms,* page 32.

40. Nehama Leibowitz, *Leader's Guide to the Book of Psalms,* pages 32-33. The passage has been altered from the original to attain gender neutrality.

41. See I Samuel 21 for a description of the event. The king there is called Akhish.

42. The Hebrew *(kefirim)* is understood by some to mean "the faithless" *(kofrim)*, in contrast to "those who seek the Lord."

43. Literally, "sons" or "children," it refers to those who are gathered near the speaker.

44. Rabbi Daniel F. Polish, *Bringing the Psalms to Life,* page 144.

45. Each half of verse six starts with words that begin with consecutive letters of the alphabet—*hei* and *vav*.

46. "A watch in the night" is even shorter than a day. In ancient times, guards divided the night into three or four periods, called "watches."

47. Part of this prayer of Moses recalls another of his pleas: "Turn from Your fierce wrath" (see Exodus 33:12).

48. David Klinghoffer, "A Deeper Understanding of Prayers," *The Jewish Week*, November 23, 2001. David Klinghoffer is the author of *The Lord Will Gather Me In: My Journey to Jewish Orthodoxy*, and the editorial director of Toward Tradition.

49. Rabbi Daniel F. Polish, *Bringing the Psalms to Life,* page 139.

50. Rabbi Lawrence A. Hoffman, *The Way Into Jewish Prayer* (Woodstock, VT: Jewish Lights, 2000), pages 111-112.

51. The lyre and the harp were played by the Levites in the Temple. See I Chronicles 15:16.

52. Psalms 104:31.

53. Psalms 113:2, 3, 4.

54. Psalms 135:13.

55. Psalms 103:19.

56. I Chronicles 16:31.

57. Psalms 10:16.

58. Psalms 33:10.

59. Proverbs 19:21.

60. Psalms 33:11, 9.

61. Psalms 132:13.

62. Psalms 135:4.

63. Psalms 94:14.

64. Psalms 78:38.

65. Psalms 20:10.

66. Rabbi Daniel Landes, *My People's Prayer Book: Traditional Prayers, Modern Commentaries, Volume 3—P'sukei D'zimrah (Morning Psalms)*, Rabbi Lawrence A. Hoffman, ed., page 121.

67. Exodus 34:6. The passage continues for a total of 13 attributes.

68. Ellen Frankel, *My People's Prayer Book, Volume 3,* page 124.

69. Some commentators interpret this verse as a prayer for God's continued sovereignty.

70. See Psalm 33: "Horses are a false hope for deliverance" (page 38).

71. Lawrence Kushner and Nehemia Polen, *My People's Prayer Book, Volume 3,* page 135.

72. *Etz Yosef* is the best-known work of Rabbi Ḥanokh Zundel ben Joseph (died 1867) of Bialystok, Poland, a commentator on the Midrash. Cited in *The Artscroll Siddur*, Rabbi Nosson Scherman, ed. (Brooklyn: Mesorah, 1987), page 74.

73. Rabbi Elliot N. Dorff, *My People's Prayer Book, Volume 3,* page 138.

74. Psalms 89:53 (this is the last verse of the psalm, which concludes Book Three of the Psalms).

75. Psalms 135:21 (this is the last verse of the psalm).

76. Psalms 72:18-19 (Psalm 72 ends with verse 20, which concludes Book Two of the Psalms).

77. This point is discussed on page 8.

78. Psalms 22:29.

79. Obadiah 1:21 (the last verse of the single chapter in the Book of Obadiah).

80. Zechariah 14:9.

81. Richard J. Israel, "How to Survive Your Synagogue" in *The Second Jewish Catalog*, Sharon Strassfeld and Michael Strassfeld, eds. (Philadelphia: Jewish Publication Society, 1976), pages 306-308.

82. Psalms 35:10.

83. Psalms 103:1.

84. Based on Isaiah 57:15.

85. Psalms 33:1.

86. Psalms 120-134. These psalms are included in many prayer books as part of the Shabbat *Minḥah* Service for recitation and reflection on Shabbat afternoon.

87. See Numbers 6:24-26. These words are recited by the leader of the service during the leader's repetition of the *Amidah*. See page 103.

Chapter

KRIAT SHEMA

We accept and bear witness to God's sovereignty

What is the most important Jewish prayer? Many people would answer: "The *Shema*." This declaration begins with the Hebrew word *Shema*: "Hear, O Israel: the Lord is our God, the Lord is One." ▦ The *Shema* is probably the best-known passage in the prayer book, but it is not a prayer. The *Shema* is verse 4 from chapter 6 in the Book of Deuteronomy. Even when included in a prayer service, it does not constitute a prayer but a reading from Scripture, from the Torah. In the Morning and Evening Services, after reciting Deuteronomy 6:4 we recite three other Biblical passages: Deuteronomy 6:5-9, Deuteronomy 11:13-21 and Numbers 15:37-41. We call this combination of Biblical verses *Kriat Shema*, Reading the *Shema*. Many prayer books print these passages with the symbols for cantillation *(trop)* that designate how to chant them, and many congregations chant Deuteronomy 6:5-9 aloud in

---

▦ Some translations of the *Shema* read: "Hear, O Israel: the Lord is our God, the Lord alone."—*JH*

unison. These practices emphasize that *Kriat Shema* is a reading, not a prayer.

Deuteronomy 6:4 clearly ranks as one of the most significant verses in Judaism, perhaps the most significant single verse that appears in the prayer book. ▨ In both the Morning Service and the Evening Service, we cover or close our eyes as we say the words slowly in a concentrated state of meditation, focused upon God. We also recite the *Shema* before going to sleep at night and at the beginning of the Torah Service, and the *Shema* is one of the verses to be recited by a Jew (or on behalf of a Jew) at the time of death.

The placement of *Kriat Shema* as the first topic in the Mishnah (the first major work of Hebrew literature after the Bible) also reflects its importance. The Mishnah opens with a question: When do we recite the *Shema* in the morning? A modern religious work probably would first present the *Shema* and then explain why Jews should recite it. The Mishnah assumes that its readers are all familiar with the *Shema* and that twice-daily recitation is required.

According to the Rabbis, reciting the *Shema* bears witness to the existence of God and to our acceptance of God's sovereignty. Saying the *Shema* thus marks "accepting the authority (literally, yoke) of the sovereignty of Heaven," *kabbalat ol malkhut shamayim* (Mishnah *Brakhot* 2:2).

The prayer book emphasizes this acceptance through the non-Biblical phrase that immediately follows: "Blessed be His glorious sovereignty forever and ever" *(Barukh shem kvod malkhuto l'olam va'ed)*. Originally, these words were said at the Temple in Jerusalem. When the High Priest

▨ What is at stake in proclaiming that God is One? The words of the *Shema* are so familiar that, despite their importance, it is easy to take them for granted. Is the purpose of the *Shema* simply to differentiate Jews from those idolatrous "others" who are so foolish as to believe in a multitude of gods? Why do we need to continue to remind *ourselves*—Hear, O Israel—that God is one, at a time when monotheism seems quite firmly established? And what does oneness *mean*? Is its significance exhausted by the rejection of paganism?

Some Jewish feminists have criticized the Jewish tendency toward hierarchical, dualistic ways of constructing the relationship between self and others. The disparaging comparisons between our God and their gods; our belief in monotheism and their idolatry; our acceptance of one, omnipotent, male ruler of the universe and their worship of many gods and goddesses, are all examples of this "over-against" thinking. But the affirmation of monotheism *can* be something that calls us to ourselves, rather than something that separates us from others. The notion that one God underlies and unifies all of existence is hardly self-evident, after all. Our *experience* of the world is fragmented and conflicting; often there seems little unity even within us, let alone between us and other persons or aspects of creation. Monotheism says that, despite appearances to the contrary, we are all connected to each other; everything is bound together in one, great, sacred, interconnected web of life. Monotheism challenges us to try to discern the One in and through the changing forms of the many. God is present in every individual and every aspect of experience, including those parts of ourselves and others we have been taught to disparage most—nature, femaleness, darkness, sexuality. "Never to despise in myself what I have been taught to despise," says poet Muriel Rukeyser, "To make this relation with the it: to know that I am it." *This* can be the meaning of monotheism. "Hear, O Israel," says poet and liturgist Marcia Falk, "The divine abounds everywhere and dwells in everything; the many are One."—*Judith Plaskow*

pronounced the ineffable name of God ❂ on Yom Kippur each year, the people assembled would fall prostrate to the ground and declare, "Blessed be His glorious sovereignty forever and ever." These words later became the response to *all* blessings uttered by the priests, somewhat similar to "Amen" today. These words also became the response to the *Shema.*

The *Shema* affirms monotheism, the belief in *one* God ("the Lord is one"). Yet we can interpret the Hebrew text in more than one way, and different English translations reflect different understandings. Some scholars prefer to translate the closing words as "the Lord alone" (is our God) rather than "the Lord is one." They understand the *Shema* not as affirming monotheism but "as describing a relationship with God, rather than His nature."[2] ❈ The medieval commentator Rashi apparently agreed with this interpretation. He wrote that "the Lord is our God now but not the God of those who are idolaters. In the future He will be recognized by everyone." ✳

Here is the text of the *Shema* (Deuteronomy 6:4) and the first of three additional passages of *Kriat Shema* (Deuteronomy 6:5–9).

Hear, O Israel: The Lord is our God, the Lord alone.[3] ❈

Blessed be His glorious sovereignty forever and ever.

Love the Lord your God with all your heart, with all your soul, and with all your might. And take to heart these words which

❂ The name recited by the High Priest probably was what we refer to as the Tetragrammaton, the name of God spelled with the four Hebrew letters *yod, hei, vav, hei.* We do not pronounce this word as it is written. When we read it as part of our prayers or as part of a Bible verse, it is pronounced *Adonai.* The word *Adonai* connotes sovereignty, as its literal meaning derives from the Hebrew word *adoni,* "my lord" or "my master."—*JH*

❈ There is another way to understand oneness and that is as inclusiveness.… God is all in all.… There can be no power other than or in opposition to God. This is the God who is male and female, both and neither, because there is no genderedness outside of God that is not made in God's image.… Despite the fractured, scattered, and conflicted nature of our experience, there is a unity that embraces and contains our diversity and that connects all things to each other.—*Judith Plaskow*[1]

✳ Rashi, commenting on Deuteronomy 6:4, cites a verse from the prophet Zechariah (14:9), which appears at the end of the *Aleinu* prayer that closes every formal prayer service: "the Lord will be King over all the earth; on that day the Lord will be One and His name One." The modern Bible scholar Jeffrey H. Tigay writes that, for all of humanity, the Lord and His name will stand alone, unrivaled. The Lord will be recognized exclusively and God's name alone will be invoked in prayer and oaths.—*JH*

❈ In his final hour, Jacob (whose other name is Israel) gathers his children to his deathbed, anxious about whether any have strayed from belief. He asks them whether in their hearts they harbor doubts about the One who spoke and brought the world into being. They respond: "**Hear Israel**, our father, just as there is no dispute in your heart, so there is none in our heart. **God is our God, God is One.**" Prostrate on his bed at the moment his soul is departing, Jacob responds: "Blessed be the Name of the Glory of God's sovereignty now and forever." Hearing this exchange, God affirms to Jacob that his name will be immortalized in the twice-daily recitation of the *Shema.* Therefore, explains this Midrash (*Sifrei Deuteronomy* 31.31.5–7), we say at night and morning *Shema Yisrael,* after Jacob's name Yisrael.

The scene provides context to the recitation of *Shema.* Not a lonely moment of proclaiming faith, the *Shema* becomes a dialogue between the dying parent and the surviving children. In a final reckoning of his ➤

I command you this day. Impress them upon your children. Speak about them when you sit at home and when you are away, when you lie down and when you rise up. Bind them as a sign upon your hand, and let them be a reminder above your eyes. Inscribe them upon the door posts of your house and at your gates.

life, Jacob does not recite his own private *Shema*. Instead he concerns himself with his children's faith. Their response is both an affirmation and a challenge: Insofar as their father is sincere in believing what he has professed, so too are the children. The answer to Jacob's concern is to be found in his own heart. If he has been true, his conscience is clear. With whatever doubt he holds, he will die. This Midrash renders the *Shema* a mutual test of faith across the generations. Belief in God is rooted in the faithfulness of children and parents, and revealed at poignant moments of reflection and mortality.

A second Midrash sets the *Shema* at the auspicious gathering of the community of Israelites at Mount Sinai. In *Midrash Rabbah, Deuteronomy* 2:31, the question is asked, "From whence did Israel attain the privilege to recite the *Shema*?" Rabbi Pinhas bar Hamma answers, "From the giving of the Torah." He explains that God's initial address to the people of Israel was: "**Hear Israel**, I am God, your God." Everyone then answered: "**God is our God, God is One.**" And Moses said: "Blessed be the Name of the Glory of his sovereignty now and forever."

The first Midrash emphasizes familial intimacy, the second establishes the *Shema* as a public exchange between God and the entire nation of Israel. God recites part, proclaiming God's commitment to be God of Israel. Israel responds, affirming and accepting God as ours, as *the* one God. The *Shema* is projected into an eternal and awesome moment of revelation, an experience of the entire people, the living along with those yet to be born, because all souls were present at Mount Sinai.

Both of these excerpts from the Midrash animate the text of Deuteronomy 6:4; they set the *Shema* as a dialogue occurring at pivotal, even monumental, moments. The atmosphere of each is frightening and foreboding, yet also infused with connection. *Shema* becomes the medium of deposing doubt and affirming commitment between intentional partners to a covenant, as children and as a nation.

For what reason then does the Talmud exempt women from what Rabbi Harlow aptly describes as this central liturgical act of the Jewish people? The *Shema* is included among positive, time-bound commandments from which women are exempt (Mishnah *Berakhot* 3:3; Babylonian Talmud, *Kiddushin* 29a), though this category is somewhat incoherent and has more exceptions than inclusions. The Abudarham argues that a woman must be exempt from twice-daily recitation of the *Shema* to avoid conflict between her duty to serve her spouse and God (*Sefer Abudarham HaShalem, Seder tefillot shel hol, 3*). God's ➤

Love is a basic Jewish value. Love of other people is stressed in Leviticus—"Love your neighbor as yourself" (19:18). The last words of the blessings recited just before *Kriat Shema* in the Morning Service and in the Evening Service stress God's love for the people Israel. Deuteronomy 6:5 stresses the need for humans to reciprocate that love with intensity, with all our heart and soul and might. How should we express this love? By teaching Torah to the next generation, and by incorporating the Torah into our daily life—writing words of the Torah on the parchment inserted into *tefillin* and *mezuzot*. The "sign upon your hand" and the "reminder above your eyes" refer to *tefillin*, ▦ visible signs of the covenant between God and the people Israel which adult Jews wear each weekday morning.[4] *Mezuzot* ✦ contain parchment scrolls and are attached to the door frames of Jewish homes.[5] "At your gates" refers to the city gates.

According to the Rabbis of the Mishnah (*Brakhot* 2:2), when we recite the following passage, Deuteronomy 11:13–21, we signify our acceptance of the authority of the commandments.

If you carefully heed My commandments that I command you this day to love the Lord your God and to serve Him with all your heart and with all your soul, then I will give rain for your land in due season, early autumn rain and late spring rain, and you will gather in your grain, your wine and your oil. I will put

grass in your fields for your cattle, and you shall eat and be satisfied. Beware lest your heart lure you to turn away and serve other gods and worship them, for then the Lord's anger will flare out against you. He will close up the skies and there will be no rain. The ground will not yield its produce and you will quickly perish from the good land that the Lord is giving you. ✖ Therefore impress these words of Mine upon your hearts and souls, bind them as a sign upon your hand and let them be a reminder above your eyes. Teach them to your children, to speak of them when you sit at home and when you are away, when you lie down and when you rise up. Inscribe them upon the door posts of your house and at your gates. Thus your days and the days of your children will endure in the land which the Lord promised to give to your fathers, so long as there is a sky over the earth.

A reader who does not understand Hebrew probably will miss a major difference between this passage and Deuteronomy 6:5-9. In English, the word "you" could refer to one person or to an entire group. Hebrew, however, differentiates between second-person singular and second-person plural. In the first passage of

sovereignty over Israel is likened to a man's sovereignty over his spouse. A woman's recitation of the *Shema*, therefore, is both the active and intentional acceptance of the sovereignty of heaven and the acknowledgment of women's full partnership in the Jewish covenant, as expressed by these two exquisite *midrashim*. Listen Israel, we recite, God is our God too. One God, of women and men.—*Bonna Devora Haberman*

▩ *Tefillin* are black leather boxes that observant Jews attach to the hand and to the head with black leather straps. The boxes hold small parchment scrolls on which a scribe has written the following passages in the special script used for the Torah: Exodus 13:1–10 and 11–16 and Deuteronomy 6:4–9 and 11:13–21. These passages contain the commandment to place "these words" of Torah "as a sign upon your hand" and as "a frontlet [*totafot*] between your eyes." In the first passage cited from Exodus, the Hebrew word translated as frontlet in other passages (*totafot*) is replaced by the word for "reminder" (*zikaron*). We do not wear *tefillin* on Shabbat or Festivals, which in themselves are reminders of the covenant.—*JH*

✺ A Jewish person comes to the door of her house. She doesn't run right in. She stops at the threshold and places a kiss on the little box on the door post.

Why? The little box is a Jewish consciousness-shifting tool. It reminds you to *Shema ve'ahavta*, "Listen so that you will love." That is what the words of Torah say that are inside that little box. A quotation from the Torah, from the book of Deuteronomy, is in there, a prayer about the unity of all which is called the *Shema*, which means listening, and the paragraph after the *Shema* which explains why we listen, *ve-ahavta*, so that you will love.

A Jewish person doesn't enter his or her home in a hurry with all the *shmutz* (dirt) of the day on their lips ready to spill out. We notice how easy it is to get blood on the door posts of our lives and so we gently and consciously enter the sacred space of our homes *Shema ve'ahavta*, listening and loving, placing a kiss full of our loving intentions upon that little box, called a *mezuzah*, on the door post.—*Rabbi Goldie Milgram*[6]

✖ I recite the *Shema* each day because it proclaims God's justice, and justice must be a critical element in the God I affirm. The calculus of reward and punishment articulated in [Deuteronomy 11:13–21] may ➤

Kriat Shema, the commandments concerning *tefillin*, *mezuzah*, and the study of Torah are directed to the individual. In the second passage, the commandments are directed to the entire people Israel, implying communal responsibility for behavior. ▨ Thus the passage emphasizes reward and punishment, which flow from the belief in God's justice. The final verse implies that the continued life of Jews in the land of Israel depends on the behavior of the total Jewish community.

be too simple and ultimately inaccurate.... Nevertheless, I find this paragraph, with all its problems, central to my beliefs, for it insists starkly (even if too starkly) that God is ultimately just. Somehow, justice is an inherent part of the world and of God; and since God is the model for human beings, the possibility of justice must be inherent in us as well. The Rabbis too had problems with the doctrine of justice announced in this paragraph, but they included it anyway, because they too had a deep faith in the ultimate justice of God as the metaphysical backdrop and support for human acts of justice.—*Rabbi Elliot N. Dorff*[7]

▨ How do we understand the second paragraph of the *Shema* [Deuteronomy 11:13–21]? ... Some people have objected to it on the grounds that it seems to promise direct rewards for good behavior and punishment for bad behavior, and thus is belied by our life experience. Indeed, it has been dropped from a number of contemporary *siddurim*, or downgraded to an "alternative" status. And even in synagogues where it survives, it is usually muttered in an undertone. The same congregations that say the first paragraph after the *Shema* with vigor and attention, and that focus on the *tzitzit* mentioned in the third paragraph with strong *kavanah* (intention), race through the second paragraph so that few worshipers actually experience its meaning.

Can we learn anew from this passage? First of all, we make many problems for ourselves if we insist on translating YHWH as "*Adonai/ Lord*" which it surely does not mean and thus treat YHWH as some power utterly separate from, above, and beyond us. To credit such an all-powerful King/Lord/Judge with punishing our every transgression and rewarding our every act of goodness certainly does not accord with what we know happens in our lives. I draw, instead, on the deep sense of YHWH as a Breathing (that is how it comes out if you try to "pronounce" it with no vowels) and hear it as the Breath of Life which is within us, between us, and beyond us. Many of us might hear it as something like "the In-Out Breath that connects all life and being."

Now, with that in mind let us look back at the text. On the one hand, at the level of individuals it is certainly true that the life-process in which we walk and breathe often does not let us [reap] what we sow. [Nonetheless,] individuals who put out love and justice into the world are somewhat more likely to bring love and justice back than those who put out anger, hatred, or fear. But it is certainly not a one-to-one certainty, as the Book of Job and the Holocaust remind us.

But at the level of societies as a whole, I think there is much more ➤

We often have difficulty accepting the concept of reward and punishment, God's providence, since we know of righteous men and women who suffer and wicked men and women who prosper. As our Sages have taught, the suffering of the righteous and the tranquility of the wicked are beyond human understanding (*Pirkei Avot* 4:19). Yet, some Jews believe that people are rewarded or punished in the world to come if not in this world.

The Bible describes the horrors inflicted upon Job, which overwhelm him for no apparent reason. Job's friends declare that his suffering must be due to grievous sins that he has committed. Most people, however, emphasizing Job's piety, correctly understand that the Book of Job teaches that such personal suffering is not the result of sinful behavior. The Rabbis taught that when people suffer, others should not tell them—as Job's friends told Job—that their affliction is proof that they have sinned (Babylonian Talmud, *Baba Metzia* 58b).

Many people ask: If we do not maintain that a connection exists between sin and suffering, why do we continue to include this passage from Numbers in our prayers? The answer to that begins in remembering that the passage is part of *Kriat Shema* (Reading the *Shema*), which is not a prayer. All the passages of *Kriat Shema* are included in the prayer book as a reading of Scripture.

For most of us, the concept of God's providence gives rise to enduring questions more than to answers. In the thirties and forties of the last century, in Buenos Aires, Argentina, German Jews who found refuge from the *Shoah* established a congregation and named it *Kehillah Kedoshah Lamrot Hakol*—Holy Congregation in Spite of Everything. Many Jews today, who desire to maintain faith while living in an imperfect, unredeemed world, are honorary members of that congregation.

The third passage of *Kriat Shema*, Numbers 15:37–41, focuses on the commandment of *tzitzit* (fringes).

The Lord said to Moses as follows: Speak to the people Israel and tell them to put fringes (*tzitzit*) on the corners of their garments throughout their generations, attaching a thread of blue-purple ✷ to the fringe at each corner. Looking upon it you will recall all the commandments of the Lord and fulfill them, ✸ so that you do not follow your heart and your eyes in lust. Thus you will be reminded to observe all of My

truth to the second paragraph of the *Shema* (and that is to whom it's directed; the pronouns are second-person plural). What's more, while most Jews are no longer farmers in the narrow sense, ALL Jews and the whole human race still take part in the great flow of rain, sun, earth, seed, which make up the rhythms of earth. And those rhythms are (a) crucial; (b) in crisis; and (c) responsive to human behavior.

I read the second paragraph as saying: If you listen, REALLY listen to the teachings of YHWH, the Breath of Life, especially the teaching that there is Unity in the world and interconnection among all its parts, then the rains will fall as they should, the rivers will run, the heavens will smile, and the good earth will feed you. BUT if you shatter the harmony of life, if you chop the world up into parts and choose one or a few to worship—like gods of wealth and power, greed, the addiction to do and make and produce, without pausing to be and make *Shabbos*—then Breath of Life will come as a hurricane to shatter your harmony. The rain won't fall (or, it will turn to acid), the rivers won't run (or, they will overflow because you have left no earth where the rain can soak in), and the heavens themselves will become your enemy (the ozone layer will cease shielding you, the carbon dioxide you pour into the air will scorch your planet), and you will perish from the good earth that the Breath of Life gives you.

So, therefore, set these words/deeds in your heart and in every breath, carry them in every act toward which you put your hands, and make them the pattern through which you see the world. Teach them to your children, to repeat them to their children; stay aware of them when you sit in your houses, when you walk on your roads, when you lie down, and when you rise up. Write them on the thresholds where you cross from world to world, the door posts of your houses, and your city-gates.—*Rabbi Arthur Waskow* [8]

✷ Violet or blue-purple indicated royalty in the ancient world. Jacob Milgrom writes that "the violet, or blue-purple, dye was extracted from the gland of the *Murex trunculus* snail found in shallow waters off the coast of northern Israel and Lebanon."[9] Since this dye was so expensive, the requirement of attaching a blue-purple thread to the fringe at each corner was suspended by the ancient Rabbis (see Mishnah *Menaḥot* 4:1).—JH

✸ The purpose of all ritual is … to lead to conviction and finally to action. The Rabbis formulated it thus: "Sight leads to memory and memory to action" (Babylonian Talmud, *Menaḥot* 43b)—*Jacob Milgrom* [10]

commandments and to be holy to Your God. I, the Lord, am your God who brought you out of the land of Egypt to be your God. I, the Lord, am your God.

Tzitzit (fringes) ▦ are attached to every *tallit* (prayer shawl). In addition, many observant Jews fulfill the commandment by always wearing a four-fringed garment under their clothing. During the Morning Service, before recitation of the *Shema*, we customarily gather together the four fringes attached to the four corners of the *tallit*. During *Kriat Shema* we hold them in our hand, and each time we read the word *tzitzit* in this passage, we kiss the gathered fringes. (We release the fringes during the blessing after *Kriat Shema*.) Just as the *tefillin* and *mezuzot* of the first passage of *Kriat Shema* remind us of the Torah and of our covenant with God, so looking upon the *tzitzit* reminds us of our commitment to fulfill all of God's commandments, ◉ which will enable us to live a life of holiness.[12] As in Numbers 15:39 above, in Exodus 19:6 God commands the people Israel to be a kingdom of priests and a holy nation. ▦ Thus each and every Jew may attain a life of holiness. The *tzitzit* are "the epitome of the democratic thrust within Judaism, which equalizes not by leveling but by elevating. All of Israel is enjoined to become a nation of priests."[13]

We are not obliged to wear *tzitzit* at night, since we cannot "look upon" any part of them in darkness. Thus, we do not wear the *tallit* during the Evening Service.[14] Nevertheless, we recite this passage at night as well as in the morning, to fulfill the obligation to remember the Exodus twice daily. ✳

Blessings precede and follow *Kriat Shema* in the Morning and Evening Services, enhancing this precious gem by providing the proper

---

▦ The blessing recited when putting on the *tallit* emphasizes *tzitzit*, the wearing of which constitutes the commandment to be fulfilled. "Blessed are You, Lord our God ... who has commanded us to wrap ourselves in *tzitzit*."—JH

◉ When we might assert that one thing is certain: Inside my skin I know what's what, but everything outside me is mysterious and alien, [when we assert that] these are two separate worlds—then we look at the *tzitzit* on the edges of our selves, we look at these fuzzy fringes made always of my own cloth and the universe's air, we look to see that not good fences but good fringes make good neighbors, we look at these threads of connection that bind us to each other and we pause at that moment to remember to remind ourselves: *Shema Yisrael YAH Eloheinu YAH ehad* [is one].—*Rabbi Arthur Waskow*[11]

▦ Leviticus 19:2 also states: "You shall be holy for I, the Lord your God, am holy."—JH

✳ We recall the liberation from the slavery of ancient Egypt as *our* redemption ("your God who brought *you* out of the land of Egypt"). This is in the spirit of the Passover Haggadah, which states: "In every generation, each person is obliged to consider himself as having gone out of Egypt." The Haggadah also discusses this passage from the Book of Numbers, quoting Mishnah *Brakhot* 1:5. Since the commandment concerning *tzitzit* does not apply at night, some early authorities had felt that the entire passage need not be included in the Evening Service. The Rabbis taught, however, that Numbers 15:37–41 must be recited in the evening as well as in the morning.—JH

setting. Mishnah *Brakhot* 1:4 teaches: "In the morning one precedes *Kriat Shema* with two blessings and follows it with one blessing. In the evening one precedes it with two blessings and follows it with two." The major themes of these blessings are creation, revelation, and redemption, thereby reviewing daily the life of the people Israel from the beginning of the world through freedom from slavery to the gift of Torah and then to our future salvation. ※

Let us first examine the blessings before and after *Kriat Shema* in the Evening Service. Unlike the blessings introduced in Chapter 1, these are long blessings, regulated by somewhat different rules than those that regulate short blessings. The word *barukh* does not begin every one of the long blessings, although each of them ends with a formal *brakhah* (including the word *barukh*). When lengthy blessings follow each other as they do here, only the first blessing requires the *brakhah* formula "blessed are You" *(barukh Attah)* at the beginning.

The first blessing before *Kriat Shema* in the Evening Service celebrates the theme of creation.

1 evening. Blessed are You, Lord our God, King of the universe who with His word brings each evening's twilight, with wisdom opens the gates of the heavens, with understanding sets the cycles of time and the succession of seasons, and arranges the stars in their set orbits in the sky according to His will. He creates day and night, rolling light away from darkness and darkness away from light, separating day from night; *Adonai tzevaot* ※ is His name. May

※ The recitation of *Shema* proclaims that God is one, there is none other. Isn't it amazing that six simple words have become the Jewish national anthem, the foundation of the Jewish faith? Just as a building cannot be built without a foundation, so Judaism can not be sustained without faith in God.

The first section of the *Shema* describes the responsibilities of the Jewish people: We must love God, teach our children, think of the words of Torah day and night, bind *tefillin*, and inscribe words of Torah on our door posts.

The second section describes the rewards and punishments contingent on the performance of *mitzvot*, cautioning us to adhere to God's commandments. This section concludes—as does the commandment to honor our parents—that those who observe the *mitzvot* will endure on the land.

The third section urges us to struggle to overcome the evil inclination. It reminds that we were slaves in Egypt—a society pervaded by the evil inclination. We were redeemed from slavery so that we would become a "kingdom of priests and a holy nation." This section exhorts each of us to overcome our own personal bondage, our own personal enslavement to evil inclination.

The six words of the first sentence of the *Shema* express the essence of Jewish faith. The last letter of the first word *(ayin)* and the last letter of the last word *(daled)* form the word *ed*, which means witness. We, the Jewish people, are witnesses that God is one and that we are faithful in serving God.

When we recite the *Shema* during morning and evening prayer services, we cover our eyes so that we can concentrate on our acceptance of the oneness of God. Only during the *Shema* do we cover our eyes. No other prayer, no other part of the service, demands that we block out interference and avoid distraction.— *Annette Labovitz*

❋ *Adonai tzevaot* literally means "Lord of hosts." Compare to Jeremiah 31:35, "Thus says the Lord, who established the sun for light by day, the laws of moon and stars for light by night, who stirs up the sea into roaring waves, whose name is Lord of Hosts."—*JH*

the living, eternal God reign over us always, forever and ever. Blessed are You, Lord who brings each evening's twilight.

The order of nature reflects God's existence. ▨ Kant states: "Two things fill the mind with ever new and increasing admiration and awe, the more often and the more steadily we reflect upon them: the starry heavens above and the moral law within."[15] Every evening we state in our prayers that God creates day and night, and twice a day we declare that the Lord alone is our God. Abraham Joshua Heschel taught what such repetition indicates. "A scientific theory, once it is announced and accepted, does not have to be repeated twice a day. The insights of wonder must be kept alive constantly. Since there is a need for daily wonder, there is a need for daily worship."[16]

The first lines of this blessing recall the power of the divine word as we read in the third verse of the Book of Genesis: "God said, 'Let there be light'; and there was light." Although this blessing is part of evening prayers, it mentions day as well as night, following the Talmud's instruction. (The same passage, in the Babylonian Talmud, *Brakhot* 11b, also teaches that night should be mentioned during the day.)

The second blessing before *Kriat Shema* in the evening celebrates revelation, God's gift of the Torah to the people Israel.

▨ Every time I *daven* the *Shema* and its blessings, I re-encounter what, for me, is the very essence of the Jewish orientation toward life in this world. The first blessing in the series, which is about Creation, helps me to re-experience the wonder that is part of every encounter with the intricacy, order, and power of the natural world. In that wonder and in my thankfulness for being among the creatures of the world, I relate to the world's wholeness, the divine presence in its unity, and my own smallness. In the second blessing, I re-encounter the love that gives humankind its sense of self-worth—the love of parents, the love of extended family and community, and the love of God. The divine love flows through each of the other loves in human lives, as it does through Torah—the moral and spiritual teaching that shapes our universe. Every encounter with Torah is thus a manifestation of the divine love.

Aware of the wonder in my own life, and made newly conscious of the love and teaching that have shaped it, I am ready to affirm my obligations, which grow out of an awareness of the divinity embodied in the universe. Being the beneficiary of that unity and of a loving community places this moral obligation on me. That is the context for reciting the *Shema*, which demands my affirmation that I will stand as a member of the Jewish people to fulfill the obligations that flow from the divine presence and from Jewish peoplehood.

The content of the paragraphs of the *Shema* varies from prayer book to prayer book. Both the Reform and Reconstructionist prayer books have avoided the explicit message of reward and punishment found in Conservative and Orthodox prayer books in favor of an emphasis on a more naturalistic approach. [The Reconstructionist *Kol Haneshamah* offers two alternatives from Deuteronomy: either the traditional 11:13–21 or 28:1–6, 30:15–19. The latter verses do not explicitly promise punishment for neglect of religious mandates. The Reform *Gates of Prayer* omits the verses that promise reward and punishment.] The rewards for accepting the yoke of heaven are, from my perspective, more intrinsic. The spiritual depth and moral strength with which I attempt to live my life can give me the meaning for which I hope.

Having accepted anew the yoke of responsibility, I am ready to serve as God's partner in the work of redeeming our troubled world. Thus, the blessing following the *Shema* emphasizes redemption. On a large scale, it is represented by the crossing of the Red Sea. But of ➤

2 evening. With love everlasting have You loved the House of Israel, Your people. Torah and *mitzvot*, statutes and laws have You taught us. Therefore, Lord our God, when we lie down and when we rise up we shall speak about Your statutes. We shall rejoice in the words of Your Torah and in Your *mitzvot* forever, for they are our life and the length of our days; ✷ we will meditate on them day and night. ✖ Never take away Your love from us. Blessed are You, Lord who loves His people Israel.

The order in nature signifies God's presence. The gift of Torah signifies God's love. We show appreciation for a gift by using it; in this case by studying Torah and making it part of our daily lives.

We turn now to the blessings that follow *Kriat Shema* in the Evening Service. The first blessing celebrates redemption from slavery. During public prayer, the leader of the service connects *Kriat Shema* to the first blessing that follows by repeating the last words of Numbers 15:41 (*Adonai Eloheikhem*, "the Lord your God") and by adding to these the first word of the blessing that follows (*emet*, "truth" or "true"). Thus, no interruption occurs between the last word of *Kriat Shema* and the following blessing.

course I usually have the opportunity to be a redeemer only on a much smaller scale. I often pause here to consider how my interactions with others and the decisions I make over the course of the day can take on a redeeming power.

In the Morning Service, the *Shema* leads directly to the *Amidah* prayer, which focuses on the messianic completion of creation. I can only be ready to offer this prayer once I have gone through the sequence of the *Shema* and its blessings. The progression here is through a series of ideas, but it is no less an emotional and spiritual journey that I take each time I pray these words. We all need the strength to act as redeemers if our world is to be redeemed, and I am grateful that we can draw such strength from our prayer books. Wonder, love, teaching, and commitment lead me daily toward redemption.—*Rabbi David A. Teutsch*

✷ The second passage before the evening *Shema* connects knowledge of Torah and observance of *mitzvot* with life. We find this theme expressed in Deuteronomy 30:19–20: "Today I call heaven and earth to witness against you that I have placed life and death before you, blessing and curse; choose life, that you and your offspring may live, by loving the Lord your God, heeding His voice, and holding fast to Him. For that is your life and the length of your days."—*JH*

✖ Our promise to meditate on the words of Torah day and night recalls Joshua's address to the people Israel soon after the death of Moses. "Let not this Book of Torah leave your lips, but meditate on it day and night, so that you may fulfill all that is written in it" (Joshua 1:8).—*JH*

✱ "The Lord your God is true" is based on Jeremiah 10:10, "the Lord God is true." Other translations read: "the Lord God is truth" and "the Lord is truly God."—*JH*

✺ "All this" refers to all that we have recited in *Kriat Shema.*—*JH*

Cantor or Leader: The Lord your God is true. ✱

3 evening. True and dependable is all this, ✺ established for us that He is the Lord our God with none besides Him and that we are His people Israel. He saves us from the hand of kings, our King redeems us from the grasp of all tyrants; He is God who delivers us from our foes and brings retribution upon

all our mortal enemies. He does great things beyond human knowledge and marvels beyond number.[17] He has given us life and has not allowed our feet to falter.[18] He guides us to triumph over our enemies and exalts our strength above all who hate us. He has wrought miracles for us, retribution for Pharaoh, signs and wonders in the land of Egypt.[19] In His wrath has He smitten all the firstborn of Egypt, bringing His people Israel out of their midst to lasting freedom. He led His children through the divided Sea of Reeds, and sank their pursuing enemies in its depths. When His children beheld His power they praised His name gratefully, gladly accepting His sovereignty. Moses and the people Israel responded to You in song very happily, all of them declaring: "Who is like You, O Lord, among the mighty? Who is like You, glorious in holiness, awesome in splendor, working wonders?" ▦ Your children beheld Your sovereignty, as You divided the Sea before Moses. "This is my God,"[20] they responded, declaring: "The Lord will reign for ever and ever."[21] And thus is it written: "For the Lord has rescued Jacob, redeeming him from one too powerful for him."[22] Blessed are You, Lord who has redeemed the people Israel.

▦ Moses and the Israelites sing this song (Exodus 15:11) after crossing the Sea of Reeds. The word translated here as "mighty" (elim) literally means "gods."—JH

The Exodus from Egypt is the classic example of redemption. Living today in an unredeemed world, we know we still need redemption, now and in the future, and the reality of our past redemption reassures us of the redemption yet to come. After the Israelites were saved at the Sea of Reeds, Moses led the people in song, which the blessing recalls by short excerpts from the Song of Moses.

The last quotation in this blessing is from the Book of Jeremiah, where it is preceded by: "He who scattered the people Israel will gather them, will guard them as a shepherd guards his flock." It is followed by the promise that the people once again will enjoy God's bounty and their mourning will turn to joy. The quotation from Jeremiah thus affirms our faith in future redemption.

The second blessing after *Kriat Shema* in the Evening Service praises God for peace and protection.

4 evening. Help us, Lord our God, to lie down in peace; and raise us up to life again, our King. Spread over us the shelter of Your peace. Improve us with Your good guidance. Save us because of Your merciful name. Shield us, and rid us of enemies, pestilence, sword, famine, and sorrow. Remove the adversary before us and behind us; shelter us in the shadow of Your wings. For You, O God, guard us and deliver us; You, O God, are a gracious and merciful King.[23] Guard our going and our coming[24] for life and for peace, now and forever. Blessed are You, Lord who guards His people Israel forever.[25]

Peace is so significant in Judaism that it constitutes one of the names of God—*Shalom*.[26] "Save us because of Your merciful name" interprets the Hebrew that literally states "Save us because of Your name." The Hebrew for "name" in this context denotes mercy. A prayer in the *Selihot* service of the High Holy Day season includes the words: "act because of Your name ... for Your name is merciful and gracious." Thus "save us because of Your name" can be understood as "save us because of Your nature." It reminds God, so to speak, pleading with Him that He live up to His name on our behalf, that He be true to Himself, to His merciful nature. ✺

In the phrase "Remove the adversary," the last word in Hebrew is *satan*, the personification of evil forces in the world, of the evil impulses in ourselves and in others. The Hebrew word *satan* provides the source of the English word "Satan," but the English name refers to an independent power at odds with God and God's goodness. In Jewish understanding, *satan* has no independent power. We pray that God will remove evil forces from the world and free us from the impulse to evil.

The last sentence of the blessing changes on Shabbat. During the Friday Evening Service, the following sentence replaces it.

✺ One of God's names in liturgy and Rabbinic literature is "the Merciful" (*Harahaman*). Though mercy is not the only meaning of God's "name," a number of sources assign it this meaning. For example, the first words of Psalm 25:11, "Because of Your name, O Lord, pardon my sin although it is great," are interpreted by commentator *Metzudat David*: "Because of Your name, which signifies mercy." He has a similar comment to Psalms 79:9, stating that God's name there signifies "You are merciful and gracious."—JH

✖ The Hebrew name for Jerusalem, *Yerushalayim*, contains the word peace, as *shalayim* derives from *shalom* or peace.—JH

Spread over us the shelter of Your peace. Blessed are You, Lord who spreads a shelter of peace over us, over all His people Israel, and over Jerusalem.

Shabbat shalom is more than a greeting or a slogan. It is a reality for which we pray, a reality that we should strive to attain in our lives. We focus our prayer for peace on Jerusalem, the city of peace. ✖

On Friday evening, in honor of Shabbat, we add two verses about creation, Exodus 31:16–17. They follow the second *brakhah* after *Kriat Shema*.

The people Israel shall observe Shabbat, maintaining Shabbat throughout their generations as an everlasting covenant. It is a sign between Me and the people Israel forever, that in six days the Lord made the heavens and the earth, and that on the seventh day He ceased from work and rested.

The Friday Evening Service then continues with *Hatzi Kaddish*[27] and the *Amidah*.[28]

We now consider the blessings that surround *Kriat Shema* in the Morning Service. The first blessing preceding *Kriat Shema* in the morning, as in the evening, celebrates creation, and it is known as *Yotzer*, "He fashions," since the first line blesses God "who fashions light and creates darkness." As in the evening, we mention both day and night in the first blessing before *Kriat Shema*. *Yotzer* is the longest of the blessings that surround *Kriat Shema*.

Yotzer elaborates on the themes of light and the mercy of God. The first sentence rephrases verse 45:7 from the Book of Isaiah. The prophet declares that God "fashions light and creates darkness, makes peace and creates evil." The Rabbis changed the phrase "creates evil" to "creates all things." Why? They certainly knew the exact wording of Isaiah's declaration and they knew about the existence of evil. Perhaps the Rabbis felt that the word "evil" would be inappropriate in a prayer, and so they chose more elegant, more elevated language (Babylonian Talmud, *Brakhot* 11b). "All things" includes evil, ※ yet avoids the intrusion of the word "evil" in a prayer stressing God's compassion.

※ The Rabbis also knew that certain religions attribute good and evil to separate divine beings. Judaism, however, views God as the source of all things, good and evil. Thus, for example, Jews are required to recite a formal blessing to God upon hearing bad news as well as upon hearing good news (see Chapter 1, pages 14–15).—*JH*

❀ This alteration in Isaiah [from "evil" to "all things"] raises the question of truth in liturgy. Do we want a liturgy that names the truths of our lives, however painful or difficult they may be, or do we want a liturgy that elevates and empowers, that focuses on the wondrous aspects of creation alone? Are these goals in conflict, or can hearing the truth be empowering?—*Judith Plaskow*[29]

[Editor's note: See Chapter 13 for Rabbi Daniel Gordis's perspective on the many different functions of prayer, at times naming the truth and at times focusing on wondrous aspects of creation.]

※ More than just male, God is portrayed as utterly exalted beyond all human power to know, approach, or even speak His glory. This liturgical picture of God is difficult to reconcile with the reciprocal notion of covenant, for all creation and power are in God's hands.... Such divine omnipotence leaves little sphere for human action, and metaphors of sovereignty, lordship, kingship, and judicial and military power convey an impression of arbitrary and autocratic rule that is quite at odds with our notion of just government, and thus with a concept of God as just governor. Feminist objections to such images stem from the sense that there is a reciprocal relationship between the symbols that a community uses for God and its social and institutional structures.—*Judith Plaskow*[31]

1 morning. Blessed are You, Lord our God, King of the universe who fashions light and creates darkness, who makes peace and creates all things. ❀ In mercy He gives light to the world and to those who dwell thereon; in His goodness He renews creation every day constantly. How numerous Your works, O Lord; in wisdom have You made them all; the earth is filled with Your creations.[30] King exalted uniquely since earliest time, praised, extolled, and glorified from ancient days, eternal God, with Your many mercies show us compassion, our mighty Master, ※ our protecting Rock, our sheltering Shield, in whom we seek refuge.

The marvels of creation inspire liturgists to burst into poetry and song. In the following poem, within the *Yotzer* prayer, the first letter of each Hebrew word is in alphabetical order. The translation fails to capture this acrostic or the poetry of the original.

Blessed God with great understanding created the rays of the sun. His goodness fashioned glory for His name, setting celestial lights round about His power. Leaders of His legions are holy beings that exalt the Almighty, constantly telling the glory of God and His sanctity. May You be blessed, Lord our God, for the excellence of Your handiwork and for the bright lights that You have made. May they always glorify You.

At the Shabbat Morning Service we replace these two passages above with the following two passages. Though they have similar themes, the uniqueness of Shabbat requires a special text.

1 morning/Shabbat. Blessed are You, Lord our God, King of the universe who fashions light and creates darkness, who makes peace and creates all things. ✳ All acknowledge You, all praise You, and all declare "None is holy as the Lord."³² All exalt You, fashioner of all, God who daily opens the gates of the east, the windows of the heavens, bringing forth the sun from its abode and the moon from its habitation. He illumines the entire world, and its inhabitants, that He created with compassion. He illumines the earth and those who dwell on it with compassion, and in His goodness always renews daily the work of creation. King, exalted alone since earliest time, praised, extolled, and exalted from time long gone,

✳ It seems almost tautological to note that the concept of "good" has no meaning without the concept of "bad"; yet it may be worth stating the obvious here. The refusal to name that with which we are uncomfortable does not make it disappear. It would seem that, in a truly inclusive monotheistic vision, the divine domain includes what is "bad"; and, at times, the "bad" needs to be named. Of course, we might debate for a long time what we mean by good and evil; Jewish teaching certainly does so, although not usually in the context of prayer. While prayer is probably not the best place to engage in theological argument, it is the right place, I believe, to name our truths and, insofar as possible, to do so inclusively—which is to say, not to name half-truths, which are, effectively, lies.

I have returned to the Biblical source for [my] new blessing, which reads ... literally, Let us bless the source of life,/source of darkness and light,/source of wholeness and chaos,/source of goodness and evil,/source of all creation." I have deliberately reversed the order of *or* and *hoshekh*, "light and darkness," from the way they appear in the original blessing, lest one infer that *or* [light] is to be identified with ... "wholeness" and ... "goodness," while *hoshekh* [darkness] is equated with ... "chaos" and ... "evil." The dualism of light and darkness is widely regarded as a value-laden opposition in Western thought, and this hierarchy has been applied in especially problematic ways to racial differences among people. If, in grappling with the images embedded in our culture, we choose to talk about light and darkness as polarities (as opposed, for example, to viewing them as points on a spectrum), I believe it important that we try to subvert the hierarchy normally associated with them.—*Marcia Falk*³³

eternal God, in Your manifold mercies show us mercy, our mighty Master, our protecting Rock, our sheltering Shield, in whom we seek refuge. You are incomparable, inimitable, peerless, and singular. You are incomparable, Lord our God, in

this world, inimitable, our King, in life of the world to come, peerless, our redeemer, in the days of the Messiah, and singular, our deliverer, in giving life to the dead.

The following poem, like the weekday poem, is an acrostic, with the first Hebrew letter of each phrase in alphabetical order. At public services the entire congregation sings the Hebrew poem. Here, too, the translation is a pale reflection of the Hebrew.

God, Master of all creation, truly blessed by all that breathes; His greatness and goodness fill the world, knowledge and wisdom surround Him. Exalted beyond His holy creatures, enhanced with glory beyond the angels. ▦ Purity and justice guard His throne, kindness and mercy attend His glory. Good are the lights that our God has created; He fashioned them with knowledge, understanding, and wisdom. Power and vigor gave He to them, that they may rule amidst the cosmos. Filled with splendor, blazing light, their splendor is beautiful throughout the world. Happily rising, joyfully setting, with awe fulfilling their Creator's will. Beauty and glory attend His name, His kingship is recalled with shouting and song. He called to the sun and light shone forth, with foresight He set the phases of the moon. All multitudes on high pay Him homage, celestial beings, sacred creatures sing of splendor and greatness

▦ The Hebrew word *merkavah*, which is translated here as "angels," means "chariot." In Rabbinic literature *merkavah* refers to groups of angels. (See Babylonian Talmud, _Hagigah_, beginning of chapter two.)—*JH*

To God who rested on the seventh day from all works of creation, ascending to His glorious throne. With splendor He robed the day of rest, calling the day of Shabbat a delight. This is the praise of the seventh day on which God rested from all of His work. The seventh day itself utters praise: "A Psalm, a song of Shabbat. It is good to give thanks, acclaiming the Lord."[34] Therefore let all that He has fashioned glorify and bless God, let them ascribe praise, honor, and greatness to God the King who fashions all, who in His holiness grants a heritage of repose to His people Israel on the holy day of Shabbat. Your name, Lord our God, will be sanctified; Your remembrance, our King, will be glorified in the heavens above and on earth below. May You be blessed, our deliverer, for the excellence of Your handiwork and for the bright lights that You have made. May they always glorify You.

On both Shabbat and weekday mornings the first blessing before *Kriat Shema* continues with the following, devoted principally to a vision of angels and other heavenly creatures as they praise the Creator.

May You be blessed, our Rock, our King, and our Redeemer, Creator of holy celestial beings. May You be praised forever, our King, fashioner of celestial

servants, all of whom stand at the peak of the universe, in unison declaring with awe words of the living God, King of the universe. All of them are beloved, all of them pure, all of them powerful, all of them with dread and awe doing the will of their Creator, and all of them opening their mouths with holiness and purity, with song and psalm, blessing and praising, glorifying and revering, sanctifying and declaring the sovereignty of God, the great, mighty, awesome King; holy is He. And all of them accept the yoke of the kingship of heaven, one from the other, and grant permission, one to the other, to hallow the one who fashioned them, with serene spirit, with pure speech and with sweet sacred song. Then all of them respond together, saying in awe: "Holy, holy, holy! The Lord of Hosts! The whole world is filled with His glory!"[35] Soaring holy crea-tures roar as they rise to other celestial beings, responding with praise: "Blessed is the glory of the Lord from His abode."[36]

To God who is blessed they chant sweet song, to the ever-living God, the King, they sing, giving voice to praise. For He alone does deeds of might, cre-ates anew, is masterful in battle, sows righteousness, reaps vic-tory, creates healing. Awesome in praise, master of wonders, He renews in His goodness every day always the work of creation, as it is written, "Praise the one who made the great lights, for His love is eternal."[37] Illumine Zion with a new light; may we all soon be privileged to share its light. ✹ Blessed are You, Lord, fashioner of lights.

The second blessing before *Kriat Shema* in the Morning Service ✴ celebrates revela-tion, God's gift of the Torah to the people Israel.

2 morning. Deep is Your love for us, ✳ Lord our God, boundless Your tender compassion. Our Father, our King, for the sake of our ancestors who trusted in You, to whom You taught the statutes of life, be gracious to us

✹ The prayer book of 10th-century Rabbi Saadia Gaon omitted: "Illumine Zion with a new light; may we all soon be privileged to share its light." Saadia stated that this sentence is extraneous to the sole theme of the blessing, which is the light of creation. In spite of his logic and his authority, however, and because of the great importance of Zion, the prayer for this type of light remains.—*JH*

✴ At one time, certain communities recited the Morning Service ver-sion of the second blessing before *Kriat Shema* ("with love abounding") both morning and evening, while other communities recited the Evening Service version (see 2 evening, "with love everlasting") both morning and evening. For example, in the prayer book of the 10th-cen-tury Rabbi Saadia Gaon "with love everlasting" *(ahavat olam)* appears both in the Morning Service and in the Evening Service, with no men-tion of "with love abounding" *(ahavah rabbah)*. Ultimately, the Ashkenazi prayer book came to use one version in the evening *(aha-vat olam)* and one in the morning *(ahavah rabbah)*. The Sefardi prayer book, however, uses "with love everlasting" *(ahavat olam)* both in the morning and in the evening, as in the prayer book of Rabbi Saadia Gaon.—*JH*

✳ The accent on God's love is noteworthy. Some versions of ancient Christian thought charged that the old covenant of Sinai (the *Old* Testament) was merely the dispensation of law, and was rendered null and void by the new covenant (or *New* Testament) of love, as manifest in Jesus. Second-century Jewish sources thus regularly identify Torah as a sign of God's ultimate love for Israel. This theme of God's love for Israel leads naturally to the *Shema*, which heralds Israel's love in return for God.—*Rabbi Lawrence A. Hoffman*[38]

and teach us. Our Father, merciful Father, whose nature is mercy, show us mercy. Inform our hearts, that we may understand and discern, obey, learn, teach, and lovingly fulfill all the words of Your Torah. Enlighten our eyes through Your Torah, that our hearts may cleave to Your commandments. ▦ Unite our hearts to love and to revere Your name, that we may never be brought to shame. For we have placed our trust in Your holy, great, and awesome name; let us therefore rejoice and be glad in Your deliverance. ◉ Bring us in peace from the four corners of the earth and lead us in dignity to our land, for You are the God who works salvation. You have chosen us among all peoples and tongues, bringing us closer to Your great name in truth, that we might give thanks to You and in love proclaim Your uniqueness. ✳ Blessed are You, Lord who chooses ✳ His people Israel with love.

▦ How then can God's giving rules [the commandments of the Torah] be a manifestation of God's love? The easiest analogy is the relationship between parents and children. Children who grow up in a home without rules experience apathy, not love. As any parent knows, it takes considerable commitment and energy to frame and enforce reasonable rules. Though rules may become an expression of paternal power exerted over the children, they may also be an act of love, demanded by parents to teach children proper behavior. In like manner, this prayer asks God to enable us to experience Torah as an expression of God's love, that we may value learning it ourselves, teaching it to others, and fulfilling its precepts in our lives.— *Rabbi Elliot N. Dorff* [39]

◉ As we recite "Let us therefore rejoice and be glad in Your deliverance," we gather up the *tzitzit* at the four corners of the *tallit*, so that we have them in our hand when we recite the next passage of the prayer, "the four corners of the earth." We then hold them during *Kriat Shema*.—JH

✳ "Your uniqueness" refers specifically to the recitation of the *Shema* (Deuteronomy 6:4) which follows, proclaiming the oneness of God, that the Lord alone is God. "In love" reflects Deuteronomy 6:5, "Love the Lord your God."—JH

✳ The Hebrew root *(b-ḥ-r)* for the verb here translated as "chooses" has different meanings depending on the tense. In the past tense it means "chose." In the present tense, however, it can mean "love." This last sentence that precedes *Kriat Shema* in the morning recalls Deuteronomy 7:7–8: "Not because you are the most numerous people did the Lord care for you and choose you, for you were the smallest of all people. It was because the Lord loved you and kept the oath that He made to your fathers that He brought you out [of Egypt]."—JH

✳ Chosenness is [a] problematic concept that appears ... throughout the prayer book. As Mordechai Kaplan, the great critic of chosenness, argued, the concept is incompatible with full citizenship in a secular ➤

One blessing follows *Kriat Shema* in the morning. Like the first blessing after *Kriat Shema* in the evening ("True and dependable," 3 evening, pages 67–68), it focuses on the redemption from Egyptian bondage. ✳ At one time some Jewish groups used "true and dependable" both morning and evening, and other groups used the text below both morning and evening. The Rabbis of the Talmud then decided to use both versions, one in the morning and one in the evening. "Rabbah bar Ḥanina said in the name of Rav: Whoever has not said (following *Kriat Shema*) 'True and certain' in the Morning Service and 'True and dependable' in the Evening Service has not fulfilled his obligation" (Babylonian Talmud, *Brakhot* 12a).

As in the Evening Service, in public prayer there is no interruption between the last words of *Kriat Shema* (from Numbers 15:41, "the Lord your God") and the blessing that follows. The leader chants aloud just after *Kriat Shema* "The Lord your God is true." Then the blessing follows.

3 morning. True and certain, established and enduring, just and dependable, beloved and cherished, pleasant and sweet, awesome and mighty, well-ordered and acceptable, and good and beautiful is this teaching to us for all time. True it is that the eternal God is our King, that the Rock of Jacob is our protecting shield. In all generations He endures and His name endures, His throne is established and His sovereignty and faithfulness will endure forever. ❋ His words live and endure, faithful and delightful throughout all time for our ancestors and for us, for our children and our generations, and for all the generations of the seed of the people Israel Your servants. From the first generations to the last His teaching is good and everlasting, true and dependable, a law that will never change.[41] True it is that You are the Lord our God and God of our ancestors, our King and King of our ancestors, our redeemer and redeemer of our ancestors, our Creator, the Rock of our deliverance; You have always helped and saved us. Your name endures forever; there is no God but You.

You always defended our ancestors, ▣ a shield and deliverer for their children after them in every generation. Though You are enthroned in heaven, Your just decrees extend to the ends of the earth. Happy the one who obeys Your commandments, who takes to heart the words of Your Torah. You are in truth Lord of Your people, mighty King to fight their cause. True, You are first and You are last. Without You we have no King, Redeemer or Deliverer. From Egypt You redeemed us, Lord our God, and from the house of bondage You delivered

democracy. Without being necessary to Jewish self-respect, it encourages notions of racial and national superiority that lead to divisions among people and foster suspicion and hatred. [As Jews, however,] we can rejoice in, offer thanks for, and seek to deepen our relationship to Torah without contrasting it to all the other ways in which the world's peoples connect to God, and without describing ourselves as singled out from among all others. The Reconstructionist liturgy, *Kol Haneshamah*, maintains its founder's suspicion of chosenness by working around the concept of election very simply. "You have chosen us from among all peoples and nations and brought us closer to Your great name" becomes "For You are the redeeming God and have brought us near to Your great name." "Blessed are You, Adonai, who chooses His people Israel with love" becomes "Blessed are You, Abundant One, who lovingly cares for Your people Israel." In this reworking, Israel's assurance of and gratitude for its own relationship to a loving God is independent of any claims to an unparalleled spiritual destiny.—*Judith Plaskow*[40]

❋ After the sentence "His throne is established and His sovereignty and faithfulness will endure forever," we release the *tzitzit* which we have held in our hand during *Kriat Shema*.—JH

▣ The literal meaning of the Hebrew *ezrat avoteinu*, translated here as "defended our ancestors," is "the help of our fathers." However, Psalm 35, which uses the verb "help" to mean defense, is the source of this language. We read in Psalms 35:1–2: "Lord, strive with those who strive against me, give battle to those who battle against me, grasp shield and buckler and rise in my defense" (*vekumah be'ezrati*).—JH

us. All of their firstborn You slew, but You redeemed Your firstborn and split the Sea of Reeds, and sank the wicked and brought out the dear ones.[42] The waters covered their oppressors; not one of them remained.[43] For this the beloved praised and exalted God,[44] and the dear ones sang songs of praise, blessings, and gratitude to the King, living, enduring God. Highly exalted, great and awesome, He brings low the arrogant and raises the downcast, ▨ releases the bound, rescues the humble, helps the poor, and answers His people when they call to Him. Praises to God supreme, ever blessed is He. Moses and the people Israel ◉ responded to You in song very happily, ▨ all of them declaring: "Who is like You, O Lord, among the mighty? Who is like You, glorious in holiness, awesome in splendor, working wonders?"[46]

The redeemed praised Your name with a new song at the shore of the Sea. Together all of them proclaimed Your sovereignty: "The Lord will reign forever and ever."[48]

▨ The imagery of this blessing is filled with reversals as God overturns the expected order of things. The proud are humbled while the meek are redeemed, and those who were enslaved go forth in freedom. There is none of the restraint that we find in the Passover Seder, where wine is removed from the second cup as the ten plagues are recited. All is celebration and thanksgiving. The mighty God has performed miracles; a lowly group of slaves is raised up and their powerful enemies are punished. This imagery is very compelling. Yet it depicts a world of "us" and "them," with God on "our" side, that makes it very difficult to confront and disentangle the complexities of oppression or the reversibility of meekness and arrogance. Perhaps the challenge confronting us is to find a way to give thanks for the "root experience" of liberation and at the same time imagine a world in which the liberation of some is not dependent on the destruction of others.—*Judith Plaskow*[45]

◉ In response to the modern demand for gender equality, a whole host of liturgies (the British *Lev Chadash*, the Reconstructionist *Kol Haneshamah*, and the Reform movement's gender-sensitive *Gates of Prayer*) have added the name of Miriam to that of Moses [at "Moses and the people Israel responded"], acknowledging Miriam's role in leading the Israelites in song and dance at the sea.—*Rabbi David Ellenson*[47]

▨ Rabbi Yochanan Muffs explains that "very happily" here means "whole-heartedly, with no strings attached," as in the idiom "gladly."[49] —*JH*

Since we have recalled the past redemption, we now ask for redemption in our time and in the future. We note the divine promise to deliver the entire Jewish people, alluded to by naming both ancient kingdoms, Judah and Israel:

Rock of Israel, rise to defend the people Israel. Keep Your promise to deliver Judah and Israel. Our Redeemer is the Lord of Hosts, the Holy One of Israel. Blessed are You, Lord who has redeemed the people Israel.

The precise wording of this prayer had not yet been fixed in Rabbinic times, as we learn from a discussion recorded in the Palestinian Talmud, *Brakhot* 1:9.

One who reads the *Shema* in the morning must mention the exodus from Egypt while saying "True and certain." Rabbi says that one must mention

God's sovereignty and others say that one must mention the splitting of the sea and the plague of death of the firstborn. Rabbi Joshua ben Levi says that one must mention all of these and also must include reference to the "Rock and Redeemer of the people Israel."

The present blessing is longer than any of the versions from the Talmud.

✳ The additions incorporate excerpts from the song that Moses and the Israelites sang after they had safely crossed the Sea of Reeds. Daily we relive that miracle by singing the same words. Though we have no precise record of the development of this blessing, we do know that Jews by the ninth century used a text nearly the same as the text we use today.

✳ The early versions of this blessing were quite brief. One such version is recorded in the Babylonian Talmud: "We gratefully acknowledge You, Lord our God, for having taken us out of the land of Egypt, saving us from the house of slavery, and for performing miracles and mighty deeds for us at the sea where we sang to You." The prayer book of Rav Amram Gaon from ninth-century Babylonia includes this blessing in a version nearly identical to our present version. A similar version is found in the prayer book of Rabbi Saadia Gaon of tenth-century Egypt.—*JH*

QUESTIONS FOR FURTHER STUDY AND REFLECTION

1. Many prayer books print the first passage of *Kriat Shema* with the *trop* to which we chant the passage when the Torah is read. Why is this done?

2. *Adonai eḥad,* the two last words of *Shema Yisrael,* are translated in two ways. Which way do you prefer, and why?

3. What is the Tetragrammaton?

4. What are your thoughts about suffering and punishment when you consider the second passage of *Kriat Shema*?

5. What thoughts should be going through our minds as we look at the *tzitzit* during our recitation of the last passage of *Kriat Shema*?

6. What does being "a kingdom of priests and a holy nation" mean? Is this too onerous a responsibility?

7. Rabbi Abraham Joshua Heschel said, "Since there is a need for daily wonder, there is a need for daily worship." Do you agree or disagree? Why? How does the first blessing before *Kriat Shema* meet this need?

8. What is the classic Jewish example of redemption? How, in addition to examples included in this chapter, does the prayer book express the idea of redemption?

---

1. Judith Plaskow on *Shema,* in *My People's Prayer Book: Traditional Prayers, Modern Commentaries, Volume 1: The Shema and Its Blessings,* Rabbi Lawrence A. Hoffman, ed. (Woodstock, VT: Jewish Lights, 1997), page 99.

2.   Jeffrey H. Tigay, *Deuteronomy* (Philadelphia: Jewish Publication Society, 1996), page 76.

3.   Deuteronomy 6:4. Another, widely used, translation reads "the Lord our God, the Lord is One."

4.   For more information about *tefillin*, see Jeffrey H. Tigay, *Deuteronomy*, pages 441-443. Also see Nahum Sarna, *Exodus* (Philadelphia: Jewish Publication Society, 1991), pages 270-273.

5.   The passages included on the parchment scrolls are Deuteronomy 6:4-9 and 11:13-21, which contain the commandment about *mezuzot*. For more information about *mezuzot*, see Jeffrey H. Tigay, *Deuteronomy*, pages 443-444.

6.   Rabbi Goldie Milgram, "The Mezuzah Story" at www.rebgoldie.com/mezuzah_story.htm.

7.   Rabbi Elliot N. Dorff, on Deuteronomy 11:13-21, in *My People's Prayer Book, Volume 1: The Shema*, page 108.

8.   Rabbi Arthur Waskow, "Sh'ma: The Second Paragraph" at www.shalomctr.org. Copyright © 2001 by Arthur Waskow. See Rabbi Waskow's writings on prayer, Torah, and *tikkun olam* on the web site of The Shalom Center, www.shalomctr.org, and in his books, *Seasons of Our Joy* (Beacon), *Godwrestling—Round 2* (Jewish Lights), and (with Phyllis Berman) *A Time for Every Purpose Under Heaven: The Jewish Life-Spiral as a Spiritual Path* (Farrar Straus & Giroux).

9.   Jacob Milgrom, ed., *Numbers* (Philadelphia: Jewish Publication Society, 1990), page 127.

10. Jacob Milgrom, ed., *Numbers*, page 128.

11. Rabbi Arthur Waskow, "At Every Boundary, the World is ONE" at www.shalomctr.org. Copyright © 2001 by Arthur Waskow. See Rabbi Waskow's writings on prayer, Torah, and *tikkun olam* on the web site of The Shalom Center, www.shalomctr.org, and in his books, *Seasons of Our Joy* (Beacon), *Godwrestling—Round 2* (Jewish Lights), and (with Phyllis Berman) *A Time for Every Purpose Under Heaven: The Jewish Life-Spiral as a Spiritual Path* (Farrar Straus & Giroux).

12. For an extensive discussion of *tzitzit*, see Jacob Milgrom, *Numbers*, pages 410-414.

13. Jacob Milgrom, *Numbers*, page 414.

14. The *Kol Nidrei* Service, when the *tallit* is worn, is no exception, because it begins before sunset. The *tallit*, having been put on during daylight, is not removed during the Yom Kippur evening service.

15. Immanuel Kant, *Critique of Practical Reason*, translated by Abbot (London, 1889), page 260.

16. Abraham Joshua Heschel, *God in Search of Man*, cited in Abraham Joshua Heschel, *Between God and Man*, Fritz Rothschild, ed. (New York: Free Press, 1965), page 43.

17. Job 9:10.

18. Psalms 66:9.

19. Literally, "in the land of the children of Ham," a son of Noah and ancestor of the Egyptians.

20. Exodus 15:2.

21. Exodus 15:18.

22. Jeremiah 31:11.

23. Compare to Nehemiah 9:31, "You, O God, are gracious and merciful."

24. Compare to Psalms 121:8, "The Lord will guard your going and your coming."

25. Compare to Psalms 121:4, "The guardian of Israel neither slumbers nor sleeps."

26. Peace will be discussed at greater length in the comments on the last blessing of the *Amidah*.

27. See Chapter 8, pages 188–189.

28. See Chapter 4, pages 81–113.

29. Judith Plaskow, on *Yotzer*, in *My People's Prayer Book, Volume 1: The Shema*, page 53.

30. Psalms 104:24.

31. Judith Plaskow, on *Yotzer*, in *My People's Prayer Book, Volume 1: The Shema*, page 53.

32. I Samuel 2:2.

33. Marcia Falk, *The Book of Blessings: New Jewish Prayers for Daily Life, the Sabbath, and the New Moon Festival* (New York: HarperCollins, 1996; paperback edition, Boston: Beacon, 1999), page 465. See also www.marciafalk.com.

34. Psalms 92:1 and 2.

35. Isaiah 6:3.

36. Ezekiel 3:12.

37. Psalms 136:7.

38. Rabbi Lawrence A. Hoffman on *Vahavi'enu*, in *My People's Prayer Book, Volume 1: The Shema*, page 81.

39. Rabbi Elliot N. Dorff, on *Ahavah rabbah ahavtanu*, in *My People's Prayer Book, Volume 1: The Shema*, page 71.

40. Judith Plaskow on *Vahavi'enu*, in *My People's Prayer Book, Volume 1: The Shema*, pages 75, 81, 82.

41. Compare to Psalms 148:6, "establishing a law that will never change."

42. The people Israel are referred to as "Your dear ones" (*yedidekha*) in Psalms 60:7.

43. Psalms 106:11.

44. *Veromemu el* (praised and exalted God) is based on words from the Song at the Sea (Exodus 15:2) which is soon to be cited here: "[and this is] the God of my father and I exalt Him" (*va'aromemenhu*).

45. Judith Plaskow on *Emet ve'yatziv*, in *My People's Prayer Book, Volume 1: The Shema*, page 129.

46. Exodus 15:11. The word translated here as "mighty" (*elim*) literally means "gods."

47. Rabbi David Ellenson on *Moshe uvenei Yisrael*, in *My People's Prayer Book, Volume 1: The Shema*, pages 130, 132.

48. Exodus 15:18.

49. Rabbi Yochanan Muffs, *Love and Joy* (New York: Jewish Theological Seminary, 1992), pages 123, 127–128.

Chapter

THE *AMIDAH*

Open my lips, and my mouth will declare Your praise

Prayer *par excellence* in Jewish tradition is the *Amidah,* also known as the *Shmoneh Esreih* and as the Silent Prayer. It is known as the Silent Prayer since we recite it silently or in a whisper. ▦ It is known as the *Amidah* ("Standing") because we must stand while reciting it. It is known as the *Shmoneh Esreih* ("Eighteen"), because originally it consisted of 18 blessings, though for nearly 2000 years it has consisted of 19. ❀ It is also known as *Tefillah* ("Prayer"). This dates from the time of the Rabbis, who referred to this collection of blessings simply as "prayer" because of its unique stature in Jewish liturgy.

▦ The Rabbis of the Talmud derive the law determining silent or whispered prayer from the behavior of Hannah, as described in the Bible: "Hannah was praying in her heart; only her lips moved, and her voice could not be heard" (I Samuel 1:13). Hannah's prayer provides the source for many Rabbinic laws about prayer.—*JH*

❀ In the ancient world, 18 vertebrae were believed to constitute the spine, with 19 connective muscles between and around them. The 19 blessings of the *Amidah* carry Divine energy through the spinal column to energize the whole body. One traditional custom is to bow deeply, stretching through all the vertebrae, at the beginning and end of the first blessing and of the 18th (or even at the close of each blessing).

These 19 blessings of praise, hope, holiness, healing, restoration, and peace form a sequence of visualizations which guide us in a process of spiritual transformation—*Rabbi Marcia Prager*[1]

Every formal service of prayer must include the *Amidah*.[2] Thus, we recite the *Amidah* three times a day, at Morning *(Shaharit)*, Afternoon *(Minhah)*, and Evening *(Maariv)* Services. On Shabbat and on Festivals we add another service, called *Musaf* (additional), with an additional *Amidah*. On Yom Kippur we add yet another service *(Ne'ilah)*, with its own *Amidah*. The *Amidah* recited on Shabbat and on Festivals differs from that recited on weekdays; it consists of only seven rather than 19 *brakhot*. Nevertheless, because of habit, many people also refer to the Shabbat or Festival *Amidah* as the *Shmoneh Esreih*.

By whatever name we know it, the origin of this collection of blessings probably dates back to the fifth century BCE. Scholars today believe that a group of sages known as Men of the Great Assembly formulated the *Amidah* blessings then. By the end of the first century, not long after the destruction of the Second Temple in the year 70, the Rabbis of the Mishnah had arranged the prayers of the *Amidah* in the form that we still use. ▦ The first three blessings concentrate on the praise of God. On weekdays, the next 13 contain a variety of requests for the physical and spiritual needs of the individual and of the community. The final three blessings emphasize gratitude. The first three and the final three are identical on all occasions. On Shabbat and Festivals, we delete the middle 13 petitions for fulfillment of needs, since we try not to disturb those days with such concerns. Accordingly, we replace the 13 petitions with one blessing that focuses on the uniqueness of Shabbat or of the Festival day.

We recite the *Amidah* while facing Israel, site of the ancient Temple. When we are in Israel, we face Jerusalem. When we are in Jerusalem, ✹ we face the Western Wall, the only surviving remnant of the ancient Temple

▦ The Babylonian Talmud, *Brakhot* 28b and *Megillah* 17b, notes that the ordering of the *Amidah* prayers was accomplished by Shimon Hapakuli following the directive of Rabban Gamliel, the leader of the authoritative body of sages.—JH

✹ Allow me to recall an "only in Jerusalem" incident. When my family and I were living in Jerusalem, we were visited by a friend from the United States on Shabbat afternoon. When it was time for the Afternoon Service *(Minhah)* we decided to *daven* (pray) on the balcony. Before we began, my friend had a question. "Excuse me, but what direction is Jerusalem?"—JH

✻ We are indeed entering a holy, separate realm when we begin the *Amidah*, but we may turn to additional metaphors to supplement the traditional image of the royal court. We might think of ourselves as having reached a clearing in the woods. Or perhaps we have reached a vista at the top of a mountain. The hike up has energized us, but nothing has prepared us for this awesome moment—the wide open expanse, the majestic beauty with no end. We straighten our spine and we stretch tall to breathe in the cool fresh air. We are still. We hear only our heart and a few distant birds. We are filled with gratitude. We are ready to begin to speak with the Holy One.—*Tamara Cohen*

✳ It is not enough to know that the word *brakhah* asks us to do a soul stretch and be a vessel. We cannot simply call to the soul and say, "OK, stretch now!" We must learn *how* to stretch. I ask myself how I can prepare for this stretch. What qualities can I cultivate to do it well? Is there a soul-exercise I could practice regularly? Can I make myself a supple enough vessel that when my soul hears the word *barukh*, it knows what to do? Another *bet-resh-khaf* word offers us key insight ➤

area. What if we are away from home in an unfamiliar place, and we cannot determine which direction faces Jerusalem? The Talmud teaches that in such circumstances we should direct our heart to our Father in Heaven (*Brakhot* 30a). Most synagogue sanctuaries are constructed with the holy Ark on the wall that faces east, so that we face Jerusalem as we face the Ark.

Our deportment while reciting the *Amidah* should be similar to the way we would behave in the presence of royalty, ✻ since Jewish prayer often refers to God as King. Of course, we should have in mind a royal court *not* from the 21st century, when kings and queens, like nostalgia, are not what they used to be. When kings held life and death in their hands, kingship symbolized God's ultimate power much more appropriately. Standing before God during the *Amidah*, we maintain a formality in the presence of unique royalty, and follow some of the conventions of a royal court. We stand erect, feet close together. We take three small steps forward before beginning the prayer and we take three small steps backward while bowing from the waist after concluding the prayer. At four specified points during the *Amidah* we bow at the knee and at the waist. ✽ We do so at the beginning and at the end of the first blessing, and again at the beginning and at the end of the 18th blessing (known as *modim* from its first Hebrew word). We do not interrupt the *Amidah* for anything except an emergency.

into becoming vessels of blessing. That word is *berekh*, which means "knee." … That the letters comprising the root of *brakhah* and *breikha*, "blessing" and "fountain," also teach us *berekh*, "knee," is therefore a very powerful teaching. For *berekh* calls to us, "Do not shut down! Know awe! Live in reverence. Allow yourself to open and fill with the miracle of it all. In joy and trembling, kneel."—*Rabbi Marcia Prager* [3]

✻ *Yod-hei-vav-hei* is translated as Lord in "O Lord, open my lips." The revised *Siddur Sim Shalom* of 1998 [4] uses the transliteration of the word *Adonai*. Using *Adonai* preserves some of the sense of meaning only itself—a name for God that cannot be reduced. [For more on *Adonai*, see pages 210–211]. These first words of the *Amidah* suggest a partnership in prayer. We say God, I need your help, you open my lips, for only then will I be able to offer words of praise.—*Tamara Cohen*

✽ The verse, "O Lord, open my lips, and my mouth will proclaim Your praise," is from Psalms 51:17 and is customarily recited prior to the *Amidah*, as prescribed in the Babylonian Talmud, *Brakhot* 4b. In the words of Abraham Joshua Heschel, we pray for the ability to pray. In the Book of Psalms, this verse is followed by: "You have no delight in sacrifice or I would give it; burnt offerings You do not desire. True sacrifice to God is a contrite spirit; God, a contrite and broken heart You will not despise" (Psalms 51:18–19).—*JH*

▩ The literal meaning of the Hebrew word *avot* is "fathers." The word "ancestors" replaces it here and elsewhere in the translation out of consideration for those who want to emphasize that our matriarchs as well as our patriarchs are included in the Hebrew word. Recently published prayer books [5] by both the Reform and the Reconstructionist movements change the Hebrew prayer from *Veilohei avoteinu* (literally "and God of our fathers") to *Veilohei avoteinu ve'imoteinu* ("God of our fathers and our mothers").—*JH*

O Lord, ✻ open my lips, and my mouth will proclaim Your praise. ✽

1. Blessed are You, Lord our God and God of our ancestors ▩, God of Abraham, God of Isaac, and God of Jacob,[6] great, mighty, and awesome God,[7] God supreme,

◻ "Most High" is the literal translation of the Hebrew for the word presented here as "supreme," in the verse: "Blessed be Abram of God Most High, Creator of heaven and earth" (Genesis 14:19).—JH

◉ The literal meaning of the word translated as "nature" is "name" (shmo). The translation follows the tradition that one of God's names is "merciful, gracious God." At this point between Rosh Hashanah and Yom Kippur, we add: "Remember us that we may live, O King who delights in life. Inscribe us in the Book of Life, for Your sake, living God."—JH

◻ Genesis 15:1 states: "Fear not, Abram, I am a shield to you." (The verse precedes the occasion when Abram's name was changed to Abraham.)—JH

✳ [Rabbi Marcia Prager has composed guided visualizations for the prayers of the weekday Amidah. Her imagery can inspire us as we pray.] Avot—We call upon our ancestors for support in our journey.

Visualize Abraham and Sarah standing before you. They can be seen as two radiant light sources. Extend from them two rays of interwoven light. The light forms a chain that comes down through the generations into you. Allow the light to grow up around you, following your spine until it comes to rest on the crown of your head. Spiral it down until you are enclosed in this light. The light is your protection.

Helping, saving, and protecting power!

You are a fountain of blessing, Holy One, protector of Abraham, supporter of Sarah.—Rabbi Marcia Prager [12]

◼ The term "God of Abraham, Isaac, and Jacob" is semantically different from a term such as "the God of truth, goodness, and beauty." Abraham, Isaac, and Jacob do not signify ideas, principles, or abstract values. Nor do they stand for teachers or thinkers, and the term is not to be understood like that of "the God of Kant, Hegel, and Schelling." Abraham, Isaac, and Jacob are not principles to be comprehended but lives to be continued. The life of one who joins the covenant of Abraham continues the life of Abraham. For the present is not apart from the past. "Abraham is still standing before God" (Genesis 18:22). Abraham endures forever. We are Abraham, Isaac, and Jacob.— Rabbi Abraham Joshua Heschel [14]

✳ Rabbinic tradition connects the silent Amidah with Hannah's silent prayer for a child. Hers is the only woman's prayer recorded in the Bible. "Now Hannah was praying in her heart: Only her lips moved, but her voice could not be heard" (1 Samuel 1:13). Eli, the High Priest, mistakes Hannah's wordless prayer for drunken babbling. He learns, however, that she has been offering a prayer of the heart.

These verses from the book of Samuel are designated as the Haftarah for the first day of Rosh Hashanah. On a day with an elaborately prescribed liturgy, Hannah reminds us that we are required to ➤

◻ who grants pure kindnesses,[8] Creator of all.[9] He remembers the kindnesses of our ancestors [10] and lovingly brings a redeemer to their children's children because of His merciful nature. ◉ He is the King who defends [11] and saves and shields. Blessed are You, Lord, Shield of Abraham. ◻

How do we address God? How do we name the ineffable? Philosophers, theologians, and poets have all posed the question. A. M. Klein, a 20th-century Canadian Jewish poet, asks:

> With what name
>   shall I call You? Where
> shall I discover the syllable,
>   the mystic word
> that shall evoke You
>   from eternity?
> Is that sweet sound a heart
>   makes, clocking life,
> Your appellation? Is the
>   noise of thunder, it?
> Is it the hush of peace,
>   the sound of strife?
> I have no title for
>   Your glorious throne,
> and for Your nearness
>   not a golden word—
> only that wanting You,
>   by that alone
> I do evoke You, knowing
>   I am heard. [13]

Such personal quests provoke and inspire us in our own search. ✳

"Lord our God and God of our ancestors, God of Abraham, God of Isaac, and God of Jacob." ◼ In prayer there are many paths, many ways. For many people, the path begun by the opening words of the *Amidah* does not lead to satisfactory fulfillment because the prayer does not include the names of the matriarchs. Many Jews who advocate changing the words of ancient prayers consider gender equality to be a principle that overrides all precedent, and after "God of Jacob" they add the names of the matriarchs to the prayer: "God of Sarah, God of Rebecca, God of Rachel, and God of Leah." ❃ ▦ No sensible person denies the importance of the matriarchs, who were partners with the patriarchs in the formation of the people Israel. However, inserting the matriarchs violates the liturgical and the literary integrity of the classic text. It also breaks the close link between the language of the Bible and the language of the prayer book. The ancient Rabbis carefully constructed this first blessing using many phrases from the Bible.

In the Book of Exodus (3:15), God reveals to Moses that one of His names is "the Lord, God of your fathers, God of Abraham, God of Isaac, and God of Jacob." The passage continues: "This is My name forever, this is how I am to be recalled for generation after generation." To add the names of the matriarchs or, indeed, any other word to this phrase from Exodus is to change God's name as revealed to Moses. To retain the classic

attend not only to the written words in the *siddur*, but to the words in our own hearts.

As important as Hannah's silent prayer is, it is no longer acceptable for women's voices not to be heard. The way women name God, out of our life experiences, from our hearts, should be added to the written words of the *siddur*.

Abraham's God was *Magen Avraham*, Shield of Abraham. Abraham, going toward a place that God would show him, understood God as Protector and Shield. Isaac's God was called *Pahad Yitzhak*, Fear of Isaac. Bound to an altar on Mount Moriah, Isaac trembled before the awesome nature of the Divine. Jacob's God is named *Avir Yaakov*, the Power of Jacob. Jacob's transformation from the twin brother of Esau to the leader of 12 sons and one daughter, the father of the 12 tribes of Israel, taught him of Divine Power.

Scholars have suggested that the reason the *Avot* blessing reads "God of Abraham, God of Isaac, God of Jacob"—repeating the word God for each of the patriarchs—is precisely that each patriarch experienced God in a different way. Isaac and Jacob did not simply receive the tradition of Abraham, they renewed it and passed it on to another generation. Just as Isaac and Jacob sought and named God from their places, so we too must search for God from our place.

Throughout Jewish tradition, people called God by many names—*Creator, Revealer, Redeemer, Rock, Teacher, Compassionate One*, even *Man of War*. Isaiah suggests the name *Mother*: "Even as a mother comforts her child, so I shall comfort you" (Isaiah 66:13).

In the Bible the only woman to name God is Hagar. When an angel of God informs her that she will bear a son and name him Ishmael, Hagar calls God *El Ro'i*—the God who sees me (Genesis 16:13).

Including the names of the matriarchs alongside the patriarchs in the first blessing of the *Amidah*, as the Reconstructionist, Reform, and the new *Siddur Sim Shalom* do, acknowledges that the ways in which our mothers knew God, the ways in which they whispered God's name, are a part of our Jewish heritage.

The ancient Rabbis, building on the Biblical text, did not include a reference to the matriarchs in their liturgical formulation—this reflects their world view. It should not constrain us, in faithfulness to our own spiritual quest, from formulating prayer in a way that builds a bridge between the classical text and our generation.

By speaking not only of the God of our fathers, God of Abraham, God of Isaac, God of Jacob, but of the God of our mothers, God of Sarah, God of Rebecca, God of Rachel, God of Leah, we place God's mirror before women and ask their names for God. Only then can the God of our ancestors become our God as well.—*Rabbi Sandy Eisenberg Sasso*

▦ The question is ... should we add the names of the *imahot*, the foremothers, to the blessing? Can we not also turn to God and claim ➤

words of the Bible here implies no hidden agenda of denigrating the matriarchs; ▣ to recite those words is to quote Scripture, nothing more and nothing less.

Those who support the inclusion of the matriarchs in the first blessing of the *Amidah* cite as a precedent the inclusion of the matriarchs in the *mi sheberakh* blessings that are recited during the Torah Service.[15] However, the long-standing practice of reciting the names of the matriarchs in those blessings constitutes no proof and provides no support for changing the wording of the first blessing of the *Amidah*. In Jewish law, the status of the *Amidah* blessings differs entirely from that of the *mi sheberakh* blessings. The latter are optional blessings recited on behalf of individuals, and their content has been flexible for centuries.

"Great, mighty, and awesome." What adjectives do we use to describe God? Because the list is endless, the Rabbis imposed a limit on adjectives, at least for this phrase in the *Amidah*. The Talmud relates that a leader of prayer embellished upon this description in the presence of Rabbi Ḥanina, adding that God is powerful, imposing, adamant, bold, confident, and honored. Rabbi Ḥanina inquired, "Have you completed all the praise of your Master? We would not be able to utter even the three adjectives that we include [that is, great, mighty, and awesome] had they not been stated by Moses in the Torah and included in the *Amidah* by the men of the Great Assembly. What you are doing could be compared to praising a mortal king for possessing some silver when he possesses thousands and thousands of gold dinars. This is belittlement, not praise" (Babylonian Talmud, *Brakhot* 33b).

"God supreme … Creator of all." These descriptions are uttered by the king and priest Melchizedek (Genesis 14:19) when greeting Abraham (known then as Abram).[18]

"Brings a redeemer *(mevi go'el)* to their children's children."

---

special treatment because of the merit stored up by them? It might be that our blessing has in mind a series of acts that only the *fathers* did (like attempting to save Sodom from destruction). But it is more likely that the special piety in question is something more general: the way (we presume) that the *avot* and the *imahot* (the foremothers) lived their lives. Surely Sarah, Rebecca, Rachel, and Leah also believed in God and did whatever God asked them to do. A reference to both would be a good way to express the totality of the Jewish people back then. When our blessing was written, mentioning only the forefathers may have been sufficient because their wives were automatically included as members of the ancient household, who, like children and slaves, were cared for by the head of household. However, to make this same point today, it is necessary to list counterparts of the *avot*—Sarah, Rebecca, Rachel, and Leah. If we are asking God to be kind to us today because of the merit of our progenitors, then mentioning the matriarchs is critical.—*Judith Hauptman*[16]

▣ Some who criticize the inclusion of the matriarchs do so because the list is incomplete. Limiting mention of the mothers of tribes to Rachel and Leah slights the two women by whom Jacob sired four progenitors of the tribes of Israel: Zilpah (the mother of Gad and Asher) and Bilhah (the mother of Dan and Naftali),[17] whose unusually good qualities are reflected in the legend that the *Shekhinah* resided in her after Rachel and Leah died (*Zohar* 1:175b). Rabbinic tradition limits the matriarchs to Sarah, Rebecca, Rachel, and Leah.—*JH*

Orthodox and Conservative Jewish prayer books incorporate the belief in a personal redeemer, the Messiah. Reconstructionist and Reform Jewish prayers, however, omit all reference to a personal redeemer, though both denominations believe in redemption. Reform and Reconstructionist prayer books have therefore changed the Hebrew as well as the English to read: "brings redemption *(mevi ge'ulah)* to their children's children."[19]

"Shield of Abraham." The Rabbis took this description of God from the Book of Genesis (15:1). Some advocates of gender equality within Hebrew prayer fault this phrase for its failure to mention Sarah, though excluding Sarah and the other matriarchs from the history of the people Israel is, of course, impossible. A recently published Conservative prayer book for Shabbat and Festivals expands the phrase to read "shield of Abraham who remembers Sarah" (*magen Avraham ufoked Sarah*). The added phrase may seem innocuous to those who read only English, but the Hebrew phrase in this context is a strange choice. The Hebrew verb in the phrase, *poked,* appears throughout the Bible in this form only in the context of punishment. For example, "He [God] remembers *(poked)* [also translated as 'visits'] the sins of the parents upon the children" (Exodus 20:5). ❁

Why, then, would the Hebrew *poked* even be considered here? Because this Hebrew verb for remember, or visit, appears in a passage about Sarah, though in another form, *pakad*. Chapter 21 of Genesis begins with the words, "And God remembered Sarah"—*pakad et Sarah*. The use of the verb in a different tense within the prayer book causes a problem, because each verb form carries different associations. The form *poked* resonates with references to sins and to punishment, and we find that form throughout the Hebrew Bible. ⌘ Hence, in both style and substance, the phrase *ufoked Sarah* is a troubling intrusion into a carefully constructed blessing.

In addition, using language that limits the role of Sarah to motherhood is a curious choice for feminists, who correctly emphasize the unlimited roles that should be open to women in our time. The roles of Abraham and Sarah in the phrase "shield of Abraham who remembers Sarah" are unbalanced, since the phrase about Abraham refers to his whole

❁ The exact phrase, "He remembers the sins of the parents upon the children" is repeated in Exodus 34:7, Numbers 14:18, and Deuteronomy 5:9, as well as Exodus 20:5. See, too, Jeremiah 29:32, "thus said the Lord: 'I am going to punish *(poked)* Shemaiah." In Jeremiah 46:25, God declares, "I will inflict punishment *(hineni foked)* on Amon."—*JH*

⌘ For those who wish to include the matriarchs in the first benediction, the *hatimah* (concluding benedictory clause), *magen Avraham ufoked Sarah* has the stylistic advantage of invoking a Biblical image ("who took note of Sarah"; refer to Genesis 21:1), on a par with "shield of Abraham" (refer to Genesis15:1). The Hebrew root *p-k-d* refers to God's providential attention; this can be for benefaction or for punishment. Rabbi Harlow correctly notes that all ten participial uses of this root in the *Tanakh* [Hebrew Bible] are negative; but many of the perfect and imperfect uses throughout the Torah are positive—so one will discern the Biblical resonance one wishes to discern.—*Richard S. Sarason*

life and the phrase about Sarah refers to one single episode. Reform and Reconstructionist prayer books add "and help of Sarah" *(ve'ezrat Sarah)* to "shield of Abraham." ⊞ This added phrase also treats Sarah unequally since, unlike the phrase about Abraham, it has no basis in the language of the Bible as related to her.

⊞ [The Reform and Reconstructionist] version of the first *brakhah* in the *Amidah* includes the matriarchs as well as the patriarchs. The phrase "help of Sarah," *ezrat Sarah,* comes from a Hebrew root *(ayin–zayin–resh)* which can mean either "save" or "be strong." This parallels the meaning of *magen*/shield…. Abraham experienced God as a shield and Sarah experienced God as a helper. Their experience and the example of their lives can enrich our own. Just as Abraham and Sarah found the strength to face the unknown physical and spiritual dangers of their journey, so we seek to find the courage and inspiration to meet the challenges of our time.—*Reena Spicehandler*[20]

✹ The Rabbis' directive (Babylonian Talmud, *Brakhot* 34a) that we remain upright recalls the words of Ecclesiastes 7:16, "Be not over-righteous." Or, in popular parlance, "Don't be such a *tzaddik*!"—*JH*

✵ On the days between Rosh Hashanah and Yom Kippur, after saying "causes salvation to blossom," we add: "Who is like You, merciful Father remembering His creatures in mercy with life?"—*JH*

While saying "blessed are You" (*barukh Attah*), we bend the knee and bow at the waist. By the time "Lord" *(Adonai)* is said, we should be standing erect again. If we indeed must humble ourselves before God, why does Jewish practice limit the bowing in the *Amidah* to the beginning and end of this *brakhah* and the 18th *brakhah*? The Rabbis taught that one must not bow at the other blessings, because we should guard against excessive humility and its display. ✹

2. You are mighty forever, Lord, You give life to the dead, You save us in many ways.

[From Shemini Atzeret to Pesaḥ, we add:

You cause the wind to blow and the rain to fall.]

He sustains the living with kindness, gives life to the dead with great mercy, supports the falling, heals the ailing, releases the bound and keeps His faith with those who sleep in dust.[21] Who is like You, Master of might, who can be compared to You, King who brings death and gives life,[22] and causes salvation to blossom?[23] ✵ Faithful are You in giving life to the dead. Blessed are You, Lord who gives life to the dead.

God gives life to the dead. Discussions and debates about the meaning of these words, though of basic importance, have obscured the main message of this *brakhah,* which affirms God's power in our lives. The ancient Rabbis who named each *brakhah* called this one "powers" *(gevurot),* ✹ not "giving life to the dead." This power includes giving and sustaining life, healing the sick, freeing the captive, and raising the fallen. This power manifests God's kindness.

We find another example of divine power in the words inserted in this blessing between Shemini Atzeret in the fall and Pesaḥ in the spring.

During this period, the first sentence of the *brakhah* is followed by "God causes the wind to blow and the rain to fall" *(mashiv haruah umorid hagashem)*. Our focus here reflects our concern for the land of Israel and its rainy season.

Jews have been engaged in controversy about the meaning of giving life to the dead since Rabbinic times. The Sadducees argued that giving life to the dead does not mean physical resurrection. Their opponents, the Pharisees, did believe in physical resurrection, and their opinion has become normative Jewish doctrine.[25] Many today continue to believe in physical resurrection. Others interpret "gives life to the dead" in a variety of ways, affirming that the death of the body does not mean the absolute end of life but only the end of life as we know it. Still others, including theologians of the Reform and Reconstructionist movements, change the words of the blessing. For example, in *Gates of Prayer,* the Reform prayer book, in both English and Hebrew, "gives life to all" or *mehayeh hakol* replaces "gives life to the dead" or *mehayeh metim*. Similarly, the Reconstructionist prayer book *Kol Haneshamah* uses the phrase "nurturing the life of every living thing" or *mehayeh kol hai*.[26] ❈ In the Conservative *Siddur Sim Shalom*, the last words of the English translation praise God as "Master of life and death," reflecting the theme that has been stated throughout the *brakhah,* God's omnipotence. At the beginning of the blessing, *Siddur Sim Shalom* retains "gives life to the dead" in both Hebrew and English. ❋

❋ [Rabbi Marcia Prager has composed guided visualizations for the prayers of the weekday *Amidah*.] Hesed and *Gevurah*—We open to Divine expansiveness and power.

See yourself in a time of your life in which you felt lost, confused, despairing. See a light come into your heart. Allow it to grow until you shine with your own source. Imagine yourself lying down at first, and gradually, as the light fills you, you come to standing.

Loyal restorer of life!

You are a fountain of blessing, Holy One, restoring life in the deadened.—*Rabbi Marcia Prager* [24]

❖ In the modern period, various reformers excised or rephrased elements of the *Amidah* that they no longer deemed credible or desirable. Thus, references to the resurrection of the dead and to angels, as well as petitions for the messianic restoration of all Jews to the land of Israel, the rebuilding of the Temple, and the reinstitution of animal sacrifices were removed, while petitions for the welfare of Jews alone were made universal. Recent generations of reformers, however, have restored much of the traditional Hebrew text, construing the more problematic elements metaphorically.—*Richard S. Sarason*

❋ An important aspect of divine power mentioned three times in [the second blessing of the *Amidah*]—once in the opening, once in the middle, and once in the eulogy—is that of "reviving the dead," *meha'yeh metim*—an attribution that has been eliminated in recent times from a number of standard prayer books…. Although understandable, the substitution of *hakol*, "all," or *kol hai*, "all that lives," for *hametim*, "the dead," seems to me misguided. Presumably, Reform and Reconstructionist objections to the phrase *meha'yeh metim* have to do with the literal interpretation of it as referring to the resurrection of the dead in messianic times. While that may once have been its primary meaning, there are a number of other ways to read it and to reconstruct the idea behind it. The selective elimination of this phrase—among only a handful of phrases seen as absolutely unacceptable by these two modern movements in Judaism—lends a tacit approval to other ➤

3. You are holy, Your name is holy and holy ones will praise You daily. Blessed are You, Lord, holy God. ▓

Who are the "holy ones"? Some authorities state that they are angels; others state that the phrase refers to the people Israel.

In public prayer, when the leader of the service repeats the *Amidah*, the *Kedushah*, which emphasizes God's holiness, replaces this short *brakhah* as the third blessing of the *Amidah*.

KEDUSHAH

This passage is recited only in the presence of a *minyan*.[27] Thus, like the *Kaddish* and the Torah Service, its recitation reflects and teaches the holiness of community. *Kedushah* means holiness or sanctification. When ten or more adult Jews are present, we add *Kedushah* to the *Amidah* during all Morning and Afternoon Services, and during the Additional *(Musaf)* Service on Shabbat and Festivals. At those times, the leader of the service chants *Kedushah* aloud as part of the third blessing of the *Amidah*. The congregation chants responses (indicated by indented lines) to the words recited by the leader (who then may repeat the congregational responses before continuing with the next phrase).

words in the liturgy that would surely seem equally preposterous today if understood in a fundamentalist way. Indeed, of all theological concepts, that of *tehiyat hametim*, "revival of the dead," seems to me one that is worth saving and grappling with. To avoid addressing it is to evade one of the monumental concerns of human life—our relationship to mortality.

My restoration of *tehiyat hametim* to [my] new *Amidah* is based on the conviction that it can be meaningfully read as an acknowledgment and even affirmation of the presence of death in our lives. For what is life without death? And what life is not part of the circle of dying, and what death is not part of the circle of living? ... In the traditional prayer, "killing" and "reviving" are acts of an agent (God) upon something else (the world). The new blessing, in contrast, speaks of the circle of life as that which kills and revives; no separate object is implied here. At first, this idea may seem puzzling. What this new blessing seeks to convey is a sense of life in continuous regenerative movement, continually dying and renewing itself:

> Let us bless the well
> eternally giving—
> the circle of life
> ever-dying, ever-living.
> —*Marcia Falk*[28]

▓ During the Ten Days of Repentance we say "holy King" rather than "holy God," since the liturgy of the Rosh Hashanah and Yom Kippur season depicts God as King on the throne of judgment.—*JH*

✸ The congregation recites these words ("We will hallow Your name") before the leader begins the recitation of *Kedushah*. We invite ourselves to join in following the mysterious model of the angelic choruses.—*JH*

Kedushah for Weekday Morning and Afternoon, and Shabbat Afternoon

We will hallow Your name in the world, ✸ **as it is hallowed in the heavens above, as written by Your prophet: They called one to the other, saying**

"Holy, holy, holy, *Adonai Tzevaot*, ※ the whole world is filled with His glory."[29]

Heavenly voices respond saying, "Blessed—

"Blessed is the glory of the Lord from His place."[30]

And in Your holy words it is written,

"The Lord shall reign forever; Your God, Zion, through all generations. Halleluyah."[31]

In all generations will we tell of Your greatness, to all eternity will we hallow Your holiness. Your praise, our God, will never leave our lips, for You are God and King, great and holy. Blessed are You, Lord, holy God. ✳

※ The Aramaic translation of this verse (from Isaiah 6:3) interprets the triple enunciation of the word "holy" to mean that God is holy in the heavens and on earth and in time. It is customary to rise on one's toes while repeating the word "holy" *(kadosh)*. Symbolically we lift ourselves out of our natural orbit to imitate actions of heavenly creatures in Isaiah's vision. The words *Adonai Tzevaot* are literally translated as "Lord of Hosts," probably meaning Lord of the heavenly array of sun, moon, stars, and planets (perhaps including angels as well).—*JH*

✳ *[Rabbi Marcia Prager has written guided imagery for the prayers of the weekday* Amidah.] *Kedushat Hashem*—We name the Holy.

Breathe in and out, seeing the purity of your breath come into your body. Breathe out slowly, allowing all impurities to leave you. Experience the wholeness and completeness of each breath. Feel its circularity, its roundness, its holiness. God's name is in each breath.

You are holy, Your name is holy. All holy beings hail You each day.

You are a fountain of blessings, Holy One, Breath-of-Life, Sacred Power.—*Rabbi Marcia Prager*[32]

The boldness of this liturgical act features mortals hallowing God's name, following the example of angels on high, far removed from human experience, as described in the visions of the prophets Isaiah and Ezekiel. In Isaiah's vision, angels surround God's divine throne and form an ecstatic chorus proclaiming, "Holy, holy, holy." Celestial beings chant in Ezekiel's vision as well: "Blessed is the glory of the Lord from His place." God's glory is everywhere; it fills the universe. Yet *Kedushah* recalls the Temple and Jerusalem, the holiest sites on earth in Judaism. It does this in a citation from Psalm 146, not ascribed to angels, affirming the eternal sovereignty of the God of Zion, a synonym for Jerusalem. Psalm 146 praises God "who brings justice to the oppressed and provides food for the hungry ... frees the bound ... gives sight to the blind ... protects the stranger, supports the orphan and the widow." The words of this psalm bring us back to earth, to help us proclaim and celebrate God's holiness as manifest not only in the heavens but also on earth in the here and now of human life.

Kedushah for Shabbat Morning

We will hallow Your name in the world, as it is hallowed in the heavens above, as written by Your prophet: They called one to the other, saying

"Holy, holy, holy *Adonai Tzevaot*, the whole world is filled with His glory."[33]

Then in a loud, thundering voice, majestic and strong in chorus resounding, lifted toward singing seraphim, heavenly voices respond saying: "Blessed—

"Blessed is the glory of the Lord from His place." [34]

From Your place, our King, appear and reign over us, for we await You. When will You reign in Zion? May it be soon in our time, and forever may You dwell there. Enhanced and hallowed may You be amidst Jerusalem Your city through all generations and for eternity. May our eyes behold Your sovereignty, as it is written in the songs of Your splendor, by David Your triumphant anointed:

"The Lord shall reign forever; Your God, Zion, through all generations. Halleluyah." [35]

In all generations will we tell of Your greatness, to all eternity will we hallow Your holiness. Your praise, our God, will never leave our lips, for You are God and King, great and holy. Blessed are You, Lord, holy God.

Kedushah for Shabbat morning, unlike *Kedushah* for a weekday morning, includes a prayer that in our lifetime we will all be united in recognizing God as the ultimate authority, a prayer that God will truly rule in Zion and throughout the world. God truly will reign as sovereign only when everyone recognizes God's sovereignty, for a King requires a kingdom. We express these hopes publicly on Shabbat, a day when we devote time and prayer to contemplating redemption and anticipating the blessings of the world to come, a day when we focus on the peace and tranquility of the world to come.

Kedushah for Shabbat Musaf

We will acclaim and hallow You, guided by the mystic meetings of holy seraphim who hallow Your name in the holy place as written by Your prophets: They called one to the other, saying

"Holy, holy, holy *Adonai Tzevaot*, the whole world is filled with His glory." [36]

His glory fills the world. When His serving angels ask each other, "Where is the place of His glory?" heavenly voices respond, saying: "Blessed—

"Blessed is the glory of the Lord from His place." [37]

From His place may He turn in mercy, with graciousness for the people who night and day, every day continually, twice daily, proclaim His uniqueness lovingly when they recite the *Shema*.

"Hear, O Israel, the Lord is our God, the Lord alone." [38]

He alone is our God, He is our Father, our King, our Redeemer, and He will tell us in mercy, once again, before all that live, "to be your God."

"I, the Lord, am your God."

And in Your holy words it is written,

"The Lord shall reign forever; Your God, Zion, through all generations. Halleluyah."[39]

In all generations will we tell of Your greatness, to all eternity will we hallow Your holiness. Your praise, our God, will never leave our lips, for You are God and King, great and holy. Blessed are You, Lord, holy God. ▩

The quotations "to be your God" and "I, the Lord, am your God" allude to the Exodus, the liberation from ancient Egyptian bondage that was God's

first redemption of the people Israel. They are among the last words of *Kriat Shema* (see page 64), taken from the Book of Numbers (15:41): "I, the Lord, am your God who brought you out of the land of Egypt to be your God. I, the Lord, am your God."

The *Musaf Kedushah* confidently asserts that "in mercy, once again, before all who live," God will redeem the people Israel, following the model of the redemption from Egypt. This assertion fuels the faith in the coming of the Messiah that will initiate the future age of redemption. A secular articulation of the Jews' persevering faith in the future is reflected in the poem that has become the national anthem of the State of Israel. This poem, written before the establishment of the State, articulates a principle that energizes the Jewish people: the hope (*hatikvah*) for fulfillment that includes Jewish life in the Holy Land as personified by Zion, Jerusalem. The reestablishment of Jewish sovereignty in the Holy Land in

▩ *Kiddush*, the blessing we say over wine to usher in the holidays and Shabbat; *kiddushin*, the ceremony that unites two people in marriage; and *Kedushah* all share a common root. What is the connection between the two ritual events, and how are they connected to the *Kedushah* in the *Amidah*?

Kedushah means sacredness, the quality that transforms and transcends the mundane, giving life meaning beyond its earthly bounds. *Kedushah* is not an inherent characteristic. It is a dynamic identity born through acts of use, love, and commitment.

We learn this from the blessings we say before every commanded act: "Blessed are You, Ruler of eternity, who has sanctified (*kiddshanu*) us with your commandments." The commandments are God's gifts, and we become sacred and beloved by God by receiving these commandments and responding to them.

Likewise, we become sacred to our husband or wife, and they in turn to us, when we declare our exclusive attention and commitment to them, and they receive our declarations and respond to them. And the holy days become sacred when we declare their special significance and relationship to us and act accordingly.

The *Kedushah* represents this dynamism of declaration and responsiveness. That is why the *Kedushah* is recited responsively and in community.

Even more, the *Kedushah* demonstrates the reflexivity of sanctification. That is, we become sacred in relationship to that which we hallow. The power of the *Kedushah* is not only that we declare God's sacredness, but that in the process, we become hallowed and sanctified. In *kiddushin*, as we sanctify our spouse to us, we in turn become sanctified to the spouse.

The result of this performance of declaration and awareness is revealed in the moment of reciting the words of the *Kedushah*. We become transformed, like angels in the presence of God. In doing so, we cause the radiance of God's light to fall more powerfully upon us, warming our souls and guiding our steps.—*Rabbi Nina Beth Cardin*

modern times contains the seeds of the promise of national redemption. Secular and religious Jews alike dream of that final redemption, even when life's realities make it appear to be unattainable. Religious Jews affirm and reaffirm the dream as a community in prayer resonating with the experiences and the words of the Bible. Shabbat itself, a reflection of our ideal life in the world to come after the redemption, provides us with an especially appropriate time to make such an affirmation.

* * *

⊠ *Tefillah* ([Petitionary] Prayer), or *Hatefillah* (The [Petitionary] Prayer) is the Talmudic designation for this set of prayers. Medieval Sefardi Jews called it the *Amidah* (Standing [Prayer]), while medieval Ashkenazim referred to it as the *Shmoneh Esreih* (Eighteen [Benedictions]). Today, the designations are interchangeable. This rubric forms the core of the fixed daily communal liturgy, because originally it was the sole element of that liturgy. (The *Kriat Shema* rubric, which may have its roots in the pre-70 period, was initially an independent liturgy with its own distinct rationale and function, based on the interpretation of Deuteronomy 6:7.) The growing consensus of contemporary scholarship is that the institution of thrice-daily communal prayer is a Rabbinic innovation from the period after the destruction of the Second Temple in 70 CE. There is no evidence that such a practice was widespread or general while the Temple stood, though it may have been the practice of some pietist groups. (We know, for example, that daily communal liturgies were recited at sunrise and sunset at Qumran, but they were different from the Rabbinic liturgies. We do not know whether other pre-70 groups, such as the Pharisees, engaged in this practice.) As a time-bound communal liturgy, the *Amidah* was intended to substitute for the time-bound daily sacrifices in the now-destroyed Temple. (That is why there is an additional—*Musaf*—recitation on Sabbaths and Festivals, corresponding to the additional offerings made on those occasions in the Temple.) Since Temple sacrifices took place twice, rather than three times, a day, the thrice-daily prayer times might be due to a conflation of customs, or might be based on the pious customs of individuals or groups before 70 (refer to Daniel 6:10 and Psalm 55:18). The disputed status of the evening prayer (obligatory or not?) partially reflects this concern.

Earliest Rabbinic literature makes clear that the overall topic and the themes of each benediction were fixed from the outset, as were the ➤

Following *Kedushah*, we recite 13 middle blessings on weekdays, and one middle blessing on Shabbat and Festivals. ⊠ Blessing 4 is the first of the middle blessings recited on weekdays, and the first of three blessings that express spiritual needs of the individual.

4. You graciously grant mortals intellect, and teach human beings understanding. ⊛ Graciously grant us intellect, understanding, and discernment that flow from You. Blessed are You, Lord who graciously grants intellect. ⊠

The gifts of intellect and understanding flow from God's grace. This is reflected in the use of the verb meaning "grants graciously" (*honen*) rather than "gives" (*noten*). This *brakhah* also calls to mind King Solomon's response when God asked him to wish for anything in the world: King Solomon requested wisdom and knowledge (II Chronicles 1:10).

At the Evening Service following Shabbat or a Festival, the fourth blessing is replaced by the following:

4 *havdalah*. You graciously grant mortals intellect, and teach human beings understanding. You graciously granted us knowledge of Your Torah, and taught

us to fulfill the laws as You have willed. You, Lord our God, have distinguished between sacred and secular, light and darkness, the people Israel and the other peoples, and between the seventh day and the six working days. Our Father, our King, begin to foster peace for the coming days, free of all sin and cleansed of all wrongdoing, clinging to reverence for You. Graciously grant us intellect, understanding, and discernment. Blessed are You, Lord who graciously grants intellect.

5. Bring us back, our Father, to Your Torah and bring us near, our King, to Your service. Help us return to You in perfect repentance. Blessed are You, Lord who desires repentance.

This *brakhah* follows the *brakhah* on understanding, just as repentance requires understanding. This *brakhah*, together with the next, addresses God as "our Father" and "our King." Jewish faith needs both descriptions, since God is both near and far, near as parents are to children and yet removed as a king in a castle beyond a moat. These images of God recur throughout Jewish liturgy.

The words of the prophet Isaiah that form part of our *Amidah* prayers on Yom Kippur reflect the Jewish emphasis on repentance: "Let the wicked forsake his path, and the unrighteous man his plotting. Let him return to the Lord, who will show him compassion. Let him return to our God, who will surely forgive him."

concluding benedictory formulas (such as *magen David, mehayeh hametim*), but evidence suggests that the precise wordings of the benedictions were initially flexible. Throughout the Talmudic period, more and more phrases became fixed. What later became the tradition of 19 daily benedictions is the custom of the Babylonian academies; the Palestinian rite retained the number 18. (In Babylonia, the "Jerusalem" and "David" benedictions were recited separately; in the land of Israel, the topics were conjoined in a single benediction.)

The content of the weekday *Amidah* is primarily petitionary, for the welfare of the Jewish people and its individual members. As Rabbi Harlow points out, both its rhetoric and its performance are governed by the etiquette of a subject approaching the sovereign. Thus, the Rabbis deemed it inappropriate to begin by making demands. Instead, one first lays forth the past basis of the relationship *(avot)*, then acknowledges the sovereign's power *(gevurot)* and majesty *(kedushah)*. Only then does the subject respectfully make requests. Before departing from the royal presence, the subject also expresses gratitude for past benefactions *(hodaah).—Richard S. Sarason*

The blessing, which thanks God for granting us knowledge, recalls the story of Adam and Havah (Eve). Havah ate the fruit of the tree of knowledge, and through that act bestowed knowledge on humanity. During this prayer, Jewish women today might focus on our gratitude to be alive in an era in history when more paths to knowledge, Jewish and secular, are open to us than at any other time in history.—*Tamara Cohen*

All other blessings that we might offer—and indeed, all requests that we might voice—depend on our ability to know ourselves and God's world in the first place. There are three kinds of knowing: *De'ah* [intellect] is factual information. *Binah* [understanding] denotes the ability to analyze things and to distinguish between them—its root, *bet-yod-nun*, means "between." *Haskel* (like the Yiddish *seikhel*) [discernment] means experiential knowledge. Had God not created us as He did, we would have no knowledge in the first place.—*Rabbi Elliot N. Dorff* [40]

6. Forgive us, our Father, for we have sinned. Pardon us, our King, for we have transgressed, because You pardon and forgive. Blessed are You, gracious Lord who freely forgives.

According to custom, we beat lightly upon the heart with a clenched fist, while saying the phrases beginning "forgive us" *(selaḥ lanu)* and "pardon us" *(meḥal lanu)*. Many Jews erroneously believe that confession plays an insignificant role in our tradition. Yet we see that Judaism's central prayer, the *Amidah*, involves daily confession.[41] Since God freely forgives, despair over our imperfections should be foreign to Jewish faith.

7. See our affliction and champion our cause. Redeem us soon because of Your nature, for You are a mighty redeemer. Blessed are You, Lord who redeems the people Israel.

The seventh blessing is the first of three blessings that express the individual's physical needs. Some people mistakenly associate the redemption in this *brakhah* with messianic deliverance. The Rabbis, however, taught specifically that redemption here means redemption from the physical adversities that afflict us. (See Babylonian Talmud, *Megillah* 17b.)

8. Heal us, O Lord, and we shall be healed. Save us and we shall be saved, for You are our glory.[42] Grant perfect healing for all of our wounds. For You, God ▨ and King, are a faithful and merciful healer. Blessed are You, Lord who heals the sick of His people Israel.

▨ [Blessing 8 uses the Hebrew word *El* for God rather than the more familiar *Elohim*.] Calling God *El* here may hark back to the name used by Moses when he prayed for Miriam's recovery (Numbers 12:13): "God *[El]* heal her." In the ancient Near East, the Canaanite god El was also a god of healing. —*Marc Brettler*[43]

❀ The traditional text does not include the father's name. Thus, for example, did King David pray: "I am Your servant, the son of Your maidservant" in Psalms 116:16. In these instances, the mother is considered to be the exemplar of those who successfully articulate pleas for mercy. —*JH*

Doctors and nurses work as partners with God in their care of the sick. The last words of the *brakhah* reflect our concern for the entire people Israel even as we confront the illness of specific individuals. This blessing, like the entire *Amidah*, focuses on the people Israel as well as the land of Israel. We express universal concern elsewhere in the prayer book.

Jewish liturgical custom encourages us to personalize this prayer, even though its text remains fixed. Thus, many prayer books note that after "Grant perfect healing for all of our wounds," we may add a prayer on behalf of someone who is ill:

May it be Your will, Lord our God and God of our ancestors, to send perfect healing, of body and of soul, to _____ [we state the Hebrew name of the one who is ill and the Hebrew name of his or her mother ❀] along with all others who are stricken.

We then conclude this *brakhah* with the words beginning "For You, God and King."

9. Bless this year for us, Lord our God, and all its varieties of produce, that it be good.

> ***(Passover to December 4)* Grant blessing to**

> ***(December 5 to Passover)* Grant dew and rain to bless**

the earth, and satisfy us with Your goodness. Bless our year as the best years. Blessed are You, Lord who blesses the years.

We must not take economic security for granted. The ancient Rabbis focused on agriculture, with different emphases for different seasons *in the land of Israel*. Why then do the dates in this blessing refer to the general calendar? Because for this purpose the seasons are calculated according to the solar calendar, though other seasons and dates in the Jewish year are calculated according to the lunar calendar. Jews in the diaspora begin to add the plea for dew and rain on the 60th day after September's autumnal equinox, a day that falls in December. Jews in the land of Israel begin to add that phrase earlier, two weeks after the end of Sukkot, in the month of Heshvan.

✖ Modern Jews have generally rejected the concept of "exile," believing instead that the diaspora countries where they enjoyed equality were their homes. They therefore found the nationalist orientation of this prayer offensive and [reworked] it in a variety of ways. One approach was to universalize the benediction into a prayer of freedom for all.... *Gates of Prayer* [Reform, 1975] says, "Sound the great horn to proclaim freedom, inspire us to strive for the liberation of the oppressed, and let the song of liberty be heard in the four corners of the earth."...

Most [mid-20th-century] Conservative prayer books, and Reconstructionist ones too, amended the line to reflect a benign American vision of Zionism, one that promoted the centrality and importance of Israel as a land of refuge for the Jewish dispossessed while simultaneously affirming the right of American Jews to remain in a diaspora that is regarded as "home" and not as "exile." Hence the *Reconstructionist Daily Prayer Book* [c.1950] changed Hebrew and English to read, "Bring the homeless of our People in peace from the four corners of the earth and enable them to march erect into our Land." The Conservative *Weekday Prayer Book* [1961] substituted "gather the dispersed" for the traditional "gather us together."

Interestingly, heightened ethnic consciousness in *Kol Haneshamah* [Reconstructionist, 1996] and *Siddur Sim Shalom* [Conservative, 1985] reverses this trend and restores the original Ashkenazi Hebrew text in its entirety. *Kol Haneshamah* even provides a lyrical translation that is faithful to the literal meaning of the Hebrew.—*Rabbi David Ellenson*[44]

10. Sound a great *shofar* announcing our freedom, raise a banner to gather our exiles, and gather us together ✖ from the four corners of the earth.[45] Blessed are You, Lord who gathers the dispersed of His people Israel.

This is the first of seven blessings that express the physical and spiritual needs of the entire people Israel. Here we pray for our people's redemption. When the Messiah appears, we will hear the sound of the *shofar,* just as the Israelites heard it during the revelation at Mount Sinai. This *brakhah* was composed after the destruction of the first Temple in the sixth century BCE. Later, after the failure of the rebellion against Rome in 135 CE, with most Jews exiled from the land of Israel, this petition became even more significant. We pray for the ingathering of Jews dispersed throughout the world, for the return of the dispersed to our holy land.

11. Bring back our judges as in early times, and our counselors as at the first.[46] Remove from us sorrow and sighing. Reign over us alone, O Lord, with kindness and mercy, and bring us righteous justice. Blessed are You, Lord, King who loves righteousness and justice. ▨

▨ During the Ten Days of Repentance, the words "King who loves righteousness and justice" are replaced by "the King of judgment."—*JH*

❋ The 11th prayer of the *Amidah* refers to good and fair judges, and is a good point to think about achieving justice in religious courts for *agunot*, chained women. These are observant Jewish women whose husbands have left them, but who are unable to remarry and begin a new life, because their husbands have not granted them a *get*, a religious divorce decree. For these women, just counselors can be the difference between freedom and continued imprisonment.—*Tamara Cohen*

✺ Rabbi David Ellenson writes: "The imprecatory tone and content of this prayer has disturbed countless prayer book editors during the last two centuries,"[47] reflecting a strong Jewish preference for less violent imagery, and for a liturgical emphasis on forgiveness rather than vengeance. After September 11, 2001, however, and as murderous attacks on civilian Jews in Israel continue to occur, the words of blessing 12 may seem both more relevant and more urgent than they did before. As Rabbi Daniel Gordis stresses in Chapter 13, our prayer book offers many images, and these images at times seem contradictory (pages 309–334).—*Claudia Chernov*

✱ In addition to prayers against heretics and slanderers, in the years of Roman rule over the land of Israel there was also a prayer directed against Jews who had converted out of the Jewish faith *(meshumadim)*, because many of them acted destructively.—*JH*

Our desire for full redemption leads us also to pray for the restoration of judges in the holy land who will follow the dictates of the Torah with wisdom and justice. We pray that sorrow will disappear with the restoration of true justice. ❊

12. And for slanderers let there be no hope; may all wickedness perish in an instant. May all of Your enemies be cut down soon. May You uproot, shatter, smash, subdue, ▨ and humble the arrogant, soon in our time. Blessed are You, Lord who shatters enemies and humbles the arrogant.

The wording of this *brakhah* has changed from the time of its first formulation until its final composition in Rabbinic times. At first the *brakhah* began with words directed against all types of Jewish heretics *(al haminim)*. Later it began with words directed against the Sadducees *(al hatzedukim)*, the opponents of the Pharisees. With the growing strength of the Christians and other sectarians, some of whom informed against Jews to the Roman rulers, the wording changed again, this time directed against sectarian slanderers *(malshinim)*. ✱ Unfortunately, we still need such a prayer today. The names and locations of informers and slanderers have changed, but their purposes remain the same.

According to some authorities, the Rabbis added this *brakhah* in the second century to the original 18 *brakhot* of the *Amidah*. Most contemporary scholars, however, hold that this *brakhah* was one of the original 18, and that the 19th came as the result of splitting one *brakhah* to make two *brakhot* (see below, on *brakhot* 14 and 15).

13. For the righteous and for the pious, for the elders of Your people Israel and for devoted scholars, for true converts and for us, may Your mercies be stirred, Lord our God. Reward generously all who truly trust in Your name, and place our destiny with them forever. Thus shall we not be ashamed, for in You have we trusted. Blessed are You, Lord, trusted sustainer of the righteous.

In the modern world, a number of Jews still exhibit prejudice against converts, men and women who have chosen to cast their lot with the Jewish people. This prejudice goes against Jewish teachings, which extend to converts the same status as Jews by birth. This *brakhah* emphasizes that true converts share the status of all other Jews.

14. To Jerusalem Your city return in mercy, and dwell in its midst as You have promised.[48] Rebuild it soon in our days, that it may last forever. Establish there soon the throne of David. Blessed are You, Lord who builds Jerusalem.

Jewish prayer has always focused on Jerusalem. The prophet Isaiah declares: "For out of Zion shall go forth Torah and the word of the Lord from Jerusalem."[49]

15. Cause the branch[50] of David Your servant to blossom soon, exalt his strength with Your salvation; we have always hoped for Your salvation. Blessed are You, Lord who causes the strength of salvation to blossom.

Scholars today maintain that the 14th and the 15th *brakhot* originally constituted one *brakhah* that concluded with words blessing the "God of David and the Builder of Jerusalem." When that original *brakhah* became two *brakhot*, the *Shmoneh Esreih*, "Eighteen," became 19. ※ Why did we need two blessings? Some suggest that the division occurred when the Rabbis decided that one *brakhah* should not conclude with two themes (Babylonian Talmud, *Brakhot* 49a). Others suggest that the Rabbis also sought to place greater emphasis on hope for the Messiah.

※ According to one theory, when the original *brakhah* that concluded with "God of David and the Builder of Jerusalem" became two *brakhot*, there were only 17 *brakhot* in the *Amidah*, since number 12 (against slanderers) had fallen out of use. When that *brakhah* was later revived, it then became the 19th. (See Jerusalem Talmud, *Brakhot* 4:3.)—*JH*

The imagery ("cause the branch of David Your servant to blossom" and "who causes the strength of salvation to blossom") recalls the end of the second *brakhah,* "who causes salvation to blossom" (see blessing 2, page 88). The Bible gives us the image of salvation as a blossoming shoot, an image that recurs throughout Jewish literature. In mystic writings, one of the names of the Messiah is *tzemah* ("shoot"). The phrase "we have always hoped for Your salvation" typifies the faith that for centuries has maintained the people Israel.

🀫 "You hear the prayer of Your people Israel with mercy"—The Spanish-Portuguese version is more universalistic: "You hear the prayer of everyone" (literally, "of every mouth," *tefillat kol peh*).—*Rabbi Lawrence A. Hoffman*[51]

⚙ [Blessing 17] is probably the most ancient part of the *Amidah* and has undergone the most change over the course of time. Originally a petition recited at the time of the Temple sacrifices, in one of its oldest extant versions it asks that God "dwell in Zion." The current version [used by Orthodox congregations] asks that God restore the Temple service (that is, the sacrifices) and concludes by praising God who "restores His Presence to Zion," *hamahazir Shekhinato leTziyon.*

Despite its seemingly archaic nature, I believe this blessing contains promising potential for re-creation. *Shekhinato,* "His [God's] Presence," is a possessive form of the word *shekhinah,* "presence" or "indwelling," which over the course of Jewish history has been used as a name for the divine and, specifically, for divine immanence. The Shekhinah (now also a term in the English language) was explicitly portrayed as a female figure in Kabbalah, although one would be hard pressed to make the claim that the kabbalistic images were liberating for women, in that they were always defined in subordinate relationship to the male God. The word *shekhinah* itself is grammatically feminine, and today the term has gained new life in some Jewish feminist circles, where it is used as a way to name divinity.

The mention of Zion in this blessing is also resonant and might be retained meaningfully in the liturgy as a reference to the Jewish homeland (rather than as a reference to the ancient Temple). Asking that the Shekhinah be restored to the Jewish homeland can be a way of seeking at least two distinct but related aims: that Israel be a place in which we live with reverence for all life; and that the sense of the divine as immanent, and the valuing of women's experience as part of the divine immanence, be honored in Israel and wherever else we make our homes. I have tried to weave these ideas together in my new blessing: *Nahazir et haShekhinah limkomah/beTziyon uvattevel kullah,* literally, "Let us restore the Shekhinah (or divine presence) to its place/in Zion and in all the world." The English version separates out the interwoven meanings of the Hebrew:

Let us restore Shekhinah to her place
in Israel and throughout the world,
and let us infuse all places
with her presence.

—*Marcia Falk*[53]

16. Hear our voice, Lord our God, have pity and mercy for us, and accept our prayer with mercy and favor. For You are God who hears prayer and supplication. Turn us not away from You unanswered, our King, for You hear the prayer of Your people Israel with mercy. 🀫 **Blessed are You, Lord who hears prayer.**

Jewish custom encourages each individual to add his or her own words during this *brakhah,* immediately after the phrase "Turn us not away unanswered, our King," and before concluding the *brakhah.*[52]

Brakhah 17 is the first of the final three *brakhot* that remain the same whenever the *Amidah* is recited.

17. Accept with favor, Lord our God, the people Israel and their prayer; restore worship to the inner sanctuary of Your House. ⚙ **May the offerings of the people Israel and their prayer**

be accepted as they are given, lovingly and freely. May the worship of Your people Israel always be acceptable to You. May we witness Your return to Zion in mercy. Blessed are You, Lord who restores His Presence to Zion.

In the ancient Temple, our ancestors worshiped God through animal sacrifice. ※ We now worship God through the words of prayer. We ask that God look with favor upon our offering of words and accept them, as the ancient priests (*kohanim*) asked God to look with favor upon their offerings and accept the sacrifices. Since the destruction of the Temple, we have replaced the concluding words of the ancient *brakhah*, "Blessed are You, Lord whom alone do we worship in awe,"[54] with a prayer for the restoration of God's presence to Zion, site of the ancient Temple. Conservative liturgy has deleted mention of "the offerings" in the second sentence,[55] retaining the petition for acceptance of prayer.

18. We gratefully acknowledge ❋ that You are Lord our God and God of our ancestors forever, Rock of our lives, Shield of our salvation in every generation. We gratefully acclaim You and we recount Your praise, evening, morning, and afternoon—for our lives that are in Your hand, for our souls that are in Your charge, for Your miracles that daily attend us, ※ and for Your wonders and favors at all seasons. You are the essence of goodness, for Your mercies have not ended. You are merciful, for Your kindnesses have not ceased. We have always placed our hope in You. ❁ Because of all these blessings, our King, Your name will be blessed and exalted forever. ▣ All life will gratefully acclaim You and truly praise Your name, God of our salvation and our help. Blessed are You, Lord whose essence is goodness, to whom grateful acclaim is befitting.

※ The word for sacrifice, *korban*, has the meaning of bringing near, which was one purpose of ancient sacrifice: bringing the worshiper nearer to God.—*JH*

❋ For those who find petitionary prayer to a personal God difficult, it may be worth citing the Rabbinic adage, "In the time to come, all prayers (of petition) will be annulled (as superfluous), but the prayer of gratitude will not be annulled" (*Midrash Rabbah, Leviticus* 9:7). The *hodaah*, "thanksgiving," benediction is a good place to discover one's religious sensibilities, for there is always reason to be thankful for the sustained gift of life. In our unredeemed world, expressions of human need remain achingly relevant; much that is heartfelt can be learned from the prayers of our ancestors; in the end our needs are not so different from theirs.—*Richard S. Sarason*

※ What does it mean to proclaim that we experience miracles daily? It requires us to reframe our definition of miracle, to think not just of Bible-size miracles like the splitting of the Red Sea or manna falling from the sky, but those miraculous experiences of our own lives: the birth of a child, the softness of another's touch, our ability to feed the hungry, the speed of a gazelle. In truth, the miracles of daily life are countless, and when we name them as miracles we can fill ourselves with gratitude and hope.—*Tamara Cohen*

❁ After "we have always placed our hope in You," we recite the prayer *al hanissim* on Hanukkah and on Purim. Conservative liturgy adds a third *al hanissim* to be recited on Israel's Independence Day.[56]—*JH*

▣ After "Your name will be blessed and exalted forever," on the days between Rosh Hashanah and Yom Kippur, we add: "Inscribe all the people of Your covenant for a good life."—*JH*

While saying "We gratefully acclaim" *(modim anaḥnu)* we bend our knees and bow at the waist. By the time "You" *(lakh)* is said, we again stand erect. At the close of this *brakhah*, while saying "Blessed are You" *(Barukh Attah)*, we bend at the knees and bow at the waist. By the time "Lord" *(Adonai)* is said, we stand erect again.

This *brakhah* also includes an extraordinary expression of Jewish theology. At first glance, the blessing may seem simplistic in proclaiming, "You are the essence of goodness, for Your mercies have not ended. You are merciful, for your kindnesses have not ceased." Do we indeed experience a world filled with kindness and mercy? This flies in the face of human experience. Apparently, the framers of this *brakhah* considered the problem, and their statement is not one of naive and untested faith. Instead of presenting their own words, they chose a quote from the Book of Lamentations, beginning "You are the essence of goodness." These are words spoken by a man who has suffered terribly at the hands of God. When we repeat these words, we follow this one man's example of maintaining faith in spite of affliction, ▦ fully aware of all that can and does happen in the world.

> ▦ The third chapter of the Book of Lamentations begins, "I am the man who has known affliction." It continues with a catalogue of an individual's suffering and sorrow. "He has worn away my flesh and skin; He has shattered my bones.... He has filled me with bitterness, sated me with wormwood ... I forgot what happiness was." The catalogue extends over 20 verses. Then we have verses 21 through 24: "But this do I call to mind, therefore I have hope. The kindness of the Lord has not ended, His mercies are not spent. They are renewed every morning; ample is Your grace. 'The Lord is my portion,' I say with full heart; therefore will I hope in Him." (The phrases in *brakhah* 18 of the *Amidah* are based on verse 22.)—JH

While the Leader recites the 18th *brakhah* during the repetition of the *Amidah*, the congregation silently reads the following version of the *brakhah*. The congregation never recites this version aloud.

We gratefully acknowledge that You are the Lord our God and God of our ancestors, God of all flesh who fashions us and all Creation. Blessings and grateful acclaim are ascribed to Your great and holy name for giving us life and for sustaining us. May You continue to give us life and to sustain us. Gather our exiles to the courts of Your sanctuary, to fulfill Your statutes, to do Your will, and to worship You wholeheartedly. For this we gratefully acclaim You. Blessed is the God of grateful acclamation.

The recitation of two versions of the same *brakhah* (known by its first Hebrew word, *modim*) results from another Rabbinic decision to compromise, to be inclusive by using both versions. The version for silent worship is called "the *modim* of our Rabbis" *(modim deRabbanan)*, since it comprises a number of short prayers recited by different Rabbis of the Talmud. (See Babylonian Talmud, *Sotah* 49a.)

At Morning Services (and at *Musaf* on Shabbat and Festivals), the leader of the service, when repeating the *Amidah* aloud, recites the priestly blessing (*birkat kohanim*) immediately before the final blessing of the *Amidah*.

Our God and God of our ancestors, bless us with the threefold blessing in the Torah written by Moses Your servant, spoken by Aaron and his sons, Your holy people: ✺

> **May the Lord bless you and keep you.**
> **May the Lord show you favor and be gracious to you.**
> **May the Lord show you kindness and grant you peace.** ✻

The priests of ancient Israel, the *kohanim*, pronounced this daily blessing for the people Israel. It ends with a prayer for peace, our most precious blessing, for one of God's names is *shalom*, peace.

At Morning Services

19 morning. Grant peace, goodness and blessing, grace, kindness, and mercy to us and to all Israel Your people. Bless us, our Father, all of us as one, with the light of Your countenance, for with that light have You given us, Lord our God, a Torah of life, love of kindness, justice and blessing, mercy, life, and peace. May it please You to bless Your people Israel in all seasons and at all times with Your peace. ✴ **Blessed are You, Lord who blesses His people Israel with peace.**

✺ Traditionally the priestly blessing was pronounced by the male descendants of the *kohanim*. In some congregations the *sheliah tzibur* (service leader) recites the blessing, and the congregation responds with *ken yehi ratzon*. In other communities, all the members of the congregation wrap arms and *tallitot* around each other and recite the blessings together. Another way to enact the priestly blessing is for each congregant to turn to a neighbor and recite the first half of each blessing, while the neighbor responds with the second half of the blessing.—*Michael M. Cohen*[57]

✻ In Numbers 6:22–27, Aaron and his descendants are commanded to bless the people Israel. Though the *kohanim* chant the blessing, the Bible makes clear in verse 27 that God alone gives the blessing.—*JH*

✴ Between Rosh Hashanah and Yom Kippur, we replace "May it please You to bless Your people Israel in all seasons and at all times with Your peace." Instead, we pray: "May we and the entire House of Israel be remembered and recorded in the book of life, blessing, sustenance, and peace. Blessed are You, Lord, Source of peace."—*JH*

At Afternoon and at Evening Services

19 afternoon and evening. Grant abundant, enduring peace to Your people Israel, for You are the supreme Sovereign of peace. May it please You to bless Your people Israel in all seasons and at all times with Your peace.[58] Blessed are You, Lord who blesses His people Israel with peace.

PERSONAL PRAYER AFTER THE *AMIDAH*

After concluding the formal, fixed blessings of the *Amidah*, we have an opportunity to personalize our prayer, to express ourselves with words of our own choosing. Our prayer books include a suggested passage. Written centuries ago, it begins: "My God, keep my tongue from evil, my lips from speaking guile."

That passage differs from the *Amidah* blessings, because it is phrased in the first-person singular, not first-person plural. Later Rabbis adapted it from the personal prayer of a sage from fourth-century Babylon, Mar the son of Ravina. Before we look at the text of his prayer as it appears in the Talmud, let us read the prayer as it appears in our prayer books:

My God, keep my tongue from evil, my lips from speaking guile. Let me be silent to those who curse me, let me be as dust to all. Open my heart through Your Torah, that I may pursue Your commandments. As for all who plot evil against me, quickly destroy their plan, defeat their designs. Do it because of Your name and Your might, do it because of Your holiness, because of Your Torah. Thus will Your loved ones be saved; through Your power deliver me, answer me.[59] May the words of my mouth and the meditation of my heart be acceptable to You, Lord, my Rock and my Redeemer. He who makes peace in His high places will make peace for us and for all the people Israel. Amen.

🈳 The time of candle lighting on a Shabbat or Festival eve, or standing before the open Ark at the beginning of the Torah Service, offer other opportunities for personal and intimate prayer.—*JH*

✵ Rabbinic law is concerned with morality as well as with ritual observance. Everyone seems to know that Rabbinic law prohibits Jews from eating pork. Considerably fewer seem to be aware that speaking ➤

Each time we complete the *Amidah* we may choose to repeat these words or to replace them with words of our own. Or we may simply reflect or meditate in silence. Many people—understandably —hesitate to add their own words or thoughts to the classic text of the prayer book. At certain points in the service, however, such as here, our own words are as appropriate and as legitimate as any classic text. We should accustom ourselves to taking advantage of this opportunity, and make at least part of our prayer experience deeply personal. 🈳 The end of the *Amidah* offers one of the fixed opportunities for doing so within a formal service.

The words in the prayer book are an adaptation of the following passage from the Babylonian Talmud, *Brakhot* 17a.

Mar the son of Ravina, after praying the *Amidah*, would say: "My God, keep my tongue from evil, my lips from speaking guile.[60] Let me be silent to those who curse me, let me be as dust to all. ✵ Open my heart through Your Torah, that I

may pursue Your commandments. Save me from evil affliction, from the evil impulse, from an evil woman, and from all evils that occur in the world. ✳ As for all who plot evil against me, quickly destroy their plan, defeat their designs. May the words of my mouth and the meditation of my heart be acceptable to You, Lord, my Rock and my Redeemer."[61]

There are six sentences in this prayer of the Rabbinic sage. Mar the son of Ravina adapted the first sentence from a verse in Psalms, and quoted a verse from Psalms in the last sentence. The authorities who compiled the prayer service, in composing the optional prayer that follows the *Amidah*, felt free to delete a sentence, to add another verse from Psalms, and to add the last sentence of the *Kaddish*, as well as to add some words of their own.

Your personal prayer after the *Amidah* can be of any length, and you can change it whenever and however you wish. In just a few words you can make it your own. You could begin by selecting words that appeal to you from the Bible, from Rabbinic literature,[63] or from other Jewish sources. Most important, express yourself with your own words. Think about your life, its blessings, and what you feel it lacks. Express in your own words what you feel, about the world in which you live and its Creator, about your life, your hopes, and those you love. ✳

maliciously, lying, and spreading gossip are equal violations of Jewish law. Just as eating pork violates the laws of *kashrut*, malicious speech violates the laws prohibiting *lashon hara*. In the words of Dr. Geoffrey Wigoder, "Judaism is more than pots and pantheism." Therefore, we pray to keep our tongues from speaking evil. Most scholars and rabbis understand the next sentence, "Let me be silent to those who curse me, let me be as dust to all," as a statement of humility. One important Talmud commentary, however, provides a different interpretation: "Just as dust can never be destroyed, so may my descendants never be destroyed, as God said to Abraham, 'your descendants shall be as the dust of the earth'" (*Tosafot* on *Brakhot* 17a).—JH

✳ The Rabbis deleted the sentence "Save me from evil affliction, from the evil impulse, from an evil woman, and from all evils that occur in the world" from the prayer book, yet retained the sentence, "As for all who plot evil against me, quickly destroy their plan, defeat their designs."[62]—JH

✳ The [*Amidah*] is an important source for understanding the mind of the Rabbis. Rather than being something apart, a pious or mystical transport, the liturgy was a vehicle for expressing the central value concepts of Talmudic civilization: *teshuvah* as the daily act of self-revision, the commitment to the establishment of justice and to the active pursuit of peace, a profound sensitivity to the power of rumor and slander in the human community. These are the same values to be found in the codes and the commentaries; the difference is that in the *siddur* these values function in a devotional rather than scholarly setting. That is, in prayer the task of the mind and the soul is not to work out the why and the how, but to form a personal link of acknowledgment and responsibility to these fundamental categories.—Alan Mintz[64]

THE MIDDLE BLESSING OF THE *AMIDAH* ON SHABBAT

Every version of the *Amidah* contains the same first three and last three blessings. We recite the *Amidah* of 19 blessings only on ordinary weekdays. The versions of the *Amidah* that we recite on Shabbat and Festivals differ substantially. On those days we do not include blessings 4 through

16. Since Shabbat and Festivals should release us from worry over the concerns expressed in these blessings, we omit the middle petitions. (Though the blessing that replaces the 13 middle petitions of the weekdays does contain several petitions, as in paragraph c below, these differ from the weekday petitions in that they request God to fulfill *spiritual* needs on behalf of the entire community.)

On Shabbat and Festivals, we recite one blessing (the fourth in number) in place of the 13 middle blessings of petition (for a total of seven blessings). Let us examine the fourth, or middle, blessing for Shabbat as it appears in the services for Shabbat evening, morning, and afternoon. The middle *brakhah* varies in each of these services, each emphasizing a different theme on a different aspect of Shabbat. Thus services on Shabbat evening, morning, and afternoon provide us with opportunities to commemorate, in order, the themes of creation, revelation, and redemption during prayer.

The middle blessing for Shabbat Evening (Theme of Creation)

a. **You sanctified the seventh day because of Your nature, the sum and substance of the creation of the heavens and the earth, blessing it beyond all other days and sanctifying it beyond all other times. And thus is it written in Your Torah:**

b. **The heavens and the earth were completed, and all their array.**[65] **On the seventh day God completed His work that He had been doing; on the seventh day He ceased all of His work that He had done. Then God blessed the seventh day and made it holy, for on it did He cease all of His work that God in creating had done.**[66]

c. **Our God and God of our ancestors, accept with favor our offering of rest. Make us holy with Your commandments and place our destiny with Your Torah. Satisfy us with Your goodness, gladden us with Your salvation and purify our hearts that we may truly serve You. Lovingly and willingly, Lord our God, grant that we inherit Your holy Shabbat. Then the people Israel who hallow Your name will find rest thereon. Blessed are You, Lord who makes Shabbat holy.**

One of the most distinguished words in the Bible is the word *kadosh* [holy or sanctified, used seven times in the Shabbat evening middle blessing], a word which more than any other is representative of the mystery and the majesty of the divine. Now what was the first holy object in the history of the world? Was it a mountain? Was it an altar? It is indeed a unique occasion at which the word *kadosh* is used for the first time: in the book of Genesis, at the end of the story of creation. How extremely significant is the fact that it is applied to time. "And God blessed the seventh day and made it *kadosh*." There is no reference in the record of creation to any object in space that would be endowed with the quality of *kedushah*, holiness.—Abraham Joshua Heschel[67]

After the silent recitation of the *Amidah* on Friday evening, the congregation chants together the passage about Creation (Genesis 2:1–3) that is included in the *Amidah* (paragraph b). We chant it aloud while standing, as an act of giving testimony. Just as we bear witness to the existence of God when we recite *Shema Yisrael*, here we bear witness to God as Creator.

So important is this passage and its recitation that even when we pray alone we should repeat these words after the *Amidah*. In presenting a reason for this practice, one of our sages taught an impressive lesson about the extraordinary potential of human beings.

Rabbi Himnuna taught that whoever utters these words from Genesis on Friday evening, *erev Shabbat*, becomes a partner of the Holy One in the work of creation. He based this lesson on a pun. The text is usually understood to mean "The heavens and the earth were completed *(va'yekhulu)*," and Rabbi Himnuna taught that it should be understood as "they (that is, God and mortals in partnership) together completed *(va'yekhalu)* the heavens and the earth" (Babylonian Talmud, *Shabbat* 119b). We face a challenge. Each Shabbat as we celebrate the creation of the world, we must ask what we have done as God's partner in creation.

The service continues as follows only in the presence of a *minyan*. The leader recites the first passage aloud.

Blessed are You, Lord our God and God of our ancestors, God of Abraham, God of Isaac, and God of Jacob, great, mighty, awesome God, God supreme, Creator of the heavens and the earth.[68]

The entire congregation usually chants the next passage aloud, and then the leader chants it aloud as well.[69]

Shield of our ancestors with His word, He gives life to the dead with His decree. Holy God, with none to compare, gives rest to His people on His holy day of Shabbat, pleased to grant them rest. We worship Him with trepidation and awe, gratefully acclaiming His name every day always with appropriate blessings. God of grateful acclaim, Lord of peace who sanctifies Shabbat, blesses the seventh day, and gives rest with holiness to the people sated with delight, recalling the work of Creation.

The leader's repetition of paragraph "c" above concludes this part of the service.

The middle blessing for Shabbat Morning (Theme of Revelation)

d. Moses rejoiced with the gift of his destiny, for You called him a faithful servant. A crown of splendor[70] did You place upon his head when he stood in Your Presence on Mount Sinai. Two tablets of stone did he bring down in his hand,[71] inscribed with Shabbat observance, and thus is it written in Your Torah.

On Friday evening the middle *brakhah* of the *Amidah* celebrates the universal emphasis of creation. On Shabbat morning it focuses on the special relationship of the people Israel to Shabbat.

Moses does not appear in the Haggadah celebrating the exodus from Egypt, though he led the people Israel to freedom. His inclusion there might have led to idolizing him. We note his joy in this part of our liturgy instead. A Rabbinic passage states: "Said the Holy One to Moses (at Sinai): I have a precious gift among My treasures, called Shabbat, and I want to give it to the people Israel. Go and tell them" (Babylonian Talmud, *Shabbat* 10b). That mission made Moses happy; it made him beam.

The service continues with an excerpt from the Torah about Shabbat observance.

e. The Israelites shall observe Shabbat, to make Shabbat an eternal covenant. Between Me and the people Israel it is a sign that in six days the Lord made the heavens and the earth, and on the seventh day He ceased from work and He rested.[72]

f. You did not give this day, Lord our God, to the other nations on earth, and You have not granted it, our King, as a heritage to those who worship idols. Nor will those outside the covenant ▣ know its rest, for to Israel Your people have You given it lovingly, to the seed of Jacob whom You have chosen, the people who make the seventh day holy. May they all be satisfied and delighted with Your goodness. The seventh day have You desired to sanctify, calling it the most precious day, a reminder of the work of creation.

▣ The Hebrew word that is here translated as "those outside the covenant" is *arelim*, literally "uncircumcised." Clearly this was intended to refer to those who are not partners to the covenant between God and the people Israel, which Shabbat commemorates and signifies. Some Hebrew versions of this passage replace the word "uncircumcised" (*arelim*) with the word "wicked" (*resha'im*). This is misleading, for the focus here is not good versus wicked behavior; it is the covenant. Neither being a member of the covenant nor being outside of the covenant ensures proper behavior. —JH

g. Our God and God of our ancestors, accept with favor our offering of rest. Make us holy with Your commandments and place our destiny with Your Torah. Satisfy us with Your goodness, gladden us with Your salvation, and purify our hearts that we may truly serve You. Lovingly and willingly, Lord our God, grant that we inherit Your holy Shabbat; then the people Israel who hallow Your name will find rest thereon. Blessed are You, Lord who makes Shabbat holy.

The middle blessing for Shabbat Afternoon (Theme of Redemption)

h. You are One, Your name is One, and who is like Your people Israel, a nation unique on earth? Great splendor, a crown of salvation, a day of rest and holiness have You given Your people. Abraham would rejoice, Isaac would exult, and

Jacob and his children would find rest therein. This rest reflects Your generous love, a truly faithful rest, a rest of tranquil peace, contentment and quietude, a perfect rest that You desire. Let Your children truly know that their rest is from You and through their rest may they sanctify Your name.

g. Our God and God of our ancestors, accept with favor our offering of rest. Make us holy with Your commandments and place our destiny with Your Torah. Satisfy us with Your goodness, gladden us with Your salvation, and purify our hearts that we may truly serve You. Lovingly and willingly, Lord our God, grant that we inherit Your holy Shabbat; then the people Israel who hallow Your name will find rest thereon. Blessed are You, Lord who makes Shabbat holy.

On Shabbat afternoon our prayers emphasize that great day in the future when everything will be Shabbat. Shabbat is a foretaste, a sampling, of the peace that will embrace everyone in the world to come. "You are One, Your name is One." Every prayer service closes with words from a vision of the prophet Zechariah, who foresaw redemption at the end of days: "The Lord shall be King over all the earth. On that day shall the Lord be One and His name One."[73]

"Great splendor, crown of salvation." This recalls the crown of splendor that adorned Moses, described in the middle blessing of the Shabbat morning *Amidah*. In this passage the crown adorns the entire people Israel. Because of the devoted labors of their ancestors, including Abraham, Isaac, and Jacob, in proclaiming God as unique in the world, the people Israel have a unique destiny.

QUESTIONS FOR FURTHER STUDY AND REFLECTION

1. Which service does not include the *Amidah*?
2. What direction do we face while reciting the *Amidah*, and why?
3. What Hebrew word do you prefer for designating God, and why?
4. Do you include the names of the matriarchs in the first *brakhah* of the *Amidah*? Why? If you do not, why not?
5. Consider men's and women's roles during your synagogue's services. Would you prefer more or less equality between men and women at your congregation? If you feel that men's and women's roles should be equal, what would be effective ways of realizing equality during services? How would you present the case to the ritual committee or Board of Directors of your congregation? How would you present the opposite case?
6. *Shmoneh Esreih*, a very common name for the *Amidah*, means 18. There are, however, 19 *brakhot*. What is the source of the inconsistency? What is the added *brakhah*? Why do scholars disagree about this?
7. The second *brakhah* includes a description of God as *mehayeh hametim*. Which of the translations of the phrase included in this chapter do you prefer? What does the phrase mean for you?

8. How does the prayer book teach about the holiness of community?

9. How does *Kedushah* relate angelic praise of God and life on earth?

10. How would you teach a high school class about Zion and redemption as reflected in the prayer book?

11. How do we personalize the formal *brakhot* of the *Amidah*?

12. Outline the structure of the 19 *brakhot* of the *Amidah*.

13. What does the *Amidah* teach about Jerusalem?

14. How does the 18th *brakhah* teach about maintaining faith in spite of affliction? How do you react to this teaching and to the manner in which the lesson is taught here?

15. Based on the note on personal prayer at the end of the *Amidah*, write two personal prayers that you would feel comfortable reciting.

16. In an interpretation of the middle *brakhah* of the Friday evening *Amidah*, we are described as God's partners in creation. Is this merely an inspiring sermon or could it become a reality? If it could, what specific actions are called for?

---

1. Rabbi Marcia Prager, *The Weekday Amidah in Guided Imagery: 20 Hand Designed Cards with Instruction Booklet* (1998) "Amidah in Movement" by Talia deLone, Ph.D. To purchase the set of cards, send a check for $25 to: Rabbi Marcia Prager, 228 West Hortter Street, Philadelphia PA 19119.

2. An exception is the midnight service on the Saturday night before Rosh Hashanah, known as *Seliḥot* (Prayers for Forgiveness).

3. Rabbi Marcia Prager, *The Path of Blessing: Experiencing the Energy and Abundance of the Divine* (New York: Bell Tower, 1998), pages 43–44.

4. *Siddur Sim Shalom for Shabbat and Festivals,* Leonard Cahan, ed. (New York: Rabbinical Assembly and United Synagogue of America, 1998).

5. See *Gates of Prayer for Shabbat: A Gender-Sensitive Prayer Book,* Chaim Stern, ed. (New York: Central Conference of American Rabbis, 1992), page 19; and *Kol Haneshamah: Shabbat Veḥagim* (Wyncote, PA: Reconstructionist Press, 1996), page 295.

6. Exodus 3:15.

7. This description is from Deuteronomy 10:17, where it is spoken by Moses.

8. Literally, "good kindnesses."

9. See Genesis 14:19, "Blessed be Abram of God Most High *(El Elyon)*, Creator *(Koneh)* of heaven and earth.

10. Literally in the Hebrew, "the patriarchs."

11. The literal meaning of *ozer,* which is translated here as "defends," is "helps." See page 75, the sidebar that refers to *ezrat avoteinu.*

12. Rabbi Marcia Prager, *Weekday Amidah in Guided Imagery* (1998). To purchase the set of cards, send a check for $25 to Rabbi Prager, 228 West Hortter Street, Philadelphia PA 19119. Rabbi Prager adapted this meditation from "Amidah in Movement" by Talia deLone, Ph.D., reprinted in *Siddur Or Chadash: A New Light* (1989, P'nai Or Religious Fellowship, now the ALEPH Alliance for Jewish Renewal).

13. A. M. Klein, *Poems* (Philadelphia: Jewish Publication Society, 1944).

14. Abraham Joshua Heschel, *God in Search of Man,* page 201; cited by Levi Weiman-Kelman, in *Kol Haneshamah: Shabbat Vehagim,* page 90.

15. Joel Rembaum, "Regarding the Inclusion of the Names of the Matriarchs in the First Blessing of the *Amidah*," page 8. This formal responsum was prepared for the Rabbinical Assembly Committee on Jewish Law and Standards, which adopted it as a position of the Committee.

16. Judith Hauptman, in *My People's Prayer Book: Traditional Prayers, Modern Commentaries, Volume 2: The Amidah,* Rabbi Lawrence A. Hoffman, ed. (Woodstock, VT: Jewish Lights, 1998), pages 68–69.

17. Marcia Falk, for example, on page 68 of *My People's Prayer Book, Volume 2: The Amidah,* edited by Rabbi Lawrence A. Hoffman.

18. See translation of Genesis 14:19 above in note 9.

19. Reform: *Gates of Prayer* (New York: Central Conference of American Rabbis, 1975). Reconstructionist: *Kol Haneshamah* (Wyncote, PA: Reconstructionist Press, 1996).

20. Reena Spicehandler, in *Kol Haneshamah Limot Hol/Daily* (Wyncote, PA: Reconstructionist Press, 1996), page 101.

21. From Daniel 12:2.

22. From I Samuel 2:6.

23. See blessing 15, page 99.

24. Rabbi Marcia Prager, *Weekday Amidah in Guided Imagery* (1998). To purchase the set of cards, send a check for $25 to Rabbi Prager, 228 West Hortter Street, Philadelphia PA 19119. Rabbi Prager adapted this meditation from "Amidah in Movement" by Talia deLone, Ph.D., reprinted in *Siddur Or Chadash: A New Light* (1989, P'nai Or Religious Fellowship, now the ALEPH Alliance for Jewish Renewal).

25. See Mishnah *Sanhedrin* 10:1.

26. The 1975 edition of *Gates of Prayer* (New York, CCAR), page 236; *Kol Haneshamah: Shabbat Vehagim* (Wyncote, PA: Reconstructionist Press, 1996), pages 298-299.

27. See Chapter 8, pages 185–186 for a fuller explanation of the *minyan.*

28. Marcia Falk, *The Book of Blessings: New Jewish Prayers for Daily Life, the Sabbath, and the New Moon Festival* (New York: HarperCollins, 1996; paperback edition, Boston: Beacon, 1999), pages 471–472, 194. See also www.marciafalk.com.

29. Isaiah 6:3.

30. Ezekiel 3:12.

31. Psalms 146:10.

32. Rabbi Marcia Prager, *Weekday Amidah in Guided Imagery* (1998). To purchase the set of cards, send a check for $25 to Rabbi Prager, 228 West Hortter Street, Philadelphia PA 19119. Rabbi Prager adapted this meditation from "Amidah in Movement" by Talia deLone, Ph.D., reprinted in *Siddur Or Chadash: A New Light* (1989, P'nai Or Religious Fellowship, now the ALEPH Alliance for Jewish Renewal).

33. Isaiah 6:3.

34. Ezekiel 3:12.

35. Psalms 146:10.

36. Isaiah 6:3.

37. Ezekiel 3:12.

38. Deuteronomy 6:5.

39. Psalms 146:10.

40. Elliot N. Dorff, in *My People's Prayer Book, Volume 2: The Amidah,* pages 100, 102.

41. Confession is not included on Shabbat and on Festivals.

42. This phrase is adapted from Jeremiah 17:14, where it is stated in the first-person singular. The phrasing of the entire *Amidah,* however, is first-person plural.

43. Marc Brettler, in *My People's Prayer Book, Volume 2: The Amidah,* page 116.

44. David Ellenson, in *My People's Prayer Book, Volume 2: The Amidah,* page 124.

45. Compare to Isaiah 11:12.

46. Compare to Isaiah 1:26, which emphasizes honest—in contrast to dishonest—judges. The blessing in the *Amidah* calls for the re-establishment of our own judges.

47. David Ellenson, in *My People's Prayer Book, Volume 2: The Amidah,* page 132.

48. See Zechariah 8:3.

49. Isaiah 2:3.

50. See Jeremiah 33:15. "I will raise up a true branch of David's line, and he shall do what is just and right in the land."

51. Lawrence A. Hoffman, in *My People's Prayer Book, Volume 2: The Amidah,* page 147.

52. For another example, see the comments on blessing 8 above.

53. Marcia Falk, *The Book of Blessings,* pages 474, 228.

54. Babylonian Talmud, *Brakhot* 11b and *Yoma* 68b. The words of this blessing are still used today to close the 17th *brakhah* on Festival days in those congregations in which the *kohanim* formally bless the community (in a ceremony known as *dukhaning*). In Reform liturgy, these words always close the 17th blessing.

55. The Conservative movement's alteration here is in keeping with its decision to *recall* the sacrificial offerings of our ancestors rather than to pray for their restoration. See Chapter 7, pages 178–182.

56. See *Siddur Sim Shalom,* pages 118–119.

57. Michael M. Cohen, *Kol Haneshamah: Shabbat Vehagim,* page 348.

58. See Babylonian Talmud, *Sotah* 40a.

59. Psalms 60:7.

60. Adapted from Psalms 34:14.

61. Psalms 19:15.

62. Refer also to David Klinghoffer (sidebar on page 32) and Daniel Gordis, Chapter 13 (pages 309–334).

63. Other examples of personal prayers by ancient Rabbis are found in Babylonian Talmud, *Brakhot* 16b–17a.

64. Alan Mintz, "Prayer and the Prayerbook," in *Back to the Sources: Reading the Classic Jewish Texts,* Barry W. Holtz, ed. (New York: Summit/Simon & Schuster, 1984), page 417.

65. Hebrew *tzevaam.* It refers to the heavenly bodies. Some interpret it to include angels.

66. Genesis 2:1–3. The *Kiddush* that we recite on Friday evening opens with this same passage.

67. Abraham Joshua Heschel, *The Sabbath: Its Meaning for Modern Man* (NY: Farrar, Straus and Young, 1951), page 9.

68. See Genesis 14:19, "Blessed be Abram of God supreme, Creator of the heavens and the earth." In the first *brakhah* of the *Amidah* generally we abridge this to "Creator of all." On Shabbat we are more expansive about Creation.

69. Practices vary from congregation to congregation.

70. See Exodus 34:29.

71. See Exodus 32:15.

72. Exodus 31:16–17.

73. Zechariah 14:9. See *Aleinu*, page 198. The translation there reads: "On that day the Lord alone shall be worshiped and shall be invoked by His singular name."

Chapter

SHABBAT

Recalling Creation: Holiness in Time

KABBALAT SHABBAT

The holiness of Shabbat is a palace in time, a moment of majesty, the radiance of joy. Shabbat can help to make us whole. Shabbat ennobles and enhances. It offers the gifts of dignity and rest, of splendor and delight. It nourishes the seed of eternity planted in our soul. On this day, we focus upon holiness in time, turning from the results of creation to the mystery of creation, from the world of creation to the creation of the world. Shabbat brings us a foretaste of future redemption.[1]

Shabbat is the only day of the week greeted with its own distinctive prayer service, called *Kabbalat Shabbat,* "Welcoming the Sabbath." We recite it just before the first full service of Shabbat, the Friday Evening Service. The brief *Kabbalat Shabbat* liturgy consists of chapters from the Book of Psalms and a medieval poem. A group of Jewish mystics, Kabbalists, who lived in Safed in northern Palestine, introduced this service at the end of the 16th century. No such service exists in the classic orders of prayer from earlier centuries.[2]

The Babylonian Talmud provides the basis for the *Kabbalat Shabbat* service. On Friday afternoon some of the Sages would formally welcome Shabbat. Rabbi Ḥanina, for example, would dress in his best clothes and declare, "Come, let us go out to greet the Sabbath queen" (*Shabbat* 119a). Rabbi Yannai, also dressed in his best, would say, "Come, O bride; come, O bride" (*Shabbat* 119a). The Rabbis of antiquity thus likened Shabbat to both a queen and a bride, imagery that appears in the medieval poem discussed below. The Kabbalists of Safed expanded on Rabbi Ḥanina's and Rabbi Yannai's examples. On Friday afternoon, groups would dress in white and go out to the fields, singing the psalms that we sing today. Then they sang a poem with the refrain, "Come, my beloved, the bride to meet; come, my beloved, the Sabbath to greet." Though the 16th-century Kabbalists sang several similar poems with this refrain composed by their contemporaries, the poem subsequently adopted for use by Jews throughout the world is *Lekha Dodi* ("Come, My Beloved"), composed by Rabbi Solomon Halevi Alkabetz.

The six psalms that begin the *Kabbalat Shabbat* service (Psalms 95–99 and 29) represent the six days of creation as well as the six working days of the week. ▨ These psalms celebrate God as both Creator and Sovereign of the world and all its creatures, a caring Sovereign whose reign demands justness and fairness.

▨ The prayers and rituals of Shabbat, the Sabbath, are designed to help us transform the 25 hours of the seventh day into "a taste of the world to come," a glimmer of life without strife, lived in harmony with nature, with other people, and with God. We are to leave behind our troubles and embrace the replenishing holiness of Shabbat.

Such a transformation is not automatic, however. We may have to work harder some weeks than others to make this transition. The mystics of 16th-century Safed created the liturgy of *Kabbalat Shabbat* to help. The six psalms that open *Kabbalat Shabbat* represent the first six days of the week. As we read these psalms in turn, we can reflect on each of the preceding week days, reviewing highlights, acknowledging and letting go of inevitable frustrations. As our review progresses through the week, we begin to shed the cares and worries we carried with us, putting them aside, at least for this 25-hour period. With the recitation of *Lekha Dodi,* we welcome within ourselves the *neshamah yetirah,* the additional soul that uplifts and energizes us on Shabbat. Only after *Lekha Dodi,* can we recite the psalm for the Sabbath day, for only then are we sufficiently prepared to enter the transcendent sanctity of Shabbat time.—*Rabbi Susan Grossman*

✸ The literal translation of "loving God" is "compassionate Father," a phrase from the liturgy (*Av haraḥaman*).—*JH*

✳ The Hebrew word *ayal* ("deer") reflects an image in Psalms 42:2–3: "Like a deer crying for water, my soul cries for You, O God; my soul thirsts for God." Though the translation uses the first person ("I") here, the Hebrew presents the petitioner as a servant, who speaks formally in the third person.—*JH*

✳ The literal translation of "dainty" is "drippings of the honeycomb," from Psalms 19:11, that describes God's judgments as "sweeter than honey, than drippings of the honeycomb."—*JH*

✳ The first word of this stanza, *Hadur,* is a name for God that means Splendid One.—*JH*

✸ The Hebrew of "my soul is weary" recalls Song of Songs 2:5, "I am faint (literally, sick) with love."—*JH*

Yedid Nefesh

A number of congregations begin by singing the 16th-century poem, *Yedid Nefesh*, which means "beloved of the soul" or "soul mate." The poem, composed by Rabbi Eleazar Azikri, a Kabbalist of Safed, celebrates the love between God the Creator and a humble creature who yearns for divine favor and the divine embrace. The first letters of each Hebrew stanza spell one of God's names: YHVH.

▣ The five short Hebrew words cited here (*El na refa na lah*—please, God, do heal her) constitute the entire prayer that Moses uttered on behalf of his sister Miriam when she was ailing (Numbers 12:13). His prayer, a classic appeal for God's mercy, here becomes a plea that the love of "my soul" (a feminine noun) be requited. Two lines later, the poet again refers to the soul as "she."—*JH*

✪ The first Hebrew word of this stanza, *Vatik*, is a name of God meaning Ancient One.—*JH*

✳ The literal translation of "we shall celebrate You" is "let us rejoice and exult in You," which recalls the language of Isaiah 25:9.—*JH*

Soul mate, loving God, ✪ compassion's gentle source,
Take my disposition and shape it to Your will.
Like a darting deer will I ▣ rush to You.
Before Your glorious Presence humbly will I bow.
Let Your sweet love delight me with its thrill,
Because no other dainty ✳ will my hunger still.

How splendid ▣ is Your light, illumining the world.
My soul is weary ✳ yearning for Your love's delight.
Please, good God, do heal her; ▣ reveal to her Your face,
The pleasure of Your Presence, bathed in Your grace.
She will find strength and healing in Your sight;
Forever will she serve You, grateful, with all her might.

What mercy stirs in You since days of old, my God. ✪
Be kind to me, Your own child; my love for You requite.
With deep and endless longing I yearned for Your embrace,
To see my light in Your light, basking in Your grace.
My heart's desire, find me worthy in Your sight.
Do not delay Your mercy, please hide not Your light.

Reveal Yourself, Beloved, for all the world to see,
And shelter me in peace beneath Your canopy.
Illumine all creation, lighting up the earth,
And we shall celebrate You ✳ in choruses of mirth.
The time, my Love, is now; rush, be quick, be bold.
Let Your favor grace me, in the spirit of days of old.[3]

Psalm 95

Come, let us sing in joy to the Lord, shout in triumph to the Rock of our salvation. Let us greet Him with gratitude, sing psalms of triumph to Him. For the Lord is a great God, a great King beyond all gods. In His hand are the depths of the earth, and the peaks of the mountains are His. His is the sea, for He made it; His is the dry land formed by His hands. Come, let us bow and kneel, bend the knee before the Lord who creates us. ▦ He is our God, and we are the people He shepherds, the flock in His hand. Today if only you would hearken to His voice. ⊛ Harden not your heart as at Meribah, as on the day of Massah in the wilderness when your ancestors tried and tested Me, even though they had witnessed My deeds. Forty years I contended with that generation, and I said, "It is a wayward people who care not for My ways." ❈ Therefore I vowed in anger that they would never reach My place of rest.

▦ The literal translation of "who creates us" is "who makes us" (*oseinu*). The word is not stated in the past tense, for God's creation is continuous. Constantly God creates us anew. Each Shabbat is an opportunity for each of us to realize this renewal.—*JH*

⊛ "Today if only you would hearken to His voice"—these words imply, "Help is yours today if only you would listen, hearken, to His voice." In commenting on this verse, Rabbi Levi declared that if the entire people Israel would observe one Shabbat properly, they would be redeemed at once (*Midrash Tehillim* on the verse).[4]—*JH*

❈ "Who care not for My ways"—Many translations of this phrase read "who have not known My ways" for the Hebrew *vehem lo yadu derakhai*. The Hebrew word *yada* does have the literal meaning of knowing, but words often signify something other than their literal meaning. For example, the same Hebrew verb appears in Exodus in a verse about a new king in Egypt who "did not know" Joseph. As Rashi points out, the new Pharaoh *did* know Joseph; but he did not care for him. The generation of Israelites in the wilderness, who had witnessed God's miracles, *did* know God's ways. This is precisely what irritated God, so to speak. The generation who had been liberated from Egypt, who had received revelation at Sinai, knew God's ways but turned out not to care for them. That quarrelsome generation tried and tested God. This leads, then, to the final verse, which reflects the fate of the adults of the wilderness generation.—*JH*

The singing of Psalm 95 begins our weekly commemoration and celebration of creation and the Creator. The sentiments articulated in the beginning of Psalm 95 also find expression in the American spiritual, "He's Got the Whole World in His Hand." In the Psalm, the word "hand" is repeated three times. "In His hand are the depths of the earth," "His is the dry land formed by His hands," "We are the people He shepherds, the flock in His hand." Repetition in the Bible, as in all oral literature, serves to emphasize an idea or a concept. All of creation, human and otherwise, has its source in God. At least once each week we should not take creation or the Creator for granted.

In the middle of Psalm 95, the mood and focus change. The psalmist begins with praise of God and proceeds to teach a lesson found in the Bible. God makes demands upon His creatures today as in ages past, and we as individuals and as a community may fail to meet the challenge, repeating the error of our ancestors. Failures of the past should sensitize us to the challenges of today. The words Meribah (literally "quarrel") and Massah (literally "trial") recall the rebellion of the Israelites in the wilder-ness. ✳ Even though the Is-raelites had witnessed God's miracles, they rebelled. Too often we, like our ancestors, fail to heed the voice of God. Too often we hear but do not care. ❂

The last Hebrew word in this Psalm, *menuḥati*, literally means "My rest." In the Bible, this word refers to the Land of Israel,[5] but when we recite this Psalm as part of *Kabbalat Shabbat,* we understand the word to mean "God's land of peace and rest." For we recite these words not strictly as a quotation from the Bible but as part of a prayer service in which we welcome Shabbat. Each week we wander the wilderness, so to speak. Some-times we wander far from the Torah and its teachings, even far from caring about Torah. Each week we must earn the right to enter the promised land of Shabbat, the land of God's peace and rest.

✳ The Israelites often were rebellious during their wanderings in the wilderness. In the specific instance recalled here, the Israelites quar-reled with Moses over the lack of water. "The place was named Massah ["Trial"] and Meribah ["Quarrel"] because the Israelites quar-reled and because they tried the Lord, saying, 'Is the Lord present among us or not?'" (Exodus 17:7).—*JH*

❂ Psalm 95 presents a dichotomy. It opens with shouts of joy and tri-umph, "Come, let us sing!"—our mood as we approach the Sabbath. Psalm 95 closes, however, with a poignant reminder of the lack of faith that our forefathers and foremothers experienced during their trek in the desert. The real message of the psalm is that we are all capable of hearing God's voice, we are all capable of experiencing ecstasy—if only we would listen.—*Carol Diament*

✳ I would like to think that the opening verse, "Sing to the Lord a new song," tells us that we should not merely recite prescribed prayers by rote but that we should also compose new prayers when we experi-ence moments of anguish, awe, gratitude, or gladness. It could also mean that we should recite prescribed prayers in new places and sit-uations. While traveling in the Canadian Rockies, I was inspired to recite the blessing that is usually recited after hearing thunder or during a storm, "Blessed are You, *Adonai* our God, Sovereign of the universe, whose power and might fill the world." Never did I feel the glory and splendor of God in a synagogue as strongly as I did on the peaks of the Rocky Mountains.—*Carol Diament*

Psalm 96

Sing to the Lord a new song; ✳ sing to the Lord, all people on earth. Sing to the Lord, bless His name, spread news of His deliverance day after day. Tell of His glory among all nations, His wonders among all peoples. For great is the Lord, and praiseworthy indeed; awesome is He beyond all gods. All the gods of the peoples are merely idols, and the Lord made the heavens. Majesty and might attend Him, strength and splendor are in His sanctuary. Ascribe to the Lord, fam-ilies of nations, ascribe to the Lord glory and strength. Ascribe to the Lord the glory due His name, lift up an offering and enter His courts. Bow to the Lord in sacred splendor; tremble in His presence, all people on earth. Proclaim among the nations that the Lord is King. The world stands firm; it cannot be shaken. He

judges the nations fairly. Let the heavens rejoice and the earth be glad. Let the sea roar, and all it contains, let the fields and all that is in them exult; then all the trees of the forest will sing for joy before the Lord who is coming, who is coming to rule the earth. ▒ He will rule the world with justice, the peoples with His faithfulness.

▒ "Who is coming to rule the earth"—The Hebrew word *lishpot* generally has been translated "to judge." Many recent translations, however, prefer "to rule." The new Jewish Publication Society translation of the Bible takes note of this on the first page of its translation of the Biblical book known as Judges *(shoftim)*. That translation still calls the book "Judges" but a footnote adds: "This is the traditional rendering of *shoftim* which, however, in the text is rendered 'chieftains.' The corresponding verb *shafat* is usually translated not 'judged' but 'ruled' or 'led.'" Indeed, the role of the Biblical *shoftim* involved ruling and leading, not judging.—JH

✺ In Psalm 96, the words "all peoples," "peoples," and "nations" are repeated eight times.—JH

✳ We can understand this passage, the "cloud and dense darkness," as describing the mystery that encloses those ways of God that we ➤

This Psalm, according to Rashi and other commentators, looks to the future. In time to come, all nations of the world will sing a new song, and all people will exclaim that the world belongs to God. No longer will idols and false gods command allegiance. The psalmist delivers a universal message, envisioning a time when all humanity ✺ will worship only God. The passage, like many passages in the *Kabbalat Shabbat* psalms, anticipates the time when all on earth will recognize God as sovereign. The prophet Isaiah connects this thought with Shabbat: "And new moon after new moon and Sabbath after Sabbath all flesh shall come to worship Me" (66:23). All the earth will glorify God, not only the people, for the exultation will include heavens, seas, fields, and forests. They all anticipate the time when the rule of God will embrace all beings.

Commentators have understood the final verses of this Psalm in different ways. One approach stresses the absolute justice of God. Thus the last words are understood to mean, "He will judge the world with righteousness, and the peoples with His equity." In this view, the whole earth will break into song, because at long last justice will prevail throughout the world. The other approach stresses God's compassion. Thus the last words are understood to mean, "He will sustain the world with kindness, provide for the peoples with graciousness." In this view, the introduction of absolute justice would be no cause for song or joy, because the application of strict justice to imperfect human beings would lead only to our destruction. We revere and celebrate God not as a strict judge who metes out punishment but as the compassionate source of forgiveness.[6]

Psalm 97

The Lord is King! Let the earth exult, let the many distant islands rejoice. Cloud and dense darkness close around Him; ✳ righteousness and justice form the base of His throne. Fire goes before Him, burning His adversaries round about. His lightning illumines the world; the earth sees it and quivers. Mountains melt like wax before the Lord, before the Master of all the earth. The heavens tell of His righteousness, all the peoples behold His glory. All who serve images will be shamed, those who take pride in idols; all gods are bowed low before Him. Zion has heard and rejoices, the cities ✳ of Judah are glad, because of Your judgments, Lord. For You, Lord, are supreme over all the earth; highly exalted beyond all gods. You who love the Lord, hate evil. He preserves the lives of His faithful; from the hand of the wicked He saves them. Light is stored for the righteous, joy for the upright in heart. Rejoice, you righteous, in the Lord; give thanks to His holy name.

cannot grasp or understand. Yet, as the verse continues, it describes a divine order of justice that informs God's governance of the world.—JH

✳ "The cities of Judah are glad"—the literal meaning of the Hebrew *bnot* is "daughters of," taken here as referring to cities.—JH

✳ "Zion" stands for Jerusalem, which was located in the territory known as Judah.—JH

✳ A Rabbinic comment declares that so long as wickedness reigns anywhere on earth, the world cannot fully rejoice, God's kingdom is not yet perfect, God is not yet wholly King (*Midrash Tehillim* on Psalm 97:1).—JH

Judaism embraces both the universal and the particular. Thus Psalm 97 focuses on distant islands, all the peoples, and all the earth, while also focusing on Zion and Judah, ✳ on the faithful and righteous among the people Israel. The Psalm opposes idolatry and foresees the destruction of God's adversaries. God will shame the evildoers. The Psalm calls on those who love the Lord to hate *evil*, not evildoers. Flashes of fire and lightning in God's battles at the beginning of the psalm prefigure another kind of light—the healing light that is stored for the righteous.

Some understand the opening words of this Psalm to mean: "Only when the Lord is acknowledged as King, does the earth exult." ✳

Psalm 98

A psalm. Sing to the Lord a new song for He has worked wonders. His right hand, His sacred arm, have won Him deliverance. The Lord has declared His triumph, in the eyes of the nations has He revealed His victory. He remembered His kindness and faithfulness to the House of Israel; all the ends of the earth have seen the victory of our God. Shout praise to the Lord, all the earth, burst into songs of praise. Sing to the Lord with the lyre, with the lyre and the sound of song. With trumpets and shofar sound sing out praise before the Lord, the King. Let the sea roar and all it contains, the world and its inhabitants. Let rivers applaud, let mountains sing as well before the Lord, for He comes to rule the earth. He shall rule the world with justice, the peoples with equity.

In spite of harsh reality that often overwhelms us and the calamities that often confront us, we continue to sing because of the history and the example set by our ancestors in the House of Israel. The faith reflected in their lives sustains us, and that faith gives us the ability to sing, to celebrate.[7] All of creation rejoices in anticipation of God's compassion and application of justice. The earth itself will sing, celebrating the entire world's redemption along with the people Israel.

Psalm 99

The Lord is King; let the peoples tremble. He is enthroned on cherubim; the earth quakes. The Lord is great in Zion, exalted beyond all the peoples. They praise Your name, great and awesome. He is holy. Mighty King who loves lawful order, You established equity, maintaining righteous judgment in Jacob.[8] Exalt the Lord our God, and bow at His footstool; He is holy. Moses and Aaron among His priests and Samuel among those who called upon Him—when they called to the Lord He would answer them, in a pillar of cloud He would speak to them; they kept His decrees, the law He gave to them. Lord our God, You answered them; for them You were a forgiving God although You rebuked them for their offenses. Exalt the Lord our God, bow to His holy mountain, for the Lord our God is holy.

⊞ I saw it in their faces the first humid summer evening that I led [Kabbalat Shabbat] services wearing a *kippah* and a large, rainbow-colored *tallit*. I saw it again when I led a wordless *niggun* (ḥasidic melody). There was a look of utter shock, a glazed stare…. Not everyone reacted in this fashion, but a core of mostly older members of Temple Beth Israel in Altoona, PA—steeped in the rituals and the "decorum" of classical Reform—responded as if the ghosts of the *shtetl* had invaded their sacred precinct.

In reflecting on the kind of congregants who are products of classical Reform, the image of Alfred Uhry's film *Driving Miss Daisy* comes to mind…. For the German Jewish families of this era and their descendants, North America was their Zion. They sought a Judaism that reflected American sensibilities and a liturgical experience that conformed to the mores of "polite" middle-class and upper-middle-class society. In contrast to what was perceived to be the "cacophony" of traditional Jewish prayer, services were to be decorous, orderly, and conducted primarily in English. The worshiper was to be silently reverent, except during responsive readings, allowing the music, the liturgy, and the rabbi's sermon to inspire with awe and sanctity. The ritual and liturgical expressions of classical Reform were perceived as a sign of arrival for Jews who had "made it" in America.

For nearly four generations, the "Miss Daisies" of the Reform Movement set the tone of congregational life…. And therein lies a fundamental challenge: How can the rabbi support these new directions [greater congregational participation, yet a lack of classical decorum; along with more mystical prayer forms, more Hebrew prayers, and greater use of symbolism] without alienating congregants whose ritual practices were once normative, but who now feel marginalized?— *Rabbi Burt E. Schuman*[9]

The Psalm presents an idealized picture of the world, even though the daily news reminds us that we live in an unredeemed world. We repeat the words of the psalmist with hope and with faith in our conviction that God is holy, as

Psalm 99 repeats three times. The word "holy" first appears in the Bible describing Shabbat.[10] The Bible and later writings constantly pair Shabbat and holiness. ⊞

Can we honestly always say that "the Lord is great in Zion"? Rabbi Samson Raphael Hirsch[11] commented that the greatness of God in Zion will be fully realized only when each and every thing in Zion, from the greatest to the smallest, bears the imprint and the inspiration of God.

The reference to Moses, Aaron, and Samuel, and God's rebuke of them, reminds us of the last part of Psalm 95, which refers to the sins of the Israelites in the wilderness. These examples of God's strictness with the people Israel call to mind the words of the prophet Amos: "You alone have I singled out among all the families on earth; therefore will I call you to account for all your iniquities"(Amos 3:2).

Jewish thought does not take at face value the saying "God's in His heaven, all's right with the world." Much that occurs on earth is imperfect. Even the Biblical heroes who serve as our models reveal imperfections. Moses, Aaron, and Samuel were devoted servants of God, yet they sinned and they needed forgiveness—Aaron because of the golden calf, Moses because he struck the rock to get water although God had commanded that he *speak* to the rock, and Samuel because he failed to teach his children to walk in the right path. God reproved each one, yet when each one called upon Him, God answered and offered forgiveness. We extol God as holy, both because He does not play favorites and because He forgives human imperfection. We should strive to make these divine attributes ours in our lives with our families as well as with others.

Psalm 29

A song of David. Ascribe to the Lord, mighty beings, ascribe to the Lord glory and might. Ascribe to the Lord the glory due His name, bow to the Lord in sacred splendor. The voice of the Lord echoes over the waters, the God of glory thunders, the Lord over mighty waters. The voice of the Lord is power, the voice of the Lord is majesty. The voice of the Lord shatters cedars, the Lord shatters the cedars of Lebanon. He makes them skip like a calf, Lebanon and Siryon like a young wild ox. The voice of the Lord kindles fiery flames. ❂ The voice of the Lord stirs ✽ the wilderness, the Lord stirs the wilderness of Kadesh. The voice of the Lord causes hinds to calve, brings ewes to early birth; while in His Temple all bespeak glory. The Lord sat enthroned at the Flood; the Lord will sit enthroned as King forever, giving strength to His people, blessing His people with peace.

❂ The cedars of Lebanon are legendary, the mightiest of trees. Siryon is identified with Mount Hermon, a constant towering presence in the north of the land of Israel. Fiery flames are kindled when rocks on the mountains of Lebanon and Siryon are split by lightning.—JH

✽ The Hebrew verb translated here as "stirs" is one associated with birth pangs of a woman in labor, preparing us for the first part of the next verse.—JH

We recite Psalm 29 while standing. This psalm depicts a storm, an example of the Creator's power, coming in from the Mediterranean Sea and hitting the fabled cedars of Lebanon. ▨ The source of this awe-inspiring power that shatters the cedars and brings animals to early birth, is also the source of the peace and serenity that inform each Shabbat.

The psalmist repeats "the voice of the Lord" seven times, corresponding to the days of the week which culminate in Shabbat. ◉ Some attach great significance to the name "Lord" appearing 18 times in this psalm, 18 being understood in Jewish mysticism as a number that points to fullness and life.

The sounds and forces of nature described here allude to the powers, all subservient to God, that were unleashed both at the creation of the world and at the Exodus from Egypt, which marked the creation of the Israelites as a people. The prayer book often recalls these two beginnings.

The worshipers in God's Temple in Jerusalem, who all "bespeak glory," may have gathered together to proclaim the final words of this psalm. They stress God's sovereignty over creation and His blessing for His people, appropriate sentiments to conclude this first part of *Kabbalat Shabbat*.

▨ When reading Psalm 29, I am reminded of our vital connection to the land of Israel. A tropical storm can be frightening and at the same time glorious. In Israel, the thunder is first heard over the Mediterranean and then over the northern mountains, which are shaken to their foundations. The storm then sweeps over the entire country, becoming most violent in the southern Aravah. The closing verse states the theme of Psalm 29: The God who brings storms to the world is also the God who restores peace and quiet. A new prayer might be that God bring peace and quiet to the land of Israel, too often mired in thunderous storm and terror.—*Carol Diament*

◉ Psalm 29, one of the most ancient in the Book of Psalms, celebrates the presence of God in the midst of a great thunderstorm. The word *kol*, which appears seven times in the psalm, here translated as 'voice,' can also mean 'thunderclap.' The psalmist concludes with mention of the great quiet that follows the storm, recalling the mythic quiet that followed God's triumph over the forces of chaos in creation. The placing of this psalm here reminds us that our weekly struggle in the world of achievement and bustle is now at an end. We have repeated the struggles of creation and now we too are called upon to achieve that great inner quiet which is the secret of true rest.—*Rabbi Arthur Green*[12]

Lekha Dodi

After we recite the songs of the psalmist enthroning God as world Sovereign, we greet Shabbat by singing a poem filled with symbolism and allusion. As mentioned above, the author, a leading mystic of the 16th century, Solomon Halevi Alkabetz, wrote the poem as an acrostic; each stanza begins with a Hebrew letter, spelling out his name. The English translation fails to replicate this acrostic feature of the poem. Translation, always an exercise in frustration, is especially incomplete in poetry. Even when translators capture most of the meaning, we often sacrifice the music of the original.[13]

In this poem, "my beloved" *(dodi)* refers to God, invited by the community of Israel to join in greeting Shabbat. The author based this use of "my beloved"※ on the use of the same Hebrew word in the Song of Songs, which Rabbi Akiba and subsequent Rabbinic interpreters have understood as a celebration of the love between God (the beloved) and Israel (the young maiden). The love between God and the people Israel pervades the Bible and medieval Hebrew poetry. The prophet Hosea, among others, portrays God as the husband of Israel.

An individual first confronting the various images that describe the people Israel and God and the Sabbath may find them confusing. The poet portrays Israel as both the bride of God the King and the husband of Shabbat, ❋ and he portrays Shabbat as both bride and queen.[14] The poem incorporates many words and phrases from the Bible, as cited in the endnotes and explained in the comments. Pointing them out in such detail may seem dry and pedantic, yet it reveals how Rabbi Alkabetz used passages from earlier sources to articulate his own thoughts and apply his Judaic knowledge to his own life and the lives of his contemporaries. Though we are not of his generation, his poetic imagination inspires us as well.

※ The Hebrew word *dodi* is sometimes translated as "my friend" or "my lover"; the gender of the Hebrew word *dodi* is masculine. The Hebrew word for God is also masculine in gender. In Hebrew, *Knesset Yisrael*, "the community of Israel," is of feminine gender.—*JH*

❋ A Rabbinic legend (Midrash, *Genesis Rabbah* 11:8) presents Shabbat as complaining to God that she alone, in all of creation, has no mate. (That is, the other six days are all paired up.) The Holy One declares that the people Israel will be her mate.—*JH*

※ The connection between Shabbat, release from exile, and redemption is based in part on the Rabbinic concept (Babylonian Talmud, *Shabbat* 57b) that Shabbat is a foretaste of the world to come.—*JH*

Of the nine stanzas, only three—the first, second, and last—mention Shabbat. In the other six stanzas the poet focuses on his people's yearnings and their hopes for release from exile and for redemption in the world to come. ※ The world to come will develop within human history and, led by the Messiah, it will include the rebuilding of Jerusalem. The poet's intense longing for redemption and release from exile arises in part out of conditions in the Jewish world of the 16th century. Rabbi Alkabetz composed *Lekha Dodi* only a few decades after the expulsion of Jews from Spain and the destruction of a substantial part of world Jewry.

Come, my beloved, the bride to meet; come, my beloved, Shabbat to greet.
"Keep" and "remember" Shabbat—both words came
As one divine utterance that God did proclaim.
The Lord is One and One is His name[15]
To His renown and praise and fame.[16]

The words "keep" and "remember" appear in the Bible's two versions of the Decalogue (popularly known as the Ten Commandments): "Keep the Sabbath day" in Deuteronomy 5:12 and "Remember the Sabbath day" in

Exodus 20:8. Rabbinic teachings explain the apparent inconsistency by pointing out that God, unlike human beings, can utter two words at one time (Babylonian Talmud, *Shavuot* 20b).

Come, my beloved, the bride to meet; come, my beloved, Shabbat to greet.
Come let us go meet Shabbat who is sought.
She is the source of the blessings God wrought;
Anointed in ancient days, divinely taught,
Although last in Creation, she was first in thought.

The poet perceives Shabbat as the source of all blessings throughout the world for all the days of the week. The third line refers to the anointing of Shabbat as queen from earliest time. Though God created Shabbat on the last day of creation, Shabbat had been first in God's plan. In Midrash, *Genesis Rabbah* 10:9, the Sages illustrate this with a parable. A king constructed and decorated a wedding canopy. Every object was in place, yet something was missing: a bride! The king, of course, had her in mind from the beginning, before he built the wedding canopy.

Come, my beloved, the bride to meet; come, my beloved, Shabbat to greet.
City, royal and sacred, to whom glory adheres,
Arise from your ruins, and the anguish of years.
Too long have you dwelt in the valley of tears;
God's mercy and pity will assuage your fears. ▦

The poet addresses the city of Jerusalem, which resembles Shabbat in its close association with the concept of redemption. The Talmud teaches: "If the people Israel would keep two consecutive Sabbaths according to the laws that govern its observance, they would be redeemed immediately" (Babylonian Talmud, *Shabbat* 118b).[17] Each week as Shabbat begins, we renew our hope for the redemption, which will include first and foremost the complete rebuilding of Jerusalem. The image of dwelling in the valley of tears describes the condition of the Jewish people during the 16th century. ✸

▦ Jeremiah 15:5 states: "But who will pity you, Jerusalem, who will console you?" The poet Alkabetz, however, turns the prophet's question into a firm declaration of hope for the future.—*JH*

✸ Ancient translators traced the image of the valley of tears to the Book of Psalms, in a verse, 84:7, which describes Israelite pilgrims going up to Jerusalem. They translated the phrase "Valley of Baca" into Aramaic as "valley of tears."—*JH*

Come, my beloved, the bride to meet; come, my beloved, Shabbat to greet.
Awake and arise from dust of the earth;
Wear splendid garments, my people, reflecting your worth.
Through David, son of Jesse who rejoiced at his birth
Bring near through Messiah my redemption and mirth.

The first two lines incorporate words from the prophet Isaiah's vision of redemption[18] to express the prayerful hope that the people Israel will break out of the misery of exile. These lines also imply that one can live in the land of Israel—as the poet did—and remain in exile, a fate that can befall even those living in Jerusalem. Many people today consider the restoration of an independent Jewish State in the Holy Land as the first stage of the final redemption, yet our world, like the world of the poet, remains unredeemed. The poet addresses the last two lines to God.[19] Jesse gave birth to David, and Jesse's descendant will give birth to the Messiah.[20]

Come, my beloved, the bride to meet; come, my beloved, Shabbat to greet.
Rouse yourself, rouse yourself[21] from the drear night;
Arise and shine, for the coming of your light.[22]
Awaken, awaken, sing out in delight;[23]
God's glory is revealed to you in splendor and might.

The poet turns to awaken the people, as well as Jerusalem, from their nighttime slumber of exile. Only then will he sing out with gratitude, anticipating the redemption. Since the reunification of Jerusalem, many congregations have adopted the custom of changing the melody of the second portion of the poem, starting with the stanza below, singing in a brighter, happier, celebratory mode.

Come, my beloved, the bride to meet; come, my beloved, Shabbat to greet.
You will not be embarrassed, you will not be ashamed.[24]
Why be downcast, why be frightened and lamed?[25]
In you will my people's poor find shelter,[26] reclaimed;
A city rebuilt on its own land,[27] not defamed.

Redemption will change the condition of the people Israel who suffer in exile.

Come, my beloved, the bride to meet; come, my beloved, Shabbat to greet.
Those who destroyed you will themselves be destroyed[28]
Your ravagers will be sent afar,[29] to live in a void.
Your God will rejoice in reclaiming you, overjoyed,
As a bridegroom with his bride,[30] in delight unalloyed. ✳

✳ In the mystical doctrine of [the Kabbalists'] teacher, Isaac Luria, the Sabbath was invested with a messianic resonance. It was a moment of union between the transcendent and immanent—masculine and feminine—aspects of God, a union that presaged the ultimate redemption. The theme of Psalms 95–99, accordingly, is the establishment of God's kingship as if it were already a present fact: "The Lord, enthroned on cherubim, is King, peoples tremble, the earth quakes" (Psalms 99.1). The *Lekha Dodi* brings the sexual metaphor to the surface. The hymn celebrates the arrival of the Sabbath, pictured as a bride and a queen, who is about to be joined to God, her consort. The scene of this union is a rebuilt Jerusalem, whom the poet addresses and exhorts to bestir herself and be ready for the redemptive events when "Your plunderers will themselves be despoiled, / Your violators will be banished; / Your God will rejoice in you / As a bridegroom takes pleasure in his bride." These mystical symbols are expressions of a religious philosophy that amounted to a major reinterpretation of Judaism and that gained wide acceptance in Jewry at the end of the 16th century.—*Alan Mintz*[31]

Come, my beloved, the bride to meet; come, my beloved, Shabbat to greet.
Break through your confinement, to the left, to the right,[32]
Show reverence for the Lord,[33] our chief delight.
The Messiah ▨ is coming, we yearn for that sight;

We shall rejoice and exult[34]
both by day and by night.

Come, my beloved, the bride to meet; come, my beloved, Shabbat to greet.

▨ The Hebrew phrase translated here as "the Messiah" is literally, "a man, the son of Peretz." This is another way of referring to the Messiah, the son of David, descended from Peretz, the child of Judah and Tamar (see Genesis 38). Peretz was also an ancestor of Boaz, the husband of Ruth, the ancestor of King David.—*JH*

✵ The poem *Lekha Dodi*, by 16th-century Safed mystic Solomon Halevi Alkabetz, evokes images of yearning for mystical union with the Divine as well as messianic redemption. It reflects the practice, common among Alkabetz's kabbalistic circle, of going out to the fields Friday evenings at sunset to welcome the Sabbath Bride and Queen.

Since Rabbinic days, these images have served as metaphors for the Jewish mystic's view of the feminine aspects of the Divine, the *Shekhinah* (Babylonian Talmud, *Shabbat* 119a). Just as a bridegroom desires his bride, the Jewish mystic desires union with the *Shekhinah*, the aspect of God that can be humanly experienced. This ardor was played out in the marital chamber of countless couples every Friday night, which mystics believed united not only husband and wife but also the masculine and feminine aspects of God, thereby facilitating the flow of Divine blessings into the world.

As women, we rejoice in the feminine imagery found in the Friday Evening Service. However, we may question what significance these images hold for us. Are we bridegroom or bride? Perhaps we see ourselves as the bride's sisters, waiting to take her hand and joyfully dance with her. Or maybe the desire for mystical union can be understood differently, in a way that transcends gender-specific roles. Perhaps there are in each of us both the bridegroom and the bride, both the masculine and the feminine, at least as those traits are defined in our society. Perhaps one of the deepest secrets of the mystical understanding of God is that men and women all share the potential to embrace both these parts of God's presence within each of us. This unity all too often remains hidden or discordant during the week, but can shine forth united on the Sabbath to fill us with a sense of wholeness. If so, then *Lekha Dodi* speaks not only to the bride and queen within each of us, but to those parts of ourselves that seem to stand outside of us, thereby awakening our own souls to find a sense of integration that is the prerequisite for a truly intimate connection with the Divine.—*Rabbi Susan Grossman*

The congregation now rises and turns to face the entrance to the sanctuary. Thus we welcome the bride, the Sabbath Queen, bowing to the left and the right[35] while singing the last line of the following stanza.

Come now in peace, her
husband's sweet pride;
In joy and rejoicing you'll
appear side by side
Midst the faithful who among
the treasured[36] people reside.
Come as we greet you: Come,
O bride; come, O bride. ✵

The final stanza returns to the theme of Shabbat, the bride of the people Israel, concluding with the phrase cited in the Talmud as the words with which Rabbi Yannai would greet Shabbat each week.

Come, my beloved, the bride to meet; come, my beloved, Shabbat to greet.

At the conclusion of *Lekha Dodi,* the congregation again faces the Ark at the front of the sanctuary. The congregation now welcomes those mourning a close relative who has died during the previous week. The mourners enter the sanctuary only after the celebratory singing of *Kabbalat Shabbat* has concluded, and the other members of the congregation greet them with the same words that visitors have used at the house of mourning: "May God comfort you among the other mourners of Zion and Jerusalem." The mourners join the congregation in reciting Psalm 92.

Psalm 92

A psalm, a song for the day of Shabbat. ✻ It is good to give thanks acclaiming the Lord, to sing to Your name, O Most High; to proclaim in the morning Your love, and Your faithfulness every night, to the music of a ten-string lute, to the chords of a lyre. You have gladdened me, Lord, with Your deeds; I sing for joy at the work of Your hands. How great are Your works, O Lord; how very deep are Your thoughts. A dullard cannot know, a fool cannot understand this: The wicked may spring up like grass and all evildoers may flourish, only to be destroyed forever. But You are exalted forever, Lord. For behold Your enemies, Lord, for behold Your enemies shall perish, all evildoers shall be scattered. You have exalted me, as You lift high the horn of a wild ox.[37] I am anointed with refreshing oil. I shall see the downfall of my enemies, my ears shall hear the defeat of the wicked who rise up against me. The righteous shall bloom like a palm tree, they shall thrive like a cedar in Lebanon. Planted in the House of the Lord, they shall flourish in the courts of our God. They still shall be fruitful in old age; fresh and fragrant shall they be, proclaiming that the Lord is just, my Rock in whom there is no flaw.

✻ At one time, before there was a *Kabbalat Shabbat* service as we know it, Shabbat was welcomed with the recitation of Psalm 92, A Psalm for Shabbat.—*JH*

✻ *[The poem below, written in 1977, welcomes Shabbat.]*

Shekhinah

Perched on our shoulders
a colorful butterfly
you whisper
into pores
shabbat's sweetness

we breathe you in
breathe the week out
take in roundness
letting go of sharp angles

we breathe in the *neshamah yetira*
the soul of the world to come
in awe
we sway   not march

As we kindle shabbat candles
you glide into our dark corners
warming us
dissolving our dense bodies
into light

—*Chana Bell*[38]

In ancient times, the Levites in the Temple recited a specific psalm for each day of the week. During Morning Services today, we continue the practice of reciting the psalm of the day. Only Psalm 92, the psalm for Shabbat, has its day designated in its text. ✻ In the Morning Service, when the congregation also recites this Psalm, the prayer book introduces it with the following: "Today is the day of holy Shabbat on which the Levites would say in the Temple."

Curiously, however, the rest of the Psalm never even mentions Shabbat. Nonetheless, the Rabbis relate Psalm 92 to Shabbat, understanding it as a song for the time to come, for the day that will be totally Shabbat and rest in life everlasting. In one ancient legend, Rabbi Levi reiterates that when Adam transgressed God's command (not to eat of the fruit of the tree), God sat in judgment of him. Then Rabbi Levi lists a schedule of events for the sixth day of Creation, on which Adam was created. In the first hour, the idea of Adam's creation occurred to God. In the second, God consulted with the ministering angels. In the third, He gathered together dust of the earth. In the fourth, He kneaded the dough, so to speak. On the fifth, God made Adam into a shapeless form. In the sixth, God gave Adam definite form. In the seventh, He breathed a soul into Adam. In the eighth, God stood Adam on his own feet. In the ninth hour, God gave Adam a commandment. In the tenth, Adam sinned; in the eleventh hour, Adam was judged in the divine court; and in the twelfth hour, Adam was expelled from the Garden. When the sentence was about to be delivered, Shabbat appeared as a defense attorney, addressing the Holy One: "Master of the universe! During the six days of creation not one person was punished and now You want to begin on *my* day?! Is this what You call my holiness and my rest?" Because of Shabbat, Adam was saved from the sentence of being sent to Gehenna. When Adam observed the power of Shabbat he wanted to sing a song to Shabbat. Shabbat, however, scolded him. "You want to sing a song to *me*? Let the two of us join in singing to the Holy One. It is good to give thanks, acclaiming the Lord." The striking image of Shabbat itself singing a song (the 92nd Psalm, "A song of Shabbat") is also incorporated into the prayers recited on Shabbat morning: "This is the praise of the seventh day on which God rested from all of His work. The seventh day itself utters praise: 'A psalm, a song for the day of Shabbat. It is good to give thanks acclaiming the Lord.'"[39]

Since ancient times it has been customary to greet Shabbat with the recitation of Psalm 93 as well.

Psalm 93

The Lord reigns, robed in majesty; the Lord is robed, girded with might. The world is set on a firm foundation; it cannot be shaken. Your throne stands firm from earliest time; You have always been. The oceans, O Lord, lift up, the oceans lift up their voice, pounding and roaring. Beyond the thunder of mighty waters, more majestic than the breakers of the sea, majestic on high is the Lord. Your decrees are enduring indeed; holiness befits Your house, O Lord, for length of days.

Psalm 93 also celebrates God's sovereign power over the majesty of creation. The Levites sang this psalm on Friday in the Temple. The prayer book for the weekday Morning Service introduces Psalm 93 with: "Today is the sixth day after Shabbat on which the Levites would say in the Temple." The Greek version of the Bible (the Septuagint) introduces this Psalm with a superscription: "For the day before the Sabbath when the earth was first inhabited,"[40] recalling the sixth day of creation, also the context of its use during *Kabbalat Shabbat*.

After Psalm 93, mourners and those observing the anniversary *(yahrzeit)* of a death recite the Mourner's *Kaddish*.

Mishnah Excerpts

Before the Shabbat *Maariv* Service, Orthodox congregations and many Conservative congregations read the entire second chapter of Mishnah *Shabbat*. Other Conservative congregations read selections from several different chapters of that Mishnah. ▓ Neither Reform nor Reconstructionist prayer books include Mishnah excerpts before *Maariv*.

With study and with prayer we welcome Shabbat in more than one way, because our tradition, like our lives, encompasses more than one dimension. We sing about passionate love of God in *Lekha Dodi* and in *Yedid Nefesh*. We chant psalms praising the Creator and creation, expressing joy and gratitude for God's gifts. We utter prayers confronting God as individuals and as members of a community. We stand in awe and reflect upon what is deepest in our hearts. To express ourselves fully, we must also study Jewish sacred texts, since study is an integral part of Jewish worship. Part of that obligation is fulfilled each time we recite passages from the Torah that constitute *Kriat Shema* in a prayer service.

▓ The Mishnah is a third-century compilation of traditions, laws, and opinions upon which the *Gemara* is based. The Mishnah and the *Gemara* together make up the Talmud.—JH

❁ The excerpts from Mishnah *Shabbat* that are recited in Orthodox and Conservative synagogues may serve to remind us of our duty to light candles every Friday night before sunset. Among the most observant Jewish communities, however, those who attend synagogue on Friday nights are mainly the men, while the women remain at home. So the women do not hear the reminder, though they are responsible for lighting the Shabbat candles. In traditional Jewish communities, husbands are supposed to instruct the wives, and indeed many do so before going to the synagogue.—Carol Diament

Mishnah *Shabbat* 2:5

Anyone who puts out the light of a candle on Shabbat eve because of fearing alien marauders, or thieves, or evil forces, or in order to let a sick person sleep, is not guilty of desecrating Shabbat. ❁ A person who does it, however, in order to save the candle, or to save the oil, or the wick, is guilty of desecrating Shabbat. Rabbi Yose does not find anyone who acts thus guilty of desecrating

Shabbat, with one exception—a person who puts out a wick, since such action produces charcoal. ▓

Mishnah *Shabbat* 16:1

All texts of Holy Scripture may be saved from fire on Shabbat, whether or not they are read in public on Shabbat. This includes Scripture written in any language, and all [that is, the burned texts that are no longer serviceable] require placement in a *genizah*. And why were sacred writings other than Torah and the Prophets not read in public on Shabbat? Out of the concern that they might come to replace the public study of Torah and Prophets on Shabbat. The container of a scroll may be saved with the scroll, and the container of *tefillin* may be saved with *tefillin*, even though money may have been stored in it. ⊛

▓ In Mishnah *Shabbat* 2:5, the Hebrew word here translated as "alien marauders" is *nokhrim*,[41] literally "strangers," which usually refers to non-Jews. According to the next sentence, an individual is guilty of desecrating Shabbat if the intention is to save the candle, oil, or wick for use at another time. Rabbi Yose asserts that only the individual who produces charcoal by putting out a wick desecrates Shabbat, because one should not be involved in activity producing a new substance on Shabbat. Note that the authorities in the ancient Jewish community disagreed on certain basic matters, and that the Mishnah preserves contrary opinions.—*JH*

⊛ Mishnah *Shabbat* 16:1 discusses saving sacred items from fire on Shabbat, even if the rescue involves work that is ordinarily forbidden. On Shabbat, we read the Torah and Prophets in public; we do not publicly read the section of the Bible called Writings, which includes Psalms and the Five *Megillot*. We may dispose of sacred books or other sacred writings only in a *genizah*, a special storage area for sacred objects that have been damaged or are no longer in use. After placement in a *genizah*, the sacred objects may later be buried in a Jewish cemetery. The Rabbis raise the question of why the Writings are not read in public on Shabbat, even though the question is not directly related to saving sacred items. Stylistically this is typical of Rabbinic literature. The discussion returns to saving sacred items. To save the *tefillin* scroll and its container, one may even hold money, which ordinarily is not to be handled in any way on Shabbat.—*JH*

Mishnah *Shabbat* 18:3

One may not deliver the young of cattle on a Festival, but one may assist the animal that is giving birth. One may deliver a child on Shabbat, and may summon a midwife for the woman from anywhere, and may desecrate Shabbat for her sake, and tie up the umbilical cord. Rabbi Yose says: One may even cut the umbilical cord. All acts required for a circumcision on Shabbat may be done on Shabbat. ▓

▓ In Mishnah *Shabbat* 18:3, the work of actually delivering a young animal involves too much physical labor to be permitted on Shabbat. At the same time, the animal must be assisted. The midwife who is summoned may walk as far as necessary, even outside the limits of the area within which one is normally allowed to walk on Shabbat. One may desecrate the Sabbath for a woman in labor, because she is in the category of an ailing person whose life could be in danger. However, most Rabbis say that the umbilical cord should be tied up, but should not be severed until after Shabbat. Rabbi Yose's disagreement is another example of the Rabbinic preservation of diverse opinion.—*JH*

After reading these and other Mishnah excerpts, we conclude our study with the following passage from the *Gemara*. Appropriately for a day on which even a personal greeting is "Shabbat Shalom," we emphasize prayers for peace.

Babylonian Talmud, *Brakhot 64a*

Rabbi Elazar said in the name of Rabbi Ḥanina: The disciples of sages increase peace in the world, as it is written [in Isaiah 54:13], "When all of your children will be learned of the Lord, great will be the peace of your children." The word for "your children" (*banayikh*) should be read as "those among you who have true understanding" (*bonayikh*). "Those who love Your Torah have great peace; they encounter no stumbling block" [Psalms 119:165]. ✳ "May there be peace within your ramparts, serenity within your citadels" [Psalms 122:7]. "For the sake of my family and my friends I speak out in prayer for your peace, for the sake of the House of the Lord our God, I will seek your welfare" [Psalms 122: 8–9]. ❋ "May the Lord give strength to His people, may the Lord bless His people with peace" [Psalms 29:13].

After the reading of the Mishnah and Talmud selections, mourners and those observing the anniversary (*yahrzeit*) of a death recite *Kaddish DeRabbanan*.[42] The congregation then begins the Shabbat Evening Service. (See Chapters 3 and 4.)

✳ Isaiah 54:13 implies that peace for the people Israel will increase along with the increase of those who study and understand sacred literature. The Rabbis often base their teachings on puns. For the Rabbis, the similarities between words reveal the deepest meaning, or real intent, of a passage. Some people prefer yet another translation of the word *bonayikh*: "The word for 'your children' should be read as 'your builders.'"—JH

❋ Psalm 122 prays for the well-being of Jerusalem, and in the Friday Evening Service, we pray that God spread a shelter of peace over Jerusalem (in *Hashkivenu*). The same prayer, when recited on weekdays, does not mention Jerusalem.—JH

✳ The Bible tells us of *ohel Sarah* (the matriarch Sarah's tent) and the *ohel mo'ed* (Tent of Meeting), where the Holy of Holies was housed during the period of desert wandering before the Children of Israel entered the Promised Land.

The Midrash states that while Sarah was alive, a light burned in her tent from one Shabbat to the next; dough for the loaves of bread was blessed; and a cloud (signifying the divine Presence) always hovered over her tent (*Midrash Rabbah, Genesis* 60:16; Rashi on Genesis 24:67). When she died, these things ceased. However, when Isaac's new wife, Rebecca, came into Sarah's tent, the light, the dough, and the cloud all returned. According to the Midrash, Sarah's tent foreshadowed the *ohel mo'ed* (Tent of Meeting) with its accompanying fire, sacrifices, and cloud of the *Shekhinah*. Sarah and Rebecca ➤

HOME RITUALS FOR SHABBAT

Candle Lighting

The lighting of candles ushers in Shabbat at home. ✳ This always has been the special obligation of women. If no women are present, however, men are obligated to light candles. (We also light candles to usher in Festivals and the High Holy Days.)

At least two Shabbat candles are lit about 18 minutes before sunset on Friday. After the candles are lit, we recite the *brakhah*.

Blessed are You, Lord our God, King of the universe who has made us holy with His commandments, commanding us to kindle Shabbat light.

As the candles burn, one may recite a brief prayer or meditation, or simply stand before the candles in a reflective mood. Some examples of what could be said follow, although one's own words and reflections are perfectly appropriate.

were precursors of the priesthood; they were the holy women of their sacred tents....

In our day, the Shabbat table is an analog to the table in the *ohel mo'ed*, where 12 *hallot* (loaves) were placed. The candles are lit, analogous to the seven-branched lampstand in the *ohel mo'ed* that always remained lit. In short, the everyday life of the house in which we dwell is elevated to the very highest level of *kedushah* (holiness) simply by carrying out preparations for Shabbat. It is no surprise to realize that many Jews define making a Jewish home in terms of making Shabbat. One way to look at homemaking, in all senses of the word, is as the elevation of the mundane into the sacred—as one cooks, cleans, celebrates, repairs, rests, studies, converses, and makes blessings.

Contemporary Shabbat preparations parallel the physical approach to the inner Holy of Holies and the *ohel mo'ed*. Even as the holiness gradually increased in intensity as one drew nearer to the Holy of Holies, so Sabbath preparations gradually intensify as the time draws closer to the moment of candle lighting, the opening ritual of Shabbat. The day of rest informs my entire week. Like a priestess, like a keeper of the Holy Temple, I prepare my home—with errands and intentionality, tasks and Torah—to be a suitable vessel for receiving Shabbat.

I enjoy bringing guests into my home on Shabbat. In so doing … I follow the tradition of my ancestors, Abraham and Sarah (Genesis, chapter 18). One of the greatest *mitzvot* (commandments, sacred obligations) is *hakhnasat orḥim* (welcoming guests). Among the Jews of Ethiopia there is a saying for bringing guests into the home: "Please come in! My house is the house of Abraham."—*Penina V. Adelman*[44]

May the light of these candles help inspire us to love You with all our hearts. May their warmth and glow radiate kindness, harmony, and peace among us all. May love and devotion bind us closer to one another and to You.[43]

Compassionate Creator of all life, embrace my life and my family's life with Your loving kindness. May my children walk in Your ways, loyal to the Torah, and adorned with good deeds. Bless our home and our family with peace and light and joy.

May the peace of Shabbat fill our hearts, fill our home, fill the world.

As I light these Shabbat candles, I feel the frenzied momentum of the week slowly draining from my body. I thank You, Creator, for the peace and relaxation of Shabbat, for moments to redirect my energies toward those treasures in my life that I hold most dear. Had You not in Your infinite wisdom created Shabbat, I may not have stopped in time.[45]

Blessing Children

At the Shabbat table, parents customarily place their hands upon the heads of their children to bless them with the following words:

For sons:
May God give you the blessings of Ephraim and Menasseh.

For daughters:
May God give you the blessings of Sarah, Rebecca, Rachel, and Leah.

Continue for all:
May the Lord bless you and guard you. May the Lord show you favor and be gracious to you. May the Lord show you kindness and grant you peace.

Singing before the Meal

Standing or seated around the table, everyone joins in song.

Shalom Aleikhem

**We wish you peace, attending angels, angels of the most sublime, ▦
the King of kings, the Holy One, blessed is He.**

***Shalom aleikhem malakhei hashareit, malakhei elyon
miMelekh malkhei hamlakhim, Hakadosh Barukh Hu.***

**Come to us in peace, angels of peace, angels of the most sublime,
the King of kings, the Holy One, blessed is He.**

**Bless us with peace, angels of peace, angels of the most sublime,
the King of kings, the Holy One, blessed is He.**

**Take your leave in peace, angels of peace, angels of the most sublime,
the King of kings, the Holy One, blessed is He.**

A Shabbat Song, *Zemer LeShabbat*

**The sun on the treetops no
longer is seen.
Come, let us welcome Shabbat,
the true queen.
Behold her descending, the holy,
the blessed,
and with her God's angels of
peace and of rest.
Come now, come now, our
queen, our bride.
*Bo'i, bo'i hamalkah, bo'i, bo'i
hakallah.*
Shalom aleikhem, angels of
peace.
*Shalom aleikhem, malakhei
hashalom.* ✳**

▦ *Shalom Aleikhem* is based on a tale in the Babylonian Talmud (*Shabbat* 119b): When a man returns home from synagogue on Friday night, he is accompanied by two angels, one good and one evil. If the house is in Sabbath order, the good angel prays that the next Sabbath will be the same as this one. If, however, the house is not properly prepared for the Sabbath, the evil angel wishes the next Sabbath will be the same as this one.

The main idea of *Shalom Aleikhem* is peace. Especially in troubled times, when Israel is in danger, we ask to be blessed with peace. Peace is of utmost importance to Jews. We pray for peace in our homes and on our streets. We want the weak and the strong, the nations large and small, to live together in peace. Our Rabbis have said that the whole world exists only for the sake of peace (Babylonian Talmud, *Gittin* 59b).—*Carol Diament*

✳ The poem "A Shabbat Song" was written by Hayyim Nahman Bialik (1873–1934), the Hebrew national poet in the 20th century.—*JH*

Eshet Hayil, A Capable Wife

In many observant homes, the husband sings the verses below from the Book of Proverbs (31:10–31) to his wife immediately before chanting *Kiddush.* ▣ In some homes, all assembled sing the verses together. Scholars maintain that the singing of these verses on Shabbat originated in the 16th century as praise for the *Shekhinah,* the manifestation of God's Presence. The word *Shekhinah* is feminine in gender, and the Kabbalists understood *Shekhinah* as the feminine aspect of God. Some scholars maintain that the singing of *Eshet Hayil* serves to praise the Torah, which in Hebrew is also feminine in gender.

Rabbinic commentary on the Book of Proverbs (*Midrash Mishlei*) identifies the verses with specific women of the Bible, as explained in the endnotes. In Hebrew, the 22 verses of *Eshet Hayil* appear as an alphabetic acrostic. "Just as the Holy One gave the Torah to the people Israel with 22 letters [the number of letters in the Hebrew alphabet], so too does He praise the worthy women using these 22 letters."

▣ One of the traditional Shabbat rituals of Friday evening is for the man to praise the "woman of the house," along with blessing the children. Obviously [from a Jewish feminist standpoint] there are some problems related to this issue, especially for women making Shabbat alone. We are accustomed to seeing ourselves as the enablers for others' experience, so that it may be hard to legitimize something we do for ourselves alone. One woman questions, "What do I do when I've lit the Shabbat candles and I look around and there's no one there?"

Yet the *Eshet Hayil* traditionally chanted by the husband has something to recommend it, in that it recognizes women's competence both at home and in the business world. The problem is that most of the work praised in the verse is directed toward the smooth running of the household, assuming homemaking as women's work, and doesn't leave much room for individual spiritual growth. And there's no parallel song of praise for the man of the house—if there is one—who might even have been the one responsible for the chicken soup.

Some people, especially if they celebrate Shabbat with the same group every week—family or friends—eliminate praise for the woman of the house and substitute a round-robin report of what each person has appreciated about other members of the group that week: what was an especially nice encounter or an especially appreciated deed. Another possibility is for women celebrating Shabbat together to sing *Eshet Hayil* to one another, as praise for womankind in general.—*Susan Weidman Schneider* [46]

A capable wife is not easily found; her value is far beyond rubies.
Her husband puts his trust in her,[47] and nothing shall he lack thereby.
She endows him with good,[48] and not evil, all the days of her life.
She seeks out wool and flax, and sets her hand to them willingly.[49]
She is like the fleet of a merchant, from afar she brings her food.[50]
She rises while it is still night, to provide food for her household, and the
    daily provision of her maids.[51]
She examines a field and buys it; with her earnings she plants a vineyard.[52]
She girds herself with strength, and puts her arms to the task with vigor.[53]
She perceives that her business thrives, her lamp burns all night.[54]
She lays her hand on the distaff, her fingers grasp the spindle.[55]

She opens her hand to the needy, and extends her hand to the poor.[56]

She fears not for her household because of snow, for all her household is clothed in crimson.[57]

Covers she makes for herself; her clothing is linen and purple.[58]

Her husband is well-known at the city gates, where he sits with the elders of the land.[59]

She makes linen cloth and sells it, a girdle she delivers to the merchant.[60]

She is clothed in strength and splendor, and cheerfully faces the future.[61]

She opens her mouth with wisdom, her tongue is guided by kindness.[62]

She attends to her household's ways, and eats not the bread of idleness.[63]

Her children come forward and call her happy; her husband sings her praise:[64]

"Many women have been admirable, but you surpass them all."[65]

Charm is deceptive and beauty is vain, but a God-fearing woman is to be praised.[66]

Honor her for the fruit of her hands; wherever people gather, her deeds speak her praise.[68] ✺ ✳

✺ Who can find a wise woman?
For her price is far above rubies.
Those in her house safely trust her
For she heeds the words of her children,
she works alongside her husband,
but outside the walls of her house,
Outside the gates of her garden,
she hears the cries in the city,
the cries of women in distress.
She is their rescuer.

She rises at dawn to organize.
She rises before light to make orderly the day.
She stretches out her hand to unchain
the chained woman,
the woman without recourse,
the women not paid their worth on this earth.
She taketh on the men at the gate,
the men of the law-making bodies,
the men of the *Bet Din*,
the Judges on high.
She looks them in the eye
and says:
>   This is unacceptable.
>   This is unjust.
>   This is cruel.
>   We demand a state
>   where there is no religious rule.

In her household she is praised.
In the state she is extolled.
Many women have done wisely
but she excels them all.

—*E. M. Broner*[67]

✳ To this day, the words *eshet ḥayil* are used to describe the finest type of Jewish homemaker and helpmate. Rabbi Harlow translates *eshet ḥayil* as "a capable wife," yet a more common translation is: "a woman of valor." Rabbi Harlow's translation, though, captures the popular understanding. When we say that a woman is a true *eshet ḥayil*, we mean that she is a devoted wife and mother who observes Jewish law to her utmost.

Jewish feminists of my generation, those of us who were raising families in the 1960s and early 1970s, strongly objected to the *Eshet Hayil* poem's representation of an ideal woman. Even though "she makes linen cloth and sells it, a girdle she delivers to the merchant" (which we can interpret as "she has a career"), ultimately she is but an enabler. Her efforts result in her husband's prominence, not her own; ➤

Kiddush

Friday Evening *Kiddush*

We recite *kiddush* in the synagogue, as a conclusion to the *Kabbalat Shabbat* and *Maariv* services, as well as in the home. ▨

---

he "is well-known at the city gates, where he sits with the elders of the land." Even though "her children come forward and call her happy; her husband sings her praise," she does not speak in her own voice. So how happy is she herself? My mother, a fervent feminist (although born too late for the first feminist movement of the early 20th century and too early for the second feminist movement of the 1970s) often remarked on the verse "Charm is deceptive, beauty is vain, but a God-fearing woman is to be praised." Perhaps, she noted, some rabbis concurred with those sentiments—but what about all the other Jewish men?

Many young women today, unlike the feminists of my generation, are opting to become the *eshet ḥayil*. Perhaps they are looking at the wounds that many in my generation endured for self-actualization—late marriage, no marriage, divorce—and blame those problems on the feminist movement. Yet, I ask them: What of all the advances in women's rights, women's careers, women's salaries, women's education—especially women's Jewish education—where would these be if the older generation had not fought the good fight?—*Carol Diament*

▨ We recite *kiddush* at the site of the meal. The custom of reciting *kiddush* in the synagogue arose in times past, when people of meager means and travelers would be invited to eat the Shabbat meal in the synagogue. When reciting *kiddush* in the synagogue, we begin with the blessing: "Blessed are You, Lord our God, King of the universe who creates the fruit of the vine."—*JH*

❂ The history of why the words, "There was evening and there was morning, the sixth day," are included in the *Kiddush* provides an example of the Kabbalists' lasting influence on the prayer book. We chant "there was evening and there was morning" softly. These words begin the last part of the last verse of Genesis chapter one, a verse that concludes with the next words, "the sixth day" *(yom hashishi)*. We chant the words "the sixth day" aloud, and continue chanting aloud the words that follow (Genesis 2:1–3). Originally this passage began with "the heavens and the earth"; that is, Jews recited only Genesis 2:1–3 before reciting the *brakhah* on the fruit of the vine. The Kabbalists, however, added *yom hashishi* (the sixth day), because of its initial Hebrew letters—*yod* and *hei*. These letters, together with *vav* and *hei*, the initial letters of the next words *va'yekhulu hashamayim* (the heavens were completed) spell out the four-letter Hebrew name of God. This name—*yod-hei-vav-hei*—is known as the tetragammaton, and special sanctity ➤

There was evening and there was morning, the sixth day. ❂ The heavens and the earth were completed, and all their array. God completed on the seventh day His work that He had done. He rested on the seventh day from all His work that He had done. Then God blessed the seventh day and hallowed it, for on it He rested from all His work that God in creating had been doing.[69]

We now raise the goblet of wine.

Blessed are You, Lord our God, King of the universe who creates the fruit of the vine.

Blessed are You, Lord our God, King of the universe who hallowed us with His *mitzvot* and cherished us, giving us the heritage of His holy Shabbat lovingly and gladly, a reminder of Creation. For it is the first of our holy gatherings,[70] a reminder of the exodus from Egypt. For You have chosen us and hallowed us from among all the peoples by giving us the heritage of Your holy Shabbat lovingly and gladly. Blessed are You, Lord who hallows Shabbat. ▨

Many people identify Shabbat with prohibitions, yet focusing only on the restrictions may blind us to the beauty and basic message of the day. Observance of Shabbat through both its rituals and its prohibitions enhances the day's significance. Many of Judaism's great teachers urge us to remember what Shabbat can add to our lives, as does Rabbi Moses ben Machir, a 16th-century contemporary of Rabbi Solomon Halevi Alkabetz, the author of *Lekha Dodi*. The following excerpt paraphrases his commentary on Jewish prayer:

It is important to participate with the community, saying Friday evening prayers together with melody and song. Thus we greet with joy the Sabbath bride who comes to us with the extra soul that is ours each Shabbat. ✳ It is appropriate to make her happy and to make ourselves happy with all that comes to hand. If someone has had an argument with a friend or with a family member, it should not be mentioned on Shabbat. The domain of Shabbat is not to be desecrated by arguments or anger. We should stress love, affection, peace, and companionship on Shabbat. We should take care to avoid anything that violates the holiness of Shabbat which stresses peace and quietude. ✵ Therefore it is appropriate for everyone to observe Shabbat with attention to its Jewish ritual requirements and to keep all sorrow and sighing at a far remove on Shabbat....

Immediately after the Evening Service, one should hurry home to make *Kiddush*, which should be done as soon as possible. (No food should be tasted after services before *Kiddush*.) Our homes should be prepared for Shabbat with the best of everything according to our means, as we would prepare for a visit from the most distinguished official in the land, an occasion for which we would have on display the

is attached to it. Since "the sixth day" consists merely of the last words from verse 1:31 in Genesis, respect for the meaning and the sense of the Biblical verses demanded that additional words from Genesis 1:31 be included. Thus, we also include "there was evening and there was morning," though these words are relegated to lesser status—and said in a soft voice. Hence, our introduction to the Friday night *Kiddush* starts with words whose initials spell out the name of God.—*JH*

✳ Women, like men, are obligated to recite *Kiddush* on Shabbat. Rabbinic teachings explain that God uttered two words at one time, obligating Jews both to remember and to keep Shabbat (Babylonian Talmud, *Shavuot* 20b). The Rabbis declare that the commandment to *remember* the Sabbath is fulfilled by reciting *Kiddush* over wine. Because the two words ("keep" and "remember" in the Bible, both referring to Shabbat) are so closely connected, the Rabbis derive the ruling that since women are obligated to *keep* (that is, observe) Shabbat, they are also obligated to *remember* it—through *Kiddush*. See *Shulhan Arukh*, *Orah Hayim* 261:2. "Women are obligated to recite *Kiddush* even though it is a positive commandment which must be fulfilled at a specific time [from which women generally are excluded] ... and they may recite it on behalf of men [so that all those who hear it fulfill their own obligation for recitation of *Kiddush*] since it is derived from the Torah that they are just as obligated as men to fulfill this *mitzvah*." Some authorities, however, do not agree that women may recite *Kiddush* on behalf of men.—*JH*

✳ This extra Shabbat soul may be viewed as the greater sensitivity allowed us by the restful and unpressured pace of Shabbat. Indeed, that extra soul may be inside us all the time, and *Lekha Dodi* may be seen as a love song that coaxes our most sensitive self to come out of hiding, in the assurance that on Shabbat it will not be harmed or threatened.—*Rabbi Arthur Green*[71]

✵ The Sabbath transforms our weekday experience of hierarchical relationships into a day of co-equal relationships. Master/slave, employer/employee, and even human/animal—all these hierarchies give way to the sanctification of relationships based on our acceptance of the other's existence. On Shabbat, we refrain from using or exploiting other people to meet our own needs. We allow each living being simply to be itself, in all its fullness. We do not judge others for what they do, but honor each being for what it is. This perspective is the seed bed for equality between women and men, as well as between groups of people.—*Rabbi Lynn Gottlieb*[72]

best and the finest in our home, with a fine table set as well. The Sabbath bride is a much more important guest, and everyone, from the richest to the poorest, should prepare as fine a welcome as their means will allow.[73]

Shabbat Morning *Kiddush*

We insert the *Kiddush* for Shabbat morning here for easy comparison with *Kiddush* for Friday night. The *Kiddush* recited before the Friday night meal differs from the *Kiddush* recited before Saturday luncheon, although both are recited over wine. After Morning Services in the synagogue, as well as at home, we raise our goblet and recite:

The people Israel shall observe Shabbat, to maintain it as an everlasting covenant through all generations. It is a sign between Me and the people Israel for all time, that in six days the Lord made the heavens and the earth, and on the seventh day He ceased from work and rested.[74]

Some individuals and some congregations omit the following paragraph that begins "Remember to hallow" and recite only the two sentences that follow it.

Remember to hallow the day of Shabbat. Six days shall you labor and do all your work, but the seventh day is a Shabbat of the Lord your God; on it you shall not do any work—you or your son or your daughter, your male or female servant, your cattle, or the stranger who is among you—for in six days the Lord made the heavens, the earth and the sea, and all they contain, and on the seventh day He rested.[75]

Therefore the Lord blessed the day of Shabbat and made it holy.[76]

Blessed are You, Lord our God, King of the universe who creates the fruit of the vine.

Netilat Yadayim

Before every meal that includes bread, observant Jews recite a blessing and ritually rinse their hands.

Blessed are You, Lord our God, King of the universe who has made us holy with His *mitzvot* and who commanded us to rinse the hands.

Brakhah over Bread

On Shabbat evening and on Shabbat morning, we recite the *brakhah* using two *ḥallot*.

Blessed are You, Lord our God, King of the universe who brings forth bread from the earth.

Zemirot

During and after Shabbat meals, we sing special songs for Shabbat, known as *zemirot*. Most complete prayer books print the lyrics of a number of *zemirot,* as do booklets containing blessings after meals. The following samples are free translations.

Yah Ribon

Ruler of all worlds, of all things, You, O Lord, are supreme, King of kings. How lovely to sing of Your wonders. At dawn and at dusk Your praise I declare, Creator of all: angels and mortals, beasts of the field, and birds of the air. Were we granted thousands of years, countless days, we could never recount all Your might, all Your praise. God of greatness and glory, save Your flock from lion's jaws; end the pain of our exile, help Your chosen in spite of our flaws. Return to Your holy of holies; then all souls will rejoice, sweet songs will they render in Jerusalem, holy city of splendor.

Yah Ribon, a beautiful Aramaic song, was written by Rabbi Israel Najara (1555–1628) of Palestine. The first letters of the stanzas form the word "Israel." This song focuses not on Shabbat but on Zion, the yearning that we be brought back to the city of Jerusalem.—*Carol Diament*

Yom Zeh Mekhubad

This day is glorified beyond all other days; as the day on which He rested, the Eternal sings its praise. Six days pursue your labors, the seventh day is God's alone; after His six days of labor He ascended to His throne. Foremost among all sacred days, Shabbat is a day of rest. At the table two loaves of ḥallah as well as wine are the best. Eat the finest food, drink the finest wine; God does provide, His faithful all assume. The best of food and nourishment, meat and fish and delicacies will you consume. Eat, and be satisfied. Lack nothing on this day. Praise the Lord who has blessed you beyond all others, the Lord whom you love, to whom you pray. The heavens declare His glory, the earth is filled with His love. Behold all His creation; perfection on earth below and in heaven above.

Blessings After the Meal

We chant *Birkat Hamazon* (Grace After Meals) after finishing the Shabbat meals. We include here only a brief passage. On Shabbat and on Festivals, we first chant Psalm 126.

A song of ascent. When the Lord restored our exiles in Zion, it was like a dream. Then our mouths were filled with laughter, joyous song was on our tongues. Then it was said among the nations: "The Lord has done great things for them." Great things indeed He did for us; therefore we rejoiced. Restore us,

Lord, as You restore streams to Israel's desert soil. Those who sow in tears shall reap in joyous song. A tearful man will plant in sadness, bearing his sack of seed. But he will come home in gladness, bearing his sheaves of grain.

On Shabbat we add the following passage to the Grace after Meals.

Strengthen us, Lord our God, with Your *mitzvot*, especially the *mitzvah* of this great and holy seventh day, that we may rest thereon lovingly, according to Your will. May it be Your will, Lord our God, to grant that our Shabbat rest be free of anguish, sorrow, and sighing. May we behold Zion Your city consoled, Jerusalem Your holy city completely rebuilt. For You are Master of deliverance and consolation.

HAVDALAH, THE CONCLUSION OF SHABBAT

We welcome Shabbat with candle lighting and a blessing; we bid Shabbat good-bye with candle lighting and blessings. After the chanting of the Evening Service, both women and men are obligated to recite *havdalah* (Hebrew for "distinction") to formally conclude Shabbat. ▓

A *havdalah* candle must have at least two wicks to conform literally with the blessing's Hebrew plural word, translated as "lights" or "flames." (For Shabbat, we light at least two candles, each with one wick.) We light the *havdalah* candle at the start of the ceremony, and all stand. We bid Shabbat good-bye with blessings in the Evening Service, before this *havdalah* ritual, when words of *havdalah* in another form are added to the fourth blessing of the *Amidah* (see pages 94–95). *Shulhan Arukh, Orah Hayyim* 296:8, states that both men and women are obligated to recite *havdalah,* but some authorities disagree, stating that women are simply obligated to hear *havdalah.* We also recite *havdalah* at the conclusion of a Festival, when it consists only of a blessing over wine and the lines of the final blessing (concluding with "between sacred and secular time"). When the Sabbath is immediately followed by a Festival, *havdalah* is incorporated into the Festival *Kiddush,* making a distinction "between holy and holy."—JH

Behold, God is my deliverance; I have trust and have no fear. For Yah[77] the Lord is my strength and might, and has been my deliverance. You shall draw water in joy from the fountain of deliverance.[78]

The Lord of Hosts is with us, the God of Jacob is our shelter.[79] Lord of Hosts, blessed the mortal who trusts in You.[80] O Lord, deliver! May the King answer us when we call.[81]

All the assembled join in chanting:

The Jews had light and joy, happiness and honor.[82] May it be the same for us.

The leader raises a cup of wine.

I raise the cup recalling deliverance, and invoke the name of the Lord.[83] Blessed are You, Lord our God, King of the universe who creates the fruit of the vine.

The leader sets the wine down and holds up the spices.

Blessed are You, Lord our God, King of the universe who creates fragrant spices. ⊛

After reciting the blessing over the spices, the leader smells the aromatic spices and then passes the spices to all assembled, who take turns inhaling the scent. The leader then chants:

Blessed are You, Lord our God, King of the universe who creates the lights of fire. ✳

After reciting the blessing over fire, we make use of the light. Some look at the reflection of light on their fingernails or at the shadow cast by their fingers onto the palms of their hands. The leader again raises the cup of wine.

Blessed are You, Lord our God, King of the universe who distinguishes between sacred and secular time, between light and darkness, between the people Israel and other people, between the seventh day and the six work days of the week. Blessed are You, Lord who distinguishes between sacred and secular time.

In keeping with the theme of redemption and deliverance, many sing about the prophet Elijah who is destined to announce the advent of the Messiah.

⊛ The spices are usually contained in a spice box. Cloves are common, but aromatic spices of any sort may be used, including sweet smelling herbs or leaves or twigs. According to one explanation, the fragrance of the spices will help to sustain us through the sadness we feel as the additional soul which had been ours on the Sabbath day departs. In the blessing, the phrase translated here as "who creates fragrant spices" literally means "who creates varieties of spices."—JH

✳ Some say that this blessing, "creates the lights of fire," is to signal the beginning of the week when work is again permitted with the departure of the Sabbath.—JH

✱ The *havdalah* liturgy and the ritual that accompanies it create one of the most theatrical ceremonies in my home. We set up an impressive collection of props on our dining room table: a flaming multi-wicked candle; a glass of wine (or sometimes juice) to drink; and spices, herbs, or fragrant flowers that we have gathered from our garden and in our travels in America and Israel. To heighten the drama, we dim the lights and sing a mystical, plaintive song of greeting to the prophet Elijah. Recently we've begun to add a song to greet the prophet Miriam as well.

Why do we get out all the "bells and whistles" for this brief but lavishly multisensory experience? I think it's because, on an unspoken level, we are terrified to leave the utopian paradise of Shabbat with its bounty of good foods and its opportunities for real rest, fellowship, intimacy, and leisurely study. How can we leap out of this perfect world that God has commanded us to imagine into being and suddenly land with a thud back in the pressures and maddening details of the everyday?

To usher us across the threshold back to reality, to cushion ourselves from its harshness, we say verses that will comfort us: When we are in danger, God will keep us safe. When we feel alone, God will be present. When we feel bleak, God will restore memories of joy and promise. And more than the words, we have the warmth and light of the candle, the fragrance of the spices, a taste of wine—all create ➤

Elijah the prophet, Elijah the Tishbite, Elijah the Gileadite. May he come to us soon, together with the Messiah, son of David.

Those assembled wish each other a good week, commonly singing "a good week" in Hebrew, English, and Yiddish.

Shavua tov. **May you have a good week.** ***A gutte vokh.*** ✱

QUESTIONS FOR FURTHER STUDY AND REFLECTION

1. The Rabbis of the Talmud would dress in their finest clothes and prepare to greet the Sabbath queen. The Kabbalists of Safed would dress in white and go out to the fields, singing psalms. How would you follow their lead in our time? How would you teach children about greeting Shabbat? How is Shabbat a queen?

2. If you do not yet know melodies for *Yedid Nefesh* or *Lekhah Dodi*, learn these in your study group. If you know only one melody for each, try to learn another one as well.

3. Based on the poems *Yedid Nefesh* and *Lekha Dodi*, as well as other texts, how would you describe the love between God and the people Israel?

4. What does Shabbat rest mean to you?

5. What do the *Kabbalat Shabbat* psalms teach about God as sovereign?

6. "God's in His heaven, all's right in the world." Many of the *Kabbalat Shabbat* psalms convey this theme, yet others convey a very different sense. How do you reconcile these?

7. Rabbi Samson Raphael Hirsch, commenting on Psalm 99, states that the greatness of God in Zion will be fully realized when each and every thing in Zion bears the imprint and the inspiration of God. Is this realization a possibility for this world, or is it to be reserved for the messianic age?

8. What is the source of a woman's obligation to recite *Kiddush* on Shabbat? What are the implications of that ruling?

9. Review the suggested prayers before candle lighting. Which aspects would you include in your own prayer or meditation? Write a prayer or meditation that you would like to add after the *brakhah*.

10. The *Eshet Ḥayil* verses have angered many Jewish feminists, yet many other Jewish women embrace them. What is your reaction? Why?

---

a brief state of altered consciousness, a state of trust as we return to the everyday. It is no less frightening, but now we are emboldened. And besides, only six more days till Shabbat! When my children were younger, we'd end the ceremony by dancing around the kitchen with them, holding their hands so they could jump as high as they could each time we sang *"Hamavdil ben kodesh leHOL! HOL! HOL!"*

Havdalah was the time when some of our women ancestors said a Yiddish supplication, *Gott fon Avraham*, in which they pleaded for their family's well-being in the week to come. Sometimes I say this prayer silently to myself, rewording it slightly:

God of Abraham, of Isaac, and of Jacob; God of Sarah, Rebecca, Rachel, and Leah; protect us at this moment as the holy and lovely Shabbat goes away. May the coming week be filled with health and life, with *mazal* and blessings, with good fortune and honor, and with acts of loving kindness. Amen.

And then it's time to answer the ringing telephone! Relatives inevitably call to shout *"Shavua Tov!" "Gutte Vokh!"* "Have a good week!" In fact, answering and making phone calls after *havdalah* feels like part of the ritual. And in some families, hopping into the car and going out for ice cream is part of the ritual as well.—*Vanessa L. Ochs*

1.   Most of these phrases about Shabbat are from the writings of Abraham Joshua Heschel. See especially *The Sabbath: Its Meaning for Modern Man* (New York: Farrar, Straus, and Young, 1951; available in paperback reprint).

2.   These include the basic compilations of prayer and commentary compiled by Rav Amram Gaon in the 9th century, Rav Saadia Gaon in the 10th, Maimonides in the 11th, and Abudarham in the 14th.

3.   The English text has been adapted from the graceful free translation of Rabbi Zalman Schachter-Shalomi.

4.   *Midrash Tehillim,* compiled between the 10th and 12th centuries, requires the proper observance of only one Shabbat. The Talmud, however, compiled in the 6th century, requires the entire Jewish people to properly observe two Sabbaths in order to bring about the messianic era. Disagreement in Jewish sources—about both large and small concerns—is common.

5.   See Rashi on this verse.

6.   For a fuller discussion of these verses, see H. L. Ginsberg, Stage Two in "A Strand in the Cord of Hebraic Hymnody," *Eretz Yisrael*, volume 10.

7.   See *Exodus Rabbah* 23:5, which cites the words "The pious person lives by his faith" (Habakuk 2:4).

8.   The name of the patriarch Jacob, whose name became Israel, is often used to stand for the entire people Israel.

9.   Rabbi Burt E. Schuman, "Synagogue: Driving Miss Daisy Crazy," *Reform Judaism* (winter 2001), pages 91, 96. Burt E. Schuman is rabbi at Temple Beth Israel, Altoona, PA.

10.   Genesis 2:3. "God blessed the seventh day and declared it holy."

11.   Samson Raphael Hirsch, 1808–1888, an outstanding German rabbi, considered one of the founders of modern Orthodoxy.

12.   Arthur Green, *Kol Haneshamah: Shabbat Vehagim* (Wyncote, PA: Reconstructionist Press, 1996), page 36.

13.   In the original, the last word of each stanza rhymes with the last Hebrew word of the refrain. "Come, my beloved, the bride to meet; come, my beloved, Shabbat to greet." (*Lekha dodi likrat kallah, pnei Shabbat nekabelah.*) The first three lines of each stanza rhyme. Sometimes they also rhyme with the first three lines of other stanzas, and three sets of them rhyme with the last word of the refrain.

14.   In Babylonian Talmud, *Baba Kama* 32b, Rabbi Hanina refers to Shabbat as both bride and queen.

15.   Zechariah 14:9, also cited at the end of the passage known as *Aleinu* at the end of every service.

16.   Deuteronomy 26:19.

17.   See endnote 4.

18.   "Awake, awake, O Zion! Clothe yourself in strength; put on your robes of splendor, Jerusalem, holy city.... Arise, shake off the dust, sit on your throne, Jerusalem!" Isaiah 52:1–2.

19.   Their literal meaning is, "Through the son of Jesse of Bethlehem bring near to my soul its redemption." According to the prophet Micah (5:1) the Messiah will come from Bethlehem.

20.   See Isaiah, chapter 11.

21. "Rouse yourself, rouse yourself; arise, Jerusalem" (Isaiah 51:17).

22. "Arise, shine, for your light has come and the glory of the Lord has shone upon you" (Isaiah 60:1).

23. "Awake, awake, take up a song" (Judges 5:12).

24. "Through the Lord has Israel won triumph everlasting. You shall not be shamed or disgraced in the ages to come" (Isaiah 45:17).

25. "Why so downcast, my soul, why disquieted within me? Have hope in God; I will yet praise Him" (Psalms 42:6).

26. "Zion has been established by the Lord. In it, the needy of His people find shelter" (Isaiah 15:32).

27. "The city shall be rebuilt on its mound" (Jeremiah 30:18).

28. "Those who despoiled you shall be despoiled" (Jeremiah 30:16).

29. "Your ravagers will stay far from you" (Isaiah 49:19).

30. "As a bridegroom rejoices over his bride, so will your God rejoice over you" (Isaiah 62:5).

31. Alan Mintz, "Prayer and the Prayerbook" in *Back to the Sources: Reading the Classic Jewish Texts,* Barry W. Holtz, ed. (New York: Summit/Simon & Schuster, 1984), pages 422-423.

32. "For you shall spread out to the right and the left" (Isaiah 54:3). The order has been reversed in the translation for the sake of rhyme.

33. "Men will hallow the Holy One of Jacob and stand in awe of the God of Israel" (Isaiah 29:23).

34. "In that day they shall say: This is our God; we trusted in Him and He delivered us. This is the Lord, in whom we trusted. Let us rejoice and exult in His deliverance" (Isaiah 25:9).

35. In bowing to royalty one bows first to the royal person's right (our left).

36. The people Israel are referred to as God's treasured people in Exodus 19:5 and elsewhere.

37. This Biblical image symbolizes great strength.

38. Chana Bell, "Shechinah" in *Women Speak to God: The Prayers and Poems of Jewish Women*, Marcia Cohn Spiegel and Deborah Lipton Kremsdorf, eds. (San Diego: Woman's Institute for Continuing Jewish Education, 1987), page 50.

39. See Chapter 3, pages 71-72.

40. Cited in Nahum M. Sarna, *Songs of the Heart: An Introduction to the Book of Psalms* (New York: Schocken, 1993), page 178.

41. One authoritative Hebrew text uses the word *nokhrim,* yet another Hebrew version uses the word *goyim.*

42. See page 190.

43. For this and for the following examples, see *Siddur Sim Shalom*, edited and translated by Rabbi Jules Harlow (New York: Rabbinical Assembly and United Synagogue of Conservative Judaism, 1985), pages 719 and 720.

44. Penina V. Adelman, "A Light Returns to Sarah's Tent: My Home Is the Sacred Tabernacle," in *Lifecycles, Volume 2: Jewish Women on Biblical Themes in Contemporary Life,* Rabbi Debra Orenstein and Rabbi Jane Rachel Litman, eds. (Woodstock, VT: Jewish Lights, 1997), pages 33, 34.

45. Composed by Navah Harlow.

46. Susan Weidman Schneider, *Jewish and Female: A Guide and Sourcebook for Today's Jewish Woman* (New York: Touchstone/Simon & Schuster, 1985), pages 89-90.

47. This refers to the matriarch Sarah, because of whom God blessed Abraham with wealth (Genesis 12:16).

48. This refers to the matriarch Rebecca, so good to Isaac when his mother Sarah died.

49. This refers to the matriarch Leah (Genesis 30:16, where she expresses her physical desire for Jacob).

50. This refers to the matriarch Rachel. Since she endured embarrassment over her barren condition, she was privileged to give birth to a son (Joseph) who would be compared to a ship filled with every good thing, and who would sustain the world with food during years of famine.

51. This refers to Pharaoh's daughter, Batya, who saved the infant Moses.

52. This refers to Yokheved, the mother of Moses, who was the equal of the entire people Israel, who are compared to a vineyard (Isaiah 5:7).

53. This refers to Miriam, who, before the birth of Moses, declared that her mother would give birth to the redeemer of the people Israel. She continued to maintain her prophecy though even her father at first disparaged her words because of the continuing slavery.

54. This refers to Hannah, who perceived the value of prayer and was privileged to give birth to a son, Samuel, who would be compared to Moses and Aaron (Psalms 99:6).

55. This refers to Yael, who slew the enemy of Israel not with military arms but with a tent peg, with the strength of her hands.

56. This refers to the widow who provided Elijah with food and water.

57. This refers to Rahav, who fearlessly sheltered the spies sent by Joshua. She and her household were saved during the Israelite attack because of the crimson cord displayed at their window, which identified her household (Joshua 2:18).

58. This refers to Bat Sheba, who gave birth to Solomon, robed as king in linen and purple.

59. This refers to Michal, wife of David, who saved his life.

60. This refers to Tzlalfonit, mother of Samson, who helped his people in battle against their enemies.

61. This refers to Elisheva bat Aminadav (Exodus 6:23), the wife of Aaron.

62. This refers to the woman who spoke with Joab and saved the city (see 2 Samuel 2:16), identified with Serach bat Asher (see Genesis 46:17).

63. This refers to the wife of Ovadiah, who saved her children and did not succumb to idol worship (not in the Biblical text, but only in the Midrash).

64. This refers to the Shunamite woman (2 Kings 4:8-37), found worthy by Elisha who saved her son.

65. This refers to Ruth the Moabite, who came under the wings of the *Shekhinah*.

66. This too refers to Ruth, who left her people and joined the people Israel, accepting the *mitzvot*.

67. E. M. Broner, in *Bringing Home the Light: A Jewish Woman's Handbook of Rituals* (Tulsa: Council Oak Books, 1999), pages 73-74. Broner writes that she recited this poem in spring 1994, in honor of Dr. Alice Shalvi, renowned Israeli educator and head of the Israeli Women's Network.

68. This too refers to Ruth, who merited being an ancestor of David, who praised the Holy One in song.

69. Genesis 1:31–2:3.

70. Shabbat is first in the list of holy gatherings, fixed times of the Lord, sacred occasions, as noted in Leviticus 23.

71. Arthur Green, *Kol Haneshamah: Shabbat Vehagim,* page 46.

72. Rabbi Lynn Gottlieb, in "It's Called a Calling: Interview with Lynn Gottlieb," *Moment* 4:5 (May 1979), page 36; adapted by Rabbi Gottlieb, 2002.

73. Moses ben Machir, *Sefer Seder Hayom* (Yoel Levenzohn: Warsaw, 1871), pages 22–23.

74. Exodus 31:16–17.

75. Exodus 20:8–11a.

76. Exodus 20:11b.

77. Two Hebrew letters, *yod* and *hei.* This is one of God's many names.

78. Isaiah 12:2–3, verses taken from a section in which the prophet describes the redemption and triumphant deliverance that will be realized by the Israelites who are living in exile.

79. Psalms 46:12.

80. Psalms 84:13.

81. Psalms 20:10.

82. Esther 8:16. Continuing the theme of hope for deliverance, this verse recalls redemption in the past.

83. Psalms 116:13.

Chapter 6

THE TORAH SERVICE

It is a tree of life for those who grasp it ...
and all its ways are peace

The Torah Service, including the Torah reading, takes place only in the presence of a *minyan*, as do the *Kaddish* and *Kedushah*.[1]

Jewish worship includes study, an obligation that we fulfill by a prescribed series of readings from the Torah.[2] Study complements prayer; through the words of the Torah, God addresses us, and through the words of prayer we address God.[3] We read the Torah publicly on Shabbat and Festival mornings, on Monday and Thursday mornings, and on Shabbat afternoons.

Public reading of the Torah presents another example of the Jewish heritage of democracy. Ever since Sinai, when the Torah was revealed to the people through Moses, the

▦ This arrangement guarantees that a Jewish community will not go three consecutive days without a formal reading of the Torah. (See Babylonian Talmud, *Baba Kama* 82a.)—JH

✺ Theoretically the public reading of the Torah is indeed an example of Jewish commitment to democracy, yet, for much of Jewish history, women's access to the Torah was severely limited. Even today in many congregations, women are still not allowed to touch the Torah despite almost universal agreement that the Torah can under no circumstance be made impure. Furthermore, prior to the last century, women were routinely forbidden to study the Torah, especially in its original language. Women's access to the Talmud—the Oral Torah—is even more recent.—*Tamara Cohen*

entire people Israel—men, women, and children—has treasured its sacred possession. ▦ No special group of religious or political leaders possesses secret knowledge of the Torah. Instead, Judaism encourages each individual to know its teachings. The Torah itself provides the earliest mention of public Torah reading. The Book of Deuteronomy commands that the entire people Israel be brought together once every seven years to hear the reading of the Torah (Deuteronomy 31:10–13). Joshua continued the public reading of the Torah (Joshua 8:34–35), as did King Josiah in the seventh century before the common era (II Kings 23:2). Approximately 200 years later, Ezra the Scribe read the Torah to the entire people on the first day of the month of Tishrei.[4] Whenever we participate in a Torah reading we continue a practice rooted in Biblical times.[6]

▦ According to Rabbinic tradition, the study of Torah is equal to the practice of all other commandments (Babylonian Talmud, *Shabbat* 127a). Some say, though, that dwelling in the land of Israel is on an even higher level.—*Carol Diament*

✸ Firstly, it may well be that [in antiquity] the Torah Service was indeed the focus (though not exclusively) of Jewish worship in the diaspora, as it was in Judaea. Secondly, this part of the service was undoubtedly the most dramatic and participatory component of the Jewish worship context and thus the one most likely to be described. Thirdly, not only was the Torah reading important in its own right, but it also served as a focus around which most, if not all, other liturgical elements revolved, that is, the *targum* [translation and explication of the Torah in Aramaic, the *lingua franca* of the day], sermon, and *Haftarah*. Fourthly … the Torah-reading ceremony and its related components reflect what was most unique and distinctive in the synagogue worship context in comparison with other religious institutions in the Greco-Roman world.—*Lee I. Levine* [5]

According to Jewish sources, Moses initiated our current practice of public Torah reading on Shabbat, Festival, and New Moon mornings, and Ezra the Scribe initiated the public readings for Monday and Thursday mornings and Shabbat afternoons. Though we lack historical proof for these attributions, they accurately associate the ritual of Torah reading with Moses and Ezra, the major leaders of ancient times who were best known for the teaching of Torah.

In ancient Palestine, public reading of the Torah on Shabbat consisted of relatively short excerpts, so that Jews completed the entire Torah once in three years. In Babylon and other diaspora communities, public reading of the Torah consisted of relatively long excerpts, so that Jews completed the entire Torah each year, ✸ and this became the standard Jewish practice throughout the world. In recent years, however, a number of congregations have revived the ancient Palestinian practice, known as the triennial cycle. The annual cycle divides the Torah into 54 portions (*sidrot* or *parashiyot;* the singular is *sidrah* or *parashah*) that we read on Shabbat. When a Festival coincides with Shabbat, the special Torah reading designated for the Festival takes precedence. Sometimes, in order to complete the public Torah reading in one year, we read two portions on a single Shabbat.[7]

In the Morning Service, the Torah Service follows the conclusion of the *Amidah*. On weekdays it then begins after the recitation of the Full *Kaddish* or *Kaddish Shalem*, and on Shabbat it begins after the recitation of Half *Kaddish* or *Hatzi Kaddish* (see Chapter 8 on the *Kaddish*). The congregation joins the leader in chanting:

There is none like You among the gods, Lord, and there is nothing like Your works.[8] Your sovereignty is everlasting, Your dominion endures for all generations.[9] The Lord is King, the Lord was King, the Lord will be King for ever and ever. The Lord will give strength to His people, the Lord will bless His people with peace.[10]

Merciful Father, may it be Your will that Zion prosper; rebuild the walls of Jerusalem.[11] For in You alone have we put our trust, King, God exalted and sublime, eternal Lord.

A member of the congregation opens the Ark. All stand and join the leader in chanting the following.

And so it was that whenever the Ark was carried forward Moses said: "Arise, Lord; let Your enemies be scattered, let those who hate You flee before You."[12] For out of Zion shall go forth Torah, the word of the Lord from Jerusalem.[13] Blessed is the one who gave Torah to His people Israel in His holiness.[14]

All remain standing while the Ark is open, and they silently recite the Aramaic meditation, *Brikh Shmeih*. In many synagogues, the leader recites part of it aloud, and, in most synagogues, the congregation chants the last words in unison (beginning *bei ana rahetz*).

Brikh Shmeih

Blessed be the name of the Master of the world, blessed be Your crown and Your abiding place. May You favor the people Israel forever. May Your redeeming power be revealed to Your people in Your sanctuary. Grant us the gift of Your good light; accept our supplications in mercy. May it be Your will to grant us a long life that we enjoy. May I be numbered among the righteous; show me mercy in watching over me and all that is mine and all that belongs to Your people Israel. You are the one who sustains and provides for all, You are the one who rules over all, You are the one who rules over sovereigns, for sovereignty is Yours.

I am the servant of the Holy One, blessed be He, before whom I bow and before whose glorious Torah do I bow at all times. Not upon mortals do I rely, nor do I depend upon angels, but upon the God of heaven who is the God of truth, whose Torah is truth, whose prophets are prophets of truth and who abounds in deeds of goodness and truth. In Him do I put my trust; to His holy, glorious

name do I utter praise. May it be Your will to open my heart to Your Torah, and to fulfill the wishes of my heart and the heart of Your entire people Israel, for goodness, for life, and for peace. ▧

▧ "May it be Your will to open my heart to Your Torah" is based on *Zohar, Vayakhel*. This is yet another example of the influence of the Kabbalah in the prayer book. According to the *Zohar*, whenever we open the Ark before a public reading of the Torah, "the heavenly gates of mercy and love are opened." This is an especially propitious time for personal prayer.—*JH*

❋ Meditation before reading Torah

We are the people of the word
and the breath of the word fills our minds with light.
We are the people of the word
and the breath of life sings through us
playing on the pipes of our bones
and the strings of our sinews
an ancient song carved in the Laurentian granite
and new as a spring azore butterfly just drying her wings
in a moment's splash of sun.
We must live the word and make it real.

We are the people of the book
and the letters march busy as ants
carrying the work of the ages through our minds.

We are the people of the book.
Through fire and mud and dust we have borne
our scrolls tenderly as a baby swaddled in a blanket,
traveling with our words sewn in our clothes
and carried on our backs.

Let us take up the scroll of Torah
and dance with it and touch it
and read it out, for the mind
touches the word and makes it light.
So does light enter us, and we shine.
    —*Marge Piercy* [15]

Jews strive to keep Shabbat free from the tensions and anxieties of life's daily concerns. For this reason, on Shabbat we generally do not recite prayers of petition or make requests of God. For example, in the weekday *Amidah* the 13 middle blessings all make requests of God; on Shabbat, we replace these middle blessings with a single blessing that hallows Shabbat. Nevertheless, any time we open the Ark or read the Torah is appropriate for making our requests, for pouring our hearts out. Therefore, even on Shabbat, the Torah Service includes prayers of petition on behalf of individuals and on behalf of the community, such as *brikh shmeih*.

After this prayer, the leader holds the Torah scroll and a member of the congregation closes the Ark. ❋ Then all on the pulpit turn to face the congregation, and the leader sings the following two passages, with the congregation repeating each one.

Hear, O Israel, the Lord is our God, the Lord alone. [16]

One is our God, great is our Lord, holy is His name.

The leader next turns to face the Ark, lifts the Torah scroll while bowing slightly, and then straightens up while singing "Let us extol."

Exalt the Lord with me, let us extol His name together. [17]

The leader turns to face the congregation once again, and begins a procession through the sanctuary with the Torah scroll. The procession gives all members of the congregation an opportunity to express their love for the Torah by kissing the covered Torah scroll as it passes near them. ⌘ As a further sign of love and reverence we adorn the Torah scroll as elaborately as our means allow. Thus, the Torah has a mantle of velvet or other special material, often embroidered, covering it and usually a crown of silver. Whenever the Ark is open and whenever the Torah scroll is being carried, lifted, or held by an individual who is standing, the congregation stands in respect. During the synagogue procession, many people turn so that they always face the Torah scroll. As the leader carries the Torah scroll, all sing:

Yours, Lord, are greatness and might, splendor, triumph and majesty; yes, all in the heavens and on earth are Yours. Yours, Lord, are sovereignty and pre-eminence over all.[18] Exalt the Lord our God, and bow at His footstool; He is holy. Exalt the Lord our God, bow to His holy mountain, for the Lord our God is holy.[19]

The procession ends at the reader's table, the lectern at which the Torah is read. The *gabbai* (who takes charge of various details during the Torah Service) ❋ removes the Torah crown and mantle, unties or unbuckles the sash that holds together the two rolls of the Torah scroll, and unrolls the parchment to the appropriate column for the first passage to be read.

While scrolling to find our place in the Torah and while reading, we never touch the parchment with our bare hands. Instead, Torah readers use a special pointer *(yad)* to keep their place. If the parchment must be handled, we hold part of a *tallit* in our hands and allow only the fabric of the *tallit* to be in direct contact with the parchment.

After the Torah scroll is placed on the lectern, the *gabbai* recites:

May the Father of mercy have mercy for the people carried since birth[20] and remember the covenant with our ancestors, saving us from evil times, rebuking the impulse to evil, favoring us as a remnant saved forever, fulfilling our requests with a good measure of salvation and mercy.[21]

Some commentators consider that the central concern here is the impulse to evil,[22] and they point out that the Torah is a life-giving antidote. The *gabbai* continues:

⌘ Some kiss the mantle directly. Most people kiss the fringes of a *tallit* or their fingers or a prayer book after touching the covered Torah scroll with them.—*JH*

❋ In most congregations, a lay member of the synagogue serves as *gabbai*. In some congregations, volunteers take turns filling this duty. In others, a rabbi or cantor or other synagogue staff member serves as *gabbai*. The *gabbai* calls the *aliyot*, follows the Torah passage in a printed Hebrew Bible to ensure accuracy while the Torah reader chants from the open scroll, covers the Torah scroll with the mantle during those prayers that are offered before and after an *aliyah*, and assists in rewinding and rewrapping the scroll after completion of the Torah reading.—*JH*

May He help and shield and save all who trust in Him. And let us say, Amen. Let us all acclaim the greatness of our God and pay honor to the Torah. Kohen: draw near. ▨ Let _____ come to the Torah. Blessed be the One who gave Torah to His people Israel in His holiness.[23]

▨ In congregations that stress egalitarianism, a Kohen (descendant of the Temple priesthood) is not necessarily called for the first *aliyah*. In such congregations, the *gabbai* usually calls for "the first." The *gabbai* then specifies the Hebrew name of the person called to the Torah. In many congregations every individual honored with an *aliyah* is called by his or her Hebrew name. Men usually have been called to the Torah using their Hebrew first name, followed by *ben* (meaning "the son of") and then the Hebrew name of their father (for example, Pinḥas *ben* David). Many congregations today use the Hebrew name of the mother as well (for example, Pinḥas *ben* David veLeah). Congregations that call women to the Torah generally use the names of both parents (for example, Sarah *bat* David veLeah). This way of naming individuals applies to other rituals and prayers as well, although prayers for the sick, even in Orthodox congregations, generally include only the Hebrew name of the individual's mother. —*JH*

❂ In Orthodox and Conservative congregations and in many Reform and Reconstructionist congregations, seven people are called to receive an *aliyah* on Shabbat mornings; three are called on Monday and Thursday mornings, on Ḥanukkah, and on Shabbat afternoons; four are called on the first of the month (Rosh Ḥodesh); five are called on Festivals, including Rosh Hashanah; and six are called on Yom Kippur. Many other Reform congregations and Reconstructionist congregations grant fewer than seven *aliyot* to the Torah on Shabbat, and fewer than five on Festivals. Some Reform congregations include a Torah service on Friday nights; the number of *aliyot* varies.—*JH*

The congregation joins the *gabbai* in declaring:

You, who cleave to the Lord your God, are all of you alive this day.[24]

Each individual called to the Torah walks by the shortest route to the reader's lectern and, after inviting the congregation to pay homage to God, chants blessings before and after the reading of Torah portion. The honor of being called to the Torah to recite these blessings is known as an *aliyah*, an ascent (plural: *aliyot*).

Orthodox congregations and some Conservative congregations call only men to the Torah to recite the Torah blessings. Most Conservative, all Reform, and all Reconstructionist congregations call both women and men to the Torah. According to the Babylonian Talmud, *Megillah* 23a, women as well as men may be called to read aloud from the Torah (and therefore to recite the Torah blessings). In the same passage, however, the Sages discourage congregations from calling women to the Torah because of its negative impact on "the dignity of the congregation." Although we have no precise definition of this dignity, different congregations perceive their dignity in different ways and have different notions of what affects their dignity negatively. In our time, the changing perceptions and self-perceptions of women have led growing numbers of congregations to grant women *aliyot* to the Torah.[25]

On Shabbat mornings, seven people receive an *aliyah*. ❂ An additional person, known as *maftir*, chants the day's assigned selection from the Prophets. Orthodox congregations and many Conservative congregations grant the first *aliyah* to a Kohen (a descendant of the priests who officiated in the Temple), the second *aliyah* to a Levi (a descendant of the tribe of Levi, who also served in the Temple), and the third through the seventh *aliyot* to a Yisrael (any Jew who is not a Kohen or a Levi). Many liberal congregations do not differentiate between these categories of Jews for *aliyot*.

The individual honored with an *aliyah* usually does not read from the Torah scroll. In most congregations, the *gabbai* or a regular Torah reader chants all portions of the *sidrah* in the special musical style designated for reading aloud from the Torah. In some congregations, however, lay members chant one or more portions. Often a young person celebrating becoming bar or a bat mitzvah chants one of the portions—or even the entire *sidrah*.

Special anniversaries, birthdays, and other significant occasions provide opportunities for honoring an individual with an *aliyah*.[26] On the Shabbat before a wedding, many congregations give the groom an *aliyah*, and congregations who consider it appropriate give the bride an *aliyah* as well, either alone or with the groom.[27] Each person called to the Torah uses the fringes of a *tallit* or the edge of a Torah scroll sash to kiss the Torah parchment at the word that begins the new portion (pointed out by the Torah reader) before the opening blessing, and at the word that ends the portion before the concluding blessing. The opening Torah blessing begins with a short phrase:

Bless the Lord, the source of blessing.

The congregation responds:

Blessed be the Lord, the source of blessing, forever and ever. ※

The person honored repeats the above line and continues:

※ The opening Torah blessing and the congregational response are the same words chanted by a leader and the congregation at the beginning of a formal public service of prayer (see page 53).—JH

✳ Saadia Gaon (10th century) noted that "Our people is a people only by virtue of the Torah" (*Beliefs and Opinions III 7*). Some translations read: "who has chosen us among all peoples and has given us His Torah." Reconstructionists substitute "who has drawn us to Your service" in place of "who has chosen us among all peoples."—JH

Blessed are You, Lord our God, King of the universe who has chosen us among all peoples by giving us His Torah. ✳ Blessed are You, Lord who gives the Torah.

A passage from the Torah is read, and the person who has been called to the Torah chants this concluding blessing:

Blessed are You, Lord our God, King of the universe who has given us a Torah of truth, planting among us life eternal. Blessed are You, Lord who gives the Torah.

▣ The Babylonian Talmud specifies that escape from danger involves recovery from serious illness, being freed from imprisonment, or return from perilous travel, such as a sea voyage or a journey in a wilderness (*Brakhot* 54b). Today we also consider those who have escaped danger to include men and women who have completed a long airplane flight and who have recovered from surgery as well as women who recently have given birth.—*JH*

✹ The Torah Service, more than any other part of the prayer service, is filled with choreography and visual stimuli. We open the Ark, parade the scrolls, and with a flourish perform *hagbah* (the elevation of the open Torah scroll in front of the congregation) and *gelilah* (the rolling and dressing of the Torah scroll in front of the congregation). During the Torah Service, in a sense, we recreate the experience of Sinai. When the Torah is revealed to us visibly, not just aurally, we feel a connection with all the generations before us that have venerated Torah.

In ancient days, the Torah Service, rather than prayer, was the focus of worship. Indeed, the first three chapters of Mishnah *Brakhot*, which deal with the recitation of the *Shema*, include directions on how to say the *Shema* correctly while on our way to work or coming home from parties—but never in the synagogue.

The *Mi Sheberakh*, a prayer recited when a person is called to ➤

Note that we state the final words of these blessings in the present tense. In Judaism, revelation is continuous: God constantly gives us the Torah, and in consequence we must constantly receive and accept it. We strive to maintain constant awareness of the uniqueness of both the gift and the Giver. We show our appreciation by using the gift and by enjoying its use. To do so is the implied challenge of every Torah Service.

A person who recently has survived or escaped danger ▣ adds the following blessing, known as *birkat hagomel*, after completing the blessings above:

Blessed are You, Lord our God, King of the universe who treats even the undeserving with kindness, who has treated me graciously with kindness.

The congregation responds:

May the One who has treated you with kindness continue to treat you graciously with kindness.

In some congregations, the *gabbai* recites the following prayer, known as *Mi Sheberakh,* for those who have been honored with *aliyot* after they all have recited the blessings. In other congregations, the *gabbai* offers a prayer for each person at the conclusion of the *aliyah*, before calling the next person to be honored.

May the One who blessed our ancestors, Abraham, Isaac, and Jacob, Sarah, Rebecca, Rachel, and Leah, bless those who have come for an *aliyah* this day, paying honor to God, the Torah, and Shabbat. May the Holy One, blessed is He, bless them and their entire families, with success in everything they do, together with all their fellow Jews. And let us say, Amen.

The Torah Service is considered to be an especially good time for offering prayers on behalf of individuals. Thus, congregations offer a version of the *Mi Sheberakh* prayer on behalf of those who are ill, on behalf of newborns and mothers of newborns, and on behalf of those soon to be wed. ❀

After the Torah reading, everyone stands while the leader chants the *Hatzi Kaddish*. Then, on Shabbat, the *gabbai* calls an additional person (*maftir*, "one who concludes") to recite the Torah blessings, and the Torah reader chants the final few verses of the day's portion once more. After the *maftir* chants the concluding blessing for the Torah reading, the *gabbai* calls two people to the lectern. The first one lifts the Torah scroll and turns it to show some of the columns on the parchment to the congregation while everyone sings:

This is the Torah that Moses set before the people Israel; ✳ by the word of the Lord through Moses.

The lifter sits down and holds the Torah scroll upright while the second person winds the wooden rollers, wraps the sash around the closed scroll, and replaces the Torah mantle, the crown, and the other adornments.

the Torah, is an important part of the Torah Service. We recite it primarily on behalf of our family members and friends who are in need of healing. We might also recite it to ask for God's help in enduring some trial or sorrow of our own. However, the *Mi Sheberakh* can also be a prayer of celebration. The person called to the Torah recites it for a special occasion, such as a bar or bat mitzvah, a forthcoming marriage, or the birth of a child. We could also recite the *Mi Sheberakh* to thank God for a baby sleeping through the night, a child's college graduation, or a job promotion.

The public recitation of this prayer is often a moment in which the community comes to know itself. It allows its members to testify to God's power in their lives. When we know each other's souls through the prism of Torah, then we truly experience Sinai anew. —*Rabbi Judith Z. Abrams*

✵ The phrase translated here as "by the word of the Lord through Moses" literally means "by the mouth of the Lord through the hand of Moses." The statement is a combination of Deuteronomy 4:44 and the last part of Numbers 9:23. —*JH*

✱ Participation of girls as *maftir* in the Torah Service occurs only in synagogues that grant *aliyot* to women. These include Reform, Reconstructionist, and most Conservative congregations. Some Orthodox congregations and some of the Conservative congregations that do not grant *aliyot* to women will, however, allow a young girl upon her coming of age to participate in other ways. For example, she might deliver a talk about the Torah or *Haftarah* readings, either in the sanctuary or at a meal celebrating the occasion (*se'udat mitzvah*). Some of these congregations may also hold women-only services outside of the main sanctuary; at these special services, women, including *bnot mitzvah* (the plural of *bat mitzvah*) are honored with *aliyot*. —*JH*

When the Torah scroll has been "dressed," the *maftir* chants a passage from one of the Biblical books of the Prophets. These verses, concluding the readings from the Torah, are called *Haftarah* (conclusion). Each Shabbat or Festival Torah reading has its own accompanying passage from one of the books of Prophets. The *maftir*, before and after chanting the passage from Prophets, recites special *Haftarah* blessings.

We customarily honor a young person becoming a bar mitzvah or a bat mitzvah with the *aliyah* as *maftir* on Shabbat. ✱ For boys, the age for full participation in Jewish ritual is 13 plus one day. For girls, it is 12 plus one day. ▨ The Shabbat morning *aliyah* as *maftir* usually represents the young person's first participation in a religious ceremony as a full member of the community. ◉

Jews become *bnei mitzvah* [28] upon reaching the appropriate birthday, whether or not they participate in a formal ceremony. Thus, simply upon reaching age 12 or 13, a Jew is obligated to fulfill the commandments and may be counted in a *minyan*. Youngsters who do not formally mark their coming of age with the ritual may do so later in their lives.[29]

The *maftir* continues the service with the additional reading (*Haftarah*), in a special chant that differs from that of the Torah reading. The following blessings, in the same special chant, precede and follow the *Haftarah* selection.

▨ Many Reform congregations consider age 13 appropriate for girls as well as for boys.—*JH*

◉ Some young people mark the occasion of becoming bar or bat mitzvah by chanting all or part of the Torah portion of the day as well as the *Haftarah*. Some young people mark the occasion simply by being called for an *aliyah* and reciting the blessings before and after the Torah reading. An individual may be called for an *aliyah* on any day when the service includes a public Torah reading. In addition to Shabbat morning, this includes Monday and Thursday mornings, Shabbat afternoon, Rosh Hodesh mornings, and Festival mornings. All of these days are appropriate for marking the occasion of becoming bar or bat mitzvah, although, in practice, calling a bar or bat mitzvah to the Torah is rare on Festival mornings.[30]—*JH*

✳ "May he come soon" refers to the Messiah.—*JH*

Before the *Haftarah*

Blessed are You, Lord our God, King of the universe who chose authentic prophets, taking delight in their words spoken in truth. Blessed are You, Lord who loves[31] the Torah, Moses His servant, Israel His people, and prophets of truth and justice.

After the *Haftarah*

Blessed are You, Lord our God, King of the universe, Rock everlasting,[32] righteous in all generations, dependable God[33] whose word is deed, whose speech is fulfillment, all of whose words are truth and justice. Dependable are You, Lord our God, and dependable Your promises; not one of them comes back unfulfilled,[34] for You are a dependable, merciful God. Blessed are You, Lord, dependable God who keeps His promises.

Have mercy on Zion, for it is the foundation of our life. Deliver the humbled spirit soon in our days. Blessed are You, Lord who causes Zion to rejoice through her children.

Bring us joy, Lord our God, through Your servant Elijah the prophet, and the kingdom of the House of David Your anointed. May he come soon, ✳ to gladden

our hearts. May no stranger sit on his throne, and may no others inherit his glory. For by Your holy name You promised him that his light never will be extinguished. Blessed are You, Lord, Shield of David.

We thank You and bless You, Lord our God, for the Torah and for worship, for the prophets, and for this Shabbat day which You have given us for holiness and rest, for dignity and splendor. For everything do we thank You and bless You. May Your name be blessed by every living creature always and forever. Blessed are You, Lord who hallows Shabbat.[35]

These blessings trace a line of transmission from Moses through the Prophets. The only prophet specified is Elijah, who according to legend will announce the arrival of the Messiah, a descendant of King David. On Shabbat we especially anticipate the time of redemption, the time when the kingdom of David will be restored. The second blessing after the *Haftarah* anticipates the return of Jews and Jewish sovereignty to Jerusalem (synonymous with Zion) in fulfillment of God's promise, as mentioned in the first blessing. Although these blessings focus on the Jews' particular history since Biblical times, the last blessing expresses an all-inclusive, universal hope that also represents an integral Jewish conviction.

After the concluding *Haftarah* blessings, the leader of the Shabbat morning service chants two Aramaic prayers known by their first two words, *Yekum Purkan*. ✳

✳ Orthodox prayer books include both *Yekum Purkan* prayers. Recent Conservative prayer books include only the first *Yekum Purkan*. Neither is included in Reform prayer books. —*JH*

✵ It has been suggested that the reference to Babylon be deleted, since it no longer applies. Others have recommended that locations of seminaries of international repute be added here. —*JH*

Prayer on Behalf of Scholars

May redemption from Heaven, graciousness and steadfast love, long life, ample sustenance, divine support, bodily health and spiritual enlightenment, and healthy children who will not break with or neglect the words of Torah be granted our masters and teachers of the holy communities in the land of Israel and in Babylon, ✵ heads of academies and leaders of the diaspora and judges at the gates, to all their disciples and the disciples of their disciples, and all engaged in the study of Torah. May the Sovereign of the universe bless them, increase their days, and grant them long life. May they be delivered from all trouble and from every harsh sickness. May our Father in Heaven be their help at all times, upon every occasion. And let us say, Amen.

Prayer on Behalf of the Congregation

May redemption from Heaven, graciousness, steadfast love and mercy, long life, ample sustenance, divine support, bodily health and spiritual enlightenment, and healthy children who will not break with or neglect the words of Torah be granted this entire holy congregation, great and small. ▦ May the Sovereign of the universe bless you, increase your days, and grant you long life. May you be delivered from all trouble and from every harsh sickness. May our Father in Heaven be your help at all times, upon every occasion. And let us say, Amen.

This prayer, in Hebrew, is also on behalf of the congregation:

May He who blessed our ancestors, Abraham, Isaac, and Jacob, bless this entire holy congregation, with all other holy congregations—them, their wives, ◉ their sons, and their daughters, and all that is theirs, together with those who establish synagogues for prayer, and those who enter them to pray, and those who provide them with light, wine for Kiddush and for *Havdalah*, food for the wayfarer, charity for the poor, and all those who faithfully devote themselves to the needs of this community. ▨ May the Holy One blessed be He reward them, remove every sickness from them, heal their whole bodies, forgive all their sins, and bless and prosper all the work of their hands, together with all the people Israel their comrades. And let us say, Amen.

▦ After the phrase "this entire holy congregation, great and small," the original Hebrew prayer continues, "including children and women."—JH

◉ Recognizing that in our time women are also members of congregations, unlike the time when this prayer was written, some contemporary prayer books have adapted this passage. For example, *Siddur Sim Shalom* reads at this point: "them, their sons and daughters, their families and all that is theirs" (page 415). *Siddur Sim Shalom* also adds the names of the matriarchs to the names of the patriarchs at the beginning of this prayer.—JH

▨ After the phrase, "all those who faithfully devote themselves to the needs of this community," Conservative prayer books add "and the Land of Israel" (*Siddur Sim Shalom*, page 415).—JH

✳ Why does our tradition place much greater value on congregational prayer in a synagogue than on prayer recited by the individual? Is not prayer highly personal, something between [an individual] and God? Yet according to Jewish teaching it is preferable to pray with a congregation rather than alone at home....

There are several answers to the question, each adding another level of meaning to the concept of *tefillah betzibbur*, prayer with the congregation.

Perhaps the most basic answer is that Judaism does not look upon prayer solely as an expression of the individual. We pray as members of the Jewish people, as descendants of Abraham, Isaac, and Jacob. We pray as members of a people that accepted the Torah at Sinai, as children of the prophets and sages, as members of a people that bases its life on a covenant with God. As Jews, our relationship to God exists through our membership in the Jewish people. The presence of fellow Jews when we pray is a visible reminder of that relationship.

Second, prayer cannot be limited to our feelings toward God. It must involve feelings toward [other individuals] and toward ourselves. As human beings, we are affected by the emotions we sense about us, ➤

Congregations may add prayers for the country (the United States of America or Canada, for example), for peace, and for the State of Israel. ✳

A Prayer for Our Country

Our God and God of our ancestors, we ask Your blessings for our country, for its government, for its leader and advisors, ▒ and for all who exercise just and rightful authority. Teach them insights of Your Torah, that they may administer all affairs of state fairly, that peace and security, happiness and prosperity, justice and freedom may forever abide in our midst.

Creator of all flesh, bless all the inhabitants of our country with Your spirit. May citizens of all races and creeds forge a common bond in true harmony to banish all hatred and bigotry and to safeguard the ideals and free institutions which are the pride and glory of our country.

May this land under Your providence be an influence for good throughout the world, uniting all people in peace and freedom and helping them to fulfill the vision of Your prophet: "Nation shall not lift up sword against nation, neither shall they experience war any more." And let us say, Amen.[37]

A Prayer for Peace

**May we see the day when
war and bloodshed cease,
when a great peace
will embrace the whole world.**

**Then nation will
not threaten nation,
and humanity will
not again know war.**

**For all who live on earth
shall realize
we have not come into being
to hate or to destroy.**

in other people. When we find ourselves in the presence of unhappy people, we cannot help but feel saddened. When we are part of a group that is celebrating, our spirits soar. When we see and hear other people praying earnestly, we become more sensitive and open to prayer.

Moreover, the synagogue is a place that is made holy by the presence of the holy Ark and the scrolls of the Torah which it contains, as well as by the people who worship there. The environment of the synagogue helps us achieve a sense of awe and holiness. If the synagogue is one that we attend regularly, it will take on yet another level of significance. It will inevitably recall to us some of the highlights of our lives....

Finally, when we pray with fellow Jews, we cannot help but think beyond our personal concerns to the needs of the community of which we are a part. We cannot really pray together with other people and at the same time harbor feelings of envy, rivalry, or ill will toward them. We become aware of common needs, of shared goals. Praying with the community is an expression of togetherness on the highest level. Praying together, like singing together—and many of our prayers are really songs that are meant to be sung in unison—creates a bond between the individual and the group.... The individual emerges from group prayer, strengthened by the bond of community.—*Rabbi Theodore Friedman*[36]

▒ When I was a teenager, I was leafing through my grandfather's *siddur*, published in Uman, Ukraine, in 1882, and I saw a prayer for the well-being of the Tsar. I was astounded to find that one year after the assassination of Alexander II—when Pobodoniestov, the foreign minister to Nicholas II, declared his infamous agenda that one-third of the Jews within the Russian Empire were to be killed, one-third were to assimilate, and one-third were to emigrate—during this, the darkest period of oppression, Jews were still praying for the health of the Tsar! This is but one example of Jewish loyalty to the diaspora countries in which Jews have lived. A Rabbinic dictum declares: *Dina demalkhuta dina*—the law of the land is the law (Babylonian Talmud, *Nedarim* 28a and elsewhere). When given the opportunity, as in the United States, Jews contribute their strength, talent, and wealth to the countries in which they reside. Yet these contributions often come at the expense of our own Jewish culture and traditions.—*Carol Diament*

We have come into being
to praise, to labor, and to love.

Compassionate God, bless the leaders of all nations
with the power of compassion.

Fulfill the promise conveyed in Scripture:

I will bring peace to the land,
and you shall lie down and no one shall terrify you.

I will rid the land of vicious beasts
and it shall not be ravaged by war.

Let love and justice flow like a mighty stream.
Let peace fill the earth as the waters fill the sea.
And let us say Amen.[38]

A Prayer for the State of Israel

Our Father in Heaven, Rock and Redeemer of the people Israel, bless the State of Israel, with its promise of redemption. Shield it with Your love; spread over it the shelter of Your peace. Guide its leaders and advisors with Your light and Your truth. Help them with Your good counsel. Unite our hearts in loving and revering You, fulfilling the words of Your Torah. Strengthen the hands of those who defend our holy land. Deliver them; crown their efforts with triumph. Bless the land with peace, and its inhabitants with lasting joy. Amen.

On the Shabbat that precedes the beginning of a new month (Rosh Hodesh),[39] we add a special prayer along with an announcement of the date of the new month. All rise as the leader lifts a Torah scroll and holds it while reciting the prayer for the new month. (See Chapter 7: Rosh Hodesh, pages 169–170.)

Many congregations add a memorial prayer for those who have been martyred (*Av Harahamim*). ▦

⊞ Some communities add a memorial prayer for those who have been martyred only on a Shabbat preceding Shavuot, Tisha B'Av, or Yom HaShoah.—*JH*

Finally, the leader and the congregation recite *Ashrei* (see pages 39–40). The leader, holding the Torah scroll, recites:

Let them praise the name of the Lord, for His name alone is exalted.[40]

The leader and congregation together recite:

His majesty encompasses earth and heaven. He exalts the strength of His people, the praise of His faithful ones, the people Israel who are close to Him. Halleluyah![41]

During the procession for returning the Torah scroll to the Ark, the congregation sings Psalm 29 (see page 123). The leader returns the Torah scroll to the Ark, and leaves the Ark open while all recite the words below. For the last lines (starting *Etz ḥayyim hi*, "It is a tree of life"), all join in song.

Whenever the Ark was set down, Moses would say: "Return, Lord, to dwell among the thousands and thousands of families of the people Israel."[42] Come, Lord, to Your resting place, You and Your mighty Ark. Let Your priests be clothed in triumph, let Your faithful sing for joy. For the sake of David Your servant, reject not Your anointed.[43] Good teaching do I give you; never forsake My Torah.[44] It is a tree of life for those who grasp it, and all who hold onto it are blessed. Its paths are pleasantness, and all its ways are peace.[45] Bring us back to You, Lord, and we shall come back; renew our days as of old.[46]

The first line of the above passage continues from the first verse chanted at the opening of the Ark at the beginning of the Torah Service. The Ark today serves as the repository of Torah scrolls, God's revelation, the most sacred objects in the sanctuary. ❀ The Ark carried by the Israelites in the wilderness also served as the repository of God's revelation—the Decalogue (the Ten Commandments). The Ark served as a focus of faith and

❀ The presentation of the Torah in the synagogue on Sabbath mornings is very different from the way in which it is studied outside a liturgical context. In the study house (*beit midrash*), the classroom, and in private study at home, the text is customarily delved into with its various commentaries; passages from many books are compared back and forth; questions are posed and answers sought; the pace of progress through the text is regulated by the incidence of problems and the acuity of discussion. In the synagogue, however, there is none of this. The Torah is read aloud at a uniform pace, with no provision for posing queries or lingering over a passage. Although individual congregants may privately peruse commentaries, the basic obligation is to listen attentively to the public reading.

The reading of the Torah, then, remains something of a special case in which the recitation of Scripture is set off as an event unto itself, yet one that is adapted to the prayer service of which it is a part. The reading of text, in short, becomes a liturgical act.

It is in the ceremonial display and treatment of the Torah as a holy object that its liturgical role is most vividly highlighted. The Torah resides in a special cabinet whose ritual curtain and perpetual lamp (*ner tamid*) recall the ancient Israelite Ark of the Law and the Holy of Holies of the Jerusalem Temple. The opening of the Ark, the retrieval of the Torah scroll, the procession with it around the synagogue, and the removal of its ornaments and vestments are dramatic rituals which attend the disclosure—literally, the unveiling—of the central symbol of Judaism. Characteristically, what lies at the sacred center of Judaism is not a hieratic mystery but the word, the possession of all Israel, whose public recitation and exposition are the main business of the Torah Service. The difference between this reading of Torah and the study of Torah is underscored by the specialness of the physical object itself. One studies from any printed and bound edition of the text. The Torah as read in the synagogue is a parchment scroll written in highly stylized calligraphy by a scribe in a state of purity. For a Torah scroll to be fit for use (*kasher*) there cannot be even one letter misshapen or out of place. The same rule of correctness applies to the public reading: any mispronunciation of the unpointed Hebrew text is quickly caught and corrected. The reading itself is undertaken in a kind of chant or cantillation, according to musical notes that appear above and below the words in the Masoretic text.—*Alan Mintz*[47]

reverence in the ancient community, a sustaining presence among the people. Whenever the Israelites moved the Ark, a ritual accompanied the beginning and the end of the journey. Thus, in the Book of Numbers we read the following: "And so it was that whenever the Ark was carried forward Moses said, 'Arise, Lord; let Your enemies be scattered, let those who hate You flee before You.' Whenever the Ark was set down, Moses would say, 'Return, Lord, to dwell among the thousands and thousands of families of the people Israel.'" Today, whenever we move the Torah scroll in procession in our sanctuaries, we chant the same words. We connect with our ancient past as we continue the journey of the people Israel, sometimes through a wilderness, sometimes beside the still waters.

The Ark is closed. We recite the Half *Kaddish*, to be followed on Shabbat and on Rosh Hodesh by the *Musaf Amidah* (see Chapters 4 and 7). ▓

▓ The Sabbath *Musaf Amidah* consists of only the silent *Amidah*, which has seven blessings. The distinctive, central blessing—the fourth blessing—has four parts. The first of these, *Tikanta Shabbat*, is a reverse acrostic that harks back to the additional sacrifices offered on the Sabbath in the ancient Temple; it also expresses hope for our return to the land of Israel. The second part is a quotation from the Book of Numbers about the Shabbat offerings, both meal and burnt offerings, made by the Temple Priests. The next two parts largely recapitulate the corresponding parts of the Shabbat morning *Amidah*.

Reform and Reconstructionist prayer books have eliminated the *Musaf* prayer, perhaps because the references to sacrifice seem outdated (refer also to pages 177–182). Nevertheless, the brevity and solemnity of this additional *Amidah* have long maintained it as a distinguished and vital part of the Sabbath liturgy.—*Carol Diament*

QUESTIONS FOR FURTHER STUDY AND REFLECTION

1. How do we show our respect and love for the Torah?
2. Do you believe that women should receive *aliyot* during the Torah Service and act as Torah readers? If so, how would you present the case to a ritual committee or to a synagogue board? If not, how would you defend your point of view?
3. The Torah Service, like the *Kedushah* and *Kaddish* prayers, requires ten Jewish adults (in Orthodox congregations, ten Jewish men). How does prayer among a congregation differ from prayer by oneself? How do the many rituals in the Torah Service affect the congregation? What are your feelings toward public and private prayer?
4. During the Torah Service and at other ritual occasions we are called by our Hebrew name. Do you know your Hebrew name? Do you know the Hebrew names of your father and your mother? How are these names significant to you? Do all members of your family know their full Hebrew names?
5. How are Moses and the ancient Israelites recalled in the Torah Service? How is Jerusalem associated with Torah in this service?

1.   See pages 185–186 for a fuller explanation of the *minyan*. Refer also to sidebar by Rabbi Theodore Friedman, pages 160–161.

2.   The obligation also is fulfilled in part by reading the passages known as *Kriat Shema* (from Deuteronomy and from Numbers) during Services.

3.   I first learned this concept from Dr. Louis Finkelstein.

4.   This is the first day of the seventh month, which we know as Rosh Hashanah. See Nehemiah 8:1–8.

5.   Lee I. Levine, *The Ancient Synagogue* (New Haven: Yale University Press, 2000), page 154.

6.   The scope of what we refer to as the Torah has changed since Biblical times; in ancient times the word Torah did not always refer to the entire Five Books of Moses.

7.   For a detailed table of Torah Readings for Shabbat and Festivals, see *Encyclopedia Judaica*, Volume 15, pages 1250–1251. A schedule of readings from the Prophets (*Haftarot*) is included there as well. On some Sabbaths, different *Haftarah* portions are read by Ashkenazi Jews and Sefardi Jews. Sometimes congregations in Israel and in the diaspora read different portions on the Sabbath because of calendrical differences introduced when the second days of Festivals are celebrated in the diaspora but not in Israel.

8.   Psalms 86:8.

9.   Psalms 145:13.

10.   Psalms 29:11.

11.   Psalms 51:20. The context of the words that immediately precede and follow this plea associates it with words of prayer as well as with sacrifices on the ancient Temple altar in Jerusalem.

12.   Numbers 10:35–36, which describes how the Ark was moved during the Israelites' wanderings in the wilderness.

13.   Isaiah 2:3. This is another example of the emphasis Jewish prayer places on Jerusalem.

14.   This should recall the message of the Torah verse: "Be holy, for I the Lord your God am holy" (Leviticus 19:2).

15.   Marge Piercy, *The Art of Blessing the Day: Poems with a Jewish Theme* (New York: Alfred A. Knopf, 1999).

16.   Deuteronomy 6:4.

17.   Psalms 34:4.

18.   I Chronicles 29:11. These are words with which King David blessed God in the presence of the community.

19.   Psalms 99:5,9. Psalm 99 is included in the service for *Kabbalat Shabbat*.

20.   See Isaiah 46:3.

21.   Some commentators state that the next two sentences (starting "May He help") form the conclusion of this prayer.

22.   These include Rabbi Eliyahu Munk.

23.   This should also recall the message of the Torah verse: "Be holy, for I the Lord your God am holy" (Leviticus 19:2).

24.   Deuteronomy 4:4. With these words Moses blessed the Israelites who remained faithful to God alone.

25. Many people maintain that contact with a menstruating woman can make a Torah Scroll impure. This opinion has no foundation in Jewish law.

26. The *gabbai* calls males with the word *yaamod* ("arise") before their Hebrew name and calls females with the word *taamod* ("arise").

27. This is known as an *aufruf*.

28. This is the plural of *bar mitzvah*, and it refers both to males and to males and females together.

29. Many communities have developed *bnei mitzvah* programs for adults.

30. For further information on bar mitzvah and bat mitzvah, see *Encyclopaedia Judaica,* volume 4, pages 243–247.

31. Many translations read: "Lord who chooses." See page 74, sidebar about the Hebrew verb *b-h-r*.

32. Isaiah 26:4.

33. Deuteronomy 7:9.

34. Adapted from Isaiah 55:11.

35. On Festivals these lines are adapted appropriately for the day being commemorated.

36. Rabbi Dr. Theodore Friedman, "Study Guide to a Prayer—Mah Tovu," *Shefa Quarterly* 1:3 (April 1978), pages 39–40.

37. Adapted from a Hebrew prayer by Dr. Louis Ginzberg (1873–1953), as it appears in *Siddur Sim Shalom*.

38. Based on the teachings of Rabbi Nahman of Bratslav of the Ukraine. Adapted and translated by Rabbi Jules Harlow from the Hebrew of Rabbi Nahman's disciple, Rabbi Nathan Sternhartz (1780–1845), from *Likutei Tefillah*, part two: 53.

39. The month of *Tishrei*, which begins with Rosh Hashanah, is not announced, because the day is so well-known.

40. Psalms 148:13.

41. Psalms 148:13, 14.

42. Numbers 10:36. The new Jewish Publication Society translation reads: "Return, O Lord, You who are Israel's myriads of thousands."

43. Psalms 132:8–10.

44. Proverbs 4:2.

45. Proverbs 3:18, 17.

46. Lamentations 5:21.

47. Alan Mintz, "Prayer and the Prayerbook" in *Back to the Sources: Reading the Classic Jewish Texts,* Barry W. Holtz, ed. (New York: Summit/Simon & Schuster, 1984), pages 420, 421.

7

Chapter

Rosh Hodesh, Beginning a New Month

Renew our lives with goodness and blessing

Most Jews know that the Hebrew year begins with the observance of Rosh Hashanah. Far fewer Jews, however, know that each Hebrew month begins with the observance of Rosh Hodesh, "the first of the month." Rosh Hodesh, or the new moon festival, had much greater significance in Biblical and Rabbinic times than it has today. The Book of Numbers 10:10 states, "On your joyous occasions—your fixed Festivals and new moon days—you shall sound the trumpets over your burnt offerings and your sacrifices of well-being." According to the Bible, the Israelites celebrated Rosh Hodesh with a festive meal (I Samuel 20:18) and refrained from all business transactions (Amos 8:5).[1] Our ancient ancestors also regarded the new moon festival as a feature of the messianic era. The prophet Isaiah declares that at redemption, "New moon after new moon and Shabbat after Shabbat all flesh shall come to worship Me, says the Lord" (Isaiah 66:23).[2]

The special stature of Rosh Hodesh derives from a Biblical verse and its interpretation. On the eve of the Exodus from Egypt, God told Moses and Aaron: "This month shall mark for you the beginning of the months;

it shall be the first of the months of the year for you" (Exodus 12:2). ▦ From the words "for you," the Rabbis determined that the date on which each month begins is to be decided not by God but by human beings, sitting as a Rabbinic court which would base its decision upon the sighting of the new moon (Babylonian Talmud, *Rosh Hashanah* 22a). Other sages declared that whoever blesses the new month at the proper time is welcoming the Divine Presence, the *Shekhinah* (Babylonian Talmud, *Sanhedrin* 42a). ❀

▦ "This month shall … be the first of the months of the year for you." This refers to the month that became known as Nisan, in which we celebrate Passover. The first month in numbering the months is Nisan, although the calendar year begins with Tishrei, the seventh month and the month of Rosh Hashanah. —JH

❀ This striking teaching, that one who blesses the new month welcomes the Divine Presence, derives from the use of the word "this" (zeh) both in Exodus 12:2, announcing the beginning of the months, and in Exodus 15:2, recalling the revelation of the *Shekhinah* at the splitting of the Sea ("this is my God"). Some say that the new moon exemplifies the creation of the world and its renewal, recalling the Creator. Thus, blessing the new month also bears witness to God as Creator. —JH

Originally, both women and men were forbidden to work on Rosh Ḥodesh. In Talmudic times, however, the Rabbis allowed men to work. For women, the prohibition against work (which included laundry and other household chores) remained in force. The Rabbis of the Talmudic era designated Rosh Ḥodesh as a semi-festival for women, in recognition of women's exemplary behavior in the wilderness of Sinai. There, the Israelite men contributed valuables for building the golden calf, while the women refused to contribute their jewelry.

The Rabbis of Talmudic times recognized the loyalty, dedication, faith, and strength of Israelite women in their refusal to help build an idol and in other instances as well. The Rabbis recognized that women played an indispensable role in the departure from Egypt. They declared that the verse in Exodus telling about "our affliction" in Egypt refers to the separation of husbands and wives. The Egyptian rulers decreed that Israelite men sleep in the fields and women sleep in the city. The women, however, would bring cooked food to their husbands, and they would comfort and encourage them, declaring that the Egyptians "will never break our spirit." Thus, in spite of the decree, the Israelite men and women came together as husbands and wives, and a new generation was born. "Through the merit of the righteous women in that generation the Israelites were redeemed from Egypt" (Babylonian Talmud, *Sotah* 11b; *Midrash Hagadol* to Deuteronomy 26:7).[3] The Rabbis also commented on Exodus 15:20, in which Miriam dances and sings after the Israelites have successfully crossed the Sea of Reeds. Miriam holds a timbrel in her hand, and the Israelite women dance with her, holding their timbrels as well. The Rabbis asked: Where did they get timbrels in the wilderness? The Rabbis and later commentators answered that even though the Israelite women left Egypt hurriedly, under great stress, they nevertheless had faith that they would be favored with God's miracles; thus they had the foresight to pack timbrels (Rashi to Exodus 15:20; *Mekhilta Shirah,* chapter 10). Such were the righteous women of that generation.

In our time, many women observe Rosh Hodesh both as a link to an ancient Jewish woman's tradition and as a special day for their own spiritual expression.[4] ✳ We find yet another association between women and the observance of the new moon in Isaiah 66:10–13, part of the assigned *Haftarah* reading when Rosh Hodesh coincides with Shabbat. God, through the prophet Isaiah, informs the people that they will be nurtured by Jerusalem as a child is nursed by a mother, drawing consolation and glory: "As a mother comforts her son so I will comfort you."

Our challenge today includes paying homage to women of the past by teaching the appropriate texts, but we must do more. We must make possible women's participation in and contribution to the ritual, spiritual, and intellectual life of the Jewish community.

✳ We the collected bless the new moon.
   We open ourselves to the new moon
   as each week we open ourselves to the flame of the candle,
   for measurement is a woman's,
   of time, of the height of the flame,
   of the passing of days.
   We are earthy and lunar,
   ordered by the calendar.
   As you reflect upon the waters,
   So our moods reflect you.

   All creatures see her in the forest,
   glinting on the waters,
   lighting the city,
   and the country road.
   Their eyes gleam with her light.
   Nocturnal creatures scurry in her path,
   The seas are shimmering robes.
   We meet where her light can shine upon us.
   As we shine upon one another.

   —E.M. Broner[5]

SHABBAT BEFORE ROSH HODESH

The Rosh Hodesh liturgy begins each month on the Shabbat immediately preceding the first of the month. After the Torah reading and before the conclusion of the Torah Service, the prayer leader formally announces the date during the following week when the new month will begin. The public announcement of Rosh Hodesh dates back to the first century before the common era. A Rabbinic court had to hear two eyewitnesses report on the appearance of the sliver of crescent moon. The court then declared that the new month had begun. Since the Jewish year is based on the lunar calendar, knowledge of the exact date of the new moon was necessary for determining the dates of the Festivals. By the fourth century, however, the Sages had established a permanent calendar through astronomical calculations. The community no longer needed to rely on sightings of the moon, and public proclamations by the court were discontinued. In our day, we recall the ancient practice in our announcement of the new month on the preceding Shabbat.

The only month for which we make no announcement is Tishrei. The first of Tishrei is Rosh Hashanah, a day so well known and anxiously anticipated that we have no need for a public proclamation about its impending arrival.

After the Torah and *Haftarah* readings on the Shabbat preceding the new moon, we announce the date on which it will occur and we also recite a special blessing. The congregation rises as the prayer leader lifts a Torah scroll and holds it at the lectern. The members of the congregation recite the following prayer and the leader then chants it aloud.

May it be Your will, Lord our God and God of our ancestors, to renew our lives this coming month with goodness and blessing. Grant us long life, a life of peace, of goodness, a life of blessing, sustenance, and bodily vitality, a life marked by piety and fear of sin, a life free of shame and censure, a life of prosperity and honor, a life in which we distinguish ourselves with love of Torah and piety, a life in which the good wishes of our hearts are fulfilled. Amen. *Selah.*

The leader, holding the Torah scroll, continues:

May the One who wrought miracles for our ancestors, redeeming them from slavery to freedom, redeem us soon and gather our dispersed from the four corners of the earth, all the people Israel united in harmony. And let us say, Amen.

⌗ On the Shabbat immediately preceding the new moon, the leader announces the name of the Hebrew month, and then specifies the day or days of the week. (Rosh Hodesh may be observed on one day or on two.) For example: "The new month of Tevet will be on the first day of the week," or "the new month of Iyar will be on the third and the fourth days of the week."—*JH*

The new month of _____ will be on _____. ⌗ May it bring blessing to us and to all the people Israel.

The congregation repeats these phrases and then continues with the following, which the leader repeats.

May the Holy One blessed be He renew the month for us and for all His people the House of Israel with life and peace, joy and gladness, deliverance and consolation. And let us say, Amen.

LITURGY ON ROSH HODESH

The Rosh Hodesh liturgy includes several additions to weekday and to Shabbat services. We add an additional *(Musaf)* service as well (see pages 177–182). In many communities, women gather on Rosh Hodesh for their own services, during which they may add special readings or prayers to supplement the formal liturgy of the day. ✺

Yaaleh Veyavo

On Rosh Hodesh during Evening, Morning, and Afternoon Services, we add a special prayer to the *Amidah*. We insert it into the 17th blessing, the first of the last three *brakhot* of the *Amidah*. The rest of the *Amidah* during these services, whether on a weekday or on Shabbat, remains the same. (Psalm 104 may be added to Morning and Evening Services.) We also add the *Yaaleh Veyavo* (literally, "may there arise and come") prayer to *Birkat Hamazon* (Blessings After Meals).

❋ Many congregations, including Orthodox congregations, sponsor prayer services exclusively for women on designated occasions throughout the year. Rosh Hodesh often is one of those occasions. Joint services involving entire families should also be encouraged because of the Jewish tradition's emphasis on the family as an entity. Women could fulfill a variety of special roles at services for the entire congregation on Rosh Hodesh. The nature and extent of their involvement, and indeed whether they could be involved at all, obviously depends on the nature of each congregation.—*JH*

❊ We recite this *Yaaleh Veyavo* prayer also on Passover, Shavuot, Sukkot, and Shemini Atzeret, with the appropriate words replacing "Rosh Hodesh."—*JH*

❋ The last six days of Passover are an exception to the entire *Hallel* rule. We recite the shortened version of *Hallel* on those days—even though Passover is a major holiday—in recognition of the suffering endured by the Egyptians during the exodus. This practice reflects Proverbs 24:17, "Rejoice not in the fall of your enemy." We do not recite *Hallel* on Rosh Hashanah or Yom Kippur, because these psalms are considered inappropriate on somber days when God is portrayed as sitting in judgment.—*JH*

Our God and God of our ancestors, may our remembrance, the remembrance of our ancestors, the remembrance of the Messiah, son of David Your servant, the remembrance of Jerusalem Your holy city, and the remembrance of Your entire people the House of Israel rise and reach You to be recalled and accepted with favor, graciousness, tenderness, mercy, and compassion for life and for peace on this day of Rosh Hodesh. ❊ Remember us this day for goodness, be mindful of us this day for blessing, and deliver us this day for life. With the promise of redemption and compassion show us mercy and grace. Have compassion and save us. For in You do we place our hope, as You are a gracious and merciful God and King.

Hallel

Before the Torah Reading on Rosh Hodesh, we recite a slightly shortened version of the collection of psalms known as *Hallel*. (Hallel consists of Psalms 113 to 118. The shortened version deletes the first 11 verses of Psalm 115 and of Psalm 116, which are included on occasions when the complete *Hallel* is recited.) The liturgy includes the short *Hallel* on Rosh Hodesh to distinguish between the new moon celebration and the major Festivals on which we recite the entire *Hallel*. ❋ We also recite the entire *Hallel* on Hanukkah and, in many congregations, on Israel's Independence Day and the day commemorating the reunification of Jerusalem. ▨ The Hebrew word *Hallel* means praise. The word "Halleluyah" calls upon the community to praise (*hallelu*) God (*Yah*).

After the morning *Amidah*, the prayer leader recites this blessing, and the members of the congregation repeat it.

Blessed are You, Lord our God, King of the universe who has made our lives holy with His *mitzvot* and commanded us to recite *Hallel*.

▨ Some Orthodox congregations do not recite *Hallel* on Israel's Independence Day or on Yom Yerushalayim. Some Orthodox congregations that do include *Hallel* on those occasions do not recite the blessing that precedes it. —JH

❀ "Servants of the Lord" refers to the members of the community in worship of God. We are servants of God, not servants of other mortals. —JH

Psalm 113

**Halleluyah!
Give praise, servants of the Lord; ❀ praise the name of the Lord.
Let the name of the Lord be blessed now and forever.
From east to west, praise the name of the Lord.
Exalted above all nations is the Lord, beyond the heavens is His glory.
Who is like the Lord our God, enthroned on high,
looking down upon the heavens and the earth,
raising the poor from dust, lifting the wretched from rubbish,
restoring them to be with the privileged, the privileged of His people,
restoring the barren woman in her home
as a happy mother of children. Halleluyah!**

All beings should bless and praise God throughout time and throughout the world. Although "enthroned on high," God shows compassion for mortals, helping those burdened with misfortune. Thus, Psalm 114, which follows, celebrates the miraculous way God shepherded the people Israel on their journey from Egyptian slavery to the promised land.

In Psalm 113, God's mercy is manifest in the lives of individuals, exemplified by helping the poor, the wretched, and the barren woman. Some prayer books, committed to gender-neutral English, present this version of the closing phrase: "turning the childless household into a home rejoicing in its children."[6] This gender inclusiveness depersonalizes the verse and dilutes the specific joy of a woman who had been barren.

Psalm 114

**When the people Israel left Egypt's land,
when the house of Jacob left a barbaric people,
Judah became His sanctuary, Israel His domain.
The sea beheld ▨ and fled, the Jordan turned backward,**

mountains skipped like rams, hills like lambs.
What happened to you, sea, that you fled; Jordan, that you turned backward,
mountains, that you skipped like rams, and hills, like lambs?
Tremble, earth, at the Lord's presence, the presence of Jacob's God,
who turns rock into pools of water, flint into fountains.

At the beginning of the exodus from Egypt, the Israelites, the descendants of the patriarch Jacob, already anticipated life in the promised land. ❋ As a result the entire land, south (called Judah) and north (called Israel), became known as God's holy land, God's domain. Jacob (whose name had been changed to Israel) and his family had journeyed to Egypt, where their descendants lived for many years. Yet despite the prominence of Jacob's son Joseph, who was second in power only to Pharaoh, and despite the Israelites' long years in the land, Egyptian culture and language remained alien to them. The phrase translated above as "a barbaric people" is often translated as "people of an alien tongue" or "people of strange speech," and Deuteronomy 28:49–50 describes the Egyptians as "a nation whose language you will not understand, a ruthless nation that will show the old no regard and the young no mercy."

❊ O, moon, who has released your elders from your pull,
O, moon, who regulates your daughters,
we are of the ocean of women,
at high and low tide.

"She made the moon for seasons.
The sun knoweth its going down.
She maketh dusk and it is night.
Yonder is the sea
great and of wide extent."

Yonder are our lives,
which we help to create.
    —E.M. Broner [7]

❋ In Exodus 6:6–8, before the Israelites have left slavery, God says: "I will free you from the labors of the Egyptians ... and I will take you to be My people.... I will bring you into the land which I promised to give to Abraham, Isaac, and Jacob."—JH

The Psalm presents two goals of the exodus from Egypt: revelation of the Torah at Sinai and life in the promised land. The Psalm begins with the exodus, follows the people Israel as they pass safely through the Sea of Reeds ("the sea beheld and fled"), and sees them reach Mount Sinai in the wilderness to receive revelation. Finally it describes the Israelites entering the holy land. The Psalm recalls physical phenomena: those that accompanied revelation, such as trembling mountains (see Exodus 19:18); those that accompanied the Israelites' entrance into the promised land in the time of Joshua, such as the backward-flowing Jordan River; and those that occurred during the Israelites' journeys in the wilderness, such as the pools of water and fountains that God supplied. At the beginning of the exodus, God turned the Sea of Reeds into dry land, enabling the Israelites to walk across it. As the Israelites wandered in the desert, God turned the dry places into pools and fountains (see, for example, Exodus 17:6 and Deuteronomy 8:15).

On Rosh Hodesh, we omit verses 1 to 11 of Psalm 115.

Psalm 115:12–18

The Lord has been mindful of us; He will bless us.
He will bless the House of Israel, He will bless the House of Aaron.
He will bless those who fear the Lord, small and great alike.
May the Lord increase your numbers, yours and your children's as well.
May you be blessed by the Lord, Creator of the heavens and the earth.
The heavens are the heavens of the Lord, and the earth He has given to mortals.
The dead cannot praise the Lord, nor can all those who descend into silence.
But we will bless the Lord, now and forever. Halleluyah!

Just as God helped the Israelites (as recalled in Psalm 114), we affirm and pray that God will bless us now. Thus we too, and future generations, will participate in a universal chorus of praise.

Psalms 113, 114, and 115 form a single unit at the beginning of *Hallel*, from the start of Psalm 113, "Let the name of the Lord be blessed now and forever," to the end of Psalm 115, "we will bless the Lord now and forever."

On Rosh Ḥodesh, we omit verses 1 to 11 of Psalm 116.

Psalm 116:12–19

How could I repay the Lord for all He has given me?
I raise the cup recalling deliverance, and invoke the Lord by name.
I pay my vows to the Lord in the presence of all His people.
Grievous in the sight of the Lord is the death of His faithful.
Please, Lord, I am Your servant, born of Your maidservant;
You have released me from chains that bound me.
To You do I offer a sacrifice of thanks, and I invoke the Lord by name.
I pay my vows to the Lord in the presence of all His people,
in the courts of the house of the Lord, in your midst, Jerusalem.
Halleluyah!

Worship in the ancient Temple consisted mainly of ritual sacrifices, as Psalm 116 recalls. These verses describe an Israelite coming to the Temple in Jerusalem to fulfill his vows to God. This section of the psalm begins with a rhetorical question (116:12), because offering adequate thanks to God is indeed impossible. The Israelite expresses his thanks symbolically, through the offering of a sacrifice in gratitude for God's blessings. Through this public ceremony, he affirms the reality of God's deliverance. The wine within the raised "cup of deliverance" will be poured on the altar as a libation, offered together with the sacrifice. "I pay my vows to the Lord in the presence of all His people." This verse appears twice—first after a cup with the libation is raised and then after the sacrifice is offered.

From a specific act of one Israelite at the Temple in Jerusalem, the focus changes to the entire world.

Psalm 117

Praise the Lord, all you nations;
laud the Lord, all you peoples.
For His love has overwhelmed us
and the faithfulness of the Lord endures forever. Halleluyah!

From an appeal to the entire world, the leader brings the focus back to the worshiping congregation. (Note that the fourth line below returns to a universal emphasis.)

Psalm 118

Acclaim the Lord for He is good; His loyal love is forever.
Let the people Israel declare: His loyal love is forever.
Let the House of Aaron declare: His loyal love is forever.
Let those who fear the Lord declare: His loyal love is forever.

Confined by distress I called to the Lord; He answered me with divine
    liberation.
The Lord is with me, I shall not fear. What can mortals do to me?
With the Lord among my helpers, I will see the defeat of my foes.
Better to take shelter with the Lord than to trust in mortals.
Better to take shelter with the Lord than to trust in the prominent.
All the nations surrounded me; with the Lord's help I overcame them.
They encircled and surrounded me; with the Lord's help I overcame them.
They encircled me like bees, they were snuffed out like a fire of thorns;
with the Lord's help I overcame them.
The enemy tried to topple me, but the Lord helped me.

The Lord is my strength and my song; He has been my deliverance.
The sounds of song and deliverance resound in the tents of the righteous;
the right hand of the Lord is triumphant.
The right hand of the Lord is exalted, the right hand of the Lord is
    triumphant.
I shall not die, but live and tell the deeds of the Lord.
The Lord surely chastened me, but He did not give me over to death.

A group of pilgrims, going up to Jerusalem to offer a sacrifice at the Temple, stands at the gates of the city. Their leader addresses the gatekeepers of Jerusalem, known as city of righteousness (see Isaiah 1:26), and the gatekeepers respond with the words of the next verse.

Open for me the gates of righteousness that I may enter them and acclaim
    the Lord.
This is the gate of the Lord; the righteous shall enter therein.

The pilgrims then enter the gate, and praise God in the verses below. In the synagogue, we recite each of the following verses twice.

I acclaim You, for You have answered me; You have been my deliverance.
The stone that the builders rejected has become the cornerstone.
This is from the Lord; it is wondrous in our sight.
This is the day made by the Lord; let us rejoice and be happy on it.

The rejected stone could be a symbol for the people Israel, at one time scorned and now restored.

The *hazzan* recites each of the following verses twice, and the congregation repeats the words each time. Having expressed gratitude for past deliverance, the pilgrims pray for their immediate future.

We beseech You, Lord, deliver us please.
We beseech You, Lord, prosper us please.

The priests (*kohanim*) of the Temple greet the leader of the pilgrims and then all of the pilgrims with words of blessing. The pilgrims answer the priests with a formula ("the Lord is God"/*El Adonai*) that expresses their acceptance of God as sovereign and that formally designates their sacrifice as an offering only to God. Light and deliverance are synonymous in this verse (see also Psalm 27, "The Lord is my light and my deliverance"). The pilgrims then request that the priests bind the sacrificial animal and place it near the corners of the altar. (The daily offering, for example, was sacrificed at the northwest corner. See Mishnah *Tamid* 4:1.)

In the name of the Lord: blessed the one who comes here.
We bless you from the House of the Lord.
The Lord is God; He has given us light.
Bind the sacrifice with cords at the horns of the altar.

The one who sacrifices the animal recites the first line below at the time of the ritual slaughter. The words "You are my God" constitute a formula of accepting God's sovereignty (see Mishnah *Sanhedrin* 7:6). In other words: I accept You as my God and to You I offer this sacrifice. The leader of the pilgrims then turns and asks that all of them acclaim the Lord. They answer with the formula: "His loyal love is forever." Thus, Psalm 118 ends as it began.

You are my God and I acclaim You, my God whom I exalt.
Acclaim the Lord for He is good; His loyal love is forever.

Closing blessing of *Hallel*

May all Your creations praise You, Lord our God. May the pious, the righteous who do Your will, and all of Your people the House of Israel, acclaim and bless You in song; may they praise, laud, exalt, extol, sanctify, and celebrate Your sovereign glory, our King. To You it is good to give thanks; to Your glory it is fitting to sing. Forever and ever You are God. Blessed are You, Lord, King acclaimed with psalms of praise.

At the conclusion of *Hallel*, the Torah Service begins (see pages 149–166). At the conclusion of the Torah Service, the Torah scroll is returned to the Ark. The leader of the service recites <u>H</u>*atzi Kaddish* before the *Musaf* Service begins.

Musaf for Rosh <u>H</u>odesh

The structure of our prayer service follows the pattern of Jewish worship in ancient times. The major mode of worship in the Temple in Jerusalem consisted of sacrificial offerings on a daily basis, leading to our practice of daily worship. On Shabbat, on Festivals, and on Rosh <u>H</u>odesh, our ancestors offered an additional sacrifice, which is why we add an additional service *(Musaf)* to our worship on those days.

The *Musaf* (Addtional) Service features its own *Amidah*. The first three and the last three *brakhot* of this *Amidah* are identical to those recited at all other times. The *Musaf Amidah* also includes a *brakhah* between the first three and the last three *brakhot* that emphasizes the themes of the day being observed.

When Rosh <u>H</u>odesh falls on a weekday, the weekday Morning *Amidah* contains 13 *brakhot* between the first three and the last three. The *Musaf Amidah* replaces those 13 *brakhot* with one *brakhah* between the first three and the last three *brakhot*, for a total of seven *brakhot*. On Shabbat and Festivals, both the Morning *Amidah* and the *Musaf Amidah* have a total of seven *brakhot*.

What is the distinction of the middle *brakhah* of the Rosh <u>H</u>odesh *Musaf Amidah*? For centuries this middle blessing has included a petition for the restoration of animal sacrifice in a rebuilt Temple in Jerusalem. Although many Jews today have difficulty imagining the attraction, solemnity, splendor, and power of animal sacrifice, our ancestors clearly valued this type of worship. Since the 19th century, however, Jews have had fundamental disagreements about the restoration of animal sacrifice. As a result, the *Musaf Amidah* differs in the prayer books used by different denominations. Orthodox prayer books continue to petition for the restoration of animal sacrifice in a rebuilt Temple in Jerusalem.[8] Conservative prayer books continue to petition for the restoration of a Temple in Jerusalem with worship services, but they do not petition for the restoration of animal sacrifice. They replace that petition with a recollection of the sacrifices offered by our ancestors. Reform and Reconstructionist prayer books omit the *Musaf* Service entirely. ▦

▦ Although this discussion of *Musaf* is part of a discussion of Rosh Hodesh, it is important to note that the different denominations maintain these differences in their *Musaf* liturgy (or in the lack of it) on Shabbat and Festivals as well. —*JH*

✪ Confession and the request for forgiveness are also part of weekday prayer, articulated in the sixth *brakhah* of the weekday *Amidah*. —*JH*

▨ Other translations of "offerings to be reconciled with You" read "acceptable offerings." "The enemy within" refers to the evil impulse, the natural urges that lead to bad behavior. Jewish thinkers assert that such urges reside within every mortal, although the degree may vary. Other translations of this passage read simply "from the enemy," referring to external foes. —*JH*

✳ After the destruction of the Second Temple, prayer replaces sacrifice as the central Jewish mode of worship. The major prayer services are the successors to the major sacrificial services in the Temple.

Sacrifice involves a flesh-and-blood animal. It is very much of this world, of the earth, of nature.

Prayer involves words. It is about God and man. It reaches for heaven.

Sacrifice seems below us, but liturgy is above and beyond us.

And yet prayer is a ritual just as sacrifice is a ritual. Liturgy is patterned, repetitious, monotonous. Ritual is composed of details. The excitement, the power of prayer is not in the words but in the ritual act of prayer.

Still, our prescribed prayers have meaning. We need to become literate about our prayers, to understand structure, nuance, rhythm, tone. The *siddur* is an anthology, something of a cross section of Jewish belief and history. Literacy about prayer requires learning and experience.

But, literacy does not mean literalism. To know what the words mean is important, but it is essential not to take those meanings *too* literally.

How does a prayer mean? A prayer is composed of words. The words express praise, petition, a sentiment, an emotion, a belief. But to pray is not just to say words. [Rabbi] Yochanan Muffs teaches his students to leave no cliché unturned in the search for meaning. Sacrifice, he reminds us, was a mystical act. Examining the traditional *Musaf,* he finds a sensuous, spiritual prayer which brings God and man together on a special day for a special purpose; perhaps for communion, perhaps mystical nearness. To recite a prayer, then, is to commit a ritual act, a prescribed, traditional, community-involved act. The prayer is composed of its words but it rises above its words. The words are but the surface level. In the wellsprings of prayer, inside us, we find prayer in its reality.

The meaning of the words is only a subset of the meaning of prayer. The words themselves are fixed and bind us to the present community ➤

Before comparing an Orthodox and a Conservative text for Rosh Ḥodesh *Musaf*, we take note that on Rosh Ḥodesh the middle *brakhah* of the *Amidah* incorporates another special theme—atonement for sin. This focus distinguishes Rosh Ḥodesh from the Festivals and Shabbat, since those days emphasize joy and their liturgy omits all mention of sin and atonement. Many Jews think of sin and forgiveness only in connection with Yom Kippur, the Day of Atonement. Yet the liturgy of Rosh Ḥodesh includes atonement for sin and forgiveness, ✪ necessary elements that precede our attainment of spiritual renewal. The waning and the waxing of the moon each month metaphorically reflect the possibility— and the need—for spiritual renewal.

When Rosh Ḥodesh occurs on a weekday, Orthodox prayer books include the following insertion within the fourth (middle) *brakhah* of the *Musaf Amidah*. (The underlined words are those altered in the Conservative *Musaf Amidah*.)

New Month festivals have You given to Your people, a time of atonement throughout their generations when they would bring offerings to be reconciled with You, as well as goats for sin-offering to attain their atonement. This was a reminder of all

the people's merit and a source of salvation from the enemy within. ✳ Establish a new altar in Zion, and a Rosh Hodesh burnt offering will we bring up upon it

and freely offer goats to You. May all of us rejoice in worship at the sanctuary, and in the songs of David Your servant that will be heard in Your city, chanted before Your altar. Everlasting love bestow upon Your people; recall the fathers' covenant on behalf of the children. Bring us to Zion Your city in song and to Jerusalem Your sanctuary with everlasting joy. <u>There shall we offer to You our obligatory sacrifices,</u> the daily offerings in their proper order and the additional offerings according to their law. And the additional offering of this New Moon day <u>shall we offer and sacrifice</u> ✳ to You lovingly according to Your commandment as You have prescribed for us in Your Torah through Moses Your servant, at Your command, ✳ as it is said:

On your New Moon festivals you shall bring a burnt offering to the Lord: two young bulls, one ram, and seven yearling lambs, without blemish. The grain offering shall be three-tenths of an ephah of choice flour mingled with oil for each bull, two-tenths of an ephah of choice flour mingled with oil for the ram, and one-tenth of an ephah of choice flour mingled with oil for each lamb. You shall bring it with the wine required for the libations, a goat for atonement, and the two daily offerings as prescribed. (Numbers 28:11–15)

and to the past. As such, they point us outward. But the words are also referents, indicators of emotion and spirituality. Here they point us inward.

Conservative Judaism does not seem to understand this. *[The author is a Conservative rabbi.—Editor]* It seems to believe that a prayer means only what its words mean. Change the words, the notion is, when we "cannot get into them." Then, it is supposed, we will really be able to pray.

On the contrary. We need the words to remain fixed, as often as possible. (We cannot keep *shelo asani ishah* [who did not make me a woman] because it is offensive in any number of ways.)

A prayer yields meaning through its words but also through its ritual function and context. Take the words too literally and one misses the point. We use words in prayer, for example, which describe God as having a face. But we do not mean that He really has a face. We speak in terms of God's human attributes so that we can place an image before our mind's eye, an image which will help us pray.

We use words that say that God rewards the righteous and punishes the wicked. We know that this is not so, that no such reality exists in the world. But the prayer is said in the hope that one day there will be justice in the world. Take these words literally, and one would have to change them. We would have to go through the *siddur* and systematically rid it of anthropomorphisms and descriptions of God's justice....

So we changed *naaseh venakriv* [we shall offer and sacrifice] to *asu vehikrivu* [they offered and sacrificed].... By altering our liturgy, we changed a traditional dream into a boring historical statement. This is backwards. The correct flow is from history to ritual. A historical event is unrepeatable. The exodus from Egypt or the revelation at Mount Sinai were unique events. But some events become definitive ones which tell us who we are. Since we cannot repeat the events, we re-enact them so that we can stay in touch with who we are supposed to be. We re-present the past. The past thus is not boring and archaic but re-enacted through ritual.

Asu vehikrivu says: We are more sophisticated than those who sacrificed. But why be so literal about it? We can say: We are just like those who sacrificed. We are in kinship with them. Their actions define our actions. Our words re-enact their now unrepeatable actions. Sacrifice is a historical event which we can re-present without literally doing sacrifice or even wanting to do it.—*Rabbi Benjamin Edidin Scolnic* [9]

✳ The literal meaning of "through Moses Your servant, at Your command" is "by the hands of Moses from the mouth of Your glory."—*JH*

Conclusion of the middle *brakhah*

Our God and God of our fathers, renew for us this month with goodness and blessedness, happiness and gladness, deliverance and consolation, sustenance and support, life and peace, with forgiveness for sin and pardon for transgression (*on leap year add:* and with atonement for wrongdoing ▩). For You have chosen Your people Israel from among all nations, setting the laws of Rosh Hodesh for them. Blessed are You, Lord who hallows the people Israel and the New Month festivals.

▩ On leap years we add one request: We ask for "atonement for wrongdoing." This addition brings the total of requests (starting with "goodness and blessedness") to 13, the number of months in a leap year (when a second month of Adar is added). In other years, only the first 12 are included, to match the 12 months.—JH

Below is a version of the same *brakhah* in the Conservative prayer book. Words that have been changed or added are underlined. Since Conservative Jews do not petition for the restoration of animal sacrifice,[10] the prayer book deletes the petition for a new altar and the description of what would happen there. Both Orthodox and Conservative versions do petition for the return of the people Israel to Jerusalem, and both petition for a central place of worship there.

New Month festivals have You given to Your people, a time of atonement throughout their generations when they would bring offerings reconciling them to You as well as goats of sin-offering to attain their atonement. This was a reminder of all the people's merit and a source of salvation from the enemy within.

Everlasting love bestow upon Your people; recall the fathers' covenant on behalf of the children. Bring us to Zion Your city in song and to Jerusalem Your sanctuary with everlasting joy. <u>There our ancestors offered their sacrifices to You,</u> the daily offerings in their proper order and the additional offerings according to their law, <u>and there shall we worship You with love and reverence as in days of old and in ancient times.</u> And the additional offering of this New Month day <u>they offered and sacrificed</u> to You lovingly, according to Your commandment, as You have prescribed for us in Your Torah through Moses Your servant, at Your command.

Some congregations include Numbers 28:11–15 here, and some omit these verses. (See page 179.)

<u>Compassionate King, accept with compassion the prayer of Your people Israel, wherever they dwell.</u>

The conclusion of the middle *brakhah* (above) is identical in Orthodox and Conservative prayer books.

When Rosh Hodesh coincides with Shabbat, the *Musaf Amidah* includes a more elaborate version of the middle *brakhah*. Here is an Orthodox version.

You formed Your universe in times of old, completing Your labors by the seventh day. You have loved and favored us, and singled us out among all nations by making us holy through Your commandments and drawing us near to Your service, our King, so that we became known by Your great and holy name. Lord our God, lovingly have You given us Sabbaths for rest and days of the New Month for atonement. Yet because we and our ancestors have sinned, our city was destroyed, our sanctuary made desolate, our splendor exiled, and the glory removed from our House of Life. We cannot fulfill our duties in Your chosen House, the great and holy House called by Your name, because of the hand sent forth against Your sanctuary.

May it be Your will, Lord our God and God of our fathers, to bring us in joy to our land and to plant us within its borders. <u>There we shall offer</u> to You our obligatory sacrifices, the daily offerings in their proper order and the additional offerings according to their law. And the additional offerings of this Shabbat day and of this Rosh Hodesh day shall <u>we offer and sacrifice</u> to You lovingly according to Your commandment as You have prescribed for us in Your Torah through Moses Your servant at Your command, as it is said:

Offerings for the day of Shabbat: two yearling lambs without blemish, together with two-tenths of an ephah of choice flour mingled with oil as a grain offering, with the proper libation; a burnt offering for every Shabbat, in addition to the daily burnt offering and its libation (Numbers 28:9–10).

Numbers 28:11–15 follows. (See page 179.)

Shabbat Conclusion

Those who keep Shabbat rejoice in Your sovereignty, calling Shabbat a delight. All of the people who hallow the seventh day find satisfaction and joy in Your goodness. For it pleased You to hallow the seventh day, calling it the most desirable day, a reminder of Creation.

Our God and God of our fathers, accept our offering of Shabbat rest. On this day of Shabbat renew for us this month for goodness and blessedness, joy and gladness, deliverance and consolation, sustenance and support, life and peace, for pardon of sin and forgiveness of wrongdoing (*on leap year add:* and atonement for wrongdoing). For You have chosen the people Israel from among all nations, proclaiming Your holy Shabbat to them, and setting the laws of Rosh Hodesh for them. Blessed are You, Lord who hallows Shabbat, the people Israel, and the New Month festivals.

A Conservative version of this *brakhah* for Shabbat *Musaf* is similar to the Orthodox version, except for the following passage, which includes changes in tense and some additional words. The changes and additions are underlined.

May it be Your will, Lord our God and God of our ancestors, <u>who restores His children to their land,</u> ▦ to bring us in joy to our land and to plant us within its borders. <u>There our ancestors offered</u> to You obligatory sacrifices, the daily offerings in their proper order and the additional offerings according to their law, <u>and there shall we worship You with love and reverence as in days of old and in ancient times.</u> And the additional offerings of this Shabbat day and of this Rosh Hodesh day <u>they offered and sacrificed</u> to You lovingly according to Your commandment as You have prescribed for us in Your Torah through Moses Your servant at Your command, as it is said.

▦ The phrase "who restores His children to their land" was added to reflect with gratitude the reality of a State of Israel in the land of Israel, a dream fulfilled in the middle of the 20th century. It is based on Jeremiah 15:17. —JH

✸ Blessing for the New Moon and New Year

Eloheinu v'Elohei avoteinu ve'imoteinu, hadesh aleinu hodesh ze veshanah zot.[11]
Dear God, God of our Mothers and Fathers
Renew us this month and this year
Direct us
Toward goodness and blessing
Toward the joyful
Toward the liberation and the challenge, as well as
Toward patience and consolation
Toward becoming ever more human beings.
Let us become capable of supporting ourselves,
Our families and friends,
Let us serve our community in dignity.

Direct us
Toward life and peace
Toward observing our blindness
Toward struggling with our goals
Toward forgiving ourselves and each other.

You chose us with an intention
You gave us the awareness of the cycles of the moon.
May we use this gift as an opportunity to understand what you intend for us.
Thank you—for inviting us to share your holiness and
This holy moment of the [New Moon and] New Year.
—*Rabbi Sheila Peltz Weinberg*[12]

Some congregations then recite Numbers 28:9–15 (see pages 181 and 179).

<u>Compassionate King, accept with compassion the prayers of Your people Israel, wherever they dwell.</u>

The Shabbat *Musaf* Conclusion for the middle *brakhah* is identical in Conservative and Orthodox prayer books (see page 181).

✳ ✳ ✳

On the first day of the month of Tishrei, Rosh Hashanah, we customarily greet the New Year in a special way. ✸ At the beginning of the festival meal, after reciting the blessings over wine and bread (*Kiddush* and *hamotzi*), everyone at the table dips an apple in honey. They then recite together the blessing before eating fruit,[13] and after that they recite, "May it be Your will, Lord our God and God of our ancestors, to renew our lives for a good and sweet year."

QUESTIONS FOR FURTHER STUDY AND REFLECTION

1. How is the new month related to the exodus from Egypt? How is it related to the role of women in the redemption from Egypt? How is the new month related to Creation?

2. Some communities sponsor Rosh Hodesh services for women only. Do you think that this should be encouraged, or do you think that women should always be part of a service that includes men and women? Explain your position.

3. Why are some verses of *Hallel* psalms deleted on the last six days of Passover? Why is there no recitation of *Hallel* on Rosh Hashanah?

4. As reflected in *Hallel* psalms, what were two goals of the exodus from Egypt? Is liberation ever a final goal in and of itself?

5. How is worship in the ancient Temple of Jerusalem recalled in Rosh Hodesh liturgy?

6. On what occasions besides Rosh Hodesh is an additional service added?

7. This chapter presents Orthodox and Conservative versions of Rosh Hodesh *Musaf*. Which do you prefer, and why? Or do you prefer deleting it, as in Reform and Reconstructionist prayer books? If so, why?

---

1. Rosh Hodesh was also a special day for visiting the prophet (II Kings 4:23).

2. This verse is included in the *Haftarah* portion of the Torah Service when Rosh Hodesh coincides with Shabbat.

3. Also refer to *The Feast of Freedom*, edited by Rachel Anne Rabinowicz (New York: Rabbinical Assembly, 1982), pages 50–51.

4. For additional consideration of Rosh Hodesh, see *Moonbeams: A Hadassah Rosh Hodesh Guide* (Woodstock, VT: Jewish Lights, 2000), especially chapter 1 and Appendix A. For additional activities and rituals, as well as background, refer to Arlene Agus, "This Month Is for You: Observing Rosh Hodesh as a Woman's Holiday," in *The Jewish Woman: New Perspectives* (New York: Schocken, 1976), edited by Elizabeth Koltun, pages 84–93. Also see sidebar by Arlene Agus, Chapter 10, pages 240–241.

5. E. M. Broner, in *Bringing Home the Light: A Jewish Woman's Handbook of Rituals* (San Francisco, Tulsa: Council Oak Books, 1999), pages 174–176. Broner includes this poem in a menopause ritual: "It is fitting that at the new moon, the wise woman, who has lived these many moons and no longer feels its pull, is honored. Thus, at her menopause, she should be enthroned, elevated, and respected."

6. *Kol Haneshamah: Shabbat Vehagim* (Wyncote, PA: Reconstructionist Press, 1995), page 358.

7. E. M. Broner, in *Bringing Home the Light,* page 176. Broner includes this poem in a menopause ritual. She notes that the passages in quotation marks "are alterations on traditional Jewish prayers said at the time of the new moon." These passages are based on Psalm 104:19–25.

8. See *Siddur: The Traditional Prayer Book for Shabbath and Festivals,* David de Sola Pool, ed. (New York: Behrman House, 1960) and *The Complete Artscroll Siddur* (Brooklyn: Mesorah, 1984).

9. Rabbi Benjamin Edidin Scolnic, *"Na'aseh Ve-nakriv:* Prayer, Sacrifice, and the Meaning of Ritual," *Conservative Judaism* 37:4 (summer 1984), pages 31–33. Rabbi Scolnic is spiritual leader of Temple Beth Shalom, Hamden, CT, and he is editor-in-chief of *Conservative Judaism.*

10. There are, however, some exceptions to this rule.

11. Our God and God of our forefathers and foremothers, renew for us this month and this year.

12. Sheila Peltz Weinberg, "Blessing for the New Moon and New Year," in Penina V. Adelman *Miriam's Well: Rituals for Jewish Women Around the Year,* 2nd ed. (New York: Biblio, 1986, 1996), pages 26–27.

13. Blessed are You, Lord our God, who creates the fruit of trees.

Chapter

THE *KADDISH*

May there be peace in abundance

Some of the most familiar words in Jewish liturgy are those of the *Kaddish*. It is not only a prayer for mourners, though that is probably its best-known form. Jewish congregations rarely, if ever, recite it in translation, though, ideally, we should understand the words that we utter in a service

of prayer. Nevertheless, for mourners, even for many who do not understand the meaning of its words, the Aramaic *Kaddish* conveys deep meaning in and of itself.

The *Kaddish* is one of the passages that Jews recite only when participating in a public worship service.[1] To be considered public, a Jewish prayer service requires a minimum of ten adults (a *minyan*). Fewer than ten fail to qualify as a *minyan*; they are merely a group of individuals. As folk wisdom observes, nine rabbis do not make a *minyan*, but ten tailors do. Every adult counts equally, just as every adult who knows how, may lead a prayer service.

In all Orthodox and in some Conservative congregations, the *minyan* is defined as ten adult male Jews, age 13 or older. In Reform, Reconstructionist, and most Conservative congregations, the *minyan* is defined as ten adult Jews, including males age 13 or older and females age 12 or older. Similarly, in all Orthodox and in some Conservative congregations, only males at least 13 years of age may lead a prayer ➤

Although individuals and groups of nine or fewer certainly may pray, we require a community to recite certain texts aloud. These texts all formally hallow God, the Holy One, who is holy by definition. Yet, it is part of the boldness and the beauty of Judaism that we mortal creatures have the ability to hallow our Creator (just as we have the ability to desecrate the name of God, who gives us such freedom). In a prayer service, this formal hallowing of God takes place only in public, only in a community. The Rabbis derived this rule from a verse in Leviticus, "I will be hallowed *in the midst* (*betokh*) of the people Israel" (22:32). The Rabbis also established ten as the minimum number that constitutes a community. ▨

In prayer, a Jew is never alone. Words of the prayer book link Jews throughout the world and throughout time. ◉ Most of Jewish prayer is phrased in first-person plural, leading us to utter "we" and "our" rather than "I" and "my," even when praying alone. In Jewish observance we attain the highest state of human holiness only when we pray as a member of a community, joining others to form a *minyan*. As individuals,

service. In Reform, Reconstructionist, and many Conservative congregations, females at least 12 years of age may also lead a prayer service. Lay leadership is common, although cantors, rabbis, or other congregational professionals usually lead services.—*JH*

▨ The Babylonian Talmud (*Berakhot* 21b) arrives at the number ten by examining a passage in the Book of Numbers. The word for community (*edah*) is applied to the ten spies in Numbers 16:21, a verse that instructs the other Israelites to separate themselves "from the midst" (*mitokh*) of that community. The Hebrew for "the midst" (*tokh*) that appears both in Numbers 16:21 and Leviticus 22:32 links the idea of hallowing God in a community with the number required to establish a community.—*JH*

◉ Even with the differences (often great and major) that do distinguish the many published prayer books from one another, all books of Hebrew prayer share a common core.—*JH*

✸ In some synagogues (generally Reform), the entire congregation stands *only* when Mourner's *Kaddish* is recited.—*JH*

✳ Contrary to popular belief, the *Kaddish*, in the shape and form that we recognize today, is a relatively late construct. Neither the notion nor the function of the *Kaddish* is mentioned in the Talmud.... Furthermore, the first complete formulation is not found until the *Seder Rav Amram* (ninth century), where it appears only as a prayer recited by the [prayer ➤

we attain that exalted state by joining others to establish congregations, by striving to help perfect the Jewish community, locally and globally, and by striving to perfect society as a whole. In Hebrew, one of the terms used to describe a congregation is *kehillah kedoshah*, holy congregation.

Whoever recites *Kaddish* does so while standing. Those who are not reciting *Kaddish* (but are only responding at the appropriate passages) are not obligated to stand during its recitation, although anyone standing when *Kaddish* begins should remain standing until the conclusion. In many congregations it is customary for everyone to stand for every recitation of *Kaddish*. ✸

Kaddish, an Aramaic word meaning "holy," originally was not part of the synagogue service. ✳ In ancient times, *Kaddish* served as a brief informal prayer that marked the end of a public lesson held at a study house or a synagogue. The teacher taught in Aramaic, the common spoken language of the time, so that all the students could understand. The *Kaddish*, also in Aramaic, closed the lesson, serving as a sacred seal. (The last line of the Mourner's *Kaddish*, and of the Full *Kaddish*, however, is in Hebrew.)

The *Kaddish*, unlike standard prayers of Jewish liturgy, does not address God directly. In addition, the *Kaddish* does not employ the Hebrew words for Lord (*Adonai*) or for God (*Elohim*), perhaps in keeping with its informal origins. We speak *about* God, who is very much present in the *Kaddish*, but we do not address God.

The ancient lessons held at study houses or synagogues featured passages from Rabbinic literature; such passages would end with a message of hope alluding to the messianic times to come. The words of *Kaddish* also give hope, as the community affirms its faith and praises God, anticipating the improvement of the human condition in this world. Those who recite the *Kaddish* maintain the hope for redemption while living in an imperfect, unredeemed world.

Mourner's *Kaddish* is the liturgical response required of all who have suffered loss through the death of a father,

leader]. Its function as *Kaddish Yatom* (Mourner's *Kaddish*) and its position as a liturgical obligation, are not mentioned until the 11th century.... Still later, when Isaac of Vienna (13th century) speaks of it in *Or Zarua*, [it] is nothing more than a simple custom.... Undoubtedly, the most striking fact is that in none of the medieval codes, even as late as the *Shulḥan Arukh* [16th century], are the rules for the recitation of the *Kaddish*, which a mourner must follow, specified in the sense that we know today.

One might ask, under such circumstances, how did a prayer that initially was not designed to render homage to the deceased and, even less, to constitute the principal commemoratory obligation of orphans, become charged with so much emotion and progressively assume such importance? The question especially merits consideration, [since] this prayer is in no way an invocation for the repose of the soul of the departed, as is the case with the *El malei raḥamim* of the Ashkenazim or the *Hashkava* of the Sephardim. Instead, it deals with the solemn glorification of God, with a strong eschatologic connotation: the confident and pressing expectation of the advent of the reign of God on earth. One notes in this regard the obvious relationship with the famous Christian credo expressed in the *Pater noster*, inspired by Matthew 6:9–10: "Our father who art in heaven, hallowed be thy name. Thy kingdom come. Thy will be done, on earth as it is in heaven." *—Rabbi Rivon Krygier*[2]

✵ In Hebrew, the term for Mourner's *Kaddish* is *Kaddish Yatom*, literally "Orphan's *Kaddish*." Although we are required to say *Kaddish* for our parents, children, spouses, or siblings, we are *permitted* to say *Kaddish* for others who have died. *Yizkor* services are held on Yom Kippur, Passover, Shavuot, and Sukkot. Customarily we recite *Kaddish* at daily prayer services in the months following the burial, and we begin to recite *Kaddish* at *Yizkor* services after the one-year anniversary of the death. *—JH*

mother, son, daughter, husband, wife, sister, or brother (including a half-brother or half-sister). According to Jewish law, the mourner is obliged to recite *Kaddish* for parents during the 11 months following burial and for the other close relatives during the 30 days following burial. In the years following, mourners recite *Kaddish* on the *yahrzeit* (the anniversary of the day of death, according to the Hebrew calendar) and at *Yizkor* Memorial Services. ✵ During the year following a death and on its anniversary, when one has strong reasons for questioning God, Judaism obligates the mourner to stand in public and reaffirm faith by praising God and by expressing hope in the future. ▨

▨ *[In 1916, women did not publicly recite* Kaddish *for their deceased relatives, but requested that a man do so on their behalf. However, when the mother of Henrietta Szold died, Szold wrote to a friend, stating her intention to say* Kaddish *herself.]*

I cannot ask you to say *Kaddish* after my mother. The *Kaddish* means to me that the survivor publicly and markedly manifests his wish and intention to assume the relation to the Jewish community which his parent had, and that so the chain of tradition remains unbroken from generation to generation, each adding its own link. You can do that for the generations of your family, I must do that for the generations of my family.

I believe that the elimination of women from such duties was never intended by our law and custom—women were freed from positive duties when they could not perform them, but not when they could. It was never intended that, if they could perform them, their performance of them should not be considered as valuable and valid as when one of the male sex performed them. And of the *Kaddish* I feel sure this is particularly true.

My mother had eight daughters and no son; and yet never did I hear a word of regret pass the lips of either my mother or my father that one of us was not a son. When my father died, my mother would not permit others to take her daughters' place in saying the *Kaddish*, and so I am sure I am acting in her spirit when I am moved to decline your offer. But beautiful your offer remains nevertheless, and, I repeat, I know full well that it is much more in consonance with the generally accepted Jewish tradition than is my or my family's conception. You understand me, don't you? —*Henrietta Szold*[4]

⊛ Another translation of the passage reflects a different understanding: "Enhanced and hallowed may His great name be in the world He has created. May His will be fulfilled and his Sovereignty revealed in the days of your life."—*JH*

✳ A Hebrew equivalent of the Aramaic prayer is found in Psalms 113:2. "May the name of the Lord be blessed now and forever." This recurring theme also appears in the words that follow the recitation of the *Shema,* "Blessed be the name of His glorious sovereignty forever" (see pages 58–59).—*JH*

✺ Recitation of the words from the *Kaddish,* "May His great name be blessed forever and ever," at the end of a lesson links the study of Torah with the hallowing of God's name.—*JH*

Kaddish emphasizes exalting and hallowing God through the redemption of life in this world and through the universal acceptance of God's sovereignty. We pray for the establishment of God's sovereignty on earth, when all people on earth will have ultimate allegiance only to God.[3]

The earliest *Kaddish* consisted only of what is now the opening passage:

Enhanced and hallowed may His great name be in the world He created as He willed. May He show His sovereignty soon, in the days of your life ⊛ and the life of the whole house of Israel. And say now, Amen.

This was followed by a congregational response, which continues to be the core of every version of the *Kaddish*:

Amen. Yehei shmeih rabba mevorakh le'alam ule'almei almaya.

Amen. May His great name be blessed forever and ever. ✳

The fourth-century sage Rabba declared that the merit gained through the recitation of this response sustains the world (Babylonian Talmud, *Sotah* 49a). ✺ The mourner (or the one who recalls the dead on a *yahrzeit* or at a *Yizkor* service), by reciting Mourner's *Kaddish*, elicits this response from the congregation. In this way, we honor the memory of the dead through the communal liturgical act of hallowing God. ▒

Even the shortest form of *Kaddish* recited today is longer than the original version. The short form, known as *Hatzi Kaddish* (Half *Kaddish*), begins with the brief prayer and response noted above, and ends with these lines:

Blessed, lauded, glorified, exalted, eminent, extolled, prominent, and praised be the name of the Holy One, beyond all blessing and song, psalm and solace uttered in the world. ✽ And say now, Amen.

We chant *Hatzi Kaddish* to separate certain sections of the service from one another.

The Full *Kaddish* (*Kaddish Shalem*) separates sections of the service too. In addition, we chant *Kaddish Shalem* toward the conclusion of a prayer service. *Kaddish Shalem* consists of the *Hatzi Kaddish* above, with the addition of the following three passages:

May the prayers and pleas of the whole House of Israel be accepted by their Father in heaven. And say now, Amen.

May there be peace in abundance from heaven, with life for us and for all the people Israel. And say now, Amen.

▒ Traditional Jewish law treats mourning sons and daughters identically in many ways.... However, in one respect men and women are treated quite differently in traditional Jewish circles—men are required to recite *Kaddish* and women are not.

Many women are deeply offended by their exclusion from public prayer after the death of a parent or relative. The recitation of *Kaddish* ... has attained a powerful symbolism for many, perhaps most, Jews. Among those of Eastern European cultures, a male child was often referred to as a *kaddishel*, a guarantee that *Kaddish* would be recited after one's death....

Even Jews who are in many other ways rather removed from formal prayer and religious rituals are often punctilious about reciting *Kaddish* during the mourning period and on the *yahrzeit*. Many women report that they simply assumed that they would recite *Kaddish* at mourning services each day—only to be told in no uncertain terms by male synagogue regulars that women were not welcome.... When these women arrived at their local Orthodox or Conservative synagogue—Reform congregations by and large do not hold daily services—they learned for the first time that many synagogue regulars regard daily prayer services as a privileged male turf....

Traditional synagogues are the most likely to have daily prayers, and they are also the most likely to be unwilling to count women for a *minyan*, posing a serious problem for the would-be female *Kaddish* reciter.... Ruth Seldin, coeditor of *The American Jewish Year Book*, tells ... about a friend who was in mourning:

"She came regularly, in fact, not just to say *Kaddish*, though that was obviously important to her. An older man was sympathetic. 'Listen,' he told her, 'You've got a brother—why don't you tell him to say *Kaddish* for your father?' The woman looked at him, barely able to control her anger. 'My brother doesn't give a damn—I want to say *Kaddish*, don't you understand?'"[5]

[For many Jewish women,] the first shock of exclusion comes only a few hours after the funeral. A 45-year-old suburban New Yorker who works as a paralegal [was told by a synagogue regular], "You can say *Kaddish* till you're blue in the face, but it won't count. If you want your father's soul to go to heaven, you better get a man to say *Kaddish* for him three times a day."

Such brutal exclusions during a time of extreme vulnerability evoke strong feelings among many women. As one professor remembers, "For me, feminism started when I was 10 and was not allowed to say *Kaddish* for my father...." Indeed, strong feelings [about] saying *Kaddish* for a parent are among the most universal experiences in the formation of Jewish feminist commitments. —*Sylvia Barack Fishman*[6]

✽ Rabbi Billy Berkowitz conceived the exercise of giving his congregants a prayer book and a red pencil and challenging them to edit out ➤

He who makes peace in His high places[7] will make peace for us and for all the people Israel. And say now, Amen.

The Mourner's *Kaddish* consists of *Kaddish Shalem*, minus the first of the preceding three passages (beginning "May the prayers and pleas"). ▦ ▧

anything they found to be untrue. I asked Billy what, if anything, *he* would retain. "Only a fragment of one line," he said, "from the *Kaddish*—'[God is] far beyond any blessings, songs, praises, and consolations that can be expressed in the world.'" There are many forms of the *Kaddish* recited in prayer services and study halls, but mourners stand and recite a special *Kaddish*. Their *Kaddish* echoes what appears eminently true for mourners, that God is far away, "beyond," that the words of most prayers may not even come close to the feelings in the speaker's heart. We tend to think of the *Kaddish* as a brave or comforting affirmation of God's glory, but from the perspective of the mourner, it may just as well be an acknowledgment of God's apparent distance.—*Rabbi Margaret Holub*[8]

▦ The Mourner's *Kaddish* may omit the passage, "May the prayers and pleas of the whole house of Israel be accepted by their Father in heaven," because prayers on behalf of those who are now mourned were not answered as anticipated. The words we utter, especially words of prayer, should not mock the unfortunate.—*JH*

▧ When I hear mourners recite *Kaddish*, I think proudly of Henrietta Szold, who many years ago refused a male friend's offer to say *Kaddish*. Or, I think lovingly of feminist leader Esther Broner, who recently said *Kaddish* for her father in an Orthodox synagogue, behind a curtain, daily, defiantly, passionately. When people rise to say *Kaddish,* I think sadly of my gay and lesbian brothers and sisters of past generations and unknown victims of pogroms and the Holocaust for whom no one was there to say *Kaddish*. But most of all, I think of my grandmother Lena, whose sweet memory reminds me why *Kaddish* is a prayer of praise for the goodness and warmth that lingers in the world even when those we love are gone.—*Rebecca Alpert*

✹ The words of the additional passage are reminiscent of words recited at the end of the Torah Service, also in Aramaic. See *Yekum Purkan*, pages 159–160.—*JH*

We recite yet another form of *Kaddish* after the public reading or teaching of a Rabbinic text. This is the Rabbis' *Kaddish* (*Kaddish DeRabbanan*), in which the three passages cited above (beginning "May the prayers and pleas") are replaced by the following:

For the people Israel and for our rabbis, for their students and for all the students of their students, and for all who engage in the study of Torah, here and everywhere, may there be peace in abundance, graciousness and steadfast love, mercy, long life, ample sustenance, and deliverance through our Father in heaven, for them and for you. And say now, Amen.

May there be peace in abundance from heaven, with good life, for us and for all the people Israel. And say now, Amen. He who makes peace in His high places will in His mercy make peace for us and for all the people Israel. And say now, Amen. ✹

When the *Kaddish*, originally recited only at the end of a lesson, had taken on other functions in the service, this special form of Rabbis' *Kaddish* became necessary as a specific response to the study or presentation of a sacred text. *Kaddish*, in any of its forms, is never recited by itself. We always attach it to a portion of the prayer service or to a Biblical or a Rabbinic text.

The following words have been adapted from a passage by the Israeli Nobel laureate, S.Y. Agnon, as an introduction to the Mourner's *Kaddish*.

Our Creator, the King of kings, delights in life. Because of His love for us, and because we are so few, each of us is important in His kingdom. Though we are flesh and blood, we are irreplaceable. When one of the House of Israel dies, there is a loss of glory in His kingdom and His grandeur is diminished. Therefore, members of the House of Israel, all of you who mourn and all of you who remember, let us fix our hearts on our Father in Heaven, our King and redeemer, and let us pray for ourselves, and for Him too, that He and His sovereignty be hallowed and enhanced, glorified and celebrated.

QUESTIONS FOR FURTHER STUDY AND REFLECTION

1. What is the origin of reciting *Kaddish*?
2. The word *Kaddish* is related to other words in the prayer book. What are they, and what is the connection?
3. Why may *Kaddish* be recited *only* in the presence of a *minyan*?
4. According to the *Kaddish*, how do we best hallow God?
5. What is *Kaddish DeRabbanan*? Why do we pray after public study of a Rabbinic text? How does public study of a Rabbinic text differ from public study of a text such as Shakespeare or Homer?
6. What are the differences between Mourner's *Kaddish* and the other forms of *Kaddish*? What do these differences reveal?
7. Sylvia Barack Fishman observes that women's exclusion from the public recitation of *Kaddish* is often deeply hurtful, and in many women it awakens Jewish feminist beliefs. What is your experience of reciting *Kaddish*?

---

1. Other passages are the *Barkhu* and the section of the *Amidah* known as *Kedushah*.

2. Rivon Krygier, "The Multiple Meanings of the Mourner's Kaddish," *Conservative Judaism* 54:2 (Winter 2002), pages 67–68.

3. It shares this theme with the prayer known as *Aleinu* (see page 198).

4. Henrietta Szold, Letter to Hayim Peretz (16 September 1916), in *Henrietta Szold: Life and Letters,* Marvin Lowenthal, ed. (New York: Viking, 1942) pages 92–93.

5. Ruth R. Seldin, "Women in the Synagogue: A Congregant's View," *Conservative Judaism* 32:2 (Winter 1979), pages 80–88; cited in Sylvia Barack Fishman, *A Breath of Life: Feminism in the American Jewish Community* (London/Hanover, NH: University Press of New England/Brandeis University Press, 1993), page 139.

6. Sylvia Barack Fishman, *A Breath of Life,* pages 138–141.

7. Job 25:2.

8. Rabbi Margaret Holub, "A Cosmology of Mourning" in *Lifecycles, Volume 1: Jewish Women on Life Passages and Personal Milestones,* Rabbi Debra Orenstein, ed. (Woodstock, VT: Jewish Lights, 1994), page 347.

Chapter

ALEINU, CONCLUDING A SERVICE

To you every knee must bow, every tongue vow loyalty

The final prayer of every service throughout the year (whether one is praying alone or with a congregation) is known by its first Hebrew word—*aleinu*. Those for whom the service seems too long feel relief when they hear the words and the melody of *Aleinu*. They may also welcome the opportunity to join others in reciting an ennobling prayer that affirms allegiance solely to God as the ultimate Sovereign and articulates a universal hope. We express the hope that all people everywhere will affirm that allegiance, aware that all of us as children of God must be concerned for each other's welfare, working for a world undivided by strife. Toward the end of each service, we pray that this Biblical vision will become a reality for all humanity.

The words of *Aleinu* reiterate the theme of God's sovereignty found throughout the prayer book. When we recite the *Shema*, for example, we accept and bear witness to God's sovereignty. (That recitation is known as *kabbalat ol malkhut Shamayim*, "accepting the yoke of the sovereignty of Heaven.") Three Biblical verses underscore this theme in *Aleinu*. The first

◈ Since the congregation follows *Aleinu* with the recitation of *Kaddish*, these verses have a liturgical function as well. *Kaddish* is never recited by itself; instead, it follows a Rabbinic lesson, a section of the service, a chapter of Psalms, or at least three Biblical verses, as is the case in *Aleinu.*—JH

◉ The first sentence of *Aleinu* recalls words in the Morning Service that appear a few passages after the initial morning blessings. "Our portion" (*helkenu*) alludes to God (compare to Psalms 16:5), and "our destiny" alludes to the Torah. The phrase "King of the king of kings" as a name for God incomparable probably was influenced by the Persians, a world power, who described their king as "the king of kings" (see Daniel 2:37).—JH

▨ *[The Aleinu lists four distinctions between Jews and non-Jews, reinforcing the concept of Jews as the chosen people. This concept has been a source of Jewish controversy for more than 100 years. Six opinions follow below.]*

Israel, in traditional Judaism, is likewise [that is, like the Catholic Church] accounted as belonging to the supernatural order.

The modern man who is used to thinking in terms of humanity as a whole can no longer reconcile himself to the notion of any people, or body of believers, constituting a type of society which may be described as belonging to a supernatural order. This is essentially what the doctrine of "election" [or chosenness] has hitherto implied. As a psychological defense to counteract the humiliation to which the Jewish people was subjected, the doctrine of "election" had its value. As an expression of the sense of spiritual achievement in the past, it had some justification in fact. But nowadays, when only present achievement tends to satisfy the human spirit, the doctrine of Israel's election in its traditional sense cannot be expected to make the slightest difference in the behavior or outlook of the Jew. From an ethical standpoint, it is deemed inadvisable, to say the least, to keep alive ideas of race or national superiority, inasmuch as they are known to exercise a divisive influence, generating suspicion and hatred. The harm which results from upholding the doctrine of "election" is not counterbalanced by the good it is supposed to do in inculcating a sense of self-respect. There are so many other ways of developing self-respect—ways that look to the future instead of to the past, to personal accomplishment rather than to collective pride—that there is no need of inviting the undesirable consequences of belief in the superiority of one's people, whichever people that be.—*Rabbi Mordecai M. Kaplan*[2]

Rabbi Mordecai Kaplan wrote in the 1930s, and the elimination of references to Jews as the chosen people remains standard in both Reform and Reconstructionist liturgy. In 2002, the web site of Congregation Kol Emet of Yardley, Pennsylvania, for instance, states: "We, as ➤

passage of *Aleinu* ends with a verse from Deuteronomy, and the second passage ends with a verse from Exodus and a verse from the prophet Zechariah. ▨

We are duty bound to praise the Lord of all, to acclaim the greatness of the One who forms creation, who did not fashion us like other nations of the world and did not establish us as other families of people on earth, who has not defined our portion like theirs, ◉ nor our destiny like that of their multitude. ▨ We bend the knee and bow, acknowledging the King of the king of kings, the Holy One, blessed be He, who stretches the heavens and lays the earth's foundations, whose glorious abode is the heavens above, whose mighty Presence inhabits the loftiest heights. He is our God, there is no other. Our King is truth, there is none but Him, as it is written in His Torah: "Know this day and take it to heart that the Lord is God in the heavens above and on the earth below. There is no other."[1]

When we chant this passage at the end of each service we continue a practice that began in about the 13th century. But the passage was composed even earlier—in the third century—for recitation on Rosh Hashanah as a poetic prelude to the verses celebrating God's sovereignty in the *Musaf* Service. ✳ Even today on Rosh Hashanah and on Yom Kippur, the leader

Reconstructionists, recognize the concept of chosenness as a cause for discrimination and, therefore, renounce that aspect of traditional Jewish belief, while focusing more on *mitzvah*, social action, and social equality."[3]—*Claudia Chernov*

The Jews' belief that they are the chosen people has often provoked antagonism from non-Jews. In the 1930s, as the Nazis were tightening the noose around the necks of German Jews, George Bernard Shaw remarked that if the Nazis would only realize how Jewish their notion of Aryan superiority was, they would drop it immediately. In 1973, in the aftermath of the Yom Kippur War, Yakov Malik, the Soviet ambassador to the United Nations, said: "The Zionists have come forward with the theory of the chosen people, an absurd ideology. That is religious racism." ...

   In light of these attacks, it is not surprising that some Jews have wanted to do away with the belief in Jewish chosenness. [Rabbi Mordecai Kaplan] advocated dropping chosenness for two reasons: to undercut accusations of the sort made by Shaw that the chosen people idea was the model for racist ideologies, and because it went against modern thinking to see the Jews as a divinely chosen people.

   But does it? After all, how did the notion of one God become known to the world? Through the Jews. And according to Jewish sources, that is the meaning of chosenness: to make God known to the world. As Rabbi Louis Jacobs has written: "We are not discussing a dogma incapable of verification, but the recognition of sober historical fact. The world owes to Israel the idea of the one God of righteousness and holiness. This is how God became known to mankind."

   Does Judaism believe that chosenness endows Jews with special rights in the way racist ideologies endow those born into the "right race"? Not at all. The most famous verse in the Bible on the subject of chosenness says the precise opposite: "You alone have I singled out of all the families of the earth. That is why I call you to account for all your iniquities" (Amos 3:2). Chosenness is so unconnected to any notion of race that Jews believe that the Messiah himself will descend from Ruth, a non-Jewish woman who converted to Judaism.—*Rabbi Joseph Telushkin*[4]

Living a Jewish life means joining a cause that is greater than ourselves. It means contributing to the betterment of the world, what some in the Jewish tradition have called *tikkun olam* (repairing the world). It means taking the secret of our soul and joining it to others who believe in redeeming the world through goodness and spiritual passion.

   This idea of mission is at the heart of the concept of chosenness. Judaism was chosen to teach Judaism, to teach the realization of and the path to one God. To be chosen is not to be better than others; it is to be called to be better than one currently is. To be chosen is to have a mission to improve the world and to feel that when we slight that task or abandon it, we are reneging on our deep purpose.—*Rabbi David J. Wolpe*[5]

The denial of our "Thou hast chosen us" vocation and singularity is a fatal blunder. Set apart from the gentiles, as evident in our incomparable history, the Jewish excellence and nobility surpasses that of any other nation. Our self-recognition implies an awareness of the Jewish grandeur; its renunciation spells a denial of the self. A people that disregards its essence, diminishes its stature. The obliteration of our exalted nature is the sole cause of our decline.—*Rabbi Abraham Isaac Kook*[6]

The chosenness of Israel relates exclusively to its spiritual vocation embodied in the Torah.... This spiritual vocation consists of two complementary functions, described as *goy kadosh*, that of a holy nation, and *mamlekhet kohanim*, that of a kingdom of priests. The first term denotes the development of communal separateness or differences in order to achieve a collective self-transcendence.... The second term implies the obligation of this brotherhood of the spiritual elite toward the rest of mankind; priesthood is defined by the prophets as fundamentally a teaching vocation.... It is the teaching of service and the service of teaching. It is concerned with the attainment of spirituality. Its particularistic aspect, while essential and indispensable, is propaedeutic [conveying preliminary instruction]; its universalist element remains the ultimate *telos*.—*Rabbi Norman Lamm*[7]

✳ *Aleinu* is usually attributed to Rav, a Sage of third-century Babylonia, though many scholars believe that it antedates Rav by a century.—*JH*

▓ For many years, a number of the members of my Reform congregation have joined the prayer leaders in prostrating themselves during the *Aleinu* prayer. As Rabbi Harlow observes, a number of Jewish communities participate in this practice on Rosh Hashanah and Yom Kippur. Traditionally, this occurs during the *Musaf* Service, an additional service long abandoned by Reform Judaism. But, in some Reform congregations, including my own, this practice has been reinstated on the High Holy Days. Congregants may be far away from the prayer leaders, yet they too stand facing the Ark, either in the sanctuary's center aisle or in front of the first row of pews.

As a Jewish feminist, whose theological understanding of the relationship between God and the Jewish people is one of partnership rather than of hierarchical domination, I have long struggled with the *Aleinu*, not just on the High Holy Days, but on Shabbat. To me, bending one's knees and bowing one's head reflect a model of faith rooted in submission—the model of Genesis 22 (Abraham's willingness to physically sacrifice his son) rather than of Genesis 18 (Abraham arguing over the justice of God's decision to kill all the inhabitants of Sodom and Gomorrah). The latter, unlike the former, is a model of shared, covenantal obligation.

In truth, my discomfort with bowing and with prostration does not simply reflect my personal theological convictions. It is also rooted in *The Union Prayerbook,* the Reform liturgy of my childhood. Its abbreviated *Aleinu* deleted the prayer's particular emphasis on God's choice of the Jewish people, while maintaining its universal hopes for the future. Identified as the "Adoration," the prayer was primarily recited in English, with two Hebrew lines remaining, usually sung by the cantor and choir, since few in the congregation knew Hebrew and no prayers were transliterated. The first of these lines, which included the phrase "We bend the knee and bow," was translated as "We bow the head in reverence." Like our Protestant neighbors, we may have bowed our heads in worship, but did not engage in an act that seemed as undignified (nor as traditionally Jewish) as moving our entire bodies in prayer.

In 1975, the Reform movement published a *New Union Prayerbook,* more commonly identified as *Gates of Prayer.* It includes three versions of the *Aleinu:* one with no translation of "We bend the knee and bow," and the others, like the *Aleinu* in the High Holy Day prayerbook, *Gates of Repentance,* replacing "We bow the head in reverence" with the more ambiguous "We therefore bow in awe." Bow what? Our heads? Or also, in some way, our bodies? Perhaps not surprisingly, the practice of falling prostrate during High Holy Day services is nowhere mentioned in *Gates of Repentance,* although other liturgical cues, such as "The Ark is opened," "The Torah is taken from the Ark," or "All are seated," are included. In part, this can be explained by the omission of the *Musaf* service, but the fact is that most Reform Jews were uncomfortable with, if not opposed to, prostrating ➤

of the service customarily bows, kneels, and stretches out fully prostrate on the floor before the Ark while chanting: "We bend the knee and bow." In some communities, members of the congregation also bow, kneel, and stretch out on the floor. ▓

Franz Rosenzweig has written,

> What distinguishes the Days of Awe from all other festivals is that here and only here does the Jew kneel. Here he does what he refused to do before the King of Persia, what no other power on earth can compel him to do, and what he need not do before God on any other day of the year, or in any other situation he may face during his lifetime. And he does not kneel to confess a fault or to pray for forgiveness of sins.... He kneels only on beholding the immediate nearness of God, hence on an occasion that transcends the earthly needs of today.[8]

Jews symbolically demonstrate ultimate allegiance during *Aleinu* throughout the year by slightly bending their knees and bowing at the waist while reciting, "We bend the knee and bow" *(va'anaḥnu korim umishtaḥavim).*

Aleinu clearly separates the people Israel from other ancient peoples. It contrasts Israel's worship of God with other nations' worship of idols. "God did not fashion us like other nations of the world and did not establish us like other families of people on earth." The original composition made the distinction even more clear by including words from the prophet Isaiah: "for they worship vanity and emptiness, and pray to a god who cannot save" (45:20). This was then followed by, "But we bend the knee and bow, acknowledging the King of the king of kings." In 14th-century Bohemia, a Jewish apostate characterized the passage from Isaiah as a slander directed against Christianity, and he so informed the Church authorities. ✹ This charge was ridiculous. Christianity did not exist at the time of Isaiah, who first spoke the words, nor did it exist in third-century Babylonia when the Rabbis incorporated Isaiah's words into the *Aleinu* prayer. Throughout late medieval and early modern times, however, many Christians believed the charge, and persecution persisted; in the early 18th century, Prussian authorities issued an edict against the use of those words, and European prayer books deleted the words. ✺ To this day, most editions of the prayer book still omit them from *Aleinu*, though some Orthodox prayer books have restored them.

The second passage of *Aleinu*, composed several centuries after the first, maintains a universal emphasis that balances the particularism of the opening passage. It articulates the hope that all who dwell on earth will join as one in the

themselves in prayer.

Thus, it was both theological conviction and religious upbringing that led me to hesitate the first time I was invited to participate in what was then an unprecedented practice either for clergy or lay members of my congregation. I looked up at the *bimah* and saw that one of the prayer leaders, who had earlier voiced opposition to this practice, not only had refrained from prostrating himself but had moved to the edge of the *bimah*, away from the other leaders. As they lay flat on the floor, he held his head high, without bowing it, as he customarily did in prayer. At that moment, a word long familiar to me from *The Union Prayerbook* ran through my mind. It was "stiff-necked," an adjective used to describe Jewish resistance to the will of God. I realized that my own resistance to bending the knee, bowing the head, and prostrating my body was similarly stiff-necked. It did not express individualism but narcissism, revealing my failure to acknowledge that I may be God's partner, but I am not God.

Quickly, I moved into the center aisle, and chanting, "We bend the knee and bow," I prostrated myself before the Ark. It was a humbling experience, instilling within me a sense of awe and obligation, leading me to recognize the importance of incorporating such moments into prayer. Rather than feeling that I had compromised my theological vision of human-divine partnership, I finally understood what it means to live in covenantal relationship with God.—*Ellen M. Umansky*

✹ In the Middle Ages, the prayer was censored by Christians as containing an implied insult to Christianity. They claimed that the verse "for they prostrate themselves before vanity and emptiness and pray to a god that saveth not" was a reference to Jesus. Pesah Peter, a 14th-century Bohemian apostate, spitefully alleged a connection between the numerical value[9] of the Hebrew word *varik*, "and emptiness," and *Yeshu*, the name of Christ.—*Editors of* Encyclopaedia Judaica[10]

✺ In spite of the historical anachronism implied by this interpretation [the connection between *Varik* and *Yeshu*], it was taken very seriously by Christians and Jews alike. The influential Jewish mystical school of German pietism (*hasidut Ashkenaz*) set great store by numerological interpretations of the liturgy, and Rabbi Jacob Moellin (*Maharil*), the renowned authority on liturgical customs, was accustomed to spit when he pronounced *varik* (the word also sounds like the Hebrew word for spitting [*yerikah*]).

When the Christians (often through the agency of apostates) heard how the Jews construed the prayer, they were understandably offended, which led to excising the offending sentence from many prayer books.—*Eliezer Segal*[11]

worship of God, but it does not imply that such worship will entail conversion to Judaism. When all people have ultimate allegiance only to God, peace and harmony will embrace the world. We pray that such a time will come soon.

⧆ *Aleinu leshabe'ah*, "We are duty bound to praise"—these words introduce a prayer whose essence might be phrased as: We give thanks to God for the chance to live a life that matters.

Aleinu begins with the somewhat problematic idea that we are not like everyone else, that our destiny is unique among the nations. This is true. "Unique," however, does not necessarily mean "better." When a child says to his or her mother, "You are the most wonderful mother in the world," the child does not intend to compare her with any other mother; the child is only speaking of adoring love. In the same way, our gratitude to God for "a destiny unique among the nations" need not be seen as a denigration of anyone else. I would hope that *every* nation would have reason to give thanks for its particular blessing to the universe.

What is true for nations is true for individuals: We each have a unique, God-given destiny to which we can rise. There is nothing more important than to live a life that matters and we give profound thanks to God for that opportunity.

The second part of the *Aleinu* is introduced by one of the most important phrases in the *siddur*. The strength of Jewish theology rests on this phrase: *al ken*, "therefore." We have affirmed God's sovereignty; we have bowed graciously before God's role as shaper of Jewish destiny. So what? Judaism requires of us that after we affirm our belief, there must be an answer to "so what," there must be a "therefore."

In this case, *"al ken"* leads immediately to a most basic premise of Jewish life: hope. We may not give up; we must always hope in the realization of our dreams of a perfected world. *Al ken nekaveh*, therefore, we hope.—*Rabbi Shira Milgrom*

⊛ "On that day the Lord alone shall be worshiped and shall be invoked by His singular name." This translation of this verse from Zechariah is based on a footnote in the new Jewish Publication Society translation of the *Tanakh*. A conventional translation reads: "On that day the Lord shall be One [*Ehad*] and His name One." Some scholars also prefer to translate the Hebrew *ehad* in *Kriat Shema* as "alone" rather than as "One."[14] —*JH*

Therefore we hope in You, ⧆ Lord our God, soon to see the splendor of Your might, removing idolatry from the earth with false gods utterly destroyed, perfecting the world with Your sovereignty so that all mortals will invoke Your name, turning back to You all the wicked of the earth. May all who dwell on earth realize that to You every knee must bend, every tongue vow loyalty. Before You, Lord our God, shall they bend and bow, paying homage to Your glory. May they all accept the yoke of Your sovereignty and may You reign over them, soon and forever. For sovereignty is Yours, and forever shall You reign in glory, as it is written in Your Torah, "The Lord shall reign for ever and ever."[12] And it is said, "The Lord shall be King of all the earth. On that day the Lord alone shall be worshiped and shall be invoked by His singular name."[13] ⊛

The focus of *Aleinu*, like that of other Hebrew prayers, moves from the particular to the universal. For centuries, tension between the particular and the universal has existed at the heart of Judaism, since non-Jews have inflicted suffering and slaughter on Jews. For example, the prayer book includes legitimate human cries for vengeance from the Book of Psalms. Nevertheless, authoritative Jewish teachers have stressed the need for balance, and they have emphasized tolerance and compassion. The prayer

Aleinu calls for the destruction of *idols*, not for the destruction of idolaters. As Rabbi Jacob Mecklenburg (1785–1865), the author of the prayer book commentary *Iyyon Tefillah*, explains:

> *Aleinu* is a kind of note to all of our prayers concerned with the destruction of the wicked. And this prayer serves to note the unworthiness of praying for the downfall of wicked people, for they are also the work of God's hand and He does not rejoice in their downfall.[15] Furthermore, Beruriah told her husband Rabbi Meir that we should not hope for the end of sinners but of sins. ※ *Aleinu* as a seal to our prayers comes to show our true intent ... namely, to pray for the end of wickedness, not of the wicked. The goal of all our prayers is that all people will return to the Lord our God and serve Him together.

The Jew in prayer focuses on God and the people Israel. We note, however, that Jews have always expressed concern not only with Jewish fate but with the fate of all humanity, even those who have oppressed Jews. All creatures on earth share the same fate. Our destinies are bound together.

We chant *Aleinu* almost immediately before concluding a prayer service. ✳ One of the greatest early Jewish legal authorities, Rabbi Jacob ben Asher (1270–1340),[18] articulated a reason: "Before leaving the synagogue for home, we chant *Aleinu* to plant in our hearts the singularity of God's sovereignty and to deepen and to strengthen the faith that He will sweep idolatry away so that false gods will be utterly destroyed."

After *Aleinu*, Mourner's *Kaddish* is recited.

※ Beruriah (in Babylonian Talmud, *Brakhot* 10a) concludes that we should not hope for the end of sinners but of sins, through an analysis of verse 104:35 from Psalms, which is the Psalm designated for Rosh Hodesh. Instead of reading "may sinners (*hotim*) be removed from the earth," Beruriah taught that the correct reading is: "may sins (*hata'im*) be removed from the earth." Beruriah taught that when no more sins exist in the world, no more sinners will exist either. Thus she understood the entire verse as: "When sins are removed from the earth, the wicked will be no more." Beruriah, wife of the distinguished Rabbi Meir, was renowned for her wit and wisdom. She was the only woman of Rabbinic times whose views on Jewish law were taken seriously. [16]—JH

✳ *[Tamara Cohen notes that a poem by the feminist artist Judy Chicago has become a popular addition after the* Aleinu *in non-traditional congregations.]*

> And then all that has divided us will merge
> And then compassion will be wedded to power
> And then softness will come to a world that is harsh and unkind
> And then both men and women will be gentle
> And then both women and men will be strong
> And then no person will be subject to another's will
> And then all will be rich and free and varied
> And then the greed of some will give way to the needs of many
> And then all will share equally in the Earth's abundance
> And then all will care for the sick and the weak and the old
> And then all will nourish the young
> And then all will cherish life's creatures
> And then all will live in harmony with each other and the Earth
> And then everywhere will be called Eden once again.
>
> —Judy Chicago[17]

Adon Olam

Many congregations sing this hymn after Mourner's *Kaddish* on Shabbat and on Festivals. Prayer books also include it in the early part of the daily Morning Service. We know neither the author nor the time of composition of this classic, although some attribute it to Solomon ibn Gabirol of Spain (11th century) or to his students. ▦

The first six lines focus solely on God's eternity, the divine presence throughout history and beyond. God's care sustains and reassures us in the uncertainties of our limited lives. The next to last line is based on verse 31:6 from Psalms: "Into Your care (literally, hand) I entrust my spirit; You redeem me, Lord, faithful God."

▦ The Artscroll *siddur* reflects the popular tradition that attributes authorship to Solomon ibn Gabirol. Rabbi Reuven Hammer, however, argues that the poem actually dates from the 15th century.[19] The *Encyclopaedia Judaica*, by contrast, suggests that the poem may be much older than even the 11th century, and may stem from Babylonia. For our purposes, the date of the poem is not significant, but it *is* interesting to note that despite its great popularity, its origins are somewhat obscure.— *Rabbi Daniel Gordis*

✸ This passage is the conclusion of tractate *Brahkot* of the Babylonian Talmud (64a). (For a translation, see Chapter 5, page 133.) On Shabbat and Holy Days it is recited after *Ein Keiloheinu* and before *Aleinu*.— JH

> The Lord eternal reigned before the birth of every living thing.
> When all was made as He ordained, then was only He known as King.
> When all is ended He will reign alone in awesome majesty.
> He was, He is, and He will be, glorious in eternity.
> Peerless and unique is He, with none at all to be compared.
> Beginningless and endless, His vast dominion is not shared.
> He is my God, my life's redeemer, my refuge in distress,
> My shelter sure, my cup of life, His goodness limitless.
> I place my spirit in His care, when I wake as when I sleep.
> God is with me, I shall not fear, body and spirit in His keep.

In many congregations, a child or a group of young children leads the singing of *Adon Olam*. Also, toward the end of a Shabbat or Festival service, before *Kaddish DeRabbanan* or before *Aleinu*, a group of children may read in unison a passage from the Talmud that stresses the association of Torah learning, peace, and children who study. ✸ Fulfilling these essential Jewish goals can assure the continued existence of our sacred tradition.

QUESTIONS FOR FURTHER STUDY AND REFLECTION

1. The first part of the *Aleinu* prayer was composed by the third century and the second part was composed several centuries later, yet only in the 13th century did *Aleinu* become the standard closing for every prayer service. What makes *Aleinu* particularly appropriate for the end of a service? What might account for its adoption as the closing prayer in the 13th century?

2. A quotation from the Book of Isaiah was deleted from the original *Aleinu*. Why? Does this deletion have any parallels in our era? Do you think that the passage from Isaiah should be restored to the *Aleinu*? Why or why not?

3. Do you bend the knee and bow during *Aleinu*? Why or why not? Do you prostrate yourself during *Aleinu* on Rosh Hashanah and Yom Kippur? Do you agree with Ellen Umansky that failure to do so indicates resistance to God's will? Why or why not?

4. Consider the arguments about the concept of the chosen people. What is your opinion? Do you agree with Mordecai Kaplan—and view Rabbi Norman Lamm, as well as Rabbis Joseph Telushkin and David Wolpe, as apologists? Or do you feel that these latter three scholars give a well-reasoned defense?

5. Rabbi Abraham Isaac Kook, the first Ashkenazi Chief Rabbi of pre-State Israel, wrote unhesitatingly: "the Jewish excellence and nobility surpasses that of any other nation." Yet he also wrote: "The obliteration of our exalted nature is the sole cause of our decline." How do you interpret these phrases?

6. Many prayers and blessings, not only *Aleinu*, include the concept of God choosing the Jewish people (for example, the Friday evening *Kiddush*). At present, Reconstructionist prayer books consistently alter those prayers to eliminate the concept of the chosen people, while Reform liturgy alters some prayers, and offers other prayers in both traditional and revised versions. Which approach do you prefer? Why?

7. What is the tension between particular and universal concerns in *Aleinu*? What themes does the second passage of Aleinu teach us?

8. The *Aleinu* envisions the end of days when God "alone shall be worshiped." A poem by Judy Chicago presents a modern vision of that day at the end of days. What would you add to (or subtract from) this poem? What does your vision encompass?

1. Deuteronomy 4:39.

2. Mordecai M. Kaplan, *Judaism as a Civilization: Toward a Reconstruction of American-Jewish Life* (New York: Macmillan, 1934), pages 43-44.

3. Congregation Kol Emet, Yardley, PA, "Statement of Principles," at www.kolemet.com, 2001.

4. Rabbi Joseph Telushkin, *Jewish Literacy* (New York: William Morrow, 1991), pages 505-506.

5. David J. Wolpe, *Why Be Jewish?* (New York: Henry Holt, 1995), pages 39-40.

6. Rabbi Abraham Isaac Kook (1865-1935), Israel's first Chief Rabbi, cited in Paul Eidelberg, "The Chosen People," *The Maccabean Online,* May 1998, at www.free-man.org/m_online/may98/eidelber.htm.

7. Rabbi Norman Lamm, *"The Condition of Jewish Belief," A Symposium Compiled by the Editors of Commentary Magazine,* 1966, cited by Hillel, The Foundation for Jewish Campus Life, in "Apologetics—Trying to Make the Problem Go Away" at www.hillel.org/Hillel/New Hille.nsf.

8. Franz Rosenzweig, *Franz Rosenzweig, His Life and Thought,* Nahum N. Glatzer, ed. (New York: Farrar, Straus and Young, 1953), page 328.

9. Each Hebrew letter has a numerical value—*alef* is 1, *bet* is 2, and so on. The numerical value of a word is the sum of the values of each of the letters. Numerical correspondences between words are important in Jewish thought.

10. From "Aleinu Le-Shabbe'ah," *Encyclopaedia Judaica,* volume 2 (Jerusalem: Keter, 1971), page 557.

11. Eliezer Segal, "From the Sources: Vanity, Emptiness and the Throne of Glory," *Jewish Free Press* (Calgary), September 28, 2000, pages 10-11.

12. Exodus 15:18.

13. Zechariah 14:9.

14. See pages 57-59 of Chapter 3.

15. See Babylonian Talmud, *Sanhedrin* 39b.

16. Refer to *Encyclopaedia Judaica*, volume 4, page 701. See *Jewish Encyclopedia* (first published in 1901), volume 3, page 109, for an interesting account of Beruriah's life written by Henrietta Szold.

17. Judy Chicago, "Merger Poem," copyright © 1979.

18. His classic work is known as the *Tur* or as the *Arba Turim*.

19. Reuven Hammer, *Entering Jewish Prayer* (New York: Schocken, 1994), page 110.

UNIT TWO:

CONTEMPORARY ISSUES

Chapter

WOMEN'S SPIRITUAL ALTERNATIVES

We bless that which is human and divine in each of us

Tamara Cohen

The beginning of the 21st century is an unprecedented era in the history of Jewish women's spirituality. Though Judaism has never been a static or monolithic religion and multiple paths of connection to the divine have always existed, the kinds of transformations introduced by Jewish feminists over the past 25 years are indeed revolutionary. And yet Jewish feminist spirituality remains rooted in ancient tradition and in dialogue with it.

Confronting God

The Hebrew prayer book includes many different texts written over the course of centuries, even millennia. Yet, until recently, the authorship of all prayers had been uniformly male and the language of the prayer book had reflected the underlying assumption that the primary speaker of the prayers was male. Furthermore, until even more recently, all Hebrew prayer books addressed a male God. Indeed, even today, every Hebrew blessing (*brakhah*) within the Conservative and Orthodox prayer book reifies God as King of the world. Speaking about God in exclusively masculine language reflects more than just the structure of the Hebrew language, in which every noun has a gender. ▦ In fact, referring to God as a male reflects and reinforces a system in which power and manhood are linked.

The Rabbis of the time of the Talmud, using the most exalted language they could, named God as King of the world. Though our world differs enormously from the Rabbis' world, we have not yet fully overturned the equation of supreme power with maleness. Changing the male imagery we use to refer to God has forced us to confront our assumptions about men and about power. Over the past decades, feminists have successfully challenged these assumptions in the human realm. We are now comfortable with women in the United States Congress, on the Supreme Court, and on the *bimah* (pulpit). God, however, has remained the final frontier. ◉

▦ No matter where a Jew prays, and no matter the gender of the worshiper, the Hebrew prayers that she or he says are sexist. Hebrew is a gender-specific language. Unlike English, in which nouns and pronouns may denote male or female (for example, king, queen), in Hebrew the parts of speech in their grammatical form have masculine or feminine endings. [In other words, English nouns and verbs are usually neutral, whereas every Hebrew noun has a masculine or a feminine gender, and Hebrew verbs also reveal gender. For example, a door and a fish are gender neutral in English, yet in Hebrew a door *(delet)* is feminine and a fish *(dag)* is masculine.] So the common beginning of countless Hebrew prayers in the daily and holiday liturgy—*Barukh Attah Adonai*—all address God as a male being. The pronoun *attah* means "you" (masculine), and *Adonai* is a noun (masculine) meaning "master."

The concept these words give us—of a God exclusively male—is theologically false to Judaism, which posits that God has male and female components and that these are made manifest in the male and female humans created in God's own image. However, the exclusively masculine appellations are one reason most of us imagine God as somehow male, and therefore perhaps [we] imagine human males as next to godliness. If we imagine Moses as Charlton Heston every Pesa<u>h</u>, we seem also to imagine God as some spiritual correlative of Michelangelo's Moses. God "looks like" the worshiper—that is, male. Rita M. Gross[1] says: "Though language about God cannot really tell us about the nature of God, because of the limitations of language and the nature of God, it can tell us a great deal about those who create and use the God-language."—*Susan Weidman Schneider*[2]

✺ In both Hebrew and English, the fact that the grammatical gender of the words "king" and *melekh* is masculine does not imply or teach that God has the characteristics of a male. Referring to God as "King" does not mean that God is a king; it is an image conveying the concept of a sovereign presence. Similarly, "the Lord is my shepherd" does not mean that God is either a shepherd or a lord; the words in this passage are images conveying the concept of a divine being who is both caring and in charge. Words naming and describing God are not to be taken literally; to do so resembles the approach of idolatry, because God is imageless and genderless. Many of those who maintain that maleness in God is implied by the word "king" substitute another English word for it; they also use gender-neutral English words as substitutes for "Lord" and for the masculine pronouns "He," "Him," and ➤

Feminists are not the first Jews to take issue with the traditional prayer book. In 1818 Abraham Geiger published a radically altered prayer book, one of the earliest acts of the Reform movement in Germany. Significant liturgical change has since become ongoing within Reform Judaism, and the prayer book has continued to evolve. In the early 20th century, Reconstructionist and Conservative prayer book editors also instituted various liturgical changes. Yet the changes begun by Jewish feminists may ultimately prove more comprehensive and far-reaching than any previous revolutions.

Feminist theologians, seekers, and thinkers have been talking about, writing about, experimenting with, and creating new ways of speaking to and about God since the 1970s. Once religious feminists recognized that accepted images of God in Jewish liturgy were incomplete, they were bound to choose their course of action. Some of them abandoned Judaism, drifting toward goddess-centered or Eastern meditative religions, either permanently or for many years. Many more religious feminists remained strongly attached to Judaism, but made varying accommodations between the time-honored Hebrew liturgy and feminist ideals. Some accepted that the power of the traditional liturgy was too strong to tamper with or to change, but they creatively interpreted the meaning behind the prayers. Some altered the English translations, but left the Hebrew liturgical texts intact. Similarly, some explored new images of God through feminist analysis, through original stories and poetry and art, and through additional ceremonies that had their own new texts; these many innovations were additions to the standard Hebrew liturgy, not replacements for it. ✳ Finally, some feminists modified the standard liturgy, and some embarked on the project of inventing new Jewish liturgy, often basing the new prayers on traditional texts as well as on feminist ideas and experiences. Here I will focus primarily on two options: new ceremonies and new liturgy.

"His." This approach provides a solution *only in translation*. In Hebrew prayer texts, all nouns, pronouns, verbs, and adjectives referring to God are grammatically masculine. The words of those who pray in Hebrew—the language of Jewish prayer, the language of revelation— are *never* gender neutral. In other words, those who demand gender neutrality are denied the opportunity to pray using traditional Hebrew texts. If maintaining gender neutrality is important, it should apply in both Hebrew and English.

The word "god," in contrast to "goddess," is masculine in gender. The word "god" does not, however, attribute male characteristics to God. Apparently because of this, those who substitute "God" for "King" or "Lord" in English-language translations understand "God" as a gender-neutral word.

Commendably, "assumptions about men and about power" are changing. Gender-language changes in prayer may have helped women to change their self-image, and may have helped men in thinking about inclusiveness as well. Changing words of prayer, however, does little if anything about "enhancing respect for women among people who do not feel any, or increase women's authority and earnings in places where prejudice is entrenched" (in the words of Jacques Barzun).[3]

God "remaining the final frontier" reflects a misunderstanding. God, unique and incomparable, is not to be included as part of some other category or agenda.—*Rabbi Jules Harlow*

✳ Rabbi Jill Hammer relates to God in a deeply personal way, [yet she] does not cry out to the King of the universe. Her God is a Her.

The images vary: There's the wise, old woman wrapped in a voluminous, black robe. There's the one Rabbi Hammer calls the "kitchen chemist," a housewife who hovers over a set of bubbling pots, supervising the creation of new potions. And there's the one she mentions first in a conversation about God—the pregnant woman, her hair long and honey-colored, her naked form bathed in a celestial glow.

She, the Blessed One with burgeoning belly, first appeared to Rabbi Hammer in a dream [and] handed Rabbi Hammer an unlit lantern with the benediction, "Don't worry, you'll understand someday." ...

Of course, many a rabbi, including Rabbi Hammer, could tell you: God is beyond gender. And yet, many a Jew could also tell you that for some people, including Rabbi Hammer, a close relationship with the Divine depends on personalizing God.

"Some people really need the female image," says Rabbi Hammer.... For other people, she says, "God is a thin man with a very different sensibility."—*Elicia Brown*[4]

Jewish feminists from all walks of life have played a role in liturgical innovation—countless Jewish studies professors and students, Rosh Hodesh group members, rabbis, and synagogue members have written their own blessings and engaged in their own explorations of feminine-gender language. Nevertheless, a few individuals stand out as leaders in the movement for liturgical change. Prominent feminist theologians who are engaged in articulating Jewish feminist spirituality include Judith Plaskow, Ellen Umansky, Lynn Gottlieb, and Marcia Falk.

The first—and perhaps the most common—type of feminist liturgical reinterpretation has involved mining Jewish sacred literature for female-oriented language. In 1976, in *Siddur Nashim*, an experimental women's prayer book, ▦ Naomi Janowitz and Maggie Wenig expand upon the meaning of *Meraḥem*—the One who has mercy—which Jews recite in *Barukh She'amar*, the opening prayer of *Pesukei DeZimra* (see page 28). Janowitz and Wenig play with the relationship between the Hebrew words *meraḥem* and *reḥem*—merciful one and womb—as the two words appear to derive from the same Hebrew root. Rather than translating *Barukh Meraḥem al ha'aretz* as "Blessed is He who has mercy on the earth," they write, "Blessed is She whose womb covers the earth."[6] ❂ Thus, Janowitz and Wenig find their female God embedded within the traditional liturgy.

▦ [*Naomi Janowitz and Maggie Wenig wrote the following introductory explanation in 1976.—Editor*] According to Jewish tradition, God has both male and female attributes. Yet, in most prayer books God is portrayed in exclusively male terms, and all the people referred to in the liturgy are men.

This distorted view of God influences the way men and women view themselves, their roles in Judaism, and even their relationships with God. As a result, women may participate in rituals, lead services, and even become rabbis, and yet still not view themselves as having been created in God's image.

To help rectify this situation, we have been working on a woman's prayer book which emphasizes the feminine aspects of God and attempts to embrace our experiences as women.

Our book is an affirmation of our choice to remain within the tradition and to sanctify our everyday lives as women. Through our prayers we define ourselves as women in terms of our relationship with God and struggle with the meaning of this relationship. Our metaphors and ideas initially come out of a wrestling with the liturgy—trying to make it embrace our experience—rather than out of an effort to develop a systematic theology. In the process, we have arrived at concepts and interpretation which we can believe in, and through which we can pray.

In addition, our liturgy assumes the inclusion of women in the *minyan* (quorum of worshipers), it assumes their full participation in the Torah service, it assumes that they will serve as "messenger of the congregation" and that they will recite the Mourners' *Kaddish*. It acknowledges their participation in these rituals by using their own words in the prayers and blessings they are to recite....

We have found that when women are reminded that they, too, are created in the image of God, they can bring forth what they carry inside—the beauty, wisdom, and strength gained as the bearers of 4,000 years of tradition.—*Naomi Janowitz and Maggie Wenig*[5]

❂ Janowitz and Wenig's interpretation—"whose womb covers the earth"—is at odds with the meaning of the classic Hebrew text. [Furthermore, even though the root letters of *meraḥem* and *reḥem* are the same (resh ḥet mem), many scholars doubt that the words actually derive from the same root.] The image itself lacks grace. A more appropriate interpretation might be "who embraces the earth" or "who nurtures the earth."—*Rabbi Jules Harlow*

Similarly, many Jewish feminists have sought to claim *Shekhinah* as a female name for the divine, rejoicing that time-honored Jewish teachings contain a feminine-gender noun for God. When Rabbi Lynn Gottlieb discovered *Shekhinah*, which she defines as "She-Who-Dwells-Within," she felt "like an orphan who uncovered documents that proved that her mother was not dead."[7] Rabbi Gottlieb continues to embrace *Shekhinah* as the immanent God, the exiled feminine seeking to return. Similarly, Judith Plaskow writes that *Shekhinah* has been hailed as "precisely that aspect of God with which we can be in relation, and it is experienced in joint study, community gatherings, lovemaking, and other moments of common and intimate human connection."[8]

Other feminists, however, express skepticism about whether *Shekhinah* offers a new name or image for God. They point out that the Kabbalists pictured *Shekhinah* as the passive female receptacle of active male divinity. ⌘ According to Rita Gross, *Shekhinah* cannot serve as the Jewish feminist answer to male God language because "almost without exception, traditional Jewish usage speaks of some variant of God and His *Shekhinah*," making it clear that *Shekhinah* was an "attachment to or appendage of the more familiar male images of God."[9]

⌘ The Rabbis of the Talmud use the feminine-gender word *Shekhinah* to mean God's presence. In early Rabbinic literature, *Shekhinah* is the aspect of the God that resides among the people and travels with them into exile. The medieval Kabbalists more fully develop the concept of *Shekhinah* as a female aspect of God. They identify *Shekhinah* as the female consort of the male Godhead.—*TC*

Other directions for new metaphors and names, also explored by Rabbi Lynn Gottlieb, stem from creative translations of ancient Hebrew words and phrases for use in the English-language prayers that she composes. For example, in "A Psalm in Praise of the *Shekhinah* for Shabbat" Rabbi Gottlieb provides new translations for words such as *Elohim*, a Biblical word usually translated as God, and *Shaddai*, usually translated as Almighty.

A Psalm in Praise of the *Shekhinah* for Shabbat

Praise Her, most awesome of the mighty!
Revere Her, She is a woman of the people.
Adore Her, She is clothed in love....

Praise Her when you come upon Her name:
Tehom, Coiled Serpent Woman;
Elat Hashahar, She Who Ascends with the Dawn;
Shaddai, Many-breasted Woman, Whose milk overflows;
Ahoti Kalah, Sister Whole unto Herself;

Em Hamerahemet, Mother Whose Womb Is Compassion;
Malkhat Shamayim, Woman of the Endless Skies;
Dayenet HaEmet, Seal of Truth;
Yehoyah, Spiritwind Woman;
Elohim, SheHe in Love with Life;
Shekhinah, Beloved Friend.

She is the breath of all living;
wild horses dance round Her moon.

Power is in Her hands;
love is in Her heart.

Praise Her
when you come upon Her name
singing inside you
Y'la la la la la la la la la la la la[10]

Marcia Prager uses Kabbalist teaching to interpret the word *Adonai* in feminist ways. Traditionally Jews have said the word *Adonai* when they encountered the Tetragrammaton, the four Hebrew letters *yod-hei-vav-hei* that form God's name. ▓ *Adonai*, however, derives from the Hebrew word *adon (ayin, dalet, vav, nun)*, which means "lord" or "master," and which bears no linguistic relation to the Hebrew Tetragrammaton. Many feminists reject the hierarchy inherent in the word *adon*, and so do not use the word *Adonai* when reciting a prayer that includes the four-letter name of God; they instead substitute Hebrew words that mean, for example, "eternal" or "all present." Prager, however, interprets the word *adon* not as a commander or ruler but as an expert or virtuoso in relationship to humanity. She uses the metaphor of a violin master who plays upon the violin while the violin itself plays upon the master: "The relationship to our *Adon* is one of intimate receptivity. To experience God in the aspect of *Adon* is to heighten our receptivity to what God is calling us to do and become."[11]

The Reconstructionist prayer book *Kol Haneshamah* (1994) employs a unique strategy for translating the four-letter name of God. Rabbi David A. Teutsch, chair of the Prayerbook Commission, writes that Reconstructionist theologians have rejected the translation "my Lord" (which is based

▓ The four Hebrew letters of God's name, *yod-hei-vav-hei*, are never pronounced in Jewish tradition. Some Christian movements do, however, translate the name as Jehovah. During prayer, Orthodox and Conservative congregations always say the word *Adonai* when the text of the prayer book reads *yod-hei-vav-hei*.

The Hebrew letters are themselves considered sacred. Many printers employ an abbreviation for the Tetragrammaton so that the book will not require the special handling that is necessary for these holy letters; the abbreviation may be *yod-yod*, a *hei* followed by an apostrophe, or a *dalet* followed by an apostrophe. During prayer, these abbreviations are also read aloud as *Adonai.—Claudia Chernov*

on the word *Adonai*) because of their commitment to gender-inclusive translation and because Lord "does not work as living imagery."[12] The Prayerbook Commission decided to print each English translation of

the Tetragrammaton in capital letters to distinguish it, and then, in the context of each individual prayer, to formulate a new name for God. *Kol Haneshamah* thus translates the Tetragrammaton in many different ways in different prayers. Some of the translations are: THE ALL MERCIFUL, GOOD ONE, KIND ONE, OMNIPRESENT, ONE EVERLASTING, THE ETERNAL ONE, ALL-KNOWING ONE, ILLUMINATOR, COMPASSIONATE ONE.

Contemporary Reform liturgies also use only gender-neutral English for the Tetragrammaton, generally either "God" or "Eternal One."

Neither Reconstructionist nor Reform prayer books translate the Hebrew word *Melekh* as "King," instead using "Sovereign" or "Ruler"—words that retain the original intent of the Hebrew but have no explicit link to man or woman.

Another type of feminist liturgical innovation has involved the creative transposition of divine names that stem from ancient Near Eastern goddess myths or the adaptation of female images from other religions into a Jewish idiom. Some feminist liturgists have written prayers using the term "Goddess" and its Hebrew equivalents *Elilah* or *Elah*.[13] ❊

Ellen M. Umansky, however, warns that within Jewish cul-

❊ "Degendered language" and "inclusive language" are not the same thing.

Degendered language replaces a gender-specific term with a non-specific one. For example, we replace "fathers" with "ancestors" when speaking of previous generations of the Jewish community....

Inclusive language is very different. It adds a feminine term where only a masculine term had been used. For example, we would use "fathers and mothers" (or "mothers and fathers") for the traditional "fathers" in speaking of the progenitors of the Jewish people. Referring to God, inclusive language uses "King and Queen" or "Father and Mother" (or vice versa) to reflect the inclusiveness of the Divinity....

I favor the use of degendered language wherever possible, to refer to both the Jewish people and to God. It respects and acknowledges the contribution of women and men to the Jewish people. It preserves the sense of relationship between humans and our God. It also respects the ultimate mystery of God's nature: God has no gender in the human sense, but when God's nature is reflected in human beings, it is found in both male and female....

Inclusive language (as defined above) is problematic and even dangerous when applied to God, because our language does affect how we think and relate to things and people. Addressing God as "Queen" or "Mother" leads to goddess religion, with serious consequences for the Jewish sense of God.

The most common understanding of the origin of things in goddess religion is that the goddess gives birth to the world and everything in it. Birth is the uniquely and exclusively feminine means of creating. Nature and all its processes are divine and reflect the divine will. These views are called "pantheism"—all that is, is divine.... Since pantheism sees nature and its processes as divine, the eternally repeated cycle of nature is viewed as an expression of divine will. There can be, and should be, no essential change in the way things are. Attempts to effect fundamental change are opposed as tampering with the divine will.

Since nature is morally neutral, viewing nature and its processes as an expression of the divine will leads necessarily to amorality. Nature's rule is kill or be killed; there is no moral distinction between predator and prey. The implications for human social relations are catastrophic:

• Dualism is rejected. The terms "good" and "evil" lose any essential significance and become irrelevant. Suffering and death are necessary so that the next stage, rebirth, can be reached.

• There are no absolute standards for human conduct, since these ➤

cannot be derived from nature. Rather, we can derive from nature that there are no such absolutes.

• Human free will is dissolved in the determinism of nature. Human choices and actions are not ultimately significant, because nature will do what it will do....

Let us use gender-neutral language to refer to God and human beings, because it more faithfully reflects reality. Let us add references to our matriarchs to our liturgy and honor their special contributions to our history. But let us not flirt with the theological dangers of paganism inherent in using feminine language for God.—*Rabbi Paula L. Reimers*[15]

▨ The Jewish renewal movement is an informal grouping (of mainly non-Orthodox Jews) rather than a denominational affiliation. Its focus is personal spiritual growth, and it relies upon many hasidic and mystical teachings, while also stressing contemporary social justice. Rabbi Arthur Waskow is a prominent renewal leader.—*Claudia Chernov*

◉ The regular use of *Elohut* or of *Yah* in Hebrew prayer breaks the unity that the prayer book still provides to Jews throughout the world. Even today, the unifying nature of Hebrew prayer acts as a kind of glue holding together the increasingly diverse and fragmented Jewish people. Feeling at home in a Hebrew prayer service anywhere in the world has a great value. True, significant liturgical differences already exist between different Jewish communities. Nevertheless, replacing the name of God in standard blessings and in liturgical readings that are still shared by the majority of world Jewry can only intensify the divisiveness and increase confusion.—*Rabbi Jules Harlow*

✻ In January 1986, *Sh'ma* magazine published a piece by Arthur Green, then academic head of the Reconstructionist Rabbinical College, entitled, "Keeping Feminist Creativity Jewish." It was followed by three responses: by D.C. economist Ronnie Levin, by Buffalo educator Drora Setel, and by me, Arlene Agus, a New York consultant. Rabbi Green's article and the three accompanying responses offer a window into Jewish feminist history.

In the early 1970s, the ideal sought by religious feminists seemed modest and attainable—equal access to all that was Jewish. We had intended to spiritually tiptoe in, gender invisible, take our places at tradition's table, and tiptoe out—leaving Judaism intact, though perhaps enhanced by our presence.

Secure in our affection for and commitment to tradition, we initially sought to transform neither ourselves nor our people. The measure of our seriousness was our desire for "more": more *mitzvot* (religious imperatives), more knowledge, a more personal relationship with sacred words, and a more personal relationship with the One to whom sacred words are addressed. In these strivings we did not see ourselves as ▶

ture the Hebrew words for a female deity are so deeply entwined with idolatry that using them might cut Jewish feminists off from *klal Yisrael*, the Jewish people. Umansky urges her fellow Jewish feminists to "suggest a naming of the Goddess that would address her as the feminine aspect of the divine, not as a separate idolatrous divine being."[14] She proposes making up a new word, or perhaps appropriating an existing word. Umansky suggests using *Elohut*, a feminine-gender word for the divine, that carries no specifically masculine or feminine connotations but that is capable of acquiring a feminist orientation. Marcia Falk, in fact, uses *Elohut*, the word suggested by Umansky, in her version of the *Shema* (see page 217).

Within Jewish renewal communities, ▨ *Yah*, a Biblical name for God, has been widely embraced as a replacement for *Adonai* when the Hebrew text reads *yod-hei-vav-hei*. ◉ *Yah* is familiar from the compound word *Halleluyah* (praise God), and the Bible treats it as a masculine noun (in Psalms 118:18, for instance). The word, however, has a feminine-sounding ending, and today many Jewish renewal activists pair it with feminine verbs. As the pronunciation of *Yah* approximates an exhalation, the name represents God as the breath of life.[16]

In short, an early and

still-ongoing Jewish feminist endeavor has been the reinterpretation of traditional images of the divine and the addition of new female images to complement the male images. For many Jewish feminists, though, gender is not the only issue. The Jewish feminist changes that began with relatively simple English-language substitutions from male to female—She instead of He, Mother instead of Father, Queen instead of King—have revealed to many that the gender of Hebrew nouns is not the only obstacle to prayer. ✳ The images themselves convey an understanding of God that violates contemporary feminists' beliefs and sense of the divine. The image of God as King is unsatisfactory both because it is masculine and because it connotes the autocratic rule by God over humanity. Queen, though feminine, also connotes autocracy. Hence, for many, a feminist critique of domination necessitates new images of God that move beyond the standard liturgy's commanding Master of All.

Consequently, feminist theologians have moved from questions of language to questions about the Jewish relationship with God. Some feminists assert that no hierarchical relationship can be a holy relationship. A social structure in which some are powerful and others are subservient has

importing an alien, secular doctrine into Judaism. Instead, we felt that we were bringing to fruition certain intrinsic and essential characteristics of Judaism itself. We saw Judaism as a legal-spiritual framework based on gender-neutral values that historically had been progressive toward the status of women. In retrospect, our naiveté was almost unfathomable. It left us prepared neither for the vehemence of the ensuing reaction, nor for the immensity of the task ahead, a task that would ultimately transform both us and our community.

Rabbi Art Green's 1986 critique of Jewish feminist liturgical changes made clear that feminist prayer creativity—once viewed as an exploratory step toward full ritual participation—had become enmeshed in the charged atmosphere of fear, mistrust, and far-reaching ideological debate. Rabbi Green was disturbed by the prayers being composed by feminists "of a more radical order" which appeared to be descending a slippery slope toward unacceptable phrases of pagan or goddess worship. He stated that the very ineffability of God required that prayer metaphors respect inviolate, time-honored boundaries reflective of the theological and linguistic uniqueness of Judaism. He presented the *Kabbalah* as a model for responsible innovation, as kabbalists had introduced a multiplicity of novel—but recognizably Jewish—male and female images. Though he claimed "that the God of Israel … is a relatively genderless male deity," he cautioned feminists to address "their needs" and "their own reality" by choosing language inoffensive to "educated Jews," language that would avoid the feminine forms, which "backfire" by "exaggerating the maleness of traditional language." Finally, he challenged feminism to avoid further fragmenting the Jewish praying community along gender lines, to act with "taste and moderation," and to "proclaim itself as spiritually and linguistically Jewish" by rejecting "new-paganism or … witchcraft."

Ronnie Levin rejected Rabbi Art Green's monolithic characterization of normative Judaism, citing the debates typically quoted in the Talmud, the evolution of Rabbinic prayer after the destruction of the Temples, the diverse authorship of the *siddur*, and the layers of liturgy added over seven centuries, for example, Mourner's *Kaddish* and *Kabbalat Shabbat*. She dismissed as "straw targets" the slippery slope toward paganism and the specter of feminist separatism. On the contrary, she asserted that women seek to penetrate, not bifurcate, the Jewish life of the synagogue, the Hebrew school, and the life-cycle ceremonies. She predicted that changes that initially appeared radical would ultimately become normative. Indeed, her words have proved to be correct 16 years later.

Drora Setel attributed Rabbi Art Green's "ahistorical naiveté" to the resistance of authority to change. She observed that such resistance resulted from a perception of the "deeply transformative nature of Jewish feminism," and she drew historic parallels between linguistic exclusion and societal oppression of women. Considering the ➤

resulted in oppression of women (as well as oppression of children and of various classes of men). The hierarchical relationship between God and Israel suggests subservience. Thus, Judith Plaskow asserts that we need not conceive of God's power as domination, and she urges us to think carefully about the type of power we ascribe to God in our attempts to understand and address divinity. Her thorough critique heightens our awareness of the different types of metaphors for power. For example, the power of a king is dominion over subjects, while the power of light does not involve any type of subjugation.

Marcia Falk, the only contemporary feminist liturgist who has compiled a complete prayer book, fiercely advocates for non-hierarchical relationships both in life and in liturgy. After many years of circulating her innovative prayers at conferences and feminist collectives, Falk published her groundbreaking *The Book of Blessings: New Jewish Prayers for Daily Life, the Sabbath, and the New Moon Festival* in 1996. Falk, an accomplished poet and translator, includes in *The Book of Blessings* her own Hebrew prayers alongside their English translations, and she also includes women's Yiddish and Hebrew poetry with her own English translations. In doing this, Falk attempts to fill the void in contemporary prayer books, which (at best) relegate women's voices to English translation yet retain male-authored, male-gender Hebrew language. Falk also gives new life to the work of Jewish women poets. In her Shabbat morning *Amidah*, for example, Falk follows the framework of the traditional *Amidah* with its seven blessings on seven themes, but she compiles each of her seven blessings through the use of women's poetry. Falk often gives the individual a choice of more than one poem that addresses the blessing's theme, such as ancestors, holiness, and peace. ▣

Falk, a devoted student of the Hebrew language, is well equipped to pioneer liturgical changes in Hebrew, not just in English. For Falk, the

Jewishness of ritual symbols, she reminded Rabbi Green of the long history of external, yet positive, influences on Jewish practice. Feminism, she hoped, like many of the other influences, could enrich and engage contemporary Jews. She characterized Rabbi Green's Judaism as monolithic, elitist, and Eastern European, and called upon him to reflect on the significance, not just the threat, of feminism.

My own 1986 response took issue with Rabbi Green's conflation of radicals and moderates. I argued that this blurring of distinctions could blind us to the real needs of real women in Jewish ritual—as well as many other spheres. Such blindness, I observed, was responsible for the slow progress in pay equity, Jewish leadership opportunities, and child care. Furthermore, it inhibited women from taking bold, original approaches to the betterment of Jewish life, in the manner of their forebears, the three heroines of Ḥanukkah. I compared Art's criticisms to a responsum by five Orthodox rabbis who had recently claimed that women's prayer groups were splitting the Jewish community and injecting alien influences into Judaism. I challenged Art to turn his thoughts away from wrong-headed solutions and toward right-headed questions on enhancing the role of women in Judaism.—*Arlene Agus*

▣ At Jewish retreats and conferences, Marcia Falk herself has led full services based entirely upon her liturgy. In addition, Congregation Beth Simchat Torah, which serves New York's lesbian, gay, bisexual, and transgendered Jewish community, holds a monthly service based entirely on Falk's *The Book of Blessings*. Many Reform, Reconstructionist, and ➤

changes needed to create useable and relevant liturgy for our era are more fundamental than the inclusion of references to Jewish women and are

even more fundamental than the use of gender-neutral language to address God.

Falk's passionately non-hierarchical spirituality translates into new images of the relationship between God and humanity, Israel and the rest of the world, Shabbat and the rest of the week, and, of course, women and men. For Falk, the dichotomies represented by such pairs are false. Difference does not imply superiority. Falk bases her theology in belief in an immanent, omnipresent divinity that "inheres in all creatures and nurtures all creation."[17] For Falk, Jewish monotheism must embrace the diverse nature of the one God.

Falk's prayers and blessings often describe God using natural metaphors, especially source or wellspring of life.

Conservative congregations also use selections from Falk's liturgy, both during Shabbat services and at special holiday or other ceremonies. In Reconstructionist and Conservative synagogues that read excerpts from *The Book of Blessings*, Marcia Falk's prayers usually do not serve as replacements for the text of the *siddur*, but as supplements to the established prayers.—*Claudia Chernov*

◉ The first time I heard a distinctly feminist version of the blessing over bread was at a conference on Judaism and gender. We broke bread with the following blessing: *Brukhah At Yah, Ruah haolam, hamotziah lehem min haaretz.* My son, sitting with me, said, "If we're going to feminize everything, why not: *Brukhah At Yah Ruah haolam hamotziah lahmaniah* [a roll] *min haadamah* [the ground]." I laughed, because for me—even though I am a feminist—changing the language and the gender of the familiar blessing evoked feelings of discomfort. Changing the Hebrew prayer was a break with tradition, with the voices from the past that have shaped my life. I champion feminist changes in English, the replacement of words such as "Lord" or "Master" for words that express the concept of God. The imagery of "Lord" is antiquated, and its use irritates me. However, changing the Hebrew blessing is troubling, because the Hebrew language ties us to Jewish people all over the world. Jews everywhere pray in Hebrew. It is the language of Jewish culture. The Hebrew language ties us to our past and, because it is the language of the State of Israel, connects us to the future.— *Carol Diament*

Blessing Before the Meal—*Hamotziah*

נְבָרֵךְ אֶת עֵין הַחַיִּים
הַמּוֹצִיאָה לֶחֶם מִן הָאָרֶץ.

Let us bless the source of life
that brings forth bread from the earth.[18] ◉

Spices—*Besamim* (from *Havdalah* Service)

נְהַלֵּל אֶת נִשְׁמַת כָּל חַי
וּנְבָרֵךְ עַל מִינֵי בְשָׂמִים.

Let us celebrate the breath
of all living things
and praise all essences.[19]

Many of Falk's blessings hint at God's presence but do not name the divine or directly refer to God at all. For example, Falk's daily morning prayer gives thanks using the traditional words *modah ani* (feminine) or *modeh ani* (masculine), but does not follow these words with the traditional *lefanekha* (before You, masculine gender) nor with *lefana'yikh*, the feminine-gender equivalent. Instead, Falk ends the phrase without directly thanking God. In leaving the prayer open-ended, Falk suggests that the process of beginning the day with gratitude is the essence of prayer, not the addressing of prayer to a higher and separate being. Such a prayer takes the feminist experience of God's presence throughout all creation and the feminist emphasis on process to radical conclusions, shifting the focus of the entire enterprise of prayer. For Falk, prayer may not be, first and foremost, about God, but about the individual Jew or the community of Jews and the way that Jews spiritually express gratitude for life.

Morning Blessing—*Birkat Hasha<u>h</u>ar*

The breath of my life
will bless,

the cells of my being
sing

in gratitude,
reawakening.[20]

נִשְׁמַת חַיַּי תְּבָרֵךְ
וְקֶרֶב לִבִּי יָשִׁיר:

כָּל עוֹד נְשָׁמָה בְּקִרְבִּי
מוֹדָה/מוֹדֶה אֲנִי.

⊞ Substituting *nevarekh* ("let us bless") for *barukh* ("blessed") separates the speaker from Jews throughout the world, because the overwhelming majority begin blessings with the word *barukh*. The word *nevarekh* also negates the basic Rabbinic principle that Jews focus on God when reciting a blessing. Shifting the focus to the community does not close "the distance between the speaker and God." In classic liturgy, we close the distance between creature and Creator by directly confronting God—addressing God as *Attah* ("You"). In contrast, the use of "let us bless" stresses empowerment, "power to the people," a concept that has an almost exalted status among many contemporary women and men.—*Rabbi Jules Harlow*

❂ "The overwhelming majority" of "Jews throughout the world" do not begin blessings with the word *barukh*; they do not say blessings at all. Offering an alternative to the formulas that so many Jews find ➤

Falk's choice of *nevarekh*, "let us bless," as the opening of certain blessings also reveals this focus. By replacing the masculine-gender *barukh*, "blessed" (and also replacing the masculine-gender *Attah*, "are You") with the gender-neutral *nevarekh*, "let us bless," Falk closes the distance between the speaker and God and shifts focus toward the community who praises. ⊞ ❂

Furthermore, Falk believes that the repeated use of any

one phrase to the exclusion of others can become idolatrous. That is, the individual at prayer may come to associate the metaphor with God's essence, so that the image itself becomes a god. Falk asserts that her aim is not merely to replace the standard masculine metaphors for God with new feminine or gender-neutral ones, but to offer a multiplicity of different metaphors, suggesting various images that relate to specific prayers.

One last example of Falk's liturgical innovation is her *Shema*.

שְׁמַע, יִשְׂרָאֵל-
לָאֱלֹהוּת אַלְפֵי פָנִים,
מְלֹא עוֹלָם שְׁכִינָתָה,
רִבּוּי פָּנֶיהָ אֶחָד.

Shema Yisrael,
la'Elohut alfei panim,
melo olam Shekhinatah,
ribui paneha ehad.

Hear, O Israel—
The divine abounds everywhere
and dwells in everything;
the many are One.[21]

Certainly, the fact that Falk has rewritten the *Shema*, ※ a Biblical declaration that has been central to Judaism for millennia, is shocking, yet it indicates Falk's unwavering commitment to comprehensive liturgical change. So catch your breath, and put your disapproval on hold! Falk's *Shema* begins like the Biblical *Shema*, with the words *Shema Yisrael*, "Hear, O Israel," but the next phrases differ markedly. Falk states in the Hebrew that divinity has many faces and that those many faces are one. Just as the Biblical *Shema* expresses the core belief of Judaism, Falk's *Shema* expresses the essence of her Jewish feminist monotheism, the multiplicity and simultaneous unity of the divine. God is one, yet no single image can describe God. ✳

Feminist emphasis on power as life-giving and compassionate has roots in the Torah itself. The Bible does at times portray God's power as destructive—God destroys the

exclusionary and alienating is not intended to disrupt the unity of the Jewish people, since no such unity in fact exists. In both the United States and Israel, only a minority of Jews accept traditional religious practice. The new liturgies that feminists and others are creating today are an attempt to make the tradition more meaningful and more welcoming to a broad spectrum of Jews who seek to express their spiritual needs honestly and with integrity in a Jewish context. —*Marcia Falk*[22]

※ Marcia Falk has not "rewritten the *Shema*"; instead she has substituted her own words for the classic text from Deuteronomy. Replacing one of the best-known verses from the Torah is both presumptuous and a break in the unifying nature of Hebrew prayer. —*Rabbi Jules Harlow*

✳ The paragraph of Falk's *Shema* that corresponds to the *Ve'ahavta* gives voice to our striving for justice, another core aspect of Jewish feminist spirituality. —*TC*

world, drowns the Egyptians, and threatens many times to wipe out the Israelites—but the Bible also presents loving and nurturing images of God. Isaiah 49:15, for instance, compares God to a mother suckling her child. ▓ The Rabbis of the Talmud expand on the Biblical crossing of the Red Sea, and portray a compassionate God who refuses to let the angels sing during the drowning of the Egyptians (*Sanhedrin* 39b). The Rabbis also describe a God who weeps at the Temple's destruction (*Eikhah Rabbah*, *Petikhta* 24). Further, the medieval Kabbalists radically re-interpret and expand the ways in which to understand and describe God, imagining and mapping out various elements of God's (male) body. ✸

▓ Loving and nurturing images of God are not only feminine. The Psalmist declares: "As a father has compassion for his children, so the Lord has compassion for those who fear Him" (Psalm 103:13). By confining the attribute of judgment to fathers and the attribute of compassion to mothers, we perpetuate a misleading cliché about men and women. The Hebrew Bible makes no such distinction. As Dr. Tikva Frymer-Kensky teaches, "The same God who directs also nurtures, the God who judges also has compassion."23

Those who insist that the model of God as mother signifies a caring parent, rather than a domineering patriarch, have apparently never heard of a domineering *matriarch*. Furthermore, newspapers and television occasionally report on mothers who neglect or abuse—or even murder—their children, or women teachers who abuse their students. Clearly, we do not reach the conclusion that women are invariably abusive or neglectful. Similarly, we should not conclude that women are invariably compassionate and caring.—*Rabbi Jules Harlow*

✸ *Sefirot* … are no more than the various attributes of God or descriptions and epithets which can be applied to Him—that is, about a continuous process of emanation. Yet at the same time this very process was described as a kind of revelation of the various Names peculiar to God in His capacity of Creator…. The first *Sefirot* [(1) *Keter*, "supreme crown"; (2) *Hokhmah*, "wisdom"; and (3) *Binah*, "intelligence"] represent the head, and, in the *Zohar*, the three cavities of the brain; the fourth [*Gedulah* or *Hesed*, "greatness" or "love"] and the fifth [*Gevurah*, "power"], the arms; the sixth [*Tiferet*, "beauty"], the torso; the seventh [*Nezah*, "lasting endurance"] and eighth [*Hod*, "majesty"], the legs; the ninth [*Tzaddik* or *Yesod Olam*, "righteous one" or "foundation of the world"], the sexual organ; and the tenth [*Malkhut*, "kingdom"] refers to the all-embracing totality of the image, or … to the female as companion to the male, since both together are needed to constitute a perfect man. In Kabbalist literature this symbolism of primal man in all its details is called *Shi'ur Komah*.—*Gershom Scholem*24

Though the particular changes that Jewish feminists are making in imagery and language are new, Jews throughout history have tried to understand and relate to God using the tools and insights of their own times. Some of today's changes will have more staying power than others. Ultimately only those that prove useful and meaningful will be transmitted to future generations, but we should treat feminist reinterpretations with respect, for they are genuine and holy strivings to communicate with the divine. Furthermore, as Judith Plaskow reminds us, "criticism of received images of God, is not, of course, criticism of God. It is criticism of ways of speaking about a reality that, in its full reality, is fully unknowable."25

Finally, if we take a step back to the Bible, we read in Genesis 1:27 that God created humankind "male and female" in the image of God. This extremely powerful and deeply affirming statement stands at the core of Jewish belief. Yet, the development of the prayer book has obscured it.

Today, after thousands of years, we seek to recover an affirmation of the holiness of both women and men. For, as Lynn Gottlieb writes, "only when women begin to speak of God She, can we finally picture ourselves as created in God's image"[26]—something that Jewish men have pictured since Biblical times. ※

Of course, when we open ourselves to new images of the divine, we also open up new avenues of connection to God. These new pathways ultimately have little to do with gender, yet they are revealed by our use of a multiplicity of images and metaphors.

Certainly we feel power in doing things the way they have always been done. We feel comfort and ease in reciting words we have learned by heart. But the avenues we follow today can create a tradition that is comfortable and powerful for generations to come. If we want our children to experience ease with feminine language and imagery—an ease that we might never experience ourselves—we must begin now, believing that there is a middle road between the rote following of custom and the radical abandonment of tradition. The middle road involves risks and challenges, yet it also involves experiencing real meaning in prayer by bringing our whole selves, as Jews and as women, to the prayer book.

※ Since the Creator created both female and male in the divine image, I have never associated God's image with either male or female. God is genderless and cannot be depicted physically. I agree with Dr. Tikva Frymer-Kensky's statement that masculine qualities of God in Biblical monotheism "are social male-gender characteristics. The monotheist God is not sexually a male."[27] Nonetheless, I can imagine that Rabbi Lynn Gottlieb's statement provides a necessary corrective—one that benefits many women. Such statements in discussions and presentations of theology may indeed be worthwhile, but I would not change the Hebrew liturgy as a result.

The poetic license of a metaphor often has been misused or misunderstood. For example, stating that God is "our Father in heaven" should articulate our thinking of God *as* Father and should not lead us to think of God as if God *were* a father. Garrett Green writes: "The logic of the *imago Dei* is not reversible. When God fashions us after His image it is called creation; when we fashion God after our image, it is called idolatry."[28]—*Rabbi Jules Harlow*

✻ The ritual impulse is very strong. Without ritual our ideas float disembodied in the ether, unable to touch our emotions; and our beliefs stay unsupported by action and experience. And, no less important, rituals create community, a sense of unity and belonging with the people ➤

Life-Cycle Rituals

As Jews, we live in at least two cycles of time, the yearly cycle and the life cycle, and both involve unique prayers and sacred texts. We mark the passage of time throughout the year and throughout our lives. Like the Yiddish *tehines* and the Judeo-Spanish songs that prior generations of Jewish women recited, new Jewish feminist rituals for life-cycle events have grown directly out of the realization that women's experiences are religiously meaningful, significant, and worthy of ceremony. ✻ Jewish feminist rituals have grown out of our recognition of the sacred in our lives and our desire to name it. They have grown out of our realization that we are not isolated individuals, but part of larger communities—a community of women and a community of Jews stretching backward and forward in time. Finally, Jewish feminist rituals have helped us to affirm that our bodies are sacred.

---

with whom we share our rituals, a sense of group identity, and of personal definition as part of this group.

For a long time, women had no access to such ritual communion. Unable to share fully in the public Jewish rituals, they lived their religious lives passively, watching the men say the prayers and read the Torah; domestically, participating in home rituals on Sabbath, Passover, Hanukkah and (to a lesser extent) Sukkot; and privately, reciting the Psalms, or books of hours, or the many *tehines*, the Yiddish devotional literature written by and for women....

All this has changed in recent years with the appearance of Jewish feminist consciousness. There have been two main thrusts of movement: toward participation in the traditional public liturgy of Judaism, and toward the creation of new women's rituals.

The traditional liturgy is hallowed precisely because it is traditional. Although some of us may rebel at certain lines of *siddur* (prayer book) that we simply cannot say, for the most part we pay little attention to the words of the prayers: it is the rhythm of the repetition, the always-sameness, the sharing with those present and those long-past, the record of Israel's yearning for God that matters. New rituals cannot count on such an automatic response and, as a result, are to some degree determined by personal taste....

I would rather say, *Berukha At Adonai*—"Blessed are You, O God," using the feminine forms—while saying the proper name of God as it is traditionally pronounced. I do not want to declare that this name, and the whole Biblical God it refers to, is a male-only image. To address my prayers to a separable female immanent presence of God, the *Shekhinah*, indicates to me that the rest of God is male....

We should try to find some way of connecting the new women's life-cycle events with traditional Jewish language and symbol so that there is a Judaic value to performing them within a Jewish setting that goes beyond what we might gain from sharing them in a non-religious or neo-pagan setting.—*Tikva Frymer-Kensky*[29]

Until recently, Ashkenazi Jewish life cycle ceremonies included only *brit milah, pidyon haben*, bar mitzvah, weddings, funerals, and mourning—and only three of these involved women: weddings, funerals, and mourning. (Sefardi Jews, however, have traditionally marked the birth of an infant daughter with the *zeved habat*—gift of the daughter—ceremony.)

The year 1922 witnessed the first synagogue ceremony in which a young American woman celebrated becoming bat mitzvah, when Rabbi Mordechai Kaplan called his daughter Judith to the Torah for an *aliyah*. Synagogue ceremonies marking girls' becoming bat mitzvah, however, did not become the norm until three to four decades later. Furthermore, until the 1970s, the American Jewish community hardly celebrated the birth of a girl at all; it certainly did not mark a baby girl's entry into the covenant with a ceremony equivalent to a *brit milah*.

Today, though, the American Jewish community has greatly enlarged its vision of life-cycle events worthy of ritual. Rabbi Debra Orenstein's 1994 compendium *Lifecycles*, for example, is full of ritual opportunities for Jewish girls, Jewish women, and Jews whose lives do not conform to conventional expectations—because they don't marry, because they adopt children, because they are gay or lesbian.

Over the past two decades, celebrations marking the birth of a Jewish girl have become almost as common as celebrations for newborn boys. At the *brit milah*, an eight-day-old boy is circumcised and he enters the covenant to begin his life as a Jew. The ceremony itself inscribes the covenant on the flesh of the boy, physically altering his body to mark him as Jewish. The ceremony also names the infant boy and initiates him into the Jewish people; it connects him both to those Jews who are present to greet the infant and to those Jews who lived in ages past. The *brit* is in no way private; indeed, as it is considered a *mitzvah* to be present at the *brit milah* of any Jew, strangers are welcome (at least in theory).

Developing a corresponding ceremony for infant girls has posed a challenge for Jewish feminists. The *brit milah* is effective because it causes the status and body of its subject to change, and thereby forces us to confront the placement of the covenant on the male body. Thus, developing a ceremony in which an infant girl enters into the covenant demands more than that the birth of a girl be recognized as of equal value to the birth of a boy. A public ceremony welcoming a girl into the Jewish people, past and present, causes us to more fully recognize that God entered into a covenant with the entire community of Jews, females as well as males.

Current Jewish ceremonies for infant girls differ, as reflected in the different names used. Four names used for the ceremony, *brit banot* (covenant for daughters), *brit bat Tzion* (covenant for a daughter of Zion), *brit ḥayyim* (covenant of life), and *brittah* (her covenant), reflect an emphasis on covenant. These rituals attempt to serve the same purposes as the *brit milah*, though they use other means than circumcision (*milah*) to welcome female infants into Jewish destiny. Other names commonly used for the ritual, *simḥat bat* (celebration of a daughter), baby naming, and *shalom bat* (welcome of a daughter), do not specifically address the entry into covenant. The lack of a standard structure for these rituals, on the one hand, reflects past neglect of girls and women and, on the other hand, has given rise today to tremendous creativity and innovation.

Creators of covenant rituals for girls have used various strategies to signify the entrance into the Jewish people. Mary Gendler has proposed the most radical idea for a ritual equivalent to circumcision: breaking the hymen.[30] As a theory, her idea is intriguing—it would reproduce the surgical and genital aspects of a circumcision, and would free the girl from the oppression of an objectified virginity—but neither Gendler herself nor other Jews have acted on the idea. Other physically-oriented suggestions have included piercing the baby girl's ears,[31] immersing her in the *mikvah*,[32] or ritually washing her feet.[33] Ear piercing recalls the entire people of Israel *hearing* the covenant at Sinai. The *mikvah* relates both to female sexuality and, from conversion rituals, to entrance into the Jewish people (male converts undergo both circumcision and ritual immersion in the *mikvah*, whereas female converts undergo only ritual immersion). Washing the infant's feet recalls Abraham washing the feet of the three messengers who visited him after his circumcision.

Others have argued that a physical ritual for infant daughters that parallels the circumcision ritual is unnecessary, because women's covenant with God differs from men's. Rabbi Laura Geller, for example, suggests that linking the ritual to Rosh Ḥodesh provides a meaningful way for infant girls to enter the covenant, as Rosh Ḥodesh itself honors Jewish women's spirituality.[34] The central blessing of Rabbi Geller's ceremony adapts the *brit milah* liturgy:

Entry into the Covenant

Barukh Attah Adonai Eloheinu Melekh ha'olam, asher kiddshanu bemitzvotav vetzivvanu lehakhnisah bivritam shel Avraham veSarah.

Blessed are you God, Ruler of the universe, Who has sanctified us with the commandments and commanded us to enter our daughter into the covenant of Abraham and Sarah.

The community responds: As this child has been entered into the covenant, so may she enter into a life enriched by Torah, and a warm and loving relationship, and a commitment to create a better world.[35]

Other baby girls' ceremonies have employed Shabbat as a sign of the covenant or made use of candles,[36] as lighting Shabbat candles is one of the three special women's commandments.[37]

Feminist mothers and fathers of sons have also struggled with the *brit milah* ceremony. How can the *brit* more accurately reflect the parents' values? Nahariyah Mosenkis read aloud the following prayer of protest at her son's circumcision ceremony:

Dear God, Thank You for sharing the creation of a healthy child with us…. We are gathered here to fulfill Your commandment of *brit milah*. But I find no joy in fulfilling this commandment. I come to You in protest as Abraham did when You told him You were going to destroy Sodom and Gomorrah….

I am offended that you command me to cause my child to suffer. How can You create us with the loving and empathetic nature which helps us to be good parents and then command us to submit our infants to the pain and distress of *brit milah*? …

Why do I submit my child to this *brit milah*? I have neither the faith in You nor knowledge of You that Abraham did. I submit my child to this because I was raised to believe that Your commandments are given to us for our benefit, and that they are righteous and just…. God, if you cannot send an angel to stop the *mohel* as you stopped Abraham from sacrificing his son Isaac, then comfort my son as he is submitted to your command.[38]

Some families opt for a private, traditional circumcision ceremony at eight days, and then invite friends and relations to a more innovative and individual ceremony at a later date. Such ceremonies are often appropriate for both boys and girls, and they tend to emphasize celebration of the birth and health of the child.[39]

Some new rituals meet modern spiritual needs while reviving ancient rites. An example is the weaning celebration, found in Genesis 21:8, "The child grew up and was weaned, and Abraham held a great feast on the day that Isaac was weaned." Only in recent years have weaning rituals been revived by women who want to mark this transition in their own and their child's lives. Maria Papacostaki and Harry Brod wrote a weaning ritual (published in 1991) that takes place at *havdalah*, a time of separation.[40]

From A Weaning Ceremony

Today we present to Artemis her own *kiddush* cup, to symbolize her increasing ability to drink from other sources. Artemis was weaned at her 18th month. Eighteen is a symbol for life, *hai,* as in the toast *lehayyim,* "to life." At this time we recite the traditional blessing for reaching a joyous time, the *sheheheyanu* [in both male and female gender language].

Barukh Attah Adonai, Eloheinu Melekh ha'olam sheheheyanu vekiyemanu vehigianu lazman hazeh.

Brukha Yah Shekhinah, Eloheinu Malkat ha'olam shehehiatnu vekiyematnu vehigiatnu lazman hazeh.

Blessed are You, *Adonai,* Ruler of the universe, who has given us life, sustained us, and enabled us to reach this season.[41]

Though baby-naming rituals and, to some extent, weaning rituals focus on the child, many recently composed rituals place the mother, or the mother to be, at the center. Indeed, from the moment of deciding to attempt conception, through the months of pregnancy, and then through the trials of childbirth and afterbirth, women and their partners can now choose to honor these passages with ritual. There are blessings for positive and negative home pregnancy tests, rituals for pregnant women and their friends, and rituals celebrating becoming a mother.[42] Rabbi Nina Beth Cardin has written a prayer for a husband to say when his wife becomes pregnant:

Master of the World, I thank You for Your kindness, for helping my wife become pregnant with our child. May the name of the Lord be blessed and exalted above all blessings and praise.

God, may it be Your will to show kindness to all pregnant women and ease the discomforts of their pregnancies. Protect them so that none of them miscarries. Guard all who are in the throes of labor, so that no harm comes to them and that they give birth to life. Include among them my wife [her name].... *El Harahaman,* God of mercy, deal with us mercifully, and not according to the laws of strict justice. Overlook our weaknesses and misdeeds, and act toward us with kindness and graciousness. Give us long life, and let my wife and me grow old together, proud of our children, watching them do Your will.[43]

Rabbi Cardin here adapts the style and some of the phrasing of the Yiddish *tehines* as well as the concepts and text of the Rosh Hashanah liturgy. Indeed, many new prayers written by women are explicitly titled *tehines*, as their authors seek a connection to authentic Jewish women's traditions.[44] Similarly, many new women's rituals make use of blessings that were originally recited in different contexts. Rabbi Sandy Eisenberg Sasso uses a blessing that the Rabbis of the Talmud prescribe when witnessing a thunderstorm. The blessing praises the Eternal as *Oseh maaseh breishit* (Doer of the deeds of creation), and Rabbi Sasso suggests that parents recite this *brakhah* after the birth of a child.[45]

New rituals also encompass infertility, miscarriage, and stillbirth—traumatic losses that women (and their partners) experience, but that lack standard Jewish mourning ceremonies. Though certain customs, including a graveside burial, are followed when a baby is stillborn, the formal service and morning rituals are omitted or curtailed. As a result, many Jews are left without a communally-sanctioned way to mourn their loss.[46]

Responding to the growing need for rituals to address infertility and miscarriage, both rabbis and lay people have developed ceremonies and compiled liturgy, including a full-length book, *Tears of Sorrow, Seeds of Hope: A Jewish Spiritual Companion for Infertility and Pregnancy Loss* by Rabbi Cardin. Many of these rituals are relatively private, for example, involving just the woman and her rabbi or just the woman and her partner. Some of the rituals include a circle of friends and family. Ceremonies may incorporate mourning customs such as the eating of round foods, especially hard boiled eggs, the tearing of clothing, and the lighting of candles. Bonnie and Lawrence Baron incorporate elements of many different ceremonies into their *seder kabbalat akarut,* written to help them accept the loss of their dream for a biological child.[47] Like the Rosh Hashanah *tashlikh* ceremony, they crumbled bread in their hands and threw it into the ocean, symbolically discarding their hopes for a biological child; like the *kriah* mourning ritual, they cut and wore ribbons, using blue and pink rather than black; like the Passover Seder, they listed the ten plagues of infertility and discarded a drop of wine for each; and like the *havdalah* ceremony, they lit a double-braided candle, raised a cup of wine, and smelled sweet spices "to distinguish between the heartbreak of infertility and the joy of transcending it."[48]

Rabbi Lynn Gottlieb's ritual for "The Fruits of Creation" recognizes a childless woman's need to acknowledge her loss yet celebrate her creativity in other ways, such as artistry, relationships, and courage in the face of hardship.[49]

For the ceremony, Deborah set up an altar made up of three bowls, which she crafted for the occasion... Using the first bowl and a washing cup, Deborah ritually washed her hands and feet. She spoke of the waters of *Shekhinah* (close-dwelling presence of God, associated with the feminine) healing and regenerating her soul.

The second bowl, the bowl of lamentations, was filled with sand from the banks of the river. [The ceremony was held on the banks of the Rio Grande.] First Deborah and then all of us performed a kind of *tashlikh* (casting out) of our losses.... Then we spontaneously formulated a litany of grief:

> **"*Shekhinah,* She who dwells within all being, I mourn the loss of the child I never bore. I mourn the loss of the mothering I envisioned. I mourn the loss of my ability to bear children. I mourn the loss of..."**

We began wailing to a tune Deborah composed until our tears flowed, our hearts were opened, and our spirits felt a release from grief. We filled the (now empty) washing bowl with water and passed it around, washing each other's faces and giving each other a blessing. Then we recited a calmer, more peaceful listing:

> **"*Shekhinah,* She who gives and takes away. I release the feelings of rage I have because I could not birth a child. I release my anger at my husband and forgive him for the times we struggled over our yearning for children. I release my feelings of inadequacy over not being physically able to conceive and forgive myself for difficult times. I release..."[50]**

Jewish women have recently developed a number of rituals to acknowledge abortion. Rabbi Leila Gal Berner and Rabbi Debra Orenstein both note the need to give shape to previously invisible life passages and to give voice to women's previous silences.[51] The rituals vary depending on the circumstances of the individuals who have undergone an abortion, for example, following sexual violence or medical recommendation, or because of psychological considerations. Rabbi Berner, who has written ceremonies for women who seek closure after an abortion and for women who have survived sexual abuse, notes that ritual can serve as a "vessel" into which a woman can "pour her most profound feelings."[52] Rabbi Nina Beth Cardin includes a prayer to be said when terminating a pregnancy in her collection *Tears of Sorrow*:

Dear one of mine,

Imagine all the good that there would be, if I could let you grow inside of me...

You'd kick and turn, and make me bloom in ways I've never known.

I'd decorate your room and guess the color of your hair.

And when you were born, I would hold you and gaze at you in wonder, in awe. I would watch you fill your tiny clothes that filled my sweetest dreams.

I could see you stand on tiptoe, stretching bravely, hard as you might to reach the bathroom light. We could have cuddled as we read the books of childhood, and stormed castles with our sock-puppets and cardboard daggers.

We could have played hide-and-seek through the house, and hugged each other when thunder roared.

And I would have heard you laugh as you talked with friends behind your bedroom door.

If only I could let you grow inside of me....

But now, before we ever say hello, we must say good-bye.

O God, hold me through my hurt, through this most awful moment. Take that which was to have been my baby and clasp her/him close to You, forever. Be with her/him, God, and be with me.[53]

Jewish feminists have also developed numerous healing rituals for women. Nancy Helman Shneiderman, following a hysterectomy, buried her womb in a pottery vessel of her own making and planted a tree over the burial site; her ceremony also included *shofar*-blowing, poetry, the *sheheheyanu* blessing, dance, and song.[54] Rabbi Sue Ann Wasserman, together with Laura Levitt, used ritual immersion in the *mikvah* as part of a healing ceremony for Laura shortly after she survived a rape.[55] And Sara Paasche Orlow wrote a ritual for the removal of a breast cyst: Women gathered at the time of the full moon to make soup, study classic Jewish writings, eat round foods, and wash each other's hands with milk, a nurturing women's liquid; this healing community of women also recited a new blessing that was to be used as part of monthly breast exams.[56]

The grandmother of feminist rituals is surely the bat mitzvah ceremony. Today, ceremonies for adolescent girls becoming bat mitzvah, like ceremonies for newborn girls, have become the norm in the liberal Jewish community. Over the past two decades, the girl's coming of age ceremony in Conservative, Reform, and Reconstructionist denominations has become the full equivalent to each denomination's bar mitzvah. ▨

Another transition to womanhood, the onset of menses, has recently achieved a measure of recognition within Jewish practice. A simple blessing at the time of one's first menstrual period praises God as *she'asani ishah*—"who has made me a woman." The words come from the morning blessing recited by Orthodox men, *shelo asani ishah*—"who has not made me a woman"—yet the new blessing inverts their meaning.[57] More elaborate rituals for the onset of menses involve the girl, her mother, and other women who offer advice and celebrate her entrance into womanhood.

Bnot mitzvah ceremonies for adult women, which celebrate a new or a renewed commitment to Judaism, have become widespread. ❀ Many synagogues hold group classes for adults, and both synagogues and Jewish organizations (including Hadassah) conduct group bat mitzvah ceremonies and celebrations. Many other adult women study and prepare one on one with a rabbi or teacher, and then celebrate their achievement in the synagogue through chanting the Torah or *Haftarah* portion and presenting a lesson or leading a discussion on the portion.

Traditional Jewish marriage and divorce rites have also been adapted by innovative Jewish feminists. Double-ring ceremonies have gained widespread acceptance, and many brides and grooms today break glasses together. Egalitarian *tena'im* (conditions) to supplement the standard *ketubah* (marriage contract) have become commonplace throughout the liberal denominations. Less common, but definitely in use, are new feminist blessings to re-interpret the *sheva brakhot,* the seven marital blessings. Rabbi Rachel Adler has gone even further, however, in her detailed critique of both the traditional *ketubah* and the traditional wedding, and she has written the *brit ahuvim*, an egalitarian covenant of lovers.[59]

▨ Reform Judaism generally neglected bar mitzvah celebrations—as well as bat mitzvah—during the early years of the 20th century, focusing instead on a confirmation ceremony at approximately age 16. Reform congregations that did hold bat mitzvah ceremonies, though, often followed the Conservative pattern. From the 1940s through the early 1980s, most Conservative congregations held bat mitzvah celebrations on Friday nights; the girl was not called up to the Torah nor did she learn Torah cantillation *(trop)*. Instead, she chanted a passage from the *Haftarah* (Prophets) in a sort of "catch up" ceremony. Neither Torah nor *Haftarah* is chanted at a standard Conservative—or Orthodox—Friday night service. Furthermore, a male reader would repeat the girl's entire *Haftarah* passage the following Saturday morning. Finally, these early bat mitzvah ceremonies did not mark the girl's entry into adult synagogue life, but were instead the ONLY opportunity offered to either adolescent girls or grown women to stand before a congregation and chant a sacred Hebrew passage.—*Claudia Chernov*

❀ I would say that three kinds of days were the highlights of my life: the day I got married, the days when my four children were born, and the day in which I had my [adult] bat mitzvah, read from the Torah, and helped to put the Torah back into the Ark. Every time I handle the Torah I want to weep with joy. I realize how much it means to me. All my life I have been Jewish, and at last I have a way to express my Jewishness.— *Suzanne Reisman*[58]

Brit Ahuvim—Lovers' Covenant

[The two individuals] confirm in the presence of witnesses a lovers' covenant between them and celebrate a partnership to establish a household among the people of Israel.

The agreement into which _____ and _____ are entering is a holy covenant like the ancient covenants of our people, made in faithfulness and peace to stand forever. It is a covenant of protection and hope like the covenant God swore to Noah and his descendants, saying, "'When the bow is in the clouds, I will see it and remember the everlasting covenant between God and all living creatures, all flesh that is on earth. That,' God said to Noah, 'shall be the sign of the covenant that I have established between me and all flesh'" (Genesis 9:16–17).

It is a covenant of distinction, like the covenant God made with Israel saying, "You shall be My people, and I shall be your God" (Jeremiah 30:22).

It is a covenant of devotion, joining hearts like the covenant David and Jonathan made, as it is said, "And Jonathan's soul was bound up with the soul of David. Jonathan made a covenant with David because he loved him as himself" (1 Samuel 18:1–3).

It is a covenant of mutual lovingkindness like the wedding covenant between God and Zion, as it is said, "I will espouse you forever. I will espouse you with the righteousness and justice and lovingkindness and compassion. I will espouse you in faithfulness and you shall know God" (Hosea 2:21–22).

The following are the provisions of the lovers' covenant into which [the two individuals] now enter:

1. _____ and _____ declare that they have chosen each other as companions, as our Rabbis teach: "'Get yourself a companion.' This teaches that a person should get a companion, to eat with, to drink with, to study Bible with, to study Mishnah with, to sleep with, to confide all one's secrets, secrets of Torah and secrets of worldly things" (*Avot DeRabbi Natan* 8).

2. _____ and _____ declare that they are setting themselves apart for each other and will take no other lover.

3. _____ and _____ hereby assume all the rights and obligations that apply to family members: to attend, care, and provide for one another [and for any children with which they may be blessed] [and for _____ child/children of _____].

4. _____ and _____ commit themselves to a life of kindness and righteousness as a Jewish family and to work together toward the communal task of mending the world.

5. _____ and _____ pledge that one will help the other at the time

of dying, by carrying out the last rational requests of the dying partner, protecting him/her from indignity or abandonment and by tender, faithful presence with the beloved until the end, fulfilling what has been written: "Set me as a seal upon your arm, for love is [strong as] death" (Song of Songs 8:6).

To this covenant we affix our signatures.[60]

Some feminist pre-wedding celebrations replace the bridal shower with ritual immersion in the *mikvah*, giving a new spin to a standard Orthodox practice. In another change, lesbians over the past 25 years have come to publicly sanctify their relationships. Same-sex couples have used a variety of ceremonies, ranging from adaptations of standard Jewish wedding rituals to affirmations of commitment using contemporary Jewish lesbian poetry and song.

New divorce rituals often seek to endorse women as active participants; such feminist rituals serve as counterweights to the acceptance of the *get*, a process that many women find alienating and marginalizing. Woman-centered rituals offset the ex-wife's passive participation in the Orthodox *bet din*, composed of three male rabbis, with the husband granting the *get* and the wife receiving it. Rabbi Vicki Hollander, for example, created a ceremony for herself which involved many aspects of Yom Kippur rituals as well as aspects of mourning rites. She fasted on the day of her appointment with the *bet din* and dressed all in white. She also wrote her own document of divorce and gave it to her ex-husband after the official *get* ceremony. She then returned home with female friends, changed her clothes to colorful ones, and ate a meal that resembled the post-funeral meal of a mourner.[61] A separation ritual by Rabbi Nina Beth Cardin interweaves Biblical passages with the ripping of a pillow case or sheet, suggesting both the symbolism of the *huppah* and the power of *kriah* (the rending of a garment in mourning).

Midlife, significant later birthdays, and aging have also become foundations for new ritual. Sometimes called *simhat hokhmah,* the celebration of wisdom, such rituals may respond to a neglect of women's aging as a process of strength, beauty, and wisdom—a neglect on the part of American as well as Jewish communal life. One such ritual, created by Phyllis Berman to mark her 50th birthday and celebrate her menopause, was loosely based on the structure of a Seder.[62] She provided four cups filled with four different liquids. Each cup symbolized a different stage of life. Participants first drank a cup of milk, indicative of childhood, then sangria for adolescence and early sexuality, champagne for marriage and partnership, and finally water for the clarity and purity of the next quarter of life. As each cup was shared, women told stories about themselves at the four periods of their lives. Barbara D. Holender, for her 65th birthday, immersed in the *mikvah* and took on a new Hebrew name. She recited: "Blessed are You, *Shekhinah*, in whose name we come into our own."[63]

Bonnie Feinman also took on a new name in a midlife ceremony that she named *Maaseh Breishit*.[64] Marcia Cohn Speigel embraced the story of Abraham and Sarah setting out on their journey to Canaan late in their lives as an inspiration for her journeys late in life.[65] The singer-songwriter Debbie Friedman wrote the song "Lekhi Lakh" for Savina Teubal, one of the first women to hold a *simhat hokhmah* ceremony.[66] This song has since been used in countless celebrations in recognition of the journeys and transitions in our own lives. Friedman's inclusive lyrics use the Biblical injunction *lekh lekha* (go forth) as well as the second-person feminine *lekhi lakh,* thus addressing both a man and a woman.

Indeed, music has been a key component of feminist spirituality and new feminist rituals. Debbie Friedman, in addition to "Lekhi Lakh," has composed "Mi Sheberakh," now a staple of healing services, and "Miriam's Song," a highlight of many women's Seders. Rabbi Shefa Gold incorporates chanting into her powerful liturgical music. Her work, and that of women such as Hana Tiferet Siegel, reveal the spiritual possibilities that arise from repetition of a few words. Two consciously feminist groups, the trio MIRAJ (Margo Stein, Geela Rayzel, and Juliet I. Spitzer) and Linda Hirshhorn's VOCOLOT, place Jewish women's lives, concerns, and voices at the center of their spiritual endeavors. Linda Hirshhorn and Fran Avni's beautiful arrangements of selections of Marcia Falk's liturgy greatly enhance its use within Jewish prayer groups.

New life-cycle rituals clearly add meaning to American Jewish life. The recent explosion of Jewish women's creativity has also affected Jewish men. The adult *bat mitzvah*, for example, originated as a ceremony for women who had never before read Torah or *Haftarah* for their congregations, but today Jewish men in their 30s to their 90s also study and prepare for a synagogue ceremony that will mean something more than it did at age 13. Many of today's new ceremonies are equally applicable to males and females, such as rituals for going away to college, for retirement, or for moving into a new home. Men today also write personal prayers. Rabbi Geoffrey Haber, using the emotional style and some of the wording of *tehines*, has written a prayer for parents to recite when their newborn child has disabilities:

O God, from the depths I cry to you, help me to feel that the ways of Your providence are wise and good, though we understand them not.

[Feminists have also written prayers for daily life, like this "Internet Prayer."]

Oh holy *Shehinah*, as I sit in front of my computer yet again today—instead of praying to You—let my time in front of this screen be considered holy. Let my fingers send out words of peace, comfort, and connection. May my work here be about *tikkun olam*, fixing and repair of the world. Help me know when I've done enough, when it is time to rest, see the outside world, and create love in other ways. Blessed be.—*Rabbi Rayzel Raphael*

In this moment, my full soul feels but little strength to pray. Yet You have given the miracle of life, and now we ask for the miracle of hope. Give us hope and strength that we may see the light at the end of this dark night. Give us the love and the commitment to advocate on behalf of our son's/daughter's needs and provide for him/her the best care, a loving home, the brightest future that we can.

May the light of love that my child [child's name], son/daughter of [name of father] and [name of mother], kindled within my heart continue to burn brightly so that as I regain strength of soul, I may bring cheer unto all my dear ones. Praised are You, O God, who gives strength to the weak, who raises the lowly, who comforts the mourner, who gives hope to those in despair.[67]

Some religious leaders fear that creating new rituals for every previously unmarked event in our lives will diminish the power of existing rituals, but others argue that not all ritual need be of equal importance. The nature of the event dictates much about the nature of the ritual—who will observe it, who will join in, where we will hold it, which prayers we will say. But we need not worry about trivializing religion. ❀ Rituals help us live life in a more conscious and gracious way. They are gifts we can give to ourselves and our communities. New rituals are also a unique legacy for the next generation who will be able to mark life passages with something Jewish

❀ There is a peculiar and inconsolable trauma in seeing a fully evolved liturgical language—even a language one could not believe in—replaced almost overnight, not by the language one *could* believe in but by a thinner version of itself with a much reduced vocabulary. The vacuity of new liturgical writing in English seems to be its hallmark, its purpose, so pervasive that even denominational boundaries are helpless to hold it back.

One need not miss the authoritarian style, the masculine focus, or the pompous delivery of old liturgy to miss its moral intensity, its heightened emotional register, its fusion of sound and sense. One need not endorse rigid traditionalism to feel that the new liturgies have excised something crucial and introduced something counterfeit.

There is no reason why the use of a modern vernacular—the lessening of a linguistic demand—should entail the lessening of an emotional demand. Even where the modern vernacular called old beliefs into question, the new liturgies might have incorporated the incisive and liberating words of the enemies of belief—William Blake, Emily Dickinson, Elias Canetti—to put worship to the test and see if it could survive. For the most part they tried nothing of the kind. They surrendered from the outset to shallow and patronizing forms of piety, as if that were the point of modernity. One might suspect that the writers simply did not care for emotional demands....

Stylistically, there is relatively little difference between what religious professionals and lay liturgists are doing, and the boundaries between categories are rather fluid. More or less by general consent—dissenting voices are assumed to belong to the right wing of religion—the liturgical vernacular of the last few decades has evolved into a smooth, non-threatening imitation of religious language, with no power to make or to break the heart.

People in the demographic profiles for whom these efforts are intended—modern skeptical people, young people, feminists, sexual outlaws—are supposed to greet this vernacular with relief. We are supposed to find it fresh and creative; it is supposed to make us "comfortable" at worship; it is supposed to compensate for centuries of oppression. If we find it galling and dispiriting we are dismissed as mere ingrates. But it is dispiriting; it is exhausting. The direct emotions of ardor and terror and inarticulate joy—the real stuff of religion—are all quite off limits; not only are they never invoked at full strength, they are scarcely alluded to in recognizable form. One has to keep holding back, pretending that prayer is not a bodily instinct, pretending that we come to religion with our problems already solved rather than out of a desperate urge to confront them. The new liturgical English ➤

to do and say—for the birth of baby girl, for the shock of discovering an illness, for the joy of becoming a grandmother.

Holiday Rituals

(Hebrew, *barukh Hashem*, remains relatively intact) assures us relentlessly that what we are doing is "meaningful," while never allowing a powerful meaning to surface.

Perhaps it's no wonder that people so intensely aware of the strong element of social control in traditional religion are so frankly controlling in their own liturgies. They have political points to advance and long-standing social patterns to break. But to use liturgy for secondary goals of this kind is to undermine its central function: the rectification of our relation with the universe in the presence of other people. Nothing is rectified—nothing is even enacted—in the new prayers: they are static, self-satisfied, an uncomprehending parroting of old forms of love and fear with all the love and fear taken out.

Often the new prayers invoke emotions outright at points where the old prayers would have encoded them in God-language; but each emotion is seized upon and displayed—generally before it can be felt—with a kind of allrightnik complacency that militates against privacy or reflection. This mood recalls nothing so much as Milan Kundera's well-known definition of kitsch in *The Unbearable Lightness of Being*:

"Kitsch causes two tears to flow in quick succession. The first tear says: How nice to see children running on the grass!

"The second tear says: How nice to be moved, together with all mankind, by children running on the grass!

"It is the second tear that makes kitsch kitsch." ...

Except when they are translating directly from older sources, modern liturgists seem overwhelmingly intent on inducing self-satisfaction.

They may not realize how close self-satisfaction is to self-contempt. Those who accept kitsch as worship must internalize the sense of being mere sheep in need of a green pasture. Those who resist it must constantly fight outright shame. The worst humiliation of contemporary religious life is the abjectness of needing God and a community badly enough *even to sit through this.—Catherine Madsen*[68]

▦ For most of Jewish history, this verse has not been translated to include both women and men. Until recently, English translations were similar to this version from the 1989 *Deluxe Edition of the Maxwell House Haggadah*: "In every generation, each individual is bound to regard *himself* as if *he* had gone personally forth from Egypt" (page 28, emphasis added). By 1997, a translation by Noam Zion and David Dishon in *A Different Night: The Family Participation Haggadah*, published by the Shalom Hartman Institute of Jerusalem, stated: "In every generation, one is obligated to see oneself as one who personally went out from Egypt" (page 114).—*Claudia Chernov*

The Passover Seder has long been the most familiar holiday ceremony observed by American Jews. Each time we celebrate Passover, we think back on the other Passovers of our lives. We also think of the Passovers celebrated before we were born, and we symbolically connect our observance of the holiday to observance throughout Jewish history, ultimately connecting ourselves to the first observance on the night of the exodus from Egypt.

At least that's the way holiday observance is supposed to work. As the Passover Haggadah says, each of us, in every generation, must see ourselves as if we personally had been freed from Egyptian slavery. ▦

Here is the problem: Even if our ancestors understood, in general, that both men and women were obligated to remember and retell the story of the exodus, the actual observance of the Passover rituals has tended to give men greater access to fulfilling the obligation. For example, women (and not men) usually spent days cleaning and cooking to prepare for Passover, so that when the holiday arrived women were often exhausted.

During the Seder, women (and not men) usually set out bowls of salt water, brought water for the washing of hands, served ḥaroset and matzah and maror, and of course served and cleared the meal itself, so that many never even heard the reading of the Haggadah. Certainly they never retold the story to their children at the Seder table, nor did they personally experience our people's liberation from slavery! Those women who, by some chance, did have the opportunity to read or hear the Haggadah experienced an almost exclusively male text: four sons, many rabbis, and no one speaking in a woman's voice.

These realizations played a role in the proliferation of women's Seders and new feminist and inclusive *Haggadot*.[69] Among the first and most influential of feminist Seders was the one that began in 1976 in New York City, described by Esther Broner in *The Telling: The Story of a Group of Jewish Women Who Journey to Spirituality through Community and Ceremony*. The Seder spoke of four daughters; it highlighted Miriam, the sister of Moses and Aaron, in the story of the exodus; it reinterpreted the salt water as the tears of women; and it listed as plagues breast cancer, sexism, and domestic violence. It used the traditional refrain *dayenu* (it is enough for us) to ask what would be "enough" for women in Judaism.

Dayenu

**If Eve had been created in the image of God
and not as helper to Adam,
it would have sufficed.
Dayenu. ❂**

**If she had been created
as Adam's equal
and not as temptress,
Dayenu.**

**If she were the first woman to
eat from the Tree of Knowledge,
who brought learning to us,
Dayenu.**

**If Sarah were recognized as a priestess,
royal in her own lineage,
Dayenu.**

**If Lot's wife had been pitied
when she turned her head
as the city swallowed her children,**

❂ This feminist "Dayenu" presents the flip side of the standard "Dayenu." It lists possibilities or potentialities that were never fulfilled, whereas the original lists actual events. When we sing "it would have been enough," in the original, we are giving thanks for gifts that we have received, gifts that in themselves would have been sufficient. In E. M. Broner and Naomi Nimrod's "Dayenu," we are pleading for equality between men and women, because men and women never attained an equality that was sufficient.—*Carol Diament*

and not mocked with the falling,
with the freezing of her tears,
Dayenu.

If our foremothers had not been considered
as hardened roots
or fruit-bearing wombs,
but as woman in themselves,
Dayenu.

If our fathers had not pitted our mothers
against each other,
like Abraham with Sarah and Hagar
or Jacob with Leah and Rachel
or Elkanah with Hannah and Penina,
Dayenu.

If Miriam were given her prophet's chair
or the priesthood,
Dayenu.

If the Just Women in Egypt
who caused our redemption
had been given sufficient recognition,
Dayenu.

If women bonding, like Naomi and Ruth,
were the tradition
and not the exception,
Dayenu.

If women were in the Tribal Council and
decided on the laws
that dealt with women,
Dayenu.

If women had been
the writers of *Tanakh*,
interpreters of our past,
Dayenu.

If women had written the Haggadah
and brought our mothers forth,
Dayenu.

If every generation of women
together with every generation of men
would continue to go out of Egypt,
Dayenu, dayenu.

Lo Dayenu

If the *Shekhinah* had brought us forth from bondage
and had not educated us,
it would not have sufficed us.

If She had educated us
and not given us opportunity to work,
it would not have sufficed us.

If She had given us the opportunity to work
and not allowed us to advance,
it would not have sufficed us.

If we were allowed to advance at work
but had to perform housewifely duties as well,
Lo Dayenu.

If we were aided by rabbinical decree
and treated with dignity,
Dayenu, dayenu. It would suffice us.[70]

Other early feminist Seders explicitly mentioned the midwives who refused to follow Pharaoh's orders, and went on to list Jewish heroines throughout history. Many feminists used the Passover themes of enslavement and liberation to explore their own identities as contemporary Jewish women. Lesbian feminist Seders, in particular, focused on themes of liberation and Jewish identity, viewing the exodus as a metaphor for openly declaring their sexual identity. Many elements of feminist Seders from the 1970s have become staples as we begin a new millennium.

The first feminist Seders tended to be intimate affairs held in living rooms or dorm rooms, lasting deep into the night. As word spread, a desire to share the experience led to the current phenomenon of women's large communal Seders. Such events, usually held shortly before Passover begins in the spring, commonly accommodate 200 to 500 women—not all of whom identify themselves as feminists. Ma'yan: The Jewish Women's Project published a feminist Haggadah and leader's guide; at least 41 different communal Seders used the Ma'yan Haggadah during the 5760/2000 Passover season. Ma'yan estimates that about 18,000 people, primarily women, attend feminist and women's Seders each year. Project Kesher has broadened the arena for women's Seders by bringing them to the former Soviet Union and Eastern Europe.

A comparison of recent and early feminist *Haggadot* reveals a shift in focus from anger at women's exclusion to celebration of women's accomplishments. In addition, recent feminist *Haggadot* tend to more closely follow the framework of the traditional Haggadah than their predecessors. Commonly found in both early and recent feminist *Haggadot* are the dedication of four cups of wine to historical Jewish women and the celebration of Miriam in the exodus from Egypt. Nearly all feminist Seders today include Miriam's cup alongside Elijah's cup. Filled with water, the cup of Miriam brings to mind Miriam's well, which, according to the Rabbis of the Talmud, provided water for the Israelites throughout their years in the desert (*Taanit* 9a). Miriam's cup also symbolically asserts women's presence during the exodus from slavery and honors women's presence today in the Seder.

Many feminists also add an orange to their Seder plates. Some artists have even designed Seder plates with a space for an orange. Jewish feminist Susannah Heschel conceived the idea after a 1979 lecture in Berkeley on women and Jewish law. When the invited speaker, an Orthodox *rebbetzin* (wife of a rabbi and a Jewish authority in her own right), was asked about the place of lesbians within Judaism, she compared it to eating bread on Passover. Some feminists adopted this symbol, and they placed a crust of bread on their Seder plates to show solidarity with lesbians. Heschel suggested substituting an orange, which was still subversive, yet was kosher for Passover and so did not transgress the ritual laws of the holiday. Heschel observed that the orange suggests fruitfulness for all Jews, and that its seeds, which must be spit out, remind us of repudiating homophobia.[71]

The Seder, with its broad-based appeal, became one of the earliest rituals reinterpreted by women. Many Jewish women quite distant from religious practice have felt connected to the Seder as a home-based gathering for family and friends. Partly because of these connections, women's Seders have played a tremendous role in Jewish feminist spirituality, both by providing a framework for the development of new rituals and by providing a setting in which these innovations can be shared.

Other holidays have also become important arenas for the development of Jewish feminist spirituality. Feminists have analyzed the difference between women's and men's experience of sin, repentance, and renewal through High Holiday rituals and discussions. Some have raised questions that bear directly on women's experiences; for example, must a rape survivor forgive her rapist? Some feminists have explored themes from the Torah and *Haftarah* readings on Rosh Hashanah and Yom Kippur. Gail Twersky Reimer and Judith Kates collected many such analyses in *Beginning Anew: A Woman's Companion to the High Holidays*. New women's ceremonies include reinterpretations of *tashlikh* with meditation, the casting away of sins against women, and discussion of alternatives to the language of sin and repentance. At one Ma'yan *tashlikh* ceremony, women threw rose petals into the water to symbolize the organic beauty of even the discarded elements of self. At another *tashlikh* ceremony, women both threw bread away and ate bread, to emphasize the need to take in as well as to discard. Songs sung at women's New Year's ceremonies include variations of the traditional High Holiday liturgy, for example,

Judith Glass's *Imenu Nafshenu* (Our Mother, Our Soul), a reinterpretation of *Avinu Malkenu* (Our Father, Our King).

Sukkot, the holiday of booths, has also become an occasion for women's celebration. In Toronto, the New Israel Fund of Canada organized an event called "Sukkah by the Water" that brought together hundreds of women by the shores of Lake Ontario to recite blessings with *lulav* and *etrog*, and also raise money for feminist projects in Israel; silk panels designed by women artists transformed the *sukkah* into a beautiful display of Jewish women's art, and a new blessing praised the *Shekhinah* "who weaves women's lives around the world into a *sukkah* of peace."[72] Penina Adelman's *Miriam's Well* describes a women's *ushpizot* ceremony, which has since been adapted and used in countless synagogues and Jewish institutions. Based on the Kabbalist ritual of welcoming the *ushpizin*, our male ancestors, into the *sukkah*, Adelman's *ushpizot* ceremony welcomes the matriarchs and other women from Jewish history into the *sukkah*—thus making Sukkot an opportunity for study about Judaism's Biblical and historical foremothers. Inspired by *ushpizin* plaques that may be hung in a *sukkah*, Ma'yan: The Jewish Women's Project has developed an *ushpizot* poster of the matriarchs that presents an innovative Sukkot blessing:

Enter hallowed mothers of our people, sisters, wise women, and prophets. Take your place with us under the protecting canopy of the *Shekhinah*. Enter those who have touched our lives and those whose names have been lost to us. As we welcome you, may we welcome into our communities the voices, visions, and leadership of all women. Blessed are You, God, the Breath of all life, who makes us holy by enjoining us to dwell together in the *sukkah*.[73]

Many liberal prayer groups have added additional verses to the Shemini Atzeret rain prayer, speaking of the matriarchs and their ties to water. The excerpt below pleads for rain in remembrance of Rebecca.

Remember the kind one who carried a pitcher of water [Genesis 24:14]
To the servant she gave water [Genesis 24:17]
In Haran for the camels, she drew water [Genesis 24:19].
For her sake, grant water.[74]

An innovative ritual for Ḥanukkah, created by Rachel Josefowitz Siegel, Amy Sheldon, and Nina Judith Katz, draws on the Ḥanukkah imagery of light amid darkness. The authors explain that they "saw darkness in the Ḥanukkah story as a metaphor for the darkness that feminists feel in the world" and the "*ḥanukkiyah* as a symbol of hope that we can find more light, energy, and power than we expect when we are in personal and spiritual darkness."[75] The excerpt below, from their revised "Ḥanukkah Blessings," speaks of women's empowerment:

Blessed are You, Divine Presence, our Goddess Illuminator of the world
who helped us with Her wonders
and sanctifies us through the kindling of Hanukah lights.

We come together to sanctify this day of Hanukah
with our love and respect for each other
and for the universe in which we dwell.
In this cold and darkening winter season,
at this time of deepening conflicts,
we kindle the lights of Hanukkah as a symbol of hope
in the pursuit of peace among all people.

We bless that which is human and divine in each of us
We bless the miracle of life and death
We bless the miracle of a light that shines beyond despair
We bless the spirit of sisterhood that enables us
to speak our wisdom and faith, in our own words.

May our eyes and hearts be open to the needs
of Jewish women and women everywhere.
May our energies be faithful to the tasks of repairing the world.

May these Hanukkah candles unite us with all peoples
who have suffered oppression and struggled for freedom
in all places, at all times.[76]

Another feminist focus for Hanukkah has been the Book of Judith. This apocryphal book, which has been associated with Hanukkah since the Middle Ages, presents a powerful female heroine who acts with courage and resolve equal to that of the Maccabees. Rabbi Leah Novick developed yet another feminist celebration for Hanukkah, the honoring of a different woman for each of the eight nights. Rabbi Novick's ritual balances the usual celebration of military heroism with recognition of non-violent or "womanly" acts of heroism.[77]

In modern Orthodox communities, women's *megillah* readings for Purim have gained popularity. Since the earliest days of the Jewish feminist movement, women have analyzed and debated the characters of Esther and Vashti. By the 1990s, Purim plays in liberal synagogues or community groups consistently presented Vashti as brave and heroic. In a twist, many feminists—who had previously eschewed the more passive Esther as a role model—are now coming around to identify with many aspects of Esther's character as well.[78] As the final touch, a feminist author, Rabbi Susan Schnur, has even re-examined the hamantaschen as a fertility cake![79]

Other holiday innovations include an *omer* calendar that offers a Biblical reading about a different woman for each day.[80] Pre-Shavuot study sessions based on the all-night *tikkun leil Shavuot* have offered women marathons of learning with feminist scholars and rabbis. Other women's

Shavuot celebrations have fused the night-long study session with something like a sleepover to create all-night women's programs of study, poetry, song, and prayer. Gail Reimer and Judith Kates have also compiled a collection of feminist essays on the Book of Ruth, which we traditionally read on Shavuot.[81]

Shabbat rituals have also been influenced by feminist creative innovation, with creative Friday night blessings for daughters and numerous feminist meditations based on *Eshet Hayil*, the verses from Proverbs in praise of the woman of valor, that are traditionally recited by a husband to his wife. (See pages 136–137.) Feminists have also written many new interpretations of the *havdalah* ceremony, which sanctifies the difference between Shabbat and the workweek. Marcia Falk has rewritten the *havdalah* blessings to emphasize the holiness that resides in the weekdays as well as in Shabbat. Others have suggested using Miriam's cup as part of the *havdalah* ritual, as the water of Miriam's well is said to fill all vessels at the end of Shabbat.[82] Rabbi Leila Gal Berner has written new Hebrew verses about "Miriam Haneviah, Miriam the Prophet," to be sung to the tune of "Eliyahu Hanavi," the traditional *havdalah* song. ▨

▨ As Shabbat fades, our people's centuries-old yearning for redemption is voiced through song. When we sing the traditional "Eliyahu Hanavi," we recall the saving message and leadership of Elijah the Prophet, harbinger of the messianic age. The contemporary lyrics of "Miriam Haneviah" parallel the traditional, offering an inspiring leadership model. Midrash tells us that Miriam helped to bolster the Israelite women's courage in taking the risk of fleeing Egypt toward freedom. A prophet in her own right, Miriam led our people in a celebration and dance after we "took the plunge" to freedom at the Reed Sea (Exodus 14:20–21).—*Rabbi Leila Gal Berner*[83]

Miriam haneviah oz vezimrah be'yadah.
Miriam tirkod itanu lehagdil zimrat olam.
Miriam tirkod itanu letaken et ha'olam.
Bimherah veyameinu hi tevi'enu
el mei ha'yeshu'a.[84]

Miriam the prophet, strength and song are in her hand. Miriam will dance with us to increase the song of the world. Miriam will dance with us to repair the world. Soon and in our day, she will bring us to the waters of redemption.

As far back as the early 1970s, Rabbi Jane Rachel Litman argued for the expansion of the Jewish liturgical "canon," which had been written by men and for men, to include women's writings, such as Greek and Roman invocations and medieval poetry, as well as Yiddish women's *tehines* (supplications). Rabbi Litman was also struck by the similarity between the *Mi Khamokha* and a 4,000-year-old Akkadian hymn to the Near Eastern deity Ishtar, which she adapted for a Shabbat service.

She pays heed to compassion and friendliness.
Cooperation is truly Her possession.

A slave, a virgin, a mother, a crone—She preserves all.
One need only call upon Her—among women Her name is powerful.

Who is like Her in greatness?
Strong, exalted, splendid are Her decrees.[85]

Rosh Ḥodesh, the first of every Hebrew month, is a semi-holiday that has long been associated with women. In pre-modern Jewish communities, women refrained from certain kinds of work on this day, and in some places they recited special personal Rosh Ḥodesh prayers. Rosh Ḥodesh was first revived as a women's holiday in the 1970s, largely because of an essay by Arlene Agus.[86] Since then women's Rosh Ḥodesh groups have sprung up in every part of North America and in every denominational setting, offering a forum in which women explore Jewish spirituality in a wide variety of ways. Some groups focus on Jewish study, others on experimental rituals to mark life passages, others on traditional prayers, and others on women's empowerment.[87]

Any discussion of women's holiday rituals raises questions about the merits of single sex celebration. What is the ultimate goal of Jewish women's celebration of the holidays? Do feminists intend to create two separate experiences for every Jewish event, one for men and one for women? Or, do feminists instead intend to influence the primary, shared male-and-female experience of Jewish events so that the joint events will ultimately reflect both women's and men's input? In other words, is the women-only celebration a temporary measure?

No clear feminist answers to these questions exist, nor should we expect any. Some believe that we are so far away from a time in which communal celebrations will truly reflect both women's and men's spirituality

⊞ Of all the feminist innovations of the past 30 years, Rosh Ḥodesh stands out for its unexpected, remarkable appeal. On six continents—from Haifa to Hong Kong, Mexico City, Sydney, and Berlin—this obscure, nearly-forgotten custom has, in 30 years, become the occasion-of-choice for women's conferences, rallies, bat mitzvah celebrations, and other rites of passage for Jewish girls and women. It crosses all boundaries separating religious from secular, conservative from liberal, personal from communal, adolescent from grandmother, and even feminist from non-feminist.

That Rosh Ḥodesh is no longer the exclusive province of observant women belies the extraordinary circumstances of its rediscovery. During the infancy of modern Jewish feminism, Conservative and liberal Orthodox women were largely stymied in their quest for greater inroads into ritual, education, and scholarship. Leadership roles were rare, backlash was strong, and recently-invented New Age alternatives felt unacceptable. It was 1971, still one year before Hebrew Union College and 12 years before the Jewish Theological Seminary would admit women to their rabbinical schools.

Feminist hopes had to rest elsewhere.

It was at this moment that Rosh Ḥodesh became manifest. The existence of an ancient holiday designated for women appeared like a missing fragment of "herstory," which we had not known to seek, but which had found us. Its affirming message seemed to bear the unmistakable handprint of God.

Many of Rosh Ḥodesh's benefits were immediately apparent. Bearing the imprimatur of respected Rabbinic authorities, this "day of good beginnings" granted inclusion without revolution. Its indisputable ➤

that the ultimate goal doesn't matter now. Many women need and want women-centered rituals today. Others feel that current women-centered rituals are a way to move beyond a history of women's exclusion, and that ultimately all Jewish rituals will be fully inclusive of women and men.

Clearly today, the women's-only ceremony provides something unique. Finding a comfortable spiritual community is difficult, and many women are able to connect to a Jewish community and a Jewish spirituality within a group of Jewish women. Both women and men should be encouraged to embrace God where they find Her, whether in mixed groups or single-sex gatherings.

Certainly Judaism is a religion of women, men, and children. Jewish feminists are most deeply concerned with creating spiritual paths that benefit women, but they ultimately aim to benefit the entire community. As the many examples of this chapter indicate, the reach of Jewish feminism has become all encompassing. Merely to have one day a lifetime or one day a year on which to celebrate as Jewish women and look at Judaism through a feminist lens, then to return to a home and a synagogue that are unchanged, would be insufficient. The goal is to enhance all of Jewish life, prayer, holidays, life cycle, and

authenticity, its documentation of women's customs, and—with few known traditions—its ability to stimulate unlimited creativity.

As the fortunes of Jewish feminism waxed and waned during the ensuing decades, Rosh Hodesh evolved to serve a multiplicity of needs. First, Rosh Hodesh became common ground for feminist mothers and their non-feminist daughters, an observance that freed girls from imitating the boys' rituals. For cautious Jewish institutions, Rosh Hodesh provided an apolitical forum for responding to women. For secular Jews, the observance of Rosh Hodesh could be appealingly non-religious. Rosh Hodesh did not threaten the traditional woman's role—in fact it enriched it—and consequently allowed college women to act feminist without the label.

Perhaps most important, Rosh Hodesh unveiled a liminal space between *keva* and *kavanah*, between the obligatory canon and creative purpose. Into this space grew feminist Seders, new study genres, *tehines,* new women's prayers, and female rites of passage.

Still, the global reach of this holiday defies explanation by these factors alone. One might conjecture that our Sages, constrained by societal norms in different periods, constructed around Rosh Hodesh a type of time capsule, a message enunciating the profound importance of women to Judaism, one that would unfold over the centuries. Proof of this hypothesis lies in the potency of the devices chosen from the Rabbinic arsenal.

One pivotal device endowed Rosh Hodesh with the three defining characteristics of the pilgrimage festivals, Passover, Shavuot, and Sukkot: a link to history, a link to nature, and a prohibition of work.

Rosh Hodesh is based on the historical Biblical episode of the golden calf; because Israelite women refused to participate, they were rewarded for their righteous acts. Rosh Hodesh is linked to nature through the celestial body, the moon. Most strikingly, it bears the hallmark of a sacred day through its work prohibition. By linking women to a cardinal category of holiness, the Sages hinted at the true, eventual, place of women in tradition.

This, then, explains the profound significance of Rosh Hodesh to Jewish women. The message once sent aloft to women now, at last, is heard.—*Arlene Agus*

beyond; to help each of us find our voices in all of Jewish life; to realize how deeply our lives can be enriched by Jewish feminist spiritual vision.

Some sections were written by Claudia Chernov.

QUESTIONS FOR FURTHER STUDY AND REFLECTION

1. From the 1970s onward, women and men within the liberal streams of Judaism have come to agree that "speaking about God in exclusively masculine language reflects more than just the structure of the Hebrew language.... Referring to God as a male reflects and reinforces a system in which power and manhood are linked." Discuss the gender-sensitive changes that have occurred in Jewish prayer over the past 30 years. In your opinion, what are the advantages and disadvantages of female-oriented language in the liturgy?

2. A number of women and men who object to exclusively masculine God language also object to language that depicts a hierarchy between God and humans. Do you agree that "no hierarchical relationship can be a holy relationship"? What *is* the nature of a holy relationship?

3. In some of her prayers and blessings, Marcia Falk has eliminated direct references to God. Do we need to invoke God directly in prayers and blessings? What is our purpose in invoking God?

4. What was your initial reaction to Falk's rendition of the *Shema?* What is your current reaction?

5. Should there be a physical ritual for newborn infant daughters to signify their entrance into the Jewish people? Or, are prayers and readings adequate?

6. Do traditional rituals and ceremonies such as the Seder and *tashlikh* need to be re-interpreted? Why or why not?

7. What are the advantages and disadvantages of single-sex celebrations?

8. Consider how you would devise a new ritual or ceremony to mark an important experience in your own life. How could you devise a personal ritual that is distinctively Jewish and welded to Jewish tradition?

---

1. Rita M. Gross, "Female God Language in a Jewish Context," *Womanspirit Rising: A Feminist Reader in Religion,* Carol P. Christ and Judith Plaskow, ed. (New York: Harper & Row, 1979), page 171.

2. Susan Weidman Schneider, *Jewish and Female: A Guide and Sourcebook for Today's Jewish Woman* (New York: Touchstone/Simon & Schuster, 1985), page 80.

3. Jacques Barzun, *From Dawn to Decadence: 500 Years of Western Cultural Life, 1500 to the Present* (New York: HarperCollins, 2000), page 83.

4. Elicia Brown, "Our Mother, Our Queen," *The Jewish Week*, September 13, 2002, page 78.

5. Naomi Janowitz and Maggie Wenig, "Selections from a Prayerbook Where God's Image is Female," *Lilith* 1:4 (Fall/Winter 1977/78), page 27.

6. Naomi Janowitz and Maggie Wenig, *Siddur Nashim* (Providence, RI: privately circulated for the women's prayer group of Brown University, 1976); cited in Judith Plaskow, *Standing Again at Sinai: Judaism From a Feminist Perspective* (New York: HarperCollins 1990), page 258.

7. Lynn Gottlieb, *She Who Dwells Within: A Feminist Vision of a Renewed Judaism* (San Francisco, CA: HarperSanFrancisco, 1995), page 20.

8. Judith Plaskow, *Standing Again at Sinai*, page 139.

9. Rita Gross, "Steps Toward Feminine Imagery of Deity in Jewish Theology," *Judaism* 30:2 (Spring, 1981), reprinted in Susannah Heschel, ed., *On Being a Jewish Feminist* (New York: Schocken, 1983), page 242.

10. Lynn Gottlieb, *She Who Dwells Within,* pages 28–30. The translation of *Shaddai* plays on the meaning of *shad* as breast.

11. Marcia Prager, *The Path of Blessing* (New York: Bell Tower, 1998), page 104.

12. David Teutsch, Preface to *Kol Haneshamah: Shabbat Vehagim,* 3rd ed. (Wynwood, PA: Reconstructionist Press, 1994), page xxii.

13. Unpublished texts from Ma'yan files, New York, NY.

14. Ellen M. Umansky, "Creating a Jewish Feminist Theology" in Judith Plaskow and Carol P. Christ, eds., *Weaving the Visions: New Patterns in Feminist Spirituality* (San Francisco: HarperSanFrancisco, 1996), page 191.

15. Paula L. Reimers, "The Problems of Feminine God Language," *United Synagogue Review,* Spring 1994, pages 15, 17. In the Fall of 2002, Rabbi Reimers commented on her *United Synagogue Review* article:

"I wrote the article excerpted here nearly a decade ago. It was—and still is, I think—a good, logical, left-brain analysis. I still believe it should be heeded as a warning. I have, however, moderated my stance.

"The Torah teaches us in Genesis 1:28: 'And Deity created adam (the earth-creature) in the Divine image, in the image of Deity did Deity create adam; male and female It created them.' And in Genesis 5:1–2, the Torah teaches: 'When Deity created adam (the earth-creature), in the Divine likeness Deity created adam; male and female Deity created them. And Deity blessed them and called their name adam in the day of their creating.' These translations are my own; they are awkward in English because I have tried to preserve the unspeakable mystery of the original verses. We cannot know Deity as Deity Is; we are beings of an infinitely lesser existence. The Torah teaches, though, that on the earthly plane, the One could only be expressed as two, male and female.

"There are times in a woman's life that she must express the truth that Deity is fully involved in her life and totally understands her in all her joys and sorrows, hopes and fears. We need to express this by calling Deity 'Mother,' 'Sister,' and 'Friend.'

"As to my concerns that the masculine pronoun protected the ethical content of Jewish monotheism, the intervening years have made me painfully aware that adherence to monotheism and *mitzvot* do not guarantee ethical behavior when fear, intolerance, and love of power grip the human heart. Only those who unswervingly follow Hillel's summary of Torah 'what is hateful to you, do not do to another' *(any other)* serve Deity and maintain the ethics at the heart of Jewish monotheism."

16. A teaching of Rabbi Arthur Waskow, shared with Tamara Cohen on many occasions.

17. Marcia Falk, "Introduction to New Blessings" in Ellen M. Umansky and Dianne Ashton, eds., *Four Centuries of Jewish Women's Spirituality: A Sourcebook* (Boston: Beacon, 1992), page 241.

18. Marcia Falk, *The Book of Blessings: New Jewish Prayers for Daily Life, the Sabbath, and the New Moon Festival* (New York: HarperCollins, 1996; paperback edition, Boston: Beacon, 1999), page 132, 133. See also www.marciafalk.com.

19. Marcia Falk, *The Book of Blessings*, pages 314, 315.

20. Marcia Falk, *The Book of Blessings*, pages 10, 11.

21. Marcia Falk, *The Book of Blessings*, pages 170, 171.

22. Marcia Falk. Copyright © 2003 by Marcia Lee Falk.

23. Tikva Frymer-Kensky, *In the Wake of the Goddesses: Women, Culture, and the Biblical Transformation of Pagan Myth* (New York/Toronto: Free Press/Maxwell Macmillan, 1992), page 164.

24. Gershom Scholem, *Encyclopaedia Judaica* (Jerusalem: Keter, 1970), volume 10, pages 565, 571.

25. Judith Plaskow, *Standing Again at Sinai*, page 135.

26. Lynn Gottlieb, *She Who Dwells Within*, page 22.

27. Tikva Frymer-Kensky, *In the Wake of the Goddesses*, page 188.

28. Garrett Green, "The Gender of God and the Theology of Metaphor" in *Speaking the Christian God: The Holy Trinity and the Challenge of Feminism*, Alvin F. Kimel, Jr., ed. (Grand Rapids: Eerdmans, 1992), page 52.

29. Tikva Frymer-Kensky, "The Ritual Impulse" (review of *Miriam's Well: Rituals for Jewish Women Around the Year* by Penina V. Adelman, published by Biblio Press, 1986), *Lilith* 16 (Spring 1987), page 27.

30. Mary Gendler, "Sarah's Seed: A New Ritual for Women," *Response* 8:4 (Winter 1974–1975), pages 65–75. Cited in Rabbi Laura Geller, "*Brit Milah* and *Brit Banot*" in *Lifecycles: Jewish Women on Life Passages and Personal Milestones*, Volume 1, Rabbi Debra Orenstein, ed. (Woodstock, VT: Jewish Lights, 1994), page 63.

31. Ceremony by Margarita Freeman and Leonard Levin, described in Sharon Strassfeld, Michael Strassfeld, Daniel Margolis, Patty Margolis, "Birth" in *The Second Jewish Catalog,* Sharon and Michael Strassfeld, eds. (Philadelphia: Jewish Publication Society, 1976), page 36.

32. Ceremony by Sharon and Michael Strassfeld, described in "Birth" in *The Second Jewish Catalog,* pages 36–37.

33. Ceremony by Rabbi Ruth Sohn and others. Rabbi Ruth Sohn, et al., "The Covenant of Washing: A Ceremony to Welcome Baby Girls into the Covenant of Israel," *Menorah* 4 (May 1983), pages 3–4. Cited in Rabbi Laura Geller, "*Brit Milah* and *Brit Banot*" in *Lifecycles*, page 64.

34. Rabbi Laura Geller, "*Brit Milah* and *Brit Banot*" in *Lifecycles*, pages 64–67.

35. Rabbi Laura Geller, "*Brit Milah* and *Brit Banot*" in *Lifecycles*, page 65. Rabbi Geller states: "The girl is entered into the covenant with a new *brakhah* based on the blessing offered at a circumcision."

36. Ceremony by Mel and Shoshana Silberman uses Shabbat as a sign of the covenant, in "Birth" in *The Second Jewish Catalog,* pages 32–33; ceremony by Rabbi Paul Swerdlow uses candles, described in "Birth" in *The Second Jewish Catalog,* page 31.

37. Pages 253–254 discuss the three women's commandments.

38. Nahariyah Mosenkis, unpublished, January 1989; from the files of American Jewish Congress Feminist Center, Los Angeles, CA.

39. See Shulamit Magnus, "*Simhat Lev:* Celebrating a Birth" and Treasure Cohen, "Creating a Tree-dition" in *Lifecycles,* pages 68–82.

40. Maria Papacostaki and Harry Brod, "Weaning Ceremony" in *A Ceremonies Sampler: New Rites, Celebrations, and Observances of Jewish Women*, Elizabeth Levine, ed. (San Diego: Women's Institute for Continuing Jewish Education, 1991), pages 39–41.

41. Maria Papacostaki and Harry Brod, page 40.

42. See "Beginnings" unit in Rabbi Debra Orenstein, ed., *Lifecycles*, and "Pregnancy, Birth, and Mothering Ceremonies" unit in Elizabeth Levine, ed., *A Ceremonies Sampler*.

43. Nina Beth Cardin, *Tears of Sorrow, Seeds of Hope: A Jewish Spiritual Companion for Infertility and Pregnancy Loss* (Woodstock, VT: Jewish Lights, 1999), page 123.

44. Chava Weissler provides an excellent analysis of modern *teḥines* in *Voices of the Matriarchs: Listening to the Prayers of Early Modern Jewish Women* (Boston: Beacon, 1998) in the chapter "American Transformation of the *Tkhines*." See especially pages 163 to 171.

45. Sandy Eisenberg Sasso, "Personal Prayers" in *A Ceremonies Sampler*, page 44.

46. Rabbi Debra Orenstein, "Infertility and Early Losses" in *Lifecycles*, page 37.

47. Bonnie and Lawrence Baron, "*Seder Kabbalat Akarut*, Accepting the Loss of the Dream for a Biological Child" in *A Ceremonies Sampler*, pages 47–53.

48. Bonnie and Lawrence Baron, page 51.

49. Lynn Gottlieb, "The Fruits of Creation" in *Lifecycles*, pages 40–44.

50. Lynn Gottlieb, "The Fruits of Creation," page 43.

51. Rabbi Debra Orenstein, "Invisible Life Passages" in *Lifecycles*, pages 117–120; Leila Gal Berner, "Our Silent Seasons," pages 121–136.

52. Leila Gal Berner, "Our Silent Seasons" in *Lifecycles*, page 122.

53. Nina Beth Cardin, *Tears of Sorrow, Seeds of Hope*, pages 97–98.

54. Nancy Helman Shneiderman, "Midlife Covenant: Healing Ritual After Hysterectomy" in *A Ceremonies Sampler*, pages 55–60. The author noted that obtaining the womb required careful and continuing collaboration with both surgeon and pathologist.

55. Laura Levitt and Sue Ann Wasserman, "*Mikvah* Ceremony for Laura (1989)" in *Four Centuries of Jewish Women's Spirituality*, pages 321–326.

56. Sara Paasche Orlow, Ritual for having a breast cyst removed, unpublished, Ma'yan ritual files.

57. Several sources invert the ancient blessing *shelo asani ishah* (who has not made me a woman), and use *she'asani ishah* (who has made me a woman) to mark the first menstrual period. The blessing "who has created me a woman" is part of a quotation from an undated broadside distributed by Bat Kol, a Jewish women's theater group, in the mid-1970s, included in Susan Weidman Schneider's discussion of menstruation in *Jewish and Female: Choices and Changes in Our Lives Today* (New York: Simon & Schuster, 1985), page 133. (Bat Kol was created by Lynn Gottlieb, Elaine Shapiro, and Eleanor Schick in 1975; *She Who Dwells Within*, page 117). The blessing "who has created me a woman" is also printed in a ceremony by Barbara Kochman Singer, "*Birkat Ha-Neetzan*: Blessing the Blossom" (*A Ceremonies Sampler*, page 83). Laura Geller includes the words *she'asani ishah* in describing her own experience of menstruating for the first time in a 1986 sermon, "Encountering the Divine Presence," printed in *Four Centuries of Jewish Women's Spirituality*, page 244. An Israeli source for inverting the male blessing is a Hebrew poem by Esther Raab (1894–1981), which uses the phrase *barukh she'asani ishah*, "Blessed [is God] who made me a woman" (page 284).

58. Sylvia Barack Fishman, *A Breath of Life: Feminism in the American Jewish Community* (New York: Free Press/Simon & Schuster, 1993), pages 130–131. Professor Fishman writes: "Suzanne Reisman, a potter and grandmother from Long Island [New York], states unequivocally that her recent bat mitzvah at her Reform temple was one of the great events of her lifetime."

59. Rachel Adler, "*B'rit Ahuvim:* A Marriage Between Subjects" in *Engendering Judaism: An Inclusive Theology and Ethics* (Philadelphia: Jewish Publication Society, 1998), pages 169–207.

60. Rachel Adler, "*B'rit Ahuvim* Lovers' Covenant" in *Engendering Judaism*, pages 214–215.

61. Vicki Hollander, "The New Improved Jewish Divorce: Her/His," *Lilith* 15:3 (Summer 1990), revised as "Weathering the Passage: Jewish Divorce" in *Lifecycles*, pages 201–205.

62. Phyllis Ocean Berman, "Recreating Menopause," *Moment*, February 1994.

63. Barbara D. Holender, "A Ceremony of Passage on My Sixty-Fifth Birthday" in *Lifecycles*, pages 332–334.

64. Bonnie Feinman, "A Midlife Celebration" in *Midlife and Its Rite of Passage Ceremony,* Irene Fine, ed. (San Diego: Woman's Institute for Continuing Jewish Education, 1983).

65. Marcia Gladys Cohn Spiegel, *Simchat Chochmah: Shabbat Chayye Sarah 5748, Saturday November 14, 1987*, unpublished, files of the American Jewish Congress Feminist Center, Los Angeles, CA.

66. Savina J. Teubal, "Simchat Hochmah" in *Four Centuries of Jewish Women's Spirituality*, pages 257–265. The ceremony was written in November 1986.

67. Rabbi Geoffrey Haber, cited in Nina Beth Cardin, *The Tapestry of Jewish Time: A Spiritual Guide to Holidays and Life-Cycle Events* (Springfield, NJ: Behrman House, 2000), page 205.

68. Catherine Madsen, "Kitsch and Liturgy," *Tikkun* 16:2 (March/April 2001), pages 41–43. Catherine Madsen is a contributing editor to the interreligious journal *CrossCurrents* and the author of a novel, *A Portable Egypt*.

69. For a comprehensive review of women's *Haggadot*, see Maida E. Solomon, "Women's *Haggadot*" in *Talking Back: Images of Jewish Women in American Popular Culture* (Brandeis Series in American Jewish History, Culture and Life), Joyce Antler, ed. (Waltham: Brandeis University, 1997).

70. E. M. Broner with Naomi Nimrod, *The Women's Haggadah*, revised from E. M. Broner, *The Telling: The Story of a Group of Jewish Women Who Journey to Spirituality Through Community and Ceremony* (New York: HarperCollins/HarperSanFrancisco, 1993), pages 211–213.

71. For further details, see Sonia Zylberberg, "Oranges and Seders: Symbols of Jewish Women's Wrestlings," *Nashim: A Journal of Jewish Women's Studies & Gender Issues,* 5 (Fall 2002/5763), pages 148–171.

72. Sukkah by the Water pamphlet, sponsored by the New Israel Fund of Canada, unpublished. Event held Sunday, September 25, 5755/1995, Toronto, Canada.

73. Ma'yan poster, undated (approximately 1990s). Available through Ma'yan (212-580-0099 or www.mayan.org).

74. See Mark Frydenberg, "Geshem: Verses for Our Mothers," translated by Rabbi Simcha Roth (1995, 1998), *Journey*, Fall 2000 (publication of Ma'yan: The Jewish Women's Project).

75. Nina Katz, Amy Sheldon, and Rachel Josefowitz Siegel, "Hanukah: Lighting the Way to Women's Empowerment" in *A Ceremonies Sampler*, page 111.

76. Rachel Josefowitz Siegel, Amy Sheldon, and Nina Katz, "Hanukkah Blessings," revised by the authors in December, 2001. Two earlier complete versions of this blessing, including a discussion and the Hebrew version of the first two lines (created by the Banoth Yerushalayim Feminist Liturgy Project), have been previously

published: Nina Katz, Amy Sheldon, and Rachel Josefowitz Siegel, "Hanukah: Lighting the Way to Women's Empowerment" in *A Ceremonies Sampler*, pages 111–114; and Nina Katz, Amy Sheldon, and Rachel Josefowitz Siegel, "Hanukah: Lighting the Way to Women's Empowerment: A Feminist Ritual of Food, Prayer, and Ourstorytelling" *Bridges* 1:2 (Fall, 1990), pages 30–31.

77. Rabbi Leah Novick, "The Peaceful Maccabee: A Ceremony for the Eight Nights of Chanukkah," *Tikkun* 14:6 (November/December 1999), part 2 of "Chanukah Insert" between pages 64–65.

78. Gail Twersky Reimer, "Eschewing Esther/Embracing Esther: The Changing Representation of Biblical Heroines" in *Talking Back*, Joyce Antler, ed.

79. Rabbi Susan Schnur, "From Prehistoric Cave Art to Your Cookie Pan: Tracing the Hamantasch Herstory," *Lilith*, Spring 1998, pages 22–24.

80. Omer Calendar published by Kolot: The Center for Women's and Gender Studies at The Reconstructionist Rabbinical College, Spring 2000.

81. Gail Reimer and Judith Kates, *Reading Ruth: Contemporary Women Reclaim A Sacred Story* (New York: Ballantine, 1994).

82. Kol Isha, 1990 (Kol Isha, P.O. Box 132, Wayland, MA 01778).

83. Rabbi Leila Gal Berner, "Commentary" in *Kol Haneshamah: Shabbat Vehagim*, page 520.

84. Rabbi Leila Gal Berner, "Miriam Haneviah," in *Kol Haneshamah: Shabbat Vehagim*, page 521. Rabbi Berner notes: "The words are meant to be sung to the same melody as 'Eliyahu Hanavi,' but 'Miriam Haneviah' has an additional line of verse. The third line is sung musically just like the second line, except that at the end the notes go down instead of up." The song "Miriam Haneviah" was conceived by Rabbi Leila Gal Berner and Rabbi Arthur Waskow; Hebrew by Rabbi Berner; it originally appeared in *Siddur Or Chadash*, published in 1989 by the P'nai Or Religious Fellowship.

85. Rabbi Jane Rachel Litman, adaptation for a Shabbat service of *Mi Khamokha* and "A Responsive Prayer to Ishtar—1600 BCE," translated from Akkadian by Ferris J. Stevens (approximately 1973), unpublished.

86. Arlene Agus, "This Month Is For You: Observing Rosh Hodesh as a Woman's Holiday," in *The Jewish Woman: New Perspectives*, Elizabeth Koltun, ed. (New York: Schocken, 1976), pages 84–93.

87. *Moonbeams: A Hadassah Rosh Hodesh Guide* (Woodstock, VT: Jewish Lights, 2000) presents Biblical and medieval Jewish sources on Rosh Hodesh, and briefly outlines modern developments. Penina Adelman's groundbreaking *Miriam's Well: Rituals for Jewish Women Around the Year* presented the experiences of one of the first modern Rosh Hodesh groups. First published in 1986 by Biblio Press of New York, the book has since been revised and reissued. *Celebrating the New Moon: A Rosh Chodesh Anthology* (Northvale, NJ: Jason Aronson, 1996), edited by Susan Berrin, offers a variety of perspectives.

Chapter

ORTHODOX WOMEN'S PRIVATE PRAYERS

May the merit of our mother Hannah protect her daughters

Leora Tanenbaum with Vanessa Paloma

Hannah, who lived in Israel in the 11th century before the common era, was a pious woman unable to bear children. In despair, she made a special visit by herself to the sanctuary in Shiloh, and she prayed there, standing and crying. She promised that if she bore a boy, she would raise him to become a servant of God. Hannah was so immersed in her heartfelt plea— moving her lips but not voicing the words aloud—that the priest Eli, who was observing her, assumed she was drunk and reprimanded her. When Hannah explained that she was entirely sober and was praying to God out of distress and conviction, Eli blessed her (I Samuel 1:1-20). Soon after, Hannah conceived and bore a son, Samuel, who grew up to become a prophet and a great leader.

The Rabbis of the Talmud regarded Hannah, a woman with a woman's unique lament, as the architect of Jewish worship. They recognized her as a role model and expressed awe at her piety. Yet they were blind to her as a *woman* who prayed. These same Rabbis prohibited women from actively participating in formal prayer services together with men. They imposed many inequities: Historically, women have not counted in the *minyan* (quorum of ten Jews necessary for communal prayer); they have not been eligible to receive an *aliyah* (the honor of reciting the blessings for the Torah reading); they have not been eligible to chant the Torah aloud; they listened to men thank God for not making them women; and they have been seated apart from men, separated by a *mehitzah* (barrier beween men's and women's sections).▣

⬚ Orthodox women sit behind a barrier, the *mehitzah*, though the degree of separation varies from synagogue to synagogue. In many synagogues, women's seating is located behind the men's, with a barrier separating the two areas. Also common is an upstairs gallery with women's seating; the gallery wall serves as the barrier. In a few Orthodox synagogues, women are completely unable to see the *bimah* (raised platform from which the Torah is read) and almost completely unable to hear the rabbi or cantor.

The origins of the *mehitzah* are in dispute, but we know that in the Second Temple, women and men were separated on at least one occasion every year—the *simhat beit hasho'evah*, the water drawing festival on the second evening of Sukkot. Today, Orthodox rabbinic authorities defend the *mehitzah* as law rather than mere custom.

Some Orthodox synagogues have seating arrangements that are relatively woman-friendly. The Hebrew Institute of Riverdale, New York, has a *mehitzah* down the center of the sanctuary, with the *bimah* in front of both the men's and women's sections, so that both women and men have equal access to the synagogue "action." The sanctuary of Lincoln Square Synagogue in New York City is in the round, with a clear, lucite *mehitzah*. The *bimah* is in the center of the men's section, and women do not have access to it, but women can easily see the men and the *bimah*. Another woman-friendly seating arrangement in some Orthodox synagogues places men in the center of the sanctuary, with women on either side in slightly raised seating, easily able to both see and hear.—*LT*

❁ All [branches of feminism,] including modern Orthodox feminism, claim that what "is" does not serve as a justification for continuing the status quo and certainly is not necessarily what "ought to be." ... So we ask: is gender inequality in Orthodox Judaism really God given? Perhaps there are other ways of conceptualizing and expressing the nature of our womanhood, our rights, our obligations, and the character of our relationships....

One of our essential dilemmas derives from our secular lives—in which we are equal and full citizens. We would not tolerate our daughter's rejection from medical school based upon her gender. If she were ➤

Many Jewish women today are guided by feminist principles, and they have successfully fought for equity in both civil and religious life. Reform, Reconstructionist, and Conservative feminists have instituted changes that allow women to participate in the synagogue exactly as men do. Orthodox feminists, in contrast, accept that women and men have different roles at synagogue. Though they seek to expand women's roles, they do not advocate mixed seating for men and women. Similarly, in the liturgical sphere, feminists from the liberal denominations and feminists in the Orthodox movement have sought divergent goals. ❁ Chapter 10 presented liturgical changes that have accompanied feminist innovations in the Reform, Reconstructionist, and Conservative movements. Orthodox women, though, generally believe that the words of the *siddur* should not be changed. Instead, they supplement traditional communal prayers with *private* prayers—a long-held Jewish practice. Just as Hannah prayed in a manner so heartfelt, so moving, and so humble that she has become a model for all Jews, so too have women throughout the centuries found their own ways to communicate powerfully, privately, and creatively with God.

Women and Communal Prayer—The Sources

Archaeological evidence and Talmudic discussion show that for as long as there have been synagogues, women have attended them to pray. Prayer is a positive commandment, and the Rabbis of the Talmud (as well as all later authorities) agree that women are obligated to pray. But, because some prayers are recited at fixed times and because women are exempt from positive commandments performed at fixed times, authorities have disagreed about which prayers are mandatory. One rationale for women's exemption from time-specific commandments has been that women, unlike men, are too busy with child-rearing and housekeeping to adhere to a rigid schedule. (Exceptions, though, have existed since the Talmudic era. For example, women are obligated to light and bless Shabbat candles immediately before sunset on Friday and to drink four cups of wine during the Passover Seder on the first night of the holiday.)

Mishnah *Brakhot* 3:3 states: "Women and slaves and minors are exempt from reciting the *Shema* and from wearing *tefillin*, but they are subject to the obligations of reciting prayers, affixing the *mezuzah*, and saying the benediction after meals." The later Rabbis of the *Gemara* reasoned in *Brakhot* 20b that women must pray even though they are exempt from *Shema* and *tefillin*, because prayer entails asking God for mercy—and women, like men, are in need of God's mercy.

Maimonides elaborated, even asserting that the obligation to pray,

to sit behind the wall in law school and not be granted the degree in the end, we would be outraged and act upon our anger.

However, with regard to our Jewish identity and practice we are largely spectators and enablers. Even those with broad and deep mastery of Judaic knowledge continue to have limited access to formal power. Women can be lawyers and judges but not *dayanot* [judges in rabbinic court]; women can be political advocates but remain *agunot* [legally married though abandoned by their husbands]; women can be public speakers but not *hazzaniot* [cantors]; women can master Torah *shebe'al peh* [Oral Torah, Talmud], but not be *poskot* [interpreters of religious law].[1] These circumscribed roles create spiritual, psychic, and social predicaments for us. They heighten dissonance in our thinking and hurt our spirits. As Orthodox feminists, we are trying to make sense of our inequality. We are giving voice to something that for so long remained unspoken.

The vehemence of our critics attests to the potency of the threat they sense to patriarchal Judaism. Beginning from the time of Rav Kook [early 20th century], rabbinic authorities perceived feminism as a secular movement.... Rabbi Meir Twersky calls our feminism "ideational assimilation." ...

Perhaps one of the striking differences between the women's movement and Orthodox feminism is that the former not only believes in change but also that women are powerful agents of change. Orthodox feminists hope that our knowledge will get us power, yet we still abide a system where change is legitimate only when sanctioned by the interpretations of *gedolim* [great sages], who seem to be reluctant to explore relevant *halakhah* even in legitimate ways.

What our critics miss is that the impetus for our feminism comes precisely from our passionate Jewish commitment. We are accused of betraying Jewish tradition by introducing alien notions into it. We are challenged to forever demonstrate our religious commitment and obedience. We are constantly proving that we are *frum* [observant, religious] enough, motherly enough, and that we also never burn the chulent [Shabbat stew].—*Tova Hartman-Halbertal with Tamar H. Miller*[2]

which is incumbent on both women and men, is mandated by God in the Torah, and not merely by the Rabbis of the Talmud, as earlier scholars had assumed. In *Mishneh Torah, Laws of Prayer* 1:2, Maimonides wrote:

> Women … are obligated to pray since it is not a time-bound commandment. The [Torah-based] obligation to pray takes the following form: that a person shall entreat and pray to God each day by declaring God's praises, then petition for his [or her] needs, as necessary, and then he [or she] is to give thanks to God for God's beneficence.

At a minimum, then, women must pray once daily, at any time. The question follows: Which prayers must a woman recite? Could a woman's private, personal prayers fulfill the obligation? Or, is she obligated to recite the fixed-time prayers that form the core of a communal service—even if she does not recite them at the fixed times? Maimonides does not address whether women must recite the daily fixed-time prayers of *Shaḥarit* and *Minḥah,* but Rabbi David Auerbach, writing in 1983, argues that, according to Maimonides's opinions, women are obligated to recite both.[3] (The Evening Service, *Maariv,* was originally voluntary, though it later became obligatory—but only for men. Women are not prohibited from reciting *Maariv,* but Orthodox rabbinic authorities consider women exempt from this obligation.) While only a minority state that women must recite the fixed-time prayers, rabbinic authorities agree that women must pray every day in some form.[4]

Yiddish Women's Prayers

Jewish ritual law requires women to pray daily, but it is not explicit about exactly which prayers a woman must say. Paradoxically, this lack of a compulsory daily liturgy may have set the stage for women's liturgical creativity.

In medieval and early modern Europe, Jewish women received only a minimal education, in part because they played no role in public life. Women were excluded not only from synagogue leadership, but also from the *beit midrash* (house of study) and the *beit din* (rabbinical court). Until our own time, the overwhelming majority of Jewish women could not read the Hebrew of the *siddur* and were unfamiliar with the structure and content of Hebrew liturgy.

Women did, however, attend synagogue on many occasions, so they routinely appointed an educated woman (for example, the rabbi's wife or daughter) to lead them in prayer in the separate women's section. In 13th-century Worms, a major German Jewish community, a woman named Urania was the cantor of the women's service, which was held in a separate room adjoining the men's service. Her tombstone calls her "the eminent and excellent lady Urania, the daughter of Rabbi Abraham, who was the chief of the synagogue singers." Likewise, a woman named Richenza led women's prayers in 13th-century Nuremberg, and Dulcie of Worms, wife of the well-known Rabbi Elazar (haRokea<u>h</u>), led prayers in the women's section of her synagogue.[5]

Throughout the Middle Ages, Jews were expelled from many parts of western European countries. Large Jewish communities arose in Eastern Europe, and the tradition of the female prayer leader became an institution there. Known as a *firzogerin* or *zogerke* (foresayer) in Yiddish, she led women's services in Russia and Poland until the early 20th century. The *firzogerin* showed the women the appropriate movements (when to rise, when to bend one's knees and bow one's head) and led the recital of the Hebrew prayers, often providing translations and commentaries so that all could connect to the words they were saying. The women's section was an emotional place; women often sobbed as they beseeched God. In a description of one *firzogerin,* Yiddish writer and satirist of the late 1800s Mendele Mokher Seforim wrote, "It was hardly possible to keep from fainting when Sarah read. She would read with great emotion, her melody melting the soul and pulling at the heart strings."[6] This is not to suggest, however, that women cried instead of praying; rather, their tears were an integral part of the process of praying.

Starting in late medieval Europe and continuing until the 20th century, some women's prayer leaders, in an effort to draw women toward Jewish spiritual expression and perhaps also to find an outlet for their own yearnings, began to write and publish their own Yiddish-language prayers, which became known as *te<u>h</u>ines* (supplications). The first *te<u>h</u>ine* to appear in print was translated from Hebrew and published in Cracow in 1577. By the 18th century, printed editions of Yiddish *te<u>h</u>ines* were widespread, often as pocket-sized books. Most *te<u>h</u>ines* were written by men, although they were intended for women. Though few women understood Hebrew, many could read Yiddish, which uses Hebrew characters.

Many women's prayers were connected with the Hebrew liturgy and were intended for recitation in the synagogue on Shabbat, Rosh <u>H</u>odesh, or the Days of Awe. Rebecca Tiktiner of Prague (died 1550), the daughter of Rabbi Meir of Tiktiner, wrote a song meant to be sung by women in synagogue as they adorned the Torah scroll in preparation for the holiday of Sim<u>h</u>at Torah.[7] Some of these synagogue *te<u>h</u>ines* were explanations and interpretations of the Hebrew prayers and were intended for recital by the *firzogerin.* Very many *te<u>h</u>ines,* however, were for private recitation. An entire category of *te<u>h</u>ines* involved the observance of the three special women's commandments. These are: 1) taking <u>h</u>allah—separating a small portion of dough when preparing bread (today the bread itself is also known as <u>h</u>allah); 2) *niddah*—separating from one's husband during the 12 days that commence with the first day of menstruation, and afterwards ritually immersing in the *mikvah* (ritual pool of water); and 3) *hadlakat nerot*—kindling Shabbat and holiday candles. The first letters of each word of the three women's commandments are often combined to form the acrostic ḥ-n-h, pronounced "Ḥannah," in recognition of the Biblical Hannah, known for her beautiful plea to God.

A prayer to be recited before separating the dough for *ḥallah* creates a complex web of meanings:

Praised are You, God our Lord, the God of our forebears. You have sanctified Your people Israel more than all the other peoples on the earth, and have commanded them Your commandments. You have commanded that when we knead the dough for our bread, (we must) separate a portion of it for You, God Almighty. You have required us to give it to the Priest, who is clean of all impurity. For You separated out a portion of the earth and created the human being from it, and gave him a pure soul from the place of the pure, where the pure High Priest stands; there is no impurity there. Now we have been punished because of our sins and the sins of our forebears, so that Jerusalem, the holy city, was destroyed.... I pray You, God, my Lord, that you grant me and my husband and my children the privilege of living to see that the holy House will be rebuilt and that Jerusalem will be once again as it was of old, and Your people Israel will once more dwell in the holy land.[8]

The woman who recites this personal prayer recalls the High Priest and Biblical rules of Temple purity, and, through taking *ḥallah*, she becomes a part of both ancient tradition and future redemption.

The following prayer was for recitation after the lighting of the Sabbath candles:

You, holy God, have hallowed Your people *Yisroel* [Israel] and the *Shabbes* [Sabbath]. You are the only God, and You have chosen only our ancestors—from among all peoples—to serve You. And You have chosen the *Shabbes* alone for rest, for honor, and for blessing, for lighting candles, and for joy and delight in Your service. Today is Your *Shabbes koydesh* [holy Sabbath], which we are obliged to maintain as a *khosn* [groom] cares for his *kale* [bride].... May we merit that You cause us to inherit that day which is wholly *Shabbes* [Mishnah, *Tamid* 7:4], which means: May we live until the time of the resurrection of the dead. Praised be You, God, who lives forever.[9]

Again, this personal prayer incorporates a web of associations. It alludes to Israel's election to God's service; to the Kabbalist concept of Shabbat as bride; and to Shabbat as a foretaste of the messianic age.

A 17th-century *teḥine* on *niddah* incorporates instruction on the proper observance of the commandment:

Jewish women [must] separate themselves from their husbands for "one full day before the onset of their menses" [Babylonian Talmud, *Shavuot* 18b].... We have included this rule in the *teḥine* so that every woman may be forewarned. Because of its merit, they will have a good reward in this world, and they will

have good and pious children and wise sons who will teach many people. Moreover, they will receive a great reward in the world-to-come. May the merit of our mother Hannah protect their daughters that they may correctly observe their *mitsves* [commandments].[10]

Many other *tehines* were also intended for private recitation. Some were connected with becoming pregnant or giving birth, others with a child's recovery from illness or a husband leaving home for a business trip.

Tehine booklets contained introductory remarks, frequently directions, for each prayer: "A pretty *tehine* to say on the Sabbath with great devotion"; "A *tehine* that the woman should pray for herself and her husband and children"; "What one says when one comes into the synagogue."[11]

Although most *tehines* were published without attribution as part of a collection, and although men commonly wrote *tehines,* evidence exists that some were indeed written by *firzogerins.* Famous female authors include Sarah bas Tovim in the 17th century, author of *Shloshe She'arim* (Three Gates), and Leah Horowitz in the 18th century, who used the pen name Sarah Rebecca Rachel Leah Horowitz and was the author of "The *Tehine* of the Matriarchs." Both were daughters of rabbis. Other *firzogerins* who composed *tehines* were Taube, wife of Jacob Pan of Prague (17th century); Bella, wife of Josepho the Hazzan Horvitz (18th century); and Serel bat Rabbi Jacob haLevi Segal of Dubnow, the wife of Rabbi Mordecai Katz Rapoport (19th century).[12]

The rise of *tehines* was aided by developments in the Jewish and the European world. In the 18th century, Israel ben Eliezer, the Baal Shem Tov, founded the hasidic movement in Eastern Europe, stressing intimate, personal connection to God. Hasidism, which incorporated mystical teachings and encouraged new methods of reaching out to God—through ecstatic behavior, corporeal worship, and music—rapidly spread throughout Europe's Jewish communities. At the same time, printed books became affordable, so that for the first time masses of people could purchase them. As the distribution of printed materials became commonplace, European rabbis began to collect and publish folklore, homiletic tales, and devotional literature in Yiddish. Hebrew religious works were translated and explained. The *Tseno Ureno* (Go Out and See), a Yiddish version of the Five Books of Moses—organized according to the weekly Torah portion and including explanatory Rabbinic legends and ethical teachings—was first published in 1622. It remained in print until the 20th century, enabling women (and men who were not literate in Hebrew) to follow the Torah portion read each week in synagogue.[13]

Chava Weissler, the pre-eminent historian of *tehines* and author of the ground-breaking *Voices of the Matriarchs,* points out several differences between *tehines* written in Western and Eastern Europe. First, Jews of Western Europe began publishing devotional collections about a hundred years earlier than Eastern European Jews. Second, in the mid-18th century, many of the individual prayers that had been printed in Western Europe were combined into one standard edition, *Seder Tehines Uvakoshes* (Order of Supplications and Petitions). It contained approximately 120 *tehines*, which ran the gamut from elaborations on the *siddur* to meditations on domestic life. This collection was reprinted many times over the next two centuries. Eastern European collections tended to be shorter, including only 8 to 12 pages. Third, Eastern European collections, unlike Western European collections, often name a woman as the author, the translator, or the transcriber of the supplications.

Finally, Eastern European *tehines* were much more connected with the synagogue than were the collections from Western Europe. Penitential *tehines* for the month preceding Rosh Hashanah and for the High Holy Days themselves were particularly numerous and popular in Eastern European collections. In addition, many printed editions of the *siddur* included *tehines,* especially prayer books that had both the Hebrew liturgy and Yiddish translations. The *tehines* might be included as introductory pieces before sections of prayer or as an appendix at the end of the prayer book. "The overall emphasis on liturgical events," Weissler believes, "suggests that, in contrast to their counterparts in Western Europe, Eastern European *tehine* authors and/or readers were more interested in women's relationship to the communal domain of men and somewhat less interested in the religious meanings of other aspects of their lives."[14]

Immediacy and Individuality of *Tehines*

Tehines differed from the prayers of the *siddur* most noticeably in the use of Yiddish—the vernacular language—rather than Hebrew, the holy language. Furthermore, *tehines* were fluid, flexible, and voluntary. Finally, many *tehines*, especially those to be recited in connection with the Hannah commandments, were intended for individual, private recitation. A woman typically recited these *tehines* alone, in the comfort of her home. Unlike the Hebrew prayers, *tehines* were most commonly written in the first person singular, making them intimate in tone. Many *tehines,* whether recited at home or in the synagogue, allowed space for the petitioner to add her own name, leading to the feeling of making a personal address to God. *Tehines*, within women's domain, presented an alternative way of communicating with God that was valid and legitimate.

Weissler notes the contrast between the way men and women welcomed in Shabbat on Friday night. Both observed "the Sabbath day to keep it holy" (Exodus 20:8), but men attended the *Kabbalat Shabbat* service in synagogue, while women lit candles at home. Women had spent the entire day cleaning their homes and preparing the food for the Friday night and Saturday afternoon meals. For each task, a woman had a *tehine* for her use.[15] These prayers lent spiritual relevance and immediacy to the mundane aspects of women's lives, infusing chores with a spark of the sacred.

When removing a piece of dough before baking a loaf of bread, women remembered through their *tehine* that the *hallah* was to be set apart because:

In former times the priest used to accept the tithe on produce, also the Levite received the tithe, and the poor man the poor man's tithe; finally, there was also for people the second tithe (consumed by the owner in Jerusalem). But nowadays, since the holy Temple was destroyed because of our many sins, all has been nullified except for the *mitzve* [commandment] of *hallah*. Therefore, *Ribono shel olam* [Lord of the universe], we ask that You accept the *mitzve of hallah* and send us great blessing in our wanderings and do not let our children become estranged [from our religious tradition]. Enable my husband and me to support them by ourselves throughout a long life. May the *mitzve of hallah* be acceptable to You as though we were fulfilling all 613 commandments.[16]

Likewise, when lighting the Shabbat candles, a woman could pray:

ly *Riboyne shel oylem* [Lord of the universe], may the *mitsve* [commandment] of my lighting the candles be accepted as equivalent to the *mitsve* of the *koyen godl* [the High Priest] when he lit the candles in the precious *beys hamikdesh* [holy Temple]. As his observance was accepted, so may mine be accepted.... May our *mitsves* be accepted as equivalent to the *mitsves* of our patriarchs and matriarchs and of the holy tribes so that we may be as pure as a child newly born of its mother.[17]

Through these *tehines,* both excerpted from *The Three Gates* by Sarah bas Tovim, women could feel part of the chain of Jewish history. They kept alive the hope for a rebuilt Temple. Just as preparing bread connected the women with the ancient tithes of the priests, kindling the Shabbat lights could be considered equivalent to the lighting of the menorah by the high priest in the Temple. The religious obligations themselves and the woman who performed them were both made holy through the invocation.

Tehines often called up the legacies of the matriarchs—Sarah, Rebecca, Rachel, and Leah—whose names are absent from almost all the prayers of the *siddur.* Thus, Eastern European women could identify with and feel a special connection with the women of the Bible. The names of the matriarchs were inserted in many *tehines* following the names of the patriarchs ("in honor of our holy fathers Abraham, Isaac, and Jacob, and our mothers Sarah, Rebecca, Rachel, and Leah"). Often the matriarchs alone were named, particularly in *tehines* related to domestic affairs. Some *tehines* focused at length on the life and deeds of a specific matriarch, and some called upon the matriarch to intercede with God on behalf of the woman reciting the *tehine*. The heart-wrenching supplication "*Tehine* of the Matriarchs," written by Leah Horowitz for recitation on Rosh Ḥodesh, provides an example:

By the merit of our mother Sarah, for whose sake You have commanded and said, "Touch not My anointed ones" (Psalms 105:15), which means in Yiddish, You nations! Do not dare to touch My righteous ones! Thus too, may no nation have any power [over] her children to touch them for evil.

By the merit of our mother Rebecca, who caused our father Jacob to receive the blessings from father Isaac. May these blessings soon be fulfilled for Israel her children!

By the merit of our faithful mother Rachel, to whom You promised that by her merit, we, the children of Israel, would come out of exile. For when the children of Israel were led into exile, they were led not far from the grave into which our mother Rachel lay. They pleaded with the foe to permit them to go to Rachel's tomb. And when the Israelites came to our mother Rachel, and began to weep and cry, "Mother, mother, how can you look on while, right in front of you, we are being led into exile?" Rachel went up before God with a bitter cry, and spoke: "Lord of the world, Your mercy is certainly greater than the mercy of any human being. Moreover, I had compassion on my sister Leah when my father switched us and gave her to my husband. He told her to expect that my husband would think that I was the one. No matter that it caused me great pain; I told her the signs [that Jacob and I had agreed upon to prevent the switch]. Thus, even more so, it is undoubtedly fitting for You, God, who are entirely compassionate and gracious, to have mercy and bring us out of this exile now." So may it come to pass, for the sake of her merit.

And for the sake of the merit of our mother Leah, who wept day and night that she not fall to the lot of the wicked Esau, until her eyes became dim. For the sake of her merit, may You enlighten our eyes out of this dark exile.[18]

In a *teḥine* for candle-lighting, a woman would ask God to "listen to my prayer as You listened to and accepted the prayer of our mother Hannah, may she rest in peace. She had been barren, but You destined her for good, pious children."[19] In a *teḥine* to be recited after lighting Ḥanukkah candles, a woman prayed to God to remember the merit "of the righteous woman Judith whom You designated to deliver Your children and behead Holofernes."[20] ⊠

🔲 Judith was a young, beautiful widow who lived during the time of the Second Temple. She seduced the Syrian commander in chief, Holofernes, and invited him to a feast where she plied him with wine; when he became drunk, she beheaded him with his own dagger. In panic, his soldiers fled. The Book of Judith is a non-canonical work written in the Second Temple period.—*LT*

Teḥines written later in the 19th century focus more closely on family events and family relations, reflecting changes in outlook that were occurring throughout Europe.[21] For Jews as well as other Europeans, the family came to be seen as meeting emotional and psychological, as well as material, needs. For example, the number of arranged marriages declined while the number of marriages based on love increased. Women of the 19th century wrote *tehines* to be recited upon becoming pregnant; upon the onset of labor and the beginning of delivery; upon nursing for the first time; upon the eruption of a baby's first tooth; when a child was sick; when a boy attended *heder* (religious school) for the first time, and so on. Such prayers allowed women to make part of their religious practice both childbirth and the awe they felt as they watched the development of their children.

Eastern European Jews coming to America in the late 19th and early 20th centuries continued to compose new *tehines* to deal with their experiences as immigrants.[22] *A naye tehine tsu hashkomes boyker* (A New *Tehine* upon Arising in the Morning), written for immigrants to North America in the early 20th century, read in part:

Although You, Lord of the universe, are our protector, yet You have written in the holy Torah that human beings should not depend on miracles, and when a person looks after himself, the Lord of the universe looks after him, too. And as it is well known that many infectious diseases come from lack of cleanliness, I therefore petition You for the strength and the wisdom to know how to keep my home and the members of my household properly clean. May You also send me the understanding to know how to preserve my health and strength, the health and strength of my husband, and the health and strength of my entire household, both with proper hygiene, and with healthful and tasty foods, so that each meal and each dish may be served on time.[23]

Weissler points out that this prayer differs markedly from the *tehines* of the 17th and 18th centuries. It reflects 20th-century concerns with maintaining a clean household, cooking proper meals, and keeping a family healthy. This *tehine* also stresses the very American ideal that God helps those who help themselves.[24] Other early American *tehines* were written in memory of the young women who died in the Triangle Shirt Waist fire in 1911, of the victims of pogroms in Russia, and of the soldiers who died in World War I.[25]

Sefardi Women's Songs

Sefardi Jewish women of Europe, Africa, and Asia, like Eastern European Jewish women, also wrote innovative prayers, and they too used the vernacular language, Ladino, a language also called Judeo-Spanish, Spagnolit, and Judezmo. The word *Ladino* was originally used by Castillian speakers in the late Middle Ages to describe Jews and Arabs who spoke Castillian; it was a pejorative word for "the others" who formed part of Spanish society but were foreigners, and it derived from the word *Latino*. After the expulsion from Spain in 1492, the word "Ladino" was appropriated by

Jews as a name for their language. Then, as now, not all Jews learned to read Hebrew, *lashon hakodesh,* the holy language—and Ladino became the Sefardi Jew's native tongue in lands such as Turkey, Bulgaria, Morocco, Tunisia, Greece, Portugal, and the Netherlands. For many Jews, it became their only Jewish language.

Many stories, prayers, and festive songs were sung in Ladino. Some harked back to Jewish life in Spain, while others reflected more recent events; some of the newer songs incorporated or adapted popular Turkish or Greek melodies. Like Yiddish songs and stories, Ladino songs and stories encompassed both religious and secular themes. Jewish life-cycle events—births, circumcisions, first immersions in the *mikvah*, and weddings—were richly embellished with music. *Coplas*, or songs with refrains, were sung primarily on Shabbat and Jewish holidays. Yet while tending to daily housework or while putting children to sleep, Sefardi Jewish women might have sung Ladino narratives about far-away lands, royal romances of Christian kings and Moorish queens, lost sisters, and men returning from war. They also sang numerous love songs, some purely romantic, and others that alluded to the relationship between God and the Jewish people and that incorporated the symbolism of Hebrew medieval poetry.

Hebrew served as the language of the synagogue and of religious life, as it did in Ashkenazi Jewish communities; however, a parallel repertoire developed, a "paraliturgy" perhaps even more striking than in the Ashkenazi Jewish world. Women were the main singers of Ladino religious songs at ceremonial gatherings and celebrations; even in gatherings when both men and women sang, *la voz cantante,* the lead singer who led the community in song, was generally a woman. Some Jewish communal institutions regularly employed semi-professional singers because of their beautiful voices and their extensive knowledge of specific songs. Women's Ladino songs thus functioned differently from Yiddish *tehines*. Although many songs employed a personal, intimate tone and were a part of women's private devotions, these songs were also routinely sung aloud at public events, both at women-only gatherings and at community-wide celebrations.

Sefardi women's prayers prior to the mid-20th century differed significantly from men's. First, women mostly prayed at home, either privately or in a group of women; most men prayed in the synagogue. Second, women almost always prayed in Ladino, because very few women could read the prescribed liturgy in Hebrew; men almost always prayed in Hebrew—though not all men understood the Hebrew prayers. For both women and men, then, Ladino was an essential element of Jewish identity. Homiletic works (most notably the outstanding, multi-volume *Me'am Lo'ez* of the 18th century), as well as complete services, such as the Passover Seder, were printed in Ladino.

In both Sefardi and Ashkenazi Jewish homes, women have long been the main bearers of culture and tradition. Among Sefardim, women's oral traditions remained strong until well into the 20th century. Through Ladino songs and prayers, mothers, aunts, sisters, and daughters came together to sing about Jewish history, family sorrows, holidays, and celebrations. Though scores of women's songs and prayers undoubtedly have been lost to us, ethnomusicologists and historians have documented and catalogued an enormous Ladino repertoire. For example, in 1932 Hajim Papo compiled a Ladino prayer book using Yugoslav orthography, which provided a glimpse into the spiritual yearnings of Sarajevan women. Some prayers were spontaneous outpourings, such as a plea for a child, health, or good fortune. Others were standards that had been sung by generations of women while performing such *mitzvot* as lighting candles.

Sefardi women prayed to *Adonai* or to *El Dio*, synthesizing one of the Hebrew names of God, *El*, with the Spanish article, *el* (the). By addressing the God of Israel as *Dio*, and not *Dios* as their Christian neighbors did, they affirmed the unity of God. By eliminating the "s" that indicates a plural noun, Sefardim emphasize that God is one.

During the 19th and 20th centuries, very many Sefardim migrated to North and South America and to Israel. In Spanish-speaking countries, Ladino merged into modern Spanish. In Israel and in the English-language countries, Hebrew became the religious language of choice. In the Balkans, the Nazi Holocaust obliterated entire Sefardi communities.

Nevertheless, Ladino prayers and songs have undergone a renaissance in recent years. As with Yiddish, many young people seek to learn of their heritage and are studying the language. Many Ladino publications have been reissued, and a new version of Ladino identity is being forged.

The following four examples of Ladino prayers reveal some of the typical functions of women's songs and show some of the liturgical themes.

Havdalah

Buena semana mos de El Dio!
Buena semana mos de El Dio,
alegres y sanos.

Para mis hijos biendecir,
que me los deje El Dio vivir,
buena semana.
 Buena semana mos de El Dio,
 alegres y sanos.

Para fadar y cercusir
para poner los tefilim,
buena semana.
 Buena semana mos de El Dio,
 alegres y sanos.

A nuestros padres bien honrar,
para los novios alegrar,
buena semana.
    Buena semana mos de El Dio,
    alegres y sanos.

Nuestra Torah venerar,
Yerushalayim ensalzar,
buena semana.
    Buena semana mos de El Dio,
    buena semana.[26]

May God give us a good week,
May God give us a good week,
with happiness and health.

A week to bless my children
that God give them life,
a good week.
    May God give us a good week,
    with happiness and health.

A week to name girls and circumcise,
to start to don *tefillin*,
a good week.
    May God give us a good week,
    with happiness and health.

A week to greatly honor our parents,
to give joy to those in love,
a good week.
    May God give us a good week,
    with happiness and health.

A week to venerate our Torah,
to praise Jerusalem,
a good week.
    May God give us a good week,
    a good week.[27]

This *havdalah* prayer was sung at the end of Shabbat. The singer asked for a good week from *El Dio*, the source of blessing, a week that would bring happiness and health to her children. The singer then asked for happiness at many life-cycle events, and she told of her intent to carry out specific commandments—honoring parents, bringing joy to newlyweds, revering the Torah, and remembering Jerusalem. This prayer could be sung by groups during a *havdalah* service. Like the following song for a *brit*, this *havdalah* song was part of the Ladino paraliturgy—a repertoire of prayers that supplemented the Hebrew liturgy of the *siddur*. Musically, both the *havdalah* song and the song for the night before a circumcision are fast-paced, light, and rhythmic.

Brit

Esta noche es alabada
de encender luz demasiada
la criatura sea guadrada
con Eliyahu hanavi.

Avram avinu el honrado,
por su zejut fue nombrado,
el brit mila por el fue allegado
con Eliyahu hanavi.[28]

This night is praised
to light a bright light
the child should be protected
by Elijah the prophet.

The honored Abraham, our father
who through his own merit was named
and the covenant came through him
with Elijah the prophet.

Ladino songs about birth and circumcision often speak of the pain of childbirth and the pride of both parents after the delivery. In *Esta noche es alabada*, though, the singer prays that Elijah the prophet will protect the baby boy and will bring him into the covenant first established by Abraham. Women would sing this song as a way to protect the infant from the evil eye, which was especially feared during the night before the *brit* ceremony. In addition, the infant was never to be left alone. Throughout the night, amulets were placed nearby, and lights were left burning to dispel evil spirits. Even so, the tune of the song was fast-paced and upbeat.

Both the Rosh Hashanah and the Yom Kippur prayer that follow have chant-like, recitative-style melodies in keeping with their more introspective tone.

Rosh Hashanah Musaf

Adonai oyi i me estremeci
Dia ke en el me vijitas
Tembli i me adolori
Dia ke en el me djuzgaz

Me arebashi i me aturvi
De kuanto en tu folor me apokas
Ki gadol yom Adonai[29]

Hashem I heard and shook
On the day in which You visit me
I trembled and was pained
On the day in which You judge me
I was enraptured and bewildered
Of how I am diminished in Your grandeur
Because great is the day of *Hashem*.

In *Adonai oyi i me estremeci*, the singer prays to God in a familiar and
intimate tone, even though the transcendence of God causes her to tremble in fear. The last line of the prayer is in Hebrew, and it summarizes the
prayer as a whole—"great is the day of *Hashem*." The incorporation of
entire phrases of Hebrew (especially much-repeated liturgical phrases)
into Ladino prayers consolidates the link with the God of Israel.
Furthermore, using the holy tongue may offer assurance to those who pray
for redemption on the Days of Awe.

La Bendision de Madre (Yom Kippur)

Padre santo
En esta klara y solemna ora
Ke esto despuesta para
Bendecir a mis fijus
Segun el dezeo de madre ke konsiento
Se, O Dio siempre pronto
A eskuchar de los altos sielos
Mi orasion I bendision ke yo
Bendigo a mis fijus
Mi Dio
Tu ke me iziste alargar la vida
En dandome fijus a mi lado
As me esta buendad
Emprezenta me los para
Buena vida
I ventura
I meresime a ver, kun mis
Ojos, sus muzal
I sus prospero inflorisido
Padre piyadoso.[30]

Mother's blessing (Yom Kippur)

Holy Father
In this clear and solemn hour
In which I find myself to
Bless my children
As a mother who feels deeply
Be, O God, always and quickly
ready to listen in the high heavens
to my prayer and the blessing that
I give my children
My God
You who lengthened my life
By giving me children to stay by my side.
Be benevolent to me and
present them with a good life
and good fortune
And may I merit to see, with my
eyes, their *mazal*
and their flowering prosperity
Merciful Father.

In this blessing from a Sarajevo *mahzor*, a mother prays on Yom Kippur, asking that God grant to her children life, *mazal* (literally, constellation) or a favorable destiny, and prosperity. Thanking the merciful God for having granted her long life and children by her side, she asks that she merit a longer life so she may see the prosperity of her children with her own eyes. As in the Rosh Hashanah prayer, the mother addresses God intimately and directly.

These Ladino prayers reveal both communal and personal concerns, from mourning the destruction of Jerusalem and venerating the Torah, to trembling and rapture before God, to the prosperity of children. A wealth of songs and prayers exist in Ladino, and these four present only a sample of the depth of this women's tradition.

In addition to songs and prayers sung together within women's gatherings, manuals of private devotions for Sefardi women were sometimes compiled. Unlike the *tehine* collections in the Yiddish-speaking world, though, Sefardi women's personal prayer books were not produced for mass consumption. The library of the Jewish Theological Seminary in New York houses a beautifully handwritten, sumptuously-bound 18th-century Italian book of Hebrew prayers and supplications, with Italian instructions for their use, compiled by a man and given to his wife, Yehudit Coen. This book has been translated into English by Rabbi Nina Beth Cardin and published with the title, *Out of the Depths I Call to You: A Book of Prayers for the Married Jewish Woman*. Like the Yiddish *tehines,* these Hebrew meditations frequently mention the four matriarchs. For example, when taking *ḥallah,* a woman reads,

May it be Your will that our dough be blessed through the work of our hands, just as blessings attended the handiwork of our mothers Sarah, Rebecca, Rachel, and Leah.[31]

The Hebrew prayer to be said during pregnancy includes this passage:

Just as You remembered Sarah, heeded Rebecca, saw Leah's sorrow, and did not forget Rachel, just as You listened to the voice of all the righteous women when they turned to You, so may You hear the sound of my plea and send the redeeming angel to protect me and to help me throughout my pregnancy.[32]

Teḥines Today

Do we need similar intimate supplications today? Observant Orthodox women in the 21st century participate in Jewish public life, read (and often speak) Hebrew, and live in ways that are generally similar to men. They understand the words of the *siddur,* and most do not feel the need for special women's prayers. In other words, Orthodox women now view the liturgy as their own, and a paraliturgy is redundant. Nevertheless, *teḥines*—or, more accurately, their descendants—are alive and well. ▨

Before looking at *teḥines* composed within the last 20 years, it is important to note that many ultra-Orthodox Ashkenazi women, like their mothers and their grandmothers before them, turn to Yiddish *teḥines* written centuries ago. Collections of such *teḥines* are available in bookstores in extremely observant Jewish communities like Brooklyn's Boro Park. In the United States, many of these collections contain the original Yiddish *teḥines* side by side with their English translations. For women in ultra-Orthodox communities, *teḥines* remain relevant in ways that the Hebrew liturgy does not.

▨ *A Teḥine for Yom Kippur*

O God, creator of heaven and earth, creator of humankind and of all living things, grant me the power to feel, the power to listen and to hear, to truly see, to touch and be touched.

Keep fresh within me the memory of my own suffering and the suffering *of klal Yisrael* [the entire Jewish people], not in order to stimulate eternal paranoia, but that I may better understand the suffering of strangers; and may that understanding lead me to do everything in my power to alleviate and to prevent such suffering.

When I see streams of refugees bearing the pathetic belongings they have salvaged from ruined homes, may I recall the wanderings of the people of Israel and may I vow never to be the cause of loss and homelessness.

Enable me to be like Yourself—to feed the hungry, clothe the naked, tend the sick, comfort the bereaved. Guide me in the ways of *tikkun olam,* of mending the world. As I delight in a loving marriage of true minds, may I never forget the thousands of women battered and beaten by their spouses. As I rejoice in the bliss of my children and ➤

Rivka Zakutinsky, a current writer of *teḥines* that are closely based on the Eastern European supplications, recalls the time her mother came to visit and forgot her little red book. "I'm lost without it!" her mother kept repeating as she searched through her suitcase for the collected *teḥines*. "Years later," writes Zakutinsky, "as I looked through the tearstained pages, I realized how precious these supplications were, and indeed, that they could truly overturn entire worlds. [My mother] communicated with God as if by telephone."[33]

Most Orthodox women, however, would not find the supplications of prior centuries spiritually uplifting. Because these private prayers reflect the immediacy, the particularity, and the individuality of day-to-day life, they also plainly reflect the biases of their times—and many pre-20th century prayers reveal prejudices against women. For example, in an 18th-century Hebrew supplication, a woman beseeches God for a male child.

grandchildren, may I never forget the pleading eyes and swollen bellies of starving infants deprived of physical and emotional nourishment. May my woman's capacities for concern, compassion, and caring never be dulled by complacency or personal contentment. May my feelings always lead me to act.

Grant me the wisdom to discern what is right and what is wrong, and inspire me with the courage to speak out whenever I see injustice, without fear of shame or fear of personal retribution. Enable me to feel pity even for my enemies. Grant me the will and the ability to be a peacemaker; so that the day may soon come when all peoples will live in friendship and Your tabernacle of peace will be spread over all the dwellers on earth. Amen.

God and God of our ancestors, forgive me my sins of pride and conceit, my obtuseness to the needs, desires, and ambitions of others, my lack of empathy, my ignorance and obliviousness to all that is going on in the world save what is directly related to my own experience and that of the Jewish people. Forgive us our arrogance and narrowness of vision; forgive us our readiness to inflict pain on those who have hurt us. Make us whole, make us holy.—*Alice Shalvi*[34]

Bestow upon me Your greatest mercies, so that the child that I carry within me may be a pure, innocent son. May he be good and kind and sacred, to serve as a blessing. Let him be a shining light to all Israel, illuminating Your Torah. Amen. So may it be Your will.[35]

Though only a son could grow up to become a Torah scholar, while a daughter could not, many women today would find this supplication offensive.

Equally troubling is the perpetuation of a distasteful feminine stereotype within the *teḥines*, as Chava Weissler has observed. In many of these Yiddish prayers, Ashkenazi Jewish women exercised their spiritual power through crying, begging, and cajoling God rather than "compelling the Godhead through theurgic activity." Weissler comments that women's power, as expressed in the *teḥines,* was quite limited.[36]

Moreover, both Yiddish *teḥines* and Ladino prayers were often recited in contexts that today are outdated (regardless of the prayers' content). For instance, *teḥines* meant to be said in the synagogue and Ladino songs that explicated the words of the *siddur* or *maḥzor* both presupposed that women did not understand Hebrew, yet observant Orthodox women today *do* know the prayers of the *siddur*. As for the *teḥines* and Ladino prayers that were recited at home, these too do not quite fit with the lives of most contemporary Orthodox women. Today, when most women are part of the paid work force, staying at home to raise children and maintain the house is generally temporary. Having prayers that validate and even valorize the hard work that goes into creating a home is wonderfully affirming, yet some of these earlier women's prayers imply that women belong *only* in the home.

Nonetheless, the spiritual needs for immediacy, for individual relevance, and for connecting to women's unique lives that were felt in prior centuries—these are still felt by Orthodox women. Renée Septimus, a mother of four and a member of an Orthodox synagogue in Queens, New York, is a pioneer in rediscovering and reclaiming Yiddish *tehines* while also writing new *tehines* in English. She notes that women's role in the Orthodox synagogue is marginal, yet her disillusionment with synagogue and ritual life "is assuaged to some extent by the flexibility of the *tehines.*" Septimus observes: "When prayers in the liturgy don't speak to [you], according to tradition, you are not personally allowed to change them. The structure and wording are mandatory. *Tehines* are open to change—you can make them personal. With *tehines,* you can rediscover the experience of being a woman in Judaism."[37]

One of Septimus's most eloquent *tehines* was written in honor of her son becoming bar mitzvah in December 1999:

Ribono shel olam [Lord of the world] I stand humbly before You, a mother like Sorah, Rivkah, Rachel, Leah, and Hannah, watching her son take steps toward adulthood and toward assuming his role and responsibility for the Jewish people.

Always I've felt intimately our partnership in the creation and maintenance of the children You have blessed me with.

But as they leave my womb and the womb of our household, I feel and need Your presence ever more as I confront the limitations of my own ability to protect them.

From the moment I knew he lived inside me, this son has inspired joy in my life and the lives of those around him.

Ribono shel olam, help him maintain his love of life and laughter, his integrity and honesty, his sensitivity and compassion. Guide him to think for himself with an open mind, seeking truth and goodness.

And keep him always safe from harm, ready to do Your sacred work, his desire and motivation always toward Torah and *mitzvot* [commandments].

Keep him strong in body, soul, and spirit so that he will have an easy life without strain or struggle. Give him the will to do Your bidding so he will be loved by You above and valued by mankind below.

And at the time help him find his *zivug* [partner] easily as You provided the *zivug* for Adam *harishon* [Adam, the first human being].

Give him his livelihood from Your outstretched, generous hand so that he will never need to depend on anyone and so that all his material needs will be fulfilled all his life.

Grant him a good old age, blessed with children who achieve good marriages, committed to Torah and *mitzvot*.

Ribono shel olam, this humble mother is filled with gratitude for all of life's blessings which You have bestowed upon me.

Watch over my beloved husband, keep him safe from any harm or illness. Grant us long life filled with love and peace so that we may see and enjoy our children, children's children, and their children.

Keep them all as close to You and as protected as a child in her mother's womb, against her mother's breast, wrapped in her mother's arms.

Help my son grow to be a good man with fine qualities, aware always of Your presence, wise and dedicated to good works, charity, and acts of loving kindness.

Dear God, I believe and I trust in You and I come before You, my soul in my hands and I beg You, my Creator, the force which sustains all life, to accept my prayer with mercy, this prayer which comes from the depths of my heart. Amen.[38]

Septimus has maintained the structure, heavy emotionalism, and rhetorical style of earlier Yiddish *tehines,* thereby connecting her supplication to authentic Jewish models. Nevertheless, this English-language *tehine* is decidedly modern. Septimus prays that her son be guided "to think for himself with an open mind" and that at the same time he remain committed to the Torah and God's commandments—a goal espoused by modern Orthodox Jews.

Like its Yiddish precursors, this prayer is exclusively for women, as it incorporates imagery of a mother's womb. Yet Septimus, unlike the women of Eastern Europe, read her *tehine* aloud in public to both the women and the men attending her son's bar mitzvah ceremony. (She reported that there were few dry eyes.)

The Israeli writer and Talmud scholar Yael Levine also composes personal prayers. Though she too calls some compositions *tehinnot* (the Hebrew word for *tehines; tehinnah* is the singular in Hebrew), Levine writes in Hebrew, she writes prayers that are to be recited by both women and men, and her concerns are strikingly modern. For instance, she prays that God remember the victims of domestic violence and that God "nullify the intentions of those who scheme to kill their wives," and, in the prayer that follows, she asks God for the wisdom and understanding to study Torah.

Tehinnah for a Woman before Torah Study

May it be Your will, Lord my God and God of my ancestors, Abraham, Isaac, Jacob, Sarah, Rebecca, Rachel, and Leah, that in Your bountiful mercy, You grant me my soul's desire, the merit to learn, teach, and immerse myself in Your Torah ▦

▦ Until the very recent past, Jewish study had been available only to boys and men. Today, however, Jewish education for girls and women is absolutely standard. Sarah Schnirer (1883–1938), from a hasidic family of Warsaw, opened the door to today's educational revolution. She established the Bais Yaakov schools for girls to "rescue Judaism for the new generation."[39] Her school offered girls an intensive Jewish curriculum, and many Orthodox luminaries, such as the Hafetz Hayyim and the Belzer Rebbe, supported her. Today, in modern American Orthodox day schools, boys and girls from kindergarten through grade 12 usually follow the identical curriculum—including Torah, Talmud, Hebrew language, Jewish philosophy, and Jewish history. In addition, post-secondary schools for Jewish women are flourishing in both the United States and Israel. After high school graduation, very many American Orthodox women study in an Israeli women's *yeshivah,* usually in a year-long program that provides an intense immersion in Torah; Talmud; the practical laws of Shabbat, holidays, *kashrut,* and family purity; and Jewish philosophy and theology. In the United States, Stern College for Women, part of Yeshiva University, the academic heart of modern American Orthodoxy, offers women a dual curriculum of religious studies and secular subjects. Drisha Institute in Manhattan, Shalhevet in Queens, and a few other institutions in the United States offer both full-time and part-time programs for women of all ages. These and other post-secondary institutions provide women with a rigorous curriculum that covers Torah and Talmud, and that often includes intricate discussions of Jewish law. Barriers to women's learning that were common even 40 or 50 years ago have virtually disappeared in modern Orthodox Jewish circles today.—*Claudia Chernov*

❈ Orthodox Judaism obligates both men and women to fulfill the *mitzvot* or the commandments. Women, however, are exempt from some of the commandments that are incumbent on men, such as Torah study. Women are exempt also from the commandment to pray daily at three set times and to dwell (in practice, to eat meals) in the *sukkah* during Sukkot. In most cases, Orthodox women are *allowed* to fulfill a commandment from which they are exempt. In some cases, such as studying Torah and eating in the *sukkah,* women are in fact encouraged.—*Claudia Chernov*

together with all Your sons and daughters. Open my heart to Your Torah, guide me in Your truth, and teach me Your laws. Lead me in this journey. Grant me wisdom and understanding, as it is written, "For God grants wisdom. From His mouth come knowledge and discernment" (Proverbs 2:6). God, create a pure heart for me, and bestow upon me the spiritual insight You gave to women so that I may perceive and comprehend Your Torah.

Listen to my prayer, God, and do not turn away from my plea. Arouse me to sanctify my time with the learning of Torah, so that I will devote many hours to study and not turn holy words into empty chatter. Endow me with the knowledge and ability to expound new interpretations of Torah that will be pleasing to You.

Strengthen me and renew my spirit so my heart will rejoice and my eyes will shine with the words of Your Torah. Let them be like a crown for my head, a necklace for my throat, more beautiful than gold, sweeter than honey and nectar. Although I was not commanded to study Torah, ❈ Your Torah is my delight, and I choose to dwell within Your gates.

Let the merits of those who stood before us act on our behalf—the prophetesses Miriam and Deborah, the mother of Samson, the Shunammite who listened to words of Torah from Elisha the

prophet, and all the other wise and righteous women of Israel who studied Torah and chose to dwell in the tent of learning. May the merit of my Torah study safeguard Your nation together with the merits of all Your sons and daughters.

Extend Your benevolence to those who cling to You, so that the words of Scripture will be realized: "Women's wisdom built her home" (Proverbs 14:1). In the same way that in the days of Hezekiah, King of Judah, a search from Dan to Beersheba could not locate an ignorant person, and from Gabbath to Antipatris there was no man, woman, or child who was not familiar with the laws of purification, so may the prophecy of Joel come true: "And afterwards I will pour My spirit upon all flesh, and your sons and daughters will prophesy, and your elders will dream dreams, and your young men will have revelations. Even on the slaves and handmaidens will I pour My spirit" (Joel 3:1-2).

Amen, may it be Your will.[40]

Levine, like Renée Septimus, maintains the structure of the Yiddish *tehines*, and her Hebrew prayer, like many of its Yiddish predecessors, interweaves passages from sacred literature and refers to both well-known and lesser-known Biblical women and men. The content of the prayer, though, differs profoundly from earlier women's prayers.

Yael Levine has also composed prayers for a man seeking a wife and for a woman seeking a husband.

Tefillah for Finding a Husband

May it be Your will, Lord my God and God of my ancestors, Abraham, Isaac, Jacob, Sarah, Rebecca, Rachel, and Leah, that in Your bountiful mercy, You provide me with a suitable life partner—a man of fine qualities who is God-fearing and who immerses himself in Torah, who is valued by others, and who is careful not to engage in harmful gossip or evil talk.

Answer my heart's prayer, and help me merit deep love and respect from my life's partner. Let him love me as much as he does himself, and let him understand and be sensitive to the secrets of my soul, a partner in all things, from whom nothing will be withheld and to whom all will be offered. Grant him a livelihood by which he will support me in the honorable way Jewish husbands provide for their wives.

Together we will set aside the time to study Torah and rejoice in Your teachings and commandments, for Torah is the source of life and longevity. May we merit to be blessed with sons and daughters who will also be dedicated to Your teachings and commandments, and may we raise them for Torah, the marriage canopy, and good deeds.

God of peace, let there always be between me and my husband love, friendship, amity, and harmony, so that we will live in joy and tranquility. Let our relationship find favor in Your eyes so that Your Presence will dwell among us. Grant us

a long life, a life of goodness and blessing, a life of richness and honor, a life of love of Torah and devotion to God.

Amen, may it be Your will.[41]

Again, Levine blends a *teḥine*-like structure and style with modern themes, including the desire for an understanding and sensitive husband. And unlike women of the past whose husbands studied with other men or alone, Levine promises that "Together we [wife and husband] will set aside the time to study Torah."

In addition to the resurgence of *teḥines*, Ladino songs have also undergone a recent revival, and they are frequently performed at weddings and bar and bat mitzvah celebrations. Some singers of Ladino music adapt existing songs to address current themes, and some also compose new songs that speak to modern concerns.

As we see, Orthodox Jewish women build upon the past as they continue to find ways to forge an intimate relationship with God. In earlier centuries, personal prayers and paraliturgical songs nourished the souls of women who were excluded from active participation in synagogue life. The supplications gave Jewish women the opportunity to reflect on both their lives and their tradition with creativity and passion. Today, modern versions of those private prayers embolden Orthodox women to make prayer relevant to their lives as well.

Women and Communal Prayer Today

Orthodox Jewish women have been publishing innovative private prayers for many centuries. Only recently have they have sought to change their status within public prayer as well. As feminist ideals have become accepted by growing numbers of Orthodox women, boundaries that once prevented women from taking part in synagogue life are increasingly breaking down. ▦ Two examples—women's *tefillah* groups and women Torah readers—indicate the hunger among Orthodox women for full participation in public prayer.

The all-women's *tefillah* (prayer) group is the most popular venue for Orthodox women who want to actively participate in synagogue but who affirm the concept of separate spheres for men and women. Orthodox women's prayer groups began meeting

▦ Although this chapter concerns the Orthodox synagogue, many non-Orthodox synagogues follow some or all of Orthodox Judaism's regulations on women's synagogue participation. For example, they do not permit women to read from the Torah or to open the Ark. Congregations affiliated with the Union for Traditional Judaism follow most of Orthodoxy's restrictions on women's synagogue participation; these congregations, however, may permit mixed seating. In addition, a handful of Conservative congregations follow most of Orthodox Judaism's regulations on women, and a larger number of Conservative congregations follow *some* Orthodox regulations on women, though Conservative congregations almost always have mixed seating. Finally, many non-denominational prayer groups, such as university campus groups and community groups, follow Orthodox Judaism's regulations on women, including separate seating for men and women, so that ➤

in the late 1970s in America and Israel, a time when large numbers of women with extensive Jewish education came of age. Participants in women's *tefillah* groups lead prayers, carry the Torah among the congregation after removing it from the Ark, kiss the Torah mantle as the Torah is carried through the room, chant the Torah portion, ✳ receive *aliyot,* and deliver scholarly speeches.

Orthodox feminists like to point out that Miriam, sister of Moses, created the first women's prayer group. When the Jews fled Egypt and prepared to cross the Red Sea, Miriam took her timbrel and led the women of Israel in dance and song, thanking God for saving them (Exodus 15:20–21). Following her lead, Jewish women from ancient times until our own have gathered together to pray. Scholars have found evidence of separate women's prayer groups in 12th-century Germany and 16th-century Italy. In the *Zohar* an angel says that righteous women who reach heaven pray to God three times daily, led by Yokheved, mother of Miriam, and by Deborah the prophet (*Zohar* 3, 167b).

An Orthodox woman's *tefillah* group does not qualify as a *minyan.* The women who participate accept the Orthodox definition of a *minyan* as ten or more adult male Jews. Therefore, women's *tefillah* groups omit all prayers for which a *minyan* is necessary—*Kaddish, Kedushah,*

Orthodox as well as non-Orthodox Jews will attend together. Nowadays, many observant men and women who follow *almost* all of Orthodox Jewish law, but who have one or two ideological differences with Orthodoxy, refer to themselves as "Conservadox."—*Claudia Chernov*

✳ Most women's *tefillah* groups read the day's Torah portion in its entirety as well as the *Haftarah* portion. According to Jewish law, public reading of the Torah requires a *minyan,* but an individual or a group of individuals may *study* the Torah privately at any time. Orthodox women's *tefillah* groups therefore consider their reading of the Torah to be private study, engaged in by a group of individuals.—*LT*

✖ There are women, albeit still a minority, who find that their participation in the male-dominated Orthodox service, however justified on halakhic [Jewish legal] grounds by the different liturgical requirements made of the two sexes, is not providing them with the spiritual inspiration and the outlet for the religiosity that they crave. By pressing for women's prayer groups conducted with the "four cubits of the *halakhah,*" they have created an acrimonious debate among Orthodox authorities, some of whom argue that whatever is legally permitted should be granted and even encouraged, while others claim that their motivation is separatist and religiously misguided and any leniency will only encourage the importation of strident feminism and other non-Jewish values into the synagogue. Where sanctioned, Orthodox women's prayer groups have scrupulously adhered to halakhic requirements and as a result have developed what is effectively a novel liturgy that removes those relatively few elements that require a quorum *(minyan)* of ten males but retains such major elements as the *Pesukei DeZimra, Shema, Amidah,* and the Torah reading on a weekday or Shabbat, and the recitation of the Scroll of Esther, the *hakkafot* of Simhat Torah, and the bat mitzvah ceremony on more specialized occasions. Should such services ultimately win universal acceptance in Orthodox synagogues rather than remain substantially restricted to a few American centers, it will be interesting to see whether or how they are given written expression in a suitable female *siddur* and whether this leads to a greater separation of the sexes at Orthodox Jewish worship than is now practiced.—*Stefan C. Reif* [42]

Barkhu, and so on. ✖ Orthodox women's *tefillah* groups are thus a supplement to, not a replacement of, the *minyan.* (Women who define *minyan* as ten adult Jews of either sex, as well as women who reject the concept of *minyan* entirely, generally choose to pray in congregations that do not divide synagogue roles according to sex.) Because many key prayers are not recited, many feel a lack at an Orthodox women's service. Besides, most groups meet only once a month, making women's prayer only an occasional alternative. Nevertheless, this grass-roots initiative has met with enormous resistance. A number of prominent Orthodox rabbis have followed Rabbi Moshe Feinstein (1895–1986), the pre-eminent Orthodox authority of the 20th century, who in 1984 denounced separate women's prayer groups. Some rabbis have gone even further and prohibited the groups. Ironically, rabbinic condemnation has, in some cases, ignited interest in the groups. Today, over 40 women's *tefillah* groups meet in the United States, many affiliated with large, urban, modern Orthodox synagogues. ▨

▨ Edah, whose mission "is to give voice to the ideology and values of modern Orthodoxy and to educate and empower the community to address its concerns," posts an on-line listing of women's *tefillah* groups. See www.edah.org/tefilla.cfm.—LT

A more revolutionary and more recent initiative is also underway. In a few congregations—such as Shira Chadashah in Israel and the Drisha Institute for Jewish Education in New York City—female Torah readers now stand at the *bimah* (reader's lectern) and face both women and men. In 2001, *The Edah Journal,* a publication of the modern Orthodox organization Edah, published a comprehensive review and analysis of Jewish ritual law concerning women's public reading of Torah together with a *minyan.* The author, Rabbi Mendel Shapiro of Jerusalem, criticized the traditional Orthodox position that Torah reading is improper for women in public, communal settings. According to Blu Greenberg, president of the Jewish Orthodox Feminist Alliance, the leading organization of Orthodox feminists, women's Torah reading "will be increasingly adopted not because there are pockets here and there within communities" that do it, "but because of the reports by people who have experienced it. Everyone who has participated in such a *minyan* reports on the experience of how natural it feels and how continuous with the tradition it feels—rather than violating traditional sensibilities."[43]

Orthodox women reading the Torah publicly in a mixed congregation will not, in all likelihood, gain as much popular acceptance as women's *tefillah* groups, because the former violates the separation between women and men that is one of the pillars of Orthodox communal prayer—while women's *tefillah* groups remain separated by sex. Still, the very fact that women's Torah reading is being explored shows something of what is possible within Orthodox Judaism. The integration of women into growing numbers of synagogue practices is made possible because of forward-thinking women—and of rabbis who agree with them. Blu Greenberg states:

When I was growing up in the 1940s and 1950s, even the word "bat mitzvah" was off-limits in Orthodoxy, signaling the celebrant as Reform or Conservative. Today, no self-respecting modern Orthodox family would refrain from marking its daughter's Jewish maturity with a bat mitzvah celebration. While changes in Orthodoxy may not seem as stark as changes in the more liberal denominations, they are more remarkable in some ways because they represent a greater shift from the status quo. In only one generation, Orthodox women's roles have shifted from exclusively private to increasingly public....

While the numbers of Orthodox feminists (including those who eschew the label) have grown, the majority of Orthodox women remain skeptical or antagonistic, even though they have integrated gender equality values into all other aspects of their lives.... Many Orthodox women remain diffident about adopting new and unfamiliar roles. I understand this because, although I advocate expanded roles, I too sometimes feel an inner, emotional resistance to the unfamiliar. Rabbis report that when they offer women in their congregations *hakkafot,* dancing with a Torah scroll on Simhat Torah, many refuse due to unease or fear.[44]

Just as private, vernacular prayers gained acceptance among our women of earlier eras, women's participation in public prayer is gaining acceptance today. The Orthodox synagogue will embrace women's participation when women themselves—along with rabbis—overcome their fear of the unfamiliar.

Some sections were written by Claudia Chernov.

QUESTIONS FOR FURTHER STUDY AND REFLECTION

1. In Eastern European synagogues, a *firzogerin* served as a sort of combined rabbi, cantor, and emcee for the women's gallery. The *firzogerin* fulfilled a necessary role, because most Jewish women were unfamiliar with the prayer book and did not know how to pray. Today, many people, men and women alike, similarly need and want guidance in the synagogue. How have different Jewish communities attempted to provide leadership and instruction? Who in today's Jewish world (if anyone) serves a role similar to the *firzogerin?*

2. *Tehines* were recited in the vernacular, and they employed an extremely personal tone. The same is true of Sefardi women's prayers. Compare the examples of Yiddish and Ladino women's prayers given in this chapter to some of the modern women's prayers given in Chapter 10. What are the advantages and disadvantages of using the vernacular language rather than Hebrew? What are the advantages and disadvantages of personalization?

3. Very many women today, Orthodox and non-Orthodox, are composing personal prayers that reflect their specifically female experiences. Overall, how do you react? List advantages and disadvantages to special women's prayers.

4. Using *tehines,* Sefardi women's songs, and the modern prayers written

by Renée Septimus and Yael Levin as guides, create your own prayer. Your prayer can mark a personal event, such as a wedding, a child's bar or bat *mitzvah,* a promotion at work, or a trip to Israel. Or, your prayer could relate to fulfilling a *mitzvah,* such as donating money or time for *tzedakah,* wrapping yourself in a *tallit,* or lighting Shabbat candles.

5. Have you prayed, or do you regularly pray, in an Orthodox synagogue? If yes, how do you react to women's exclusion from the *bimah?* Does it hamper your ability to pray with devotion? Or, conversely, does it allow you to concentrate on prayer particularly well? That is, by knowing that you will not be asked or expected to recite the Torah blessings, open the Ark, and so on, are you able to immerse yourself more fully in prayer?

---

1.   The Hebrew words *dayanot, agunot, ḥazzaniot,* and *poskot* are in the feminine plural form. With the exception of *agunot,* these words are commonly used in the masculine plural form: *dayanim, ḥazzanim,* and *poskim.*

2.   Tova Hartman-Halbertal with Tamar H. Miller, "Our Tradition, Ourselves," *JOFA: Jewish Orthodox Feminist Alliance Journal,* supplement to *The Jewish Week,* Spring 2001, page 6.

3.   David ben Avraham Dov Auerbach, *Haliḥot Bayta: Otzar Dinim Uminhagim al Mitzvot ha'Ishah beYisrael* (Jerusalem: Machon Sharei Ziv, 1983), pages 35–37. Cited in Irwin Haut, "Are Women Obligated to Pray?" in *Daughters of the King: Women and the Synagogue* (Philadelphia: Jewish Publication Society, 1992), page 94.

4.   Irwin Haut, "Are Women Obligated to Pray?" pages 89–101.

5.   Emily Taitz, "Women's Voices, Women's Prayers: Women in the European Synagogues of the Middle Ages," in Susan Grossman and Rivka Haut, eds., *Daughters of the King,* pages 62–65.

6.   Mendele Mokher Seforim, "Of Bygone Days," in Ruth Wisse, ed. and trans., *A Shtetl and Other Yiddish Novellas* (New York: Behrman, 1973), pages 300–301; cited in Emily Taitz, "Women's Voices, Women's Prayers," page 67.

7.   Emily Taitz, "Women's Voices, Women's Prayers," pages 65–68.

8.   Excerpt from *Seder tkhines u-vakoshes* (Furth, 1762), no. 45; translated by Chava Weissler, *Voices of the Matriarchs: Listening to the Prayers of Early Modern Jewish Women* (Boston: Beacon, 1998), pages 30–31.

9.   Excerpt from *"Tkhine* for Lighting Candles" (Vilna, 1869); translated by Tracy Guren Klirs, Ida Cohen Selavan, and Gella Schweid Fishman, *The Merit of Our Mothers: A Bilingual Anthology of Jewish Women's Prayers,* Tracy Guren Klirs, ed. (Cincinnati: Hebrew Union College Press, 1992), page 88.

10. Excerpt from *Shloshe She'arim (Three Gates)* by Sarah Bas Tovim (Vilna, 1865); translated by Tracy Guren Klirs, Ida Cohen Selavan, and Gella Schweid Fishman, *The Merit of Our Mothers,* pages 16, 18.

11. Chava Weissler, *Voices of the Matriarchs,* page 6.

12. Emily Taitz, "Women's Voices, Women's Prayers," page 67.

13. Chava Weissler, *Voices of the Matriarchs,* page 5; Ellen M. Umansky, "Piety, Persuasion, and Friendship: A History of Jewish Women's Spirituality" in Ellen M. Umansky and Dianne Ashton, eds., *Four Centuries of Jewish Women's Spirituality* (Boston:

Beacon, 1992), page 4.

14. Chava Weissler, *Voices of the Matriarchs*, page 25.

15. Chava Weissler, *Voices of the Matriarchs*, page 9.

16. Excerpt from *Shloshe She'arim (Three Gates)* by Sarah Bas Tovim, translated by Norman Tarnor, *A Book of Jewish Women's Prayers: Translations from the Yiddish* (Northvale, NJ: Jason Aronson, 1995), page 28.

17. Excerpt from *Shloshe She'ar*im *(Three Gates)* by Sarah Bas Tovim (Vilna, 1865), translated by Tracy Guren Klirs, Ida Cohen Selavan, and Gella Schweid Fishman, *The Merit of Our Mothers*, page 20.

18. Excerpt from "*Teḥine* of the Matriarchs" by Leah Horowitz; translated by Chava Weissler, *Voices of the Matriarchs*, pages 121–123.

19. Excerpt from a collection of *teḥines* published in Vilna in the early 20th century; translated by Norman Tarnor, *A Book of Jewish Women's Prayers*, page 45.

20. Excerpt from a collection of *teḥines* published in Vilna in the early 20th century; translated by Norman Tarnor, *A Book of Jewish Women's Prayers*, page 51.

21. Chava Weissler, *Voices of the Matriarchs*, page 152.

22. Chava Weissler, *Voices of the Matriarchs*, page 153.

23. "A New *Teḥine* upon Arising in the Morning," in *Shas Teḥine Rav Peninim (The Six Orders Teḥine Full of Pearls)* (New York: Hebrew Publishing Company, c. 1916), pages 6–7, quoted in Yitskhok Shloyme Mayer, "Amerikaner *tkhines*," *YIVO bleter* 39 (1955), page 272; cited in Chava Weissler, *Voices of the Matriarchs*, page 154.

24. Chava Weissler, *Voices of the Matriarchs*, pages 154–155.

25. Chava Weissler, *Voices of the Matriarchs*, page 155.

26. *Havdalah* song, "*Buena semana mos de El Dio!*" from *Un Vergel Vedre* compiled by Susana Weich-Shahak (Spain: IberCaja, 1995). The song was originally published as "*Noche de Alhad.*"

27. *Havdalah* song, English translation by Vanessa Paloma. All translations from the Ladino and Spanish are by Vanessa Paloma.

28. Song for a *brit*, "*Esta noche es alabada*" from *Musica y tradiciones Sefardies* compiled by Susana Weich-Shahak (Spain: Centro de Cultura Tradicional, Diputaction de Salamanca, 1992).

29. Rosh Hashanah *Musaf* prayer, "*Adonai oyi i m'estremeci*" from *Maagalim* (Israel: Renanot, HaMachon L'Musika Yehudit), 1991.

30. "La Bendision de Madre" from *The Flory Jagoda Songbook* (New York: Tara Publications, 1993).

31. Excerpt from Hebrew supplications compiled for Yehudit Coen; translated by Nina Beth Cardin, *Out of the Depths I Call to You: A Book of Prayers for the Married Jewish Woman*, Nina Beth Cardin, ed. (Northvale, NJ: Jason Aronson, 1995), page 4.

32. Excerpt from Hebrew supplications compiled for Yehudit Coen; translated by Nina Beth Cardin, *Out of the Depths I Call to You*, page 72.

33. Rivka Zakutinsky, *Techinas: A Voice From The Heart "As Only A Woman Can Pray"* (Brooklyn: Aura Press, 1992), page 13.

34. Alice Shalvi, "A Techine for Yom Kippur" in *Beginning Anew: A Woman's Companion to the High Holy Days*, Gail Twersky Reimer and Judith A. Kates, eds. (New York: Touchstone/Simon & Schuster, 1997), pages 274–275.

35. Excerpt from Hebrew prayers and supplications compiled for Yehudit Coen; English translation by Nina Beth Cardin, *Out of the Depths I Call to You*, page 70.

36. Chava Weissler, *Voices of the Matriarchs,* page 178.

37. Private communication, Leora Tanenbaum and Renée Septimus, July 2001.

38. Renée Septimus, unpublished manuscript. Copyright © 2003 Renée Septimus.

39. Sarah Schnirer, cited in Sylvia Barack Fishman, *A Breath of Life: Feminism in the American Jewish Community* (New York: Free Press, 1993), page 190.

40. Yael Levine, *Tehinnah* for a Woman before Torah Study, translated by Yael Levine, Renée Septimus, and Mordehi Horowitz. Original Hebrew prayer first published in Yael Levine, *Si'ah Sefatayim* (Jerusalem: Old City Press 2002).

41. Yael Levine, *Tefillah* for a Finding a Husband, translated by Yael Levine, Renée Septimus, and Mordehi Horowitz. Original Hebrew prayer first published in Yael Levine, *Si'ah Sefatayim* (Jerusalem: Old City Press 2002).

42. Stefan C. Reif, *Judaism and Hebrew Prayer: New Perspectives on Jewish Liturgical History* (Great Britain: Cambridge University Press, 1993) page 314.

43. Blu Greenberg, cited in Rachel Pomerance, "In Modern Orthodox Circles, Idea of Female Torah Readers Catching On," Jewish Telegraphic Agency electronic bulletin, November 12, 2002.

44. Blu Greenberg, "Orthodox Feminism and the Next Century," *Sh'ma* online (www.shma.com), January 2000.

Chapter

ISRAELI POETRY AS PRAYER

The Lord is near to all who call upon Him,
to all who call upon Him in truth

Rochelle Furstenberg

In *To Pray As A Jew*, the late Rabbi Hayim Halevi Donin passionately describes the experience of praying and the occasions when we turn to God in prayer—an experience that applies to Hebrew poetry as well. Rabbi Donin writes:

> I pray because I want to cry out to the Supreme Being, communicate with Him as I can communicate with no one else. Such moments come occasionally when I am in distress or when I feel lonely and isolated from the world. Sometimes, it is when I feel anxious about the safety or health of loved ones, or when my people are being threatened.... Sometimes, it's when a great sense of relief comes over me, or when truly joyous news exhilarates me and makes me ecstatic ... a sense of exuberance and a feeling of gratefulness.... People pray without realizing it's prayer, not in a structured way.[1]

Rabbi Donin points out that the Hebrew verb *lehitpalel* (to pray) derives from the root *p-l-l,* which means to judge, and so the reflexive *lehitpalel* implies to judge oneself or to contemplate. These qualities can be found in much of modern Hebrew poetry and song. Hillel Weiss, in *Ve'Ani Tefilati,* an analysis of Hebrew poetry, distinguishes between the different themes of traditional Hebrew prayer and illustrates those same themes in contemporary Israeli poetry: praise of God and awe of God's world; petition; protest; national songs of triumph; and lamentations for the destruction of Jews.[2]

While Jews in the United States (and Israel too) reveal great creativity as they devise new forms for their prayers and also fill old forms with more compelling content, this chapter focuses on poems that function as prayers. These Hebrew poems are certainly not conventional prayers, but within the secular Zionist milieu, poetry and song often acquire the role of prayer. In Israel, poetry elicits the emotions that Rabbi Donin describes, and it often parallels the form and the content of Hebrew prayer. The impulse to prayer and the impulse to poetry are often similar, stemming from a heightened awareness of one's being. A *brakhah,* a blessing, is exactly this: It focuses on the mundane—waking up in the morning, eating, looking at a mountain—and it raises the everyday to an intense appreciation of the world, an appreciation that radiates spirituality. In her essay *"HaOmetz LeHulun—*The Courage for the Mundane," poet and literary critic Leah Goldberg (1911-1970) portrays the poet as one who is privileged to feel the eternal and infinite immanent in the everyday, secular world: "The real creator does not flee the everyday. He raises it to a higher reality."[3] What is this but a definition of a blessing? As Psalm 145:18 states, "God is near to ... all who call upon Him in truth." Truth occurs when the writer throws off all affectation and posturing, and so penetrates to the most authentic self.

The question of "secular prayer" is, however, theologically complex. The first condition for prayer is that an individual sees him or herself as standing in the presence of God, that we as human beings acknowledge and address our Maker. According to Rabbi Joseph B. Soloveitchik (1903-1993), one of the most important Orthodox thinkers in the 20th century, this condition is a crucial one. No one could honestly claim that most contemporary secular Israeli poets experience a direct awareness of God's presence. Yet, as shall become evident, among Hebrew poets of earlier generations, some do address God directly, among them the non-observant writers Esther Raab and Amir Gilboa. Furthermore, very many Hebrew poets reveal an amorphous feeling of being in God's presence, a heightened sense of the spiritual. More often than not, the address is tentative. Leah Goldberg asks God, "Teach me to pray." That is, she asks God, teach me to address You, to know that You are listening to me. Indeed, in times of joy and sorrow, humankind must reach out beyond the limited self. The poet suspends disbelief, and assumes that a Creator, a Supreme Being, is listening.

In *Body of Prayer*—a thoughtful discussion between writer and theater director Michal Govrin, poet David Shapiro, and French philosopher

Jacques Derrida—Govrin asserts that prayer, like prophecy, projects a future and brings that future about through the power of language and the power of performance.

> Both [both prayer and prophecy] bring, or believe to bring a projected future into reality by the mere power of saying it, as a curse, as a wish, as a blessing, as an oath. Like magic. Yet the most intense expectation of the prayer is for the listener—an expectation and an outrageous confidence—of being listened to. Without the addressing there wouldn't be a prayer. Even wordless, before the first word, the prayer is already addressing. The prayer itself has the power to establish the space of address—to create, to open it. And in a way it does not only create an "I" who has the power to address, but also the addressee.
>
> Although it sounds heretical, it's a very central, traditional Jewish attitude that prayer does create the listening God at the moment of saying the name of "God" in the prayer.[4]

Similarly, in 20th-century Hebrew poetry—which emerged from a long tradition of Hebrew prayer—the secular poet calls upon God and, therefore, creates a listening God. The Hebrew itself enables the poet to create the listening God, as the language resounds with the echoes of traditional prayers and Biblical passages.

Secular Prayer

It is commonly understood that the early Zionists rebelled against religion. In attempting to create a "new Jew" who would be productive and self-sufficient, the first Zionists broke with the tradition of their fathers and mothers. But their choice of a Zionist ideology reveals that they did not throw out the whole tradition. Instead, they selected certain strands of Jewish tradition and expanded upon them. First and foremost, they emphasized love for the land of Israel, a love that Jews have expressed in prayer for 2000 years. The early Zionists also emphasized the Bible (while de-emphasizing the Talmud). The Bible connected them to the era of King David and King Solomon, the era of Jewish sovereignty. And they revitalized the Hebrew language, which bears layers of Jewish heritage. However much the Zionist pioneers rebelled against their *shtetl* upbringing, they nonetheless harbored strong ties to the homes from which they came, and they carried memories of the prayers and songs that their parents and grandparents had sung. Inevitably, phrases from these prayers and chants entered the poems and songs of the pioneers. Community singing, which continues to thrive in Israel, particularly in *kibbutzim*, almost always includes lyrics from liturgical poems, prayers, and Shabbat and holiday songs.

Today, many popular singers create hit songs based on traditional prayers. Gil Hitman sings *Adon Olam*, Boaz Sharabi has put *piyyutim* (liturgical poems) to music, and Chava Alberstein sings, *"Mi Ha'Ish?"* from Psalms 34:13, "Who is the man who desires life?"

Praise and Wonder of God's World

Zionist love for the land of Israel combined with a heightened awareness of nature also imbued Hebrew poetry with a religious sensibility. This celebration of the land of Israel and of the transcendent in nature is particularly evident among the women poets who became prominent in the 1920s. Influenced by the ideas of A. D. Gordon, they sought an unmediated relationship to the divine through their contact with the land, and they became keen observers of nature. No doubt they were influenced by 19th-century romanticism, the heritage of poets like William Wordsworth:

> There was a time when meadow, grove and stream,
> The earth and every common sight.
> To me did seem
> Appareled in celestial light.[5]

For those writing in Hebrew the celestial in nature often evokes the words of Psalms and prayers. The poet Esther Raab (1894–1981) has said, "Every poem is a prayer."[6] Raab has recently been re-discovered. Perhaps her reputation had been eclipsed by the more tragic story of the poet Rachel who died of tuberculosis, while Raab's strong, less feminine tone worked against her. She is unique in being the only woman writer of the second *aliyah* period (1904–1914) who was born and grew up in the land of Israel, the only one who did not emerge from a Russian literary tradition. She relates naturally to the language and landscape of the country. At the same time, her poetry incorporates the phrases of traditional prayer which she imbibed as a child. Her work provides an example of the relationship between intense contemplation of the landscape of *eretz Yisrael* and transcendence. Literary critic Zvi Luz describes how hidden spiritual messages and mystical insights break through her observations of nature.[7] This is evident in her prose-poem "Prayer" in "Notebooks of Hell":

My God, receive my soul which rises to You—You have known it from the time I came forth from my mother, from the time I used to awaken at night and go out to the garden to see Your miracles, to see the eucalyptuses standing in the silence, to see how they move slightly, as though You had blown into them—to see the dewdrops on the lilies—and the moonbeams shattering against them into splinters recoiling from Your spirit which passes over my head, You hovered in space over my head, I felt You with all my being—Remember this for me—gather me up in Your hand and I will not fear—You to whom the Truth is known.[8]

This piece expresses an awe of God, whose presence is palpable, immanent in nature. "To see the eucalyptuses standing in the silence, to see how they move slightly, as though You had blown into them ... You hovered in space over my head. I felt You with all my being." The poet is describing a mystical experience. Rabbi Donin has noted that feelings of awe and admiration well up in our hearts when we observe great natural scenes, and that these feelings bring forth prayer, like the Psalm, "O Lord, how great are Your works." For Raab, the feelings of wonder are accompanied by a feeling of creatureliness: "receive my soul ... gather me up in Your hand and I will not fear." She implies here that God has created the human being and so will protect God's creation. This echoes the conventional prayer preceding the morning blessings, "My God, the soul which You have given me is pure. You created it in me, You breathed it into me and You maintain it within me."

Ultimately, Raab's prose-poem expresses her connection to the Creator. The poet expresses total dependence, begging for God's grace. Rabbi David Hartman, discussing Rabbi Soloveitchik's philosophy of prayer, explains that "the fundamental driving force in approaching the Master is need and dependency ... the existential awareness that one lives in the presence of God in a personal and intimate way and that the divine presence can be addressed through direct and warm speech."[9] Rabbi Soloveitchik, however, argues that reflecting on the impersonal God of nature does not lead to prayer, because the essence of prayer is relational intimacy. Such intimacy emerges from membership in the covenantal community, from being a part of the Jewish people—and that means accepting the Torah and observing *mitzvot*. This is clearly not the aim of most 20th-century Hebrew poetry. Nonetheless, identification with the covenantal community is implicit.

Rabbi Donin asks, "What makes Jewish prayer Jewish?" He responds: "[It] uses the idiom of the Hebrew Bible and reflects the Jewish soul. It ... expresses the basic values of the Jewish people and affirms the central articles of Jewish faith. It ... reflects our historical experience and gives expression to our future aspirations."[10] Much in contemporary Hebrew poetry meets these qualifications. In addition, Hebrew poetry explicitly borrows the wording of traditional prayers. By incorporating phrases and themes of Hebrew prayers, a poem conjures images of religious life in the past and at the same time testifies commitment to the national ethos. The poem creates a link to the past while transforming the meaning of the prayer toward a more modern sensibility.

Esther Raab's poem "*Shirat Ishah*—Woman's Song" uses the structure of the woman's morning blessing to celebrate women's status in Judaism. Orthodox women recite the daily morning blessing, "Blessed are You, Lord our God, King of the universe who has created me according to His will," while men recite, "Blessed are You, Lord our God, King of the universe who has not made me a woman," which seems to minimize women's status. Raab, though, praises both the unique position of women and the God who created her.

Blessed He who made me a woman—
that I'm earth and Adam
and a tender rib;
Blessed who made me
circles upon circles—
like wheels of planets
and like circles of fruits—
who gave me living flesh
which blossoms
and made me like plant of the field—
that bears fruit;

so that Your cloud-tatters
slide like silk
on my face and thighs;
and I am big
and want to be a girl,
weeping from sorrow,
and laughing, and singing with a voice,
thinner than thin—
like a wee cricket
in the chorus of your lofty
cherubs—
smallest of the small—
I play
at Your feet—
my Creator![11]

בָּרוּךְ שֶׁעֲשָׂנִי אִשָּׁה-
שֶׁאֲנִי אֲדָמָה וְאָדָם,
וְצֵלַע רַכָּה;
בָּרוּךְ שֶׁעֲשִׂיתַנִי
עֲגוּלִים עֲגוּלִים-
כְּגַלְגַּלֵּי מַזָּלוֹת
וּכְעִגּוּלֵי פֵּרוֹת-
שֶׁנָּתַתָּ לִי בָּשָׂר חַי
פּוֹרֵחַ,
וַעֲשִׂיתַנִי כְּצֶמַח הַשָּׂדֶה-
נוֹשֵׂא פְּרִי;

שֶׁקִּרְעֵי עֲנָנֶיךָ,
מַחֲלִיקִים כְּמֶשִׁי
עַל פָּנַי וִירֵכַי;
וַאֲנִי גְדוֹלָה
וּמְבַקֶּשֶׁת לִהְיוֹת יַלְדָּה,
בּוֹכִיָּה מִצַּעַר,
וְצוֹחֶקֶת, וְשָׁרָה בְּקוֹל,
דַּק מִן הַדַּק-
כְּצַרְצַר זָעִיר
בְּמַקְהֵלַת כְּרוּבֶיךָ
הַנַּעֲלָה-
קְטַנָּה שֶׁבַּקְּטַנּוֹת-
אֲנִי מְשַׂחֶקֶת
לְרַגְלֶיךָ-
בּוֹרְאִי![12]

Anne Lapidus Lerner points out that Esther Raab takes the morning blessing *shelo asani ishah* (who has not made me a woman) and turns it around to make it a paean to womanhood. Subtle changes of language allow Raab to counter the prejudice against women without being strident. Lerner claims that the title *"Shirat Ishah"* implies that the poem is not exclusively personal, but, like the *brakhah* that it inverts, is about everywoman. However, Raab sees woman both as *adamah,* earth, and Adam, primal man. Raab sees woman as equal to man, yet possessing unique mother-earth qualities. The term "tender rib" highlights woman's uniqueness on the one hand and her humanity on the other. The first woman was made from Adam's rib, but it was a "tender" rib. God has made women softer than men, round, without sharp edges, like the sensual circularity of fruit and the orbits of the heavenly spheres. Woman connects heaven and earth. The celestial is perceived in the sensual, in women bearing fruit, and also in caresses. Raab yearns again to be young, a free spirit, spontaneously expressing sorrow, laughter, and song. The phrase "like a wee cricket" seems to indicate a low self-image, and indeed Raab is humble before God. Yet she calls her poem *shirah* rather than *shir.* The former alludes to Moses' Song at the Sea and the prophetess Deborah's Song, both national songs of praise to God upon deliverance, whereas *shir* refers to a more intimate, personal poem.

Although Raab modifies the morning prayer, she does not struggle with women's rights. She sees herself as one of God's creatures, sitting at God's feet, though not, as one *midrash* says about righteous women, at her learned husband's feet! Both the prose-poem "Prayer" and *"Shirat Ishah*—Woman's Song" reveal Raab's intense relationship to God through nature, particularly through woman's sensuality. Her perspective is that of the body and the earth: she is a creature in God's chorus.

This outpouring of praise for God's creation dovetails with both a romantic vision of nature and with love of the land of Israel. Such praise arises again and again in poems and songs of the pioneering generation, and it continues today. The Eternal radiates forth from a specific reality, from the earthly and particular. This especially characterizes the women poets Rachel, Yocheved Bat-Miriam, Esther Raab, and Leah Goldberg.

A transmutation of religious emotion and liturgy into other Zionist values also takes place in modern Hebrew poetry. In the following poem, Abraham Shlonsky (1900–1973) suffuses the ideology of labor with religious symbolism. Shlonsky, born in the Ukraine and influenced by symbolist European poetry, set the tone for a whole generation of Israeli poets.[13] The following poem was written in the early 1920s, while he worked as a road builder in the valley of Jezreel.

[TOIL]

Dress me, good mother, in a glorious robe of many colors, and at dawn lead me to [my] toil.

My land is wrapped in light as in a prayer shawl. The houses stand forth like frontlets; and the roads paved by hand, stream down like phylactery straps.

Here the lovely city says the morning prayer to its Creator. And among the creators is your son Abraham, a road-building bard of Israel.

And in the evening twilight, father will return from his travails, and, like a prayer, will whisper joyfully: "My dear son Abraham, skin, sinews and bones—hallelujah."

Dress me, good mother, in a glorious robe of many colors, and at dawn lead me to toil.[14]

[עָמָל]

הַלְבִּישִׁינִי, אִמָּא כְּשֵׁרָה, כְּתֹנֶת פַּסִּים לְתִפְאֶרֶת
וְעִם שַׁחֲרִית הוֹבִילִינִי אֱלֵי עָמָל.

עוֹטְפָה אַרְצִי אוֹר כַּטַּלִּית,
בָּתִּים נִצְבוּ כַטּוֹטָפוֹת,
וְכִרְצוּעוֹת תְּפִלִּין גּוֹלְשִׁים כְּבִישִׁים,סָלְלוּ כַּפַּיִם.

תְּפִלַּת שַׁחֲרִית פֹּה תִּתְפַּלֵּל קִרְיָה נָאָה אֱלֵי בּוֹרְאָהּ.
וּבַבּוֹרְאִים-בְּנֵךְ אַבְרָהָם,
פַּיְטָן-סוֹלֵל בְּיִשְׂרָאֵל.

וּבָעֶרֶב בֵּין הַשְּׁמָשׁוֹת יָשׁוּב אַבָּא מִסַּבְלוֹתָיו
וְכִתְפִלָּה יִלְחַשׁ נַחַת:
-הַבֵּן יַקִּיר לִי אַבְרָהָם,
עוֹר וְגִידִים וַעֲצָמוֹת-
הַלְלוּיָהּ.

הַלְבִּישִׁינִי, אִמָּא כְּשֵׁרָה, כְּתֹנֶת פַּסִּים לְתִפְאֶרֶת
וְעִם שַׁחֲרִית הוֹבִילִינִי
אֱלֵי עָמָל. [15]

Abraham Shlonsky sees the handiwork of man side by side with the handiwork of nature as a stimulus for the worship of God and as an ingredient of prayer. Physical labor has replaced the old religion's emphasis on Torah study, which many early Zionists perceived as sterile and fruitless. "The robe of many colors" refers to Joseph's robe (Genesis 27:3), suggesting princeliness and the favorite son. He who works the land is princely; in this new scale of values, the laborer is the preferred one. The very landscape prays to God, for it is "wrapped in a prayer shawl." The houses in this new land are the frontlets of the *tefillin*, and the roads are the straps.

The city sings forth a morning prayer to the Creator, and Abraham (Shlonsky himself), like the patriarch Abraham, forges a new religion of road-building and writing poetry in the land of Israel. He alludes to the sentence, "My son dear to me Efraim," from the Book of Jeremiah (31:19) that is found in the Rosh Hashanah liturgy. His father creates the Evening Service out of praise for his son's physicality, for his body devoted to toil. Most of all, the intense energy that Shlonsky exudes is indeed a religious ecstasy. The whole physical world, both natural and man-made, is in praise of God.

Shlonsky's praying world is congruent with Rabbi Abraham Isaac Kook's view that the soul is engaged in ongoing prayer. The soul's prayer is striving to emerge from muteness into existence; it strives to spread to all the energies of life, those both of the individual soul and of the whole nation. The belief that the soul constantly prays, but that only when articulated does the prayer reveal itself, is here reflected in poetry.

The praying soul enables us to experience the world intensely, as Leah Goldberg expresses in the following poem.

Teach Me, God, To Pray

Teach me, God, to pray, to praise
the splendor of ripe fruit, the wonder of a wrinkled leaf,
the freedom to see, to feel, to breathe,
to know, to hope, and even to know grief.

Teach my lips blessing, song, and praise
when You renew Your time each night, each dawn,
so that my days will not repeat my yesterdays,
to save my life from mere routine of all days gone.[16]

לַמְּדֵנִי, אֱלֹהַי

לַמְּדֵנִי, אֱלֹהַי, בָּרֵךְ וְהִתְפַּלֵּל
עַל סוֹד עָלֶה קָמֵל, עַל נֹגַהּ פְּרִי בָּשֵׁל,
עַל הַחֵרוּת הַזֹּאת: לִרְאוֹת, לָחוּש, לִנְשׁם
לָדַעַת, לְיַחֵל, לְהִכָּשֵׁל.

לַמֵּד אֶת שְׂפְתוֹתַי בְּרָכָה וְשִׁיר הַלֵּל
בְּהִתְחַדֵּשׁ זְמַנְּךָ עִם בֹּקֶר וְעִם לֵיל,
לְבַל יִהְיֶה יוֹמִי הַיּוֹם כִּתְמוֹל שִׁלְשׁוֹם.
לְבַל יִהְיֶה עָלַי יוֹמִי הֶרְגֵּל.[17]

Asking God to teach a human to pray to God—it seems to be a paradox. The traditional liturgy, though, includes many prayers that prepare us for the encounter with God. The *Amidah*, the central prayer of every service, opens with *Adonai sefatai tiftah ufi yagid tehilatekha*—"O Lord, open my lips, and my mouth will proclaim Your praise." In contemporary times, when belief in God is not automatic, Goldberg is also asking God to help her believe. She asks God to help her pray, so that she can articulate her intense experience of the world: "the splendor of ripe fruit, the wonder of a wrinkled leaf." She wants to celebrate youth and ripeness of being, and also "the wrinkled leaf," the processes of dehydration and death. She seeks the freedom to see and feel, to know everything, but also to fail, to know grief. She knows that without God the world will be less intense. She again requests God to "teach my lips blessing, song, and praise" so she can experience daily renewal, and not be doomed to mere routine, numb to the world around her.

Leah Goldberg was well aware of the tension of praying to a God about whom she had doubts. She was a poet of universal orientation, steeped in the culture of Europe. Born in Konigsberg, she grew up in Kovno, Lithuania. After receiving her doctorate from the University of Bonn, she came to Palestine in 1935. She became chair of the Department of Comparative Literature at the Hebrew University, and she translated Tolstoy's "War and Peace" and Petrarch's sonnets into Hebrew. The subject matter of her poems is not predominantly Jewish; two of primary concerns are unrequited love and nature. Yet Goldberg recognizes the Godhead in nature. In the poem *"Nisayon"* ("Trial"), she describes an overwhelming spiritual ecstasy—which can only be understood as revelation—and she asks God "how shall I stand up to the test / of such complete bliss?" Although she recognizes prayer as a universal expression of humanity's suffering and joy in "Courage of the Mundane," she also claims that Hebrew is the particular "soul language" of the Jewish people, the medium for its dialogue with God. She herself often uses language from the liturgy and Bible in her poetry.

Petition and Protection

The most heartfelt poems have entered the Israeli song repertoire, among them, "Going to Caesarea" by Hannah Senesh.

Going To Caesarea

God—may there be no end,
To sea, to sand,
Water's splash,
Lightning's flash,
The prayer of man.[18]

הֲלִיכָה לְקֵיסַרְיָה

אֵלִי, אֵלִי, שֶׁלֹּא יִגָּמֵר לְעוֹלָם
הַחוֹל וְהַיָּם
רִשְׁרוּשׁ שֶׁל הַמַּיִם,
בְּרַק הַשָּׁמַיִם,
תְּפִלַּת הָאָדָם. [19]

Hannah Senesh (1921–1944), who parachuted behind Nazi lines to save Jews in her birthplace, Hungary, had been a member of Kibbutz Sdot Yam near Caesarea. She was caught and killed by the Nazis. Her shimmering experience of the seaside near her kibbutz is recorded here. The senses are entirely engaged: the sound of water, the flash of light across the sky, the graininess of sand. Senesh does not plead, "Let the world continue." Instead she says, "may there be no end." By structuring her plea in the negative, Senesh conjures up the threat of loss. The objects of nature so intensely felt at this moment—sea, sand, lightning, sky—are made more precious by the fear of losing them. There is an intense yearning to hold onto the moment, onto life, a yearning that becomes especially poignant when considering Hannah Senesh's tragic fate.

As often occurs in Hebrew prayers, praise of God's wondrous world transforms into petition. Human praise of God leads to the plea that God, who has the power to create the world, also protect it and help humanity. Hannah Senesh stands in awe before nature, and, more than that, she petitions God that the created world will endure.

In *Biblical Prose Prayer*, Moshe Greenberg points out that the Bible includes many spontaneous prayers of petition. Such prayer opens with an address that invokes God's name; this address may also include descriptive attributes of God. A specific request of God then follows. Petitionary prayer in the Bible may also contain a motivating sentence, "offering what is hoped will be a persuasive reason for God to comply."[20] Rabbi David Hartman writes that, according to Rabbi Soloveitchik's vision of prayer, petitioning God in prayer leads us toward self-discovery. By articulating our pains and needs in meaningful linguistic structures, humanity, according to Rabbi Soloveitchik, comes to understand what those pains and needs are.[21] The poets in Israel can be seen as modern *paytanim,* liturgical poets, expressing appreciation of everyday life and begging God to protect it.

Call for Redemption

Amir Gilboa's poem "Great are my God's works" is a song of praise to God, written at the time of his marriage to his wife Gabriella. The poem reveals the exuberance of a person in love and the experience of rebirth as a consequence of love. The literary critic Ida Tzurit notes the influence of Gilboa's hasidic background, his exposure to mystical conceptions of the universe in which the human merges with the eternal flow, the "source of life." The poet feels thankfulness for God's gifts and abundance, and this thankfulness is reinforced when the poet fuses with his beloved. He goes beyond himself and is overwhelmed by the abundance of the other person. He feels renewed, reborn. The phrase "my God's works" expresses an intimate relationship to God, an intimacy that the poet also feels with his bride. At the same time, the poem uses an acrostic, a traditional Hebrew poetic structure, to spell out the name "Gabriella."

The poem works on many levels, interweaving this personal moment with the fate of the Jewish people. Amir Gilboa (1917–1984) was born in the Ukraine and raised in Poland. In 1937 he secretly joined a He-halutz group making its way to Palestine illegally.[22] He never said good-bye to his family, who were destroyed in the Holocaust, and he expressed great guilt about this. Gilboa's well-known poem "Isaac" describes the sacrifice not of the son, but of the father, an image of what happened to those left behind in Europe.

In the poem "Great are my God's works" Gilboa suggests that in this eternal moment, he stands above time, with God, looking backward and forward. God sees his fears and accompanies him to the terrible sights of the Holocaust—sights that continue to live in his imagination and that cause the cells of his body to weep. The phrase "He accompanies me / to all the terrible sights" plays on the Hebrew word *hamoraot*, literally, "the fears." This word also suggests the Hebrew word *marot*, "terrible sights." Gilboa has lived with anxieties created by the terrible sights of the Holocaust, which he imagines his family experienced. Nonetheless, he's confident that the joy he feels at the moment of his marriage will continue to flow, become the reality of his life, replace the images of the past, and lift him from past sorrows and fears to a life of abundance. He hints that this personal redemption is also at work in a larger sense in the Jewish people.

In other poems, the poet fuses pictures of Israel's renewal with memories of the Holocaust. His poems carry a messianic strand: The Jewish nation is reborn out of the ashes. But Gilboa is rarely heavy-handed or histrionic; instead, he employs a unique whimsical mode. Although Amir Gilboa is the same age as the realistic writers called the "Palma<u>h</u> generation,"[23] he defies easy categorization. Gilboa creates his poetic world out of childlike wonder and linguistic play—which always contains the language of the Bible and the prayer book that he absorbed as a child.

Great are my God's works

**Great are my God's works. He accompanies me
to all the terrible sights, and all the weeping cells.
Sees the sorrows with me, and confident in my joy that
one day will become a reality
forever. Great are my God's works
since the day I knew him. I thank you, My God,
here comes my joy. Here it comes descending upon me.**[24]

גְּדוֹלִים מַעֲשֵׂי אֱלֹהַי

גְּדוֹלִים מַעֲשֵׂי אֱלֹהַי. הוּא בָּא עִמִּי
בְּכָל הַמּוֹרָאוֹת וּבְכָל תָּאֵי הַבֶּכִי.
רוֹאֶה עִמִּי בַּתּוּגוֹת וּבוֹטֵחַ בְּשִׂמְחָתִי
יוֹם אֶחָד כִּי תָבוֹא לִהְיוֹת קַיֶּמֶת
אֶל תָּמִיד. גְּדוֹלִים מַעֲשֵׂי אֱלֹהַי
לְמִן יוֹם בּוֹ הִכַּרְתִּיהוּ. אוֹדְךָ, אֱלֹהַי,
הִנֵּה בָּאָה שִׂמְחָתִי. הִנֵּה בָּאָה וְיוֹרְדָה עָלַי. 25

In this poem, Amir Gilboa alludes to a Yom Kippur verse praising God, "God's Works."[26] Here, though, the poet places God and man on equal footing. Both observe the good and the evil as God "accompanies" the poet. Yet the poet sustains hope that redemption ("joy") will come. He casually says, "and confident in my joy that / one day will become a reality"—as if God has nothing to do with the poet's joy, as if the joy is accidental or random. The poet implies the terrible dilemma: How can God's world be good when God has been with him in his fears, his terrible visions of the Holocaust? The personal and collective are also invoked through the word *taei*, cells, which literally mean the cells of the body and which the poet describes as "weeping." The word *taei,* though, can also refer to chambers, particularly gas chambers. At the same time, Gilboa declares that joy is coming. Just as he has found a personal renewal in a sweep of cosmic and earthly love, the people of Israel find a cosmic renewal through the birth and existence of the State of Israel. Gilboa does not try to understand or explain the destruction, and, by the same token, he does not explain the blessing of redemption. Instead it is a gift that rains down on him. "Here comes my happiness. Here it comes descending upon me." The final sentences of the poem convey the childlike joy that characterizes Gilboa. Effortlessly, naturally, a beautiful object seems to float down from the sky. No wonder the poet still believes that God's works are great.

The experience of war—like the devastation of the Holocaust—is threaded throughout the fabric of Israeli consciousness, and inevitably many poets have written lamentations for those who suffered and died. Hayim Gouri was born in Tel Aviv in 1923, studied at an agricultural school, and served in the elite Palmah combat forces.[27] He saw active duty during the Israeli war of independence. This poem is a heart-rending, almost innocent cry to God to watch over the soldiers.

Prayer

The battle—it'll take place tonight
Bless these boys—because the time has come.
See them, they are silent and willing—their eyes afire.
See the night descends, there's a wind in the treetops, the pine tree quivers.
The battle will be tonight. And there are few of them.

Bless them, God, because the time has come.
The stars are aflame. And many camps are gathered on the other side.
For who will see the light of day? And who will fall, who will die?
Will there be victory or defeat and the grave?

Oh my God, bless them. Bless those going out to war.
Bless their weapons, that shouldn't miss the target.... Bless their homes.
Bless this, the nation, its boys, its defenders
Until the battle ends.

Behold they went silently, their footsteps disappear.
And the heavy darkness, and the night is in the hills
Bless them—because the time has come
Bring blessing to the boys.[28]

קְרָב יְהִי הַלַּיְל
הָבֵא בְּרָכָה לַנְּעָרִים--כִּי בָאָה עֵת.
רְאֵה אוֹתָם שׁוֹתְקִים וּנְכוֹנִים--וְעֵינֵיהֶם דּוֹלְקוֹת.
רְאֵה יוֹרֵד הָעֶרֶב, רוּחַ בַּצַּמָּרוֹת, הָאֹרֶן מְרַטֵּט.
קְרָב יְהִי הַלַּיְל. וְהֵמָּה מְעַטִּים מְאֹד.

בָּרְכֵם, אֵלִי, כִּי בָאָה עֵת.
כּוֹכָבִים הֻצַּתּוּ וּמַחֲנוֹת רַבִּים נֶאֱסָפִים מֵעֵבֶר.

כִּי מִי יִרְאֶה אוֹר-יוֹם? וּמִי נָפַל וָמֵת?
הֲנִצָּחוֹן יֻשַּׂג אוֹ אִם תְּבוּסָה וָקֶבֶר?

בָּרְכֵם, אֵלִי, בָּרֵךְ יוֹצְאֵי לַמִּלְחָמָה.
בָּרֵךְ נִשְׁקָם לְבַל יַחֲטִיא ... בָּרֵךְ בֵּיתָם.
בָּרֵךְ אֶת זֶה הָעָם, אֶת נְעָרָיו וְלוֹחֲמָיו,
עַד קְרָב יִתַּם.

הִנֵּה יָצְאוּ שְׁקֵטִים וְצַעֲדָם אוֹבֵד,
וַעֲלָטָה כְּבֵדָה וְלַיְל בֶּהָרִים,
בָּרְכֵם--כִּי בָאָה עֵת.
הָבֵא בְּרָכָה לַנְּעָרִים. [29]

Gouri uses the word *ne'arim* to emphasize the soldiers' youth. These men are still boys. It also hints at the conflict in II Samuel 2:14, "Let the young men *(ne'arim)* arise and play [that is, duel] before us," in which young warriors fight in pairs to determine the outcome of the battle. In Gouri's poem, the boys are tense and silent, but willing to go into combat. Their eyes afire might imply a heroic spirit, but the tension increases as the night falls. And most telling: The boys who have never experienced war are ready, yet the pine tree shivers. Nature, which has witnessed battle, knows what lies ahead. The poet fears too, because the soldiers are very few. The word *et* ("time") brings to mind Ecclesiastes 3:2–8, "a time to be born and a time to die … a time for war and a time for peace." The poet again observes nature's reaction as the stars flame, and he fearfully weighs the outcome, for many enemy camps are gathering. He recalls the Yom Kippur prayer, *Unetaneh Tokef*—"Who will live, and who will die?" Here the poet asks, "who will see the light of day? And who will fall, who will die?"

Gouri repeats again and again the basic plea: "Bless them." He calls upon God to bless the soldiers' arms, bless their homes, bless the nation. The repetition highlights the poet's fear and emotion. He is at a loss for words, holding onto God's coattails, praying and begging God to bless these men.

Poems of Protest

A strong tradition in Judaism, from Biblical times to the present, involves humanity demanding justice of God. Abraham challenges God when God intends to destroy Sodom (Genesis 18:24–25): "Perhaps there are fifty innocent within the city, will You really sweep it away? … The Judge of all the world—will God not do what is just?" There is also the hasidic tale that Rabbi Levi Yitzhak of Berdichev stood up in the synagogue on Yom Kippur and said, "Today it is You who shall be judged. By Your children who suffer for You. Who die for You and the sanctification of Your name."[30] The very act of accusing God, however, is a form of prayer. Mortals may protest God's actions in the world, but we have no one else to turn to— so our protest too becomes a prayer.

In our era of loss of faith, many Hebrew poems challenge God's design, God's indifference, and God's apathy during the Holocaust. Dan Pagis (1930–1986) goes one step further. He points to the creation of a human who is capable of such obscene cruelty, and he accuses God of sharing in the atrocity of the Nazis who themselves were created in God's image.

Dan Pagis was born in Radautz (Bukovina). During the Second World War he was interred in a Ukrainian concentration camp. He escaped in 1944 and two years later came to Israel. He was a professor of Hebrew literature at the Hebrew University, specializing in medieval Hebrew poetry. Pagis's own poetry refers to his Holocaust experience, and "Testimony" establishes him as a witness to the evil. He indicates that those who were created "in the image"—ostensibly of God—were the ones who wore boots and uniforms, while

I was a shadow.
I had a different Maker,
And He in His Mercy left nothing in me to die.[31]

Pagis says that he rose in smoke, becoming part of the bodiless God that has no body or form. In "Another Testimony," the poet again accuses God.

Another Testimony

You are the first, and You remain the last,
if You're not able to judge between plea and plea,
between blood and blood,
listen to my heart, hardened in judgment, see my plight:
Michael, Gabriel,
Your angel collaborators,
stand and admit
that You said: Let us make Man
and they said Amen.[32]

עֵדוּת אַחֶרֶת

אַתָּה הָרִאשׁוֹן וְאַתָּה הַנִּשְׁאָר אַחֲרוֹן,
כִּי יִפָּלֵא מִמְּךָ מִשְׁפָּט בֵּין דִּין לְדִין
בֵּין דָּם לְדָם,
הַקְשֵׁב לְלִבִּי הַקָּשֶׁה בַּדִּין, רְאֵה אֶת עָנְיִי.
מְשֻׁתְּפֵי-הַפְּעֻלָּה שֶׁלְּךָ, מִיכָאֵל, גַּבְרִיאֵל,
עוֹמְדִים וּמוֹדִים
שֶׁאָמַרְתָּ: נַעֲשֶׂה אָדָם,
וְהֵם אָמְרוּ אָמֵן. [33]

The first line has its source in *Adon Olam*, which states that God has no beginning and no end. Pagis, however, ridicules God. Why does God exist forever? Because all others have been destroyed. God sits in judgment, yet there is no justice. No distinctions are made between "plea and plea" or "blood and blood." God destroys both the guilty and the innocent. Pagis's verses ironically invert the Biblical phrase "they are to judge the people with equitable justice" (Deuteronomy 16:18), which was the basis for establishing the Sanhedrin, the Jewish high court of ancient Israel.

Pagis calls out to God to listen to him, for his heart has been "hardened" by God's arbitrary judgment. This hints at God's hardening of Pharaoh's heart (Exodus 7:14, 9:12, and elsewhere), suggesting again that God does not distinguish between the oppressors of the Jewish people and the Jewish people themselves. The poet points to God's collaborators, the angels who helped God create man, and he quotes Genesis 1:26, in which God says, "Let us make man" *(Naaseh adam)*. For Pagis, this is the greatest injustice of all—God made man and the angels approved.

From protesting God's injustice to blaspheming is but a small step. Michal Govrin's 1995 novel, *Hashem (The Name)*, is one long prayer by Amalia, a young woman who has recently become intensely religious. She seeks to mystically heal the rift between God and humanity, a rift made evident in the Holocaust. She begins praying, and she counts the *omer*—the 49 days from Pesaḥ to Shavuot, the holiday that celebrates God's revelation of the Torah. Amalia, on the verge of madness, numbers the days until the divine manifestation, the day on which she seeks to attain a consummation and union with God and thereby heal the rift in the universe. Govrin explains her feelings while writing the novel:

> Amalia's ecstatic submission and prayer became for me imprisoning, bare and unbearable hypocrisy in the wake of destruction. I could not contain myself, I had to push her to hurl words against heaven, to blaspheme.... Blasphemy, that might be one of the strongest forms of address, of prayer.[34]

Amalia waits for Shavuot to surrender herself entirely and fuse with God. Yet in Amalia's mind, submission and union with God imply self annihilation, and she thinks of sacrificing herself by jumping off a cliff. Yet she stops short.

And the storm has not yet vanished. As if something is still revealed, clarified for the first time....

As if a barrier was removed from the eye. The destruction exposed on the slopes, caustic, uncovered, as if this is the Covenant, and also the consolation. The break hidden between us, King who causes death and restores life....

As if everything that was, was only to reveal to me, on the verge of the end of the Counting, the great tenderness hidden here between us in the destruction.[35]

Instead of the fusion with God, she finds a human resurrection in the Sabbath.

The time has come. Just to go on turning now, with no expectations anymore, for an answer.... Just to go on turning, that's the prayer. Just to go on turning in the expanding space.

And the voice speaking between us is enough. Enough the words of the prayer muttered from my lips.[36]

Blasphemy, anger at God for the irreconcilable gap between human and God, the incomprehensibility of God's ways, particularly in the Holocaust —these are transformed into the acceptance of a limited, contingent world, where all one can do is to seek out a means of communication with God. Michal Govrin has depicted a character whose intense desire to fuse with God had created a perverted vision of Judaism. In discussing her novel, Govrin also notes that the rift in the universe created by the horror of the Holocaust *cannot* be healed. We can, though, perceive God's tenderness in the rift and accept our earthly, human world, which includes both destruction and restoration.

The late Yehuda Amichai (1924–1999) used the language of prayer and the Bible to criticize God and religion, albeit in a lighthearted manner. Born in Wurzberg, Germany, he came to Jerusalem with his family in 1936, served in the Jewish Brigade in the Second World War, and fought in the War of Independence. Amichai came from an Orthodox home and acquired a deep knowledge of Judaism. He had a special affection for his father, and he struggled with the rupture from his father's tradition. Despite Amichai's secular outlook, his poetry constantly refers to the Jewish tradition, extensively citing classic Jewish texts. Influenced as well by English poetry, Amichai created a new poetic style, transforming Hebrew through his colloquial, often ironic, iconoclastic tone.

God Full of Mercy

God-Full-of-Mercy, the prayer for the dead.
If God was not full of mercy,
Mercy would have been in the world,
Not just in Him.
I, who plucked the flowers in the hills
And looked down into all the valleys,
I, who brought corpses down from the hills,
Can tell you that the world is empty of mercy.

I, who was King of Salt at the seashore,
Who stood without a decision at my window,
Who counted the steps of angels,
Whose heart lifted weights of anguish
In the horrible contests.

I, who use only a small part
Of the words in the dictionary.

I, who must decipher riddles
I don't want to decipher,
Know that if not for the God-full-of-mercy
There would be mercy in the world,
Not just in Him.[37]

אֵל מָלֵא רַחֲמִים

אֵל מָלֵא רַחֲמִים,
אִלְמָלֵא הָאֵל מָלֵא רַחֲמִים
הָיוּ הָרַחֲמִים בָּעוֹלָם וְלֹא רַק בּוֹ.
אֲנִי, שֶׁקָּטַפְתִּי פְּרָחִים בָּהָר
וְהִסְתַּכַּלְתִּי אֶל כָּל הָעֲמָקִים,
אֲנִי, שֶׁהֵבֵאתִי גְּוִיּוֹת מִן הַגְּבָעוֹת,
יוֹדֵעַ לְסַפֵּר שֶׁהָעוֹלָם רֵיק מֵרַחֲמִים.

אֲנִי שֶׁהָיִיתִי מֶלֶךְ הַמֶּלַח לְיַד הַיָּם,
שֶׁעָמַדְתִּי בְּלִי הַחְלָטָה לְיַד חַלּוֹנִי,
שֶׁסָּפַרְתִּי צַעֲדֵי מַלְאָכִים,
שֶׁלִּבִּי הֵרִים מִשְׁקָלוֹת כְּאֵב
בַּתַּחֲרִיּוֹת הַנּוֹרָאוֹת.

אֲנִי, שֶׁמִּשְׁתַּמֵּשׁ רַק בְּחֵלֶק קָטָן
מִן הַמִּלִּים שֶׁבַּמִּלּוֹן.

אֲנִי, שֶׁמֻּכְרָח לִפְתּוֹר חִידוֹת בְּעַל כָּרְחִי
יוֹדֵעַ כִּי אִלְמָלֵא הָאֵל מָלֵא רַחֲמִים
הָיוּ הָרַחֲמִים בָּעוֹלָם
וְלֹא רַק בּוֹ. [38]

Amichai plays with images, in this poem using images of death and mourning. The poem's title refers to the prayer, *El Malei Raḥamim*, the prayer affirming God's mercy that is said at funerals, but Amichai understands the phrase *El malei raḥamim*, "God is full of mercy," to mean that God has a monopoly on mercy, leaving none for the rest of the world. Amichai then recalls his own awakening to the cruelty, the lack of mercy in the world. He begins as a youth wandering in the hillsides, plucking "flowers in the hills, and [looking] down into all the valleys." Although this existence sounds idyllic, the intimation of human aggression is present in the picking of flowers. The trauma, the great realization that there is no mercy in the world, comes when the youth goes to war and must bring back the corpses of his comrades killed in battle.

His carefree immersion in nature is again traced at the seashore, where he is "King of Salt," a carefree youth "who counted the steps of angels." Like Jacob who saw the angels going up and down the ladder to heaven (Genesis 28:12), Amichai experienced the transcendental. But again he turns to the lack of mercy when—parallel to carrying corpses—he carries "weights of anguish," wounded soldiers in pain. He might also be expressing the anguish he feels. Amichai then says that he uses "only a small part of the words in the dictionary." He uses only material-world, modern words, not the metaphorical language of the prophets. Nor does he use the words of those modern poets who echo the prophets. He doesn't have the belief, the prophetic inspiration, to decipher the lack of mercy in the world. He implies, though, that by projecting all kindness and mercy onto a God of mercy, we humans limit our own kindness and mercy.

Confession

In addition to secular Israeli poets who refer to Hebrew prayers and use the forms of prayer in their work, a number of observant Israelis also write poetry. Often they write about the same subjects and raise the same questions about faith as contemporary non-religious poets, but some of the poems of observant Israeli writers achieve a religious intensity and mystical insight. This can be said about the poetry of Zelda Schneersohn Mishkovsky (1914–1984), who signed her poems as Zelda. Born in the Ukraine, she came from a family of prominent hasidic scholars. In 1925 she immigrated to the land of Israel with her family and settled in Jerusalem. After her studies she worked as a teacher, and in 1950 married Haim Mishkovsky, who encouraged her to devote herself to her poetry. Her first book of poems appeared in 1967 and was enthusiastically received by avant garde poets as well as religious and non-religious readers. Some of her poems have been put to music.

Zelda's poetry is characterized by the fear and trembling of the religious sensibility, and by a realization of human vulnerability and fragility that is coupled with a deep empathy for people. She calls upon traditional prayers and Biblical phrases, and she weaves them into her poems.

In This Moment of Reflection

In this moment of reflection,
Cut off from everything,
I reveled in the beauty of grape leaves on a vine—
Only when a shadow of peace
Abides in the hills of Jerusalem
And the awakening sounds of birds
And infants surround me,
And I have not betrayed
And I have not spoken falsely
And dark terror has not possessed
My senses—
Then my soul absorbs a very slight quiver
That passes through the leaves as they greet
The light of dawn.

O hidden, secret God,
Save me from evil rumors
That fling into the darkness
The delicate stillness
Of a heart that looks on from the side.
For what is my home and what is my life
On a day, alas,
This chaotic day
That hurls to the ground
With blinding fury
The delight of the grapevine
And all my meditations.[39]

בְּשָׁעָה מְהֻרְהֶרֶת זוֹ

בְּשָׁעָה מְהֻרְהֶרֶת זוֹ
מְנֻתֶּקֶת מִכֹּל
הִתְעַנַּגְתִּי עַל יְפִי עֲלֵי הַגֶּפֶן-
רַק כַּאֲשֶׁר צֵל שֶׁל שָׁלוֹם
שָׁרוּי בְּהָרֵי יְרוּשָׁלַיִם
וְקוֹלוֹת יְקִיצָה שֶׁל צִפֳּרִים
וְתִינוֹקוֹת מַקִּיפִים אוֹתִי,
וְלֹא בָּגַדְתִּי
וְלֹא דִּבַּרְתִּי דֹּפִי,
וְאֵימָה חֲשֵׁכָה לֹא כִשְׁפָה
אֶת חוּשִׁי-
קוֹלֶטֶת נַפְשִׁי רֶטֶט רָפֶה עַד מְאֹד
שֶׁעוֹבֵר בֶּעָלִים בְּפָגְשָׁם
אוֹר שֶׁל שַׁחֲרִית.

יָהּ טָמִיר וְנֶעְלָם
הַצִּילֵנִי מִשְּׁמוּעוֹת רָעוֹת
שֶׁהוֹדְפוֹת לָאֹפֶל
אֶת הַשֶּׁקֶט הַדַּק
שֶׁל לֵב מִסְתַּכֵּל מִן הַצַּד.
כִּי מַה בֵּיתִי וּמַה חַיַּי
בְּיוֹם שֶׁל אֲהָהּ
זֶה הַיּוֹם הַפְּרָאִי
שֶׁמַּשְׁלִיךְ לָאָרֶץ
בְּחֵמָה מְעַוֶּרֶת
אֶת עֶדְנַת הַגֶּפֶן
וְכָל הֲגִיגִי.[40]

Zelda meditates on God's world at dawn, but her emotion here differs from the ecstatic praise of life found in her poem, "I flowered in a house of stone, / Without care, without goal, / like an innocent fantasy, / a cyclamen bursting from stone."[41] This poem depicts her sense of terror in the world. The poet stands before an awe-inspiring God, whose ways are concealed from humanity. "O hidden, secret God" suggests the Kabbalist concept of an enigmatic God.

At first, the poet simply reflects on nature; she delights in the beauty of the grapevine as dawn approaches. Her solitary contemplation of beauty is interrupted by the daybreak; the peaceful shadows of the Jerusalem hills and the chirping of birds disturb her revelry. The crying of infants also breaks the early morning silence. With the awakening to the world, a sudden guilt constricts her, and she blurts out phrases from the Confession *(Vidui)* of Yom Kippur: "I have not betrayed / I have not spoken falsely," *Velo bagadti, velo dibbarti dofi.* Zelda exhibits profound psychological insight, as "dark terror" seizes her as she awakens to life fearing that she has sinned. But the phrase "dark terror" is used in Genesis 15:12 to describe Abraham's emotions at the *Brit Ben Habtarim*, his covenant with God. The awe that Zelda feels is frequently discussed in Jewish literature, from the Bible to medieval Hebrew liturgists to the present. The poet's awe reflects the long history of Jews' relationship to God—a relationship of joy and praise as in the *Hallel* prayer, yet an ominous relationship as well. This same sense of awe causes even the grape leaves to quiver.

In the next verse, Zelda is increasingly aware of the threatening world, and she appeals to the awesome God, whose ways are concealed, to save her from "evil rumors" and from bad news. She describes herself as an observer, one who watches "from the side." But with the sounds of life around her at the break of dawn, Zelda realizes that the chaos of the world must affect her, must penetrate her solitariness. She alludes to the Yom Kippur prayer, "What are we? What is our life? What is our piety?" How can we stand up against the chaos of life that destroys all the simple pleasures of contemplation? The urge for confession comes upon the believer in times of sudden fear, and she asks herself, what have I done that might destroy the life I know?

Zelda is a forerunner of the religious poets who have come to prominence in the last decade. As might be expected, Israel's modern religious poets use the structures and phrases of traditional prayer in their poetry. In addition, though, they often integrate into their poems both contemporary values and contemporary means of expression.

Chava Pinchas Cohen, a well-known religious poet and the editor of *Dimui*, a religious arts magazine, uses the style of traditional prayer in the poem below, in which she prays for the ability to efficiently and lovingly accomplish her mundane, everyday tasks.

A Mother's Morning Prayer

At this time as I stand cooking oatmeal,
Remove all sorts of alien thoughts from me
And when I touch the baby's back and take his temperature
May all sorts of problems disappear,

May they not confuse my thoughts.
And give me the strength to scrub my face
So that each one of my children
Can see his face in mine
As in a mirror washed for a festival.

And the darkness sunk within
My face—cover it with light
So that I don't lose my patience, and I won't be hoarse
From coarse, insistent screaming.
May I not experience weakness
Before the unknowable
And may it never end, even for a moment,
The touch of flesh upon flesh, my children's and mine.

Give me so much of Your love
That I can stand at the door and hand it out
With the simplicity of someone slicing bread
And smearing butter every morning.
Renew the sweet offering of boiling milk bubbling over
And the smell of coffee hovering above
The thanksgiving sacrifice and the daily sacrifice
That I never learned how to give.[42]

תְּפִילָה לָאֵם בְּטֶרֶם שַׁחֲרִית

בְּשָׁעָה שֶׁאֲנִי עוֹמֶדֶת לְבַשֵּׁל דַּיְסַת סֹלֶת
הָסֵר מִמֶּנִּי כָּל מִינֵי מַחֲשָׁבוֹת זָרוֹת
וּכְשֶׁאֲנִי נוֹגַעַת בְּגֵו הַתִּינוֹק וּמַדָּה חֻמּוֹ
שֶׁיֵּלְכוּ מִמֶּנִּי כָּל מִינֵי טְרָדוֹת
שֶׁלֹּא יְבַלְבְּלוּ מַחְשְׁבוֹתַי.
וְתֵן לִי אֹמֶץ לְזַכֵּךְ פָּנַי
שֶׁיּוּכַל כָּל אֶחָד מִילָדַי
לִרְאוֹת פָּנָיו בְּתוֹךְ פָּנַי
כְּמוֹ בְּמַרְאֶה רְחוּצָה לִקְרַאת חַג

וְאֶת הַחֹשֶׁךְ הַמֻּשְׁקָע מִפְּנִים
פָּנַי-כַּסֵּה בָּאוֹר.
שֶׁלֹּא תִפְקַע סַבְלָנוּתִי וְלֹא יֵחַר גְּרוֹנִי
מִצְּעָקָה מִתְחַבֶּטֶת וּמִתְעַבָּה
שֶׁלֹּא יִהְיֶה לִי רִפְיוֹן יָדַיִם
מוּל הַבִּלְתִּי נוֹדָע
וְשֶׁלֹּא יִפָּסֵק אַף לֹא לְרֶגַע
מַגָּע בָּשָׂר בְּבָשָׂר בֵּינִי לְבֵין יְלָדַי

תֵּן בִּי אַהֲבָתְךָ שֶׁיְּהֵא בִּי דַּי לַעֲמֹד בְּפֶתַח הַבַּיִת וּלְחַלְּקָה
בְּפַשְׁטוּת בָּהּ פּוֹרְסִים לֶחֶם וּמוֹרְחִים חֶמְאָה כָּל בֹּקֶר
מְחֻדָּשׁ נִיחוֹחַ חָלָב רוֹתֵחַ וְגוֹלֵשׁ וְרֵיחַ הַקָּפֶה מְכַסִּים
עַל קָרְבַּן תּוֹדָה וְקָרְבַּן תָּמִיד
שֶׁאֵינִי יוֹדַעַת אֵיךְ נוֹתְנִים. 43

Pinchas-Cohen has written a domestic prayer, elevating the household activity of mothers, but the prayer also humanizes the liturgy. The poet suggests the ancient ritual that consisted of the weekly offering of the shewbread, the *leḥem hapanim,* on the table in the Holy Temple—thereby creating the effect of a home. Pinchas-Cohen here substitutes her own prayer for the traditional morning prayer. Hers is the prayer of a mother who must tend to children, one who cannot devote herself to praying at set times. She prays for the harmony of domestic labor, just as Abraham Shlonsky prayed for the harmony of labor on the land, and she begs that no evil thoughts or foreign concerns dampen her intensity. She prays that she succeed in fulfilling both the creaturely needs of her children—cooking oatmeal, healing their illness—and their emotional needs. She prays that she be attuned to each child. Her face must not be closed to her children; instead her face should reflect each one. The poet's play on the word *panim* also hints at the idea of God addressing Moses "face to face," and it provides theological insight: God was not only revealed to Moses, but Moses found himself reflected in God's countenance. Pinchas-Cohen knows that her tasks are not easy, and she seeks to conceal from her children her own darkness. She prays that light cover her and radiate out to the children. She also prays that she be strong enough to confront the unknown dangers that lurk in the dark—harking back to Zelda's terror of the new day. And she begs that she never forget that they are flesh of her flesh. In asking God to bestow love upon her, she is also asking that she—the mother who has created children out of her flesh—be able to imitate God in her relationship with her children. Just as God looked face to face at Moses and bestowed love, may she do so. She likens her preparation of her family's breakfast to the sacrifices made in the Temple in Jerusalem, especially the sacrifice of thanksgiving, which expresses love and appreciation. Again, the domestic enriches the spiritual, and the spiritual enriches the domestic.

Among the secular Israeli poets, the use of traditional prayers hardly forms a dominant trend in their work. Nonetheless, a surprising number of young poets do employ traditional prayer structures and phrasing to express spiritual needs. As Eyal Megged, a poet and novelist, indicates in the following poem, hidden emotions can unexpectedly surface when he encounters traditional Hebrew prayers.

Maariv

I passed near a broken down synagogue
In the Montefiore neighborhood at the evening prayer
And I heard from it, "Blessed be God, the blessed"
I continued and the darkness grew.
And only the abundance of purple-flowered vines
Still astounded me with its lively color
As if the light of day was growing
And I heard myself say,
Blessed be God, the blessed
And I repeated and said,
Blessed be God, the blessed.[44]

מַעֲרִיב

עָבַרְתִּי לְיַד בַּית כְּנֶסֶת רָעוּעַ
בִּשְׁכוּנַת מוֹנְטִיפְיוֹרִי בִּתְפִלַּת מַעֲרִיב
וְשָׁמַעְתִּי מִתּוֹכוֹ בָּרוּךְ ה' הַמְּבֹרָךְ
הִמְשַׁכְתִּי הָלְאָה וְהָאֹפֶל גָּבַר
וְרַק שִׁפְעַת פִּרְחֵי מְטַפֵּס סְגֻלִּים
עוֹד הִדְהִימָה בְּחִיּוּת צִבְעָהּ
כְּאִלּוּ אוֹר הַיּוֹם גּוֹבֵר
וְשָׁמַעְתִּי אֶת עַצְמִי אוֹמֵר
בָּרוּךְ ה' הַמְּבֹרָךְ
וְחוֹזֵר וְאוֹמֵר
בָּרוּךְ ה' הַמְּבֹרָךְ. [45]

Eyal Megged chances upon a run-down synagogue in a deteriorating neighborhood. The poet considers religion outmoded and run-down as well, yet he carries within him a remembrance of the evening prayer. The poem emphasizes the evening, and the deepening darkness indicates that the poet too is going into the darkness toward death. If he is not heading toward actual death, he is in danger of the death of the senses that Leah Goldberg feared—a fear that led her to pray that God teach her to pray, that she stay alive to the world.

Megged is shocked to the life of the senses by the sight of bright purple-flowered vines. He describes a radiant vision that lights up the world as if it is day, and the words of the Evening Service in praise of God rise to his lips. The blessing that echoed in his head may have helped to awaken his senses; recalling the praise of God may have caused him to stop and appreciate the flowers. Although Megged describes one specific experience, we can understand the poem more generally to mean that, in spite of the alienation of young Israelis from religion (that is, the run-down synagogue), the Jewish heritage still reverberates and is still capable of enriching their lives.

Her Jewish heritage has clearly influenced Rachel Chalfi (born 1945). A Tel Aviv poet known for her feminist voice, Chalfi has published six volumes of poetry and has also worked as a writer, director, and producer for Israeli radio and television. A number of her poems have religious overtones, and the style is often colloquial. The following poem presents an image of humanity in its relation to God and prayer.

Prayer

pillars of water
go downward
to infinite blue
go upward
to infinite white
striving, straining
to connect me
with the higher power
to whom yearns
the innermost stone
of my being.

A hard rock
Neglected
At the roadside
A stone of the ancient ruins
A stone
Only when she prays
Drops from these pillars of water
Pour over her
Make her shine
Like a pearl
Lying on the bottom
Of this dark
Enigmatic
Inner sea.[46]

תְּפִלָּה

עַמּוּדֵי הַמַּיִם
הוֹלְכִים לְמַטָּה
עַד אֵינְסוֹף כְּחֻלִּים
הוֹלְכִים לְמַעְלָה
עַד אֵינְסוֹף הַלֹּבֶן
מְנַסִּים מִתְאַמְּצִים
לְהַבְּרֵנִי עִם
הַכֹּחַ הָעֶלְיוֹן
שֶׁאֵלָיו נוֹהָה
הָאֶבֶן הַפְּנִימִית
בְּיוֹתֵר שֶׁלִּי

אֶבֶן קָשָׁה
זְנוּחָה
בְּצִדֵּי דְרָכִים
אֶבֶן מֵאַבְנֵי הָעִיִּים
אֶבֶן
שֶׁרַק כְּשֶׁהִיא מִתְפַּלֶּלֶת
זוֹלְגוֹת עָלֶיהָ טִפּוֹת
עַמּוּדֵי הַמַּיִם הַלָּלוּ
וּמַבְהִיקוֹת אוֹתָהּ
מָשָׁל הָיְתָה פְּנִינָה
מֻנַּחַת עַל קַרְקַע
הַיָּם הַפְּנִימִי
הָאָפֵל הַסָּתוּם הַזֶּה [47]

Rachel Chalfi portrays the contemporary soul yearning for the infinite, which is depicted as blue and white waters streaming upward and downward. The soul is the innermost stone that is usually forgotten in the everyday world. It is the rock formation neglected by the roadside. The stone's exterior is tough, seemingly indifferent, but the "innermost stone" brings to mind the foundation stone of the Temple in Jerusalem, the stone located at the center of the innermost Holy of Holies, that underlies all Jewish worship. The soul-stone of the poet is connected to the stones of the Temple, for only in prayer do the waters of infinity pour over the stone, cleanse it, make it radiant like a pearl in the dark, murky, impenetrable floor of the inner sea. There can be no better depiction of the contemporary condition and the human need for prayer.

QUESTIONS FOR FURTHER STUDY AND REFLECTION

1. What are similarities between traditional Jewish liturgy and contemporary Hebrew poetry?
2. Can a poem that does not address God be considered a prayer?
3. How is Esther Raab's poem on womanhood similar to and different from the morning blessing in which a woman thanks God for creating her according to God's will?
4. What does Abraham Shlonsky's poem celebrate? What role do the *tefillin* play in the poem?
5. Why does Leah Goldberg beg God to teach her to pray?
6. How are praise and petition connected?
7. What do the poems by Hannah Senesh and Zelda have in common?
8. What image of God does Amir Gilboa present? To which "terrible sights" does he refer? What redemption does he suggest? What is the tone of the poem?
9. What protests to God exist in classic Jewish literature? Does the traditional liturgy include any prayers of protest? What national calamity has Pagis witnessed? What causes Pagis to accuse God of injustice? What is the greatest injustice?
10. Consider the play on words in Yehuda Amichai's *El Malei Rahamim*, and trace Amichai's fall from innocence.
11. According to Michal Govrin, why should Amalia abandon her submission to God? Why should Amalia no longer seek to become one with God in ecstasy? What human resolution does Amalia find?
12. Zelda's poem "In This Moment of Reflection" begins with an innocent contemplation of nature at dawn. How does the poet change emotionally? Why do the sounds of the morning cause the poet to confess? How does Zelda's confession allude to the Yom Kippur confession?
13. How does Chava Pinchas-Cohen's domestic prayer use the words and ideas of traditional prayers? How does Pinchas-Cohen borrow from the

teḥines of earlier centuries? What is the poet praying for? What is Pinchas-Cohen's attitude toward motherhood?

14. How does Eyal Megged view Jewish worship? Why causes him to begin to pray?

15. How does Rachel Chalfi describe the infinite? The soul? What does the "innermost stone" suggest? What images does Chalfi use to describe the process of prayer?

---

1. Rabbi Hayim Halevy Donin, *To Pray As A Jew* (New York: Basic Books, 1980) pages 3–5.

2. Hillel Weiss, ed., *Ve'Ani Tefillati Antologia: Shirat HaTefillah Shel Meshorerim Bnei Zmanenu* (Bet El: Bet El Publishers, 1991), page i. Translated by Rochelle Furstenberg. (All translations from Hebrew into English, within Chapter 12, are by Rochelle Furstenberg, unless otherwise indicated.)

3. Leah Goldberg, in *"HaOmetz LeHulun"* ["The Courage for the Mundane"], Turim, April 15, 1938, reprinted in *The Writings of Leah Goldberg, Volume of Essays* (Tel Aviv: Sifriat Hapoalim, undated), page 166.

4. Shapiro, David; Govrin, Michal; and Derrida, Jacques, *Body of Prayer* (New York: Irwin S. Chanin School of Architecture of the Cooper Union for the Advancement of Science and Art, 2001), page 35. *Body of Prayer* is based on a symposium that took place upon the publication of the English translation of Michal Govrin's novel, *The Name*. (The Hebrew novel *Hashem* was published in 1995 by Sifriya Hahadasha/Hakibbutz Hameuchad of Tel Aviv. In 1998, the novel was translated into English by Barbara Harshav and published as *The Name* by Riverhead Books of New York. English was also the language used at the symposium.)

5. William Wordsworth, "Intimations of Immortality from Recollections of Early Childhood" in *Selected Poetry of William Wordsworth* (New York: Modern Library/Random House, 1950), page 541.

6. Cited in Zvi Luz, *Shirat Esther Raab [The Poetry of Esther Raab]* (Tel Aviv: Hakibbutz Hameuchad, 1997). Luz mentions a poem titled *"Kol HaShir Hu Tefillah."*

7. Zvi Luz, *Shirat Esther Raab,* pages 80–83.

8. Esther Raab, "Prayer," English translation in Anne Lapidus Lerner, "A Woman's Song: The Poetry of Esther Raab," in *Gender and Text in Modern Hebrew and Yiddish Literature,* Naomi B. Sokoloff, Anne Lapidus Lerner, and Anita Norich, eds. (New York/Cambridge: Jewish Theological Seminary/Harvard University Press, 1992), page 31. The Hebrew prose-poem *"Tefillah"* ("Prayer") is from the collection *"Gehinnom"* ("Notebooks of Hell"); now available in *Esther Raab, Collected Prose,* Ehud Ben-Ezer, ed. (Israel: Astrolog, 2001).

9. David Hartman, *Love and Terror in the God Encounter: The Theological Legacy of Rabbi Joseph B. Soloveitchik* (Northvale, NJ: Jason Aronson, 2001), pages 173–174.

10. Rabbi Hayim Halevy Donin, pages 6, 7.

11. Esther Raab, "A Woman's Song," translated by Harold Schimmel, in Esther Raab, *Thistles: Collected Poems* (Jerusalem: Ibis, 2001).

12. Esther Raab, *"Shirat Ishah"* in *Kol Hashirim Shel Esther Raab [The Collected Poetry of Esther Raab]* (Tel Aviv: Zmora-Bitan, 1994), page 197.

13. Abraham Shlonsky rebelled against Hayyim Nahman Bialik's literary hegemony in the 1920s, and together with Nathan Alterman set the tone for a new generation of younger Hebrew poets. Shlonsky's influence waned in the 1960s, when poets such as Nathan Zach called for a less metaphorical, more colloquial tone.

14. Abraham Shlonsky, "[Toil]," translated by T. Carmi, *The Penguin Book of Hebrew Verse*, T. Carmi, ed. (New York: Penguin, 1981), page 534.

15. Abraham Shlonsky, *"[Amal]"* in *Shirim, Volume 2* (Tel Aviv: Sifriat Hapoalim, 1971), page 11.

16. Leah Goldberg, "Teach Me, God, To Pray," translated by Rabbi Jules Harlow.

17. Leah Goldberg, *"Lamdeni, Elohai,"* from *"Shirei Sof Haderekh"* ["Poems at the End of the Road"] in *Barak Baboker [Lightning in the Morning]* (Jerusalem: Sifriat Hapoalim, 1955).

18. Hannah Senesh, "Going to Caesarea," translated by Eitan Senesh and Rochelle Furstenberg.

19. Hannah Senesh, *"Halikhah LeKaisaryah"* in Hillel Weiss, ed., *Ve'Ani Tefillati Antologia,* page 20.

20. Moshe Greenberg, *Biblical Prose Prayer* (Berkeley: University of California Press, 1983), pages 10–11.

21. David Hartman, pages 178–179.

22. He-halutz comes from the Hebrew word for pioneer. He-halutz was a Jewish youth group, created in the aftermath of the 1881 Russian pogroms. Its purpose was to spread the Zionist message to Jewish youth throughout the world and to encourage emigration to Palestine.

23. Writers of the Palmah generation are known for their depictions of the heroics of the War of Independence and the establishment of the State of Israel. See note 27 below for information on the Palmah combat units.

24. Amir Gilboa, "Great are my God's works," translated by Gili and Tali Gilboa.

25. Amir Gilboa, *"Gedolim Maasei Elohai"* in *Shirim [Poems]: Kehulim Ve'Adumim [The Red and the Blue]* (Tel Aviv: Am Oved, 1963), page 329.

26. The cantor recites "God's Works" as a part of the *Musaf Amidah* service. The congregation and cantor together state, "Great are the works of our God." (Refer to *The Complete Artscroll Machzor: Yom Kippur*, Rabbi Nosson Scherman, ed. [Brooklyn: Mesorah, 1986], pages 524–527.)

27. Palmah units were created by emergency order in May 1942, and these units acted as the mobilized striking force of the Haganah's national command during World War II and then later during the war of independence. The Palmah was absorbed into the Israel Defense Forces in 1948.

28. Hayim Gouri, "Prayer," translated by Rochelle Furstenberg.

29. Hayim Gouri, *"Tefillah"* in *Pirkhei Esh [Flowers of Flame]* (Tel Aviv: Sifriat Hapoalim, 1949), page 64; reprinted in Hillel Weiss, ed., *Ve'Ani Tefillati Antologia,* page 125.

30. The tale about Rabbi Levi Yitzhak is found in Eli Wiesel, *Souls on Fire: Portraits and Legends of Hasidic Masters,* translated by Marion Wiesel (New York: Random, 1972), page 110.

31. Dan Pagis, "Testimony," translated by Warren Bargad and Stanley F. Chyet in *Israeli Poetry: A Contemporary Anthology,* Warren Bargad and Stanley F. Chyet, eds. (Bloomington, IN: Indiana University Press/Institute for the Translation of Hebrew Literature, 1985), page 111. The Hebrew poem "Edut" was published in 1970 in *Gilgul [Transformations],* by Masada Press of Ramat Gan (page 24).

32. Dan Pagis, "Another Testimony," translated by Warren Bargad and Stanley F. Chyet in *Israeli Poetry*, page 111.

33. Dan Pagis, *"Edut Aheret"* in *Gilgul [Transformations]* (Ramat Gan: Masada Press), page 25. Also in Hillel Weiss, ed., *Ve'Ani Tefillati Antologia*, page 137.

34. Shapiro, Govrin, Derrida, *Body of Prayer*, pages 51, 53.

35. Michal Govrin, *The Name*, page 364.

36. Michal Govrin, *The Name*, page 367.

37. Yehuda Amichai, "God Full of Mercy" in *Yehuda Amichai: A Life of Poetry 1948-1994,* translated by Benjamin and Barbara Harshav (New York: HarperCollins, 1994), page 31.

38. Yehuda Amichai, *"El Malei Rahamim"* in *Mivhar Shirim: Shirim, 1948-1961* (Tel Aviv: Schocken, 1981), page 10.

39. Zelda, "In This Moment of Reflection," translated by Rochelle Furstenberg and Rabbi Jules Harlow.

40. Zelda, *"Beshaah Mehurheret Zo"* in *Shirei Zelda: Hao Har, Halo Eish* (Tel Aviv: Hakibbutz Hameuchad, 1985), page 140. Also in Hillel Weiss, ed., *Ve'Ani Tefillati Antologia*, page 95.

41. Zelda, "I flowered in a house of stone," translated by Rochelle Furstenberg.

42. Chava Pinchas-Cohen, "A Mother's Morning Prayer," translated by Rochelle Furstenberg and Rabbi Jules Harlow.

43. Chava Pinchas-Cohen, *"Tefillah Le'em Beterem Shaharit,"* in *Masah Ayala [Voyage of a Doe]* (Tel Aviv: Hakibbutz Hameuchad, 1994), page 33.

44. Eyal Megged, *"Maariv,"* translated by Rochelle Furstenberg.

45. Eyal Megged, *"Maariv"* in *Shalosh Shanim [Three Years]* (Tel Aviv: Sifriat Hapoalim, 1980), page 86; reprinted in Hillel Weiss, ed., *Ve'Ani Tefillati Antologia*, page 101.

46. Rachel Chalfi, "Prayer," translated by Rachel Chalfi and Rochelle Furstenberg.

47. Rachel Chalfi, *"Tefillah,"* in *Homer [Matter]* (Tel Aviv: Hakibbutz Hameuchad, 1990), page 79.

Chapter

Prayer as a Response to Evil and Suffering

From the depths I call you

Rabbi Daniel Gordis

Two years after our family made *aliyah* and began our new lives in Jerusalem, two years after we moved to what had seemed an idyllic place to live, to raise children, and to become part of the Jewish dream of rebuilding Zion, the tragedy known as the "second intifada" started, bringing despair to Jews living in Israel and to Jews around the world. Dreams of peace had collapsed into realities of war. Though we had anticipated a radically different future, we had suddenly been restored to the days of violence, death, and destruction that we believed had been relegated to Israel's past.

The months that followed the outbreak of the second intifada (a euphemism, since what we faced was a war and not a popular uprising) held more than their share of difficulty and pain.

One day in May 2001 is vividly seared into my memory, when the Versailles wedding hall in the Talpiyot section of Jerusalem collapsed in the middle of a wedding celebration. As the upper floor of the building gave way, dozens of people were swept into the cavernous, gaping hole in the middle of the building, and many were crushed by the cement, metal, furniture, and people that landed on them. Twenty-three people were killed, and hundreds were badly hurt. It was one of the saddest days in Israel's short history and one that will always live with me. But along with the dramatic and horrifying events of the days themselves, I will always remember what happened in *shul* the night after the tragedy.

The wedding hall collapsed late on a Thursday night, so the next night was *erev* Shabbat and, coincidentally, just two days before Shavuot. Ordinarily, it would have been a joyous weekend as people prepared to celebrate receiving the Torah at Mount Sinai. This particular year, however, no one we knew was in the mood to celebrate. The events of the day had been too painful, the harrowing loss too great and too close to home. But, most of us obediently trudged off to *shul* and dutifully recited the traditional liturgy for the beginning of Shabbat. We did what we were supposed to do, but without the joy that usually attends such worship. *Maariv* was quiet and rather subdued, but uneventful—until the singing of *Yigdal* at the very end of the service.

The person leading the service had selected a beautiful British melody for *Yigdal*, a melody both regal and uplifting. We sang through to the final two lines:[1]

God will send our Messiah by the end of days
To redeem those who await God's final salvation
God will revive the dead in abundant kindness
Blessed forever is God's praised Name.

With this melody, the congregation had the option of repeating the last two lines, and, this particular evening, we chose to do so. After the last lines had been sung twice, though, we did not disband as usual. This time, we continued singing those lines over and over. The notions that God will send our Messiah, that God will redeem us, and that God will revive the dead, were too powerful that particular night to sing only one time. The message of hope in the prayer book, which we often ignore or do not realize is there, was at that moment exactly what we needed. Without anyone coordinating or planning the singing, we found ourselves, along with friends and neighbors, singing these lines again and again, and the passion and volume of the singing increased each time.

Eventually, of course, the singing came to an end, and we all filed out of *shul* and made our way home to Shabbat dinner. But I heard many people humming the melody as we fanned out across the neighborhood of Bakk'a on that clear Jerusalem night. We had been transformed. Having entered *shul* after one of the worst days that any of us could remember, we walked home feeling hopeful, feeling redeemed. The *siddur* had not only *spoken* of redemption; it had actually *brought* us redemption. True, this had not been the full redemption for which we pray, but it was a start. In that communal singing and that spontaneous bonding with one another, being part of a community of worshipers had brought us to a place that, just an hour earlier, none of us could have imagined. ▨

That experience, for me, encapsulates much of what is wonderful about prayer. We come together as Jews joined by a shared liturgy and a common setting, but divided by radically different beliefs about what prayer is. Some of us believe that God hears our prayers, others are not certain, and still others are convinced that God does not hear our prayers. ❂ Some Jews believe very literally in a God whose power transcends humanity and nature, a God who gave the world its beginning, a God to whom our prayers are directed. Others believe that God is a metaphor—a valuable, even an essential, idea, but not a being who can be said in any meaningful way to exist. All too often, we imagine that these differences in belief and outlook make praying together impossible. ▨

On that *erev* Shabbat in Jerusalem, after the collapse of the Versailles wedding hall, we learned that our differing theologies do not prevent us from praying together. The experience that we had with our friends and neighbors taught us that, at times, prayer gives us an opportunity to reach out—to heaven and to fellow human beings—when life seems unbearably difficult and hope seems impossible to maintain. At such moments, our beliefs about God and about prayer do not really matter. Instead we recognize that, at its most effective, prayer binds us to one another. By giving us an opportunity to express our pain, our loss, our confusion, and our sadness, prayer re-instills in us a belief in a better tomorrow.

Versailles was only one of the tragedies that Jews have faced over the past months. Israel has faced many attacks during this period and they

▨ Judaism values community as a higher order of human existence. At Sinai, Jews entered into a covenant with God to bring about a sacred people that would jointly achieve what individuals cannot. Communal prayer builds a sense of unity; it makes manifest communal values; it bonds people in mutual love and support of one another; and it commits an entire community to values that its members vow to live by.—*Rabbi Lawrence Hoffman*[2]

❂ In prayer we are united less by theology than by any other factor. The *siddur* has allowed modern Jews to come together despite our differences, partly by weight of tradition, and partly by the diversity of world-views found in it. In the same service a traditional congregation may sing that God has no body (in the credo known as the *Yigdal*) or that he has gray hair and wears *tefillin* (in the "Hymn of Glory," *Shir HaKavod*). One congregant may wince at the first song, and another at the latter. But neither comes to the synagogue for the purpose of defining God.—*Michael Swartz*[3]

▨ Differences in belief and outlook do not, in theory, make praying together impossible, but, at least among American Jews, these differences do result in *de facto* separations. Although Jews with conflicting beliefs may come together to celebrate certain religious events (the wedding of a friend or relative, for example) or to attend a *Yizkor* service on Yom Kippur, Jews who are indifferent to God's existence generally avoid synagogue prayer. Praying together unites only those Jews who already seek to be part of a religious community. Though communal prayer has the capacity to unite Jews of divergent beliefs, praying together does not—except for rare occasions—unite those Jews who place substantially different values on the importance of synagogue attendance.—*Claudia Chernov*

have resulted in terrible loss of life. But Israel was not alone. In the United States, the attacks of September 11, 2001, and particularly the devastating loss of life at the World Trade Center, created a sense of loss so deep that we could barely give it expression. We mourned for the innocent individuals who lost their lives, and perhaps even more we mourned for a way of life that we had believed was synonymous with America. The United States had been the place where terrible things did not happen, the place where we were safe and secure. On that September 11, we learned that no such place exists on earth. We learned about vulnerability and about hatred that can stalk us anywhere. As Jews, many of us asked ourselves, "Where can we turn at moments like these? What can we do? What can we believe when such things happen? What can Judaism offer? Can my Jewish heritage help me to address this sadness? Can it lend me support as I cope with this grief?"

Judaism offers many ways of responding to grief and sorrow. It creates community, and it begs us to study the words of our predecessors who wrestled with questions about God and with feelings of loss and rage. Judaism also urges us to become activists, to make the world a better place than it was when we were born into it. Joining with others, studying, and taking action are only a few Jewish responses; indeed, there are many more. One of the most critical ways in which our tradition encourages us to grapple with evil and with suffering is through prayer and worship. That is the response that we will examine in this chapter.

The prayer book seeks to help us respond to evil and to the helplessness, sadness, and anger that evil often engenders, and it provides a variety of ways in which to respond—including some ways that seem contradictory. The first thing that we will examine is the prayer book's acknowledgment of our fear of evil. The *siddur* readily attests to the existence of evil, and it helps us pray that we will be spared the harm that evil brings.

I. Accepting the Existence of Evil, Acknowledging Our Fear, and Praying To Be Spared

Suffering, unfortunately, is part of the universe in which we live. It may be caused by natural disasters, in which humanity played no role, and it may be caused by environmental destruction or industrial accidents, in which humans were partly responsible. Suffering is also directly caused by other people, and we will call that "evil" in this chapter.

The Torah, particularly the Book of Genesis, seeks to explain the existence of certain forms of suffering. For example, the Torah asks, why should women experience pain in childbirth when that process is essential to the preservation of our species? The Torah's answer: Eve and the sin of the serpent and the apple in the Garden of Eden. To take another example, why do many people struggle to earn enough for basic subsistence when they have done nothing wrong and deserve life's basic sustenance no less than anyone else? The Torah's answer: the punishment of Adam and God's declaration to Adam as he is evicted from the Garden of Eden that "by the sweat of your brow will you eat bread."

The Torah then asks the most difficult question of all: Why is there evil in which people cause each other harm and suffering? The Torah responds to this query in the tale of Cain and Abel. We might have expected this tale to explain why human beings behave with cruelty to other people. In this case, the Torah provides few answers. It offers no explanation as simple as Eve's sinning with the serpent or Adam's eating the apple and then trying to hide from God. The Torah does provide one explanation: Cain was jealous because God accepted Abel's offering and rejected his, but that is only a partial answer. We know why Cain wishes to kill Abel, but we do not know why God allows the evil to happen. ▣ True, God punishes Cain and through the Torah teaches us that we are all "our brothers' keepers," but that is hardly compensation to Abel, whose life has been cut short. The Torah offers no other explanation in this story (though the Rabbis in the Midrash offer numerous solutions to the problem). The question may not be: "Why do people suffer?" Instead, the question may be: "Given that innocent people suffer, how do we create lives of meaning?" That is where the *siddur* begins.

▣ Rabbi Gordis mentions another crucial question that we confront in the story of Cain and Abel, namely, how can a just and benevolent God allow evil in the world which God has created? Since antiquity, theologians have defined human suffering either as punishment for misconduct, as a test of the sufferer's faith, or as a divine lesson inspiring the sufferer to improve. The crux of the problem is reconciling the presence of evil with an omnipotent God who does only good and who acts only justly. Maimonides (1135–1204) in *Guide of the Perplexed* proves that God is all-powerful and all-good; human understanding, however, is so limited that we cannot fathom God's ways. Maimonides states: "This lesson is the principal object of the whole Book of Job ... that we should not fall into the error of imagining God's knowledge to be similar to ours, or God's intention, providence, and rule similar to ours." The 17th-century Christian philosopher René Descartes in *Meditations on First Philosophy* also proves that an all-powerful and all-good God exists, and he deduces that evil must result from human error. Thus, in a Cartesian universe, evil occurs when humans misunderstand or misconstrue God's world. In our era, some thinkers have argued that God first created the natural universe according to God's immutable laws, but the universe now runs without God's direct intervention and the universal laws include the possibility for evil. Yet another contemporary argument is that evil arises because God has granted humans free will; if human actions are never evil, then humans do not truly have the choice to sin. All of these positions find some support within Jewish thought today, although, as Rabbi Gordis notes, Judaism tends to focus more on what to do about evil (how to comfort the sufferer, for instance) than on what to think about evil.—*Claudia Chernov*

After the initial blessings of the Morning Service, the prayer book introduces a personal petition. According to the Talmud (*Brakhot* 16b), Rabbi Judah HaNasi uttered this petition after concluding his recitation of *Shaharit*.

May it be Your will, Lord, my God, and the God of my ancestors, that You rescue me today and every day from brazen men and from brazenness, from an evil man, an evil companion, an evil neighbor, an evil mishap, the destructive spiritual impediment, a harsh trial and a harsh opponent, whether he be a member of the covenant or whether he not be a member of the covenant.

Note what this prayer does and does not ask for. Though other prayers express the desire for a redeemed world in which there is no evil and no suffering, this prayer situates us in *this* world, in the reality that we actually occupy. It accepts as givens that suffering occurs, that evil people exist, and that we must share our world with them. The most that we can hope for, is to be spared their evil. We pray that we will not be touched by evil companions, neighbors, or mishaps. The prayer also acknowledges that danger can come to us from people of various sorts, whether or not they are "members of the covenant." The problem of evil is not one of Jews or non-Jews; it is universal, endemic, omnipresent. We know that danger lurks in hidden places, and we pray simply and honestly that we will be able to avoid it.

In offering us his personal plea, Rabbi Judah teaches us something very important about Jewish prayer: It may simply express what is in our heart. Rather than transforming the world or imagining an alternate reality, Jewish worship may provide opportunities to admit to ourselves that there are things that we fear. More important, perhaps, than expecting God to change the world is joining together as a faith community to reflect honestly and to speak openly about these fears.

Honesty. That is how prayer builds community; that is how prayer encourages us to seek God's presence. Perhaps we seek God when we plead during the High Holy Days, "Do not cast us aside as we grow old. As our strength ebbs, please do not abandon us." We know that we will grow old and that we will become weak. We acknowledge our fear of that process, and we pray that as we age we will be as comfortable as possible. Similarly, at the start of our day, the prayer book urges us first and foremost to be honest, to acknowledge our fear, and to express to God, to our community of fellow worshipers, and to ourselves the deep and unavoidable truth—we want to be spared the wrath of evil.

Rabbi Judah's petition is only one example of prayers that acknowledge the existence of evil. The verses that the *siddur* borrows from the Bible, especially from the Book of Psalms, often make the same point. The psalmist shares certain perspectives with Rabbi Judah HaNasi, but also presents slightly different views. Rabbi Judah's plea is stark: "There is terrifying evil in the world, and I pray that You protect me from it." The Psalms also acknowledge the presence of evil, but the psalmist often declares that because of God's power, God's protection is nearly guaranteed. Psalm 94, the psalm for Wednesday, offers an example of this approach.[4]

God of retribution, Lord, God of retribution, appear! Rise up, Judge of the earth, give the arrogant their deserts! How long shall the wicked—O Lord— how long shall the wicked exult? Shall they utter insolent speech, shall all evil- doers vaunt themselves? They crush Your people, O Lord, they afflict Your very own; they kill the widow and the stranger, they murder the orphan.

After this acknowledgement of evil, the tone of the Psalm eventually changes. The Biblical poet assures us that God will ultimately triumph, that God will not cast off the Jewish people. That assurance leads the psalmist to find comfort in the presence of God, and the Psalm continues:

But the Lord is my haven, my God is my sheltering rock. God will make their evil recoil upon them, annihilate them through their own wickedness; the Lord our God will annihilate them.

This Psalm exemplifies a thematic pattern that we find in the liturgy: an awareness of evil's existence, the hope that God will spare us from the ravages of evildoers, and, finally, the renewed closeness to God that emerges after we have expressed our sorrow and fear. The purpose of worship in these instances is not to have our petitions answered, but to gain insight, comfort, and even faith from the open admission that the evil in the world frightens us.

What could possibly be a more appropriate way to respond to our world than this openness, this honesty? Given the tragic events in Israel in 2000 and 2001 and the horrifying attacks on American soil in September 2001, what more could we ask of Judaism than to provide us a setting for admitting our fears, for expressing our anger, for venting our frustration? Did Jews across America attend synagogue services by the thousands on the Shabbat after September 11 ▦ because they believed that God would protect them and that praying with a *minyan* would make them safer? That almost certainly was not the case. In confronting evil, many of us rely on our faith in God. Some of us, however, find that our faith can be shaken when tragedy strikes. Then, more than ever, we need each other. Prayer is a response to the horrors of evil not because it pretends that it can change the world in which we live, but because it enables us to find each other in the darkness that pervades our lives. Our prayer book insists, however subtly, that the way to

▦ The phenomenon of increased synagogue attendance and religious interest after September 11 has been much discussed. As only one example, see "Reform Jews Mark a Post-9/11 Upsurge," in *The Forward* (November 3, 2001, page 3). The paper notes that "many of the [Reform] movement's synagogues drew unusually large crowds in the weeks immediately following the terrorist attacks. Interest in the movement's rabbinical school and communal service program is also up, leaders say, and the Web site of the Religious Action Center of Reform Judaism, the movement's public policy arm, has been attracting 85 percent more visitors since the attacks." The article notes that increased attendance and interest were noted in the other movements, as well.—DG

315

build community and relationships with each other is through honesty and through an open acceptance of a world that we cannot control, but is the only one in which we are given an opportunity to live. ▓

For some of us, as was true of Rabbi Judah HaNasi, acknowledgement of evil's existence leads to the stark prayer that we ourselves be spared. For others, as with the psalmist in Psalm 94, the reality of evil can actually lead to intensified faith. Both approaches begin with the evil that abides in the world. In our day, the notion that the religious soul accepts the horror of the world may allow us to turn these moments of desperation into opportunities to engage our tradition and its liturgy seriously. Some of us imagine that the truly religious soul does not feel abandoned or that people of genuine faith never feel lost or alone, but the *siddur* tells us that is not true. All of us can be overwhelmed by the world's evil, and the prayer book assures us that the best way to begin is to pray with complete honesty. We can enter prayer simply by saying, "I am afraid—please let me be spared." Even that simple thought, the *siddur* tells us, is genuine prayer.

▓ Rabbi Gordis conflates communal bonding with honesty in prayer. Yet, as Rabbi Jules Harlow notes, modern society offers us many non-religious ways to honestly and openly come together as a community. Prayer, Rabbi Harlow observes, does create relationships between human beings, but its primary purpose is to create relationships with God. Communal prayer creates a relationship between God and community as well as relationships between God and each member of the community—even as it creates relationships among human beings. Judaism mandates a quorum of ten or more adults (for Orthodox Jews, ten or more men) to recite certain prayers, among them *Kaddish Yatom* or Mourner's *Kaddish*. This suggests that one Jewish response to suffering is indeed the recognition of our need for public prayer within a community. Nonetheless, as Rabbi Gordis discusses in the following sections of this chapter, communal prayer may certainly fulfill other purposes than honest acceptance of painful reality. Furthermore, honest acceptance of reality may occur even in individual prayer (as well as in non-religious settings). Throughout the Bible we find examples of individual prayers that are honest and heartfelt. Samuel I offers an especially moving example of individual prayer when Hannah beseeches God to give her a son. Yet Hannah's personal prayer becomes, for the Rabbis of the Talmud, the quintessential example of all prayer, both individual and communal. What is the relationship between prayer, community, and honesty as we respond to evil? The question is intriguing.—*Rebecca Boim Wolf, Claudia Chernov*

❂ We often use "mythical" to connote something that is not true. But serious religious life asks us to think about "truth" in a less simplistic way. There are truths in myth that may not be scientifically validated. If they order our universe, and give expression to truths that the rational world cannot, they are no less "true" than anything else. As the famous Protestant theologian Paul Tillich puts it, "There is no substitute for the use of symbols and myths: they are the language of faith."[5]—*DG*

II. Alternate Spiritual Realities, Creating a World of Faith, Bringing Us Closer to God

The prayer book offers a number of other approaches to the problem of evil, as well as an acknowledgment of evil's reality. At times we, as seekers of God, need a restoration of our faith that a different, more perfect reality can exist. We need to believe in a religious or mythical reality ❂ in which human beings do not contend with evil, for evil is simply not there.

We often recite these sections of the liturgy just as we are entering a frightening or potentially frightening period. As our first example of this approach, let's consider the poem *Yedid Nefesh*, recited at the beginning of Shabbat services on Friday evening. As we rush to synagogue on Friday night, many of us are tired from a week's toil and stress. We may feel very distant from God; God's presence and God's salvation may seem the farthest things possible from our state of mind. Because of that, many of us fear that we are somehow illegitimate. We might suspect, as we look around the synagogue, that everyone else feels more spiritually attuned. We might imagine that we are the only ones feeling distant from God. Precisely to counter this suspicion, this beautiful poem enters our consciousness. As the sun sets and as we begin our Shabbat worship, we recite the following lines:[6]

Beloved soul mate, merciful Father, draw your servant close to You. Majestic one, beautiful and radiant, my soul is ill, desperate for Your love. Please, God, heal my soul, showing her the sweetness of Your radiance. Then she will be strengthened and healed, and she will enjoy eternal satisfaction.... Hurry, my beloved, because the time has come, care for me as You used to, in days of old.

What is the poet, Elazar Azikri, saying? Despite the opulent language, the poem concerns very human emotions. Just as we often say to a human being whom we love but from whom we feel estranged, "Hold me—I am alone, but I do not want to be," the poet says, "Draw Your servant close to You." He then declares that his soul is sick with love. We know that feeling—we are so in love with someone that we feel ill if we suspect our love is not reciprocated. "Heal my soul," the poet continues. Make me whole again by bringing me back to You. Please help us find our way back to Your presence. Help us to overcome the loneliness that evil and suffering have created for us. Even in these dark hours, we see, prayer can be about drawing us back to God.

Yedid Nefesh is hardly the only example of this. Consider *Adon Olam*, a deceivingly simple poem that we recite when we are about to go to sleep—a time when we lose control of our bodies and our thoughts, a time when physical darkness is about to overtake us. *Adon Olam* concludes the Shabbat morning service and also serves as part of a service recited at bedtime.

Master of the Universe who reigned before any form was created.
At the time when God's will brought all into being, then as "King" was God's name proclaimed.
After all has ceased to be, God the awesome one will reign alone.
It is God who was, who is, and who will remain in splendor.
God is one. There is no second to compare to God, to declare as God's equal.
Without beginning, without conclusion, God's is the power and the dominion.

**This is my God, my living Redeemer, rock of my pain in time of distress. God
     is my banner, a refuge for me, the portion in my cup on the day I call.**
**Into God's hand I shall entrust my spirit, when I go to sleep and when I
     awaken**
And with my spirit, my body, too; God is with me, I shall not fear.

The first six lines describe God in abstract terms, calling God transcendent, far-removed from us, reflecting eternal truths and power. God is not governed by time, and God's power knows no bounds. This is the God of philosophers and theologians, the idea of God we're taught from a very early age.

In the final four lines, the poet describes the imminent God, a more intimate and personal God, a God who touches our lives. As important as the philosophic approach to the transcendent God may be, it is not an approach that most of us seek. The imminent God touches our own souls. In the last four lines, God is "rock" and "redeemer" and "the portion in my cup." Because of the closeness of this God, the poet confidently entrusts his soul and his body to God. The poem ends, "God is with me, I shall not fear."

This poem differs greatly from the prayer of Rabbi Judah HaNasi and from Psalm 94. *Adon Olam* does not even mention evil or what is wrong with the world. (Of course, proclaiming that we have no fear does suggest that the world is indeed a fearful place, but that fear is hardly the focus of *Adon Olam* or of *Yedid Nefesh*.) Just as we are about to go to sleep, just as our worries and sorrows are likely to surface in our dreams, we recite a poem that describes God as both timeless and intimate, transcendent and imminent. This is a God in whom we can have complete trust. Our faith in God is so complete that any mention of evil is out of place. This is the God in whose shadow all is well, all fear is banished. This God creates a world we would love to inhabit. As we sing the poem and transport ourselves to a different reality, we actually create and inhabit that world for a few blissful moments.

Yigdal is another prayer that restores both God's closeness and our faith that God will redeem our world. In *Yigdal* (mentioned at the beginning of this chapter) we focus on a God who will send the Messiah, who will revive the dead, and who deals with us in abundant kindness.

God will send our Messiah by the end of days
To redeem those who await the final salvation
God will revive the dead in abundant kindness
Blessed forever is God's praised Name.

The *Havdalah* prayers that we recite at the conclusion of Shabbat offer yet another example of an alternate spiritual reality in which evil has no existence. To understand the profound claim that *Havdalah* makes, we need first to understand the spiritual world that we entered when Shabbat began. On Shabbat we abstain from starting a fire, from building, from destroying—all in order to live in harmony (to as great an extent as is possible) with the natural world. We do not use money or acquire material possessions. We do not work or engage in business. ▨ Instead we focus on the creation of a spiritual reality in which we have everything that is truly necessary. We attempt to create a setting in which the people and the experiences that we all too often disregard—our spouse, our children, sitting around the table and singing—can claim the center of our attention. In the world of the Kabbalists, Shabbat takes on the aura of a wedding, the union of humanity and God that results in a perfected reality.

▨ The reasons for these prohibitions are actually much more complicated. Indeed, the ultimate reasons for certain Shabbat prohibitions are not always clear, even though this part of Jewish law is highly developed. This brief excursus on the spiritual focus of Shabbat, however, serves only to explain the context of *Havdalah*, and so will not expand on this complex section of Jewish law.—*DG*

Until the Messiah comes, though, Shabbat must end as the sun sets on Saturday night. Perhaps one day we will experience the redemption—the everlasting Shabbat of the end of days. Until then, however, we must leave this idyllic reality at sunset. We acknowledge our sadness even before Shabbat is over, as the melody of the *Minḥah* service moves to a minor key and takes on a mournful quality. Our sadness and our fear reach their apex when the stars appear, when it is time to recite *Maariv* and *Havdalah*. We fear returning to the world of competition and of commerce, but we say something very different as we light the braided candle, prepare the spices, and lift the cup of wine.

Behold! God is my salvation, I shall trust and not fear—for God is my might and my praise.... For the Jews there was light, gladness, joy and honor—so may it be for us. I will raise the cup of salvation, and invoke the name of God.

The *Havdalah* service makes no mention of evil. To the contrary, it actually seems to deny the fear that we feel upon leaving the cocoon of Shabbat and returning to the world we normally inhabit. In the *Havdalah brakhot*—as in *Adon Olam* and *Yigdal*—fear, evil, and suffering are expunged from the religious lexicon. To be a Jew is to enjoy moments when prayer aids us in creating mythic new worlds, in framing new realities where evil is nowhere to be found.

We find a blatant example of the *siddur* eradicating evil from its lexicon in *Yotzer*, the first blessing before *Kriat Shema* in the morning service: "Blessed are You, Lord our God, King of the universe, who fashions light and creates darkness, who makes peace and creates all things." As Rabbi Harlow notes (page 70), this blessing differs radically from Isaiah 45:7, the verse on which it is based. The Biblical verse reads, "who fashions light and creates darkness, who makes peace and creates evil." The *Yotzer* blessing thus affords us another glimpse into the spiritual world that the Rabbis sought to create, a world in which evil is not a focus. This critical blessing does not deny evil, but it certainly ignores it.

At this stage, two questions might come to mind. The first is whether the *siddur*, in taking two such radically opposed approaches to evil, is inconsistent and, therefore, less intellectually serious than we have a right to expect. The second question is whether—after we have witnessed undeniable evil—a prayer book that denies evil deserves our attention.

Before answering the first question, we need to understand that the *siddur* is not a theological treatise. Theology—as a rigorous intellectual discipline that demands consistency—is foreign to the religious world of the early Rabbis. Interestingly, the Hebrew language has no word that means precisely what the Western world means with the word "theology"; systematic theology as it developed in the Greco-Roman world, and later in Christianity, is simply not part of our natural vocabulary as Jews. In the Rabbinic period when much of the liturgy was composed, the Rabbis lived comfortably with inconsistencies in prayer, in *Midrash*, and even in belief. The liturgy, rather than offering one rigorous and systematic approach, is a compendium of differing and often conflicting material. As such, our prayer book mirrors the differing and changing feelings that are found in any community of Jews. ▨

The feelings that we each have about suffering, evil, and God result from the experiences each of us have had. As all of us have lived different lives, our beliefs and our feelings will necessarily differ. Were the *siddur* to validate only one set of views, large numbers of Jews would find the *siddur*—or at least significant sections of it—completely unapproachable. That option was unacceptable to the Rabbis, who therefore built a varying and flexible array of viewpoints into the prayer book. Thus, the contradictory views of evil in the *siddur* do not indicate intellectual sloppiness, but the desire to validate many different approaches.

Before answering the second question, whether we can take Jewish liturgy seriously when it describes a world in which evil does not exist,

▨ Maimonides (1135–1204) presents a prominent example of the desire for a more consistent and unified stance. Judaism's greatest medieval philosopher, Maimonides thought that Judaism ought to have something akin to the Catholic catechism, a series of faith statements that would succinctly define Jewish belief. He therefore composed the *Thirteen Principles of Faith*, enumerating the basic theological convictions that every Jew ought to share. Yet as important as Maimonides was, Judaism simply does not demand the sort of theological conviction that he espoused. Though many Jewish thinkers have long advocated precisely the certainty that Maimonides sought, and though the Torah and much of Rabbinic literature take God's existence for granted, those dimensions of Jewish thought are not the only way in which Jews have viewed the world. Although Maimonides attempted to impose a consistent philosophic approach, he was ultimately unsuccessful. His *Thirteen Principles* to this day are found in many prayer books, but they never became a "catechism" in Jewish communities. They are studied and discussed, but personal acceptance of the principles of Maimonides never became a *sine qua non* for Jewish legitimacy. —DG[7]

we need to reflect for a moment on the purpose of prayer. If the only purpose were to petition God and ask for the repair of our world, descriptions of a world lacking in evil would make little sense. But in the difficult and complex times in which we live, we must understand that petitioning God is not the only purpose of prayer.

Another important dimension of *tefillah* (prayer) is creating images of the world in which we would like to live, images that can strengthen us and give us hope. Throughout the ages, Jews observed Shabbat and entered an alternate reality without pain and suffering, where poverty was banished and competitiveness was set aside, yet surely our predecessors were never deluded into thinking that the evils of the real world had vanished. Rather, Shabbat offered them a respite and a refuge, a chance to dream and to imagine a different and better world, even if that better world had yet to be created. The retreat into that refuge did not blind the Jew to the inadequacies of the real world, as Marx claimed when he spoke of religion as an "opiate of the masses." Instead, Shabbat awakened Jews to the reality that we would like to create; it strengthened our conviction that the world we labor to create can, in fact, be created. One purpose of prayer is to keep the image of what we are trying to create fresh and foremost in our minds, so that we do not become discouraged or succumb to despair. When we think of prayer "working," we sense that praying together with our community has fortified us, strengthened us and given us faith even in times of darkness.

III. The Political Dimension of Jewish Prayer

Prayer, as we have seen, includes a spiritual response to the evil in our world. The prayer book has moments in which we accept evil as part of our world, but we nonetheless struggle to strengthen our faith as we confront that evil. At other times, the *siddur* helps us create alternate spiritual realities in which evil, in effect, does not exist. The prayer book includes yet more of the Jewish people's responses to evil. One of these additional responses to evil in the pages of the *siddur* is political. This response clearly refers to those who do us harm, and it plainly asks God to help us

❀ Judaism, as a general rule, focuses on both the material and the spiritual worlds, while Christianity focuses almost entirely on the spiritual world. Christian theological emphasis on heaven, for example, far exceeds Jewish emphasis. As another example, many Christian teachings place celibacy on a higher spiritual plane than marital sexuality, while hardly any Jewish teachings at all recommend ➤

defeat our enemies. In this sort of prayer, we recognize that the only possible solution is a victory of good over evil; only the defeat of evil will allow us to live the lives that we were meant to live.

At times, and especially because of the influence of Christianity, ❀ we feel that a political dimension to prayer—one that asks God to cause harm to other people—violates what a truly religious moment ought to be. The Jewish view, however, differs. Though Jewish prayer envisions spiritual worlds in which evil does not exist, it also acknowledges that we have enemies who must be defeated. This response to evil asks us to think not about what we have done to bring suffering on ourselves or what led our enemies to attack us; instead, this element of the *siddur* simply insists that our enemies be seen as enemies and it expresses our hope that they will be destroyed. Our prayer, in this instance, asks God to help us destroy those who do us harm.

celibacy. Similarly, Judaism regulates many aspects of daily life that Christianity largely ignores, such as the preparation of meat. Many of us today, living in a Christian cultural milieu, tend to view all religions as primarily other-worldly, even though we may know that Judaism focuses very strongly upon this world.—*Claudia Chernov*

Consider the *Av Harahamim* prayer which we recite after the reading of the Torah on Shabbat mornings. I first began paying serious attention to this prayer when I was in rabbinical school at the Jewish Theological Seminary. One of our most revered teachers would recite this prayer in a piercing voice. This man, whose piety and kindness were a model for us, was a survivor of the *Shoah*.[8] He had lost his entire family in the Nazi atrocities. Each Shabbat morning, as the congregation recited *Av Harahamim* relatively quietly, I heard his voice at the front of the sanctuary, emphasizing the numerous times in which the word *dam* or "blood" was mentioned. In the quiet hum of the room, his call for vengeance, even decades after the *Shoah*, brought chills to my spine. Now on Shabbat mornings, living thousands of miles away, I still think of him and the poignancy of his prayer. It was a chilling plea for revenge, and it is most definitely part of the Jewish approach to prayer. We should think seriously about what we are saying, as we recite:

Father of compassion ... recall with compassion the devout, the upright, and the perfect ones; the holy congregations who gave their lives for the sanctification of Your name.... May God remember them for good.... May God, before our eyes, exact retribution for the spilled blood of God's servants, as is written in the Torah of Moses, the man of God: "O nations, sing the praise of God's people for God will avenge the blood of God's servants, and God will bring retribution upon God's foes."[9] And in the Holy Writings, it is said, "Why should the nations say, 'Where is their God?' Let there be known among the nations, before our eyes, revenge for Your servants' spilled blood."[10]

One could not begin to imagine a much more direct plea than that.

Av Harahamim is only one example in the *siddur* of a plea for God's intervention and the punishment of our enemies. In the weekday *Amidah*, we find a distinct element of *realpolitik* in a few of the central passages. The 13 middle blessings begin with prayers for insight, repentance, and forgiveness. We then turn from our inner needs to outer necessities, beginning with the prayer for redemption (the 7th blessing of the weekday *Amidah*):

Behold our affliction, wage our battles, and redeem us speedily for Your name's sake, for You are a powerful redeemer. Blessed are You, Lord, Redeemer of Israel.

This blessing follows the blessing in which we ask forgiveness for our sins (a passage which I will discuss further). In asking God to see our affliction immediately after we have requested God's forgiveness, the *siddur* seems to say that even if we have sinned, God still cares about our survival. Even if we have sinned, our enemies must stop tormenting us. We ask God, the "Redeemer of Israel," to rescue us from our enemies, to wage our battles. In other words, we ask God to destroy our enemies. We pray that God redeem us from our tribulations and sufferings, both day-to-day troubles and virulent attacks on our very survival.

The focus on our survival continues just a few passages later in the 10th blessing of the *Amidah*.

Sound a great *shofar* for our freedom, and raise a banner to gather our exiles, and gather us together from the four corners of the earth. Blessed are You, Lord, who gathers together the dispersed people of Israel.

This prayer does not specifically mention evil; however, throughout Jewish history, rabbis and other Jewish leaders have seen the dispersion itself as a major cause of Jewish suffering. The Rabbis of the Talmud saw the exile as a punishment for the Jews' sins (a subject we discuss below), a perspective that some religious Jews share to this very day. Moreover, non-religious Jews have also seen exile as a source of Jewish suffering. At the close of the 19th century many non-religious Jews began to feel that exile—regardless of how the exile came about—had produced a weak, anemic, fearful, and powerless Jew who could be redeemed only by the creation of a Jewish state that would "gather together the dispersed people of Israel." Some of modern Jewry's most famous men and women espoused this opinion, including Herzl (after witnessing the Dreyfus affair), Bialik (after reporting on the aftermath of the Kishinev pogrom), Natan Altermann, and many, many others. Thus, both religious Jews and non-religious Jews have long seen exile as the cause of Israel's suffering and, therefore, believed that the key dimension of Jewish redemption would be the return of exiled Jews and the re-establishment of a national Jewish state in the land of Israel.

In the next blessing, we pray for the restoration of justice, and this prayer follows naturally from our prayer for the gathering of the exiles. One result of living in exile, in lands where the Jews were scarcely tolerated, was that Jews suffered continual injustice. When we think of the

Dreyfus affair and the responses of men like Theodor Herzl and Emile Zola, we can understand that the prayer asking God to "bring back our judges as in early times" is more than a prayer for abstract justice—it is a prayer that God change the political status of the Jew and create a world in which our suffering dramatically diminishes. Indeed, the language of the 11th blessing makes this intention clear.

Restore our judges as they used to be, and our counselors as at the beginning, and remove from us sorrow and suffering, and rule over us—You alone, Lord—with justice and mercy, sustain our cause.[11] Blessed are You, Lord, the King who loves righteousness and judgment.

Commentators have asked, why would restoring our judges result in God's removing sorrow and suffering from us? What is the connection? By gaining "our judges," we avoid the power of the enemies who rule over us. One scholar even notes that ancient manuscripts of this prayer read not "remove from us sorrow and suffering," but, "remove from us the rule of Greece and Rome"![12] Though our version is less direct, this prayer for justice is a subtle plea for God's political redemption of the Jews.

The prayer "against heretics" follows immediately afterward, and it makes the same plea overtly. The vociferousness of this prayer and the vehemence of its plea that the enemy be destroyed are noteworthy.

Frustrate the hopes of all those who malign us; let all evil very soon disappear. Let all Your enemies soon be destroyed. May You quickly uproot and crush the arrogant; may You subdue and humble them in our time. Blessed are You, Lord, who destroys our enemies and humbles the arrogant.[13]

What is extraordinary about this passage is that the enemies against which it rails are Jews! According to traditional interpretations, this passage was added to the *Amidah* during the time of Yavneh, shortly after the destruction of the Second Temple, when Jewish society was beset by great civil strife and passionate religious divisiveness. Some Jews had conspired with the Roman authorities and had turned over those Jews who had violated Roman edicts banning the study and teaching of Torah and forbidding Jewish observances. This blessing asked God's help in undermining the work of these heretics and political traitors. Perhaps it was also a section of the *Amidah* that traitors were not willing to utter, thus assisting Jews to determine who was and was not a traitor.

How exactly this prayer was meant to work, and who precisely the "enemies" and the "arrogant" were, are not entirely clear. These questions are the subject of intense scholarly debate. What is undeniable, however, is that the enemies mentioned in the prayer were Jews who were undermining Jewish causes and even collaborating with those who oppressed the Jews. This facet of life has followed us into modernity. Many of us have heard stories of Jews who collaborated with the Nazis or with other Axis powers during World War II, of Jews who slandered fellow Jews to the authorities in the days of the Soviet Union, and even of Israeli soldiers who sold their guns or other weapons to Israel's Arab enemies. Whether they acted out of selfishness, fear, or even misguided principle, such cases have been rare, but they have occurred. Thus, in the twelfth prayer of the *Amidah*, we see yet another response to evil: We ask God to enable us to subvert the work of enemies among our own ranks.

This politically aware dimension of the *Amidah* continues with a few final passages, which I will summarize and quote in part below. These are the sections about the rebuilding of Jerusalem, the restoration of the Davidic line to the throne, and finally the restoration of the Temple service to Jerusalem. These passages share a plea for the restoration of full Jewish life to Jerusalem, and with it a more secure and less dependent Jewish community there than that exists in exile. The plain meaning of these prayers has more to do with religious issues than political ones, yet the prayers to restore Jewish life in Zion were rarely exclusively religious. The political implications of such a restoration were obvious to both Jews and non-Jews throughout the medieval and modern periods. Jews have prayed that, with the restoration of Jewish sovereign life to Jerusalem, much of the suffering that Jews have endured in exile will come to an end.

Blessing 14 of the Amidah prays for the rebuilding of Jerusalem:

And to Jerusalem, Your city, may You return in compassion, and may You rest within it, as You have spoken. May You rebuild it soon in our days as an eternal structure, and may You speedily establish the throne of David within it. Blessed are You, Lord, the builder of Jerusalem.

Then comes blessing 15, the prayer for the restoration of David's throne:

The offspring of Your servant David may You speedily cause to flourish, and enhance his pride through Your salvation, for we hope for Your salvation all day long. Blessed are You, Lord, who causes the pride of salvation to flourish.

And after we pray that our prayers will be accepted (blessing 16), we recite blessing 17, which closes:

May our eyes behold Your return to Zion in compassion. Blessed are You, Lord, who restores His Presence to Zion.

This concludes a distinctly political segment of the *Amidah*, a very different response from those we saw in the first two sections of this chapter.

Prayers that ask God to help us uproot our enemies are recited elsewhere in the daily service. A full listing of such prayers would be beyond the purview of this chapter but I will mention a few of the best known examples. Perhaps the most commonly recognized instance of this political response to evil is recited in synagogue as the congregation prepares to remove to the Torah from the Ark. When the Ark is opened, the congregation sings a verse taken from the Torah, Numbers 10:35. As the Israelites traveled through the desert, Moses would recite this verse each time the Ark of the Tabernacle was raised up for the next stage of its journey:

Whenever the Ark was about to set out, Moses would say, "Rise up, O Lord, may Your enemies be scattered, and those who hate You flee before You."

As we open our Arks today, we are reminded of that Ark and its meandering in the desert; we are also reminded of Moses' prayer for victory over his people's enemies. As we prepare to read the Torah that Moses set before us, we reiterate that very same plea today.

We see a similar theme in sections of the *Maariv* service as well. In the first blessing that follows *Kriat Shema*, known as *Emet Ve'emunah* (true and dependable), we describe God as One who "redeems us from the power of kings, our King who delivers us from the hand of all the cruel tyrants. God is the God who exacts vengeance for us from our foes and who brings just retribution upon all enemies of our soul," and we conclude, "Blessed are You, Lord, who redeemed Israel."

Our faith in a God who intervenes in history, who saves us and who will continue to save us, continues in *Hashkiveinu*, the second blessing after *Kriat Shema*. As we are about to go to sleep, with all the uncertainty and introspection that evening, night, and dark bring, we pray:[14]

Shield us, remove from us enemies and pestilence, remove starvation, sword, and sorrow. Remove the evil forces that surround us; shelter us in the shadow of Your wings, for You, O God, are our guardian and our deliverer.... Blessed are You, Lord, who guards His people Israel forever.

As these examples teach us, Jewish prayer has a third response to evil. In addition to accepting the existence of evil and creating spiritual realities in which no evil dwells, prayer also allows us to acknowledge that we have enemies and to ask for God's help in destroying them. Those are intensely harsh words for a religious setting, but Jews have survived, our liturgy seems to suggest, by facing reality. When we cannot deny that we have enemies, we must be willing to fight and defeat them. There is no alternative. Pacifism is a luxury of the powerful or of those who have no enemies; Jews living in exile have fallen into neither of these categories, and our liturgy has reflected the world in which we have lived and the steps we have taken to survive.

Though our survival may depend on defeating our enemies, we do not relish the obligation to wage war, nor do we take pleasure in our enemies' destruction. By taking pleasure in destroying others, we violate our own souls. ▓ We are no longer who we were meant to be. We are meant to be a people of peace; we envision a world united by faith in God and we pray for a messianic era that will end the conflicts that surround us. Nowhere is this expressed more beautifully than in the *Kedushah* for Shabbat morning. We call out to God:[15]

Throughout Your universe reveal Yourself, our King, and reign over us, for we await You. When will You reign in Zion? Let it be soon, and in our days; and dwell there forever. Then You will be exalted and sanctified in the midst of Jerusalem, Your own city, forever and to all eternity.

▓ The customs of Passover offer a beautiful example of the concept that we do not take pleasure in the destruction of our enemies. At the Seder, we spill drops of wine as we list the plagues, decreasing our joy as we recall the suffering of the Egyptians. Then, on the last day of the holiday, we do not recite the full *Hallel*, the praises recited on Festivals. The last day of Passover is indeed a Festival, yet it also marks the day that the Egyptians drowned in the Red Sea. Because we do not seek to gloat over victory, we recite an abridged *Hallel.—Rebecca Boim Wolf*

Who takes part in the messianic era, when conflict no longer reigns and enemies are removed? Is this vision only for Jews? Hardly. The second passage of the *Aleinu* prayer, a concluding part of almost all Jewish services, makes the point clearly:

Therefore, it is our hope, O Lord our God, that we may speedily see the glory of Your power, when You will remove the abominations from the earth, and the idols will be cut off…. All humankind will call upon Your name, and all the wicked of the earth will be drawn to You…. Then shall all accept the yoke of Your kingdom, and You will reign over them speedily and forever…. And it is said: And God shall be King over all the earth; on that day God shall be One and God's name One.

Thus, suggests the *siddur*, our challenge when we survey the world is two-fold. We must be honest about the enemies we have and, despite our difficulty with violence and warfare as a religious mandate, we must wage the battles that are necessary for our survival. We must, however, remain constantly aware that warfare is but a means to a sacred end, the survival of the Jewish people. We must wage our battles while at every moment we seek the glimmering hope of peace, the prospect of coming to terms with a former enemy. The purpose of our war is to bring the Messiah, to create an era devoid of battle and bloodshed. This delicate balance—to believe in the necessity of war and to love peace—is terribly difficult to maintain. That is precisely why taking this portion of the liturgy seriously is so critical for the Jewish people in our time.

IV. Evil as an Opportunity for Self-Examination

In the previous section, I noted that the *Amidah*'s prayer for redemption, the plea that God "behold our affliction, wage our battles," follows immediately after the prayer for forgiveness. Praying for redemption immediately after praying for forgiveness might well suggest that, even if we have sullied our relationship with God, we nonetheless hope and pray that God will heed our prayers and deliver us from our enemies. We claim, therefore, that even if we are not perfect, we do not deserve to suffer.

As plausible as that interpretation is, it ignores another possible response to evil, namely, that we have either caused it or brought suffering upon ourselves through sin. Though many Jews today are uncomfortable espousing this position, any discussion of the prayer book's approach to evil would be terribly incomplete if it did not mention those passages that lay responsibility for our suffering at our own feet. With that in mind, let's turn to a few of the most commonly cited passages that reflect this view.

The notion that an individual's suffering is rooted in his or her misdeed is found throughout Jewish history. The Talmud at *Brakhot* 5a, for example, notes that when we suffer, we should examine our deeds carefully. ▣ This view is found earlier in the Torah, and the Rabbis selected Torah passages that make this point as central elements of the liturgy. Perhaps none is more famous than the middle passage of the *Shema* (Deuteronomy 11:13–21).

▣ The same phrase, *yefashpesh bemaasav*, urging us to examine our deeds carefully, also appears in the Babylonian Talmud at *Eiruvin* 13b, in a famous argument between the schools of Hillel and Shammai as to whether human beings would be better off having been created or not having been created.—DG

If, then, you obey the commandments that I enjoin upon you this day, loving the Lord your God and serving Him with all your heart and soul, I will grant the rain for your land in season ... and thus shall you eat your fill. Take care not to be lured away to serve other gods and bow to them. For the Lord's anger will flare up against you, and God will shut up the skies so that there will be no rain and the ground will not yield its produce; and you will soon perish from the good land that the Lord is assigning to you.

Many of us have difficulty with this perspective. All of us can think of instances of suffering—illness and death of innocent young children, natural disasters in which people are randomly injured and killed, and many more—in which a correlation between a person's character and life span cannot be discovered. Indeed, it is precisely at these instances of suffering, when God's world seems most random and cruel, that we find our faith most seriously tested. For that reason, many of us focus on other dimensions of the *siddur* and stay away from confrontations with texts that correlate our suffering with our sinfulness.

Many Jews, however, struggle to make sense of this section of the *Shema*. Some genuinely believe that our fates are recompense for how we have lived, and they claim that even if *we* cannot see justice in the picture, God still can. Divine justice is beyond humanity's ability to comprehend, they claim, but justice does exist. Others find this claim untenable. Some people read this passage more narrowly, noting that the specific sin described is idolatry and the punishment for idolatry is the destruction of the natural world. Therefore, one way of understanding this passage is that idolatry—putting our faith in things that we believe will save us, but that ultimately cannot (such as weapons of mass destruction)—can indeed destroy our world.

No matter which solutions we seek, the second passage of the *Shema* is difficult. Yet that passage is by no means unique. Later compositions in the prayer book make similar points. Consider the central section of the *Musaf Amidah* for festivals. Discussing the trauma of exile, the *siddur* says:

Because of our sins we have been exiled from our land and sent far from our soil. Therefore, we cannot ascend to appear and to prostrate ourselves before You, and to perform our obligations in ... the holy House upon which Your name was proclaimed, because of the hand that was dispatched against Your sanctuary. ✺

✺ As an indication of how troubling this passage is, consider that the Conservative movement's original *Siddur Sim Shalom* prayer book, which leaves virtually all the liturgy in its original form, changes the language of this paragraph almost completely. The second edition of *Sim Shalom*, responding to criticism about this change, restores the original Hebrew but renders an English translation that radically alters the meaning of the text.—*DG*

The passage continues with a prayer that God show us mercy and restore us to Jerusalem, but, by that point, the central claim has been made: The exile, and all the suffering that it has caused, are the result of our sins.

Before we dismiss this claim as outlandish, we should remind ourselves that Jewish historical accounts suggest that one of the reasons for the destruction of the two Temples was infighting among the Jews; this social collapse made attention to affairs of state virtually impossible. Thus, even if we reject that the Babylonian invasion or the Roman destruction of Jerusalem occurred because God decided to punish the Jews, we should at least consider the claim that we lost our sovereignty because of our own sin. But that will not resolve the entire problem. Those who struggled with the *Shema* will struggle with this passage as well. Some of the more liberal movements in American Judaism have, in fact, removed this passage from the Festival *Amidah*.

Other passages in the prayer book focus on our sinfulness, without specifically claiming that we cause our suffering. Blessing six of the weekday *Amidah* is a classic example:

Forgive us, our Father, for we have sinned, pardon us, our King, for we have transgressed, for You pardon and forgive. Blessed are You, Lord, who pardons abundantly.

This says nothing about our suffering resulting from our sin, but it suggests that our sinfulness is deeply ingrained. Similarly, the *Ashamnu* prayer, which we recite on the High Holy Days (and also as part of the confessional on our deathbed and before our marriage) suggests that sinfulness is ingrained. ▓ As we confess aloud that we have committed the *Ashamnu*'s alphabetically listed sins, we beat our chests with a closed fist.

What is the import of this sort of material in the *siddur*? In the aftermath of the dramatic and horrifying evil of September 11, 2001, should we blame ourselves for the suffering? Or should we comfort ourselves with the notion that the injured and the dead must have brought the suffering on themselves? Certainly not! That viewpoint is not a legitimate or tenable approach to God, religion, or the synagogue. Yet at the same time, the prayer book *is* meant to be sobering. It does ask us, even as we cry out in pain and pray for comfort and healing, whether we have contributed to the events at hand and whether we could have prevented them. Were we vigilant enough? Did we recognize that we had enemies even before they struck us? When the Taliban destroyed statues of the Buddha, did we ignore the attack, because we remained safe? Did we relax our security precautions because we enjoyed the freedoms that America provided?

Similar questions confront us about the Mideast situation and the horrible suffering of the Jewish people that terrorism has caused. Did we avail ourselves of all our opportunities to improve relations—or even reach peace—with Israel's Arab neighbors? Have we treated the Arab populations as we should have over the 35 years that have passed since Israel conquered the West Bank and Gaza? Though the Six-Day War was forced upon us, have we perhaps contributed to the Arabs' frustration and anger?

We will disagree strongly, perhaps even passionately, about many of the answers to these questions, and that is exactly the point. The purpose of prayer is not to beseech God for magical solutions to our problems. Rather, prayer makes us think, encourages us to depend on each other and to build communities of Jews who feel, worry, hope, and pray together. Asking ourselves—and each other—what responsibility *we* have for what

▓ We recite *Ashamnu* in the first-person plural, as "we." When we confess our sins on the High Holy Days, we do so as a community, with one voice. We admit to God, "We are guilty … we have sinned." We do not say, "I have sinned." We admit to sins as an entire community, indicating that each one of us is responsible for the others and no one of us can be singled out for blame. The communal listing indicates as well, as Rabbi Gordis suggests, that sinfulness is an inherent part of our nature.
—Rebecca Boim Wolf

has occurred does not mean that we accept all the blame, for that makes no sense. It suggests, however, that our world is extraordinarily complex and that we, too, must examine ourselves as we pray to God for comfort and protection. Prayer at its best strengthens us while it causes us to reflect. None of us grow without being asked difficult, uncomfortable questions. Here, too, the genius of the *siddur* shines brightly.

Ultimately, Jewish prayer is not about self-flagellation, self-deprecation, or about claiming that we are worthless. Indeed, even when the *siddur* begins with claims that our lives are of limited meaning, it almost immediately seems to respond, "Yes, we are limited, but we are made great by our relationship with God." And especially in times of great suffering, prayer nurtures our relationship with God. Consider the following passage from the beginning of the *Shaḥarit* service:

Master of all the worlds! Not in the merit of our righteousness do we cast our supplications before You, but in the merit of Your abundant mercy. What are we? What is our life? What is our kindness? What is our righteousness? … Are not all the heroes like nothing before You, the famous as if they never existed, the wise as if devoid of wisdom, and the perceptive as if devoid of intelligence? For most of their deeds are nothingness, and the days of their lives are empty before You. The preeminence of human beings over beast is non-existent, for all is vain. But we are Your people, members of Your covenant, children of Abraham, Your beloved, to whom You took an oath at Mount Moriah.

The *siddur* does ask us to consider our shortcomings openly and honestly, but it never asks us to wallow in self-denigration or to consider ourselves meaningless or valueless. Instead, the prayer book urges us to recall that we are blessed through our covenant with God, that we are part of a glorious history of accomplishment and of seeking God's presence. In our most painful moments, the liturgy does ask us to analyze our past actions and motivations, but it reminds us that we are part of a larger and more noble story, a story in which human dignity has triumphed, a story in which the Jewish people have survived, grown, and flourished. If our encounter with the liturgy can give us, even in our darkest moments, the faith to believe that we will triumph once again, then we can genuinely say that our prayers have been heard.

Conclusion: The Urge to Pray and the Need Not to be Alone

Jewish prayer, as we have seen, functions on many levels, saying many different and competing things. Prayer encourages us and chastises us. It asks God to defeat our enemies, yet it also denies that any wrong exists in the world. Prayer bonds us together as we confront the harsh reality of our world, and it ushers us into mythical worlds in which suffering is entirely banished.

These many different approaches are not designed to be confusing or inconsistent. Instead they are designed to offer us different emotional and intellectual ways of grappling with our world. By wrestling with the prayer book, we can grow in directions we had not thought possible. Yet these various approaches to evil and suffering all focus on God. The *siddur* suggests that whether we can or cannot make sense of the world, at the end of the day we are not alone. To paraphrase *Adon Olam*, the prayer book says to each of us, "you are not alone, you have no reason to fear."

Of course that is exactly why we pray. We need reassurance and a sense of community. Even if we are not certain what we believe, we reach out for God's presence. On Shabbat, for instance, we are not to petition God. What, then, should we do on Shabbat when we need to petition God on behalf of those who are ill and in need of our prayers? Should we ignore the no-petition rule? That is impossible. Should we ignore those who need our prayers? Should we ignore those for whom we feel a desperate need to pray? That, too, is impossible.

The ingenious solution to this problem is the addition of a line to the *Mi Sheberakh*, the prayer for the ill, on Shabbat: "It is Shabbat, and thus we do not petition [God], and we are confident that healing will come speedily." This strange line might seem like a surreptitious way of petitioning when we are not supposed to, but it acknowledges a powerful truth about human beings and, particularly, about Jews: We pray not only because we are commanded to, but because we need to. In the face of evil, in the darkest of times, we reach out to feel God's presence. Even when we know that we must not petition God, we do. Reaching out to God in petition and in prayer is a human need, something that Judaism tells us is both legitimate and necessary.

In the season of the High Holy Days, for a full month before Rosh Hashanah, many congregations recite Psalm 27 at the conclusion of both the morning and evening services. The psalmist says quite beautifully

One thing I ask of the Lord, only that do I seek: to live in the house of the Lord all the days of my life, to gaze upon the beauty of the Lord, to frequent God's Temple.

To dwell in God's presence—that, our prayer book genuinely believes, is what we want. Particularly in times of suffering, dwelling in God's presence can seem impossible, and so we pray. We pray when we feel confident in our relationship with God, but even more we pray to renew, restore, and rebuild our relationship with God. We pray to reach out to God, and we pray to reach out to each other. Will prayer eradicate evil? Perhaps not. But our tradition insists that if prayer helps us open the gates to God's presence and helps connect us to others, it genuinely alleviates our suffering. It helps us light a small candle to ward off the seemingly endless darkness.

Do the various models that we have seen in this chapter—models of how prayer responds to evil and suffering—exhaust all the possibilities? Of course not. What we see in the *siddur* is, in many respects, in the eye of the beholder. Our challenge is to learn to use the *siddur* as a rich and varied resource and perhaps to discover models we have not discussed in these pages. Prayer is not about right and wrong, nor is prayer about fitting a preconceived notion of what it must mean. Prayer may be about discovery, about hope.

We live in difficult and painful times, and often as we gaze at our children and grandchildren we fear for the world they will inherit. We will change that world by working together to build a better society, but also by reminding ourselves through prayer that a better tomorrow is possible. We turn to the *siddur* for comfort, for consolation, and for hope. We turn to God, and we call out, in the words of the psalmist, "Out of the depths I call you, O Lord ... listen to my cry, heed my plea for mercy." [16] We do so knowing that the answer to our prayer can mean very different things, all of them important. We do so in anticipation of an era when the vision that we recite during the Grace after Meals will be fulfilled: "God will gird God's nation with strength, and God will bless the Jewish people with peace."

QUESTIONS FOR FURTHER STUDY AND REFLECTION

1. Given the many different purposes of prayer in Judaism, why do we value praying with a *minyan*, a community, over praying alone? What must happen in the synagogue to allow participants to achieve the goals of communal prayer?

2. The prayer book responds to evil in various ways. Which way speaks to you most compellingly? Can you think of examples from the *siddur* which are not mentioned in this chapter, that fall into the various categories? Which prayers move you most at times of distress?

3. Do you feel comfortable with prayers that ask God to destroy our enemies? Does that sentiment seem appropriate in a synagogue? Why?

4. What sorts of additional prayers might you compose, if you were adding prayers to the *siddur* today?

5. When asked what we have done to bring suffering upon ourselves, how should we answer? For ourselves? For our community? For our country?

1. Unless otherwise noted, all translations of the liturgy are Rabbi Daniel Gordis's adaptations of the translations in *The Complete Artscroll Siddur*, edited by Rabbi Nosson Scherman (New York: Mesorah, 1984). Rabbi Gordis has removed references to God as "He," "His," and "Him." However, Rabbi Gordis retains metaphors such as King, Ruler, and the like, despite their common masculine associations, in order to remain faithful to the language of the *siddur*.

2. Lawrence A. Hoffman, *The Way Into Jewish Prayer* (Woodstock, VT: Jewish Lights, 2000), page 98.

3. Michael Swartz, "Models for New Prayer," *Response* 13:1,2 (Fall–Winter 1982), page 36.

4. This translation, and the translations of many other Biblical passages cited in this chapter, are taken from *Tanakh: The Holy Scriptures* (Philadelphia: Jewish Publication Society, 1985).

5. Paul Tillich, *Dynamics of Faith* (New York: Harper Colophon, 1957), page 51.

6. This translation, intentionally not literal, is by Rabbi Gordis.

7. Rabbi Gordis has discussed this issue at greater length in *God Was Not in the Fire: The Search for a Spiritual Judaism* (New York: Scribner, 1995), especially in Chapter Two, "Judaism and Belief in God—Can the Skeptic Embark on the Journey?"

8. *Shoah* is the word that many Jews use for Holocaust. The Hebrew word *Shoah* means "calamity." Holocaust is an English word that means "burnt offering" or "sacrifice to God." The Jews of Europe in the thirties and forties were not sacrificed. They were murdered. There is a tremendous difference; Rabbi Gordis uses the word *Shoah* in order to take that difference seriously.

9. Deuteronomy 32:43.

10. Deuteronomy 32:43; Psalms 79:10.

11. Rabbi Gordis adapts this translation from *Siddur Sim Shalom*, edited by Rabbi Jules Harlow (New York: Rabbinical Assembly, 1975), page 113.

12. See Barukh HaLevi Epstein, *Barukh She'Amar* (Tel Aviv: Am Olam), page 131.

13. The translation by Rabbi Gordis is adapted from both the *Artscroll Siddur* and the *Siddur Sim Shalom*.

14. The translation by Rabbi Gordis is adapted from *Siddur Sim Shalom*.

15. The translation by Rabbi Gordis is adapted from *Siddur Sim Shalom*.

16. Psalms 130:1. The translation by Rabbi Gordis is based on the Jewish Publication Society translation.

AFTERWORD

Sandra King

Hadassah exemplified "Jewish feminism" decades before that expression was coined. Throughout the 20th century Hadassah, an organization conceived and led by Jewish women, taught women—many of whom had been denied the same access to education that their brothers, fathers, and sons had enjoyed—about Judaism and Zionism. Then, beginning in the 1970s, Jewish feminist activists and scholars led a movement to gain gender equality within Jewish public and private life.

Yet, at the end of the century, there remained a need for accessible, comprehensive publications that would bring Jewish feminist perspectives to the fore. Hadassah's National Jewish Education Department heard the call and began to produce what has now become a trilogy of study guides. In 1997 Hadassah published *Jewish Women Living the Challenge,* a compendium of articles and essays on contemporary issues. The book was enormously successful throughout North America, and it was also studied by both American and Israeli women as they prepared to celebrate their religious coming of age at Hadassah's National Convention in an adult bat mitzvah ceremony, today known as the Hadassah *Eishet Mitzvah* ceremony.

Following that success, a sequel that would provide deeper awareness of classic and modern Jewish sources became the logical next step. Hadassah took note of the growing numbers of Rosh Hodesh groups— women gathering to pray on the festival of the New Moon and to claim the monthly celebration as their own. Why was there no curriculum for Jewish study each month? Hadassah responded in 2000 by publishing

Moonbeams. Like its predecessor, *Moonbeams* has inspired countless women—in the United States, Israel, and other countries—to further their connection to Judaism through rigorous study of sacred texts and modern commentaries.

You have in your hands the final book in our trilogy. *Pray Tell* is a response to the overwhelming need for rigorous explanation, analysis, and commentary on the *siddur.* The genius of world-renowned scholar Rabbi Jules Harlow, together with modern polemical insights, provide a frame for the prayer book. Provocative and intriguing, *Pray Tell* helps us sustain an intimate, accessible dialogue with the Almighty.

Hadassah's trilogy is complete, but this is not the end of the project. Rather, it is the beginning of Jewish scholarship as a way of life. *Eishet Mitzvah* and Rosh H̲odesh study groups are two suggested pathways. Many other avenues are also open. We know that exciting study fuels the desire to continue learning at higher and higher levels. As the ancient Jewish philosopher Philo of Alexandria observed, "Love of learning is by nature curious and inquisitive … prying into everything, reluctant to leave anything, material or immaterial, unexplored." Let us all leave nothing unexplored.

ABOUT TRANSLITERATION

Many Hebrew words and phrases have been included in *Pray Tell,* written with the English alphabet. In transliterating, the Hadassah Jewish Education Department generally follows the practice of the *Encyclopaedia Judaica.* The list below indicates the pronunciation of transliterated Hebrew.

a   father or mama

e   celebrate

ei   weight

i   magazine

o   stone

u   Ruth or blue

kh   "ch" as the Scottish word loch or the German name Bach

<u>h</u>   "ch" as the Scottish word loch or the German name Bach

tz   ts as in hats

All other letters have the same pronunciations in Hebrew and English.

About Our Contributors

Hadassah's National Jewish Education Department gratefully acknowledges the authors who wrote chapters and commentary specifically for inclusion in *Pray Tell*.

Abrams, Rabbi Judith Z., Ph.D., is founder and director of Maqom: A School for Adult Talmud Study. Life coaching and classes are available through the web site: www.maqom.com.

Agus, Arlene is a founder of the Jewish feminist movement and its first organization, Ezrat Nashim. She has taught Jewish theology and ethics at numerous institutions, such as the Skirball Center for Adult Jewish Learning; City University of New York Graduate Center, School of Continuing Education; and the 92nd Street "Y." Her writings have appeared in numerous books and journals, including *The Jewish Woman: New Perspectives* (Schocken), *What Happens After I Die?* (UAHC Press), *Lifecycles,* volumes 1 and 2 (Jewish Lights Publishing), and *The Jerusalem Report.*

Alpert, Rebecca T. is the co-director of the Women's Studies Program and assistant professor of Religion and Women's Studies at Temple University. She is the co-author of *Exploring Judaism: A Reconstructionist Approach* (rev. 2000), author of *Like Bread on the Seder Plate: Jewish Lesbians and the Transformation of Tradition* (Columbia University Press, 1997), and editor of *Voices of the Religious Left: A Contemporary Sourcebook* for (Temple University Press, 2000).

Brown, Erica is currently a Jerusalem Fellow and the former scholar-in-residence of the Boston Federation of the CJP. She lives in Israel with her husband and four children.

Cardin, Rabbi Nina Beth is the director of Jewish Life at the JCC of Greater Baltimore. Her most recent books are *Tears of Sorrow, Seeds of Hope:*

A Jewish Spiritual Companion for Infertility and Pregnancy Loss (Jewish Lights Publishing) and *A Tapestry of Jewish Time: A Spiritual Guide to the Holidays and Life-Cycle Events* (Behrman).

Chernov, Claudia is senior editor of the National Department of Jewish Education at Hadassah. She has written and edited portions of such Hadassah study guides as *Moonbeams: A Hadassah Rosh Hodesh Guide* (Jewish Lights Publishing), *Judaism and Ecology, Jewish Women Living the Challenge, Ribcage: Israeli Women's Fiction,* and *Zionism: The Sequel.* Claudia lives in New York, and is a member of Ansche Chesed, where ever-increasing numbers of *minyanim* (meaning, in this case, separate Shabbat morning prayer services) reflect differing attitudes toward prayer and liturgy. She is grateful for this opportunity to work with Rabbi Jules Harlow.

Cohen, Tamara is a Jewish feminist educator, writer, and activist. She is a past Program Director of Ma'yan: The Jewish Women's Project of the Jewish Community Center in Manhattan. She has also worked with Project Kesher and Kolot: The Center for Women and Gender Studies at the Reconstructionist Rabbinical College, and she is the spiritual leader of the Coalition for Jewish Life of Washington, Connecticut. Tamara served as editor of *The Journey Continues: Ma'yan's Passover Haggadah* and as contributing author to numerous journals and anthologies, including *The Women's Passover Companion: Women's Reflections on the Festival of Freedom* (Jewish Lights Publishing), *Jewish Women Living the Challenge* (Hadassah), and *Beginning Anew: A Woman's Companion to the High Holidays* (Simon & Schuster). She serves on the founding board of Brit Tzedek V'Shalom: The Jewish Alliance for Justice and Peace, and she is a former board member of Jews for Racial and Economic Justice and a founder of Jewish Activist Gays and Lesbians. Tamara lives in Gainesville, Florida, with her partner.

Diament, Carol is director of the National Department of Jewish Education at Hadassah, a post she has held since July 1986. In 1991, under her guidance, the Department was awarded the Shazar Prize for Excellence in Jewish Education in the Diaspora from the President of the State of Israel. Dr. Diament is the first woman to have completed a doctorate in Jewish studies at Yeshiva University; her dissertation examined the Eastern European Hebrew press and its role in Zionism. She received the Simon Rockower award for excellence in journalism for "How Holy Is the Holy Land?" published in *Hadassah Magazine.* She has edited *Moonbeams: A Hadassah Rosh Hodesh Guide* (Jewish Lights Publishing), *Jewish Women Living the Challenge, Ribcage: Israeli Women's Fiction,* and *Zionism: The Sequel,* among others.

Furstenburg, Rochelle is a Jerusalem-based writer who specializes in social, cultural, and literary topics. She writes a column on Israeli life for *Hadassah Magazine* and is a frequent contributor to *The Jerusalem Report*. Her work has also appeared in *The Jerusalem Post, Washington Post, San Francisco Chronicle,* and *Modern Hebrew Literature.* She wrote *Images of Jerusalem: City of David in Modern Hebrew Literature* for the National Department of Jewish Education at Hadassah in 1995, and she wrote bi-annual overviews of "Culture in Israel" for the *American Jewish Yearbook* from 1993 to 1999. She has written about Israeli and American feminist movements and about post-Zionism, and she was director of the Senior Center at the Whole-Family internet site. She was born and raised in Chicago. Rochelle Furstenberg has a B.A. degree from Douglass College of Rutgers University and an M.A. degree in Philosophy from Boston University. She has lived in Israel since 1965. She is married and has five children.

Gordis, Rabbi Daniel is director of the Jerusalem Fellows Program at the Mandel School for Educational and Social Leadership in Jerusalem, Israel. He is the author of several books, including *God Was Not In The Fire* (Scribner), about Judaism as a spiritual search, and *If A Place Can Make You Cry—Dispatches from an Anxious State* (Crown Publishers; excerpted in *The New York Times Magazine*) about Israeli life after the collapse of the Oslo peace accords. Rabbi Gordis and his family came to Israel in 1998, and they live in Jerusalem. He can be reached at www.danielgordis.org.

Grossman, Rabbi Susan is spiritual leader of Congregation Beth Shalom in Columbia, Maryland. She is one of the editors of *Etz Hayim Torah and Commentary* (The Rabbinical Assembly and The United Synagogue), and she is co-editor of *Daughters of the King: Women and the Synagogue* (Jewish Publication Society). Her articles on women and Judaism have appeared in many anthologies and publications. Rabbi Grossman currently serves on the Committee of Jewish Law and Standards for the Conservative movement.

Haberman, Bonna Devora is Resident Scholar in women's studies and lecturer in Near Eastern and Judaic studies at Brandeis University, where she also serves as Director of Mistabra: The Israel-Diaspora Institute for Jewish Textual Activism. She previously served as associate researcher and lecturer at Harvard Divinity School, and she is a founder of Women of the Wall, an Israeli movement supporting women's freedom to pray at the Kotel (the Western Wall). She has also organized a Jewish movement to liberate women from trafficking in prostitution. She is the mother of five.

Hanauer, Courtney is assistant director of the National Department of Jewish Education at Hadassah. She received a bachelor's degree, *summa cum laude,* from Queens College in psychology and sociology, with a minor in Jewish studies. She is a past Flatow Scholar.

Harlow, Rabbi Jules, a native of Iowa, was ordained by the Jewish Theological Seminary of America in 1959. From that year until his retirement in 1994, he served on the executive staff of the Rabbinical Assembly—the international association of Conservative rabbis—notably as Director of Publications, specializing as editor and translator of liturgy. Prominent among Rabbi Harlow's contributions are *Siddur Sim Shalom* (Rabbinical Assembly and the United Synagogue of Conservative Judaism) and *Maḥzor for Rosh Hashanah and Yom Kippur* (Rabbinical Assembly). Other liturgical publications include *The Bond of Life* for mourners and *The Feast of Freedom*, the Rabbinical Assembly's Haggadah, for which he served as a translator and member of the editorial committee. Rabbi Harlow also participated in editing and translating the Rabbinical Assembly's *Weekday Prayer Book* and *Seliḥot* service.

Rabbi Harlow is the Literary Editor of *Etz Hayim Torah and Commentary* (The Rabbinical Assembly and The United Synagogue, 2001), which was awarded first prize in non-fiction by the National Jewish Book Council in 2002 and designated the book of the year.

His translations of stories by Nobel Laureate S. Y. Agnon have appeared in *Commentary, Midstream,* and *Conservative Judaism* magazines and in collections of stories published by Schocken Books. The National Academy of Television Arts and Sciences nominated for an Emmy his interview of Isaac Bashevis Singer on NBC "for outstanding achievement in religious programming." The University of Notre Dame Press has included his essay, "Peace in Traditional Jewish Expression," in *Liturgical Foundations of Social Policy in the Catholic and Jewish Traditions,* and his essay, "Revising the Liturgy for Conservative Jews," in *The Changing Face of Jewish and Christian Worship in North America.* In addition, Rabbi Harlow has edited textbooks for children, including *Lessons from Our Living Past, Stories from Our Living Past,* and *Exploring Our Living Past* (Behrman).

He has lectured and preached in congregations throughout the United States and Canada. For more than 20 years he has officiated at High Holy Day services in Omaha, Nebraska. In 1996 through 1998, he served as Rabbi of The Great Synagogue in Stockholm, Sweden. Other interests include chamber music and jazz.

Horowitz, Mordehi is an Israeli-born American citizen. Before coming to the United States, he served as a paratrooper in the Israeli army. He takes an interest in music, politics, and reading.

King, Sandra is the chair of the National Department of Jewish Education at Hadassah, and is a Vice-President of Hadassah's National Board. She is a licensed professional counselor and a certified professional grief counselor. In addition to her private practice, she is the facilitator of bereavement support groups in the Delaware Valley, and she has taught psychology courses at Philadelphia-area colleges.

Labovitz, Annette is an innovative Jewish educator whose learning materials are used nationwide. Dr. Labovitz wrote her doctoral dissertation for Chicago's Spertus College of Judaica on "The Enrichment of Jewish Education Through the Effective Use of Holy Stories." She and her husband, Rabbi Eugene Labovitz, are known as "The Legendary *Maggidim*." They live in the New York area and frequently appear together as scholars-in-residence using stories from their five anthologies: *A Touch of Heaven: Spiritual and Kabbalistic Stories for Jewish Living* (Jason Aronson); *Time for My Soul: A Treasury of Jewish Stories for Our Holy Days* (Jason Aronson); *A Sacred Jewish Trust: Stories for Our Heritage and History* (Isaac Nathan); *Secrets of the Past, Bridges to the Future* (CAJE, Miami); and *The Legendary Maggidim: Stories of Soul and Spirit* (Targum/Feldheim).

Levine, Yael holds a Ph.D. from the Talmud department of Bar-Ilan University, and she frequently publishes articles on women and Judaism in academic journals. She also composes Hebrew prayers, among them *Teḥinnat haNashim leVinyan haMikdash* (The Supplication of the Mothers for the Rebuilding of the Temple), which is recited in various communities on Tisha Be'Av as an extra-liturgical text. She is engaged in independent research, and resides in Jerusalem. Levine is also owner and webmaster of an educational site in English on Naomi Shemer's song "Jerusalem of Gold."

Milgrom, Rabbi Shira is spiritual leader of Congregation Kol Ami in White Plains, New York. A graduate of Hebrew Union College-Jewish Institute of Religion, she is the author of articles on Jewish spirituality, education, and healing, and the editor of a *siddur* now used across North America. Rabbi Milgrom travels as an educator, and she passionately creates encounters with Jewish texts, rituals, and traditions—merging the intimate and personal with the grand vision of Judaism and the Jewish people. Rabbi Milgrom and husband Dr. David Elcott are the parents of four children.

Ochs, Vanessa L. teaches Jewish studies and anthropology of religion in the Department of Religious Studies of the University of Virginia. She is the author of *Words on Fire* (Harcourt Brace Jovanovich), and co-author, wiht Elizabeth Ochs, of *The Jewish Dream Book: The Key to Opening the Inner Meaning of Your Dreams* (Jewish Lights Publishing). A CLAL Senior Associate, Ochs is co-editor, with Rabbi Irwin Kula, of *The Book of Jewish Sacred Practices: CLAL's Guide to Everyday and Holiday Rituals and Blessings* (Jewish Lights Publishing).

Paloma, Vanessa is a singer and performer who specializes in Ladino music. She has performed as a soloist throughout the United States, Latin America, Israel, and the Orient. Ms. Paloma received a master's degree from Indiana University in early music performance with an emphasis on medieval Spain. For more information, go to www. vanessapaloma.com.

Plaskow, Judith is professor of religious studies at Manhattan College and author of *Standing Again at Sinai: Judaism from a Feminist Perspective* (Harper).

Raphael, Rabbi Rayzel is Rabbinic Director of Faithways, an Interfaith Family Support Network of the Jewish Family and Children's Service of Greater Philadelphia. She also directs the Jewish Creativity Project, which uses music and the arts, through New Legends and Jewish Outreach Institute. In her spare time Rabbi Raphael sings with MIRAJ, an *a cappella* trio, and with Shabbat Unplugged; teaches; and performs weddings. Married to Dr. Simcha Raphael, her primary job is *ima* to Yigdal and Hallel.

Sarason, Richard S. is professor of Rabbinic literature and thought at Hebrew Union College–Jewish Institute of Religion in Cincinnati, Ohio. Jewish liturgy is one of his ongoing research interests and the subject of some of his teaching.

Sasso, Rabbi Sandy Eisenberg, the first woman to be ordained by the Reconstructionist Rabbinical College, has been rabbi of Congregation Beth El Zedeck in Indianapolis since 1977. She writes extensively about the religious imagination of children and about women's spirituality. Rabbi Sasso is the author of many children's books including *God's Paintbrush, In God's Name,* and *God Said Amen* (all Jewish Lights Publishing).

Septimus, Renée graduated from Barnard College with a degree in philosophy and from New York University with a degree in counseling. Currently a social worker, she also teaches, lectures, and writes about Jewish topics, particularly women's spirituality. She is married and is the mother of four.

Tanenbaum, Leora is associate editor of the National Department of Jewish Education at Hadassah, for which she has co-written several books, including *Moonbeams: A Hadassah Rosh Ḥodesh Guide* (Jewish Lights Publishing). In her other life, she is the author of *Catfight: Women and Competition* and *Slut! Growing Up Female with a Bad Reputation* (both Seven Stories Press). Tanenbaum has been featured on the *Today* show, *Oprah*, National Public Radio, and in the pages of *Redbook*, *The Washington Post,* and *The Forward*.

Teutsch, Rabbi David A. is the Wiener Professor of Contemporary Jewish Civilization and Director of the Ethics Center at the Reconstructionist Rabbinical College. He edited the groundbreaking eight-volume *Kol*

Haneshamah Reconstructionist prayer book series. Rabbi Teutsch has previously served as President of the Reconstructionist Rabbinical College and Executive Vice President of the Jewish Reconstructionist Federation.

Umansky, Ellen M. is the Carl and Dorothy Bennett Professor of Judaic Studies at Fairfield University in Fairfield, Connecticut. She has written on modern Jewish history and thought, Jewish women's spirituality, and contemporary Jewish theology. She is the co-editor of *Four Centuries of Jewish Women's Spirituality: A Sourcebook* (Beacon) and the author of two books on Lily Montagu, founder of the Liberal Jewish movement in England. Professor Umansky is currently completing the book *From Christian Science To Jewish Science: Spiritual Healing and American Jews* (Oxford University Press).

Wolf, Rebecca Boim served as associate editor of the National Department of Jewish Education at Hadassah in the spring and summer of 2002. She is currently pursuing her Ph.D. in Jewish history at New York University. Her dissertation focuses on Hadassah, its image and identity throughout the organization's history. Rebecca graduated from Barnard College in 1996 and served as the Assistant Director for International Concerns for the Jewish Council for Public Affairs before beginning graduate work.

Acknowledgment of Sources

Hadassah's National Jewish Education Department gratefully acknowledges the authors and the authors' representatives who granted us permission to reprint their copyrighted work in *Pray Tell*.

"*Buena semana mos de El Dio*" ("*Noche de Alhad*") from Susana Weich-Shahak, *Un vergel vedre* published by IberCaja, of Zaragoza, Spain. Reprinted with the permission of IberCaja.

"*Ad-nai oyi i m'estremeci,*" from Maagalim, published by Renanot, Hamachon L'Musika Yehudit of Jerusalem. Reprinted with the permission of Renanot, Hamachon L'Musika Yehudit.

"*La Bendision de Madre.*" Reprinted from the *Flory Jagoda Songbook,* Tara Publications. Permission to reprint granted by Tara Publications of New York.

Penina V. Adelman, from "A Light Returns to Sarah's Tent." Excerpt from *Lifecycles Volume 2: Jewish Women on Biblical Themes in Contemporary Life* © 1997 Debra Orenstein and Rachel Jane Litman, editors (Woodstock, VT: Jewish Lights Publishing). $19.95+$3.75 s/h. Order by mail or call 800-962-4544 or on-line at www.jewishlights.com. Permission granted by Jewish Lights Publishing, P.O. Box 237, Woodstock, VT 05091.

Rachel Adler, commentary in *Kol Haneshamah: Shabbat Vehagim,* The Reconstructionist Press, 7804 Montgomery Ave, Suite #9, Elkins Park, PA 19027-2649 e-mail press@jrf.org. Reprinted with permission from the Reconstructionist Press.

Rachel Adler, from "*B'rit Ahuvim* Lovers' Covenant." Reprinted from *Engendering Judaism: An Inclusive Theology and Ethics,* copyright © 1998 by Rachel Adler. With permission of the publisher, The Jewish Publication Society.

Yehuda Amichai, "God Full of Mercy" an English translation by Benjamin and Barbara Harshav of "*El Malei Rahamim.*" Poem from YEHUDA AMICHAI: A LIFE OF POETRY 1948–1994 by YEHUDA AMICHAI. Copyright © 1994 by HarperCollins Publishers, Inc. Hebrew-language version copyright © 1994 by Yehuda Amichai. Reprinted by permission of HarperCollins Publishers, Inc.

Yehuda Amichai, "*El Malei Rahamim.*" World copyright © Schocken Publishing House Ltd., Tel Aviv, Israel. Reprinted by permission of Schocken Publishing House.

Chana Bell, "Shechinah." Copyright © 1977 by Chana Bell. Reprinted by permission of the author. Chana Bell, M.A., is a learning disabilities specialist.

Rabbi Leila Gal Berner, "Miriam Haneviah" (Hebrew) and commentary in *Kol Haneshamah: Shabbat Vehagim,* The Reconstructionist Press. Hebrew poem copyright © Leila Gal Berner, reprinted by permission of the author. Commentary reprinted with permission from the Reconstructionist Press, 7804 Montgomery Ave, Suite #9, Elkins Park, PA 19027-2649 e-mail press@jrf.org.

Marc Brettler, excerpt from *My People's Prayer Book: Traditional Prayers, Modern Commentaries*—Volume 2: The Amidah, copyright © 1998 Rabbi Lawrence A. Hoffman, ed. (Woodstock, VT: Jewish Lights Publishing). $23.95+$3.75 s/h. Order by mail or call 800-962-4544 or on-line at www.jewishlights.com. Permission granted by Jewish Lights Publishing, P.O. Box 237, Woodstock, VT 05091.

E. M. Broner, excerpts from *Bringing Home the Light: A Jewish Woman's Handbook of Rituals* by E. M. Broner, copyright © 1999 by E. M. Broner. Used by permission of Council Oak Books, 1290 Chestnut Street, San Francisco, CA 94109. Toll-free order number 800-247-8850.

E. M. Broner, "Dayenu" and "Lo Dayenu." Two and one-half pages of verse from THE TELLING by E. M. Broner. Copyright © 1993 by E. M. Broner. Reprinted by permission of HarperCollins Publishers, Inc.

Elicia Brown, "Our Mother, Our Queen," *The Jewish Week,* September 13, 2002. Reprinted by permission of Elicia Brown and The Jewish Week.

Nina Beth Cardin, excerpts from *Tears of Sorrow, Seeds of Hope: A Jewish Spiritual Companion for Infertility and Pregnancy Loss,* copyright © 1999 by Nina Beth Cardin (Woodstock, VT: Jewish Lights Publishing). $19.95+$3.75 s/h. Order by mail or call 800-962-4544 or on-line at www.jewishlights.com. Permission granted by Jewish Lights Publishing, P.O. Box 237, Woodstock, VT 05091.

Nina Beth Cardin, translations from Hebrew prayers. From OUT OF THE DEPTHS I CALL TO YOU: A BOOK OF PRAYERS FOR THE MARRIED JEWISH WOMAN. Edited and translated by Rabbi Nina Beth Cardin. Copyright © 1995, 1992 by Nina Beth Cardin. Excerpts from pages 70, 72. Reprinted by permission of Jason Aronson Inc.

Rachel Chalfi, *"Tefillah."* Copyright © Rachel Chalfi and ACUM. Reprinted by permission of ACUM Ltd., Society of Authors, Composers, and Music Publishers in Israel, and by permission of Rachel Chalfi.

Rachel Chalfi, "Prayer" an English translation by Rachel Chalfi and Rochelle Furstenberg of *"Tefillah."* Used by permission of ACUM Ltd., Society of Authors, Composers, and Music Publishers in Israel, and by permission of Rachel Chalfi.

Judy Chicago, "Merger Poem," copyright © Judy Chicago, 1979. Reprinted with the permission of Through the Flower, 101 N. Second Street, Belen, NM 87002.

Michael M. Cohen, commentary in *Kol Haneshamah: Shabbat Vehagim,* The Reconstructionist Press, 7804 Montgomery Ave, Suite #9, Elkins Park, PA 19027-2649 e-mail press@jrf.org. Reprinted with permission from the Reconstructionist Press.

Rabbi Hayim Halevy Donin, from TO PRAY AS A JEW by RABBI HAYIM HALEVY DONIN. Copyright © 1980 by Rabbi Hayim Halevy Donin. Reprinted by permission of Basic Books, a member of Perseus Books, L.L.C.

Rabbi Elliot N. Dorff, excerpts from *My People's Prayer Book: Traditional*

Prayers, Modern Commentaries—Volume 1: The Sh'ma and Its Blessings © 1997 Rabbi Lawrence A. Hoffman, ed. (Woodstock, VT: Jewish Lights Publishing). $23.95 + $3.75 s/h. Order by mail or call 800-962-4544 or on-line at www.jewishlights.com. Permission granted by Jewish Lights Publishing, P.O. Box 237, Woodstock, VT 05091.

Rabbi Elliot N. Dorff, excerpt from *My People's Prayer Book: Traditional Prayers, Modern Commentaries*—Volume 2: The Amidah © 1998 Rabbi Lawrence A. Hoffman, ed. (Woodstock, VT: Jewish Lights Publishing). $23.95+$3.75 s/h. Order by mail or call 800-962-4544 or on-line at www.jewishlights.com. Permission granted by Jewish Lights Publishing, P.O. Box 237, Woodstock, VT 05091.

Rabbi Elliot N. Dorff, excerpt from *My People's Prayer Book: Traditional Prayers, Modern Commentaries*—Volume 3: P'sukei D'zimrah © 1999 Rabbi Lawrence A. Hoffman, ed. (Woodstock, VT: Jewish Lights Publishing). $24.95+$3.75 s/h. Order by mail or call 800-962-4544 or on-line at www.jewishlights.com. Permission granted by Jewish Lights Publishing, P.O. Box 237, Woodstock, VT 05091.

Amy Eilberg, "The Gifts of First Fruits" in *Four Centuries of Jewish Women's Spirituality*, Ellen M. Umansky and Dianne Ashton, eds. (Boston: Beacon Press, 1992), page 284. Copyright © Rabbi Amy Eilberg. Reprinted with permission of the author.

David Ellenson, excerpt from *My People's Prayer Book: Traditional Prayers, Modern Commentaries*—Volume 1: The Sh'ma and Its Blessings © 1997 Rabbi Lawrence A. Hoffman, ed. (Woodstock, VT: Jewish Lights Publishing). $23.95 + $3.75 s/h. Order by mail or call 800-962-4544 or on-line at www.jewishlights.com. Permission granted by Jewish Lights Publishing, P.O. Box 237, Woodstock, VT 05091.

David Ellenson, excerpt from *My People's Prayer Book: Traditional Prayers, Modern Commentaries*—Volume 2: The Amidah, copyright © 1998 Rabbi Lawrence A. Hoffman, ed. (Woodstock, VT: Jewish Lights Publishing). $23.95+$3.75 s/h. Order by mail or call 800-962-4544 or on-line at www.jewishlights.com. Permission granted by Jewish Lights Publishing, P.O. Box 237, Woodstock, VT 05091.

Marcia Falk, comment on pages 216–217. Copyright © 2003 by Marcia Lee Falk.

Marcia Falk, excerpts from *The Book of Blessings: New Jewish Prayers for Daily Life, the Sabbath, and the New Moon Festival* (HarperCollins, 1996; paperback edition, Beacon, 1999). Copyright © 1996 by Marcia Lee Falk. Reprinted with permission from the author. More information about Marcia Falk's work can be found at www.marciafalk.com.

Rabbi Dr. Theodore Friedman, excerpt from "Study Guide to a Prayer," *Shefa Quarterly*. Reprinted with permission.

Sylvia Barack Fishman, excerpt from *A Breath of Life*. Reprinted with the permission of The Free Press, a Division of Simon & Schuster Adult Publishing Group, from A BREATH OF LIFE: *Feminism in the American Jewish Community* by Sylvia Barack Fishman. Copyright © 1993 by Sylvia Barack Fishman.

Ellen Frankel, excerpt from *My People's Prayer Book: Traditional Prayers, Modern Commentaries*—Volume 3: P'sukei D'zimrah, copyright © 1999 Rabbi Lawrence A. Hoffman, ed. (Woodstock, VT: Jewish Lights Publishing). $24.95+$3.75 s/h. Order by mail or call 800-962-4544 or on-line at www.jewishlights.com. Permission granted by Jewish Lights Publishing, P.O. Box 237, Woodstock, VT 05091.

Tikva Frymer-Kensky, "The Ritual Impulse," *Lilith* 16 (Spring 1987). Reprinted with permission from Tikva Frymer-Kensky. Professor Frymer-Kensky's most recent book is *Reading the Women of the Bible*.

Rabbi Laura Geller, from "Brit Milah and Brit Banot." Excerpt from *Lifecycles Volume 1: Jewish Women on Life Passages & Personal Milestones,* copyright © 1994. Edited by Debra Orenstein (Woodstock, VT: Jewish Lights Publishing). $19.95+$3.75 s/h. Order by mail or call 800-962-4544 or on-line at www.jewish-lights.com. Permission granted by Jewish Lights Publishing, P.O. Box 237, Woodstock, VT 05091.

Rabbi Leonard B. Gewirtz, excerpt from "Jewish Theology in One Sentence: The B'rakhah," *Shofar,* June 2001. Reprinted by permission of Rabbi Leonard B. Gewirtz.

Amir Gilboa, *"Gedolim Maasei Adonai."* Copyright © Gabriella Gilboa and ACUM. Reprinted by permission of ACUM Ltd., Society of Authors, Composers, and Music Publishers in Israel, and by permission of Gabriella Gilboa.

Amir Gilboa, "Great are my God's works," English translation by Gili and Tali Gilboa of *"Gedolim Maasei Adonai."* Used by permission of ACUM Ltd., Society of Authors, Composers, and Music Publishers in Israel, and by permission of Gabriella Gilboa.

Leah Goldberg, *"Lamdeni, Elohai."* Hebrew poem reprinted by permission of Hakibbutz Hameuchad, Bnai Brak, Israel. English translation of *"Lamdeni, Elohai"* by Rabbi Jules Harlow, reprinted by permission of Rabbi Jules Harlow and Hakibbutz Hameuchad.

Rabbi Lynn Gottlieb, from "The Fruits of Creation." Excerpt from *Lifecycles Volume 1: Jewish Women on Life Passages & Personal Milestones,* copyright © 1994. Edited by Debra Orenstein (Woodstock, VT: Jewish Lights Publishing). $19.95+$3.75 s/h. Order by mail or call 800-962-4544 or on-line at www.jewish-lights.com. Permission granted by Jewish Lights Publishing, P.O. Box 237, Woodstock, VT 05091.

Rabbi Lynn Gottlieb, from "It's Called a Calling: Interview with Lynn Gottlieb," *Moment* May 1979; adapted by Rabbi Lynn Gottlieb 2002. Copyright © Lynn Gottlieb. Reprinted with the permission of the author.

Rabbi Lynn Gottlieb, "A Psalm in Praise of the *Shekhinah* for Shabbat." From SHE WHO DWELLS WITHIN by LYNN GOTTLIEB. Copyright © 1995 by Lynn Gottlieb. Reprinted by permission of HarperCollins Publishers Inc.

Hayim Gouri, "Prayer," English translation by Rochelle Furstenberg of *"Tefillah."* Used by permission of ACUM Ltd., Society of Authors, Composers, and Music Publishers in Israel, and by permission of Hayim Gouri.

Hayim Gouri, *"Tefillah."* Copyright © Hayim Gouri and ACUM. Reprinted by permission of ACUM Ltd., Society of Authors, Composers, and Music Publishers in Israel, and by permission of Hayim Gouri.

Michal Govrin, excerpts from *Body of Prayer,* a symposium with David Shapiro, Michal Govrin, and Jacques Derrida. Copyright © 2001 by The Irwin S. Chanin School of Architecture Archive of The Cooper Union, and by Michal Govrin. Reprinted by permission.

Michal Govrin, from *The Name,* translated by Barbara Harshav. Reprinted by permission of Riverhead Books.

Rabbi Arthur Green, commentary in *Kol Haneshamah: Shabbat Veḥagim,* 3rd ed. (Wyncote, PA: Reconstructionist Press, 1996). Copyright © Rabbi Arthur Green. Used with permission of Rabbi Arthur Green.

Rabbi Arthur Green and Barry W. Holtz, excerpts from *Your Word is Fire: The Hasidic Masters on Contemplative Prayer* edited and translated by Arthur Green and Barry W. Holtz, published by Paulist Press. Copyright © 1977. Used with permission of Paulist Press. www.paulistpress.com.

Blu Greenberg, excerpt from HOW TO RUN A TRADITIONAL JEWISH HOUSE-HOLD by Blu Greenberg. Copyright © 1989, 1983 by Blu Greenberg. Reprinted by permission of the publisher, Jason Aronson Inc.

Blu Greenberg, excerpt from "Orthodox Feminism and the Next Century." Reprinted with permission from *Sh'ma: A Journal of Jewish Responsibility,* January 2000. For more information visit www.shma.com.

Rabbi Geoffrey J. Haber, prayer from *The Tapestry of Jewish Time: A Spiritual Guide to Holidays and Life-Cycle Events,* edited by Nina Beth Cardin (Behrman House, 2000). Reprinted with permission of Rabbi Haber. Copyright © Behrman House Inc., reprinted with permission. www.behrmanhouse.com.

Tova Hartman-Halbertal with Tamar H. Miller, excerpt from "Our Tradition, Ourselves" in *JOFA: Jewish Orthodox Feminist Alliance Journal,* supplement to the *Jewish Week,* spring 2001. Reprinted with permission of JOFA, the Jewish Orthodox Feminist Alliance.

Rabbi Jules Harlow, translations of Hebrew prayers. From *Siddur Sim Shalom, A Prayerbook for Shabbat, Festivals and Weekdays,* edited with translations by Rabbi Jules Harlow. Copyright © 1985 by The Rabbinical Assembly. Reprinted by permission of The Rabbinical Assembly.

Judith Hauptman, excerpt from *My People's Prayer Book: Traditional Prayers, Modern Commentaries*—Volume 2: The Amidah © 1998 Rabbi Lawrence A. Hoffman, ed. (Woodstock, VT: Jewish Lights Publishing). $23.95+$3.75 s/h. Order by mail or call 800-962-4544 or on-line at www.jewishlights.com. Permission granted by Jewish Lights Publishing, P.O. Box 237, Woodstock, VT 05091.

Abraham Joshua Heschel, "The God of Abraham" from "A Religion of Time" from GOD IN SEARCH OF MAN by Abraham Joshua Heschel. Copyright © 1955 by Abraham Joshua Heschel. Copyright renewed © 1983 by Sylvia Heschel. Reprinted by permission of Farrar, Straus and Giroux, LLC.

Abraham Joshua Heschel, excerpt from "On Prayer." Reprinted with permission from *Conservative Judaism,* volume 25, number 1, Fall 1970, pages 1–13, copyright © the Rabbinical Assembly.

Abraham Joshua Heschel, excerpt from THE SABBATH: ITS MEANING FOR MODERN MAN by Abraham Joshua Heschel. Copyright © 1951 by Abraham Joshua Heschel. Copyright renewed 1979 by Sylvia Heschel. Reprinted by permission of Farrar, Straus and Giroux, LLC.

Rabbi Lawrence A. Hoffman, excerpt from *My People's Prayer Book: Traditional Prayers, Modern Commentaries*—Volume 1: The Sh'ma and Its Blessings © 1997 Rabbi Lawrence A. Hoffman, ed. (Woodstock, VT: Jewish Lights Publishing). $23.95 + $3.75 s/h. Order by mail or call 800-962-4544 or on-line at www.jewishlights.com. Permission granted by Jewish Lights Publishing, P.O. Box 237, Woodstock, VT 05091.

Lawrence A. Hoffman, excerpt from *My People's Prayer Book: Traditional Prayers, Modern Commentaries*—Volume 2: The Amidah, copyright © 1998 Rabbi Lawrence A. Hoffman, ed. (Woodstock, VT: Jewish Lights Publishing). $23.95+$3.75 s/h. Order by mail or call 800-962-4544 or on-line at www.jewish-lights.com. Permission granted by Jewish Lights Publishing, P.O. Box 237, Woodstock, VT 05091.

Rabbi Lawrence A. Hoffman, excerpts from *The Way Into Jewish Prayer,* copyright © 2000 by Rabbi Lawrence A. Hoffman (Woodstock, VT: Jewish Lights Publishing). $21.95 + $3.75 s/h. Order by mail or call 800-962-4544 or on-line at www.jewishlights.com. Permission granted by Jewish Lights Publishing, P.O. Box 237, Woodstock, VT 05091.

Rabbi Margaret Holub, from "A Cosmology of Mourning." Excerpt from *Lifecycles Volume 1: Jewish Women on Life Passages & Personal Milestones,* copyright © 1994 Debra Orenstein, editor (Woodstock, VT: Jewish Lights Publishing). $19.95 + $3.75 s/h. Order by mail or call 800-962-4544 or on-line at www.jewishlights.com. Permission granted by Jewish Lights Publishing, P.O. Box 237, Woodstock, VT 05091.

Rabbi Richard J. Israel, from "How to Survive Your Synagogue." From *The Second Jewish Catalog,* copyright © date 1976, Michael Strassfeld and Sharon Strassfeld, editors, by the Jewish Publication Society, used by permission.

Naomi Janowitz and Maggie Wenig, "Selections from a Prayerbook Where God's Image is Female," *Lilith* 1:4 (Fall/Winter 1977/78). Reprinted with the permission of Rabbi Margaret Moers Wenig. Today, Naomi Janowitz, Ph.D., is professor of Religious Studies at the University of California, Davis. Margaret Moers Wenig is Rabbi Emerita of Beth Am, The People's Temple of New York City.

Rabbi Mordecai M. Kaplan, from *Judaism as a Civilization: Toward a Reconstruction of American-Jewish Life.* Originally published, New York: Macmillan, 1934. Excerpts from *Judaism as a Civilization* by Mordecai Kaplan, copyright © date 1981. Used by permission of The Jewish Publication Society.

A. M. Klein, from *Poems,* copyright date © 1944, Abraham M. Klein, by The Jewish Publication Society, used by permission.

David Klinghoffer, from "A Deeper Understanding of Prayers," *The Jewish Week,* November 23, 2001. Reprinted with the permission of the author. David Klinghoffer's latest book is *The Discovery of God: Abraham and the Birth of Monotheism,* to be published by Doubleday in April 2003.

Tracy Guren Klirs, Ida Cohen Selavan, and Gella Schweid Fishman, translations from Yiddish prayers. From *The Merit of Our Mothers: A Bilingual Anthology of Jewish Women's Prayers,* edited by Tracy Guren Klirs. Copyright © 1992 by the Hebrew Union College Press. Reprinted with the permission of Hebrew Union College Press.

Rivon Krygier, from "The Multiple Meanings of the Mourner's Kaddish." Reprinted with permission from *Conservative Judaism,* volume 54 number 2, Winter 2002, pages 67–68, copyright © the Rabbinical Assembly.

Lawrence Kushner and Nehemia Polen, excerpt from *My People's Prayer Book: Traditional Prayers, Modern Commentaries*—Volume 3: P'sukei D'zimrah © 1999 Rabbi Lawrence A. Hoffman, ed. (Woodstock, VT: Jewish Lights Publishing). $24.95 + $3.75 s/h. Order by mail or call 800-962-4544 or on-line at www.jewishlights.com. Permission granted by Jewish Lights Publishing, P.O. Box 237, Woodstock, VT 05091.

Rabbi Norman Lamm, excerpt from "The Condition of Jewish Belief," a symposium compiled by the editors of *Commentary Magazine,* 1966. Reprinted by permission of Rabbi Norman Lamm.

Rabbi Daniel Landes, excerpt from *My People's Prayer Book: Traditional Prayers, Modern Commentaries*—Volume 3: P'sukei D'zimrah © 1999 Rabbi Lawrence A. Hoffman, ed. (Woodstock, VT: Jewish Lights Publishing). $24.95+$3.75 s/h. Order by mail or call 800-962-4544 or on-line at www.jewishlights.com. Permission granted by Jewish Lights Publishing, P.O. Box 237, Woodstock, VT 05091.

Lee I. Levine, excerpt from *The Ancient Synagogue* published by Yale University Press Copyright © 2000. Used by permission of Yale University Press.

Yael Levine, original Hebrew prayers from *Si'ah Sefatayim*, published by Old City Press of Jerusalem, 2002. Used in translation by permission of Yael Levine.

C. S. Lewis, excerpt from REFLECTIONS ON THE PSALMS, copyright © 1958 by C. S. Lewis PTE Ltd. and renewed 1986 by Arthur Owen Barrfield, reprinted by permission of Harcourt, Inc.

Rabbi Jane Rachel Litman, prayer for Shabbat. Copyright © Jane Rachel Litman. Reprinted with the permission of the author.

Catherine Madsen, excerpt from "Kitsch and Liturgy," first published in *Tikkun,* March/April 2001. Copyright © Catherine Madsen. Reprinted with the permission of the author. Catherine Madsen is a contributing editor to the interreligious journal *CrossCurrents* and the author of a novel, *A Portable Egypt*.

Eyal Megged, "Maariv" English translation by Rochelle Furstenberg of Hebrew original. Used by permission of ACUM Ltd., Society of Authors, Composers, and Music Publishers in Israel, and Eyal Megged.

Eyal Megged, *"Maariv."* Copyright © Eyal Megged and ACUM. Reprinted by permission of ACUM Ltd., Society of Authors, Composers, and Music Publishers in Israel, and by permission of Eyal Megged.

Rabbi Goldie Milgram, "The Mezuzah Story" by Rabbi Goldie Milgram, from her web site, "Reclaiming Judaism as a Spiritual Practice," www.reclaimingjudaism.org. Reprinted with the permission of the author.

Alan Mintz, from "Prayer and the Prayerbook." Reprinted with permission of Simon & Schuster Adult Publishing Group from BACK TO THE SOURCES: READING THE CLASSICAL JEWISH TEXTS, edited by Barry W. Holtz, pages 403–429. Copyright © 1984 by Barry W. Holtz.

Nahariyah Mosenkis, prayer of protest on her son's circumcision. Copyright © Nahariyah Mosenkis. Reprinted with the permission of the author.

Dan Pagis, *"Edut Aheret."* Copyright © estate of Dan Pagis and ACUM. Reprinted by permission of ACUM Ltd., Society of Authors, Composers, and Music Publishers in Israel, and by permission of the estate of Dan Pagis.

Dan Pagis, "Another Testimony" and excerpt from "Testimony," English translation by Warren Bargad and Stanley F. Chyet of *"Edut Aheret"* and *"Edut"* in *Israeli Poetry: A Contemporary Anthology,* edited by Warren Bargad and Stanley F. Chyet. Used by permission of ACUM and the estate of Dan Pagis. Reprinted by permission of Indiana University Press.

Maria Papacostaki and Harry Brod from "Weaning Ceremony." Reprinted from *A Ceremonies Sampler: New Rites, Celebrations, and Observances of Jewish Women,* edited by Elizabeth Levine, published by the Woman's Institute for Continuing Jewish Education of San Diego, California. Reprinted with the permission of Harry Brod.

Marge Piercy, from THE ART OF BLESSING THE DAY by Marge Piercy, copyright © 1999 by Middlemarsh, Inc. Used by permission of Alfred A. Knopf, a division of Random House, Inc.

Chava Pinchas-Cohen, "A Mother's Morning Prayer," English translation by Rabbi Jules Harlow and Rochelle Furstenberg of *"Tefillah La'em Beterem Shaharit."* Used by permission of ACUM Ltd., Society of Authors, Composers, and Music Publishers in Israel, and by permission of Chava Pinchas-Cohen.

Chava Pinchas-Cohen, *"Tefillah La'em Beterem Shaharit."* Copyright © Chava Pinchas-Cohen and ACUM. Reprinted by permission of ACUM Ltd., Society of Authors, Composers, and Music Publishers in Israel, and by permission of Chava Pinchas-Cohen.

Judith Plaskow, excerpts from *My People's Prayer Book: Traditional Prayers, Modern Commentaries*—Volume 1: The Sh'ma and Its Blessings © 1997 Rabbi Lawrence A. Hoffman, ed. (Woodstock, VT: Jewish Lights Publishing). $23.95 + $3.75 s/h. Order by mail or call 800-962-4544 or on-line at www.jewishlights.com. Permission granted by Jewish Lights Publishing, P.O. Box 237, Woodstock, VT 05091.

Rabbi Daniel F. Polish, excerpt from *Bringing the Psalms to Life: How to Understand and Use the Book of Psalms,* copyright © 2000 Daniel F. Polish (Woodstock, VT: Jewish Lights Publishing). $21.95hc/$16.95pb + $3.75 s/h. Order by mail or call 800-962-4544 or on-line at www.jewishlights.com. Permission granted by Jewish Lights Publishing, P.O. Box 237, Woodstock, VT 05091.

Rabbi Marcia Prager, from Cards of *The Weekday Amidah in Guided Imagery.* The text of the blessings is adapted by Rabbi Prager from "Amidah in Movement" by Talia deLone, from *Siddur Or Chadash,* published by P'nai Or, 1989. Copyright © P'nai Or Religious Fellowship. The *Amidah* meditation cards can be purchased by sending a check for $25 to Rabbi Marcia Prager, 228 West Hortter Street, Philadelphia, PA 19119. Reprinted with the permission of Rabbi Marcia Prager.

Esther Raab, "Prayer," English translation by Ann Lapidus Lerner of *"Tefillah"* (from the collection *"Gehinnom"*) in Ann Lapidus Lerner, "A Woman's Song: The Poetry of Esther Raab," *Gender and Text in Modern Hebrew and Yiddish Literature,* edited by Naomi B. Sokoloff, Anne Lapidus Lerner, and Anita Norich. Copyright © 1992. Reprinted by permission of the Jewish Theological Seminary of America. The translation of *"Tefillah"* by Esther Raab is used by permission of ACUM Ltd., Society of Authors, Composers, and Music Publishers in Israel, and by permission of Ehud Ben-Ezer. *"Tefillah"* is included in the book *Esther Raab, Collected Prose* (Israel: Astrolog Publlishers, 2001).

Esther Raab, *"Shirat Ishah."* Copyright © estate of Esther Raab and ACUM. Reprinted by permission of ACUM Ltd., Society of Authors, Composers, and Music Publishers in Israel, and by permission of Ehud Ben-Ezer.

Esther Raab, "Woman's Song," English translation by Harold Schimmel of *"Shirat Ishah."* © Copyright in the original Hebrew version ACUM and Ehud Ben-Ezer. English translation ©copyright the Institute for the Translation of Hebrew Literature.

Stefan Reif, excerpt from *Judaism and Hebrew Prayer: New Perspectives on Jewish Liturgical History*. Copyright © 1993 by Cambridge University Press, Great Britain. Reprinted with the permission of Cambridge University Press.

Rabbi Paula Reimers, from "The Problems of Feminine God Language," *United Synagogue Review,* Spring 1994. Reprinted with permission of Rabbi Paula Reimers and the United Synagogue of Conservative Judaism. The United Synagogue of Conservative Judaism promotes the role of the synagogue in Jewish life in order to motivate Conservative Jews to perform *mitzvot* encompassing ethical behavior, spirituality, Judaic learning, and ritual observance.

Rabbi Paula Reimers, comment on page xvi. Copyright © 2003 by Paula Reimers.

Steven Sager, commentary in *Kol Haneshamah: Shabbat Vehagim,* The Reconstructionist Press, 7804 Montgomery Ave, Suite #9, Elkins Park, PA 19027-2649 e-mail press@jrf.org. Reprinted with permission from the Reconstructionist Press.

Rabbi Nosson Scherman, commentary on "Blessings." Reproduced from *The ArtScroll Siddur: Weekday/Sabbath/Festival* with translation and commentary by Rabbi Nosson Scherman, with permission from the copyright holders ARTSCROLL/MESORAH PUBLICATIONS, LTD. Copyright © Mesorah Publications, Ltd.

Susan Weidman Schneider, excerpts from *Jewish and Female: A Guide and Sourcebook for Today's Jewish Woman.* Copyright © by Susan Weidman Schneider. Reprinted by permission of the author. Susan Weidman Schneider is editor of *Lilith,* the award-winning independent Jewish women's magazine. *Lilith* can be reached at 800-783-4903 or 212-757-0818, by email at LilithMag@aol.com, or by mail at 250 West 57 Street, Suite 2432, New York, NY 10107.

Rabbi Burt E. Schuman, from "Synagogue: Driving Miss Daisy Crazy." Excerpted with permission from the Winter 2001 issue of *Reform Judaism* magazine, published by the Union of American Hebrew Congregations. Reprinted with the permission of Rabbi Burt E. Schuman.

Rabbi Benjamin Edidin Scolnic, excerpt from *"Na'aseh Ve-nakriv:* Prayer, Sacrifice, and the Meaning of Ritual." Reprinted with permission from *Conservative Judaism*, volume 37, number 4, Summer 1984, pages 31–33, copyright © the Rabbinical Assembly.

Eliezer Segal, excerpt from "From the Sources: Vanity, Emptiness and the Throne of Glory," *Jewish Free Press* (Calgary), September 28, 2000. Reprinted with the permission of Eliezer Segal.

Ruth Seldin, excerpt from "Women in the Synagogue: A Congregant's View." Reprinted with permission from *Conservative Judaism*, volume 32, number 2, Winter 1979, pages 80–88, copyright © the Rabbinical Assembly.

Hannah Senesh, "Going to Caesarea," English translation by Eitan Senesh and Rochelle Furstenberg of *"Halikah Lekaisaryah."* Used by permission of ACUM Ltd., Society of Authors, Composers, and Music Publishers in Israel, and by permission of Eitan Senesh.

Hannah Senesh, *"Halikah Lekaisaryah."* Copyright © Eitan Senesh and ACUM. Reprinted by permission of ACUM Ltd., Society of Authors, Composers, and Music Publishers in Israel, and by permission of Eitan Senesh.

Alice Shalvi, "A Techine for Yom Kippur." Copyright © by Alice Shalvi. Reprinted with the permission of the author.

Rabbi Judy Shanks, from "Ask The Rabbi." Excerpted with permission from the Winter 2000 issue of *Reform Judaism* magazine, published by the Union of American Hebrew Congregations. Reprinted with the permission of Rabbi Judy Shanks.

Abraham Shlonsky, *"[Amal]."* Copyright © estate of Abraham Shlonsky and ACUM. Reprinted by permission of ACUM Ltd., Society of Authors, Composers, and Music Publishers in Israel, and by permission of the estate of Abraham Shlonsky.

Abraham Shlonsky, "[Toil]" an English translation by T. Carmi of *"[Amal]."* Used by permission of ACUM Ltd., Society of Authors, Composers, and Music Publishers in Israel, and by permission of estate of Abraham Shlonsky. Translation by T. Carmi, from *The Penguin Book of Hebrew Verse*, edited by T. Carmi, first published in Great Britain by Allen Lane and Penguin Books, 1981, page 534. Copyright © T. Carmi, 1981. Reproduced by permission of Penguin Books Ltd.

Rachel Josefowitz Siegel, Amy Sheldon, Nina Judith Katz, "Hanukah Blessings." Copyright © 2001. Reprinted with the permission of the authors.

Henry Slonimsky, excerpt from *Essays* (Cincinnati/Chicago: Hebrew Union College Press/Quadrangle, 1967). Reprinted with the permission of Hebrew Union College Press.

Reena Spicehandler, commentary in *Kol Haneshamah Limot Hol, Daily Prayerbook,* The Reconstructionist Press, 7804 Montgomery Ave, Suite #9, Elkins Park, PA 19027-2649 e-mail press@jrf.org. Reprinted with permission from the Reconstructionist Press.

Rabbi Adin Steinsaltz, excerpts from *A Guide to Jewish Prayer* by Rabbi Adin Steinsaltz, copyright © 2000 by Israel Institute for Talmudic Publications. Used by permission of Schocken Books, a division of Random House, Inc.

Michael Swartz, excerpt from "Models for New Prayer," *Response*, Fall-Winter 1982. Reprinted with the permission of the author. Michael Swartz is a professor of Jewish Studies at Ohio State University.

Henrietta Szold, excerpt from a letter. From HENRIETTA SZOLD: LIFE AND LETTERS by Marvin Lowenthal, copyright 1942 The Viking Press, renewed © 1970 by Harold C. Emer and Harry L. Shapiro, Executors of the Estate. Used by permission of Viking Penguin, a division of Penguin Putnam Inc.

Norman Tarnor, translations from Yiddish prayers. From A BOOK OF JEWISH WOMEN'S PRAYERS. Translations from the Yiddish. Selected and with commentary by Norman Tarnor. Copyright © 1995 by Norman Tarnor. Excerpt from page 28. Reprinted by permission of Jason Aronson Inc.

Rabbi Joseph Telushkin, excerpt on pages 505-6 from JEWISH LITERACY by Rabbi Joseph Telushkin. Copyright © 1991 by RABBI JOSEPH TELUSHKIN. Reprinted by permission of HarperCollins Publishers Inc.

Rabbi Arthur Waskow, commentary on prayer. Copyright © 2001 by Arthur Waskow. See Rabbi Waskow's writings on prayer, Torah, and *tikkun olam* on the web site of The Shalom Center, www.shalomctr.org, and in his books *Seasons of Our Joy* (Beacon); *Godwrestling—Round 2* (Jewish Lights Publishing); and, with Phyllis Berman, *A Time for Every Purpose Under Heaven: The Jewish Life-Spiral as a Spiritual Path* (Farrar, Straus and Giroux).

Sheila Peltz Weinberg, "Blessings for the New Moon and New Year," in Penina V. Adelman, *Miriam's Well: Rituals for Jewish Women Around the Year,* 2nd edition. (New York: Biblio, 1996). Copyright © Sheila Peltz Weinberg. Reprinted with the permission of the author.

Dvora E. Weisberg, from "On Wearing *Tallit* and *Tefillin*." From *Daughters of the King: Women and the Synagogue*, copyright © date 1992, Susan Grossman and Rikva Haut, editors, by the Jewish Publication Society, used by permission.

Chava Weissler, excerpts from *Voices of the Matriarchs* by Chava Weissler. Copyright © 1998 by Chava Weissler. Reprinted by permission of Beacon Press, Boston.

Rabbi David J. Wolpe, excerpt from *Why Be Jewish?* Copyright © 1995 by David J. Wolpe. Reprinted by permission of Henry Holt and Company.

Zelda, *"Beshaah Mehurheret Zo."* Copyright © ACUM and the estate of Zelda (Mishkovsky). Reprinted by permission of ACUM Ltd., Society of Authors, Composers, and Music Publishers in Israel, and by permission of the estate of Zelda (Mishkovsky).

Zelda, "In This Moment of Reflection," English translation by Rabbi Jules Harlow and Rochelle Furstenberg and Jules Harlow of *"Beshaah Mehurheret Zo."* Used by permission of ACUM Ltd., Society of Authors, Composers, and Music Publishers in Israel, and by permission of the estate of Zelda (Mishkovsky).

Every reasonable effort has been made to trace the owners of copyrighted materials that are reprinted in this book, but in some instances this has been impossible. Hadassah, the Women's Zionist Organization of America, will be glad to receive information leading to more complete acknowledgments in subsequent printings of the book and in the meantime extends sincere apologies for any omissions.

About Hadassah

Hadassah, the Women's Zionist Organization of America, is dedicated to enhancing the quality of American Jewish life, to improving health care in Israel, and to forging stronger connections between America and Israel. Founded by Henrietta Szold in 1912, Hadassah continues to follow her exhortation: "Dream great dreams, and then take practical steps to make them a reality."

Hadassah's work ranges from international projects to individual enrichment, from the founding and maintaining of state-of-the-art hospitals in Israel to organizing adult bat mitzvah ceremonies throughout the United States.

Hadassah is the largest Zionist organization and the largest women's organization in America. Its more than 300,000 members come from all walks of American Jewish life to participate in Hadassah's programs. Examples of the educational programs include Hebrew classes, adult study groups on Jewish themes, preparation for adult bat mitzvah ceremonies, Jewish family education programs, and Zionist youth groups. Hadassah also works to increase health awareness and to advocate for political change on issues of importance to American Jewish women.

Hadassah's publications include an award-winning monthly magazine, *Hadassah Magazine,* that deals with a broad variety of topics of concern to the American Jewish community. Hadassah also publishes educational books and the curricula for its educational programs.

Through its diverse programs, Hadassah encourages members to strengthen their partnership with Israel, enhance their own Jewish commitment, and realize their potential as a dynamic force in American society.

ADDITIONAL HADASSAH PUBLICATIONS

True to its roots as a study circle, Hadassah encourages its members to explore the many facets of Jewish history and culture, and, to aid members in doing so, the National Jewish Education Department publishes study guides and other resources on a wide variety of topics. Unless indicated otherwise, for purchase, call the National Hadassah Order Department at 1-800-880-9455.

Moonbeams: A Hadassah Rosh Ḥodesh Guide

Leora Tanenbaum, Claudia R. Chernov, and Hadassah Tropper; edited by Carol Diament
Course of study for a woman's monthly Rosh Ḥodesh (Festival of the New Moon) group. Included are extensive Biblical and Talmudic passages, Rabbinic commentaries, and modern works discussing issues and conflicts crucial to the Jewish woman today. Order #R989. $15 Hadassah members, $20 non-members.

Jewish Women Living the Challenge: A Hadassah Compendium

Carol Diament, editor; programming ideas by Claudia R. Chernov and Leora Tanenbaum
Collection of essays on Jewish women's issues, with extensive programming ideas. Order #R797. $15 Hadassah members, $20 non-members.

Ribcage: Israeli Women's Fiction

Carol Diament and Lily Rattok, editors
Study guide contains short stories in English translation. Order #R492. $10 Hadassah members, $15 non-members.

Judaism and Ecology

Carol Diament, editor

Study guide on Jewish environmental values.
Order #R229. $7 Hadassah members,
$11 non-members.

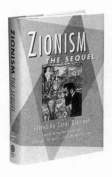

Zionism: The Sequel

Carol Diament, editor

Essays on the meanings of contemporary Zionism.
Part I, "The Israel-Diaspora Debate," introduced by
Gideon Shimoni, analyzes the relationship of diaspora
Jews to the State of Israel. Part II, "Zionism For and
Against Itself," introduced by Arnold Eisen, presents
personal statements from Israeli and American Jewish
thinkers—from the extreme Right to the extreme Left,
from the secular to the ultra-Orthodox, and more.
Order #R795. $18 Hadassah members,
$25 non-members

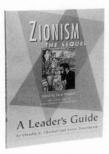

Zionism: The Sequel: A Leader's Guide

Claudia Chernov and Leora Tanenbaum

The *Leader's Guide* to *Zionism: The Sequel* provides
step-by-step instructions for leading a year-long study
group. Order #R915. $10.

Israeli and American Jews: Understanding and Misunderstanding

Carol Diament, editor

Study guide addresses the seemingly irreconcilable
differences between the two leading Jewish populations
of the world. Order #R222. $8 Hadassah members,
$12 non-members.

An American Zionist Tapestry

Lawrence Grossman

Study guide on the leaders of American Zionism. Order #R252. $4 Hadassah members, $6 non-members.

A Zionist Tapestry

Monty Penkower

Study guide presents the major thinkers and ideas of Zionism and their implications for contemporary Zionist thought and action. Order #R251. $4 Hadassah members, $6 non-members.

Images of Jerusalem: City of David in Modern Hebrew Literature

Rochelle Furstenberg

Study guide in honor of the 3000th anniversary of Jerusalem as the capital of the Jewish people. Order #R613. $10 Hadassah members, $13 non-members.

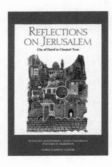

Reflections on Jerusalem: City of David in Classical Texts

N. Rothenberg, L. Tanenbaum, and S. Silverman

Study guide in honor of the 3000th anniversary of Jerusalem as the capital of the Jewish people. Order #R614. $6 Hadassah members, $9 non-members.

Understanding the Holocaust: How It Happened

Jack Wertheimer

Study unit focuses on the Holocaust itself and on the factors that permitted this tragedy to occur. Order #R221. $2 Hadassah members, $3 non-members.

The Talmud and You

Aaron Kirschenbaum

Two-book series on the Talmud's relevance to daily life. Order #R232 for Book 1 (Units I and II) and #R233 for Book 2 (Units III and IV). Each book $2 Hadassah members, $3 non-members.

Leader's Guide to the Book of Samuel

Naomi Sarlin

The first study guide in Hadassah's Bible series. Order #R199. $1.50 Hadassah members, $2.50 non-members.

Leader's Guide to the Book of Jeremiah

Aaron Kirschenbaum

Study the prophetic tradition in Judaism. Order #R197. $3 Hadassah members, $5 non-members.

Leader's Guide to the Book of Psalms

Nehama Leibowitz

Study one of Judaism's most beloved texts with our era's great Bible scholar. Order #R198. $3 Hadassah members, $5 non-members.

Jewish Marital Status

Carol Diament, editor

Anthology of essays offering Jewish viewpoints on dating, sex, intimate relationships, marriage, and the end of marriage. Special price $25. Call Hadassah National Jewish Education Department at 1-212-303-8167.

A Companion Guide to Jewish Marital Status

Ellen Singer

Programming and activities on *Jewish Marital Status.* Order #R226. $3 Hadassah members, $5 non-members.

About JEWISH LIGHTS Publishing

People of all faiths and backgrounds yearn for books that attract, engage, educate, and spiritually inspire.

Our principal goal is to stimulate thought and help all people learn about who the Jewish People are, where they come from, and what the future can be made to hold. While people of our diverse Jewish heritage are the primary audience, our books speak to people in the Christian world as well and will broaden their understanding of Judaism and the roots of their own faith.

We bring to you authors who are at the forefront of spiritual thought and experience. While each has something different to say, they all say it in a voice that you can hear.

Our books are designed to welcome you and then to engage, stimulate, and inspire. We judge our success not only by whether or not our books are beautiful and commercially successful, but by whether or not they make a difference in your life.

We at Jewish Lights take great care to produce beautiful books that present meaningful spiritual content in a form that reflects the art of making high quality books. Therefore, we want to acknowledge those who contributed to the production of this book.

Stuart M. Matlins, Publisher

PRODUCTION
Sara Dismukes, Tim Holtz,
Martha McKinney & Bridgett Taylor

EDITORIAL
Rebecca Castellano, Amanda Dupuis, Polly Short Mahoney,
Lauren Seidman & Emily Wichland

COVER / TEXT PRINTING & BINDING
Versa Press, East Peoria, Illinois

AVAILABLE FROM BETTER BOOKSTORES.
TRY YOUR BOOKSTORE FIRST.

The Way Into... Series

A major multi-volume series to be completed over the next several years, **The Way Into... provides an accessible and usable "guided tour" of the Jewish faith, its people, its history and beliefs—in total, an introduction to Judaism for adults that will enable them to understand and interact with sacred texts.** Each volume is written by a major modern scholar and teacher, and is organized around an important concept of Judaism.

The Way Into... will enable all readers to achieve a real sense of Jewish cultural literacy through guided study. Available volumes:

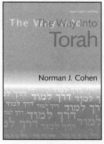  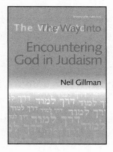 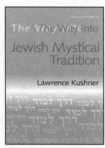

The Way Into Torah
by *Dr. Norman J. Cohen*

What is "Torah"? What are the different approaches to studying Torah? What are the different levels of understanding Torah? For whom is study intended? Explores the origins and development of Torah, why it should be studied and how to do it. An easy-to-use, easy-to-understand introduction to an ancient subject.
6 x 9, 176 pp, HC, ISBN 1-58023-028-8 **$21.95**

The Way Into Jewish Prayer
by *Dr. Lawrence A. Hoffman*

Opens the door to 3,000 years of the Jewish way to God by making available all you need to feel at home in Jewish worship. Provides basic definitions of the terms you need to know as well as thoughtful analysis of the depth that lies beneath Jewish prayer.
6 x 9, 224 pp, HC, ISBN 1-58023-027-X **$21.95**

The Way Into Encountering God in Judaism
by *Dr. Neil Gillman*

Explains how Jews have encountered God throughout history—and today—by exploring the many metaphors for God in Jewish tradition. Explores the Jewish tradition's passionate but also conflicting ways of relating to God as Creator, relational partner, and a force in history and nature.
6 x 9, 240 pp, HC, ISBN 1-58023-025-3 **$21.95**

The Way Into Jewish Mystical Tradition
by *Rabbi Lawrence Kushner*

Explains the principles of Jewish mystical thinking, their religious and spiritual significance, and how they relate to our lives. A book that allows us to experience and understand the Jewish mystical approach to our place in the world.
6 x 9, 224 pp, HC, ISBN 1-58023-029-6 **$21.95**

Or phone, fax, mail or e-mail to: **JEWISH LIGHTS Publishing**
Sunset Farm Offices, Route 4 • P.O. Box 237 • Woodstock, Vermont 05091
Tel: (802) 457-4000 • Fax: (802) 457-4004 • www.jewishlights.com
Credit card orders: (800) 962-4544 (8:30AM–5:30PM ET Monday–Friday)
Generous discounts on quantity orders. SATISFACTION GUARANTEED. Prices subject to change.

Jewish Meditation

Aleph-Bet Yoga
Embodying the Hebrew Letters for Physical and Spiritual Well-Being
by *Steven A. Rapp*; Foreword by *Tamar Frankiel & Judy Greenfeld*; Preface by *Hart Lazer*

Blends aspects of hatha yoga and the shapes of the Hebrew letters. Connects yoga practice with Jewish spiritual life. Easy-to-follow instructions, b/w photos.
7 x 10, 128 pp, Quality PB, b/w photos, ISBN 1-58023-162-4 **$16.95**

The Rituals & Practices of a Jewish Life
A Handbook for Personal Spiritual Renewal
by *Rabbi Kerry M. Olitzky* and *Rabbi Daniel Judson*; Foreword by *Vanessa L. Ochs*; Illustrated by *Joel Moskowitz*

This easy-to-use handbook explains the why, what, and how of ten specific areas of Jewish ritual and practice: morning and evening blessings, covering the head, blessings throughout the day, daily prayer, tefillin, tallit and *tallit katan*, Torah study, kashrut, *mikvah*, and entering Shabbat. 6 x 9, 272 pp, Quality PB, Illus., ISBN 1-58023-169-1 **$18.95**

Discovering Jewish Meditation: *Instruction & Guidance for Learning an Ancient Spiritual Practice* by Nan Fink Gefen 6 x 9, 208 pp, Quality PB, ISBN 1-58023-067-9 **$16.95**

The Handbook of Jewish Meditation Practices: *A Guide for Enriching the Sabbath and Other Days of Your Life* by Rabbi David A. Cooper
6 x 9, 208 pp, Quality PB, ISBN 1-58023-102-0 **$16.95**

Meditation from the Heart of Judaism: *Today's Teachers Share Their Practices, Techniques, and Faith* Ed. by Avram Davis 6 x 9, 256 pp, Quality PB, ISBN 1-58023-049-0 **$16.95**

The Way of Flame: *A Guide to the Forgotten Mystical Tradition of Jewish Meditation* by Avram Davis 4½ x 8, 176 pp, Quality PB, ISBN 1-58023-060-1 **$15.95**

Minding the Temple of the Soul: *Balancing Body, Mind, and Spirit through Traditional Jewish Prayer, Movement, and Meditation* by Tamar Frankiel and Judy Greenfeld
7 x 10, 184 pp, Quality PB, Illus., ISBN 1-879045-64-8 **$16.95**

Entering the Temple of Dreams: *Jewish Prayers, Movements, and Meditations for the End of the Day* by Tamar Frankiel and Judy Greenfeld
7 x 10, 192 pp, Illus., Quality PB, ISBN 1-58023-079-2 **$16.95**

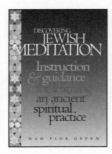 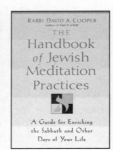  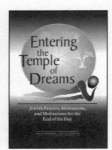 

Ecology

Torah of the Earth: *Exploring 4,000 Years of Ecology in Jewish Thought*
In 2 Volumes Ed. by *Rabbi Arthur Waskow*

An invaluable key to understanding the intersection of ecology and Judaism. Leading scholars provide a guided tour of Jewish ecological thought.
Vol. 1: *Biblical Israel & Rabbinic Judaism*, 6 x 9, 272 pp, Quality PB, ISBN 1-58023-086-5 **$19.95**
Vol. 2: *Zionism & Eco-Judaism*, 6 x 9, 336 pp, Quality PB, ISBN 1-58023-087-3 **$19.95**

Ecology & the Jewish Spirit: *Where Nature & the Sacred Meet* Ed. and with Intros.
by Ellen Bernstein 6 x 9, 288 pp, Quality PB, ISBN 1-58023-082-2 **$16.95**

Healing/Wellness/Recovery

Jewish Paths toward Healing and Wholeness
A Personal Guide to Dealing with Suffering
by *Rabbi Kerry M. Olitzky*; Foreword by *Debbie Friedman*

Why me? Why do we suffer? How can we heal? Grounded in personal experience with illness and Jewish spiritual traditions, this book provides healing rituals, psalms and prayers that help readers initiate a dialogue with God, to guide them along the complicated path of healing and wholeness. 6 x 9, 192 pp, Quality PB, ISBN 1-58023-068-7 **$15.95**

Healing of Soul, Healing of Body
Spiritual Leaders Unfold the Strength & Solace in Psalms
Ed. by *Rabbi Simkha Y. Weintraub, CSW*, for The National Center for Jewish Healing

For those who are facing illness and those who care for them. Inspiring commentaries on ten psalms for healing by eminent spiritual leaders reflecting all Jewish movements make the power of the psalms accessible to all.
6 x 9, 128 pp, Quality PB, Illus., 2-color text, ISBN 1-879045-31-1 **$14.95**

Jewish Pastoral Care
A Practical Handbook from Traditional and Contemporary Sources
Ed. by *Rabbi Dayle A. Friedman*

Gives today's Jewish pastoral counselors practical guidelines based in the Jewish tradition.
6 x 9, 464 pp, HC, ISBN 1-58023-078-4 **$35.00**

Twelve Jewish Steps to Recovery: *A Personal Guide to Turning from Alcoholism & Other Addictions—Drugs, Food, Gambling, Sex . . .* by Rabbi Kerry M. Olitzky & Stuart A. Copans, M.D. Preface by Abraham J. Twerski, M.D.; "Getting Help" by JACS Foundation 6 x 9, 144 pp, Quality PB, ISBN 1-879045-09-5 **$14.95**

One Hundred Blessings Every Day: *Daily Twelve Step Recovery Affirmations, Exercises for Personal Growth & Renewal Reflecting Seasons of the Jewish Year*
by Rabbi Kerry M. Olitzky 4½ x 6½, 432 pp, Quality PB, ISBN 1-879045-30-3 **$14.95**

Recovery from Codependence: *A Jewish Twelve Steps Guide to Healing Your Soul*
by Rabbi Kerry M. Olitzky 6 x 9, 160 pp, Quality PB, ISBN 1-879045-32-X **$13.95**

Renewed Each Day: *Daily Twelve Step Recovery Meditations Based on the Bible*
by Rabbi Kerry M. Olitzky & Aaron Z. *Vol. I: Genesis & Exodus*; *Vol. II: Leviticus, Numbers and Deuteronomy*
Vol. I: 6 x 9, 224 pp, Quality PB, ISBN 1-879045-12-5 **$14.95**
Vol. II: 6 x 9, 280 pp, Quality PB, ISBN 1-879045-13-3 **$14.95**

Children's Spirituality

ENDORSED BY CATHOLIC, PROTESTANT, AND JEWISH RELIGIOUS LEADERS
MULTICULTURAL, NONDENOMINATIONAL, NONSECTARIAN

Cain & Abel   AWARD WINNER!
Finding the Fruits of Peace
by *Sandy Eisenberg Sasso*
Full-color illus. by *Joani Keller Rothenberg*

For ages 5 & up

A sensitive recasting of the ancient tale shows we have the power to deal with anger in positive ways. Provides questions for kids and adults to explore together. "Editor's Choice"—American Library Association's *Booklist*

9 x 12, 32 pp, HC, Full-color illus., ISBN 1-58023-123-3   **$16.95**

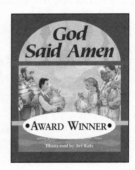

For Heaven's Sake   AWARD WINNER!
by *Sandy Eisenberg Sasso*; Full-color illus. by *Kathryn Kunz Finney*

For ages 4 & up

Everyone talked about heaven, but no one would say what heaven was or how to find it. So Isaiah decides to find out.   9 x 12, 32 pp, HC, Full-color illus., ISBN 1-58023-054-7   **$16.95**

God Said Amen   AWARD WINNER!
by *Sandy Eisenberg Sasso*; Full-color illus. by *Avi Katz*

For ages 4 & up

Inspiring tale of two kingdoms: one overflowing with water but without oil to light its lamps; the other blessed with oil but no water to grow its gardens. The kingdoms' rulers ask God for help but are too stubborn to ask each other. Shows that we need only reach out to each other to find God's answer to our prayers.   9 x 12, 32 pp, HC, Full-color illus., ISBN 1-58023-080-6   **$16.95**

God in Between   AWARD WINNER!
by *Sandy Eisenberg Sasso*; Full-color illus. by *Sally Sweetland*

For ages 4 & up

If you wanted to find God, where would you look? This magical, mythical tale teaches that God can be found where we are: within all of us and the relationships between us.
9 x 12, 32 pp, HC, Full-color illus., ISBN 1-879045-86-9   **$16.95**

Noah's Wife: *The Story of Naamah*
by *Sandy Eisenberg Sasso*; Full-color illus. by *Bethanne Andersen*   AWARD WINNER!

For ages 4 & up

Opens religious imaginations to new ideas about the story of the Flood. When God tells Noah to bring the animals onto the ark, God also calls on Naamah, Noah's wife, to save each plant on Earth.   9 x 12, 32 pp, HC, Full-color illus., ISBN 1-58023-134-9   **$16.95**

But God Remembered   AWARD WINNER!
Stories of Women from Creation to the Promised Land
by *Sandy Eisenberg Sasso*; Full-color illus. by *Bethanne Andersen*

For ages 8 & up

Vibrantly brings to life four stories of courageous and strong women from ancient tradition; all teach important values through their actions and faith.
9 x 12, 32 pp, HC, Full-color illus., ISBN 1-879045-43-5   **$16.95**

Children's Spirituality

ENDORSED BY CATHOLIC, PROTESTANT, AND JEWISH RELIGIOUS LEADERS
MULTICULTURAL, NONDENOMINATIONAL, NONSECTARIAN

In Our Image
God's First Creatures AWARD WINNER!
by *Nancy Sohn Swartz*
Full-color illus. by *Melanie Hall*

(For ages 4 & up)

A playful new twist on the Creation story—from the perspective of the animals. Celebrates the interconnectedness of nature and the harmony of all living things. "The vibrantly colored illustrations nearly leap off the page in this delightful interpretation." —*School Library Journal*
9 x 12, 32 pp, HC, Full-color illus., ISBN 1-879045-99-0 **$16.95**

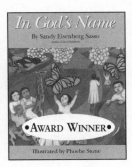

God's Paintbrush AWARD WINNER!
by *Sandy Eisenberg Sasso*; Full-color illus. by *Annette Compton*

(For ages 4 & up)

Invites children of all faiths and backgrounds to encounter God openly in their own lives. Wonderfully interactive; provides questions adult and child can explore together at the end of each episode. 11 x 8½, 32 pp, HC, Full-color illus., ISBN 1-879045-22-2 **$16.95**

Also available: **A Teacher's Guide: A Guide for Jewish & Christian Educators and Parents**
8½ x 11, 32 pp, PB, ISBN 1-879045-57-5 **$8.95**

God's Paintbrush Celebration Kit 9½ x 12, HC, Includes 5 sessions/40 full-color Activity Sheets and Teacher Folder with complete instructions, ISBN 1-58023-050-4 **$21.95**

In God's Name AWARD WINNER!
by *Sandy Eisenberg Sasso*; Full-color illus. by *Phoebe Stone*

(For ages 4 & up)

Like an ancient myth in its poetic text and vibrant illustrations, this award-winning modern fable about the search for God's name celebrates the diversity and, at the same time, the unity of all people. 9 x 12, 32 pp, HC, Full-color illus., ISBN 1-879045-26-5 **$16.95**

What Is God's Name? (A Board Book)

(For ages 0–4)

An abridged board book version of award-winning *In God's Name.*
5 x 5, 24 pp, Board, Full-color illus., ISBN 1-893361-10-1 **$7.95** A SKYLIGHT PATHS Book

The 11th Commandment: *Wisdom from Our Children*
by *The Children of America* AWARD WINNER!

(For all ages)

"If there were an Eleventh Commandment, what would it be?" Children of many religious denominations across America answer this question—in their own drawings and words. "A rare book of spiritual celebration for all people, of all ages, for all time."—*Bookviews*
8 x 10, 48 pp, HC, Full-color illus., ISBN 1-879045-46-X **$16.95**

Children's Spirituality

ENDORSED BY CATHOLIC, PROTESTANT, AND JEWISH RELIGIOUS LEADERS

Because Nothing Looks Like God

by *Lawrence and Karen Kushner*
Full-color illus. by *Dawn W. Majewski*

For ages
4 & up

MULTICULTURAL, NONDENOMINATIONAL, NONSECTARIAN

What is God like? The first collaborative work by husband-and-wife team Lawrence and Karen Kushner introduces children to the possibilities of spiritual life. Real-life examples of happiness and sadness—from goodnight stories, to the hope and fear felt the first time at bat, to the closing moments of life—invite us to explore, together with our children, the questions we all have about God, no matter what our age.

11 x 8½, 32 pp, HC, Full-color illus., ISBN 1-58023-092-X **$16.95**

*Also available: **Teacher's Guide**, 8½ x 11, 22 pp, PB, ISBN 1-58023-140-3 **$6.95** For ages 5–8*

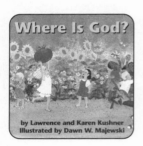

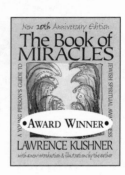

Where Is God?
What Does God Look Like?
How Does God Make Things Happen? (Board Books)

For ages
0–4

by *Lawrence and Karen Kushner*; Full-color illus. by *Dawn W. Majewski*

Gently invites children to become aware of God's presence all around them. Three board books abridged from *Because Nothing Looks Like God* by Lawrence and Karen Kushner.
Each 5 x 5, 24 pp, Board, Full-color illus. **$7.95** SKYLIGHT PATHS Books

Sharing Blessings
Children's Stories for Exploring the Spirit of the Jewish Holidays

For ages
6 & up

by *Rahel Musleah* and *Rabbi Michael Klayman*; Full-color illus.

What is the spiritual message of each of the Jewish holidays? How do we teach it to our children? Through stories about one family's life, *Sharing Blessings* explores ways to get into the *spirit* of thirteen different holidays.
8½ x 11, 64 pp, HC, Full-color illus., ISBN 1-879045-71-0 **$18.95**

The Book of Miracles   AWARD WINNER!
A Young Person's Guide to Jewish Spiritual Awareness

For ages
9 & up

by *Lawrence Kushner*

Introduces kids to a way of everyday spiritual thinking to last a lifetime. Kushner, whose award-winning books have brought spirituality to life for countless adults, now shows young people how to use Judaism as a foundation on which to build their lives.
6 x 9, 96 pp, HC, 2-color illus., ISBN 1-879045-78-8 **$16.95**

Life Cycle & Holidays

The Jewish Family Fun Book: *Holiday Projects, Everyday Activities, and Travel Ideas with Jewish Themes*
by *Danielle Dardashti* & *Roni Sarig*; Illustrated by *Avi Katz*

With almost 100 easy-to-do activities to re-invigorate age-old Jewish customs and make them fun for the whole family, this complete sourcebook details activities for fun at home and away from home, including meaningful everyday and holiday crafts, recipes, travel guides, enriching entertainment and much, much more. Illustrated.
6 x 9, 288 pp, Quality PB, Illus., ISBN 1-58023-171-3 **$18.95**

The Book of Jewish Sacred Practices
CLAL's Guide to Everyday & Holiday Rituals & Blessings
Ed. by *Rabbi Irwin Kula* & *Vanessa L. Ochs, Ph.D.*

A meditation, blessing, profound Jewish teaching, and ritual for more than one hundred everyday events and holidays. 6 x 9, 368 pp, Quality PB, ISBN 1-58023-152-7 **$18.95**

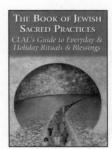  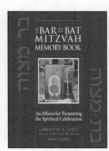  

Celebrating Your New Jewish Daughter: *Creating Jewish Ways to Welcome Baby Girls into the Covenant—New and Traditional Ceremonies*
by Debra Nussbaum Cohen; Foreword by Rabbi Sandy Eisenberg Sasso
6 x 9, 272 pp, Quality PB, ISBN 1-58023-090-3 **$18.95**

The New Jewish Baby Book AWARD WINNER!
Names, Ceremonies & Customs—A Guide for Today's Families
by Anita Diamant 6 x 9, 336 pp, Quality PB, ISBN 1-879045-28-1 **$18.95**

Parenting As a Spiritual Journey
Deepening Ordinary & Extraordinary Events into Sacred Occasions
by Rabbi Nancy Fuchs-Kreimer 6 x 9, 224 pp, Quality PB, ISBN 1-58023-016-4 **$16.95**

Putting God on the Guest List, 2nd Ed. AWARD WINNER!
How to Reclaim the Spiritual Meaning of Your Child's Bar or Bat Mitzvah
by Rabbi Jeffrey K. Salkin 6 x 9, 224 pp, Quality PB, ISBN 1-879045-59-1 **$16.95**

The Bar/Bat Mitzvah Memory Book: *An Album for Treasuring the Spiritual Celebration* by Rabbi Jeffrey K. Salkin and Nina Salkin
8 x 10, 48 pp, Deluxe HC, 2-color text, ribbon marker, ISBN 1-58023-111-X **$19.95**

For Kids—Putting God on Your Guest List
How to Claim the Spiritual Meaning of Your Bar or Bat Mitzvah
by Rabbi Jeffrey K. Salkin 6 x 9, 144 pp, Quality PB, ISBN 1-58023-015-6 **$14.95**

Bar/Bat Mitzvah Basics, 2nd Ed.: *A Practical Family Guide to Coming of Age Together*
Ed. by Cantor Helen Leneman 6 x 9, 240 pp, Quality PB, ISBN 1-58023-151-9 **$18.95**

Hanukkah, 2nd Ed.: *The Family Guide to Spiritual Celebration*—The Art of Jewish Living
by Dr. Ron Wolfson 7 x 9, 240 pp, Quality PB, Illus., ISBN 1-58023-122-5 **$18.95**

Shabbat, 2nd Ed.: *Preparing for and Celebrating the Sabbath*—The Art of Jewish Living
by Dr. Ron Wolfson 7 x 9, 320 pp, Quality PB, Illus., ISBN 1-58023-164-0 **$19.95**

Passover, 2nd Ed.: *The Family Guide to Spiritual Celebration*—The Art of Jewish Living
by Dr. Ron Wolfson 7 x 9, 352 pp, Quality PB, ISBN 1-58023-174-8 **$19.95**

Life Cycle/Grief/Divorce

Divorce Is a Mitzvah: *A Practical Guide to Finding Wholeness and Holiness When Your Marriage Dies*

by *Rabbi Perry Netter;*

Afterword—"Afterwards: New Jewish Divorce Rituals"—by *Rabbi Laura Geller*

What does Judaism tell you about divorce? This first-of-its-kind handbook provides practical wisdom from biblical and rabbinic teachings and modern psychological research, as well as information and strength from a Jewish perspective for those experiencing the challenging life-transition of divorce. 6 x 9, 224 pp, Quality PB, ISBN 1-58023-172-1 **$16.95**

Against the Dying of the Light
A Parent's Story of Love, Loss and Hope

by *Leonard Fein*

The sudden death of a child. A personal tragedy beyond description. Rage and despair deeper than sorrow. What can come from it? Raw wisdom and defiant hope. In this unusual exploration of heartbreak and healing, Fein chronicles the sudden death of his 30-year-old daughter and reveals what the progression of grief can teach each one of us.
5½ x 8½, 176 pp, HC, ISBN 1-58023-110-1 **$19.95**

Mourning & Mitzvah, 2nd Ed.: *A Guided Journal for Walking the Mourner's Path through Grief to Healing* with *Over 60 Guided Exercises*

by *Anne Brener, L.C.S.W.*

For those who mourn a death, for those who would help them, for those who face a loss of any kind, Brener teaches us the power and strength available to us in the fully experienced mourning process. Revised and expanded. 7½ x 9, 304 pp, Quality PB, ISBN 1-58023-113-6 **$19.95**

Grief in Our Seasons: *A Mourner's Kaddish Companion*

by *Rabbi Kerry M. Olitzky*

A wise and inspiring selection of sacred Jewish writings and a simple, powerful ancient ritual for mourners to read each day, to help hold the memory of their loved ones in their hearts. Offers a comforting, step-by-step daily link to saying Kaddish.
4½ x 6½, 448 pp, Quality PB, ISBN 1-879045-55-9 **$15.95**

  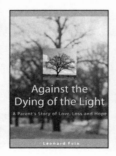  

Tears of Sorrow, Seeds of Hope
A Jewish Spiritual Companion for Infertility and Pregnancy Loss
by Rabbi Nina Beth Cardin   6 x 9, 192 pp, HC, ISBN 1-58023-017-2 **$19.95**

A Time to Mourn, A Time to Comfort
A Guide to Jewish Bereavement and Comfort
by Dr. Ron Wolfson   7 x 9, 336 pp, Quality PB, ISBN 1-879045-96-6 **$18.95**

When a Grandparent Dies
A Kid's Own Remembering Workbook for Dealing with Shiva and the Year Beyond
by Nechama Liss-Levinson, Ph.D.
8 x 10, 48 pp, HC, Illus., 2-color text, ISBN 1-879045-44-3 **$15.95**   For ages 7–13

Theology/Philosophy

Love and Terror in the God Encounter
The Theological Legacy of Rabbi Joseph B. Soloveitchik
by *Dr. David Hartman*

Renowned scholar David Hartman explores the sometimes surprising intersection of Soloveitchik's rootedness in halakhic tradition with his genuine responsiveness to modern Western theology. An engaging look at one of the most important Jewish thinkers of the twentieth century.
6 x 9, 240 pp, HC, ISBN 1-58023-112-8 **$25.00**

These Are the Words: *A Vocabulary of Jewish Spiritual Life*
by *Arthur Green*

What are the most essential ideas, concepts and terms that an educated person needs to know about Judaism? From *Adonai* (My Lord) to *zekhut* (merit), this enlightening and entertaining journey through Judaism teaches us the 149 core Hebrew words that constitute the basic vocabulary of Jewish spiritual life. 6 x 9, 304 pp, Quality PB, ISBN 1-58023-107-1 **$18.95**

Broken Tablets: *Restoring the Ten Commandments and Ourselves*
Ed. by *Rabbi Rachel S. Mikva*; Intro. by *Rabbi Lawrence Kushner* AWARD WINNER!

Twelve outstanding spiritual leaders each share profound and personal thoughts about these biblical commands and why they have such a special hold on us.
6 x 9, 192 pp, Quality PB, ISBN 1-58023-158-6 **$16.95**; HC, ISBN 1-58023-066-0 **$21.95**

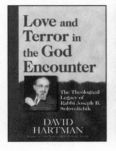    

A Heart of Many Rooms: *Celebrating the Many Voices within Judaism* AWARD WINNER!
by Dr. David Hartman 6 x 9, 352 pp, Quality PB, ISBN 1-58023-156-X **$19.95**;
HC, ISBN 1-58023-048-2 **$24.95**

A Living Covenant: *The Innovative Spirit in Traditional Judaism* AWARD WINNER!
by Dr. David Hartman 6 x 9, 368 pp, Quality PB, ISBN 1-58023-011-3 **$18.95**

Evolving Halakhah: *A Progressive Approach to Traditional Jewish Law*
by Rabbi Dr. Moshe Zemer 6 x 9, 480 pp, HC, ISBN 1-58023-002-4 **$40.00**

The Death of Death: *Resurrection and Immortality in Jewish Thought* AWARD WINNER!
by Dr. Neil Gillman 6 x 9, 336 pp, Quality PB, ISBN 1-58023-081-4 **$18.95**

The Last Trial: *On the Legends and Lore of the Command to Abraham to Offer Isaac as a Sacrifice* by Shalom Spiegel 6 x 9, 208 pp, Quality PB, ISBN 1-879045-29-X **$17.95**

Tormented Master: *The Life and Spiritual Quest of Rabbi Nahman of Bratslav*
by Dr. Arthur Green 6 x 9, 416 pp, Quality PB, ISBN 1-879045-11-7 **$18.95**

The Earth Is the Lord's: *The Inner World of the Jew in Eastern Europe*
by Abraham Joshua Heschel 5½ x 8, 128 pp, Quality PB, ISBN 1-879045-42-7 **$14.95**

A Passion for Truth: *Despair and Hope in Hasidism* by Abraham Joshua Heschel
5½ x 8, 352 pp, Quality PB, ISBN 1-879045-41-9 **$18.95**

Your Word Is Fire: *The Hasidic Masters on Contemplative Prayer* Ed. by Dr. Arthur Green and Dr. Barry W. Holtz 6 x 9, 160 pp, Quality PB, ISBN 1-879045-25-7 **$15.95**

Spirituality—The Kushner Series
Books by Lawrence Kushner

The Way Into Jewish Mystical Tradition
Explains the principles of Jewish mystical thinking, their religious and spiritual significance, and how they relate to our lives. A book that allows us to experience and understand the Jewish mystical approach to our place in the world.
6 x 9, 224 pp, HC, ISBN 1-58023-029-6 **$21.95**

Jewish Spirituality: *A Brief Introduction for Christians*
Addresses Christian's questions, revealing the essence of Judaism in a way that people whose own tradition traces its roots to Judaism can understand and appreciate.
5½ x 8½, 112 pp, Quality PB, ISBN 1-58023-150-0 **$12.95**

Eyes Remade for Wonder: *The Way of Jewish Mysticism and Sacred Living*
A Lawrence Kushner Reader Intro. by *Thomas Moore*

Whether you are new to Kushner or a devoted fan, you'll find inspiration here. With samplings from each of Kushner's works, and a generous amount of new material, this book is to be read and reread, each time discovering deeper layers of meaning in our lives.
6 x 9, 240 pp, Quality PB, ISBN 1-58023-042-3 **$18.95**; HC, ISBN 1-58023-014-8 **$23.95**

   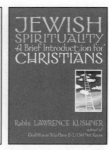 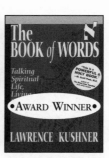

Invisible Lines of Connection: *Sacred Stories of the Ordinary* AWARD WINNER!
5½ x 8½, 160 pp, Quality PB, ISBN 1-879045-98-2 **$15.95**

Honey from the Rock: *An Introduction to Jewish Mysticism* SPECIAL ANNIVERSARY EDITION
6 x 9, 176 pp, Quality PB, ISBN 1-58023-073-3 **$15.95**

The Book of Letters: *A Mystical Hebrew Alphabet* AWARD WINNER!
Popular HC Edition, 6 x 9, 80 pp, 2-color text, ISBN 1-879045-00-1 **$24.95**; *Deluxe Gift Edition,* 9 x 12, 80 pp, HC, 4-color text, ornamentation, slipcase, ISBN 1-879045-01-X **$79.95**; *Collector's Limited Edition,* 9 x 12, 80 pp, HC, gold-embossed pages, hand-assembled slipcase. With silkscreened print. Limited to 500 signed and numbered copies, ISBN 1-879045-04-4 **$349.00**

The Book of Words: *Talking Spiritual Life, Living Spiritual Talk* AWARD WINNER!
6 x 9, 160 pp, Quality PB, 2-color text, ISBN 1-58023-020-2 **$16.95**; HC, ISBN 1-879045-35-4 **$21.95**

God Was in This Place & I, i Did Not Know: *Finding Self, Spirituality and Ultimate Meaning*
6 x 9, 192 pp, Quality PB, ISBN 1-879045-33-8 **$16.95**

The River of Light: *Jewish Mystical Awareness* SPECIAL ANNIVERSARY EDITION
6 x 9, 192 pp, Quality PB, ISBN 1-58023-096-2 **$16.95**

Because Nothing Looks Like God
by Lawrence and Karen Kushner; Full-color illus. by Dawn W. Majewski
11 x 8½, 32 pp, HC, Full-color illus., ISBN 1-58023-092-X **$16.95** **For ages 4 & up**

Spirituality & More

The Jewish Lights Spirituality Handbook
A Guide to Understanding, Exploring & Living a Spiritual Life
Ed. by *Stuart M. Matlins, Editor in Chief, Jewish Lights Publishing*

Rich, creative material from over fifty spiritual leaders on every aspect of Jewish spirituality today: prayer, meditation, mysticism, study, rituals, special days, the everyday, and more.
6 x 9, 456 pp, Quality PB, ISBN 1-58023-093-8 **$18.95**; HC, ISBN 1-58023-100-4 **$24.95**

The Story of the Jews: *A 4,000-Year Adventure—A Graphic History Book*
Written and illustrated by *Stan Mack*

Through witty cartoons and accurate narrative, illustrates the major characters and events that have shaped the Jewish people and culture. For all ages.
6 x 9, 304 pp, Quality PB, Illus., ISBN 1-58023-155-1 **$16.95**

The Jewish Prophet: *Visionary Words from Moses and Miriam to Henrietta Szold and A. J. Heschel*
by *Rabbi Dr. Michael J. Shire*

This beautifully illustrated collection of Jewish prophecy features the lives and teachings of thirty men and women, from biblical times to modern day. Provides an inspiring and informative description of the role each played in their own time, and an explanation of why we should know about them in our time. Illustrated with illuminations from medieval Hebrew manuscripts.
6½ x 8½, 128 pp, HC, 123 full-color illus., ISBN 1-58023-168-3 **$25.00**

  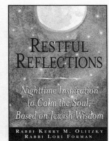  

The Enneagram and Kabbalah: *Reading Your Soul*
by Rabbi Howard A. Addison 6 x 9, 176 pp, Quality PB, ISBN 1-58023-001-6 **$15.95**

Cast in God's Image: *Discover Your Personality Type Using the Enneagram and Kabbalah*
by Rabbi Howard A. Addison 7 x 9, 176 pp, Quality PB, ISBN 1-58023-124-1 **$16.95**

Mystery Midrash: *An Anthology of Jewish Mystery & Detective Fiction* AWARD WINNER!
Ed. by Lawrence W. Raphael 6 x 9, 304 pp, Quality PB, ISBN 1-58023-055-5 **$16.95**

Criminal Kabbalah: *An Intriguing Anthology of Jewish Mystery & Detective Fiction*
Ed. by Lawrence W. Raphael; Foreword by Laurie R. King
6 x 9, 256 pp, Quality PB, ISBN 1-58023-109-8 **$16.95**

Sacred Intentions: *Daily Inspiration to Strengthen the Spirit, Based on Jewish Wisdom*
by Rabbi Kerry M. Olitzky & Rabbi Lori Forman
4½ x 6½, 448 pp, Quality PB, ISBN 1-58023-061-X **$15.95**

Restful Reflections: *Nighttime Inspiration to Calm the Soul, Based on Jewish Wisdom*
by Rabbi Kerry M. Olitzky & Rabbi Lori Forman
4½ x 6½, 448 pp, Quality PB, ISBN 1-58023-091-1 **$15.95**

Embracing the Covenant: *Converts to Judaism Talk About Why & How* Ed. by Rabbi
Allan Berkowitz & Patti Moskovitz 6 x 9, 192 pp, Quality PB, ISBN 1-879045-50-8 **$16.95**

Wandering Stars: *An Anthology of Jewish Fantasy & Science Fiction* Ed. by Jack Dann;
Intro. by Isaac Asimov 6 x 9, 272 pp, Quality PB, ISBN 1-58023-005-9 **$16.95**

Israel—A Spiritual Travel Guide: *A Companion for the Modern Jewish Pilgrim* AWARD WINNER!
by Rabbi Lawrence A. Hoffman 4¾ x 10, 256 pp, Quality PB, ISBN 1-879045-56-7 **$18.95**

Spirituality

Ehyeh: *A Kabbalah for Tomorrow*
by *Arthur Green*

Distills a forty-year search for wisdom by one of the world's leading interpreters of the Jewish mystical tradition who shares the fundamental ideas and spiritual teachings of Kabbalah. Explains how the ancient language of Kabbalah can be retooled to address the needs of our generation. 6 x 9, 224 pp, HC, ISBN 1-58023-125-X **$21.95**

The Dance of the Dolphin
Finding Prayer, Perspective and Meaning in the Stories of Our Lives
by *Karyn D. Kedar*

Helps you decode the three "languages" we all must learn—prayer, perspective, meaning—to weave the seemingly ordinary and extraordinary together.
6 x 9, 176 pp, HC, ISBN 1-58023-154-3 **$19.95**

Does the Soul Survive?
A Jewish Journey to Belief in Afterlife, Past Lives & Living with Purpose
by *Rabbi Elie Kaplan Spitz*; Foreword by *Brian L. Weiss*, M.D.

Spitz relates his own experiences and those shared with him by people he has worked with as a rabbi, and shows us that belief in afterlife and past lives, so often approached with reluctance, is in fact true to Jewish tradition.
6 x 9, 288 pp, Quality PB, ISBN 1-58023-165-9 **$16.95**; HC, ISBN 1-58023-094-6 **$21.95**

The Gift of Kabbalah
Discovering the Secrets of Heaven, Renewing Your Life on Earth
by *Tamar Frankiel, Ph.D.*

Makes accessible the mysteries of Kabbalah. Traces Kabbalah's evolution in Judaism and shows us its most important gift: a way of revealing the connection between our "everyday" life and the spiritual oneness of the universe. 6 x 9, 256 pp, HC, ISBN 1-58023-108-X **$21.95**

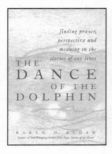    

God Whispers: *Stories of the Soul, Lessons of the Heart*
by Karyn D. Kedar 6 x 9, 176 pp, Quality PB, ISBN 1-58023-088-1 **$15.95**

Bringing the Psalms to Life: *How to Understand and Use the Book of Psalms*
by Rabbi Daniel F. Polish
6 x 9, 208 pp, Quality PB, ISBN 1-58023-157-8 **$16.95**; HC, ISBN 1-58023-077-6 **$21.95**

The Empty Chair: *Finding Hope and Joy—*
Timeless Wisdom from a Hasidic Master, Rebbe Nachman of Breslov AWARD WINNER!
4 x 6, 128 pp, Deluxe PB, 2-color text, ISBN 1-879045-67-2 **$9.95**

The Gentle Weapon: *Prayers for Everyday and Not-So-Everyday Moments*
Adapted from the Wisdom of Rebbe Nachman of Breslov
4 x 6, 144 pp, Deluxe PB, 2-color text, ISBN 1-58023-022-9 **$9.95**